Environmental Philosophy

SECOND EDITION

Environmental Philosophy

From Animal Rights to Radical Ecology

GENERAL EDITOR

Michael E. Zimmerman
Tulane University

ASSOCIATE EDITORS

J. Baird Callicott
University of North Texas

George Sessions
Sierra College

Karen J. Warren
Macalester College

John Clark
Loyola University, New Orleans

Prentice Hall, Upper Saddle River, New Jersey 07458

Library of Congress Cataloging-in-Publication Data

Environmental philosophy : from animal rights to radical ecology / general editor, MICHAEL E. ZIMMERMAN ; associate editors, J. BAIRD CALLICOTT . . . [et al.] — 2nd ed.
p. cm.
Includes bibliographical references and index.
ISBN 0-13-778366-3 (pbk. : alk. paper)
1. Human ecology—Philosophy. 2. Environmental ethics.
I. Zimmerman, Michael E., [date]
GF21.E56 1998
179'.1—DC21 97-33443

Editorial director: Charlyce Jones Owen
Editorial/production: Edie Riker
Cover design: Wendy Alling Judy
Cover art: Leaves and Lappet 1996, Jeremy Stratford 1959, British. The Grand Design/Superstock Inc.
Buyer: Tricia Kenny
Director of Marketing: Gina Sluss

This book was set in 10/12 New Baskerville by Pub-Set, Inc. and was printed and bound by Courier Companies, Inc. The cover was printed by Phoenix Color Corp.

Simon & Schuster/A Viacom Company
Upper Saddle River, New Jersey 07458

Printed in the United States of America
10 9 8 7 6 5 4 3 2 1

ISBN 0-13-778366-3

Prentice-Hall International (UK) Limited, *London*
Prentice-Hall of Australia Pty. Limited, *Sydney*
Prentice-Hall Canada Inc., *Toronto*
Prentice-Hall Hispanoamericana, S.A., *Mexico*
Prentice-Hall of India Private Limited, *New Delhi*
Prentice-Hall of Japan, Inc., *Tokyo*
Simon & Schuster Asia Pte. Ltd., *Singapore*
Editora Prentice-Hall do Brasil, Ltda., *Rio de Janeiro*

Contents

Preface to the Second Edition

Encouraged by the very positive response generated by the first edition of this anthology, we have made changes that we believe make this anthology even better. Although some essays from the original edition have been deleted, others have been added to increase the scope of our coverage of environmental philosophy.

To his environmental ethics section, J. Baird Callicott has added his important new essay about how environmental ethicists can respond to scientific challenges to the ecosystem paradigm. In addition to writing a new introduction to the deep ecology section, George Sessions has added an essay by Harold Glasser, an important new voice in the deep ecology movement. Karen J. Warren has provided a revised introduction to her section on ecofeminism. The most significant changes in the anthology have occurred in John Clark's section, now called political ecology. This entirely new section includes essays on free-market environmentalism, sustainable development, liberal environmentalism, socialist environmentalism, social ecology, bioregionalism, and ecotage.

My thanks go to all the associate editors for their ideas, hard work, and continuing participation. In particular, I would like to commend John Clark for having done such a fine job of redefining his section, which includes his original essay on social ecology.

On behalf of all the editors, I would like to thank the anonymous referees, who provided useful suggestions for improving the anthology, and Angela Stone, our editor at Prentice Hall, who supported us all the way.

Michael E. Zimmerman

Preface to the Second Edition

Environmental Philosophy

General Introduction

Michael E. Zimmerman

Michael E. Zimmerman is professor of philosophy at Tulane University and clinical professor of psychology at Tulane University Medical School. He is also cochair of Tulane's Environmental Studies program. Author of many essays on environmental philosophy and two books on Heidegger, he has also written Contesting Earth's Future: Radical Ecology and Postmodernity.

Thirty years ago, most Anglo-American philosophers were studying epistemology, linguistic usage, and meta-ethics, while Americans studying continental philosophy were focused on phenomenology and existentialism. Postwar American philosophers, unlike the public-minded philosophers of the pre–World War II era, usually did not conduct research or teach about major cultural, social, or political issues. In the 1960s and 1970s, however, the countercultural revolution—including the antiwar movement, the civil rights movement, the women's movement, the animal rights movement, and the environmental movement—introduced a host of issues that were so compelling and politically polarizing that they could not be ignored by philosophers, who were teaching on the same campuses that were harboring many of these insurgents. A new generation of American philosophers, influenced by one or another of these movements, began seeking ways to introduce consideration of them into classrooms and professional journals.

Philosophers concerned about environmental issues raised basic questions about humanity's relationship with nature. Are humans the only inherently valuable beings in the known universe, or does the natural world—plants, animals, bioregions—have its own worth, independent of the use to which it can be put by human beings? Do humans have moral obligations only to other humans, or do we also have moral obligations to animals, to plants, and even to whole ecosystems? To what extent do ecological problems arise from anthropocentrism and from humanity-nature dualism? Do humans have any obligations to future generations? Is it morally wrong to exterminate a species of plant or animal? When we are told that industrial technology furthers man's progress, what is meant by "man"? Is it merely an illusion that wealthy groups seem to gain the most from technological innovation, often at the expense of poor or dispossessed people? To what extent do technological innovations free people, and to what extent do those innovations generate serious social and ecological problems? Is human freedom compatible with the disappearance of everything wild and free in nature? How do we know that history has any direction at all, much less a "progressive" one? If there is a progressive trend in history, on what basis do we assume that it requires in almost every instance that humans dominate nonhumans?

Some of these questions had already been raised by previous American theologians, philosophers, and naturalists, including Jonathan Edwards, Ralph Waldo Emerson, Henry David Thoreau, John Muir, John Burroughs, and Aldo Leopold. Their celebration of the beauty of the natural world and their concern about its fate at the hands of a rapidly expanding and industrious American population, however, were heeded only irregularly, especially when the North American continent seemed too vast ever to be overrun or substantially harmed by human settlements and activity. Although it has been a century since Frederick Jackson Turner proclaimed the end of the American frontier era, the better part of the twentieth century saw Americans "developing" the continent with reckless abandon. During the Great Depression, World War II, and the postwar industrial boom, a number of Americans counseled their fellow citizens to conserve natural resources and to respect the land, but the time was not yet ripe for a dramatic reevaluation of accepted attitudes toward the nonhuman realm.

Many commentators point to Rachel Carson's best-selling book, *Silent Spring* (1962), as the catalyst for the environmental movement, which took the nation by storm within a decade. Maintaining that widespread use of the pesticide DDT had killed millions of America's beloved songbirds by weakening their eggs (hence, the "silent spring"), Carson urged her fellow citizens to examine critically their taken-for-granted attitudes toward living nature. Her cautionary tale not only demonstrated that birds were dying from misguided human practices but also implied that people might be next. Today, public opinion polls clearly demonstrate that the great majority of Americans take seriously the possibility that a combination of industrialization, on the one hand, and the growing human population, on the other, could lead to problems so serious that they might undermine the future well-being of humankind. Moreover, a great many Americans believe that the natural world is valuable in and of itself, not simply because of its utility for humans.

To understand how dramatic are the changes that have taken place in public and academic attitudes toward environmental issues, the reader need only contemplate the fact that a college anthology like this one—now in its second edition—would have been completely unthinkable a little over a generation ago. At that time, few philosophers, no matter what their conceptual orientation and intellectual interests, would have regarded the very idea of environmental philosophy as anything other than absurd. Although some philosophers may still look askance at this idea, its success can be measured by the substantial number of college-level courses now offered in environmental ethics and environmental philosophy. Moreover, numerous academic departments offer courses and concentrations in environmentally related topics, and interdisciplinary environmental studies programs are a common feature of American colleges and universities.

Environmental philosophy is often regarded as identical to environmental ethics, that is, as an effort to examine critically the notion that nature has inherent worth and to inquire into the possibility that humans have moral duties to animals, plants, and ecosystems. As the questions posed earlier indicate, however, the scope of environmental philosophy reaches beyond ethical issues and includes diverse metaphysical, epistemological, cultural, and political issues as well. In the mid-1980s, I had become frustrated by the lack of anthologies dealing with the particular issues that I wanted to address in my own course, Humanity's Place in Nature, which I first offered at Tulane University in 1981. It was not until 1990, however, that I decided to devise an anthology that would be suitable for advanced undergraduates and graduate students and that would provide coverage of areas that were, in my view, particularly important for understanding environmental philosophy. To provide the best possible coverage of areas in which I had an interest but had not necessarily mastered, I decided to assemble a team of experts, each of whom would edit his or her own section of the anthology. Four deservedly well-known environmental philosophers—J. Baird Callicott (environmental ethics), George Sessions (deep ecology), Karen J. Warren (ecofeminism), and John Clark (political ecology)—graciously agreed to my proposal to compose the anthology now before you. Because these philosophers have provided excellent introductions to their own sections, I will not duplicate their efforts here. I would, however, like to offer the following general observations, the aim of which is both to provide a brief overview of my own understanding of the current state of affairs in environmental philosophy and to explain the reason for the changes that have been made in this second edition.

In the first edition, I maintained that environmental philosophy may be roughly divided into three major fields. The first field, environmental ethics, asserts that progress could be made in ending the ecological crisis by challenging anthropocentric ethical norms and extending moral considerability to nonhuman beings. Like other experts confronted with a new problem that they have not been trained to solve, some ethicists seek to use their own available tools—that is, modern moral theories—to address the environmental crisis. Many environmental ethicists envision the following possibility: just as today one is morally and legally obligated to refrain from abusing or killing humans, so tomorrow one may be morally and legally obligated to refrain from abusing or killing many kinds of living beings—except, of course, for nontrivial reasons. Unfortunately, however, because moral theory focuses primarily on individuals, because human individuals differ in important respects from nonhuman beings, and because many ecologists are more concerned with species and ecosystems than with individual plants and animals, moral extensionism has run into some difficulties.

Some environmental ethicists are sharply critical of Western anthropocentrism and humanity-nature dualism, but others adhere to a less radical position, sometimes known as "weak" anthropocentrism. According to this position, humans are intrinsically more valuable than nonhumans, but at least *some* nonhuman beings have a worth of their own and thus ought not to be treated merely as means for human ends. A weak anthropocentrist would justify protecting wild habitats from development or defending an endangered species, not simply because doing so might benefit some group of humans, but also because the habitat and species are somehow good in themselves, or inherently valuable. Just what this "good" might be and just what groups of entities (animals? plants? ecosystems?) are deserving of moral considerability have been the subjects of extensive debate among environmental ethicists.

The second field of environmental philosophy, radical ecology, often associated with the countercultural movement, includes deep ecology, ecofeminism, and social ecology, among others. Radical ecophilosophers consider themselves radical for at least two reasons. First, they claim that their analyses disclose the conceptual, attitudinal, social, political, and cultural origins of the ecological crisis. Second, they argue that only a revolution or a cultural paradigm shift can save the planet from ecological devastation. Although acknowledging that reforming current practices (e.g., requiring tighter controls on industrial pollution or encouraging recycling) may help matters in the short run, radical ecologists generally believe that such reforms will be insufficient in the long run because they address only the symptoms, not the roots, of the ecological crisis.

Despite agreeing in many respects about the limitations of environmental reformism, radical ecophilosophers have different views about what constitutes the roots of the ecological crisis. A number of deep ecologists think that one of its roots is anthropocentrism: the view that humans alone are the origin and measure of all value. Presumably, such a view breeds an arrogance that leads people to treat nonhuman beings as nothing but raw material for satisfying human needs and desires. Many ecofeminists think that the major root of the ecological crisis is patriarchy: an oppressive social structure that justifies the exploitation of women and nature because it regards both as somehow inferior to men. In some cases, ecofeminists maintain that oppressive hierarchies in general are responsible for exploitative behavior, whether such behavior is directed at women, lower-class people, animals, or ecosystems. Similarly, many social ecologists assert that the principal root of the ecological crisis is the social hierarchy. Authoritarian social structures allow some people to dominate others and also to waste, despoil, and needlessly harm nonhuman beings. One reason that I decided to develop this anthology was that no anthology available in the 1980s provided decent coverage of radical ecology, although I myself regarded it as very important.

The third field in environmental philosophy, anthropocentric reformism, argues that the root of our environmental problems is not anthropocentric and patriarchal attitudes, not the institutions and practices that embody them, and not the moral obtuseness that prevents people from discerning the moral considerability or inherent value of nonhuman beings. Rather, air and water pollution, the wasteful use of natural resources, and other environmentally harmful practices stem from ignorance, greed, illegal behavior, and shortsightedness. Such imprudent and morally blameworthy practices may be curbed by enacting legislation, changing public policy, increasing education, altering tax laws, returning public lands to private ownership, emphasizing moral obligations to future generations, promoting wise stewardship of nature, and otherwise encouraging more prudent use of natural resources. According to anthropocentric reformers, though nature has value only as an instrument for human ends, those ends are complex and numerous, ranging from the food provided by plants and animals to the aesthetic pleasure evoked by a wild landscape. Anthropocentric reformers, then, see no need either for revolutionary cultural and political changes or for alterations in human-centered moral theory.

When contemplating the possible fields to be covered in the first edition of this anthology and when taking into account the amount of space available, I concluded that the first two fields—environmental ethics and radical ecology—deserved extensive coverage but that the third—anthropocentric reformism—could be omitted because it was already sufficiently well known and understood. Moreover, I concluded that by limiting radical ecology to deep ecology, ecofeminism, and social ecology, I would have provided sufficient coverage of this topic. In choosing editors who would focus on these three branches of radical ecology, I had hoped to encourage constructive conversations among deep ecologists, ecofeminists, and social ecologists because some representatives from each of these branches were engaging in what I regarded as fruitless and often intemperate debates.

Responses from a variety of readers and reviewers encouraged me to reevaluate these two conclusions about the content of the anthology. Some readers wanted coverage of anthropocentric reformism, for example, free-market and government regulatory (liberal) approaches to environmental problems. Warning that young people feel despair not only in the face of the grim future envisioned by some radical ecologists but in the face of the unlikely prospects of the revolutionary changes purportedly needed to avert such a future, reformists maintain that significant improvements to current and future environmental conditions can take place if, for example, markets are freed from unnecessary government constraints and public lands are sold to private citizens. Other readers, skeptical of what can be achieved by such reformism, maintained that there are other kinds of radical ecology, for example, socialism, biogregionalism, and "direct action" (including ecotage) that were not represented in the first edition. Finally, still other readers maintained that the first edition had defined social ecology too narrowly and needed to take into account other forms. Within the constraints imposed by considerations of space, the new edition reflects our efforts to respond to those readers who wanted the anthology to include essays about environmental reformism and about other kinds of radical ecophilosophy.

Believing that John Clark's section, originally entitled Social Ecology, was the place in which such changes could most effectively be introduced, I approached him about the possibility. Exhibiting great energy and insight, he selected six essays, composed an essay on social ecology, and wrote a fine introduction for his section, which has been completely changed and bears the title Political Ecology. This section includes essays by leading thinkers on free-market environmentalism, sustainable economic development, political liberalism, socialist environmentalism, social ecology, bioregionalism, and ecotage. We hope that readers will agree that these changes significantly improve the anthology's quality and coverage.

Other changes have been made as well. To the environmental ethics section, J. Baird Callicott has added his own essay about how environmental ethicists can respond to scientific challenges to the ecosystem paradigm. In recent decades the ecosystem approach to environmental science has been eclipsed by population dynamics. As opposed to the ecosystem approach, which emphasizes natural harmony, balance, rhythm, and cycles, the latter approach emphasizes discord, perturbations, heterogeneity, and fluctuation. Since federal environmental legislation has been bolstered by scientific claims that human industry and population growth are upsetting the "delicate balance of nature," and since contemporary environmental science suggests that there is no such balance, environmental philosophers have good reason to grapple with changes in how science interprets the natural environment.

In addition to writing a new introduction to the deep ecology section, George Sessions has added an essay by Harold Glasser, an important new voice in this movement. Finally, Karen J. Warren has revised her introduction to the section on ecofeminism. Several essays from the first edition have been omitted, not because of concern for their quality, but rather because of the decision to emphasize fields that had not received adequate coverage in the first edition. My thanks go to all my associate editors for their ideas, hard work, and continuing participation in this anthology.

On behalf of all the editors, I would like to thank the anonymous referees, who provided useful suggestions for improvement, and Angela Stone, our editor at Prentice Hall, who has supported us all the way.

PART ONE

Environmental Ethics

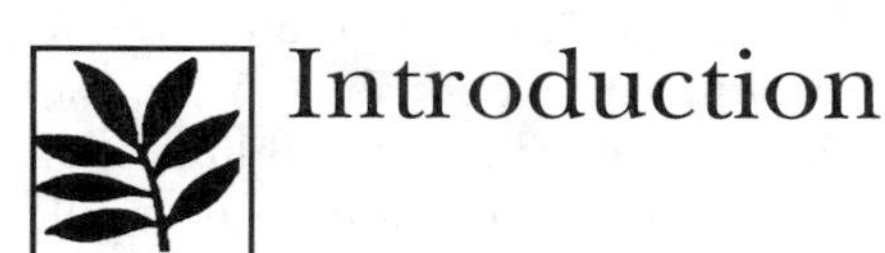

Introduction

J. Baird Callicott

J. Baird Callicott is professor of philosophy and religion studies at the University of North Texas. He is the author of In Defense of the Land Ethic: Essays in Environmental Philosophy, Beyond the Land Ethic: More Essays in Environmental Philosophy, *and* Earth's Insights: A Multicultual Survey of Ecological Ethics from the Mediterranean Basin to the Australian Outback, *and more than a hundred book chapters, journal articles, and book reviews in environmental philosophy.*

In 1973, with the publication of three seminal papers, environmental ethics made its formal debut on the staid and conservative stage of professional philosophy. That spring, the young Australian philosopher Peter Singer published "Animal Liberation" in *The New York Review of Books.* That summer, "The Shallow and the Deep, Long Range Ecology Movement: A Summary" by the distinguished Norwegian philosopher and mountaineer Arne Naess appeared in the international philosophy journal *Inquiry.* That fall, another young Australian philosopher, Richard Sylvan (then Routley), addressed his colleagues at the Fifteenth World Congress of Philosophy in Varna, Bulgaria, with a question: "Is There a Need for a New, an Environmental, Ethic?"

Over the next several years, a few more papers in this novel and exciting area of research appeared in such professional journals as *Ethics* and the *Journal of Philosophy.* Then, in 1979, Eugene C. Hargrove established a new quarterly, *Environmental Ethics,* and the floodgates opened. Articles in environmental ethics poured forth. College courses began to be offered in the subject. By the middle of the next decade a number of book-length discussions had appeared. Thus a whole new field of philosophy has come into being.

The three seminal papers of 1973 stand at the fountainhead not of one but of three increasingly divergent streams of thought. Deep ecology, flowing from the paper by Naess, has now solidified into an eight-point "platform," which has been adopted by members of the radical green movement, including its covert operatives, the "ecowarriors" of Earth First! Moreover, deep ecology has become a "practice" aimed at directly *experiencing* connectedness with nature. Deep ecology seems, accordingly, vaguely anti-intellectual and overtly hostile to the impersonal (as the deep ecologists think of it) "ethical reduction" of what they believe should be a more intimate relationship to the natural world than that typical of morality. The ethical theory of animal liberation and animal rights has become the philosophical wing of an even more visible and increasingly militant movement. The goals of that movement, however, have been not only different from but also often in conflict with the goals of the environmental movement. And as moral philosophies, animal liberation/rights and environmental ethics are now recognized as separate fields of study, each with its own agenda.

Accordingly, in this anthology, deep ecology has its own section, while this first part is divided into two distinct groups of essays: individualistic approaches and holistic approaches. Since the conflict between animal liberation/rights and environmental ethics has been more profound or at least longer standing than the internecine disputes among ecofeminism, deep ecology, and social ecology, one might suppose that essays in animal welfare ethics might be excluded from this anthology. But there are good reasons for including some of those essays here.

Historically, animal liberation/rights and environmental ethics were conflated. Even today, although the schism between the two occurred in the early 1980s, most philosophers, let alone laypeople, regard them as being pretty much the same thing. Because we are large vertebrates ourselves, thoughts of other large vertebrates understandably come to mind when we consider the natural environment. Wild animals *are* a significant part of the natural environment, but domestic animals—who get the lion's share of attention from animal welfare ethicists—are not. And the natural environment comprises much, much more than just our furry friends.

Practically, animal liberation/rights and environmental ethics often overlap and, as just noted, often conflict. For example, domestic cattle and sheep, feral rabbits, goats, pigs, and the like often threaten to destroy delicate ecosystems and to extinguish endangered plant species. The ethics of most environmentalists would require preserving ecosystems and certainly plant species at all costs, even if that should mean assassinating the commonplace herbivorous mammals, while the ethics of animal liberationists and animal rights activists would favor the mammals, even if that should mean further ecological degradation and the erosion of biodiversity.

Methodologically, however, animal liberation/rights and environmental ethicists are united by a resolute commitment to the methods of traditional Western philosophy. Both spin their theories out of the strands of thought found in the history of European and Euro-American thought. Both develop moral philosophies that ground ethical theories, which in turn imply practical precepts. Both believe in the power of reason to persuade and to engender consensus. And both believe in the power of ideas to direct individual action, to change social values, and to forge new cultural ideals.

Theoretically, and most important for our purposes here, animal liberation/rights broke new ground in moral philosophy by taking a step beyond the species barrier. The very able and persuasive articulation of animal liberation by Singer and animal rights by Tom Regan—both decidedly nonanthropocentic (nonhuman centered) moral philosophies—blazed a path followed by a second wave of philosophers with wider concerns. Thus while animal liberation/rights is an end point in support of the agenda of the very popular animal welfare movement, it can be regarded, as it is here, as only the first step toward a more encompassing environmental ethic oriented to all living things severally or individually.

We begin Part One of this anthology with Sylvan's summons to the global community of philosophers to focus philosophy's formidable powers of conceptual analysis and cognitive creativity on the environmental problematique. In 1973, an adequate, nonanthropocentric environmental ethic simply did not exist in Western intellectual traditions, Sylvan argues, although one had been prophetically envisioned by the great American conservationist Aldo Leopold at midcentury. So he urged contemporary philosophers to take up Leopold's mantle and make it their business to provide one.

The principal deficiency, as Sylvan's arresting "last people" and "last man" ethical thought experiments at the heart of his paper are intended to drive home, is that the "base class" of traditional Western ethics is coextensive with the class of human beings. Adapting a term from liberal feminism (ecofeminism by then had not emerged as such), traditional Western ethical theory has been guilty of "human [as well as male] chauvinism." Hence, the principal theoretical problem that Sylvan sets out for the philosophers who would respond to his challenge is how to enlarge the ethical base class so that it will include nonhuman, as well as human, beings.

Notice that Sylvan mentions, among the large class of ethically disenfranchised beings, that an eventual environmental ethic might embrace, both individual plants (trees) and animals (dingoes), on the one hand, and environmental collectives or wholes such as species (*the* blue whale) and ecosystems, on the other. As he is simply sketching the problem, not attempting to solve it, he is rather casual about what nonhuman beings ought and ought not to be included in the moral base class of an adequate environmental ethic or how theoretically to go about expanding the base class.

We may regard Peter Singer's paper, "All Animals Are Equal," as an attempt to address the philosophical problem as Sylvan has set it out, though Singer was, of course, not deliberately responding to Sylvan's plea. In traditional Western moral philosophy, human chauvinism, or what Singer and Richard Ryder (also drawing on the rhetoric of contemporaneous feminism) call "speciesism" (an analogy with sexism), is not simply asserted without defense. Moral philosophers from Plato to Rawls have spent considerable energy explaining what makes human beings so special and what makes us and us alone worthy of moral treatment. Singer exploits this ubiquitous feature of classic Western moral philosophy and poses the following dilemma for any human chauvinist ethics.

If what entitles a human being to be a member of the moral base class (call it the philosopher's preferred "criterion for moral standing") is pitched high enough to exclude other animals, then it will also exclude the human "marginal cases"—human infants, the severely retarded, and abjectly senile people. If we are serious about the possession of a certain capacity—say the capacity to reason or to speak—demarcating the difference between those who do deserve moral consideration and those who don't, and if we are self-consistent, then we should permit treating the marginal cases just as we treat other morally disenfranchised beings: without qualms, researchers might perform painful medical experiments and test products on unwanted babies, state fish and game departments might open a hunting season on the retarded, and Purina might make dog food out of the senile.

Outrageous, to be sure. That's just the point. But to bring the marginal cases into the moral base class, we shall have to lower the entry requirement. To what level? Singer turns for an answer to the criterion proposed by Jeremy Bentham: sentience, the capacity to experience pleasure and pain. Sentience is arguably a more relevant criterion for moral treatment than some more exclusive alternative since the minimum consideration one asks of others is not to be harmed by them. And one may suppose that to be harmed, in the last analysis, means to be hurt, to be caused to suffer. Where exactly the "insuperable line," as Bentham calls it, falls between those animals who are and those who are not sentient is far from clear, but it *is* entirely clear that at the very least all vertebrates ought to be included in the moral base class as so delineated.

The enormous appeal of Singer's animal liberation ethic stems, ironically, from the fact that he has really put forth nothing new. Rather, he has simply demanded that the value theory—pleasure is good and pain is evil—of classical utilitarianism be consistently applied. Classical utilitarianism insisted on the *impartial* accounting of pleasures and pains but arbitrarily limited it to the pleasures and pains of human beings. Remove this ad hoc limitation and *voilà*, one has animal liberation.

That, however, exposed Singer's animal liberation ethic to all the problems that classical utilitarianism's ingenious critics had worked out over two centuries. Singer is an advocate of vegetarianism for purely moral reasons, but even this basic practical implication of the ethical enfranchisement of animals is suspect on purely utilitarian grounds. We might raise animals in comfort, slaughter them painlessly, and still enjoy our steaks, chops, and bacon and eggs.

Such considerations as these led Tom Regan to counter Singer's animal liberation ethic with the equally familiar and classical antidote—rights (animal rights in this case). According to Regan, those animals who are subjects of a life, which from their own point of view may be better or worse, have "inherent value" and therefore rights, which "trump" the "principle of utility" that roughly directs us to do whatever would produce a greater balance on average of pleasure over pain among all the sentient creatures whom one's actions affect.

For Singer and Regan, the ethical entitlement of "animals" is a philosophical goal in and of itself. If, however, our goal is to develop the more inclusive environmental ethic originally envisioned by Sylvan, animal liberation and animal rights are at best a way station.

Obviously, plants are left totally out of account by animal liberation/rights, to say nothing of the nonliving parts of ecosystems about which we environmentalists are concerned, such as the soil, water, and air. Moreover, despite this title, "All Animals Are Equal," for Singer not even *all* animals are included in his charmed circle of moral patients since many kinds of animals may not be sentient. The animals to which Regan's theory would extend rights are even more narrowly restricted—indeed, much more so.

In a 1978 paper, "On Being Morally Considerable," Kenneth E. Goodpaster tentatively took moral philosophy beyond animal liberation/rights into environmental ethics proper. He agreed with Bentham and Singer that withholding ethical entitlement from entities that fail to meet the more restrictive of historically proposed criteria (such as being rational) for "moral considerability" was neither intellectually honest nor ultimately warranted. But he disagreed with them that the insuperable line should be drawn by the sentience criterion. From a biological point of view sentience is a means, not an end—a means to life. Hence, not sentience but "being alive" should be the criterion for moral considerability. Furthermore, such a criterion is arguably more relevant to the benefit for which it selects since nonsentient living things may also intelligibly be said to have interests, and if so, they may be directly benefited or harmed—even though harming them may not hurt them, may not cause them consciously to suffer. But Goodpaster's reasoning clearly follows the form classically established by Bentham and recently elaborated by Singer.

Goodpaster's "life-principle" ethic is minimalistic. He expressly avoids the issue of how much weight we ought to give the interests of plants and other barely living beings. And he even admits that while technically they may be morally considerable, practically they may fall well below the human "threshold" of moral sensitivity. Thus we may forever be unable actually to take the interests of all the living things that our actions affect into account as we make our day-to-day practical decisions.

Three years later, the distinguished American philosopher Paul W. Taylor proffered a much stronger version of biocentrism (literally, a "life-centered" ethical theory). According to Taylor, all living things are "teleological centers of life." An organism's *telos* (Greek for "end, goal") is to reach a state of maturity and to reproduce. Our actions can interdict the fulfillment of an organism's *telos,* and to do just that is to harm it. Taylor agrees with Goodpaster that all living things have interests and thus a good of their own, quite regardless of the uses to which we might put them and quite independently of whether they are sentient or care. While Taylor withholds rights from nonhuman natural entities, he argues that *all* wild organisms have *equal* inherent worth. (Taylor's limitation of moral considerability to *wild* telelogical centers of life appears to be theoretically unjustified, however.)

The idea that all wild organisms (from fruit flies to sperm whales) are of equal moral worth runs counter to our considered ethical intuitions according to which long-lived, conscious beings are intrinsically more valuable than ephemeral, insentient beings. However, even if we were persuaded by Taylor's bioegalitarianism, the resulting environmental ethic would be beside the point, not to mention diabolically difficult to practice. The welfare of grubs, bugs, and shrubs is simply not the focus of environmental concern. As Sylvan's programmatic paper suggests, environmental concern focuses less on individual living things (though their well-being is not ignored entirely) than on species and other "holistic" entities, on biotic communities, ecosystems, wilderness, and the planetary biosphere as a whole.

There are many important differences between the individualistic and holistic approaches to nonanthropocentric moral philosophy. It's not just that the animal welfare ethics do not go far enough, rather they run in a different and often contrary direction to environmental concerns. In addition to conflicts between the welfare of domestic or feral sentient animals and endangered plant species or overall ecosystem health, there are also conflicts of interest between domestic and feral animals, on the one hand, and wild animals on the other. In "Animal Rights, Human Wrongs," Regan expresses a concern for both whales and gibbon apes. But most of the concern of animal liberation/rights has been lavished on animals like cattle (especially veal calves or "bobby calves," as Regan refers to them), chickens, and the like that are factory farmed. While factory farming is environmentally destructive because of the depletion of the irrechargable aquifers, the erosion of the soil, and the pollution by chemicals, the well-being of domestic creatures themselves—plants included, certainly, as well as animals—is just not an environmental issue. Environmentally speaking, wild animal and plant *populations* are the important issue, and they are often severely affected adversely by competition from domestic and feral types.

In sum, environmental concerns are predominantly holistic, not individualistic. Thus the exclusively individualistic approach to environmental ethics inadequately addresses these concerns. Environmental concerns and exclusively individualistic environmental ethics pass one another by, like the proverbial ships in the night, without meeting or making contact.

Well, what to do? Perhaps we can get a clue by diagnosing the problem. Singer, Regan, Goodpaster, and Taylor all provide variations on a common theoretical theme that could be called the standard paradigm of traditional moral philosophy. The standard paradigm identifies and justifies a property or characteristic that entitles the possessor to moral considerability. The principal difference between the theories of Singer, Regan, Goodpaster, and Taylor and those of their anthropocentric predecessors lies in the choice of the ethically enfranchising property or characteristic. Most traditional exponents of the standard paradigm carefully select a property or characteristic that they believe only human beings possess. Singer, Regan, Goodpaster, and Taylor have deliberately chosen theirs to include not only all human beings but also a wide range of nonhuman beings. All vertebrates possess Singer's, all mammals possess Regan's, and all living things possess Goodpaster's and Taylor's.

Attempts have been made to attribute unconscious interests—similar to those attributed to plants and insentient animals by Goodpaster and Taylor—to environmental wholes, such as species and ecosystems. And attempts have been made to argue that mere existence is a property warranting moral consideration. But such attempts have not been taken seriously. Biocentrism thus represents the end point of this simple line of argument. It stretches this familiar pattern of moral reasoning to its limit. Like a rubber band asked to encircle too big a bundle, attempts to stretch it further have snapped its credibility.

The holistic approach to environmental ethics would seem, therefore, to require either a different theoretical paradigm or some theoretical means of cogently augmenting biocentrism. Basing his theory on hints and suggestions offered by Aldo Leopold, J. Baird Callicott has pursued the former alternative, while Holmes Rolston III has pursued the latter. Leopold claims that "a land ethic changes the role of *Homo sapiens* from conqueror of the land community to plain member and citizen of it. It implies respect for his fellow-members and also respect for the *community as such.*" Indeed, as "The Land Ethic" progresses, "fellow-members" recede farther and farther from the author's attention and concern for the "community as such" looms ever larger in importance. When Leopold finally comes to write the summary moral maxim or golden rule of the land ethic, he seems to have forgotten about individual plants and animals altogether, and only the ecosystem as a whole remains as the object of moral considerability: "A thing is right when it tends to preserve the integrity, stability, and beauty of the biotic community. It is wrong when it tends otherwise."

Because of the perfect fit of the land ethic with their holistic concerns, contemporary environmentalists have made it their ethic of choice. But Leopold was a forester by training and wildlife ecologist by profession, not a philosopher. Hence his brief but suggestive foray into ethics is not theoretically well formed or fully argued. In "The Conceptual Foundations of the Land Ethic," J. Baird Callicott attempts explicitly to construct the theoretical superstructure that occasionally shows through the informal texture of Leopold's prose.

The standard paradigm requires us to grant moral considerability to whatever the philosopher's preferred (and justified) criterion of moral considerability identifies as morally considerable—no matter how we may *feel* about such beings. Callicott argues that Leopold's land ethic belongs to the tradition of moral philosophy classically articulated in the eighteenth century by David Hume and Adam Smith, in which ethics are rooted precisely in altruistic feelings like benevolence, sympathy, and loyalty. According to Callicott, Charles Darwin suggested that such feelings were naturally selected in many species, including our prehuman ancestors, because without them individuals could not bond together into mutually beneficial societies and communities. Rudimentary ethics emerged as human beings evolved to the point where they could articulate codes of conduct conforming to their social sentiments. As human societies grew in scope and complexity, so did our ethics. By now, we have reached the point where the enlightened among us regard all human persons as members of one world community, the "global village," subject to a common ethics of humanity, the "human rights" ethic.

Leopold envisions the land ethic to be the next stage of human moral evolution, for presently ecology portrays terrestrial nature to be a biotic community composed of plants and animals, soils and waters. A universal ecological literacy would trigger sympathy and fellow-feeling for *fellow members* of the biotic community *and* feelings of loyalty and patriotic regard for the *community as a whole,* Callicott suggests. How to balance human interests against those of nonhuman natural entities and nature as a whole is as big a problem for the feeling-based land ethic as for any other environmental ethic. Callicott defends the land ethic against the charge that it amounts to "environmental fascism," which some of its exclusively individualistic critics have, in retaliation for his very generous critique of their views, leveled against it.

If the biocentrism of Goodpaster and Taylor errs in being exclusively individualistic, the ecocentrism (short for ecosystem-centered ethic) of Leopold and Callicott may err in being excessively—though by no means exclusively—holistic. Rolston has attempted a different synthesis of individualism and holism. At the foundation of his theory lies the core claim of biocentrism—that any and every living thing is intrinsically valuable and thus morally considerable. But for his approach to be more plausible than that of Goodpaster and Taylor, he must somehow reconcile the moral considerability of individual plants (from the lowliest shrub to the most magnificent sequoia) and animals (from gnats to mountain gorillas) with common sense, and he must also somehow make his theory reach environmental wholes. Rolston has been working at this project since the publication of his 1975 essay, "Is There an Ecological Ethic?" which was as seminal as the slightly earlier paper by Sylvan reprinted here. His "Challenges in Environmental Ethics" summarizes the fruits of nearly two decades of inquiry.

To the equal baseline intrinsic value of living things, each with a good of its own, Rolston adds a value premium, so to speak, for sentience and an additional value premium for self-consciousness. Thus sentient animals possess more intrinsic value than plants and insentient animals; and we self-conscious rational animals possess the most intrinsic value of all individual natural entities. Therefore, in cases of conflict, human interests take precedence over those of individual animals and plants, as most sensible people believe; and, by the same token, the interests of sentient animals take precedence over those of insentient animals and plants. Rolston then awards a value dividend, as it were, to species, the perpetuation of which is the reproductive end of specimens, and to ecosystems as the matrix in which baseline intrinsically valuable living things evolved and on which they remain dependent for their flourishing. In Rolston's essentially biocentric system, like the moon that shines by a borrowed light, natural wholes, such as species and ecosystems, possess an intrinsic value derived from the baseline intrinsic value of living organisms and thus enjoy only derivative moral considerability. Furthermore, it is not clear how applying Rolston's system might adjudicate conflicts of interest between wholes and individuals. That problem, however, is endemic to all ethics that go beyond traditional anthropocentrism, and so it would be unfair to suggest that Rolston's environmental ethic is any less decisive, in respect to such practical conundrums, than are any of its competitors.

Recent developments in ecology, the science that inspires and informs holistic environmental ethics, may undermine some of the assumptions common to the Leopold-Callicott and the Rolston approaches. Most fundamentally, doubts about the very existence of biotic communities and ecosystems have been increasingly forthcoming in ecology. If biotic communities and ecosystems do not exist as such, then claims that they have intrinsic value and the creation of a nonanthropocentric environmental ethic to protect them would be otiose. Most people today, similarly, would consider a nonanthropocentric ethic that provided moral considerability for leprechauns to be beside the point—because most people do not believe that leprechauns actually exist. And if they do exist, both biotic communities and ecosystems change, not only because of the impact of human activities on them, but also because they are naturally, inherently dynamic. Moreover such violent occurrences in biotic communities and ecosystems as hurricanes and tornadoes, wildfires, and floods are normal, routine, and in the long run often, apparently, beneficial. Assuming that biotic communities and ecosystems as such do actually exist, why should violent anthropogenic (human-induced) changes be singled out for moral censure? In the final essay of Part One, "Do Deconstructive Ecology and Sociobiology Undermine Leopold's Land Ethic?" J. Baird Callicott addresses the unexpected challenges to holistic, nonanthropocentric environmental ethics presented by contemporary ecology.

Callicott argues that biotic communities are no less real than human communities; nor are they any more dynamic and unstable. If human communities are sufficiently robust to generate duties and obligations to families and family members, municipalities and fellow citizens, nation-states and compatriots, then biotic communities are sufficiently robust to engender analogous duties to fellow members—to soils and waters, plants and animals—and to the community as such. But what duties and obligations? If nature is inherently dynamic and violent natural events are normal and often beneficial, then our efforts to preserve or restore the ecological status quo ante—the way the world was before we human beings began to transform it—might be counterproductive. Callicott argues that anthropogenic disturbances of nature, per se, are neither unnatural nor environmentally unethical. What is wrong, rather, with most human environmental impacts is their scope and rate. The current rate of anthropogenic species extinction, for example, is thousands of times faster than the "background" rate that persisted for millions of years before human beings came on the scene. And while forests may suddenly be destroyed by localized events like volcano eruptions, wildfires, tornadoes, or hurricanes, anthropogenic deforestation is going on everywhere at once. The crucial consideration in morally evaluating anthropogenic change in nature, Callicott argues, is the ecological concept of "scale"—both temporal and spatial scale. We cannot, nor should we try, to simply leave nature alone. Rather we should try to limit the way we disturb nature, as we pursue our economic interests, to normal temporal and spatial scales.

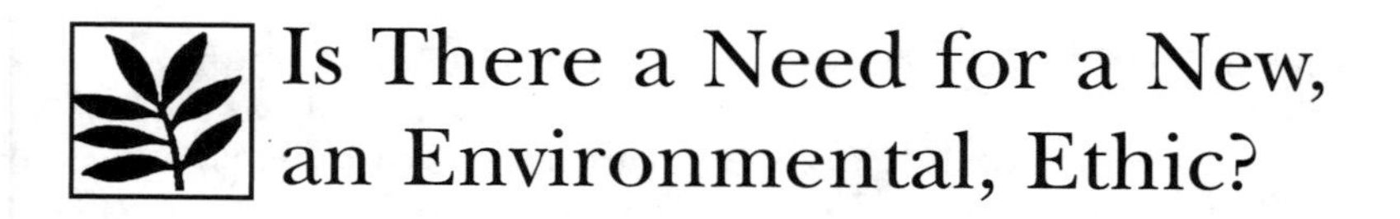

Is There a Need for a New, an Environmental, Ethic?

Richard Sylvan (Routley)

Richard Sylvan (formerly Routley) was a fellow with the Research School of Social Sciences at the Australian National University in Canberra. With Don Mannison and Michael McRobbie, he edited Environmental Philosophy.

1

It is increasingly said that civilization, Western civilization at least, stands in need of a new ethic (and derivatively of a new economics) setting out people's relations to the natural environment, in Leopold's words "an ethic dealing with man's relation to land and to the animals and plants which grow upon it."[1] It is not of course that old and prevailing ethics do not deal with man's relation to nature; they do, and on the prevailing view man is free to deal with nature as he pleases, i.e., his relations with nature, insofar at least as they do not affect others, are not subject to moral censure. Thus assertions such as "Crusoe ought not to be mutilating those trees" are significant and morally determinate but, inasmuch at least as Crusoe's actions do not interfere with others, they are false or do not hold—and trees are not, in a good sense, moral objects.[2] It is to this, to the values and evaluations of the prevailing ethics, that Leopold and others in fact take exception. Leopold regards as subject to moral criticism, as wrong, behavior that on prevailing views is morally permissible. But it is not, as Leopold seems to think, that such behavior is beyond the scope of the prevailing ethics and that an *extension* of traditional morality is required to cover such cases, to fill a moral void. If Leopold is right in his criticism of prevailing conduct what is required is a *change* in the ethics, in attitudes, values and evaluations. For as matters stand, as he himself explains, men do not feel morally ashamed if they interfere with a wilderness, if they maltreat the land, extract

This essay was originally published in *Proceedings of the XV World Congress of Philosophy*, No. 1. Varna, Bulgaria, 1973, pp. 205–210. Reprinted with permission of author.

from it whatever it will yield, and then move on; and such conduct is not taken to interfere with and does not rouse the moral indignation of others. "A farmer who clears the woods off a 75% slope, turns his cows into the clearing, and dumps its rainfall, rocks, and soil into the community creek, is still (if otherwise decent) a respected member of society."[3] Under what we shall call *an environmental ethic* such traditionally permissible conduct would be accounted morally wrong, and the farmer subject to proper moral criticism.

Let us grant such evaluations for the purpose of the argument. What is not so clear is that a *new* ethic is required even for such radical judgments. For one thing it is none too clear what is going to count as a new ethic, much as it is often unclear whether a new development in physics counts as a new physics or just as a modification or extension of the old. For, notoriously, ethics are not clearly articulated or at all well worked out, so that the application of identity criteria for ethics may remain obscure.[4] Furthermore we tend to cluster a family of ethical systems which do not differ on core or fundamental principles together as one ethic; e.g. the Christian ethic, which is an umbrella notion covering a cluster of differing and even competing systems. In fact then there are two other possibilities, apart from a new environmental ethic, which might cater for the evaluations, namely that of an extension or modification of the prevailing ethics or that of the development of principles that are already encompassed or latent within the prevailing ethic. The second possibility, that environmental evaluations can be incorporated within (and ecological problems solved within) the framework of prevailing Western ethics, is open because there isn't a single ethical system uniquely assumed in Western civilization: on many issues, and especially on controversial issues such as infanticide, women's rights, and drugs, there are competing sets of principles. Talk of a new ethic and prevailing ethics tends to suggest a sort of monolithic structure, a uniformity, that prevailing ethics, and even a single ethic, need not have.

Indeed Passmore has mapped out three important traditions in Western ethical views concerning man's relation to nature; a dominant tradition, the despotic position, with man as despot (or tyrant), and two lesser traditions, the stewardship position, with man as custodian, and the co-operative position with man as perfecter.[5] Nor are these the only traditions; primitivism is another, and both romanticism and mysticism have influenced Western views.

The dominant Western view is simply inconsistent with an environmental ethic; for according to it nature is the dominion of man and he is free to deal with it as he pleases (since—at least on the mainstream Stoic-Augustine view—it exists only for his sake), whereas on an environmental ethic man is not so free to do as he pleases. But it is not quite so obvious that an environmental ethic cannot be coupled with one of the lesser traditions. Part of the problem is that the lesser traditions are by no means adequately characterized anywhere, especially when the religious backdrop is removed, e.g. *who* is man steward for and responsible to? However both traditions are inconsistent with an environmental ethic because they imply policies of complete interference, whereas on an environmental ethic some worthwhile parts of the earth's surface should be preserved from substantial human interference, whether of the "improving" sort or not. Both traditions would in fact prefer to see the earth's land surfaces reshaped along the lines of the tame and comfortable north-European small farm and village landscape. According to the co-operative position man's proper role is to develop, cultivate and perfect nature—all nature eventually—by bringing out its potentialities, the test of perfection being primarily usefulness for human purposes; while on the stewardship view man's role, like that of a farm manager, is to make nature productive by his efforts though not by means that will deliberately degrade its resources. Although these positions both depart from the dominant position in a way which enables the incorporation of some evaluations of an environmental ethic, e.g. some of those concerning the irresponsible farmer, they do not go far enough: for in the present situation of expanding populations confined to finite natural areas, they will lead to, and enjoin, the perfecting, farming and utilizing of all natural areas. Indeed these lesser traditions lead to, what a thoroughgoing environmental ethic would reject, a principle of total use, implying that every natural area should be cultivated or otherwise used for human ends, "humanized."[6]

As the important Western traditions exclude an environmental ethic, it would appear that such an ethic, not primitive, mystical or romantic, would be new all right. The matter is not so straightforward; for the dominant ethic has been substantially qualified by the rider that one is not always entitled to do as one pleases where this physically interferes with others. Maybe some such proviso was implicit all along (despite evidence to the contrary), and it was simply assumed that doing what one pleased with natural items would not affect others (the non-interference assumption). Be this as it may, the *modified* dominant position appears, at least for many thinkers, to have supplanted the dominant position; and the modified position can undoubtedly go much further towards an environmental ethic. For example, the farmer's polluting of a community stream may be ruled immoral on the grounds that it physically interferes with others who use or would use the streams. Likewise business enterprises which destroy the natural environment for no satisfactory returns or which cause pollution deleterious to the health of future humans, can be criticized on the sort of welfare basis (e.g. that of Barkley and Seckler) that blends with the modified position; and so on.[7] The position may even serve to restrict the sort of family size one is entitled to have since in a finite situation excessive population levels will interfere with future people. Nonetheless neither the modified dominant position nor its Western variants, obtained by combining it with the lesser traditions, is adequate as an environmental ethic, as I shall try to show. A new ethic *is* wanted.

2

As we noticed (an) *ethic* is ambiguous, as between a specific ethical system, a *specific* ethic, and a more generic notion, a super ethic, under which specific ethics cluster.[8] An ethical system S is, near enough, a propositional system (i.e.

a structured set of propositions) or theory which includes (like individuals of a theory) a set of values and (like postulates of a theory) a set of general evaluative judgments concerning conduct, typically of what is obligatory, permissible and wrong, of what are rights, what is valued, and so forth. A general or lawlike proposition of a system is a principle; and certainly if systems S_1 and S_2 contain different principles, then they are different systems. It follows that any environmental ethic differs from the important traditional ethics outlined. Moreover if environmental ethics differ from Western ethical systems on some *core* principle embedded in Western systems, then these systems differ from the Western super ethic (assuming, what seems to be so, that it can be uniquely characterized)—in which case if an environmental ethic *is* needed then a new ethic is wanted. It suffices then to locate a core principle and to provide environmental counter examples to it.

It is commonly assumed that there are what amount to core principles of Western ethical systems, principles that will accordingly belong to the super ethic. The fairness principle inscribed in the Golden Rule provides one example. Directly relevant here, as a good stab at a core principle, is the commonly formulated liberal principle of the modified dominance position. A recent formulation runs as follows:

"The liberal philosophy of the Western world holds that one should be able to do what he wishes, providing (1) that he does not harm others and (2) that he is not likely to harm himself irreparably."[9]

Let us call this principle *basic (human) chauvinism*—because under it humans, or people, come first and everything else a bad last—though sometimes the principle is hailed as a *freedom* principle because it gives permission to perform a wide range of actions (including actions which mess up the environment and natural things) providing they do not harm others. In fact it tends to cunningly shift the onus of proof to others. It is worth remarking that *harming others* in the restriction is narrower than a restriction to the (usual) interests of others; it is not enough that it is in my interests, because I detest you, that you stop breathing; you are free to breathe, for the time being anyway, because it does not harm me. There remains a problem however as to exactly what counts as harm or interference. Moreover the width of the principle is so far obscure because "other" may be filled out in significantly different ways: it makes a difference to the extent, and privilege, of the chauvinism whether "other" expands to "other human"—which is too restrictive—or to "other person" or to "other sentient being"; and it makes a difference to the adequacy of the principle, and inversely to its economic applicability, to which class of others it is intended to apply, whether to future as well as to present others, whether to remote future others or only to non-discountable future others and whether to possible others. The latter would make the principle completely unworkable, and it is generally assumed that it applies at most to present and future others.

It is taken for granted in designing counter examples to basic chauvinist principles, that a semantical analysis of permissibility and obligation statements stretches out over ideal situations (which may be incomplete or even inconsistent), so that what is permissible holds in some ideal situation, what is obligatory in every ideal situation, and what is wrong is excluded in every ideal situation. But the main point to grasp for the counter examples that follow, is that ethical principles if correct are universal and are assessed over the class of ideal situations.

(i) The *last man* example. The last man (or person) surviving the collapse of the world system lays about him, eliminating, as far as he can, every living thing, animal or plant (but painlessly if you like, as at the best abattoirs). What he does is quite permissible according to basic chauvinism, but on environmental grounds what he does is wrong. Moreover one does not have to be committed to esoteric values to regard Mr. Last Man as behaving badly (the reason being perhaps that radical thinking and values have shifted in an environmental direction in advance of corresponding shifts in the formulation of fundamental evaluative principles).

(ii) The *last people* example. The last man example can be broadened to the last people example. We can assume that they know they are the last people, e.g. because they are aware that radiation effects have blocked any chance of reproduction. One considers the last people in order to rule out the possibility that what these people do harms or somehow physically interferes with later people. Otherwise one could as well consider science fiction cases where people arrive at a new planet and destroy its ecosystems, whether with good intentions such as perfecting the planet for their ends and making it more fruitful or, forgetting the lesser traditions, just for the hell of it.

Let us assume that the last people are very numerous. They humanely exterminate every wild animal and they eliminate the fish of the seas, they put all arable land under intensive cultivation, and all remaining forests disappear in favor of quarries or plantations, and so on. They may give various familiar reasons for this, e.g. they believe it is the way to salvation or to perfection, or they are simply satisfying reasonable needs, or even that it is needed to keep the last people employed or occupied so that they do not worry too much about their impending extinction. On an environmental ethic the last people have behaved badly; they have simplified and largely destroyed all the natural ecosystems, and with their demise the world will soon be an ugly and largely wrecked place. But this conduct may conform with the basic chauvinist principle, and as well with the principles enjoined by the lesser traditions. Indeed the main point of elaborating this example is because, as the last man example reveals, basic chauvinism may conflict with stewardship or co-operation principles. The conflict may be removed it seems by conjoining a further proviso to the basic principle, the effect (3) that he does not willfully destroy natural resources. But as the last people do not destroy resources willfully, but perhaps "for the best of reasons," the variant is still environmentally inadequate.

(iii) The *great entrepreneur* example. The last man example can be adjusted so as to not fall foul of clause (3). The last man is an industrialist; he runs a giant complex of automated factories and farms which he proceeds to extend. He produces automobiles among other things, from renewable and recyclable resources of course, only he dumps and recycles these shortly after manufacture and sale to a dummy buyer instead of putting them on the road for a short time as we do. Of course he has the best of reasons for his activity, e.g. he is increasing gross world product, or he is improving output to fulfill some plan, and he will be increasing his own and general welfare since he much prefers increased output and productivity. The entrepreneur's behavior is on the Western ethic quite permissible; indeed his conduct is commonly thought to be quite fine and may even meet Pareto optimality requirements given prevailing notions of being "better off."

Just as we can extend the last man example to a class of last people, so we can extend this example to the *industrial society* example: the society looks rather like ours.

(iv) The *vanishing species* example. Consider the blue whale, a mixed good on the economic picture. The blue whale is on the verge of extinction because of his qualities as a private good, as a source of valuable oil and meat. The catching and marketing of blue whales does not harm the whalers; it does not harm or physically interfere with others in any good sense, though it may upset them and they may be prepared to compensate the whalers if they desist; nor need whale hunting be willful destruction. (Slightly different examples which eliminate the hunting aspect of the blue whale example are provided by cases where a species is eliminated or threatened through destruction of its habitat by man's activity or the activities of animals he has introduced, e.g. many plains-dwelling Australian marsupials and the Arabian oryx.) The behavior of the whalers in eliminating this magnificent species of whale is accordingly quite permissible—at least according to basic chauvinism. But on an environmental ethic it is not. However, the free-market mechanism will not cease allocating whales to commercial uses, as a satisfactory environmental economics would; instead the market model will grind inexorably along the private demand curve until the blue whale population is no longer viable—if that point has not already been passed.[10]

In sum, the class of permissible actions that rebound on the environment is more narrowly circumscribed on an environmental ethic than it is in the Western super ethic. But aren't environmentalists going too far in claiming that these people, those of the examples and respected industrialists, fishermen and farmers are behaving, when engaging in environmentally degrading activities of the sort described, in a morally impermissible way? No, what these people do is to a greater or lesser extent evil, and hence in serious cases morally impermissible. For example, insofar as the killing or forced displacement of primitive peoples who stand in the way of an industrial development is morally indefensible and impermissible, so also is the slaughter of the last remaining blue whales for private profit. But how to reformulate basic chauvinism as a satisfactory freedom principle is a more difficult matter. A tentative, but none too adequate beginning might be made by extending (2) to include harm to or interference with others who would be so affected by the action in question were they placed in the environment and (3) to exclude speciecide. It may be preferable, in view of the way the freedom principle sets the onus of proof, simply to scrap it altogether, and instead to specify classes of rights and permissible conduct, as in a bill of rights.

3

A radical change in a theory sometimes forces changes in the meta-theory; e.g. a logic which rejects the Reference Theory in a thoroughgoing way requires a modification of the usual meta-theory which also accepts the Reference Theory and indeed which is tailored to cater only for logics which do conform. A somewhat similar phenomenon seems to occur in the case of a meta-ethic adequate for an environmental ethic. Quite apart from introducing several environmentally important notions, such as *conservation, pollution, growth* and *preservation,* for meta-ethical analysis, an environmental ethic compels re-examination and modified analyses of such characteristic actions as *natural right, ground* of right, and of the relations of obligation and permissibility to rights; it may well require re-assessment of traditional analyses of such notions as *value* and *right,* especially where these are based on chauvinist assumptions; and it forces the rejection of many of the more prominent meta-ethical positions. These points are illustrated by a very brief examination of accounts of *natural right* and then by a sketch of the species bias of some major positions.[11]

Hart accepts, subject to defeating conditions which are here irrelevant, the classical doctrine of natural rights according to which, among other things, "any adult human . . . capable of choice is at liberty to do (i.e. is under no obligation to abstain from) any action which is not one coercing or restraining or designed to injure other persons."[12] But this sufficient condition for a human natural right depends on accepting the very human chauvinist principle an environmental ethic rejects, since if a person has a natural right he has a right; so too the *definition* of a natural right adopted by classical theorists and accepted with minor qualifications by Hart presupposes the same defective principle. Accordingly an environmental ethic would have to amend the classical notion of a natural right, a far from straightforward matter now that human rights with respect to animals and the natural environment are, like those with respect to slaves not all that long ago, undergoing major re-evaluation.

An environmental ethic does not commit one to the view that natural objects such as trees have rights (though such a view is occasionally held, e.g. by pantheists. But pantheism is false since artefacts are not alive). For moral prohibitions forbidding certain actions with respect to an object do not award that object a correlative right. That it would be wrong to mutilate a given tree or piece of property does not entail that the tree or piece of property has a correlative right not to be mutilated (without seriously stretching the notion of a right). Environmental views can stick with mainstream theses according to which rights are coupled with corresponding responsibilities and so with bearing obligations, and with corresponding interests and concern; i.e. at least, whatever has a right also has responsibilities and therefore obligations, and whatever has a right has interests. Thus although any person may have a right by no means every living thing can (significantly) have rights, and arguably most sentient objects other than persons cannot have rights. But persons can relate morally, through obligations, prohibitions and so forth, to practically anything at all.

The species bias of certain ethical and economic positions which aim to make principles of conduct or reasonable economic behavior calculable is easily brought out. These positions typically employ a single criterion *p*, such as preference or happiness, as a *summum bonum;* characteristically each individual of some *base* class, almost always humans, but perhaps including future humans, is supposed to have an ordinal *p* ranking of the states in question (e.g. of affairs, of the economy); then some principle is supplied to determine a collective *p* ranking of these states in terms of individual *p* rankings, and what is best or ought to be done is determined either directly, as in act-utilitarianism under the Greatest Happiness principle, or indirectly, as in rule-utilitarianism, in terms of some optimization principle applied to the collective ranking. The species bias is transparent from the selection of the base class. And even if the base class is extended to embrace persons, or even some animals (at the cost, like that of including remotely future humans, of losing testability), the positions are open to familiar criticism, namely that the whole of the base class may be prejudiced in a way which leads to unjust principles. For example if every member of the base class detests dingoes, on the basis of mistaken data as to dingoes' behavior, then by the Pareto ranking test the collective ranking will rank states where dingoes are exterminated very highly, from which it will generally be concluded that dingoes ought to be exterminated (the evaluation of most Australian farmers anyway). Likewise it would just be a happy accident, it seems, if collective demand (horizontally summed from individual demand) for a state of the economy with blue whales as a mixed good, were to succeed in outweighing private whaling demands; for if no one in the base class happened to know that blue whales exist or cared a jot that they do then "rational" economic decision-making would do nothing to prevent their extinction. Whether the blue whale survives should not have to depend on what humans know or what they see on television. Human interests and preferences are far too parochial to provide a satisfactory basis for deciding on what is environmentally desirable.

These ethical and economic theories are not alone in their species chauvinism; much the same applies to most going meta-ethical theories which, unlike intuitionistic theories, try to offer some rationale for their basic principles. For instance, on social contract positions obligations are a matter of mutual agreements between individuals of the base class; on a social justice picture rights and obligations spring from the application of symmetrical fairness principles to members of the base class, usually a rather special class of persons, while on a Kantian position which has some vague obligations somehow arise from respect for members of the base class persons. In each case if members of the base class happen to be ill-disposed to items outside the base class then that is too bad for them: that is (rough) justice.

NOTES

1. Aldo Leopold, *A Sand Country Almanac with Essays on Conservation from Round River* (New York: Ballantine, 1966), p. 238.
2. A view occasionally tempered by the idea that trees house spirits.
3. Leopold, *Sand County*, p. 245.
4. To the consternation no doubt of Quineans. But the fact is that we can talk perfectly well about inchoate and fragmentary systems the identity of which may be indeterminate.
5. John Passmore, *Man's Responsibility for Nature: Ecological Problems and Western Traditions* (New York: Scribner's, 1974).
6. If "use" is extended, somewhat illicitly, to include use for preservation, this total use principle is rendered innocuous at least as regards its actual effects. Note that the total use principle is tied to the resource view of nature.
7. P. W. Barkley and D. W. Seckler, *Economic Growth and Environmental Decay: The Solution Becomes the Problem* (New York: Harcourt, Brace, Jovanovich, 1972).
8. A *meta-ethic* is, as usual, a theory about ethics, super ethics, their features and fundamental notions.
9. Barkley and Seckler, *Economic Growth and Environmental Decay*, p. 58. A related principle is that (modified) free enterprise can operate within similar limits.
10. The tragedy of the commons type reasons are well explained in Barkley and Seckler, *Economic Growth and Environmental Decay.*
11. Some of these points are developed by those protesting about human maltreatment of animals; see especially the essays collected in S. and R. Godlovitch and J. Harris, eds., *Animals, Men and Morals: An Enquiry into the Maltreatment of Non-humans* (New York: Grove Press, 1971).
12. H. L. A. Hart, "Are There any Natural Rights?" reprinted in A. Quinton, ed., *Political Philosophy* (London: Oxford University Press, 1967).

All Animals Are Equal[1]

Peter Singer

Peter Singer is professor of philosophy and director of the Centre for Human Bioethics at Monash University in Melbourne, Australia. He is the author of Animal Liberation: A New Ethics for Our Treatment of Animals *and* Practical Ethics.

In recent years a number of oppressed groups have campaigned vigorously for equality. The classic instance is the Black Liberation movement, which demands an end to the prejudice and discrimination that has made blacks second-class citizens. The immediate appeal of the black liberation movement and its initial, if limited success made it a model for other oppressed groups to follow. We became familiar with liberation movements for Spanish-Americans, gay people, and a variety of other minorities. When a majority group—women—began their campaign, some thought we had come to the end of the road. Discrimination on the basis of sex, it has been said, is the last universally accepted form of discrimination, practiced without secrecy or pretense even in those liberal circles that have long prided themselves on their freedom from prejudice against racial minorities.

One should always be wary of talking of "the last remaining form of discrimination." If we have learnt anything from the liberation movements, we should have learnt how difficult it is to be aware of latent prejudice in our attitudes to particular groups until this prejudice is forcefully pointed out.

A liberation movement demands an expansion of our moral horizons and an extension or reinterpretation of the basic moral principle of equality. Practices that were previously regarded as natural and inevitable come to be seen as the result of an unjustifiable prejudice. Who can say with confidence that all his or her attitudes and practices are beyond criticism? If we wish to avoid being numbered amongst the oppressors, we must be prepared to re-think even our most fundamental attitudes. We need to consider them from the point of view of those most disadvantaged by our attitudes, and the practices that follow from these attitudes. If we can make this unaccustomed mental switch we may discover a pattern in our attitudes and practices that consistently operates so as to benefit one group—usually the one to which we ourselves

This essay originally appeared in *Philosophic Exchange,* Vol. 1, No. 5 (Summer, 1974), 243–257. Reprinted with permission.

belong—at the expense of another. In this way we may come to see that there is a case for a new liberation movement. My aim is to advocate that we make this mental switch in respect of our attitudes and practices towards a very large group of beings: members of species other than our own—or, as we popularly though misleadingly call them, animals. In other words, I am urging that we extend to other species the basic principle of equality that most of us recognise should be extended to all members of our own species.

All this may sound a little far-fetched, more like a parody of other liberation movements than a serious objective. In fact, in the past the idea of "The Rights of Animals" really has been used to parody the case for women's rights. When Mary Wollstonecroft, a forerunner of later feminists, published her *Vindication of the Rights of Women* in 1792, her ideas were widely regarded as absurd, and they were satirized in an anonymous publication entitled *A Vindication of the Rights of Brutes*. The author of this satire (actually Thomas Taylor, a distinguished Cambridge philosopher) tried to refute Wollstonecroft's reasonings by showing that they could be carried one stage further. If sound when applied to women, why should the arguments not be applied to dogs, cats and horses? They seemed to hold equally well for these "brutes"; yet to hold that brutes had rights was manifestly absurd; therefore the reasoning by which this conclusion had been reached must be unsound, and if unsound when applied to brutes, it must also be unsound when applied to women, since the very same arguments had been used in each case.

One way in which we might reply to this argument is by saying that the case for equality between men and women cannot validly extended to non-human animals. Women have a right to vote, for instance, because they are just as capable of making rational decisions as men are; dogs, on the other hand, are incapable of understanding the significance of voting, so they cannot have the right to vote. There are many other obvious ways in which men and women resemble each other closely, while humans and other animals differ greatly. So, it might be said, men and women are similar beings, and should have equal rights, while humans and non-humans are different and should not have equal rights.

The thought behind this reply to Taylor's analogy is correct up to a point, but it does not go far enough. There *are* important differences between humans and other animals, and these differences must give rise to *some* differences in the rights that each have. Recognizing this obvious fact, however, is no barrier to the case for extending the basic principle of equality to non-human animals. The differences that exist between men and women are equally undeniable, and the supporters of Women's Liberation are aware that these differences may give rise to different rights. Many feminists hold that women have the right to an abortion on request. It does not follow that since these same people are campaigning for equality between men and women they must support the right of men to have abortions too. Since a man cannot have an abortion, it is meaningless to talk of his right to have one. Since a pig can't vote, it is meaningless to talk of its right to vote. There is no reason why either Women's Liberation or Animal Liberation should get involved in such nonsense. The extension of the basic principle of equality from one group to another does not imply that we must treat both groups in exactly the same way, or grant exactly the same rights to both groups. Whether we should do so will depend on the nature of the members of the two groups. The basic principle of equality, I shall argue, is equality of consideration; and equal consideration for different beings may lead to different treatment and different rights.

So there is a different way of replying to Taylor's attempt to parody Wollstonecroft's arguments, a way which does not deny the differences between humans and non-humans, but goes more deeply into the question of equality, and concludes by finding nothing absurd in the idea that the basic principle of equality applies to so-called "brutes". I believe that we reach this conclusion if we examine the basis on which our opposition to discrimination on grounds of race or sex ultimately rests. We will then see that we would be on shaky ground if we were to demand equality for blacks, women, and other groups of oppressed humans while denying equal consideration to non-humans.

When we say that all human beings, whatever their race, creed or sex, are equal, what is it that we are asserting? Those who wish to defend a hierarchical, inegalitarian society have often pointed out that by whatever test we choose, it simply is not true that all humans are equal. Like it or not, we must face the fact that humans come in different shapes and sizes; they come with differing moral capacities, differing intellectual abilities, differing amounts of benevolent feeling and sensitivity to the needs of others, differing abilities to communicate effectively, and differing capacities to experience pleasure and pain. In short, if the demand for equality were based on the actual equality of all human beings, we would have to stop demanding equality. It would be an unjustifiable demand.

Still, one might cling to the view that the demand for equality among human beings is based on the actual equality of the different races and sexes. Although humans differ as individuals in various ways, there are no differences between the races and sexes *as such*. From the mere fact that a person is black, or a woman, we cannot infer anything else about that person. This, it may be said, is what is wrong with racism and sexism. The white racist claims that whites are superior to blacks, but this is false—although there are differences between individuals, some blacks are superior to some whites in all of the capacities and abilities that could conceivably be relevant. The opponent of sexism would say the same: a person's sex is no guide to his or her abilities, and this is why it is unjustifiable to discriminate on the basis of sex.

This is a possible line of objection to racial and sexual discrimination. It is not, however, the way that someone really concerned about equality would choose, because taking this line could, in some circumstances, force one to accept a most inegalitarian society. The fact that humans differ as individuals, rather than as races or sexes, is a valid reply to someone who defends a hierarchical society like, say, South Africa, in which all whites are superior in status to all blacks. The existence of individual variations that cut across the lines of race or sex, however, provides us with no defence at all against a more sophisticated opponent of equality, one who proposes that, say, the interests of those with I.Q. ratings above 100 be preferred to the interests of those I.Q.s below 100. Would a hierarchical society of this sort really be so much better than one based on race or sex? I think not. But if we tie the moral principle of equality to the factual equality of the different races or sexes, taken as a whole, our opposition to racism and sexism does not provide us with any basis for objecting to this kind of inegalitarianism.

There is a second important reason why we ought not to base our opposition to racism and sexism on any kind of factual equality, even the limited kind which asserts that variations in capacities and abilities are spread evenly between the different races and sexes: we can have no absolute guarantee that these abilities and capacities really are distributed evenly, without regard to race or sex, among human beings. So far as actual abilities are concerned, there do seem to be certain measurable differences between both races and sexes. These differences do not, of course, appear in each case, but only when averages are taken. More important still, we do not yet know how much of these differences is really due to the different genetic endowments of the various races and sexes, and how much is due to environmental differences that are the result of past and continuing discrimination. Perhaps all of the important differences will eventually prove to be environmental rather than genetic. Anyone opposed to racism and sexism will certainly hope that this will be so, for it will make the task of ending discrimination a lot easier; nevertheless it would be dangerous to rest the case against racism and sexism on the belief that all significant differences are environmental in origin. The opponent of, say, racism who takes this line will be unable to avoid conceding that if differences in ability did after all prove to have some genetic connection with race, racism would in some way be defensible.

It would be folly for the opponent of racism to stake his whole case on a dogmatic commitment to one particular outcome of a difficult scientific issue which is still a long way from being settled. While attempts to prove that differences in certain selected abilities between races and sexes are primarily genetic in origin have certainly not been conclusive, the same must be said of attempts to prove that these differences are largely the result of environment. At this stage of the investigation we cannot be certain which view is correct, however much we may hope it is the latter.

Fortunately, there is no need to pin the case for equality to one particular outcome of this scientific investigation. The appropriate response to those who claim to have found evidence of genetically-based differences in ability between the races or sexes is not to stick to the belief that the genetic explanation must be wrong, whatever evidence to the contrary may turn up: instead we should make it quite clear that the claim to equality does not depend on intelligence, moral capacity, physical strength, or similar matters of fact. Equality is a moral ideal, not a simple assertion of fact. There is no logically compelling reason for assuming that a factual difference in ability between two people justifies any difference in the amount of consideration we give to satisfying their needs and interests. The principle of the equality of human beings is not a description of an alleged actual equality among humans: it is a prescription of how we should treat humans.

Jeremy Bentham incorporated the essential basis of moral equality into his utilitarian system of ethics in the formula: "Each to count for one and none for more than one." In other words, the interests of every being affected by an action are to be taken into account and given the same weight as the like interests of any other being. A later utilitarian, Henry Sidgwick, put the point in this way: "The good of any one individual is of no more importance, from the point of view (if I may say so) of the Universe, than the good of any other."[2] More recently, the leading figures in contemporary moral philosophy have shown a great deal of agreement in specifying as a fundamental presupposition of their moral theories some similar requirement which operates so as to give everyone's interests equal consideration—although they cannot agree on how this requirement is best formulated.[3]

It is an implication of this principle of equality that our concern for others ought not to depend on what they are like, or what abilities they possess—although precisely what this concern requires us to do may vary according to the characteristics of those affected by what we do. It is on this basis that the case against racism and the case against sexism must both ultimately rest; and it is in accordance with this principle that speciesism is also to be condemned. If possessing a higher degree of intelligence does not entitle one human to use another for his own ends, how can it entitle humans to exploit non-humans?

Many philosophers have proposed the principle of equal consideration of interests, in some form or other, as a basic moral principle; but, as we shall see in more detail shortly, not many of them have recognised that this principle applies to members of other species as well as to our own. Bentham was one of the few who did realize this. In a forward-looking passage, written at a time when black slaves in the British dominions were still being treated much as we now treat non-human animals, Bentham wrote:

> The day *may* come when the rest of the animal creation may acquire those rights which never could have been witholden from them but by the hand of tyranny. The French have already discovered that the blackness of the skin is no reason why a human being should be abandoned without redress to the caprice of a tormentor. It may one day come to be recognised that the number of the legs, the villosity of the skin, or the termination of the *os sacrum,* are reasons equally insufficient for abandoning a sensitive being to the same fate. What else is it that should trace the insuperable line? Is it the faculty of reason, or perhaps the faculty of discourse? But a full-grown horse or dog is beyond comparison a more rational, as well as a more conversable animal, than an infant of a day, or a week, or even a month, old. But suppose they were otherwise, what would it avail? The question is not, Can they reason? nor Can they *talk*? but, *Can they suffer*?[4]

In this passage Bentham points to the capacity for suffering as the vital characteristic that gives a being the right to equal consideration. The capacity for suffering—or more strictly, for suffering and/or enjoyment or happiness—

is not just another characteristic like the capacity for language, or for higher mathematics. Bentham is not saying that those who try to mark "the insuperable line" that determines whether the interests of a being should be considered happen to have selected the wrong characteristic. The capacity for suffering and enjoying things is a pre-requisite for having interests at all, a condition that must be satisfied before we can speak of interests in any meaningful way. It would be nonsense to say that it was not in the interests of a stone to be kicked along the road by a schoolboy. A stone does not have interests because it cannot suffer. Nothing that we can do to it could possibly make any difference to its welfare. A mouse, on the other hand, does have an interest in not being tormented, because it will suffer if it is.

If a being suffers, there can be no moral justification for refusing to take that suffering into consideration. No matter what the nature of the being, the principle of equality requires that its suffering be counted equally with the like suffering—in so far as rough comparisons can be made—of any other being. If a being is not capable of suffering, or of experiencing enjoyment or happiness, there is nothing to be taken into account. This is why the limit of sentience (using the term as a convenient, if not strictly accurate, shorthand for the capacity to suffer or experience enjoyment or happiness) is the only defensible boundary of concern for the interests of others. To mark this boundary by some characteristic like intelligence or rationality would be to mark it in an arbitrary way. Why not choose some other characteristic, like skin color?

The racist violates the principle of equality by giving greater weight to the interests of members of his own race, when there is a clash between their interests and the interests of those of another race. Similarly the speciesist allows the interests of his own species to override the greater interests of members of other species.[5] The pattern is the same in each case. Most human beings are speciesists. I shall now very briefly describe some of the practices that show this.

For the great majority of human beings, especially in urban, industrialized societies, the most direct form of contact with members of other species is at meal-times: we eat them. In doing so we treat them purely as means to our ends. We regard their life and well-being as subordinate to our taste for a particular kind of dish. I say "taste" deliberately—this is purely a matter of pleasing our palate. There can be no defense of eating flesh in terms of satisfying nutritional needs, since it has been established beyond doubt that we could satisfy our need for protein and other essential nutrients far more efficiently with a diet that replaced animal flesh by soy beans, or products derived from soy beans, and other high-protein vegetable products.[6]

It is not merely the act of killing that indicates what we are ready to do to other species in order to gratify our tastes. The suffering we inflict on the animals while they are alive is perhaps an even clearer indication of our speciesism than the fact that we are prepared to kill them.[7] In order to have meat on the table at a price that people can afford, our society tolerates methods of meat production that confine sentient animals in cramped, unsuitable conditions for the entire durations of their lives. Animals are treated like machines that convert fodder into flesh, and any innovation that results in a higher "conversion ratio" is liable to be adopted. As one authority on the subject has said, "cruelty is acknowledged only when profitability ceases."[8] So hens are crowded four or five to a cage with a floor area of twenty inches by eighteen inches, or around the size of a single page of the *New York Times*. The cages have wire floors, since this reduces cleaning costs, though wire is unsuitable for the hens' feet; the floors slope, since this makes the eggs roll down for easy collection, although this makes it difficult for the hens to rest comfortably. In these conditions all the birds' natural instincts are thwarted: they cannot stretch their wings fully, walk freely, dust-bathe, scratch the ground, or build a nest. Although they have never known other conditions, observers have noticed that the birds vainly try to perform these actions. Frustrated at their inability to do so, they often develop what farmers call "vices," and peck each other to death. To prevent this, the beaks of young birds are often cut off.

This kind of treatment is not limited to poultry. Pigs are now also being reared in cages inside sheds. These animals are comparable to dogs in intelligence, and need a varied, stimulating environment if they are not to suffer from stress and boredom. Anyone who kept a dog in the way in which pigs are frequently kept would be liable to prosecution, in England at least, but because our interest in exploiting pigs is greater than our interest in exploiting dogs, we object to cruelty to dogs while consuming the produce of cruelty to pigs. Of the other animals, the condition of veal calves is perhaps worst of all, since these animals are so closely confined that they cannot even turn around or get up and lie down freely. In this way they do not develop unpalatable muscle. They are also made anaemic and kept short of roughage, to keep their flesh pale, since white veal fetches a higher price; as a result they develop a craving for iron and roughage, and have been observed to gnaw wood off the sides of their stalls, and lick greedily at any rusty hinge that is within reach.

Since, as I have said, none of these practices cater for anything more than our pleasures of taste, our practice of rearing and killing other animals in order to eat them is a clear instance of the sacrifice of the most important interests of other beings in order to satisfy trivial interests of our own. To avoid speciesism we must stop this practice, and each of us has a moral obligation to cease supporting the practice. Our custom is all the support that the meat-industry needs. The decision to cease giving it that support may be difficult, but it is no more difficult than it would have been for a white Southerner to go against the traditions of his society and free his slaves; if we do not change our dietary habits, how can we censure those slaveholders who would not change their own way of living?

The same form of discrimination may be observed in the widespread practice of experimenting on other species in order to see if certain substances are safe for human beings, or to test some psychological theory about the effect of severe punishment on learning, or to try out various new compounds just in case something turns up. People sometimes think that all this experimentation is for vital medical purposes, and so will reduce suffering overall. This comfortable belief is very wide of the mark. Drug companies test new shampoos and cosmetics that they are intending to put on the market by dropping them into the eyes of rabbits, held open by metal clips, in order to observe what damage results. Food additives, like artificial colorings and preservatives, are tested by what is known as the "LD_{50}"—a test designed to find the level of consumption at which 50% of a group of animals will die. In the process, nearly all of the animals are made very sick before some finally die, and others pull through. If the substance is relatively harmless, as it often is, huge doses have to be force-fed to the animals, until in some cases sheer volume or concentration of the substance causes death.

Much of this pointless cruelty goes on in the universities. In many areas of science, non-human animals are regarded as an item of laboratory equipment, to be used and expended as desired. In psychology laboratories experimenters devise endless variations and repetitions of experiments that were of little value in the first place. To quote just one example, from the experimenter's own account in a psychology journal: at the University of Pennsylvania, Perrin S. Cohen hung six dogs in hammocks with electrodes taped to their hind feet. Electric shock of varying intensity was then administered through the electrodes. If the dog learnt to press its head against a panel on the left, the shock was turned off, but otherwise it remained on indefinitely. Three of the dogs, however, were required to wait periods varying from 2 to 7 seconds while being shocked before making the response that turned off the current. If they failed to wait, they received further shocks. Each dog was given from 26 to 46 "sessions" in the hammock, each session consisting of 80 "trials" or shocks, administered at intervals of one minute. The experimenter reported that the dogs, who were unable to move in the hammock, barked or bobbed their heads when the current was applied. The reported findings of the experiment were that there was a delay in the dogs' responses that increased proportionately to the time the dogs were required to endure the shock, but a gradual increase in the intensity of the shock had no systematic effect in the timing of the response. The experiment was funded by the National Institutes of Health, and the United States Public Health Service.[9]

In this example, and countless cases like it, the possible benefits to mankind are either non-existent or fantastically remote; while the certain losses to members of other species are very real. This is, again, a clear indication of speciesism.

In the past, argument about vivisection has often missed this point, because it has been put in absolutist terms: would the abolitionist be prepared to let thousands die if they could be saved by experimenting on a single animal? The way to reply to this purely hypothetical question is to pose another: would the experimenter be prepared to perform his experiment on an orphaned human infant, if that were the only way to save many lives? (I say "orphan" to avoid the complication of parental feelings, although in doing so I am being overfair to the experimenter, since the non-human subjects of experiments are not orphans.) If the experimenter is not prepared to use an orphaned human infant, then his readiness to use non-humans is simple discrimination, since adult apes, cats, mice and other mammals are more aware of what is happening to them, more self-directing and, so far as we can tell, at least as sensitive to pain, as any human infant. There seems to be no relevant characteristic that human infants possess that adult mammals do not have to the same or higher degree. (Someone might try to argue that what makes it wrong to experiment on a human infant is that the infant will, in time and if left alone, develop into more than the non-human, but one would then, to be consistent, have to oppose abortion, since the fetus has the same potential as the infant—indeed, even contraception and abstinence might be wrong on this ground, since the egg and sperm, considered jointly, also have the same potential. In any case, this argument still gives us no reason for selecting a non-human, rather than a human with severe and irreversible brain damage, as the subject for our experiments.)

The experimenter, then, shows a bias in favor of his own species whenever he carries out an experiment on a non-human for a purpose that he would not think justified him in using a human being at an equal or lower level of sentience, awareness, ability to be self-directing, etc. No one familiar with the kind of results yielded by most experiments on animals can have the slightest doubt that if this bias were eliminated the number of experiments performed would be a minute fraction of the number performed today.

Experimenting on animals, and eating their flesh, are perhaps the two major forms of speciesism in our society. By comparison, the third and last form of speciesism is so minor as to be insignificant, but it is perhaps of some special interest to those for whom this paper was written. I am referring to speciesism in contemporary philosophy.

Philosophy ought to question the basic assumptions of the age. Thinking through, critically and carefully, what most people take for granted is, I believe, the chief task of philosophy, and it is this task that makes philosophy a worthwhile activity. Regrettably, philosophy does not always live up to its historic role. Philosophers are human beings and they are subject to all the preconceptions of the society to which they belong. Sometimes they succeed in breaking free of the prevailing ideology: more often they become its most sophisticated defenders. So, in this case, philosophy as practiced in the universities today does not challenge anyone's preconceptions about our relations with other species. By their writings, those philosophers who tackle problems that touch upon the issue reveal that they make the same unquestioned assumptions as most other humans, and what they say tends to confirm the reader in his or her comfortable speciesist habits.

I could illustrate this claim by referring to the writings of philosophers in various fields—for instance, the attempts that have been made by those interested in rights to draw the boundary of the sphere of rights so that it runs parallel to the biological boundaries of the species *homo sapiens*, including infants and even mental defectives, but excluding those other beings of equal or greater capacity who are so useful to us at mealtimes and in our laboratories. I think it would be a more appropriate conclusion to this paper, however, if I concentrated on the problem with which we have been centrally concerned, the problem of equality.

It is significant that the problem of equality, in moral and political philosophy, is invariably formulated in terms of human equality. The effect of this is that the question of the equality of other animals does not confront the philosopher, or student, as an issue in itself—and this is already an indication of the failure of philosophy to challenge accepted beliefs. Still, philosophers have found it difficult to discuss the issue of human equality without raising, in a paragraph or two, the question of the status of other animals. The reason for this, which should be apparent from what I have said already, is that if humans are to be regarded as equal to one another, we need some sense of "equal" that does not require any actual, descriptive equality of capacities, talents or other qualities. If equality is to be related to any actual characteristics of humans, these characteristics must be some lowest common denominator, pitched so low that no human lacks them—but then the philosopher comes up against the catch that any such set of characteristics which covers *all* humans will not be possessed *only by humans.* In other words, it turns out that in the only sense in which we can truly say, as an assertion of fact, that all humans are equal, at least some members of other species are also equal—equal, that is, to each other and to humans. If, on the other hand, we regard the statement "All humans are equal" in some non-factual way, perhaps as a prescription, then, as I have already argued, it is even more difficult to exclude non-humans from the sphere of equality.

This result is not what the egalitarian philosopher originally intended to assert. Instead of accepting the radical outcome to which their own reasonings naturally point, however, most philosophers try to reconcile their beliefs in human equality and animal inequality by arguments that can only be described as devious.

As a first example, I take William Frankena's well-known article "The Concept of Social Justice."[10] Frankena opposes the idea of basing justice on merit, because he sees that this could lead to highly inegalitarian results. Instead he proposes the principle that:

> . . . all men are to be treated as equals, not because they are equal, in any respect but simply because they are human. They are human because they have emotions and desires, and are able to think, and hence are capable of enjoying a good life in a sense in which other animals are not.

But what is this capacity to enjoy the good life which all humans have, but no other animals? Other animals have emotions and desires, and appear to be capable of enjoying a good life. We may doubt that they can think—although the behavior of some apes, dolphins and even dogs suggest that some of them can—but what is the relevance of thinking? Frankena goes on to admit that by "the good life" he means "not so much the morally good life as the happy or satisfactory life," so thought would appear to be unnecessary for enjoying the good life; in fact to emphasise the need for thought would make difficulties for the egalitarian since only some people are capable of leading intellectually satisfying lives, or morally good lives. This makes it difficult to see what Frankena's principle of equality has to do with simply being *human*. Surely every sentient being is capable of leading a life that is happier or less miserable than some alternative life, and hence has a claim to be taken into account. In this respect the distinction between humans and non-humans is not a sharp division, but rather a continuum along which we move gradually, and with overlaps between the species, from simple capacities for enjoyment and satisfaction, or pain and suffering, to more complex ones.

Faced with a situation in which they see a need for some basis for the moral gulf that is commonly thought to separate humans and animals, but can find no concrete difference that will do the job without undermining the equality of humans, philosophers tend to waffle. They resort to high-sounding phrases like "the intrinsic dignity of the human individual."[11] They talk of the "intrinsic worth of all men" as if men (humans?) had some worth that other beings did not,[12] or they say that humans, and only humans, are "ends in themselves" while "everything other than a person can only have value for a person."[13]

This idea of a distinctive human dignity and worth has a long history; it can be traced back directly to the Renaissance humanists, for instance to Pico della Mirandola's *Oration on the Dignity of Man*. Pico and other humanists based their estimate of human dignity on the idea that man possessed the central, pivotal position in the "Great Chain of Being" the led from the lowliest forms of matter to God himself; this view of the universe, in turn, goes back to both classical and Judeo-Christian doctrines. Contemporary philosophers have cast off these metaphysical and religious shackles and freely invoke the dignity of mankind without needing to justify the idea at all. Why should we not attribute "intrinsic dignity" or "intrinsic worth" to ourselves? Fellow-humans are unlikely to reject the accolades we so generously bestow on them, and those to whom we deny the honor are unable to object. Indeed, when one thinks only of humans, it can be very liberal, very progressive, to talk of the dignity of all human beings. In so doing, we implicitly condemn slavery, racism, and other violations of human rights. We admit that we ourselves are in some fundamental sense on a par with the poorest, most ignorant members of our own species. It is only when we think of humans as no more than a small sub-group of all the beings that inhabit our planet that we may realize that in elevating our own species we are at the same time lowering the relative status of all other species.

The truth is that the appeal to the intrinsic dignity of human beings appears to solve the egalitarian's problems only as long as it goes unchallenged. Once we ask *why* it should be that all humans—including infants, mental defectives, psychopaths, Hitler, Stalin and the rest—have some kind of dignity or worth that no elephant, pig or chimpanzee can ever achieve, we see that this question is as difficult to answer as our original request for some relevant fact that justifies the inequality of humans and other animals. In fact, these two questions are really one: talk of intrinsic dignity or moral worth only takes the problem back one step, because any satisfactory defence of the claim that all and only humans have intrinsic dignity would need to refer to some relevant capacities or characteristics that all and only humans possess. Philosophers frequently introduce ideas of dignity, respect and worth at the point at which other reasons appear to be lacking, but this is hardly good enough. Fine phrases are the last resource of those who have run out of arguments.

In case there are those who still think it may be possible to find some relevant characteristic that distinguishes all humans from all members of other species, I shall refer again, before I conclude, to the existence of some humans who quite clearly are below the level of awareness, self-consciousness, intelligence, and sentience, of many non-humans. I am thinking of humans with severe and irreparable brain damage, and also of infant humans. To avoid the complication of the relevance of a being's potential, however, I shall henceforth concentrate on permanently retarded humans.

Philosophers who set out to find a characteristic that will distinguish humans from other animals rarely take the course of abandoning these groups of humans by lumping them in with the other animals. It is easy to see why they do not. To take this line without re-thinking our attitudes to other animals would entail that we have the right to perform painful experiments on retarded humans for trivial reasons; similarly it would follow that we had the right to rear and kill these humans for food. To most philosophers these consequences are as unacceptable as the view that we should stop treating non-humans in this way.

Of course, when discussing the problem of equality it is possible to ignore the problem of mental defectives, or brush it aside as if somehow insignificant.[14] This is the easiest way out. What else remains? My final example of speciesism in contemporary philosophy has been selected to show what happens when a writer is prepared to face the question of human equality and animal inequality without ignoring the existence of mental defectives, and without resorting to obscurantist mumbo-jumbo. Stanley Benn's clear and honest article "Egalitarianism and Equal Consideration of Interests"[15] fits this description.

Benn, after noting the usual "evident human inequalities" argues, correctly I think, for equality of consideration as the only possible basis for egalitarianism. Yet Benn, like other writers, is thinking only of "equal consideration of human interests." Benn is quite open in his defence of this restriction of equal consideration:

> . . . not to possess human shape *is* a disqualifying condition. However faithful or intelligent a dog may be, it would be a monstrous sentimentality to attribute to him interests that could be weighed in an equal balance with those of human beings . . . if, for instance, one had to decide between feeding a hungry baby or a hungry dog, anyone who chose the dog would generally be reckoned morally defective, unable to recognize a fundamental inequality of claims.

> This is what distinguishes our attitude to animals from our attitude to imbeciles. It would be odd to say that we ought to respect equally the dignity or personality of the imbecile and of the rational man . . . but there is nothing odd about saying that we should respect their interests equally, that is, that we should give to the interests of each the same serious consideration as claims to considerations necessary for some standard of well-being that we can recognize and endorse.

Benn's statement of the basis of the consideration we should have for imbeciles seems to me correct, but why should there be any fundamental inequality of claims between a dog and a human imbecile? Benn sees that if equal consideration depended on rationality, no reason could be given against using imbeciles for research purposes, as we now use dogs and guinea pigs. This will not do: "But of course we do distinguish imbeciles from animals in this regard," he says. That the common distinction is justifiable is something Benn does not question; his problem is how it is to be justified. The answer he gives is this:

> . . . we respect the interests of men and give them priority over dogs not *insofar* as they are rational, but because rationality is the human norm. We say it is *unfair* to exploit the deficiencies of the imbecile who falls short of the norm, just as it would be unfair, and not just ordinarily dishonest, to steal from a blind man. If we do not think in this way about dogs, it is because we do not see the irrationality of the dog as a deficiency or a handicap, but as normal for the species. The characteristics, therefore, that distinguish the normal man from the normal dog make it intelligible for us to talk of other men having interests and capacities, and therefore claims, of precisely the same kind as we make on our own behalf. But although these characteristics may provide the point of the distinction between men and other species, they are not in fact the qualifying conditions for membership, or the distinguishing criteria of the class of morally considerable persons; and this is precisely because a man does not become a member of a different species, with its own standards of normality, by reason of not possessing these characteristics.

The final sentence of this passage gives the argument away. An imbecile, Benn concedes, may have no characteristics superior to those of a dog; nevertheless this does not make the imbecile a member of "a different species" as the dog is. *Therefore* it would be "unfair" to use the imbecile for medical research as we use the dog. But why? That the imbecile is not rational is just the way things have worked out, and the same is true of the dog—neither is any more responsible for their mental level. If it is unfair to take advantage of an isolated defect, why is it fair to take advantage of a more general limitation? I find it hard to see anything in this argument except a defence of preferring the interests of members of our own species because they are members of our own species. To those who think there might be more to it, I suggest the following mental exercise. Assume that it has been proven that there is a difference in the average, or normal, intelligence quotient for two different races, say whites and blacks. Then substitute the term "white" for every occurrence of "men" and "black" for every occurrence of "dog" in the passage quoted; and substitute "high I.Q." for "rationality" and when Benn talks of "imbeciles" replace this term by "dumb whites"—that is, whites who fall well below the normal white I.Q. score. Finally, change "species" to "race". Now re-read the passage. It has become a defence of a rigid, no-exceptions division between whites and blacks, based on I.Q. scores, *not withstanding an admitted overlap* between whites and blacks in this respect. The revised passage is, of course, outrageous, and this is not only because we have made fictitious assumptions in our substitutions. The point is that in the original passage Benn was defending a rigid division in the amount of consideration due to members of different species, despite admitted cases of overlap. If the original did not, at first reading, strike us as being as outrageous as the revised version does, this is largely because although we are not racists ourselves, most of us are speciesists. Like the other articles, Benn's stands as a warning of the ease with which the best minds can fall victim to a prevailing ideology.

NOTES

1. Passages of this article appeared in a review of *Animals, Men and Morals*, edited by S. and R. Godlovitch and J. Harris (Gollancz and Taplinger, London 1972) in *The New York Review of Books*, April 5, 1973. The whole direction of my thinking on this subject I owe to talks with a number of friends in Oxford in 1970–71, especially Richard Keshen, Stanley Godlovitch, and, above all, Roslind Godlovitch.
2. *The Methods of Ethics* (7th Ed.) p. 382.
3. For example, R.M. Hare, *Freedom and Reason* (Oxford, 1963) and J. Rawls, *A Theory of Justice* (Harvard, 1972); for a brief account of the essential agreement on this issue between these and other positions, see R.M. Hare, "Rules of War and Moral Reasoning," *Philosophy and Public Affairs*, vol. 1, no. 2 (1972).
4. *Introduction to the Principles of Morals and Legislation*, ch. XVII.
5. I owe the term "speciesism" to Dr. Richard Ryder.
6. In order to produce 1 lb. of protein in the form of beef or veal, we must feed 21 lbs. of protein to the animal. Other forms of livestock are slightly less inefficient, but the average ratio in the U.S. is still 1:8. It has been estimated that the amount of protein lost to humans in this way is equivalent to 90% of the annual world protein deficit. For a brief account, see Frances Moore Lappe, *Diet for a Small Planet* (Friends of The Earth/Ballantine, New York 1971) pp. 4–11.
7. Although one might think that killing a being is obviously the ultimate wrong one can do to it, I think that the infliction of suffering is a clearer indication of speciesism because it might be argued that at least part of what is wrong with killing a human is that most humans are conscious of their existence over time, and have desires and purposes that extend into the future—see, for instance, M. Tooley, "Abortion and Infanticide," *Philosophy and Public Affairs*, vol. 2, no. 1 (1972). Of course, if one took this view one would have to hold—as Tooley does—that killing a human infant or mental defective is not in itself wrong, and is less serious than killing certain higher mammals that probably do have a sense of their own existence over time.
8. Ruth Harrison, *Animal Machines* (Stuart, London, 1964). This book provides an eye-opening account of intensive farming methods for those unfamiliar with the subject.
9. *Journal of the Experimental Analysis of Behavior*, vol. 13, no. 1 (1970). Any recent volume of this journal, or of other journals in the field, like the *Journal of Compara-*

tive and Physiological Psychology, will contain reports of equally cruel and trivial experiments. For a fuller account, see Richard Ryder, "Experiments on Animals" in *Animals, Men and Morals.*

10. In R. Brandt (ed.) *Social Justice* (Prentice Hall, Englewood Cliffs, 1962); the passage quoted appears on p. 19.
11. Frankena, *op. cit.* p. 23.
12. H.A. Bedau, "Egalitarianism and the Idea of Equality" in *Nomos IX: Equality*, ed. J.R. Pennock and J.W. Chapman, New York 1967.
13. G. Vlastos, "Justice and Equality" in Brandt, *Social Justice*, p. 48.
14. E.G. Bernard Williams, "The Idea of Equality," in *Philosophy, Politics and Society* (second series) ed. P. Laslett and W. Runciman (Blackwell, Oxford, 1962) p. 118; J. Rawls, *A Theory of Justice*, pp. 509–10.
15. *Nomos IX: Equality*; the passages quoted are on pp. 62ff.

Animal Rights, Human Wrongs

Tom Regan

Tom Regan is professor of philosophy and university alumni distinguished professor at North Carolina State University. He is the author of The Case for Animal Rights, *and with Peter Singer, he edited* Animal Rights and Human Obligations.

THE KANTIAN ACCOUNT

It is a commonplace to say that morality places some limits on how animals may be treated. We are not to kick dogs, set fire to cats' tails, torment hamsters or parakeets. Philosophically, the issue is not so much *whether* but *why* these acts are wrong.

An answer favored by many philosophers, including Thomas Aquinas and Immanuel Kant, is that people who treat animals in these ways develop a habit which, in time, inclines them to treat humans similarly.[1] People who torment animals will, or are likely to, torment people. It is this spillover effect that makes mistreating animals wrong. We are not concerned directly with the ill-treatment that the animals themselves receive. Rather, our concern is that this bodies ill for humankind. So, on this Kantian account, the moral principle runs something like this: don't treat animals in ways that will lead you to mistreat human beings.

One need have no quarrel with this principle itself. The real quarrel lies with the grounds on which this principle is allegedly based. Peter Singer argues that there is a close parallel between this view and those of the racist and sexist, a view which, following Richard Ryder, he denominates speciesism.[2] The racist believes that the interests of others matter only if they happen to be members of his own race. The speciesist believes that the interests of others matter only if they happen to be members of his own species. Racism has been unmasked for the prejudice that it is. The color of one's skin cannot be used to determine the relevance of an individual's interests. Singer and Ryder both argue that neither can the number of one's legs, whether one walks upright or on all fours, lives in the trees, the sea or the suburbs. Here they recall Ben-

This essay originally appeared in *Environmental Ethics*, Vol. 2, No. 2 (Summer 1980), 99–120. Reprinted with permission.

tham.[3] There is, they argue forcefully, no rational, unprejudiced way to exclude the interests of nonhuman animals just because they are not the interests of human beings. Because the Kantian account would have us think otherwise, we are right to reject it.

THE CRUELTY ACCOUNT

A second view about constraints on how animals may be treated involves the idea of cruelty. The reason we are not to kick dogs is that we are not to be cruel to animals and kicking dogs is cruel. It is the prohibition against cruelty which covers and conveniently sums up our negative duties to animals, duties concerning how animals are *not* to be treated.

The prohibition against cruelty can be given a distinctively Kantian twist. This happens when the grounds given are that cruelty to animals leads people to be cruel to other people. John Locke suggests, but does not clearly endorse, this view:

> One thing I have frequently observed in Children, that when they have got possession of any poor Creature, they are apt to use it ill: They often *torment*, and treat very roughly, young Birds, Butterflies, and such other poor Animals, which fall into their Hands, and that with a seeming kind of Pleasure. This I think should be watched in them, and if they incline to any such *Cruelty*, they should be taught the contrary Usage, For the Custom of Tormenting and Killing of Beasts, will, by Degrees, harden their Minds even towards Men; and they who delight in the Suffering and Destruction of Inferior Creatures, will not be apt to be very compassionate, or benign to those of their own kind.[4]

Locke's position suggests the speciesism which characterizes the Kantian account and will not do for the same reasons. However, Locke's understanding of what cruelty is—tormenting a sentient creature or causing it to suffer, "with a seeming kind of Pleasure"—seems correct and has important implications. Many thinkers, including many persons active in the humane movement, champion the prohibition against cruelty to animals because it is wrong to be cruel to the animals themselves. This way of grounding the prohibition against cruelty, which I call "the cruelty account," deserves our critical attention.

It is difficult to overestimate the importance the idea of preventing cruelty has played, and continues to play, in the movement to secure better treatment for animals. Entire societies are devoted to this cause, the Society for the Prevention of Cruelty to Animals (SPCA) in the United States and the Royal Society for the Prevention of Cruelty to Animals (RSPCA) in Great Britain being perhaps the best known examples. I do not wish to deny the importance of preventing cruelty nor to deprecate the crusading work done by these organizations, but I must conclude that to stake so much on the prevention of cruelty both clouds the fundamental moral issues and runs a serious risk of being counterproductive.

Cruel is a term of moral appraisal used to refer either to the character of a person or to an individual action. Persons are cruel who are inclined to delight in or, in Locke's phrase, to take "a seeming kind of Pleasure" in causing pain. An individual action is cruel if one takes pleasure in making another suffer. It is clear that someone's being cruel is distinct from someone's causing pain. Surgeons cause pain. Dentists cause pain. Wrestlers, boxers, football players cause pain. But it does not follow that they are cruel people or that their individual actions are cruel. To establish cruelty we need to know more than that someone caused pain; we also need to know the state of mind of the agent, whether he/she took "a seeming kind of Pleasure" in the pain inflicted. It is faulty to reason in this way:

> Those who cause pain are cruel. Surgeons (football players, etc.) cause pain. Therefore, surgeons (football players, etc.) are cruel.

But just as clearly, it is faulty to reason in the following way:

> Those who cause pain are cruel. Those who experiment on animals (or kill whales, or raise veal calves in isolation, etc.) cause pain. Therefore those who treat animals in these ways are cruel.

Those who are inclined to march under the banner of anti-cruelty must soon recognize the speciousness of this line of reasoning, if their thought, however well intentioned, is not to cloud the issues.

Once cruelty is understood in the way Locke saw that it should be, we can understand why more is needed. Take the case of the use of animals in the Draize test. Increasingly people want to object morally to this, to say it is wrong. However, if this required establishing cruelty, the weight of the evidence would be on the side of the experimenters and against the objectors, for there is no adequate evidence for believing that people who administer the Draize test are cruel people or that they are cruel when they administer this test. Do they take "a seeming kind of Pleasure" in causing the animals pain? That they cause *pain* to the animals is certain. But causing pain does not establish cruelty. Except for a few sadists in the scientific community, there is good reason to believe that researchers are no more cruel than are most persons.

Does this mean that using animals in the Draize test is right? Precisely not. Rather, to ask whether this is right is logically distinct from, and should not be confused with, asking whether someone is cruel. Cruelty has to do with a person's state of mind. The moral rightness or wrongness of a person's actions is different. Persons can do what is right or wrong whatever their state of mind. Researchers using the Draize test can be doing what is wrong, whether or not they enjoy causing animals to suffer. If they do enjoy this, we shall certainly think less of them as persons. But even if they enjoy the pain it will not follow that the pain is unjustified, any more than it will follow that the pain is justified if they feel sorry for the animals or feel nothing all. The more we are able to keep in view how the morality of what a person does is distinct from his/her state of mind, distinct from the presence or absence of taking pleasure in pain, the better the chances will be for significant dialogue between vivisectors and anti-vivisectionists.

To charge vivisectors with cruelty *can* only serve to call forth all their defenses, because the charge will be taken as a denunciation of *what they are* (evil people) rather than of *what they do*. It will also give them an easy way out. After all, *they* are in privileged position to know their own mental states; *they* can take a sober moment and see whether in fact they do take a "seeming kind of Pleasure" in causing pain. If, as will usually be the case, they find that they honestly do not, then they can reply that they are not cruel (evil) people. So we see now where the well-intentioned efforts of those defending animals can be and often are counterproductive. If it's cruelty they are charged with, and they are not cruel, then they can come away with a feeling that their hands are clean. They win, and the litany of accusations about cruelty is so much water off their backs. It is no good trying to improve the lot of animals by trying to convince persons who are not cruel that they are.

Some will complain that my argument is "too picky." They might say that cruelty has been interpreted too narrowly: what is meant is treating animals badly in ways they don't deserve, harming or wronging them. In practice this is what anti-cruelty charges often come to. But then this is the way the charges should be made, lest they be misunderstood or be counterproductive. To ask for more care in the charges leveled is not to strain at gnats. It is to begin to make the charges more difficult to answer. Perhaps a name like "The Society for the Prevention of Maltreatment of Animals" is not as euphonious as "The Anti-Cruelty Society," but a lack of euphony is a price those laboring for animal welfare should gladly pay.

THE UTILITARIAN ACCOUNT

Utilitarians give a different account of the constraints regarding how animals ought to be treated. The utilitarian account, or one version of it, involves two principles.[5] The first is a principle of equality. This principle declares that the desires, needs, hopes, etc. of different individuals, when these are of equal importance *to* these individuals, *are* of equal importance or value no matter who the individuals are, prince or pauper, genius or moron, white or black, male or female, *human or animal*. This equality of interests principle seems to provide a philosophical basis for avoiding the grossest forms of prejudice, including racism, sexism and, following Ryder and Singer, speciesism. Whether it succeeds is an issue which we shall take up below.

The second principle is that of utility itself. Roughly speaking, according to this principle, we are to act so as to bring about the greatest possible balance of good over evil, for example, the greatest possible balance of satisfaction over dissatisfaction, taking the interests of everyone affected into account *and* counting equal interests equally. Now, since animals have interests, *their* interests must be taken into account, and because their interests are frequently as important to them as comparable interests are to human beings, *their* interests must be given the same weight as comparable human interests. It is because kicking dogs and setting fire to cats' tails run counter to the principles of equality and utility that, on this utilitarian account, they are wrong.

Granted, this is a very rough sketch; nonetheless, it enables us to understand the main features of the utilitarian account, and also to find points of resemblance and contrast between it and the other accounts so far described. Like the Kantian account, but unlike the cruelty account, the utilitarian account emphasizes results or consequences, but unlike the Kantian account, and resembling the cruelty account, the utilitarian account recognizes the moral status of animals in their own right. We are not to measure morality by the speciesist yardstick of human interest alone. Finally, unlike the cruelty account, but in concert with the Kantian, the utilitarian does not conflate the morality of an act with the mental state of the agent. The utilitarian can be as opposed to cruelty as anyone else, but within the utilitarian theory right and wrong are determined by consequences, not feelings and intentions: the ordinary moral constraints placed on how we may treat animals are accounted for because they are necessary if we are not to violate the equality of interests principle *or* if we are to succeed in bringing about the greatest possible balance of good over bad.

The utilitarian account has much to recommend it. How far can it take us in challenging the way in which animals are routinely treated, for example, as subjects in scientific research? Peter Singer, a utilitarian whose work has well deserved influence, holds that utilitarianism leads to far-reaching consequences here. Singer argues that we become vegetarians *and* that we oppose much (even if not quite all) research involving animal subjects. Singer's main argument is that the intensive rearing of animals as well as their routine use in experimentation violates the equality of interests principle. The animals involved, we have reason to believe, have an interest in not being made to suffer, and this interest, we have further reason to believe, is as important to them as is the comparable interest in the case of human beings. This being so, Singer contends, it is wrong to do to animals what we would not do to humans. It cannot be right to raise animals intensively or use them in research if we would morally oppose doing these things to human beings. We do condemn cannibalism and the coerced use of humans in research and we must, Singer argues, morally condemn the comparable treatment of animals. We have a moral obligation to become vegetarians and oppose much, if not quite all, vivisection.

As clear and powerful as this argument is, I do not believe that Singer succeeds in making a fully convincing case. He shows that animals are treated differently than human beings, but not that this differential treatment violates either the equality of interests principle or the principle of utility. Consider the equality of interests principle first. We can count equal interests equally, no matter whose interests they are, and still treat individuals quite differently. For example, I might correctly regard my son's and my neighbor's son's interests in receiving a medical education as being equal and yet help only my son. I treat them differently but I do *not* necessarily count their equal interests differently, and neither do I thereby do anything that is in any obvious sense morally reprehensible. I have duties to my son which I do not have to the children of others.

The general point is this: the differential treatment of individuals with equal interests does not by itself violate the equality of interests principle. Singer has to give an *argument* which shows *more* than that they are treated differently. What argument does he give and how adequate is it? Singer proceeds by asking whether we would do to humans what we allow to be done to animals.[6] For example, would a researcher use an orphaned, profoundly retarded human baby in the sort of painful experiment in which he is willing to use a more intellectually and emotionally developed animal? If the researcher says no, Singer charges him with speciesism, with violating the equality of interests principle. The animal's interest in avoiding pain is just as important to it as is the infant's interest to him/her.

This argument begs the question. It assumes that by treating the involved individuals differently, we count their equal interests differently. As I have explained, however, this is not always true. Whether it is true in any particular case, therefore, is something which must be established, not simply assumed on the basis of differential treatment. Singer, I believe, assumes just this, and thus begs the question.

Singer's argument has a further deficiency, which involves the principle of utility. First, Singer does not show that the differential treatment of animals runs counter to the utilitarian objective of bringing about the greatest possible balance of good over evil. To show this Singer would have to give an elaborate, detailed description, not only of how animals are treated, a part of the task which he does complete with great skill, but an analysis of what, all considered, are the consequences for everyone involved. He would have to inquire how the world's economy depends on present levels of productivity in the animal industry, how many people's lives are directly and indirectly involved with the maintenance or growth of this industry, etc. Even more, he would have to show in detail what would probably be the consequences of a collapse or slowdown of the animal industry's productivity.

Secondly, Singer needs to make a compelling case for the view that *not* raising animals intensively or *not* using them routinely in research leads to better consequences, all considered, than those which now result from treating animals in these ways. Singer is required to show that better consequences *would* result, or at last that it is *very probable* that they would. Showing that it is possible or conceivable that they might is insufficient. It comes as a disappointment, therefore, that we do not find anything approaching this kind of required empirical data. What we find, instead, are passages where he bemoans (rightly, I believe) the fact that animals are fed protein-rich grains which could be fed to malnourished human beings.[7] The point, however, is not whether these grains *could* be fed to the malnourished; it is whether we have solid empirical grounds for believing that they *would* be made available to and eaten by these people, if they were not fed to animals, *and* that the consequences resulting from this shift would be better, all considered. I hope I am not unfair to Singer in observing that these calculations are missing, not only here, but, to my knowledge, throughout the body of his published writings.

This, then, is the first thing to note regarding Singer and the principle of utility: *he fails to show, with reference to this principle, that it is wrong* to treat animals as they are now being treated in modern farming and scientific research. The second thing to note is that, for all we know and so long as we rely on the principle of utility, the present treatment of animals might actually be justified. The grounds for thinking so are as follows.

On the face of it, utilitarianism seems to be the fairest, least prejudicial view available. Everyone's interests count, and no one's counts for more or less than the equal interests of anyone else. The trouble is, as we have seen, that there is no necessary connection, no preestablished harmony between respect for the equality of interests principle *and* promoting the utilitarian objective of maximizing the balance of good over bad. On the contrary, the principle of utility might be used to justify the most radical kinds of differential treatment between individuals or groups of individuals, and thus it might justify forms of racism and sexism, for these prejudices can take different forms and find expression in different ways. One form consists in not even taking the interests of a given race or sex into account at all; another takes these interests into account but does not count them equally with those of the equal interests of the favored group. Another does take their interests into account equally, but adopts laws and policies, engages in practices and customs which give greater opportunities to the members of the favored group, because doing so promotes the greatest balance of good over evil, all considered.

Thus, forms of racism or sexism, which seem to be eliminated by the utilitarian principle of equality of interests, could well be resurrected and justified by the principle of utility. If a utilitarian here replies that denying certain humans an equal opportunity to satisfy or promote their equal interests on racial or sexual grounds must violate the equality of interests principle and so, on his position, is wrong, we must remind him that differential treatment is not the same as, and does not entail, violating the equality of interests principle. It is quite possible, for example, to count the equal interests of blacks and whites the same (and thus to honor the equality principle) and still discriminate between races when it comes to what members of each race are permitted to do to pursue those interests, on the grounds that such discrimination promotes the utilitarian objective. So, utilitarianism, despite initial appearances, does not provide us with solid grounds on which to exclude all forms of racism or sexism.

Similarly with speciesism. The same kind of argument can show a possible utilitarian justification of an analogous speciesism. We count the equal interests of animals and humans equally; it just so happens that the consequences of treating animals in ways that humans are not treated, such as intensively raising animals, but not humans, are better, all considered, than are other arrangements. Thus, utilitarianism might provide a basis for speciesist practices. Whether it *actually* does depends on whether the consequences are better, all considered, if animals continue to be treated as they are. Since Singer fails to provide us with empirical data showing that the consequences would be better if we changed, it follows that, for all we know, the present speciesist way of treating animals might actually be justified, given his version of utilitarianism.

ANIMAL RIGHTS

Our results to this point are mainly negative. I have thus far argued (1) that the moral principles we seek cannot refer to the agent's state of mind, to whether the agent takes a "seeming kind of Pleasure" in causing animal suffering. (2) These principles cannot refer only to consequences that harm or benefit human beings, since this prejudicially leaves out of account the harms and benefits to the animals themselves. (3) These principles cannot refer only to the utilitarian objective of maximizing the balance of good over evil, even if animal harms and benefits are taken into account. What is wanted, then, is an account which avoids each of these shortcomings. This account is to be found, I believe, by postulating the existence of animal rights. Indeed, I believe that only if we postulate human rights can we provide a theory which adequately guards humans against the abuses which utilitarianism might permit.

Various analyses of the concept of a right have been proposed. We will bypass the nooks and crannies of these competing analyses so as to focus attention on the role that moral rights play in our thinking about the status of the individual, relative to the interests of the group. Here the truth seems to lie where Ronald Dworkin sees it: the rights of the individual trump the goals of the group.[8]

What does this mean? It means that the moral rights of the individual place a justifiable limit on what the group can do to the individual. Suppose a group of people stand to gain enjoyment by arranging for others to be harmed. Imagine, for example, the Romans enjoying how the Christians go up against lions. Such a group does wrong because they allow their interests to override the individual's moral rights. This does not mean that there are no circumstances in which an individual's rights must give way to the collective interest. Imagine that Bert has inadvertently swallowed the microfilmed code which we must have in order to prevent a massive nuclear explosion in New Zealand. Bert sits safely in Tucson, Arizona. We explain the situation but Bert refuses to consent to our request that we operate, retrieve the code, and prevent the explosion. He cites his right to determine what is to be done to his body. In such a case it is not implausible to say that Bert's right must give way to the collective interests of others.

Individual rights then normally, but not always, trump collective interests. To give a precise statement of the conditions which determine which ought to prevail is very difficult indeed, but the following conditions, which deal only with the right not to be harmed, at least seem to incorporate necessary conditions for overriding this right.[9]

An individual's right not to be harmed can justifiably be overridden only if—

a. we have very good reason to believe that overriding the individual's right by itself will prevent, and is the only realistic way to prevent, vastly greater harm to other innocent individuals; or
b. we have very good reason to believe that allowing the individual to be harmed is a necessary link in a chain of events which collectively will prevent vastly greater harm to innocent individuals, *and* we have very good reason to believe that this chain of events is the only realistic way to prevent this vastly greater harm; or
c. we have very good reason to believe that it is only if we override the individual's right that we can have a reasonable hope of preventing vastly greater harm to other innocent individuals.

There is much that is vague in these conditions, e.g., "vastly greater harm," "innocent individuals," "reasonable hope." At present, however, we will have to make do with them as they stand. Even so we can see that these conditions attempt to do justice to the complexity of conflicts of interest. In particular, they attempt to explain how, in a principled way, we might justify overriding an individual's right not to be harmed even though *just* doing this will not guarantee the prevention of vastly greater harm. Condition (b) brings this out—harming an individual is only one part of a more complex series of events which we have very good reason to believe will prevent vastly greater harm, or because—as (c) brings out—we simply do not know how things will turn out, but do have very good reason to believe that we have no reasonable hope of preventing some catastrophe unless we allow an individual to be harmed. Possibly some will find these conditions too liberal. Condition (c) in particular might seem too lenient. Even (b) might go too far. I am not certain what to say here and beg to leave this issue unresolved, except to say that the case for not harming animals is proportionately greater the more one is inclined to restrict the above set just to condition (a). For reasons that will become clearer, however, even the more liberal view, that harm can not be justified unless one of the three conditions is met, is sufficient to make a strong case against our routine abuse of animals.

These conditions share an extremely important feature. Each specifies what we must know or have good reason to believe if we are justified in overriding an individual's right not to be harmed. Each requires anyone who would harm an individual to show that this does not involve violating the individual's right. Part of the importance of the question, whether animals have rights, specifically, the right not to be harmed, now comes into clear focus. *If* they have this right, then it will be violated whenever animals are harmed and condition (a), (b), or (c) is not satisfied. Moreover, the onus of justification is always on those who harm animals to explain how they are not violating the right of animals not to be harmed, if animals have this right. So, the question continues to press itself upon us. Do animals have the right not to be harmed?

This is not an easy question to answer. One is reminded of Bentham's observation that the idea of moral rights is "nonsense on stilts." Bentham meant this in the case of *human* moral rights. One can only speculate regarding what he might have thought concerning the moral rights of *animals*! So, how is one to procede? The circuitous path we must cautiously travel, I think, is in broad outline as follows.[10]

We begin by asking about our reasons for thinking that human beings have the moral right not to be harmed; then we go on to ask whether, given these reasons, a case can be made for saying that animals have this right as well. Let us go back to the idea that individual human beings have this right and that, except in extreme cases, this right trumps collective interest. Why? What is there about being a human being to which we can point and say, "*That's* why you must not harm the individual even if the group benefits"?

The heart of the answer lies, I believe, in thinking that human beings have a certain kind of value, inherent value. By this I mean that each human being has value logically independently of whether he/she is valued by anyone else (or, what perhaps comes to the same thing, whether he/she is the object of anyone else's interest).[11] The view that human beings have inherent value implies that the kind of value properly attributable to them is not exclusively instrumental. Humans have value not just because, and not just so long as, they are good for something. They have value distinct from their utility and skill.

If this is true, we can explain, in general terms reminiscent of Kant, what is involved in mistreating human beings. Humans are mistreated if they are treated as valuable only if they forward the interests of other beings. To treat a human being thus is to show a lack of proper respect for the sort of value humans have. In Kant's terms, what has value in itself must always be treated as an end, never merely as a means. However, this is precisely what we are doing if we harm an individual so that others might gain pleasure or profit; we are treating the individual merely as a means, as valuable only to the extent he/she contributes to the collective interest.

Now, *if* we accept the postulate that human beings have inherent value, we can press on and ask how rights enter the picture. They enter in being grounded in inherent value. In other words, it is individuals who have inherent value who have moral rights, and it is *because* they have value of this kind that they have a moral right not to be treated in ways that deny their having this kind of value. Rather than rights being connected with the *value of consequences* which affect individuals for good or ill, rather than rights being justified by the utility of recognizing them, rights are based on *the value of individuals.* In the case of the right not to be harmed, then, what we can say is that individuals who have inherent value have the right not to be harmed, which precludes treating them merely as a means. This would fail to treat these individuals with that respect to which, because of the kind of value they have, they are entitled.

Now, certainly the foregoing is not a definitive account of the view that individuals having inherent value have basic moral rights, in particular the right not to be harmed. One omission is especially conspicuous. What is there about being a human being that underlies this inherent value? Any answer is controversial, and a sustained defense of the answer proposed here is not possible.[12] But here is the answer I would give: human beings not only are alive; *they have a life.*[13] What is more, we are the subjects of a life that is better or worse for us, logically independently of anyone else's valuing us or finding us useful.

I do not mean that others cannot contribute to or detract from the value of our lives. On the contrary, the great goods of life (love, friendship, and, in general, fellow feeling) and its great evils (hatred, enmity, loneliness, alienation) all involve our relationships with other persons. What I mean, rather, is that our being *the subject* of a life that is better or worse for us does not depend logically on what others do or do not do. This fact, I believe, provides the illumination we seek. Humans have inherent value because we are ourselves the subjects of a life that is more or less valuable to us. In sum:

> Human beings have inherent value because, logically independently of the interest of others, each individual is the subject of a life that is better or worse for that individual. Because of the type of value that human beings have, it is wrong (a sign of disrespect and a violation of rights) to treat humans as if they had value merely as a means (e.g., to use humans merely to advance the pleasures of the group). In particular, to harm human beings for the sake of the profit or pleasure of any group is to violate their right not to be harmed.

The question now arises whether this same line of argument can be developed in the case of animals. It can, at least in the case of those animals who are the subjects of a life that is better or worse for them, logically independently of whether they are valued by anyone else. And there can be no rational doubt that there *are* numerous species of animals of which this is true. . . . They too have a distinctive kind of value in their own right, if we do; therefore, they too have a right not to be treated in ways that fail to respect this value, if we do. And, like humans, this right of theirs will be overridden unjustifiably if they are harmed merely to advance the profits or pleasures of others.

CONCLUSION

Two final philosophical points are in order, before I bring the results of my argument to bear on how animals are treated in the world at large. First, it is important to realize that I have not *proven* that animals have rights, or even that *human* beings have rights. Rather, I have argued that if humans have rights, so do many animals. More particularly, I have argued for what appears to be the most promising line of argument for explaining human rights, the view that we have inherent value, and that this can rationally be extended to animals of some kinds. So, while I admit that I have not proven that animals (or humans) have rights, I hope at least to have made clear the direction in which future argument ought to proceed. Erecting pointers, to be sure, is not the same as constructing proofs, but pointers are the best I can do here.

Second, the history of moral philosophy teaches us that utilitarianism dies hard. Just when one thinks it has been forced off the stage for good, one finds it loitering in the wings, awaiting yet another curtain call. The utilitarian can be counted on to say that there is nothing introduced by the idea of rights for which he cannot account.[14] One has only to see that the utilitarian objective is promoted if we recognize a strict obligation not to harm individuals except in extreme cases, *and* that, furthermore, utility is promoted by saying that individuals have the right not to be harmed, this invocation of a right functioning as an especially forceful way of conveying the idea that we ought not to harm individuals.

I am not convinced by this attempt to resurrect utilitarianism, and here I raise my final and most fundamental objection to it. The utilitarian is in no position to say that he knows that the utilitarian objective is promoted by talk of individuals having rights. But even if it is true that talk of rights helps promote the utilitarian objective, and for this reason such talk ought to be encouraged and honored, there can only be a *contingent* connection between any right, such as the right not to be harmed, and the fact that respecting this right forwards the utilitarian objective. The most that the utilitarian can say is that recognizing the right not to be harmed *as a matter of fact* fits in with forwarding his goal of maximizing the balance of good over evil.[15] The utilitarian must also accept that things could have been (and could become) otherwise. He must accept the possibility that it could have been or might become all right to harm individuals if this ever happened to forward the utilitarian objective. But neither the wrongness of harming individuals nor the right not to be harmed can change in the ways utilitarian theory implies they can. They are not contingent upon *utility*. Neither depends on the value of consequences. Instead, each depends on *the value of individuals.*

Let us put this in perspective before applying it. . . . Making an informed judgment about the morality of whaling or the use of the Draize test we must know both facts and moral principles. Otherwise, we cannot know which facts are morally relevant; and without this preliminary knowledge, we do not know what moral judgments to make. To determine what these principles are . . . is one of the distinctive tasks of moral philosophy. Three positions were examined and found wanting: the Kantian account, the cruelty account, and the utilitarian account. We then considered an account ascribing rights to animals, a position which meets the objections which were fatal to the views examined earlier. Unlike the Kantian account, the rights account insists upon the moral status of animals in their own right; unlike the cruelty account, the rights account does not confuse the morality of acts with the mental states of agents;

and unlike utilitarianism, this account closes the door to the justification of prejudices which merely happen to bring about the best consequences. This emphasis on the value of individuals becomes prominent now as we turn at last to the task of applying the rights account to the whale, the veal calf, and the others.

It would be grotesque to suggest that the whale, the rabbit, the gibbon, the bobbie calf, the millions of animals brought so much pain and death at the hands of humans are not harmed, for harm is not restricted to human beings. They are harmed, harmed in a literal, not a metaphorical sense. They are made to endure what is detrimental to their welfare, even death. Those who would harm them, therefore, must justify doing so. Thus, members of the whaling industry, the cosmetics industry, the farming industry, the network of hunters-exporters-importers must justify the harm they bring animals in a way that is consistent with recognizing the animals' right not to be harmed. To produce such a justification it is not enough to argue that people profit, satisfy their curiosity, or derive pleasure from allowing animals to be treated in these ways. These facts are not the morally relevant ones. Rather, what must be shown is that overriding the right of animals not to be harmed is justified because of further facts. For example, because we have very good reason to believe that overriding the individual's right prevents, and is the only realistic way to prevent, vastly greater harm to other innocent individuals.

Let us ask the whaling industry whether they have so justified their trade. Have they made their case in terms of the morally relevant facts? Our answer must be: no! And the cosmetic industry? No! The farmers who raise veal calves? No! The retailer of exotic animals? No! A thousand times we must say: no! I do not say that they cannot possibly justify what they do. The individual's right not to be harmed, we have argued, almost always trumps the interests of the group, but it is possible that such a right must sometimes give way. Possibly the rights of animals must sometimes give way to human interests. It would be a mistake to rule this possibility out. Nevertheless, the onus of justification must be borne by those who cause the harm to show that they do not violate the rights of the individuals involved.

We allow then that it is *possible* that harming animals might be justified; but we also maintain that those harming animals typically fail to show that the harm caused is *actually* justified. A further question we must ask ourselves is what, morally speaking, we ought to do in such a situation? Reflection on comparable situations involving human beings will help make the answer clear.

Consider racism and sexism. Imagine that slavery is an institution of the day and that it is built on racist or sexist lines. Blacks or women are assigned the rank of slave. Suppose we are told that in extreme circumstances even slavery might conceivably be justified, and that we ought not to object to it or try to bring it down, even though no one has shown that it is actually justified in the present case. Well, I do not believe for a moment that we would accept such an attempt to dissuade us from toppling the institution of slavery. Not for a moment would we accept the general principle involved here, that an institution actually is justified because it might conceivably be justified. We would accept the quite different principle that we are morally obligated to oppose any practice which appears to violate rights unless we are shown that it really does not do so. To be satisfied with anything less is to cheapen the value attributable to the victims of the practice.

Exactly the same line of reasoning applies in the case where animals are regarded as so many dispensable commodities, models, subjects, etc. We ought not to back away from bringing these industries and related practices to a halt just because it is *possible* that the harm caused to the animals *might* be justified. If we do, we fail to mean it when we say that animals are not mere things, that they are the subjects of a life that is better or worse for them, that they have inherent value. As in the comparable case involving harm to human beings, our duty is to act, to do all that we can to put an end to the harm animals are made to endure. The fact that the animals themselves cannot speak out on their own behalf, the fact that they cannot organize, petition, march, exert political pressure, or raise our level of consciousness—all this does not weaken our obligation to act on their behalf. If anything, their impotence makes our obligation the greater.[16] . . .

NOTES

1. Relevant selections from both St. Thomas and Kant are included in Regan and Singer, *Animal Rights and Human Obligations.* What I call the Kantian account is critized further in my "Exploring the Idea of Animal Rights" in D. Paterson and R. Ryder, eds., *Animal Rights: A Symposium* (London: Centaur Press, 1979). Kant's views are criticized at length by Elizabeth Pybus and Alexander Broadie, "Kant's Treatment of Animals," *Philosophy* 49 (1974): 375–83. I defend Kant against their objections in my "Broadie and Pybus on Kant," *Philosophy* 51 (1976): 471–72. Broadie and Pybus reply in their "Kant on the Maltreatment of Animals," *Philosophy* 53 (1978): 560–61. At present I am persuaded that Broadie and Pybus are correct in arguing that Kant cannot account for the idea that animals themselves can be maltreated.
2. Singer, *Animal Liberation,* and Ryder, *Victims of Science.*
3. The famous passage from Bentham reads as follows (from *The Principles of Morals and Legislation* (1789), chap. 17, Sect. 1, reprinted in Regan and Singer, *Animal Rights and Human Obligations*): "The day has been, I grieve to say in many places it is not yet past, in which the greater part of the species, under the denomination of slaves, have been treated by the law exactly upon the same footing as, in England for example, the inferior races of animals are still. The day may come, when the rest of the animal creation may acquire those rights which never could have been withholden from them but by the hand of tyranny. The French have already discovered that the blackness of the skin is no reason why a human being should be abandoned without redress to the caprice of a tormentor. It may come one day to be recognized, that the number of the legs, the villosity of the skin, or the termination of the os sacrum, are reasons equally insufficient for abandoning a sensitive being to the same fate. What else is it that should trace the insuperable line? Is it the faculty of reason, or, perhaps, the faculty of discourse? But a full-grown horse or dog is beyond comparison a more rational, as well as a more conversable

animal, than an infant of a day, or a week, or even a month, old. But suppose the case were otherwise, what would it avail? The question is not, Can they reason? nor, Can they talk? but, Can they suffer?"

4. John Locke, *Some Thoughts Concerning Education*, 5th ed. (London, 1905). See also James Axtell, ed., *The Educational Writings of John Locke* (Cambridge: Cambridge University Press, 1968), sec. 116, pp. 225–26.
5. The utilitarian position I consider is the one associated with Bentham and forcefully presented by Peter Singer. That Singer is a utilitarian is made unmistakably clear in his "The Fable of the Fox and the Unliberated Animals" *Ethics* 88 (1978): 119–25.
6. See Singer, *Animal Liberation*, especially pp. 78–83.
7. Ibid., chap. 4.
8. Ronald Dworkin, *Taking Rights Seriously* (Cambridge: Harvard University Press, 1977).
9. The present statement of these conditions deviates somewhat from my earlier effort in "The Moral Basis of Vegetarianism," *Canadian Journal of Philosophy* 5 (1975): 181–214. I believe the inclusion of conditions (b) and (c) marks an improvement over the earlier formulation. However, a fuller statement has to include more than simply the idea of *preventing* vastly greater harm; for example, *reducing* already existing harm also has a place.
10. See my "An Examination and Defense of One Argument Concerning Animal Rights," *Inquiry* 22 (1979): 189–219.
11. Whether sense can be made of including irreversibly comatose human beings in the class of beings having inherent value is a troublesome question indeed.
12. I do not believe it is absurd to think of natural objects which lack consciousness, or collections of such objects, as having inherent value, in the sense in which I use this expression. An *X* has inherent value if it has value logically independently of anyone's valuing *X*. I do not say this is easy to clarify or to defend, and it may be wrongheaded. At present, however, I believe it is a view that must be held, if we are to develop an environmental ethic, as distinct from an ethic for the use of the environment.
13. The distinction between being alive and having a life is one James Rachels frequently makes. See, for example, his "Euthanasia" in Tom Regan, ed., *Matters of Life and Death* (New York: Random House, 1980). Rachels does not, so far as I am aware, relate this distinction to the idea of inherent value.
14. It is possible that Mill meant to give rights a utilitarian basis. On this see David Lyons, "Human Rights and the General Welfare," *Philosophy and Public Affairs* 6 (1977): 113–29, reprinted in David Lyons, ed., *Rights* (Belmont, California: Wadsworth Publishing Co., 1979). The principal objection to this enterprise is the third objection I raise against utilitarianism here.
15. I do not believe utilitarianism is alone in implying that the duty not to harm an individual (or the individual's right not to be harmed) are *contingent* moral truths, which *might* have been otherwise (or *might* become otherwise). Certain aspects of Kant's theory as well as ethical egoism arguably imply this as well. This is absolutely fatal to these theories, a point I argue in my "Utilitarianism, Vegetarianism, and Animal Rights," in *Philosophy and Public Affairs.*
16. For a more complete list of recent philosophical work relating to the topics discussed in the present essay, see Charles Magel and Tom Regan, "Animal Rights and Human Obligations: A Select Bibliography," *Inquiry* 22 (1979): 243–47.

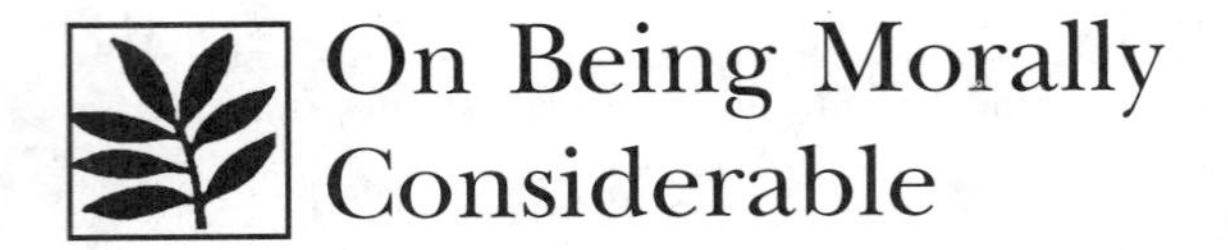

On Being Morally Considerable

Kenneth E. Goodpaster

Kenneth E. Goodpaster holds the David and Barbara Koch chair in business ethics at the University of St. Thomas, St. Paul, Minnesota. With Kenneth M. Sayre, he edited Ethics and Problems of the 21st Century.

> A thing is right when it tends to preserve the integrity, stability, and beauty of the biotic community. It is wrong when it tends otherwise.
>
> —*Aldo Leopold*

What follows is a preliminary inquiry into a question which needs more elaborate treatment than an essay can provide. The question can be and has been addressed in different rhetorical formats, but perhaps G.J. Warnock's formulation of it[1] is the best to start with:

> Let us consider the question to whom principles of morality apply from, so to speak, the other end—from the standpoint not of the agent, but of the "patient." What, we may ask here, is the condition of moral *relevance*? What is the condition of having a claim to be *considered*, by rational agents to whom moral principles apply? (148)

In the terminology of R. M. Hare (or even Kant), the same question might be put thus: In universalizing our putative moral maxims, what is the scope of the variable over which universalization is to range? A more legalistic idiom, employed recently by Christopher D. Stone,[2] might ask: What are the requirements for "having standing" in the moral sphere? However the question gets formulated, the thrust is in the direction of necessary and sufficient conditions on *X* in

(1) For all *A*, *X* deserves moral consideration from *A*. where *A* ranges over rational moral agents and moral 'consideration' is construed broadly to include the most basic forms of practical respect (and so is not restricted to "possession of rights" by *X*).

This essay originally appeared in *The Journal of Philosophy*, LXXV, 6 (June 1978), 308–25. Reprinted with permission.

I

The motivation for addressing such a question stems from several sources. The last decade has seen a significant increase in the concern felt by most persons about "the environment." This new awareness manifests itself in many ways. One is a quest for methods of "technology assessment," for criteria for social choice that capture the relevant costs and benefits (be they quantifiable or not). On another front, heated controversies have arisen over endangered species and our treatment of animals generally (both as sources of food and as sources of experimental knowledge). The morality of abortion and, in general, the proper uses of medical technology have also tried our ethical sensitivities about the scope and nature of moral considerability.

These developments emphasize the importance of clarity about the *framework* of moral consideration as much as about the *application* of that framework. We need to understand better, for example, the scope of moral respect, the sorts of entities that can and should receive moral attention, and the nature of the "good" which morality (since it at least *includes* beneficence) is supposed to promote. In addition, we need principles for weighing or adjudicating conflicting claims to moral consideration.

The question focused on here is therefore only a first step toward the larger task. It is a framework question more than an application question—though its practical relevance is not so remote as to be purely a matter of logical speculation. My convictions about the proper answer to the question are sketched in another place,[3] but they can be summarized more explicitly as follows.

Modern moral philosophy has taken ethical egoism as its principal foil for developing what can fairly be called a *humanistic* perspective on value and obligation. That is, both Kantian and Humean approaches to ethics tend to view the philosophical challenge as that of providing an epistemological and motivational generalization of an agent's natural self-interested concern. Because of this preoccupation with moral "takeoff," however, too little critical thought has been devoted to the flight and its destination. One result might be a certain feeling of impotence in the minds of many moral philosophers when faced with the sorts of issues mentioned earlier, issues that question the breadth of the moral enterprise more than its departure point. To be sure, questions of conservation, preservation of the environment, and technology assessment *can* be approached simply as application questions, e.g., "How shall we evaluate the alternatives available to us instrumentally in relation to humanistic satisfactions?" But there is something distressingly uncritical in this way of framing such issues—distressingly uncritical in the way that deciding foreign policy solely in terms of "the national interest" is uncritical. Or at least, so I think.

It seems to me that we should not only wonder about, but actually follow "the road not taken into the wood." Neither rationality nor the capacity to experience pleasure and pain seem to me necessary (even though they may be sufficient) conditions on moral considerability. And only our hedonistic and concentric forms of ethical reflection keep us from acknowledging this fact.

Nothing short of the condition of *being alive* seems to me to be a plausible and nonarbitrary criterion. What is more, this criterion, if taken seriously, could admit of application to entities and systems of entities heretofore unimagined as claimants on our moral attention (such as the biosystem itself). Some may be inclined to take such implications as a *reductio* of the move "beyond humanism." I am beginning to be persuaded, however, that such implications may provide both a meaningful ethical vision and the hope of a more adequate action guide for the long-term future. Paradigms are crucial components in knowledge—but they can conceal as much as they reveal. Our paradigms of moral considerability are individual persons and their joys and sorrows. I want to venture the belief that the universe of moral consideration is more complex than these paradigms allow.

II

My strategy, now that my cards are on the table, will be to spell out a few rules of the game (in this section) and then to examine the "hands" of several respected philosophers whose arguments seem to count against casting the moral net as widely as I am inclined to (sections III, IV, and V). In the concluding section (VI), I will discuss several objections and touch on further questions needing attention.

The first (of four) distinctions that must be kept clear in addressing our question has already been alluded to. It is that between moral *rights* and moral *considerability*. My inclination is to construe the notion of rights as more specific than that of considerability, largely to avoid what seem to be unnecessary complications over the requirements for something's being an appropriate "bearer of rights." The concept of rights is used in wider and narrower senses, of course. Some authors (indeed, one whom we shall consider later in this paper) use it as roughly synonymous with Warnock's notion of "moral relevance." Others believe that being a bearer of rights involves the satisfaction of much more demanding requirements. The sentiments of John Passmore[4] are probably typical of this narrower view:

> The idea of "rights" is simply not applicable to what is non-human . . . It is one thing to say that it is wrong to treat animals cruelly, quite another to say that animals have rights (116/7).

I doubt whether it is so clear that the class of rights-bearers is or ought to be restricted to human beings, but I propose to suspend this question entirely by framing the discussion in terms of the notion of moral considerability (following Warnock), except in contexts where there is reason to think the widest sense of 'rights' is at work. Whether beings who deserve moral consideration in themselves, not simply by reason of their utility to human beings, also possess moral *rights* in some narrow sense is a question which will, therefore, remain open here—and it is a question the answer to which need not be determined in advance.

A second distinction is that between what might be called a *criterion of moral considerability* and a *criterion of moral significance.* The former represents the central quarry here, while the latter, which might easily get confused with the former, aims at governing *comparative* judgments of moral "weight" in cases of conflict. Whether a tree, say, deserves any moral consideration is a question that must be kept separate from the question of whether trees deserve more or less consideration than dogs, or dogs than human persons. We should not expect that the criterion for having "moral standing" at all will be the same as the criterion for adjudicating competing claims to priority among beings that merit that standing. In fact, it may well be an insufficient appreciation of this distinction which leads some to a preoccupation with rights in dealing with morality. I suspect that the real force of attributions of "rights" derives from comparative contexts, contexts in which moral considerability is presupposed and the issue of strength is crucial. Eventually, of course, the priority issues have to be dealt with for an operational ethical account—this much I have already acknowledged—but in the interests of clarity, I set them aside for now.

Another important distinction, the third, turns on the difference between questions of intelligibility and questions of normative substance. An adequate treatment of this difficult and complicated division would take us far afield,[5] but a few remarks are in order. It is tempting to assume, with Joel Feinberg,[6] that we can neatly separate such questions as

(2) What sorts of being can (logically) be *said* to deserve moral consideration?

from questions like

(3) What sorts of beings do, as a matter of "ethical fact" deserve moral consideration?

But our confidence in the separation here wanes (perhaps more quickly than in other philosophical contexts where the conceptual/substantive distinction arises) when we reflect upon the apparent *flexibility* of our metamoral beliefs. One might argue plausibly, for example, that there were times and societies in which the moral standing of blacks was, as a matter of *conceptual analysis,* deniable. Examples could be multiplied to include women, children, fetuses, and various other instances of what might be called "metamoral disenfranchisement." I suspect that the lesson to be learned here is that, as William Frankena has pointed out,[7] metaethics is, and has always been, a partially normative discipline. Whether we are to take this to mean that it is really impossible ever to engage in morally neutral conceptual analysis in ethics is, of course, another question. In any case, it appears that, with respect to the issue at hand, keeping (2) and (3) apart will be difficult. At the very least, I think, we must be wary of arguments that purport to answer (3) *solely* on the basis of "ordinary language"–style answers to (2).

Though the focus of the present inquiry is more normative than conceptual [hence aimed more at (3) than at (2)], it remains what I called a "framework" inquiry nonetheless, since it prescinds from the question of relative weights (moral significance) of moral considerability claims.

Moreover—and this brings us to the fourth and last distinction—there is another respect in which the present inquiry involves framework questions rather than questions of application. There is clearly a sense in which we are subject to *thresholds* of moral sensitivity just as we are subject to thresholds of cognitive or perceptual sensitivity. Beyond such thresholds we are "morally blind" or suffer disintegrative consequences analogous to "information overload" in a computer. In the face of our conative limitations, we often will distinguish between moral demands that are relative to those limitations and moral demands that are not. The latter demands represent claims on our consideration or respect which we acknowledge as in some sense ideally determinative if not practically determinative. We might mark this distinction by borrowing Ross's categories of "prima facie vs. actual duty" except that (A) these categories tend to map more naturally onto the distinction mentioned earlier between considerability and significance, and (B) these categories tend to evoke conditionality and lack thereof of a sort which is rooted more in a plurality of "external" moral pressures than in an agent's "internal" capacities for practical response. Let us, then, say that the moral considerability of *X* is *operative* for an agent *A* if and only if the thorough acknowledgement of *X* by *A* is psychologically (and in general, causally) possible for *A*. If the moral considerability of *X* is defensible on all grounds independent of operativity, we shall say that it is *regulative.* An agent may, for example, have an obligation to grant regulative considerability to all living things, but be able psychologically and in terms of his own nutrition to grant operative consideration to a much smaller class of things (though note that capacities in this regard differ among persons and change over time).

Using all these distinctions, and the rough and ready terminology that they yield, we can now state the issue in (1) as a concern for a relatively substantive (vs. purely logical) criterion of moral considerability (vs. moral significance) of a regulative (vs. operative) sort. As far as I can see, *X*'s being a living thing is both necessary and sufficient for moral considerability so understood, whatever may be the case for the moral *rights* that rational agents should acknowledge.

III

Let us begin with Warnock's own answer to the question, now that the question has been clarified somewhat. In setting out his answer, Warnock argues (in my view, persuasively) against two more restrictive candidates. The first, what might be called the *Kantian principle,* amounts to little more than a reflection of the requirements of moral *agency* onto those of moral considerability:

(4) For *X* to deserve moral consideration from *A*, *X* must be a rational human person.

Observing that such a criterion of considerability eliminates children and mentally handicapped adults, among others, Warnock dismisses it as intolerably narrow.

The second candidate, actually a more generous variant of the first, sets the limits of moral considerability by disjoining "potentiality":

(5) For all *A*, *X* deserves moral consideration from *A* if and only if *X* is a rational human person or is a potential rational human person.

Warnock's reply to this suggestion is also persuasive. Infants and imbeciles are no doubt potentially rational, but this does not appear to be the reason why we should not maltreat them. And we would not say that an imbecile reasonably judged to be incurable would thereby reasonably be taken to have no moral claims (151). In short, it seems arbitrary to draw the boundary of moral *considerability* around rational human beings (actual or potential), however plausible it might be to draw the boundary of moral *responsibility* there.[8]

Warnock then settles upon his own solution. The basis of moral claims, he says, may be put as follows:

> . . . just as liability to be judged as a moral agent follows from one's general capability of alleviating, by moral action, the ills of the predicament, and is for that reason confined to rational beings, so the condition of being a proper "beneficiary" of moral action is the capability of *suffering* the ills of the predicament—and for that reason is not confined to rational beings, nor even to potential members of that class (151).

The criterion of moral considerability then, is located in the *capacity to suffer*:

(6) For all *A*, *X* deserves moral consideration from *A* if and only if *X* is capable of suffering pain (or experiencing enjoyment).

And the defense involves appeal to what Warnock considers to be (analytically) the *object* of the moral enterprise: Amelioration of "the predicament."

Now two issues arise immediately in the wake of this sort of appeal. The first has to do with Warnock's own over-all strategy in the context of the quoted passage. Earlier on in his book, he insists that the appropriate analysis of the concept of morality will lead us to an "object" whose pursuit provides the framework for ethics. But the "object" seems to be more restrictive:

> . . . the general object of moral evaluation must be to contribute in some respects, by way of the actions of rational beings, to the amelioration of the human predicament—that is, of the conditions in which *these* rational beings, humans, actually find themselves (16; emphasis in the original).

It appears that, by the time moral considerability comes up later in the book, Warnock has changed his mind about the object of morality by enlarging the "predicament" to include nonhumans.

The second issue turns on the question of analysis itself. As I suggested earlier, it is difficult to keep conceptual and substantive questions apart in the present context. We can, of course, stipulatively *define* 'morality' as both having an object and having the object of mitigating suffering. But, in the absence of more argument, such definition is itself in need of a warrant. Twentieth-century preoccupation with the naturalistic or definist fallacy should have taught us at least this much.

Neither of these two observations shows that Warnock's suggested criterion is wrong, of course. But they do, I think, put us in a rather more demanding mood. And the mood is aggravated when we look to two other writers on the subject who appear to hold similar views.

W. K. Frankena, in a recent paper,[9] joins forces:

> Like Warnock, I believe that there are right and wrong ways to treat infants, animals, imbeciles, and idiots even if or even though (as the case may be) they are not persons or human beings—just because they are capable of pleasure and suffering, and not just because their lives happen to have some value to or for those who clearly are persons or human beings.

And Peter Singer[10] writes:

> If a being is not capable of suffering, or of experiencing enjoyment or happiness, there is nothing to be taken into account. This is why the limit of sentience (using the term as a convenient, if not strictly accurate, shorthand for the capacity to suffer or experience enjoyment or happiness) is the only defensible boundary of concern for the interests of others (154).

I say that the mood is aggravated because, although I acknowledge and even applaud the conviction expressed by these philosophers that the capacity to suffer (or perhaps better, *sentience*) is sufficient for moral considerability, I fail to understand their reasons for thinking such a criterion necessary. To be sure, there are hints at reasons in each case. Warnock implies that nonsentient beings could not be proper "beneficiaries" of moral action. Singer seems to think that beyond sentience "there is nothing to take into account." And Frankena suggests that nonsentient beings simply do not provide us with moral reasons for respecting them unless it be potentially for sentience.[11] Yet it is so clear that there *is* something to take into account, something that is not merely "potential sentience" and which surely does qualify beings as beneficiaries and capable of harm—namely, *life*—that the hints provided seem to me to fall short of good reasons.

Biologically, it appears that sentience is an adaptive characteristic of living organisms that provides them with a better capacity to anticipate, and so avoid, threats to life. This at least suggests, though of course it does not prove, that the capacities to suffer and to enjoy are ancillary to something more important rather than tickets to considerability in their own right. In the words of one perceptive scientific observer:

> If we view pleasure as rooted in our sensory physiology, it is not difficult to see that our neurophysiological equipment must have evolved via variation and selective retention in such a way as to record a positive signal to adaptationally satisfactory conditions and a negative signal to adaptationally unsatisfactory conditions. . . . The pleasure signal is only an evolutionarily derived indicator, not the goal itself. It is the applause which signals a job well done, but not the actual completion of the job.[12]

Nor is it absurd to imagine that evolution might have resulted (indeed might still result?) in beings whose capacities to maintain, protect, and advance their lives did not depend upon mechanisms of pain and pleasure at all.

So far, then, we can see that the search for a criterion of moral considerability takes one quickly and plausibly beyond humanism. But there is a tendency, exhibited in the remarks of Warnock, Frankena, and Singer, to draw up the wagons around the notion of sentience. I have suggested that there is reason to go further and not very much in the way of argument not to. But perhaps there is a stronger and more explicit case that can be made for sentience. I think there is, in a way, and I propose to discuss it in detail in the section that follows.

IV

Joel Feinberg offers (51) what may be the clearest and most explicit case for a restrictive criterion on moral considerability (restrictive with respect to life). I should mention at the outset, however, that the context for his remarks is

(I) the concept of "rights", which, we have seen, is sometimes taken to be narrower than the concept of "considerability"; and

(II) the *intelligibility* of rights-attributions, which, we have seen, is problematically related to the more substantive issue of what beings deserve moral consideration.

These two features of Feinberg's discussion might be thought sufficient to invalidate my use of that discussion here. But the context of his remarks is clearly such that 'rights' is taken very broadly, much closer to what I am calling moral considerability than to what Passmore calls "rights." And the thrust of the arguments, since they are directed against the *intelligibility* of certain rights attributions, is *a fortiori* relevant to the more substantive issue set out in (1). So I propose to treat Feinberg's arguments as if they were addressed to the considerability issue in its more substantive form, whether or not they were or would be intended to have such general application. I do so with due notice to the possible need for scare-quotes around Feinberg's name, but with the conviction that it is really in Feinberg's discussion that we discover that the clearest line of argument in favor of something like sentience, an argument which was only hinted at in the remarks of Warnock, Frankena, and Singer.

The central thesis defended by Feinberg is that a being cannot intelligibly be said to possess moral rights (read: deserve moral consideration) unless that being satisfies the "interest principle," and that only the subclass of humans and higher animals among living beings satisfies this principle:

> . . . the sorts of beings who can have rights are precisely those who have (or can have) interests. I have come to this tentative conclusion for two reasons: (1) because a right holder must be capable of being represented and it is impossible to represent a being that has no interests, and (2) because a right holder must be capable of being a beneficiary in his own person, and a being without interests is a being that is incapable of being harmed or benefited, having no good or "sake" of its own (51).

Implicit in this passage are the following two arguments, interpreted in terms of moral considerability:

(A1) Only beings who can be represented can deserve moral consideration.
Only beings who have (or can have) interests can be represented.
Therefore, only beings who have (or can have) interests can deserve moral consideration.

(A2) Only beings capable of being beneficiaries can deserve moral consideration.
Only beings who have (or can have) interests are capable of being beneficiaries.
Therefore, only beings who have (or can have) interests can deserve moral consideration.

I suspect that these two arguments are at work between the lines in Warnock, Frankena, and Singer, though of course one can never be sure. In any case, I propose to consider them as the best defense of the sentience criterion in recent literature.

I am prepared to grant, with some reservations, the first premises in each of these obviously valid arguments. The second premises, though, are *both* importantly equivocal. To claim that only beings who have (or can have) interests can be represented might mean that "mere things" cannot be represented because they have nothing to represent, no "interests" as opposed to "usefulness" to defend or protect. Similarly, to claim that only beings who have (or can have) interests are capable of being beneficiaries might mean that "mere things" are incapable of being benefited or harmed—they have no "well-being" to be sought or acknowledged by rational moral agents. So construed, Feinberg seems to be right; but he also seems to be committed to allowing any *liv-*

ing thing the status of moral considerability. For as he himself admits, even plants

> . . . are not "mere things"; they are vital objects with inherited biological propensities determining their natural growth. Moreover we do say that certain conditions are "good" or "bad" for plants, thereby suggesting that plants, unlike rocks, are capable of having a "good" (51).

But Feinberg pretty clearly wants to draw the nets tighter than this—and he does so by interpreting the notion of "interests" in the two second premises more narrowly. The contrast term he favors is not 'mere things' but 'mindless creatures'. And he makes this move by insisting that "interests" logically presuppose *desires* or "wants" or "aims", the equipment for which is not possessed by plants (nor, we might add, by many animals or even some humans?).

But why should we accept this shift in strength of the criterion? In doing so, we clearly abandon one sense in which living organisms like plants do have interests that can be represented. There is no absurdity in imagining the representation of the needs of a tree for sun and water in the face of a proposal to cut it down or pave its immediate radius for a parking lot. We might of course, on reflection, decide to go ahead and cut it down or do the paving, but there is hardly an intelligibility problem about representing the tree's interest in our deciding not to. In the face of their obvious tendencies to maintain and heal themselves, it is very difficult to reject the idea of interests on the part of trees (and plants generally) in remaining alive.[13]

Nor will it do to suggest, as Feinberg does, that the needs (interests) of living things like trees are not really their own but implicitly *ours*: "Plants may need things in order to discharge their functions, but their functions are assigned by human interests, not their own" (54). As if it were human interests that assigned to trees the tasks of growth or maintenance! The interests at stake are clearly those of the living things themselves, not simply those of the owners or users or other human persons involved. Indeed, there is a suggestion in this passage that, to be capable of being represented, an organism must *matter* to human beings somehow—a suggestion whose implications for human rights (disenfranchisement) let alone the rights of animals (inconsistently for Feinberg, I think)—are grim.

The truth seems to be that the "interests" that nonsentient beings share with sentient beings (over and against "mere things") are far more plausible as criteria of *considerability* than the "interests" that sentient beings share (over and against "mindless creatures"). This is not to say that interests construed in the latter way are morally irrelevant—for they may play a role as criteria of moral *significance*—but it is to say that psychological or hedonic capacities seem unnecessarily sophisticated when it comes to locating the minimal conditions for something's deserving to be valued for its own sake. Surprisingly, Feinberg's own reflections on "mere things" appear to support this very point:

> . . . more things have no conative life: no conscious wishes, desires, and hopes; or urges and impulses; or unconscious drives, aims, and goals; or latent tendencies, direction of growth, and natural fulfillments. Interests must be compounded somehow out of conations; hence mere things have no interests (49).

Together with the acknowledgment, quoted earlier, that plants, for example, are not "mere things," such observations seem to undermine the interest principle in its more restrictive form. I conclude, with appropriate caution, that the interest principle either grows to fit what we might call a "life principle" or requires an arbitrary stipulation of psychological capacities (for desires, wants, etc.) which are neither warranted by (A1) and (A2) nor independently plausible.

V

Thus far, I have examined the views of four philosophers on the necessity of sentience or interests (narrowly conceived) as a condition on moral considerability. I have maintained that these views are not plausibly supported, when they are supported at all, because of a reluctance to acknowledge in nonsentient living beings the presence of independent needs, capacities for benefit and harm, etc. I should like, briefly, to reflect on a more general level about the roots of this reluctance before proceeding to a consideration of objections against the "life" criterion which I have been defending. In the course of this reflection, we might gain some insight into the sources of our collective hesitation in viewing environmental ethics in a "nonchauvinistic" way.[14]

When we consider the reluctance to go beyond sentience in the context of moral consideration—and look for both explanations and justifications—two thoughts come to mind. The first is that, given the connection between beneficence (or nonmaleficence) and morality, it is natural that limits on moral considerability will come directly from limits on the range of beneficiaries (or "maleficiaries"). This is implicit in Warnock and explicit in Feinberg. The second thought is that, if one's conception of the good is *hedonistic* in character, one's conception of a beneficiary will quite naturally be restricted to beings who are capable of pleasure and pain. If pleasure or satisfaction is the only ultimate gift we have to give, morally, then it is to be expected that only those equipped to receive such a gift will enter into our moral deliberation. And if pain or dissatisfaction is the only ultimate harm we can cause, then it is to be expected that only those equipped for it will deserve our consideration. There seems, therefore, to be a noncontingent connection between a hedonistic or quasi-hedonistic[15] theory of value and a response to the moral-considerability question which favors sentience of interest possession (narrowly conceived).

One must, of course, avoid drawing too strong a conclusion about this connection. It does not follow from the fact that hedonism leads naturally to the sentience criterion either that it entails that criterion or that one who holds that criterion must be a hedonist in his theory of value. For one might be a hedonist with respect to the good and yet think that moral consideration was, on other grounds, restricted to a subclass of the beings capable of enjoyment or pain. And one might hold to the sentience criterion for considerability while denying that pleasure, for example, was the only intrinsically good thing in the life of a human (or nonhuman) being. So hedonism about value and the sentience criterion of moral considerability are not logically equivalent. Nor does either entail the other. But there is some sense, I think, in which they mutually support each other—both in terms of "rendering plausible" and in terms of "helping to explain." As Derek Parfit is fond of putting it, "there are not entailments, but then there seldom are in moral reasoning."[16]

Let me hazard the hypothesis, then, that there is a nonaccidental affinity between a person's or a society's conception of value and its conception of moral considerability. More specifically, there is an affinity between hedonism or some variation on hedonism and a predilection for the sentience criterion of considerability or some variation on it. The implications one might draw from this are many. In the context of a quest for a richer moral framework to deal with a new awareness of the environment, one might be led to expect significant resistance from a hedonistic society unless one forced one's imperatives into an instrumental form. One might also be led to an appreciation of how technology aimed at largely hedonistic goals could gradually "harden the hearts" of a civilization to the biotic community in which it lives—at least until crisis or upheaval raised some questions.[17]

VI

Let us now turn to several objections that might be thought to render a "life principle" of moral considerability untenable quite independently of the adequacy or inadequacy of the sentience or interest principle.

(O1) A principle of moral respect or consideration for life in all its forms is mere Schweitzerian romanticism, even if it does not involve, as it probably does, the projection of mental or psychological categories beyond their responsible boundaries into the realms of plants, insects, and microbes.

(R1) This objection misses the central thrust of my discussion, which is *not* that the sentience criterion is necessary, but applicable to all life forms—rather the point is that the possession of sentience is not necessary for moral considerability. Schweitzer himself may have held the former view—and so have been "romantic"—but this is beside the point.

(O2) To suggest seriously that moral considerability is coextensive with life is to suggest that conscious, feeling beings have no more central role in the moral life than vegetables, which is downright absurd—if not perverse.

(R2) This objection misses the central thrust of my discussion as well, for a different reason. It is consistent with acknowledging the moral considerability of all life forms to go on to point out differences of moral significance among these life forms. And as far as perversion is concerned, history will perhaps be a better judge of our civilization's treatment of animals and the living environment on that score.

(O3) Consideration of life can serve as a criterion only to the degree that life itself can be given a precise definition; and it can't.

(R3) I fail to see why a criterion of moral considerability must be strictly decidable in order to be tenable. Surely rationality, potential rationality, sentience, and the capacity for or possession of interests fare no better here. Moreover, there do seem to be empirically respectable accounts of the nature of living beings available which are not intolerably vague or open-textured:

> The typifying mark of a living system . . . appears to be its persistent state of low entropy, sustained by metabolic processes for accumulating energy, and maintained in equilibrium with its environment by homeostatic feedback processes.[18]

Granting the need for certain further qualifications, a definition such as this strikes me as not only plausible in its own right, but ethically illuminating, since it suggests that the core of moral concern lies in respect for self-sustaining organization and integration in the face of pressures toward high entropy.

(O4) If life, as understood in the previous response, is really taken as the key to moral considerability, then it is possible that larger systems besides our ordinarily understood "linear" extrapolations from human beings (e.g., animals, plants, etc.) might satisfy the conditions, such as the biosystem as a whole. This surely would be a *reductio* of the life principle.

(R4) At best, it would be a *reductio* of the life principle in this form or without qualification. But it seems to me that such (perhaps surprising) implications, if true, should be taken seriously. There is some evidence that the biosystem as a whole exhibits behavior approximating to the definition sketched above,[19] and I see no reason to deny it moral considerability on that account. Why should the universe of moral considerability map neatly onto our medium-sized framework of organisms?

(O5) There are severe epistemological problems about imputing interests, benefits, harms, etc. to nonsentient beings. What is it for a tree to have needs?

(R5) I am not convinced that the epistemological problems are more severe in this context than they would be in numerous others which the objector would probably not find problematic. Christopher Stone has put this point nicely:

> I am sure I can judge with more certainty and meaningfulness whether and when my lawn wants (needs) water than the Attorney General can judge whether and when the United States wants (needs) to take an appeal from an adverse judgment by a lower court. The lawn tells me that it wants water by a certain dryness of the blades and soil—immediately obvious to the touch—the appearance of bald spots, yellowing, and a lack of springiness after being walked on; how does "the United States" communicate to the Attorney General? (24).

We make decisions in the interests of others or on behalf of others every day—"others" whose wants are far less verifiable than those of most living creatures.

(O6) Whatever the force of the previous objections, the clearest and most decisive refutation of the principle of respect for life is that one cannot *live* according to it, nor is there any indication in nature that we were intended to. We must eat, experiment to gain knowledge, protect ourselves from predation (macroscopic and microscopic), and in general deal with the overwhelming complexities of the moral life while remaining psychologically intact. To take seriously the criterion of considerability being defended, all these things must be seen as somehow morally wrong.

(R6) This objection, if it is not met by implication in (R2), can be met, I think, by recalling the distinction made earlier between regulative and operative moral consideration. It seems to me that there clearly are limits to the operational character of respect for living things. We must eat, and usually this involves killing (though not always). We must have knowledge, and sometimes this involves experimentation with living things and killing (though not always). We must protect ourselves from predation and disease, and sometimes this involves killing (though not always). The regulative character of the moral consideration due to all living things asks, as far as I can see, for sensitivity and awareness, not for suicide (psychic or otherwise). But it is not vacuous, in that it does provide a *ceteris paribus* encouragement in the direction of nutritional, scientific, and medical practices of a genuinely life-respecting sort.

As for the implicit claim, in the objection, that since nature doesn't respect life, we needn't, there are two rejoinders. The first is that the premise is not so clearly true. Gratuitous killing in nature is rare indeed. The second, and more important, response is that the issue at hand has to do with the appropriate moral demands to be made on rational moral agents, not on beings who are not rational moral agents. Besides, this objection would tell equally against *any* criterion of moral considerability so far as I can see, if the suggestion is that nature is a moral.

I have been discussing the necessary and sufficient conditions that should regulate moral consideration. As indicated earlier, however, numerous other questions are waiting in the wings. Central among them are questions dealing with how to balance competing claims to consideration in a world in which such competing claims seem pervasive. Related to these questions would be problems about the relevance of developing or declining status in life (the very young and the very old) and the relevance of the part-whole relation (leaves to a tree; species to an ecosystem). And there are many others.

Perhaps enough has been said, however, to clarify an important project for contemporary ethics, if not to defend a full-blown account of moral considerability and moral significance. Leopold's ethical vision and its implications for modern society in the form of an environmental ethic are important—so we should proceed with care in assessing it.

NOTES

1. *The Object of Morality* (New York: Methuen, 1971); parenthetical page references to Warnock will be to this book.
2. *Should Trees Have Standing?* (Los Altos, Calif.: William Kaufmann, 1974); parenthetical page references to Stone will be to this book.
3. "From Egoism to Environmentalism," in Goodpaster and K. M. Sayre, eds., *Ethics and Problems of the 21st Century* (Notre Dame, Ind.: University Press, 1978).
4. *Man's Responsibility for Nature* (New York: Scribner's, 1974).
5. Cf. R. M. Hare, "The Argument from Received Opinion," in *Essays on Philosophical Method* (New York: Macmillan, 1971), p. 117.

6. "The Rights of Animals and Unborn Generations," in Blackstone, *Philosophy and Environmental Crisis* (University of Georgia, 1974), p. 43; parenthetical page references to Feinberg will be to this paper.
7. "On Saying the Ethical Thing," in Goodpaster, ed., *Perspectives on Morality* (Notre Dame, Ind.: University Press, 1976), pp. 107–124.
8. Actually, it seems to me that we ought not to draw the boundary of moral responsibility just here. See my "Morality and Organizations," in *Proceedings of the Second National Conference on Business Ethics* (Waltham, Mass.: Bentley College, 1978).
9. "Ethics and the Environment," in Goodpaster and Sayre, *op. cit.*
10. "All Animals Are Equal," in Tom Regan and Peter Singer, *Animal Rights and Human Obligations* (Englewood Cliffs, N.J.: Prentice-Hall, 1976). See p. 316.
11. "I can see no reason, from the moral point of view, why we should respect something that is alive but has no conscious sentiency and so can experience no pleasure or pain, joy or suffering, unless perhaps it is potentially a consciously sentient being, as in the case of a fetus. Why, if leaves and trees have no capacity to feel pleasure or to suffer, should I tear no leaf from a tree? Why should I respect its location any more than that of a stone in my driveway, if no benefit or harm comes to any person or sentient being by my moving it?" ("Ethics and the Environment").
12. Mark W. Lipsey, "Value Science and Developing Society," paper delivered to the Society for Religion in Higher Education, Institute on Society, Technology and Values (July 15–Aug. 4, 1973), p. 11.
13. See Albert Szent-Gyorgyi, *The Living State* (New York; Academic Press, 1972), esp. ch. VI, "Vegetable Defense Systems."
14. Cf. R. and V. Routley, "Not for Humans Only," in Goodpaster and Sayre, note 3. R. Routley is, I think, the originator of the phrase "human chauvinism".
15. Frankena uses the phrase "quasi-hedonist" in *Ethics* (Englewood Cliffs, N.J.: Prentice-Hall, 1973), p. 90.
16. "Later Selves and Moral Principles," in A. Montefiori, ed., *Philosophy and Personal Relations* (Boston: Routledge & Kegan Paul, 1973), p. 147.
17. There is more, but much depends, I think, on defending claims about the value theory at work in our society and about the need for noninstrumental approaches to value change. Value theory, like scientific theory, tends to evolve by trying to accommodate to the conventional pattern any new suggestions about what is good or should be respected. I suspect that the analogy holds true for the explanations to be given of ethical revolutions—a new and simpler way of dealing with our moral sense emerges to take the place of the old contrivances—be they egoistic, utilitarian, or in the present case hedonistic (if not humanistic). Such topics are, of course, not the topics of this essay. Perhaps I can be excused for raising them here by the contention that a line of argument in ethics (indeed, in philosophy generally) needs not only to be criticized—it needs to be *understood.*
18. K. M. Sayre, *Cybernetics and the Philosophy of Mind* (New York: Humanities, 1976), p. 91.
19. See J. Lovelock and S. Epton, "The Quest for Gaia," *The New Scientist,* LXV, 935 (Feb. 6, 1975): 304–309.

The Ethics of Respect for Nature

Paul W. Taylor

Paul W. Taylor is professor emeritus of philosophy at Brooklyn College, City University of New York. He is the author of Respect for Nature: A Theory of Environmental Ethics.

HUMAN-CENTERED AND LIFE-CENTERED SYSTEMS OF ENVIRONMENTAL ETHICS

When the basic characteristics of the attitude of respect for nature are made clear, it will be seen that a life-centered system of environmental ethics need not be holistic or organicist in its conception of the kinds of entities that are deemed the appropriate objects of moral concern and consideration. Nor does such a system require that the concepts of ecological homeostasis, equilibrium, and integrity provide us with normative principles from which could be derived (with the addition of factual knowledge) our obligations with regard to natural ecosystems. The "balance of nature" is not itself a moral norm, however important may be the role it plays in our general outlook on the natural world that underlies the attitude of respect for nature. I argue that finally it is the good (well-being, welfare) of individual organisms, considered as entities having inherent worth, that determines our moral relations with the Earth's wild communities of life.

In designating the theory to be set forth as life-centered, I intend to contrast it with all anthropocentric views. According to the latter, human actions affecting the natural environment and its nonhuman inhabitants are right (or wrong) by either of two criteria: they have consequences which are favorable (or unfavorable) to human well-being, or they are consistent (or inconsistent) with the system of norms that protect and implement human rights. From this human-centered standpoint it is to humans and only to humans that all duties are ultimately owed. We may have responsibilities *with regard to* the natural ecosystems and biotic communities of our planet, but these responsibilities are

This essay originally appeared in *Environmental Ethics*, Vol. 3, No. 3 (Fall 1981), pp. 197–218. Reprinted with permission.

in every case based on the contingent fact that our treatment of those ecosystems and communities of life can further the realization of human values and/or human rights. We have no obligation to promote or protect the good of nonhuman living things, independently of this contingent fact.

A life-centered system of environmental ethics is opposed to human-centered ones precisely on this point. From the perspective of a life-centered theory, we have prima facie moral obligations that are owed to wild plants and animals themselves as members of the Earth's biotic community. We are morally bound (other things being equal) to protect or promote their good for *their* sake. Our duties to respect the integrity of natural ecosystems, to preserve endangered species, and to avoid environmental pollution stem from the fact that these are ways in which we can help make it possible for wild species populations to achieve and maintain a healthy existence in a natural state. Such obligations are due those living things out of recognition of their inherent worth. They are entirely additional to and independent of the obligations we owe to our fellow humans. Although many of the actions that fulfill one set of obligations will also fulfill the other, two different grounds of obligation are involved. Their well-being, as well as human well-being, is something to be realized *as an end in itself.*

If we were to accept a life-centered theory of environmental ethics, a profound reordering of our moral universe would take place. We would begin to look at the whole of the Earth's biosphere in a new light. Our duties with respect to the "world" of nature would be seen as making prima facie claims upon us to be balanced against our duties with respect to the "world" of human civilization. We could no longer simply take the human point of view and consider the effects of our actions exclusively from the perspective of our own good. . . .

We can think of the good of an individual nonhuman organism as consisting in the full development of its biological powers. Its good is realized to the extent that it is strong and healthy. It possesses whatever capacities it needs for successfully coping with its environment and so preserving its existence throughout the various stages of the normal life cycle of its species. The good of a population or community of such individuals consists in the population or community maintaining itself from generation to generation as a coherent system of genetically and ecologically related organisms whose average good is at an optimum level for the given environment. (Here *average good* means that the degree of realization of the good of *individual organisms* in the population or community is, on average, greater than would be the case under any other ecologically functioning order of interrelations among those species populations in the given ecosystem.)

The idea of a being having a good of its own, as I understand it, does not entail that the being must . . . take an interest in what affects its life for better or for worse. We can act in a being's interest or contrary to its interest without its being interested in what we are doing to it in the sense of wanting or not wanting us to do it. It may, indeed, be wholly unaware that favorable and unfavorable events are taking place in its life. I take it that trees, for example, have no knowledge or desires or feelings. Yet is is undoubtedly the case that trees can be harmed or benefited by our actions. We can crush their roots by running a bulldozer too close to them. We can see to it that they get adequate nourishment and moisture by fertilizing and watering the soil around them. Thus we can help or hinder them in the realization of their good. It is the good of trees themselves that is thereby affected. . . .

When construed in this way, the concept of a being's good is not coextensive with sentience or the capacity for feeling pain. William Frankena has argued for a general theory of environmental ethics in which the ground of a creature's being worthy of moral consideration is its sentience. I have offered some criticisms of this view elsewhere, but the full refutation of such a position, it seems to me, finally depends on the positive reasons for accepting a life-centered theory of the kind I am defending in this essay. . . .[1]

Since I am concerned only with human treatment of wild organisms, species populations, and communities of life as they occur in our planet's natural ecosystems, it is to those entities alone that the concept "having a good of its own" will here be applied. I am not denying that other living things, whose genetic origin and environmental conditions have been produced, controlled, and manipulated by humans for human ends, do have a good of their own in the same sense as do wild plants and animals. It is not my purpose in this essay, however, to set out or defend the principles that should guide our conduct with regard to their good. It is only insofar as their production and use by humans have good or ill effects upon natural ecosystems and their wild inhabitants that the ethics of respect for nature comes into play. . . .

THE BIOCENTRIC OUTLOOK ON NATURE

[The] belief system underlying the attitude of respect for nature I call (for want of a better name) "the biocentric outlook on nature." Since it is not wholly analyzable into empirically confirmable assertions, it should not be thought of as simply a compendium of the biological sciences concerning our planet's ecosystems. It might best be described as a philosophical world view, to distinguish it from a scientific theory or explanatory system. However, one of its major tenets is the great lesson we have learned from the science of ecology: the interdependence of all living things in an organically unified order whose balance and stability are necessary conditions for the realization of the good of its constituent biotic communities.

Before turning to an account of the main components of the biocentric outlook, it is convenient here to set forth the overall structure of my theory of environmental ethics as it has now emerged. The ethics of respect for nature is made up of three basic elements: a belief system, an ultimate moral attitude, and a set of rules of duty and standards of character. These elements are connected with each other in the following manner. The belief system provides a certain outlook on nature which supports and makes intelligible an autonomous agent's adopting, as an ultimate moral attitude, the attitude of respect for nature. It supports and makes intelligible the attitude in the sense that, when an autonomous agent understands its moral relations to the natural world in terms of this outlook, it recognizes the attitude of respect to be the only *suitable* or *fitting* attitude to take toward all wild forms of life in the Earth's biosphere. Living things are now viewed as *the appropriate objects of the attitude of respect* and are accordingly regarded as entities possessing inherent worth. One then places intrinsic value on the promotion and protection of their good. As a consequence of this, one makes a moral commitment to abide by a set of rules of duty and to fulfill (as far as one can by one's own efforts) certain standards of good character. Given one's adoption of the attitude of respect, one makes that moral commitment because one considers those rules and standards to be validly binding on all moral agents. They are seen as embodying forms of conduct and character structures in which the attitude of respect for nature is manifested.

This three-part complex which internally orders the ethics of respect for nature is symmetrical with a theory of human ethics grounded on respect for persons. Such a theory includes, first, a conception of oneself and others as persons, that is, as centers of autonomous choice. Second, there is the attitude of respect for persons as persons. When this is adopted as an ultimate moral attitude it involves the disposition to treat every person as having inherent worth or "human dignity." Every human being, just in virtue of her or his humanity, is understood to be worthy of moral consideration, and intrinsic value is placed on the autonomy and well-being of each. This is what Kant meant by conceiving of persons as ends in themselves. Third, there is an ethical system of duties which are acknowledged to be owed by everyone to everyone. These duties are forms of conduct in which public recognition is given to each individual's inherent worth as a person.

This structural framework for a theory of human ethics is meant to leave open the issue of consequentialism (utilitarianism) versus nonconsequentialism (deontology). That issue concerns the particular kind of system of rules defining the duties of moral agents toward persons. Similarly, I am leaving open in this paper the question of what particular kind of system of rules defines our duties with respect to the natural world.

The biocentric outlook on nature has four main components. (1) Humans are thought of as members of the Earth's community of life, holding that membership on the same terms as apply to all the nonhuman members. (2) The Earth's natural ecosystems as a totality are seen as a complex web of interconnected elements, with the sound biological functioning of each being dependent on the sound biological functioning of the others. (This is the component referred to above as the great lesson that the science of ecology has taught us.) (3) Each individual organism is conceived of as a teleological center of life, pursuing its own good in its own way. (4) Whether we are concerned with standards of merit or with the concept of inherent worth, the claim that humans by their very nature are superior to other species is a groundless claim and, in the light of elements (1), (2), and (3) above, must be rejected as nothing more than an irrational bias in our own favor.

The conjunction of these four ideas constitutes the biocentric outlook on nature. In the remainder of this paper I give a brief account of the first three components, followed by a more detailed analysis of the fourth. I then conclude by indicating how this outlook provides a way of justifying the attitude of respect for nature.

HUMANS AS MEMBERS OF THE EARTH'S COMMUNITY OF LIFE

We share with other species a common relationship to the Earth. In accepting the biocentric outlook we take the fact of our being an animal species to be a fundamental feature of our existence. We consider it an essential aspect of "the human condition." We do not deny the differences between ourselves and other species, but we keep in the forefront of our consciousness the fact that in relation to our planet's natural ecosystems we are but one species population among many. Thus we acknowledge our origin in the very same evolutionary process that gave rise to all other species and we recognize ourselves to be confronted with similar environmental challenges to those that confront them. The laws of genetics, of natural selection, and of adaptation apply equally to all of us as biological creatures. In this light we consider ourselves as one with them, not set apart from them. We, as well as they, must face certain basic conditions of existence that impose requirements on us for our survival and well-being. Each animal and plant is like us in having a good of its own. Although our human good (what is of true value in human life, including the exercise of individual autonomy in choosing our own particular value systems) is not like the good of a nonhuman animal or plant, it can no more be realized than their good can without the biological necessities for survival and physical health.

When we look at ourselves from the evolutionary point of view, we see that not only are we very recent arrivals on Earth, but that our emergence as a new species on the planet was originally an event of no particular importance to the entire scheme of things. The Earth was teeming with life long before we appeared. Putting the point metaphorically, we are relative newcomers, entering a home that has been the residence of others for hundreds of millions of years, a home that must now be shared by all of us together.

The comparative brevity of human life on Earth may be vividly depicted by imagining the geological time scale in spatial terms. Suppose we start with algae, which have been around for at least 600 million years. (The earliest protozoa actually predated this by several *billion* years.) If the time that algae have been here were represented by the length of a football field (300 feet), then the period during which sharks have been swimming in the world's oceans and spiders have been spinning their webs would occupy three quarters of the length of the field; reptiles would show up at about the center of the field; mammals would cover the last third of the field; hominids (mammals of the family *Hominidae*) the last two feet; and the species *Homo sapiens* the last six inches.

Whether this newcomer is able to survive as long as other species remains to be seen. But there is surely something presumptuous about the way humans look down on the "lower" animals, especially those that have become extinct. We consider the dinosaurs, for example, to be biological failures, though they existed on our planet for 65 million years. One writer has made the point with beautiful simplicity:

> We sometimes speak of the dinosaurs as failures; there will be time enough for that judgment when we have lasted even for one tenth as long. . . .[2]

The possibility of the extinction of the human species, a possibility which starkly confronts us in the contemporary world, makes us aware of another respect in which we should not consider ourselves privileged beings in relation to other species. This is the fact that the well-being of humans is dependent upon the ecological soundness and health of many plant and animal communities, while their soundness and health does not in the least depend upon human well-being. Indeed, from their standpoint the very existence of humans is quite unnecessary. Every last man, woman, and child could disappear from the face of the Earth without any significant detrimental consequence for the good of wild animals and plants. On the contrary, many of them would be greatly benefited. The destruction of their habitats by human "developments" would cease. The poisoning and polluting of their environment would come to an end. The Earth's land, air, and water would no longer be subject to the degradation they are now undergoing as the result of large-scale technology and uncontrolled population growth. Life communities in natural ecosystems would gradually return to their former healthy state. Tropical forests, for example, would again be able to make their full contribution to a life-sustaining atmosphere for the whole planet. The rivers, lakes, and oceans of the world would (perhaps) eventually become clean again. Spilled oil, plastic trash, and even radioactive waste might finally, after many centuries, cease doing their terrible work. Ecosystems would return to their proper balance, suffering only the disruptions of natural events such as volcanic eruptions and glaciation. From these the community of life could recover, as it has so often done in the past. But the ecological disasters now perpetrated on it by humans—disasters from which it might never recover—these it would no longer have to endure.

If, then, the total, final, absolute extermination of our species (by our own hands?) should take place and if we should not carry all the others with us into oblivion, not only would the Earth's community of life continue to exist, but in all probability its well-being would be enhanced. Our presence, in short, is not needed. If we were to take the standpoint of the community and give voice to its true interest, the ending of our six-inch epoch would most likely be greeted with a hearty "Good riddance!"

THE NATURAL WORLD AS AN ORGANIC SYSTEM

To accept the biocentric outlook and regard ourselves and our place in the world from its perspective is to see the whole natural order of the Earth's biosphere as a complex but unified web of interconnected organisms, objects, and events. The ecological relationships between any community of living things and their environment form an organic whole of functionally interdependent parts. Each ecosystem is a small universe itself in which the interactions of its various species populations comprise an intricately woven network of cause-effect relations. Such dynamic but at the same time relatively stable structures as food chains, predator-prey relations, and plant succession in a forest are self-regulating, energy-recycling mechanisms that preserve the equilibrium of the whole.

As far as the well-being of wild animals and plants is concerned, this ecological equilibrium must not be destroyed. The same holds true of the well-being of humans. When one views the realm of nature from the perspective of the biocentric outlook, one never forgets that in the long run the integrity of the entire biosphere of our planet is essential to the realization of the good of its constituent communities of life, both human and nonhuman.

Although the importance of this idea cannot be overemphasized, it is by now so familiar and so widely acknowledged that I shall not further elaborate on it here. However, I do wish to point out that this "holistic" view of the Earth's ecological systems does not itself constitute a moral norm. It is a factual aspect of biological reality, to be understood as a set of causal connections in ordinary empirical terms. Its significance for humans is the same as its significance for nonhumans, namely, in setting basic conditions for the realization of the good of living things. Its ethical implications for our treatment of the natural environment lie entirely in the fact that our *knowledge* of these causal connections is an essential *means* to fulfilling the aims we set for ourselves in adopting the attitude of respect for nature. In addition, its theoretical implications for the ethics of respect for nature lie in the fact that it (along with the other elements of the biocentric outlook) makes the adopting of that attitude a rational and intelligible thing to do.

INDIVIDUAL ORGANISMS AS TELEOLOGICAL CENTERS OF LIFE

As our knowledge of living things increases, as we come to a deeper understanding of their life cycles, their interactions with other organisms, and the manifold ways in which they adjust to the environment, we become more fully aware of how each of them is carrying out its biological functions according to the laws of its species-specific nature. But besides this, our increasing knowledge and understanding also develop in us a sharpened awareness of the uniqueness of each individual organism. Scientists who have made careful studies of particular plants and animals, whether in the field or in laboratories, have often acquired a knowledge of their subjects as identifiable individuals. Close observation over extended periods of time has led them to an appreciation of the unique "personalities" of their subjects. Sometimes a scientist may come to take a special interest in a particular animal or plant, all the while remaining strictly objective in the gathering and recording of data. Nonscientists may likewise experience this development of interest when, as amateur naturalists, they make accurate observations over sustained periods of close acquaintance with an individual organism. As one becomes more and more familiar with the organism and its behavior, one becomes fully sensitive to the particular way it is living out its life cycle. One may become fascinated by it and even experience some involvement with its good and bad fortunes (that is, with the occurrence of environmental conditions favorable or unfavorable to the realization of its good). The organism comes to mean something to one as a unique, irreplaceable individual. The final culmination of this process is the achievement of a genuine understanding of its point of view and, with that understanding, an ability to "take" that point of view. *Conceiving of it as a center of life, one is able to look at the world from its perspective.*

This development from objective knowledge to the recognition of individuality, and from the recognition of individuality to full awareness of an organism's standpoint, is a process of heightening our consciousness of what it means to be an individual living thing. We grasp the particularity of the organism as a teleological center of life, striving to preserve itself and to realize its own good in its own unique way.

It is to be noted that we need not be falsely anthropomorphizing when we conceive of individual plants and animals in this manner. Understanding them as teleological centers of life does not necessitate "reading into" them human characteristics. We need not, for example, consider them to have consciousness. Some of them may be aware of the world around them and others may not. Nor need we deny that different kinds and levels of awareness are exemplified when consciousness in some form is present. But conscious or not, all are equally teleological centers of life in the sense that each is a unified system of goal-oriented activities directed toward their preservation and well-being.

When considered from an ethical point of view, a teleological center of life is an entity whose "world" can be viewed from the perspective of *its* life. In looking at the world from that perspective we recognize objects and events occurring in its life as being beneficent, maleficent, or indifferent. The first are occurrences which increase its powers to preserve its existence and realize its good. The second decrease or destroy those powers. The third have neither of these effects on the entity. With regard to our human role as moral agents, we can conceive of a teleological center of life as a being whose standpoint we can take in making judgments about what events in the world are good or evil, desirable or undesirable. In making those judgments it is what promotes or protects the being's own good, not what benefits moral agents themselves, that sets the standard of evaluation. Such judgments can be made about anything that happens to the entity which is favorable or unfavorable in relation to its good. As was pointed out earlier, the entity itself need not have any (conscious) *interest* in what is happening to it for such judgments to be meaningful and true.

It is precisely judgments of this sort that we are disposed to make when we take the attitude of respect for nature. In adopting that attitude those judgments are given weight as reasons for action in our practical deliberation. They become morally relevant facts in the guidance of our conduct.

THE DENIAL OF HUMAN SUPERIORITY

This fourth component of the biocentric outlook on nature is the single most important idea in establishing the justifiability of the attitude of respect for nature. Its central role is due to the special relationship it bears to the first three components of the outlook. This relationship will be brought out after the concept of human superiority is examined and analyzed.[3]

In what sense are humans alleged to be superior to other animals? We are different from them in having certain capacities that they lack. But why should these capacities be a mark of superiority? From what point of view are they judged to be signs of superiority and what sense of superiority is meant? After all, various nonhuman species have capacities that humans lack. There is the speed of a cheetah, the vision of an eagle, the agility of a monkey. Why should not these be taken as signs of *their* superiority over humans?

One answer that comes immediately to mind is that these capacities are not as *valuable* as the human capacities that are claimed to make us superior. Such uniquely human characteristics as rational thought, aesthetic creativity, autonomy and self-determination, and moral freedom, it might be held, have a higher value than the capacities found in other species. Yet we must ask: valuable to whom, and on what grounds?

The human characteristics mentioned are all valuable to humans. They are essential to the preservation and enrichment of our civilization and culture. Clearly it is from the human standpoint that they are being judged to be desirable and good. It is not difficult here to recognize a begging of the question. Humans are claiming human superiority from a strictly human point of view, that is, from a point of view in which the good of humans is taken as the standard of judgment. All we need to do is to look at the capacities of nonhuman animals (or plants, for that matter) from the standpoint of *their* good to find a contrary judgment of superiority. The speed of the cheetah, for example, is a sign of its superiority to humans when considered from the standpoint of the good of its species. If it were as slow a runner as a human, it would not be able to survive. And so for all the other abilities of nonhumans which further their good but which are lacking in humans. In each case the claim to human superiority would be rejected from a nonhuman standpoint.

When superiority assertions are interpreted in this way, they are based on judgments of *merit*. To judge the merits of a person or an organism one must apply grading or ranking standards to it. (As I show below, this distinguishes judgments of merit from judgments of inherent worth.) Empirical investigation then determines whether it has the "good-making properties" (merits) in virtue of which it fulfills the standards being applied. In the case of humans, merits may be either moral or nonmoral. We can judge one person to be better than (superior to) another from the moral point of view by applying certain standards to their character and conduct. Similarly, we can appeal to nonmoral criteria in judging someone to be an excellent piano player, a fair cook, a poor tennis player, and so on. Different social purposes and roles are implicit in the making of such judgments, providing the frame of reference for the choice of standards by which the nonmoral merits of people are determined. Ultimately such purposes and roles stem from a society's way of life as a whole. Now a society's way of life may be thought of as the cultural form given to the realization of human values. Whether moral or nonmoral standards are being applied, then, all judgments of people's merits finally depend on human values. All are made from an exclusively human standpoint.

The question that naturally arises at this juncture is: why should standards that are based on human values be assumed to be the only valid criteria of merit and hence the only true signs of superiority? This question is especially pressing when humans are being judged superior in merit to nonhumans. It is true that a human being may be a better mathematician than a monkey, but the monkey may be a better tree climber than a human being. If we humans value mathematics more than tree climbing, that is because our conception of civilized life makes the development of mathematical ability more desirable than the ability to climb trees. But is it not unreasonable to judge nonhumans by the values of human civilization, rather than by values connected with what it is for a member of *that* species to live a good life? If all living things have a good of their own, it at least makes sense to judge the merits of nonhumans by standards derived from *their* good. To use only standards based on human values is already to commit oneself to holding that humans are superior to nonhumans, which is the point in question.

A further logical flaw arises in connection with the widely held conviction that humans are *morally* superior beings because they possess, while others lack, the capacities of a moral agent (free will, accountability, deliberation, judgment, practical reason). This view rests on a conceptual confusion. As far as moral standards are concerned, only beings that have the capacities of a moral agent can properly be judged to be *either* moral (morally good) *or* immoral (morally deficient). Moral standards are simply not applicable to beings that lack such capacities. Animals and plants cannot therefore be said to be morally inferior in merit to humans. Since the only beings that can have moral merits *or be deficient in such merits* are moral agents, it is conceptually incoherent to judge humans as superior to nonhumans on the ground that humans have moral capacities while nonhumans don't.

Up to this point I have been interpreting the claim that humans are superior to other living things as a grading or ranking judgment regarding their comparative merits. There is, however, another way of understanding the idea of human superiority. According to this interpretation, humans are superior to nonhumans not as regards their merits but as regards their inherent worth. Thus the claim of human superiority is to be understood as asserting that all humans, simply in virtue of their humanity, have *a greater inherent worth* than other living things.

The inherent worth of an entity does not depend on its merits.[4] To consider something as possessing inherent worth, we have seen, is to place intrinsic value on the realization of its good. This is done regardless of whatever particular merits it might have or might lack, as judged by a set of grading or ranking standards. In human affairs, we are all familiar with the principle that one's worth as a person does not vary with one's merits or lack of merits. The same can hold true of animals and plants. To regard such entities as possessing inherent worth entails disregarding their merits and deficiencies, whether they are being judged from a human standpoint or from the standpoint of their own species.

The idea of one entity having more merit than another, and so being superior to it in merit, makes perfectly good sense. Merit is a grading or ranking concept, and judgments of comparative merit are based on the different degrees to which things satisfy a given standard. But what can it mean to talk about one thing being superior to another in inherent worth? In order to get at what is being asserted in such a claim it is helpful first to look at the social origin of the concept of degrees of inherent worth.

The idea that humans can possess different degrees of inherent worth originated in societies having rigid class structures. Before the rise of modern democracies with their egalitarian outlook, one's membership in a hereditary class determined one's social status. People in the upper classes were looked up to, while those in the lower classes were looked down upon. In such a society one's social superiors and social inferiors were clearly defined and easily recognized.

Two aspects of these class-structured societies are especially relevant to the idea of degrees of inherent worth. First, those born into the upper classes were deemed more worthy of respect than those born into the lower orders. Second, the superior worth of upper class people had nothing to do with their merits nor did the inferior worth of those in the lower classes rest on their lack of merits. One's superiority or inferiority entirely derived from a social position one was born into. The modern concept of a meritocracy simply did not apply. One could not advance into a higher class by any sort of moral or nonmoral achievement. Similarly, an aristocrat held his title and all the privileges that went with it just because he was the eldest son of a titled nobleman. Unlike the bestowing of knighthood in contemporary Great Britain, one did not earn membership in the nobility by meritorious conduct.

We who live in modern democracies no longer believe in such hereditary social distinctions. Indeed, we would wholeheartedly condemn them on moral grounds as being fundamentally unjust. We have come to think of class systems as a paradigm of social injustice, it being a central principle of the democratic way of life that among humans there are no superiors and no inferiors. Thus we have rejected the whole conceptual framework in which people are judged to have different degrees of inherent worth. That idea is incompatible with our notion of human equality based on the doctrine that all humans, simply in virtue of their humanity, have the same inherent worth. (The belief in universal human rights is one form that this egalitarianism takes.)

The vast majority of people in modern democracies, however, do not maintain an egalitarian outlook when it comes to comparing human beings with other living things. Most people consider our own species to be superior to all other species and this superiority is understood to be a matter of inherent worth, not merit. There may exist thoroughly vicious and depraved humans who lack all merit. Yet because they are human they are thought to belong to a higher class of entities than any plant or animal. That one is born into the species *Homo sapiens* entitles one to have lordship over those who are one's inferiors, namely, those born into other species. The parallel with hereditary social classes is very close. Implicit in this view is a hierarchical conception of nature according to which an organism has a position of superiority or inferiority in the Earth's community of life simply on the basis of its genetic background. The "lower" orders of life are looked down upon and it is considered perfectly proper that they serve the interests of those belonging to the highest order, namely humans. The intrinsic value we place on the well-being of our fellow humans reflects our recognition of their rightful position as our equals. No such intrinsic value is to be placed on the good of other animals, unless we choose to do so out of fondness or affection for them. But their well-being imposes no moral requirement on us. In this respect there is an absolute difference in moral status between ourselves and them.

This is the structure of concepts and beliefs that people are committed to insofar as they regard humans to be superior in inherent worth to all other species. I now wish to argue that this structure of concepts and beliefs is completely groundless. If we accept the first three components of the biocentric outlook and from that perspective look at the major philosophical traditions which have supported that structure, we find it to be at bottom nothing more than the expression of an irrational bias in our own favor. The philosophical traditions themselves rest on very questionable assumptions or else simply beg the question. I briefly consider three of the main traditions to substantiate the point. These are classical Greek humanism, Cartesian dualism, and the Judeo-Christian concept of the Great Chain of Being.

The inherent superiority of humans over other species was implicit in the Greek definition of man as a rational animal. Our animal nature was identified with "brute" desires that need the order and restraint of reason to rule them (just as reason is the special virtue of those who rule in the ideal state). Rationality was then seen to be the key to our superiority over animals. It enables us to live on a higher plane and endows us with a nobility and worth that other creatures lack. This familiar way of comparing humans with other species is deeply ingrained in our Western philosophical outlook. The point to consider here is that this view does not actually provide an argument *for* human superiority but rather makes explicit the framework of thought that is implicitly used by those who think of humans as inherently superior to nonhumans. The Greeks who held that humans, in virtue of their rational capacities, have a kind of worth greater than that of any nonrational being, never looked at rationality as but one capacity of living things among many others. But when we consider rationality from the standpoint of the first three elements of the ecological outlook, we see that its value lies in its importance for *human* life. Other creatures achieve their species-specific good without the need of rationality, although they often make use of capacities that humans lack. So the humanistic outlook of classical Greek thought does not give us a neutral (non-question-begging) ground on which to construct a scale of degrees of inherent worth possessed by different species of living things.

The second tradition, centering on the Cartesian dualism of soul and body, also fails to justify the claim to human superiority. That superiority is supposed to derive from the fact that we have souls while animals do not. Animals are mere automata and lack the divine element that makes us spiritual beings. I won't go into the now familiar criticisms of this two-substance view. I only add the point that, even if humans are composed of an immaterial, unextended soul and a material, extended body, this in itself is not a reason to deem them of greater worth than entities that are only bodies. Why is a soul substance a thing that adds value to its possessor? Unless some theological reasoning is offered here (which many, including myself, would find unacceptable on epistemological grounds), no logical connection is evident. An immaterial something which thinks is better than a material something which does not think only if thinking itself has value, either intrinsically or instrumentally. Now it is intrinsically valuable to humans alone, who value it as an end in itself, and it is instrumentally valuable to those who benefit from it, namely humans.

For animals that neither enjoy thinking for its own sake nor need it for living the kind of life for which they are best adapted, it has no value. Even if "thinking" is broadened to include all forms of consciousness, there are still many living things that can do without it and yet live what is for their species a good life. The anthropocentricity underlying the claim to human superiority runs throughout Cartesian dualism.

A third major source of the idea of human superiority is the Judeo-Christian concept of the Great Chain of Being. Humans are superior to animals and plants because their Creator has given them a higher place on the chain. It begins with God at the top, and then moves to the angels, who are lower than God but higher than humans, then to humans, positioned between the angels and the beasts (partaking of the nature of both), and then on down to the lower levels occupied by nonhuman animals, plants, and finally inanimate objects. Humans, being "made in God's image," are inherently superior to animals and plants by virtue of their being closer (in their essential nature) to God.

The metaphysical and epistemological difficulties with this conception of a hierarchy of entities are, in my mind, insuperable. Without entering into this matter here, I only point out that if we are unwilling to accept the metaphysics of traditional Judaism and Christianity, we are again left without good reasons for holding to the claim of inherent human superiority.

The foregoing considerations (and others like them) leave us with but one ground for the assertion that a human being, regardless of merit, is a higher kind of entity than any other living thing. This is the mere fact of the genetic makeup of the species *Homo sapiens.* But this is surely irrational and arbitrary. Why should the arrangement of genes of a certain type be a mark of superior value, especially when this fact about an organism is taken by itself, unrelated to any other aspect of its life? We might just as well refer to any other genetic makeup as a ground of superior value. Clearly we are confronted here with a wholly arbitrary claim that can only be explained as an irrational bias in our own favor.

That the claim is nothing more than a deep-seated prejudice is brought home to us when we look at our relation to other species in the light of the first three elements of the biocentric outlook. Those elements taken conjointly give us a certain overall view of the natural world and of the place of humans in it. When we take this view we come to understand other living things, their environmental conditions, and their ecological relationships in such a way as to awake in us a deep sense of our kinship with them as fellow members of the Earth's community of life. Humans and nonhumans alike are viewed together as integral parts of one unified whole in which all living things are functionally interrelated. Finally, when our awareness focuses on the individual lives of plants and animals, each is seen to share with us the characteristic of being a teleological center of life striving to realize its own good in its own good in its own unique way.

As this entire belief system becomes part of the conceptual framework through which we understand and perceive the world, we come to see ourselves as bearing a certain moral relation to nonhuman forms of life. Our ethical role in nature takes on a new significance. We begin to look at other species as we look at ourselves, seeing them as beings which have a good they are striving to realize just as we have a good we are striving to realize. We accordingly develop the disposition to view the world from the standpoint of their good as well as from the standpoint of our own good. Now if the groundlessness of the claim that humans are inherently superior to other species were brought clearly before our minds, we would not remain intellectually neutral toward that claim but would reject it as being fundamentally at variance with our total world outlook. In the absence of any good reasons for holding it, the assertion of human superiority would then appear simply as the expression of an irrational and self-serving prejudice that favors one particular species over several million others.

Rejecting the notion of human superiority entails its positive counterpart: the doctrine of species impartiality. One who accepts that doctrine regards all living things as possessing inherent worth—the *same* inherent worth, since no one species has been shown to be either "higher" or "lower" than any other. Now we saw earlier that, insofar as one thinks of a living thing as possessing inherent worth, one considers it to be the appropriate object of the attitude of respect and believes that attitude to be the only fitting or suitable one for all moral agents to take toward it.

Here, then, is the key to understanding how the attitude of respect is rooted in the biocentric outlook on nature. The basic connection is made through the denial of human superiority. Once we reject the claim that humans are superior either in merit or in worth to other living things, we are ready to adopt the attitude of respect. The denial of human superiority is itself the result of taking the perspective on nature built into the first three elements of the biocentric outlook.

Now the first three elements of the biocentric outlook, it seems clear, would be found acceptable to any rational and scientifically informed thinker who is fully "open" to the reality of the lives of nonhuman organisms. Without denying our distinctively human characteristics, such a thinker can acknowledge the fundamental respects in which we are members of the Earth's community of life and in which the biological conditions necessary for the realization of our human values are inextricably linked with the whole system of nature. In addition, the conception of individual living things as teleological centers of life simply articulates how a scientifically informed thinker comes to understand them as the result of increasingly careful and detailed observations. Thus, the biocentric outlook recommends itself as an acceptable system of concepts and beliefs to anyone who is clear-minded, unbiased, and factually enlightened, and who has a developed capacity of reality awareness with regard to the lives of individual organisms. This, I submit, is as good a reason for making the moral commitment involved in adopting the attitude of respect for nature as any theory of environmental ethics could possibly have.

MORAL RIGHTS AND THE MATTER OF COMPETING CLAIMS

I have not asserted anywhere in the foregoing account that animals or plants have moral rights. This omission was deliberate. I do not think that the reference class of the concept, bearer of moral rights, should be extended to include nonhuman living things. My reasons for taking this position, however, go beyond the scope of this paper. I believe I have been able to accomplish many of the same ends which those who ascribe rights to animals or plants wish to accomplish. There is no reason, moreover, why plants and animals, including whole species populations and life communities, cannot be accorded *legal* rights under my theory. To grant them legal protection could be interpreted as giving them legal entitlement to be protected, and this, in fact, would be a means by which a society that subscribed to the ethics of respect for nature could give public recognition to their inherent worth.

There remains the problem of competing claims, even when wild plants and animals are not thought of as bearers of moral rights. If we accept the biocentric outlook and accordingly adopt the attitude of respect for nature as our ultimate moral attitude, how do we resolve conflicts that arise from our respect for persons in the domain of human ethics and our respect for nature in the domain of environmental ethics? This is a question that cannot adequately be dealt with here. My main purpose in this paper has been to try to establish a base point from which we can start working toward a solution to the problem. I have shown why we cannot just begin with an initial presumption in favor of the interests of our own species. It is after all within our power as moral beings to place limits on human population and technology with the deliberate intention of sharing the Earth's bounty with other species. That such sharing is an ideal difficult to realize even in an approximate way does not take away it's claim to our deepest moral commitment.

NOTES

1. See W. K. Frankena, "Ethics and the Environment," in K. E. Goodpaster and K. M. Sayre, eds., *Ethics and Problems of the 21st Century* (Notre Dame, University of Notre Dame Press, 1979), pp. 3–20. I critically examine Frankena's views in "Frankena on Environmental Ethics," *Monist,* Vol. 64, No. 3 (July 1981), pp. 313–324.
2. Stephen R. L. Clark, *The Moral Status of Animals* (Oxford: Clarendon Press, 1977), pp. 112.
3. My criticisms of the dogma of human superiority gain independent support from a carefully reasoned essay by R. and V. Routley showing the many logical weaknesses in arguments for human-centered theories of environmental ethics. R. and V. Routley, "Against the Inevitability of Human Chauvinism," in K. E. Goodpaster and K. M. Sayre, eds., *Ethics and Problems of the 21st Century* (Notre Dame: University of Notre Dame Press, 1979), pp. 36–59.
4. For this way of distinguishing between merit and inherent worth, I am indebted to Gregory Vlastos, "Justice and Equality," in R. Brandt, ed., *Social Justice* (Englewood Cliffs, N.J.: Prentice-Hall, 1962), pp. 31–72.

The Land Ethic

Aldo Leopold

Aldo Leopold (1887–1949) was professor of wildlife management at the University of Wisconsin from 1933 until his death. He is the author of A Sand County Almanac, *often called the bible of the contemporary environmental movement.*

When god-like Odysseus returned from the wars in Troy, he hanged all on one rope a dozen slave-girls of his household whom he suspected of misbehavior during his absence.

This hanging involved no question of propriety. The girls were property. The disposal of property was then, as now, a matter of expediency, not of right and wrong.

Concepts of right and wrong were not lacking from Odysseus' Greece: witness the fidelity of his wife through the long years before at last his black-prowed galleys clove the wine-dark seas for home. The ethical structure of that day covered wives, but had not yet been extended to human chattels. During the three thousand years which have since elapsed, ethical criteria have been extended to many fields of conduct, with corresponding shrinkages in those judged by expediency only.

THE ETHICAL SEQUENCE

This extension of ethics, so far studied only by philosophers, is actually a process in ecological evolution. Its sequences may be described in ecological as well as in philosophical terms. An ethic, ecologically, is a limitation on freedom of action in the struggle for existence. An ethic, philosophically, is a differentiation of social from anti-social conduct. These are two definitions of one thing. The thing has its origin in the tendency of interdependent individuals or groups to evolve modes of co-operation. The ecologist calls these symbioses. Politics and economics are advanced symbioses in which the original free-for-all competition has been replaced, in part, by co-operative mechanisms with an ethical content.

The complexity of co-operative mechanisms has increased with population density, and with the efficiency of tools. It was simpler, for example, to define the anti-social uses of sticks and stones in the days of the mastodons than of bullets and billboards in the age of motors.

The first ethics dealt with the relation between individuals; the Mosaic Decalogue is an example. Later accretions dealt with the relation between the individual and society. The Golden Rule tries to integrate the individual to society; democracy to integrate social organization to the individual.

There is as yet no ethic dealing with man's relation to land and to the animals and plants which grow upon it. Land, like Odysseus' slave-girls, is still property. The land-relation is still strictly economic, entailing privileges but not obligations.

The extension of ethics to this third element in human environment is, if I read the evidence correctly, an evolutionary possibility and an ecological necessity. It is the third step in a sequence. The first two have already been taken. Individual thinkers since the days of Ezekiel and Isaiah have asserted that the despoliation of land is not only inexpedient but wrong. Society, however, has not yet affirmed their belief. I regard the present conservation movement as the embryo of such an affirmation.

An ethic may be regarded as a mode of guidance for meeting ecological situations so new or intricate, or involving such deferred reactions, that the path of social expediency is not discernible to the average individual. Animal instincts are modes of guidance for the individual in meeting such situations. Ethics are possibly a kind of community instinct in-the-making.

THE COMMUNITY CONCEPT

All ethics so far evolved rest upon a single premise: that the individual is a member of a community of interdependant parts. His instincts prompt him to compete for his place in that community, but his ethics prompt him also to co-operate (perhaps in order that there may be a place to compete for).

The land ethic simply enlarges the boundaries of the community to include soils, waters, plants, and animals, or collectively: the land.

This sounds simple: do we not already sing our love for and obligation to the land of the free and the home of the brave? Yes, but just what and whom do we love? Certainly not the soil, which we are sending helter-skelter downriver. Certainly not the waters, which we assume have no function except to turn turbines, float barges, and carry off sewage. Certainly not the plants, of which we exterminate whole communities without batting an eye. Certainly not the animals, of which we have already extirpated many of the largest and most beautiful species. A land ethic of course cannot prevent the alteration, management, and use of these "resources," but it does affirm their right to continued existence, and, at least in spots, their continued existence in a natural state.

In short, a land ethic changes the role of *Homo sapiens* from conqueror of the land-community to plain member and citizen of it. It implies respect for his fellow-members, and also respect for the community as such.

In human history, we have learned (I hope) that the conqueror role is eventually self-defeating. Why? Because it is implicit in such a role that the conqueror knows, *ex cathedra,* just what makes the community clock tick, and just what and who is valuable, and what and who is worthless, in community life. It always turns out that he knows neither, and this is why his conquests eventually defeat themselves.

In the biotic community, a parallel situation exists. Abraham knew exactly what the land was for: it was to drip milk and honey into Abraham's mouth. At the present moment, the assurance with which we regard this assumption is inverse to the degree of our education.

The ordinary citizen today assumes that science knows what makes the community clock tick; the scientist is equally sure that he does not. He knows that the biotic mechanism is so complex that its workings may never be fully understood.

That man is, in fact, only a member of a biotic team is shown by an ecological interpretation of history. Many historical events, hitherto explained solely in terms of human enterprise, were actually biotic interactions between people and land. The characteristics of the land determined the facts quite as potently as the characteristics of the men who lived on it.

Consider, for example, the settlement of the Mississippi valley. In the years following the Revolution, three groups were contending for its control: the native Indian, the French and English traders, and the American settlers. Historians wonder what would have happened if the English at Detroit had thrown a little more weight into the Indian side of those tipsy scales which decided the outcome of the colonial migration into the cane-lands of Kentucky. It is time now to ponder the fact that the cane-lands, when subjected to the particular mixture of forces represented by the cow, plow, fire, and axe of the pioneer, became bluegrass. What if the plant succession inherent in this dark and bloody ground had, under the impact of these forces, given us some worthless sedge, shrub, or weed? Would Boone and Kenton have held out? Would there have been any overflow into Ohio, Indiana, Illinois, and Missouri? Any Louisiana Purchase? Any transcontinental union of new states? Any Civil War?

Kentucky was one sentence in the drama of history. We are commonly told what the human actors in this drama tried to do, but we are seldom told that their success, or the lack of it, hung in large degree on the reaction of particular soils to the impact of the particular forces exerted by their occupancy. In the case of Kentucky, we do not even know where the bluegrass came from—whether it is a native species, or a stowaway from Europe.

Contrast the cane-lands with what hindsight tells us about the Southwest, where the pioneers were equally brave, resourceful, and persevering. The impact of occupancy here brought no bluegrass, or other plant fitted to withstand the bumps and buffetings of hard use. This region, when grazed by livestock, reverted through a series of more and more worthless grasses, shrubs, and weeds to a condition of unstable equilibrium. Each recession of plant types bred erosion; each increment to erosion bred a further recession of plants. The result today is a progressive and mutual deterioration, not only of plants and soils, but of the animal community subsisting thereon. The early settlers did not expect this: on the ciénegas of New Mexico some even cut ditches to hasten it. So subtle has been its progress that few residents of the region are aware of it. It is quite invisible to the tourist who finds this wrecked landscape colorful and charming (as indeed it is, but it bears scant resemblance to what it was in 1848).

This same landscape was "developed" once before, but with quite different results. The Pueblo Indians settled the Southwest in pre-Columbian times, but they happened *not* to be equipped with range livestock. Their civilization expired, but not because their land expired.

In India, regions devoid of any sod-forming grass have been settled, apparently without wrecking the land, by the simple expedient of carrying the grass to the cow, rather than vice versa. (Was this the result of some deep wisdom, or was it just good luck? I do not know.)

In short, the plant succession steered the course of history; the pioneer simply demonstrated, for good or ill, what successions inhered in the land. Is history taught in this spirit? It will be, once the concept of land as a community really penetrates our intellectual life.

THE ECOLOGICAL CONSCIENCE

Conservation is a state of harmony between men and land. Despite nearly a century of propaganda, conservation still proceeds at a snail's pace; progress still consists largely of letterhead pieties and convention oratory. On the back forty we still slip two steps backward for each forward stride.

The usual answer to this dilemma is "more conservation education." No one will debate this, but is it certain that only the *volume* of education needs stepping up? Is something lacking in the *content* as well?

It is difficult to give a fair summary of its content in brief form, but, as I understand it, the content is substantially this: obey the law, vote right, join some organizations, and practice what conservation is profitable on your own land; the government will do the rest.

Is not this formula too easy to accomplish anything worth-while? It defines no right or wrong, assigns no obligation, calls for no sacrifice, implies no change in the current philosophy of values. In respect of land-use, it urges only enlightened self-interest. Just how far will such education take us? An example will perhaps yield a partial answer.

By 1930 it had become clear to all except the ecologically blind that southwestern Wisconsin's topsoil was slipping seaward. In 1933 the farmers were told that if they would adopt certain remedial practices for five years, the public would donate CCC labor to install them, plus the necessary machinery and materials. The offer was widely accepted, but the practices were widely forgotten when the five-year contract period was up. The farmers continued only those practices that yielded an immediate and visible economic gain for themselves.

This led to the idea that maybe farmers would learn more quickly if they themselves wrote the rules. Accordingly the Wisconsin Legislature in 1937 passed the Soil Conservation District Law. This said to farmers, in effect: *We, the public, will furnish you free technical service and loan you specialized machinery, if you will write your own rules for land-use. Each county may write its own rules, and these will have the force of law.* Nearly all the counties promptly organized to accept the proffered help, but after a decade of operation, *no county has yet written a single rule.* There has been visible progress in such practices as strip-cropping, pasture renovation, and soil liming, but none in fencing woodlots against grazing, and none in excluding plow and cow from steep slopes. The farmers, in short, have selected those remedial practices which were profitable anyhow, and ignored those which were profitable to the community, but not clearly profitable to themselves.

When one asks why no rules have been written, one is told that the community is not yet ready to support them; education must precede rules. But the education actually in progress makes no mention of obligations to land over and above those dictated by self-interest. The net result is that we have more education but less soil, fewer healthy woods, and as many floods as in 1937.

The puzzling aspect of such situations is that the existence of obligations over and above self-interest is taken for granted in such rural community enterprises as the betterment of roads, schools, churches, and baseball teams. Their existence is not taken for granted, nor as yet seriously discussed, in bettering the behavior of the water that falls on the land, or in the preserving of the beauty or diversity of the farm landscape. Land-use ethics are still governed wholly by economic self-interest, just as social ethics were a century ago.

To sum up: we asked the farmer to do what he conveniently could to save his soil, and he has done just that, and only that. The farmer who clears the woods off a 75 per cent slope, turns his cows into the clearing, and dumps its rainfall, rocks, and soil into the community creek, is still (if otherwise decent) a respected member of society. If he puts lime on his fields and plants his crops on contour, he is still entitled to all the privileges and emoluments of his Soil Conservation District. The District is a beautiful piece of social machinery, but it is coughing along on two cylinders because we have been too timid, and too anxious for quick success, to tell the farmer the true magnitude of his obligations. Obligations have no meaning without conscience, and the problem we face is the extension of the social conscience from people to land.

No important change in ethics was ever accomplished without an internal change in our intellectual emphasis, loyalties, affections, and convictions.

The proof that conservation has not yet touched these foundations of conduct lies in the fact that philosophy and religion have not yet heard of it. In our attempt to make conservation easy, we have made it trivial.

SUBSTITUTES FOR A LAND ETHIC

When the logic of history hungers for bread and we hand out a stone, we are at pains to explain how much the stone resembles bread. I now describe some of the stones which serve in lieu of a land ethic.

One basic weakness in a conservation system based wholly on economic motives is that most members of the land community have no economic value. Wildflowers and songbirds are examples. Of the 22,000 higher plants and animals native to Wisconsin, it is doubtful whether more than 5 per cent can be sold, fed, eaten, or otherwise put to economic use. Yet these creatures are members of the biotic community, and if (as I believe) its stability depends on its integrity, they are entitled to continuance.

When one of these non-economic categories is threatened, and if we happen to love it, we invent subterfuges to give it economic importance. At the beginning of the century songbirds were supposed to be disappearing. Ornithologists jumped to the rescue with some distinctly shaky evidence to the effect that insects would eat us up if birds failed to control them. The evidence had to be economic in order to be valid.

It is painful to read these circumlocutions today. We have no land ethic yet, but we have at least drawn nearer the point of admitting that birds should continue as a matter of biotic right, regardless of the presence or absence of economic advantage to us.

A parallel situation exists in respect of predatory mammals, raptorial birds, and fish-eating birds. Time was when biologists somewhat over-worked the evidence that these creatures preserve the health of game by killing weaklings, or that they control rodents for the farmer, or that they prey only on 'worthless' species. Here again, the evidence had to be economic in order to be valid. It is only in recent years that we hear the more honest argument that predators are members of the community, and that no special interest has the right to exterminate them for the sake of a benefit, real or fancied, to itself. Unfortunately this enlightened view is still in the talk stage. In the field the extermination of predators goes merrily on: witness the impending erasure of the timber wolf by fiat of Congress, the Conservation Bureaus, and many state legislatures.

Some species of trees have been 'read out of the party' by economics-minded foresters because they grow too slowly, or have too low a sale value to pay as timber crops: white cedar, tamarack, cypress, beech, and hemlock are examples. In Europe, where forestry is ecologically more advanced, the non-commercial tree species are recognized as members of the native forest community, to be preserved as such, within reason. Moreover some (like beech) have been found to have a valuable function in building up soil fertility. The interdependence of the forest and its constituent tree species, ground flora, and fauna is taken for granted.

Lack of economic value is sometimes a character not only of species or groups, but of entire biotic communities: marshes, bogs, dunes, and 'deserts' are examples. Our formula in such cases is to relegate their conservation to government as refuges, monuments, or parks. The difficulty is that these communities are usually interspersed with more valuable private lands; the government cannot possibly own or control such scattered parcels. The net effect is that we have relegated some of them to ultimate extinction over large areas. If the private owner were ecologically minded, he would be proud to be the custodian of a reasonable proportion of such areas, which add diversity and beauty to his farm and to his community.

In some instances, the assumed lack of profit in these 'waste' areas has proved to be wrong, but only after most of them had been done away with. The present scramble to reflood muskrat marshes is a case in point.

There is a clear tendency in American conservation to relegate to government all necessary jobs that private landowners fail to perform. Government ownership, operation, subsidy, or regulation is now widely prevalent in forestry, range management, soil and watershed management, park and wilderness conservation, fisheries management, and migratory bird management, with more to come. Most of this growth in governmental conservation is proper and logical, some of it is inevitable. That I imply no disapproval of it is implicit in the fact that I have spent most of my life working for it. Nevertheless the question arises: What is the ultimate magnitude of the enterprise? Will the tax base carry its eventual ramifications? At what point will governmental conservation, like the mastodon, become handicapped by its own dimensions? The answer, if there is any, seems to be in a land ethic, or some other force which assigns more obligation to the private landowner.

Industrial landowners and users, especially lumbermen and stockmen, are inclined to wail long and loudly about the extension of government ownership and regulation to land, but (with notable exceptions) they show little disposition to develop the only visible alternative: the voluntary practice of conservation on their own lands.

When the private landowner is asked to perform some unprofitable act for the good of the community, he today assents only with outstretched palm. If the act costs him cash this is fair and proper, but when it costs only forethought, open-mindedness, or time, the issue is at least debatable. The overwhelming growth of land-use subsidises in recent years must be ascribed, in large part, to the government's own agencies for conservation education: the land bureaus, the agricultural colleges, and the extension services. As far as I can detect, no ethical obligation toward land is taught in these institutions.

To sum up: a system of conservation based solely on economic self-interest is hopelessly lopsided. It tends to ignore, and thus eventually to eliminate, many elements in the land community that lack commercial value, but that are (as far as we know) essential to its healthy functioning. It assumes, falsely, I think, that the economic parts of the biotic clock will function without the uneconomic parts. It tends to relegate to government many functions eventually too large, too complex, or too widely dispersed to be performed by government.

An ethical obligation on the part of the private owner is the only visible remedy for these situations.

THE LAND PYRAMID

An ethic to supplement and guide the economic relation to land presupposes the existence of some mental image of land as a biotic mechanism. We can be ethical only in relation to something we can see, feel, understand, love, or otherwise have faith in.

The image commonly employed in conservation education is 'the balance of nature.' For reasons too lengthy to detail here, this figure of speech fails to describe accurately what little we know about the land mechanism. A much truer image is the one employed in ecology: the biotic pyramid. I shall first sketch the pyramid as a symbol of land, and later develop some of its implications in terms of land-use.

Plants absorb energy from the sun. This energy flows through a circuit called the biota, which may be represented by a pyramid consisting of layers. The bottom layer is the soil. A plant layer rests on the soil, an insect layer on the plants, a bird and rodent layer on the insects, and so on up through various animal groups to the apex layer, which consists of the larger carnivores.

The species of a layer are alike not in where they came from, or in what they look like, but rather in what they eat. Each successive layer depends on those below it for food and often for other services, and each in turn furnishes food and services to those above. Proceeding upward, each successive layer decreases in numerical abundance. Thus, for every carnivore there are hundreds of his prey, thousands of their prey, millions of insects, uncountable plants. The pyramidal form of the system reflects this numerical progression from apex to base. Man shares an intermediate layer with the bears, raccoons, and squirrels which eat both meat and vegetables.

The lines of dependency for food and other services are called food chains. Thus soil-oak-deer-Indian is a chain that has now been largely converted to soil-corn-cow-farmer. Each species, including ourselves, is a link in many chains. The deer eats a hundred plants other than oak, and the cow a hundred plants other than corn. Both, then, are links in a hundred chains. The pyramid is a tangle of chains so complex as to seem disorderly, yet the stability of the system proves it to be a highly organized structure. Its functioning depends on the co-operation and competition of its diverse parts.

In the beginning, the pyramid of life was low and squat; the food chains short and simple. Evolution has added layer after layer, link after link. Man is one of thousands of accretions to the height and complexity of the pyramid. Science has given us many doubts, but it has given us at least one certainty: the trend of evolution is to elaborate and diversify the biota.

Land, then, is not merely soil; it is a fountain of energy flowing through a circuit of soils, plants, and animals. Food chains are the living channels which conduct energy upward; death and decay return it to the soil. The circuit is not closed; some energy is dissipated in decay, some is added by absorption from the air, some is stored in soils, peats, and long-lived forests; but it is a sustained circuit, like a slowly augmented revolving fund of life. There is always a net loss by downhill wash, but this is normally small and offset by the decay of rocks. It is deposited in the ocean and, in the course of geological time, raised to form new lands and new pyramids.

The velocity and character of the upward flow of energy depend on the complex structure of the plant and animal community, much as the upward flow of sap in a tree depends on its complex cellular organization. Without this complexity, normal circulation would presumably not occur. Structure means the characteristic numbers, as well as the characteristic kinds and functions, of the component species. This interdependence between the complex structure of the land and its smooth functioning as an energy unit is one of its basic attributes.

When a change occurs in one part of the circuit, many other parts must adjust themselves to it. Change does not necessarily obstruct or divert the flow of energy; evolution is a long series of self-induced changes, the net result of which has been to elaborate the flow mechanism and to lengthen the circuit. Evolutionary changes, however, are usually slow and local. Man's invention of tools has enabled him to make changes of unprecedented violence, rapidity, and scope.

One change is in the composition of floras and faunas. The larger predators are lopped off the apex of the pyramid; food chains, for the first time in history, become shorter rather than longer. Domesticated species from other lands are substituted for wild ones, and wild ones are moved to new habitats. In this world-wide pooling of faunas and floras, some species get out of bounds as pests and diseases, others are extinguished. Such effects are seldom intended or foreseen; they represent unpredicted and often untraceable readjustments in the structure. Agricultural science is largely a race between the emergence of new pests and the emergence of new techniques for their control.

Another change touches the flow of energy through plants and animals and its return to the soil. Fertility is the ability of soil to receive, store, and release energy. Agriculture, by overdrafts on the soil, or by too radical a substitution of domestic for native species in the superstructure, may derange the channels of flow or deplete storage. Soils depleted of their storage, or of the organic matter which anchors it, wash away faster than they form. This is erosion.

Waters, like soil, are part of the energy circuit. Industry, by polluting waters or obstructing them with dams, may exclude the plants and animals necessary to keep energy in circulation.

Transportation brings about another basic change: the plants or animals grown in one region are now consumed and returned to the soil in another. Transportation taps the energy stored in rocks, and in the air, and uses it elsewhere; thus we fertilize the garden with nitrogen gleaned by the guano birds from the fishes of seas on the other side of the Equator. Thus the formerly localized and self-contained circuits are pooled on a world-wide scale.

The process of altering the pyramid for human occupation releases stored energy, and this often gives rise, during the pioneering period, to a deceptive exuberance of plant and animal life, both wild and tame. These releases of biotic capital tend to becloud or postpone the penalties of violence.

This thumbnail sketch of land as an energy circuit conveys three basic ideas:

(1) That land is not merely soil.
(2) That the native plants and animals kept the energy circuit open; others may or may not.
(3) That man-made changes are of a different order than evolutionary changes, and have effects more comprehensive than is intended or foreseen.

These ideas, collectively, raise two basic issues: Can the land adjust itself to the new order? Can the desired alterations be accomplished with less violence?

Biotas seem to differ in their capacity to sustain violent conversion. Western Europe, for example, carries a far different pyramid than Caesar found there. Some large animals are lost; swampy forests have become meadows or plow-land; many new plants and animals are introduced, some of which escape as pests; the remaining natives are greatly changed in distribution and abundance. Yet the soil is still there and, with the help of imported nutrients, still fertile; the waters flow normally; the new structure seems to function and to persist. There is no visible stoppage or derangement of the circuit.

Western Europe, then, has a resistant biota. Its inner processes are tough, elastic, resistant to strain. No matter how violent the alterations, the pyramid, so far, has developed some new *modus vivendi* which preserves its habitability for man, and for most of the other natives.

Japan seems to present another instance of radical conversion without disorganization.

Most other civilized regions, and some as yet barely touched by civilization, display various stages of disorganization, varying from initial symptoms to advanced wastage. In Asia Minor and North Africa diagnosis is confused by climatic changes, which may have been either the cause or the effect of advanced wastage. In the United States the degree of disorganization varies locally; it is worst in the Southwest, the Ozarks, and parts of the South, and least in New England and the Northwest. Better land-uses may still arrest it in the less advanced regions. In parts of Mexico, South America, South Africa, and Australia a violent and accelerating wastage is in progress, but I cannot assess the prospects.

This almost world-wide display of disorganization in the land seems to be similar to disease in an animal, except that it never culminates in complete disorganization or death. The land recovers, but at some reduced level of complexity, and with a reduced carrying capacity for people, plants, and animals. Many biotas currently regarded as 'lands of opportunity' are in fact already subsisting on exploitative agriculture, i.e. they have already exceeded their sustained carrying capacity. Most of South America is overpopulated in this sense.

In arid regions we attempt to offset the process of wastage by reclamation, but it is only too evident that the prospective longevity of reclamation projects is often short. In our own West, the best of them may not last a century.

The combined evidence of history and ecology seems to support one general deduction: the less violent the manmade changes, the greater the probability of successful readjustment in the pyramid. Violence, in turn, varies with human population density; a dense population requires a more violent conversion. In this respect, North America has a better chance for permanence than Europe, if she can contrive to limit her density.

This deduction runs counter to our current philosophy which assumes that because a small increase in density enriched human life, that an indefinite increase will enrich it indefinitely. Ecology knows of no density relationship that holds for indefinitely wide limits. All gains from density are subject to a law of diminishing returns.

Whatever may be the equation for men and land, it is improbable that we as yet know all its terms. Recent discoveries in mineral and vitamin nutrition reveal unsuspected dependencies in the up-circuit: incredibly minute quantities of certain substances determine the value of soils to plants, of plants to animals. What of the down-circuit? What of the vanishing species, the preservation of which we now regard as an esthetic luxury? They helped build the soil; in what unsuspected ways may they be essential to its maintenance? Professor Weaver proposes that we use prairie flowers to reflocculate the wasting soils of the dust bowl; who knows for what purpose cranes and condors, otters and grizzlies may some day be used?

LAND HEALTH AND THE A-B CLEAVAGE

A land ethic, then, reflects the existence of an ecological conscience, and this in turn reflects a conviction of individual responsibility for the health of the land. Health is the capacity of the land for self-renewal. Conservation is our effort to understand and preserve this capacity.

Conservationists are notorious for their dissensions. Superficially these seem to add up to mere confusion, but a more careful scrutiny reveals a single plane of cleavage common to many specialized fields. In each field one group (A) regards the land as soil, and its function as commodity-production; another group (B) regards the land as a biota, and its function as something broader. How much broader is admittedly in a state of doubt and confusion.

In my own field, forestry, group A is quite content to grow trees like cabbages, with cellulose as the basic forest commodity. It feels no inhibition against violence; its ideology is agronomic. Group B, on the other hand, sees forestry as fundamentally different from agronomy because it employs natural species, and manages a natural environment rather than creating an artificial one. Group B prefers natural reproduction on principle. It worries on biotic as well as economic grounds about the loss of species like chestnut, and the threatened loss of the white pines. It worries about a whole series of secondary forest functions: wildlife, recreation, watersheds, wilderness areas. To my mind, Group B feels the stirrings of an ecological conscience.

In the wildlife field, a parallel cleavage exists. For Group A the basic commodities are sport and meat; the yardsticks of production are ciphers of take in pheasants and trout. Artificial propagation is acceptable as a permanent as well as a temporary recourse—if its unit costs permit. Group B, on the other hand, worries about a whole series of biotic side-issues. What is the cost in predators of producing a game crop? Should we have further recourse to exotics? How can management restore the shrinking species, like prairie grouse, already hopeless as shootable game? How can management restore the threatened rarities, like trumpeter swan and whooping crane? Can management principles be extended to wildflowers? Here again it is clear to me that we have the same A-B cleavage as in forestry.

In the larger field of agriculture I am less competent to speak, but there seem to be somewhat parallel cleavages. Scientific agriculture was actively developing before ecology was born, hence a slower penetration of ecological concepts might be expected. Moreover the farmer, by the very nature of his techniques, must modify the biota more radically than the forester or the wildlife manager. Nevertheless, there are many discontents in agriculture which seem to add up to a new vision of 'biotic farming.'

Perhaps the most important of these is the new evidence that poundage or tonnage is no measure of the food-value of farm crops; the products of fertile soil may be qualitatively as well as quantitatively superior. We can bolster poundage from depleted soils by pouring on imported fertility, but we are not necessarily bolstering food-value. The possible ultimate ramifications of this idea are so immense that I must leave their exposition to abler pens.

The discontent that labels itself 'organic farming,' while bearing some of the earmarks of a cult, is nevertheless biotic in its direction, particularly in its insistence on the importance of soil flora and fauna.

The ecological fundamentals of agriculture are just as poorly known to the public as in other fields of land-use. For example, few educated people realize that the marvelous advances in technique made during recent decades are improvements in the pump, rather than the well. Acre for acre, they have barely sufficed to offset the sinking level of fertility.

In all of these cleavages, we see repeated the same basic paradoxes: man the conqueror *versus* man the biotic citizen; science the sharpener of his sword *versus* science the search-light on his universe; land the slave and servant *ver-*

sus land the collective organism. Robinson's injunction to Tristram may well be applied, at this juncture, to *Homo sapiens* as a species in geological time:

> Whether you will or not
> You are a King, Tristram, for you are one
> Of the time-tested few that leave the world,
> When they are gone, not the same place it was.
> Mark what you leave.

THE OUTLOOK

It is inconceivable to me that an ethical relation to land can exist without love, respect, and admiration for land, and a high regard for its value. By value, I of course mean something far broader than mere economic value; I mean value in the philosophical sense.

Perhaps the most serious obstacle impeding the evolution of a land ethic is the fact that our educational and economic system is headed away from, rather than toward, an intense consciousness of land. Your true modern is separated from the land by many middlemen, and by innumerable physical gadgets. He had no vital relation to it; to him it is the space between cities on which crops grow. Turn him loose for a day on the land, and if the spot does not happen to be a golf links or a 'scenic' area, he is bored stiff. If crops could be raised by hydroponics instead of farming, it would suit him very well. Synthetic substitutes for wood, leather, wool, and other natural land products suit him better than the originals. In short, land is something he has 'outgrown.'

Almost equally serious as an obstacle to a land ethic is the attitude of the farmer for whom the land is still an adversary, or a taskmaster that keeps him in slavery. Theoretically, the mechanization of farming ought to cut the farmer's chains, but whether it really does is debatable.

One of the requisites for an ecological comprehension of land is an understanding of ecology, and this is by no means co-extensive with 'education'; in fact, much higher education seems deliberately to avoid ecological concepts. An understanding of ecology does not necessarily originate in courses bearing ecological labels; it is quite as likely to be labeled geography, botany, agronomy, history, or economics. This is as it should be, but whatever the label, ecological training is scarce.

The case for a land ethic would appear hopeless but for the minority which is in obvious revolt against these 'modern' trends.

The 'key-log' which must be moved to release the evolutionary process for an ethic is simply this: quit thinking about decent land-use as solely an economic problem. Examine each question in terms of what is ethically and esthetically right, as well as what is economically expedient. A thing is right when it tends to preserve the integrity, stability, and beauty of the biotic community. It is wrong when it tends otherwise.

It of course goes without saying that economic feasibility limits the tether of what can or cannot be done for land. It always has and it always will. The fallacy the economic determinists have tied around our collective neck, and which we now need to cast off, is the belief that economics determines *all* land-use. This is simply not true. An innumerable host of actions and attitudes, comprising perhaps the bulk of all land relations, is determined by the land-users' tastes and predilections, rather than by his purse. The bulk of all land relations hinges on investments of time, forethought, skill, and faith rather than on investments of cash. As a land-user thinketh, so is he.

I have purposely presented the land ethic as a product of social evolution because nothing so important as an ethic is ever 'written.' Only the most superficial student of history supposes that Moses 'wrote' the Decalogue; it evolved in the minds of a thinking community, and Moses wrote a tentative summary of it for a 'seminar.' I say tentative because evolution never stops.

The evolution of a land ethic is an intellectual as well as emotional process. Conservation is paved with good intentions which prove to be futile, or even dangerous, because they are devoid of critical understanding either of the land, or of economic land-use. I think it is a truism that as the ethical frontier advances from the individual to the community, its intellectual content increases.

The mechanism of operation is the same for any ethic: social approbation for right actions: social disapproval for wrong actions.

By and large, our present problem is one of attitudes and implements. We are remodeling the Alhambra with a steamshovel, and we are proud of our yardage. We shall hardly relinquish the shovel, which after all has many good points, but we are in need of gentler and more objective criteria for its successful use.

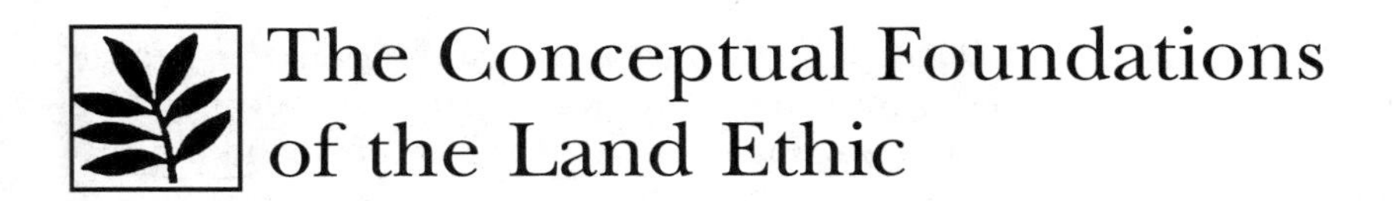

The Conceptual Foundations of the Land Ethic

J. Baird Callicott

J. Baird Callicott is professor of philosophy and religious studies at the University of North Texas. He is the author of In Defense of the Land Ethic: Essays in Environmental Philosophy, Beyond the Land Ethic: More Essays in Environmental Philosophy, Earth's Insights: A Multicultural Survey of Ecological Ethics from the Mediterranean Basin to the Australian Outback, *and more than a hundred book chapters, journal articles, and book reviews in environmental philosophy.*

> The two great cultural advances of the past century were the Darwinian theory and the development of geology. . . . Just as important, however, as the origin of plants, animals, and soil is the question of how they operate as a community. That task has fallen to the new science of ecology, which is daily uncovering a web of interdependencies so intricate as to amaze—were he here—even Darwin himself, who, of all men, should have least cause to tremble before the veil.
>
> —*Aldo Leopold, fragment 6B16, no. 36, Leopold Papers, University of Wisconsin—Madison Archives*

As Wallace Stegner observes, *A Sand County Almanac* is considered "almost a holy book in conservation circles," and Aldo Leopold a prophet, "an American Isaiah." And as Curt Meine points out, "The Land Ethic" is the climactic essay of *Sand County*, "the upshot of 'The Upshot.' "[1] One might, therefore, fairly say that the recommendation and justification of moral obligations on the part of people to nature is what the prophetic *A Sand County Almanac* is all about.

But, with few exceptions, "The Land Ethic" has not been favorably received by contemporary academic philosophers. Most have ignored it. Of those who have not, most have been either nonplussed or hostile. Distinguished Australian philosopher John Passmore dismissed it out of hand, in the first book-length academic discussion of the new philosophical subdiscipline called "environmental ethics."[2] In a more recent and more deliberate discussion, the equally distinguished Australian philosopher H. J. McCloskey patron-

This essay originally in *Companion to a Sand County Almanac*. Reprinted with permission from the University of Wisconsin Press.

ized Aldo Leopold and saddled "The Land Ethic" with various far-fetched "interpretations." He concludes that "there is a real problem in attributing a coherent meaning to Leopold's statements, one that exhibits his land ethic as representing a major advance in ethics rather than a retrogression to a morality of a kind held by various primitive peoples."[3] Echoing McCloskey, English philosopher Robin Attfield went out of his way to impugn the philosophical respectability of "The Land Ethic." And Canadian philosopher L. W. Sumner has called it "dangerous nonsense."[4] Among those philosophers more favorably disposed, "The Land Ethic" has usually been simply quoted, as if it were little more than a noble, but naive, moral plea, altogether lacking a supporting theoretical framework—i.e., foundational principles and premises which lead, by compelling argument, to ethical precepts.

The professional neglect, confusion, and (in some cases) contempt for "The Land Ethic" may, in my judgment, be attributed to three things: (1) Leopold's extremely condensed prose style in which an entire conceptual complex may be conveyed in a few sentences, or even in a phrase or two; (2) his departure from the assumptions and paradigms of contemporary philosophical ethics; and (3) the unsettling practical implications to which a land ethic appears to lead. "The Land Ethic," in short, is, from a philosophical point of view, abbreviated, unfamiliar, and radical.

Here I first examine and elaborate the compactly expressed abstract elements of the land ethic and expose the "logic" which binds them into a proper, but revolutionary, moral theory. I then discuss the controversial features of the land ethic and defend them against actual and potential criticism. I hope to show that the land ethic cannot be ignored as merely the groundless emotive exhortations of a moonstruck conservationist or dismissed as entailing wildly untoward practical consequences. It poses, rather, a serious intellectual challenge to business-as-usual moral philosophy.

"The Land Ethic" opens with a charming and poetic evocation of Homer's Greece, the point of which is to suggest that today land is just as routinely and remorsely enslaved as human beings then were. A panoramic glance backward to our most distant cultural origins, Leopold suggests, reveals a slow but steady moral development over three millennia. More of our relationships and activities ("fields of conduct") have fallen under the aegis of moral principles ("ethical criteria") as civilization has grown and matured. If moral growth and development continue, as not only a synoptic review of history, but recent past experience suggest that it will, future generations will censure today's casual and universal environmental bondage as today we censure the casual and universal human bondage of three thousand years ago.

A cynically inclined critic might scoff at Leopold's sanguine portrayal of human history. Slavery survived as an institution in the "civilized" West, more particularly in the morally self-congratulatory United States, until a mere generation before Leopold's own birth. And Western history from imperial Athens and Rome to the Spanish Inquisition and the Third Reich has been a disgraceful series of wars, persecutions, tyrannies, pogroms, and other atrocities.

The history of moral practice, however, is not identical with the history of moral consciousness. Morality is not descriptive; it is prescriptive or normative. In light of this distinction, it is clear that today, despite rising rates of violent crime in the United States and institutional abuses of human rights in Iran, Chile, Ethiopia, Guatemala, South Africa, and many other places, and despite persistent organized social injustice and oppression in still others, moral consciousness is expanding more rapidly now than ever before. Civil rights, human rights, women's liberation, children's liberation, animal liberation, etc., all indicate, as expressions of newly emergent moral ideals, that ethical consciousness (as distinct from practice) has if anything recently accelerated—thus confirming Leopold's historical observation.

Leopold next points out that "this extension of ethics, so far studied only by philosophers"—and therefore, the implication is clear, not very satisfactorily studied—"is actually a process in ecological evolution" (202). What Leopold is saying here, simply, is that we may understand the history of ethics, fancifully alluded to by means of the Odysseus vignette, in biological as well as philosophical terms. From a biological point of view, an ethic is "a limitation on freedom of action in the struggle for existence" (202).

I had this passage in mind when I remarked that Leopold manages to convey a whole network of ideas in a couple of phrases. The phrase "struggle for existence" unmistakably calls to mind Darwinian evolution as the conceptual context in which a biological account of the origin and development of ethics must ultimately be located. And at once it points up a paradox: Given the unremitting competitive "struggle for existence" how could "limitations on freedom of action" ever have been conserved and spread through a population of *Homo sapiens* or their evolutionary progenitors?

For a biological account of ethics, as Harvard social entomologist Edward O. Wilson has recently written, "the central theoretical problem . . . [is] how can altruism [elaborately articulated as morality or ethics in the human species], which by definition reduces personal fitness, possibly evolve by natural selection?"[5] According to modern sociobiology, the answer lies in kinship. But according to Darwin—who had tackled this problem himself "exclusively from the side of natural history" in *The Descent of Man*—the answer lies in society.[6] And it was Darwin's classical account (and its divers variations), from the side of natural history, which informed Leopold's thinking in the late 1940s.

Let me put the problem in perspective. How, we are asking, did ethics originate and, once in existence, grow in scope and complexity?

The oldest answer in living human memory is theological. God (or the gods) imposes morality on people. And God (or the gods) sanctions it. A most vivid and graphic example of this kind of account occurs in the Bible when Moses goes up on Mount Sinai to receive the Ten Commandments directly from God. That text also clearly illustrates the divine sanctions (plagues, pestilences, droughts, military defeats, etc.) for moral disobedience. Ongoing revelation of the divine will, of course, as handily and as simply explains subsequent moral growth and development.

Western philosophy, on the other hand, is almost unanimous in the opinion that the origin of ethics in human experience has somehow to do with human reason. Reason figures centrally and pivotally in the "social contract theory" of the origin and nature of morals in all its ancient, modern, and contemporary expressions from Protagoras, to Hobbes, to Rawls. Reason is the wellspring of virtue, according to both Plato and Aristotle, and of categorical imperatives, according to Kant. In short, the weight of Western philosophy inclines to the view that we are moral beings because we are rational beings. The ongoing sophistication of reason and the progressive illumination it sheds upon the good and the right explain "the ethical sequence," the historical growth and development of morality, noticed by Leopold.

An evolutionary natural historian, however, cannot be satisfied with either of these general accounts of the origin and development of ethics. The idea that God gave morals to man is ruled out in principle—as any supernatural explanation of a natural phenomenon is ruled out in principle in natural science. And while morality might *in principle* be a function of human reason (as, say, mathematical calculation clearly is), to suppose that it is so *in fact* would be to put the cart before the horse. Reason appears to be a delicate, variable, and recently emerged faculty. It cannot, under any circumstances, be supposed to have evolved in the absence of complex linguistic capabilities which depend, in turn, for their evolution upon a highly developed social matrix. But we cannot have become social beings unless we assumed limitations on freedom of action in the struggle for existence. Hence we must have become ethical before we became rational.

Darwin, probably in consequence of reflections somewhat like these, turned to a minority tradition of modern philosophy for a moral psychology consistent with and useful to a general evolutionary account of ethical phenomena. A century earlier, Scottish philosophers David Hume and Adam Smith had argued that ethics rest upon feelings or "sentiments"—which, to be sure, may be both amplified and informed by reason.[7] And since in the animal kingdom feelings or sentiments are arguably far more common or widespread than reason, they would be a far more likely starting point for an evolutionary account of the origin and growth of ethics.

Darwin's account, to which Leopold unmistakably (if elliptically) alludes in "The Land Ethic," begins with the parental and filial affections common, perhaps, to all mammals.[8] Bonds of affection and sympathy between parents and offspring permitted the formation of small, closely kin social groups, Darwin argued. Should the parental and filial affections bonding family members chance to extend to less closely related individuals, that would permit an enlargement of the family group. And should the newly extended community more successfully defend itself and/or more efficiently provision itself, the inclusive fitness of its members severally would be increased, Darwin reasoned. Thus, the more diffuse familial affections, which Darwin (echoing Hume and Smith) calls the "social sentiments," would be spread throughout a population.[9]

Morality, properly speaking—i.e., morality as opposed to mere altruistic instinct—requires, in Darwin's terms, "intellectual powers" sufficient to recall the past and imagine the future, "the power of language" sufficient to express "common opinion," and "habituation" to patterns of behavior deemed, by common opinion, to be socially acceptable and beneficial.[10] Even so, ethics proper, in Darwin's account, remains firmly rooted in moral feelings or social sentiments which were—no less than physical faculties, he expressly avers—naturally selected, by the advantages for survival and especially for successful reproduction, afforded by society.[11]

The protosociobiological perspective on ethical phenomena, to which Leopold as a natural historian was heir, leads him to a generalization which is remarkably explicit in his condensed and often merely resonant rendering of Darwin's more deliberate and extended paradigm: Since "the thing [ethics] has its origin in the tendency of interdependent individuals or groups to evolve modes of co-operation . . . all ethics so far evolved rest upon a single premise: that the individual is a member of a community of interdependent parts" (202–3).

Hence, we may expect to find that the scope and specific content of ethics will reflect both the perceived boundaries and actual structure or organization of a cooperative community or society. *Ethics and society or community are correlative.* This single, simple principle constitutes a powerful tool for the analysis of moral natural history, for the anticipation of future moral development (including, ultimately, the land ethic), and for systematically deriving the specific precepts, the prescriptions and proscriptions, of an emergent and culturally unprecedented ethic like a land or environmental ethic.

Anthropological studies of ethics reveal that in fact the boundaries of the moral community are generally coextensive with the perceived boundaries of society.[12] And the peculiar (and, from the urbane point of view, sometimes inverted) representation of virtue and vice in tribal society—the virtue, for example, of sharing to the point of personal destitution and the vice of privacy and private property—reflects and fosters the life way of tribal peoples.[13] Darwin, in his leisurely, anecdotal discussion, paints a vivid picture of the intensity, peculiarity, and sharp circumscription of "savage" mores: "A savage will risk his life to save that of a member of the same community, but will be wholly indifferent about a stranger."[14] As Darwin portrays them, tribes people are at once paragons of virtue "within the limits of the same tribe" and enthusiastic thieves, manslaughterers, and torturers without.[15]

For purposes of more effective defense against common enemies, or because of increased population density, or in response to innovations in subsistence methods and technologies, or for some mix of these or other forces, human societies have grown in extent or scope and changed in form or structure. Nations—like the Iroquois nation or the Sioux nation—came into being upon the merger of previously separate and mutually hostile tribes. Animals and plants were domesticated and erstwhile hunter-gatherers became herders and farmers. Permanent habitations were established. Trade, craft, and (later) industry flourished. With each change in society came corresponding and correlative changes in ethics. The moral community expanded to become coextensive with the newly drawn boundaries of societies and the representation of virtue and vice, right and wrong, good and evil, changed to accommodate, foster, and preserve the economic and institutional organization of emergent social orders.

Today we are witnessing the painful birth of a human super-community, global in scope. Modern transportation and communication technologies, international economic interdependencies, international economic entities, and nuclear arms have brought into being a "global village." It has not yet become fully formed and it is at tension—a very dangerous tension—with its predecessor, the nation-state. Its eventual institutional structure, a global federalism or whatever it may turn out to be, is, at this point, completely unpredictable. Interestingly, however, a corresponding global human ethic—the "human rights" ethic, as it is popularly called—has been more definitely articulated.

Most educated people today pay lip service at least to the ethical precept that all members of the human species, regardless of race, creed, or national origin, are endowed with certain fundamental rights which it is wrong not to respect. According to the evolutionary scenario set out by Darwin, the contemporary moral ideal of human rights is a response to a perception—however vague and indefinite—that mankind worldwide is united into one society, one community—however indeterminate or yet institutionally unorganized. As Darwin presciently wrote:

> As man advances in civilization, and small tribes are united into larger communities, the simplest reason would tell each individual that he ought to extend his social instincts and sympathies to all the members of the same nation, though personally unknown to him. This point being once reached, there is only an artificial barrier to prevent his sympathies extending to the men of all nations and races. If, indeed, such men are separated from him by great differences of appearance or habits, experience unfortunately shows us how long it is, before we look at them as our fellow-creatures.[16]

According to Leopold, the next step in this sequence beyond the still incomplete ethic of universal humanity, a step that is clearly discernible on the horizon, is the land ethic. The "community concept" has, so far, propelled the development of ethics from the savage clan to the family of man. "The land ethic simply enlarges the boundary of the community to include soils, waters, plants, and animals, or collectively: the land" (204).

As the foreword to *Sand County* makes plain, the overarching thematic principle of the book is the inculcation of the idea—through narrative description, discursive exposition, abstractive generalization, and occasional preachment—"that land is a community" (viii). The community concept is "the basic concept of ecology" (viii). Once land is popularly perceived a biotic community—as it is professionally perceived in ecology—a correlative land ethic will emerge in the collective cultural consciousness.

Although anticipated as far back as the mid-eighteenth century—in the notion of an "economy of nature"—the concept of the biotic community was more fully and deliberately developed as a working model or paradigm for ecology by Charles Elton in the 1920s.[17] The natural world is organized as an intricate corporate society in which plants and animals occupy "niches," or as Elton alternatively called them, "roles" or "professions," in the economy of nature.[18] As in a feudal community, little or no socioeconomic mobility (upward or otherwise) exists in the biotic community. One is born to one's trade.

Human society, Leopold argues, is founded, in large part, upon mutual security and economic interdependency and preserved only by limitations on freedom of action in the struggle for existence—that is, by ethical constraints. Since the biotic community exhibits, as modern ecology reveals, an analogous structure, it too can be preserved, given the newly amplified impact of "mechanized man," only by analogous limitations on freedom of action—that is, by a land ethic (viii). A land ethic, furthermore, is not only "an ecological necessity," but an "evolutionary possibility" because a moral response to the natural environment—Darwin's social sympathies, sentiments, and instincts translated and codified into a body of principles and precepts—would be automatically triggered in human beings by ecology's social representation of nature (203).

Therefore, the key to the emergence of a land ethic is, simply, universal ecological literacy.

The land ethic rests upon three scientific cornerstones: (1) evolutionary and (2) ecological biology set in a background of (3) Copernican astronomy. Evolutionary theory provides the conceptual link between ethics and social organization and development. It provides a sense of "kinship with fellow-creatures" as well, "fellow-voyagers" with us in the "odyssey of evolution" (109). It establishes a diachronic link between people and nonhuman nature.

Ecological theory provides a synchronic link—the community concept—a sense of social integration of human and nonhuman nature. Human beings, plants, animals, soils, and waters are "all interlocked in one humming community of cooperations and competitions, one biota."[19] The simplest reason, to paraphrase Darwin, should, therefore, tell each individual that he or she ought to extend his or her social instincts and sympathies to all the members of the biotic community though different from him or her in appearance or habits.

And although Leopold never directly mentions it in *A Sand County Almanac*, the Copernican perspective, the perception of the Earth as "a small planet" in an immense and utterly hostile universe beyond, contributes, perhaps subconsciously, but nevertheless very powerfully, to our sense of kinship, community, and interdependence with fellow denizens of the Earth household. It scales the Earth down to something like a cozy island paradise in a desert ocean.

Here in outline, then, are the conceptual and logical foundations of the land ethic: Its conceptual elements are a Copernican cosmology, a Darwinian protosociobiological natural history of ethics, Darwinian ties of kinship among all forms of life on Earth, and an Eltonian model of the structure of biocenoses all overlaid on a Humean-Smithian moral psychology. Its logic is that natural selection has endowed human beings with an affective moral response to perceived bonds of kinship and community membership and identity; that today the natural environment, the land, is represented as a community, the biotic community; and that, therefore, an environmental or land ethic is both possible—the biopsychological and cognitive conditions are in place—and necessary, since human beings collectively have acquired the power to destroy the integrity, diversity, and stability of the environing and supporting economy of nature. In the remainder of this essay I discuss special features and problems of the land ethic germane to moral philosophy.

The most salient feature of Leopold's land ethic is its provision of what Kenneth Goodpaster has carefully called "moral considerability" for the biotic community per se, not just for fellow members of the biotic community:[20]

> In short, a land ethic changes the role of *Homo sapiens* from conqueror of the land-community to plain member and citizen of it. It implies respect for his fellow-members, *and also respect for the community as such.* (204, emphasis added)

The land ethic, thus, has a holistic as well as an individualistic cast.

Indeed, as "The Land Ethic" develops, the focus of moral concern shifts gradually away from plants, animals, soils, and waters severally to the biotic community collectively. Toward the middle, in the subsection called Substitutes for a Land Ethic, Leopold invokes the "biotic rights" of *species*—as the context indicates—of wildflowers, songbirds, and predators. In The Outlook, the climactic section of "The Land Ethic," nonhuman natural entities, first appearing as fellow members, then considered in profile as species, are not so much as mentioned in what might be called the "summary moral maxim" of the land ethic: "A thing is right when it tends to preserve the integrity, stability, and beauty of the biotic community. It is wrong when it tends otherwise" (224–25).

By this measure of right and wrong, not only would it be wrong for a farmer, in the interest of higher profits, to clear the woods off a 75 percent slope, turn his cows into the clearing, and dump its rainfall, rocks, and soil into the community creek, it would also be wrong for the federal fish and wildlife agency, in the interest of individual animal welfare, to permit populations of deer, rabbits, feral burros, or whatever to increase unchecked and thus to threaten the integrity, stability, and beauty of the biotic communities of which they are members. The land ethic not only provides moral considerability for the biotic community per se, but ethical consideration of its individual members is preempted by concern for the preservation of the integrity, stability, and beauty of the biotic community. The land ethic, thus, not only has a holistic aspect; it is holistic with a vengeance.

The holism of the land ethic, more than any other feature, sets it apart from the predominant paradigm of modern moral philosophy. It is, therefore, the feature of the land ethic which requires the most patient theoretical analysis and the most sensitive practical interpretation.

As Kenneth Goodpaster pointed out, mainstream modern ethical philosophy has taken egoism as its point of departure and reached a wider circle of moral entitlement by a process of generalization:[21] I am sure that *I*, the enveloped ego, am intrinsically or inherently valuable and thus that *my* interests ought to be considered, taken into account, by "others" when their actions may substantively affect *me*. My own claim to moral consideration, according to the conventional wisdom, ultimately rests upon a psychological capacity—rationality or sentiency were the classical candidates of Kant and Bentham, respectively—which is arguably valuable in itself and which thus qualifies *me* for moral standing.[22] However, then I am forced grudgingly to grant the same moral consideration I demand from others, on this basis, to those others who can also claim to possess the same general psychological characteristic.

A *criterion* of moral value and consideration is thus identified. Goodpaster convincingly argues that mainstream modern moral theory is based, when all the learned dust has settled, on this simple paradigm of ethical justification and logic exemplified by the Benthamic and Kantian prototypes.[23] If the criterion of moral values and consideration is pitched low enough—as it is in Bentham's criterion of sentiency—a wide variety of animals are admitted to moral entitlement.[24] If the criterion of moral value and consideration is pushed lower still—as it is in Albert Schweitzer's reverence-for-life ethic—all minimally conative things (plants as well as animals) would be extended moral considerability.[25] The contemporary animal liberation/rights, and reverence-for-life/life-principle ethics are, at bottom, simply direct applications of the modern classical paradigm of moral argument. But this standard modern model of ethical theory provides no possibility whatever for the moral consideration of wholes—of threatened *populations* of animals and plants, or of endemic, rare, or endangered *species*, or of biotic *communities*, or most expansively, of the *biosphere* in its totality—since wholes per se have no psychological experience of any kind.[26] Because mainstream modern moral theory has been "psychocentric," it has been radically and intractably individualistic or "atomistic" in its fundamental theoretical orientation.

Hume, Smith, and Darwin diverged from the prevailing theoretical model by recognizing that altruism is as fundamental and autochthonous in human nature as is egoism. According to their analysis, moral value is not identified with a natural quality objectively present in morally considerable beings—as reason and/or sentiency is objectively present in people and/or animals—it is, as it were, projected by valuing subjects.[27]

Hume and Darwin, furthermore, recognize inborn moral sentiments which have society as such as their natural object. Hume insists that "we must renounce the theory which accounts for every moral sentiment by the principle of self-love. We must adopt a more *public affection* and allow that the *interests of society* are not, *even on their own account,* entirely indifferent to us."[28] And Darwin, somewhat ironically (since "Darwinian evolution" very often means natural selection operating exclusively with respect to individuals), sometimes writes as if morality had no other object than the commonweal, the welfare of the community as a corporate entity:

> We have now seen that actions are regarded by savages, and were probably so regarded by primeval man, as good or bad, solely as they obviously affect the welfare of the tribe,—not that of the species, nor that of the individual member of the tribe. This conclusion agrees well with the belief that the so-called moral sense is aboriginally derived from social instincts, for both relate at first exclusively to the community.[29]

Theoretically then, the biotic community owns what Leopold, in the lead paragraph of The Outlook, calls "value in the philosophical sense"—i.e., direct moral considerability—because it is a newly discovered proper object of a specially evolved "public affection" or "moral sense" which all psychologically normal human beings have inherited from a long line of ancestral social primates.[30]

In the land ethic, as in all earlier stages of social-ethical evolution, there exists a tension between the good of the community as a whole and the "rights" of its individual members considered severally. While The Ethical Sequence section of "The Land Ethic" clearly evokes Darwin's classical biosocial account of the origin and extension of morals, Leopold is actually more explicitly concerned, in that section, with the interplay between the holistic and individualistic moral sentiments—between sympathy and fellow-feeling on the one hand, and public affection for the commonweal on the other:

> The first ethics dealt with the relation between individuals; the Mosaic Decalogue is an example. Later accretions dealt with the relation between the individual and society. The Golden Rule tries to integrate the individual to society; democracy to integrate social organization to the individual. (202–3)

Actually, it is doubtful that the first ethics dealt with the relation between individuals and not at all with the relation between the individual and society. (This, along with the remark that ethics replaced an "original free-for-all competition," suggests that Leopold's Darwinian line of thought has been uncritically tainted with Hobbesean elements. [202]. Of course, Hobbes's "state of nature," in which there prevailed a war of each against all, is absurd from an evolutionary point of view.) A century of ethnographic studies seems to confirm, rather, Darwin's conjecture that the relative weight of the holistic com-

ponent is greater in tribal ethics—the tribal ethic of the Hebrews recorded in the Old Testament constitutes a vivid case in point—than in more recent accretions. The Golden Rule, on the other hand, does not mention, in any of its formulations, society per se. Rather, its primary concern seems to be "others," i.e., other human individuals. Democracy, with its stress on individual liberties and rights, seems to further rather than countervail the individualistic thrust of the Golden Rule.

In any case, the conceptual foundations of the land ethic provide a well-formed, self-consistent theoretical basis for including both fellow members of the biotic community and the biotic community itself (considered as a corporate entity) within the purview of morals. The preemptive emphasis, however, on the welfare of the community as a whole, in Leopold's articulation of the land ethic, while certainly *consistent* with its Humean-Darwinian theoretical foundations, is not *determined* by them alone. The overriding holism of the land ethic results, rather, more from the way our moral sensibilities are informed by ecology.

Ecological thought, historically, has tended to be holistic in outlook.[31] Ecology is the study of the *relationships* of organisms to one another and to the elemental environment. These relationships bind the *relata*—plants, animals, soils, and waters—into a seamless fabric. The ontological primary of objects and the ontological subordination of relationships, characteristic of classical Western science, is, in fact, reversed in ecology.[32] Ecological relationships determine the nature of organisms rather than the other way around. A species is what it is because it has adapted to a niche in the ecosystem. The whole, the system itself, thus, literally and quite straightforwardly shapes and forms its component parts.

Antedating Charles Elton's community model of ecology was F. E. Clements' and S. A. Forbe's organism model.[33] Plants and animals, soils and waters, according to this paradigm, are integrated into one superorganism. Species are, as it were, its organs; specimens its cells. Although Elton's community paradigm (later modified, as we shall see, by Arthur Tansley's ecosystem idea) is the principal and morally fertile ecological concept of "The Land Ethic," the more radically holistic superoganism paradigm of Clements and Forbes resonates in "The Land Ethic" as an audible overtone. In the peroration of Land Health and the A-B Cleavage, for example, which immediately precedes The Outlook, Leopold insists that

> in all of these cleavages, we see repeated the same basic paradoxes: man the conqueror *versus* man the biotic citizen; science the sharpener of his sword *versus* science the searchlight on his universe; land the slave and servant *versus* land the collective organism. (223)

And on more than one occasion Leopold, in the latter quarter of "The Land Ethic," talks about the "health" and "disease" of the land—terms which are at once descriptive and normative and which, taken literally, characterize only organisms proper.

In an early essay, "Some Fundamentals of Conservation in the Southwest," Leopold speculatively flirted with the intensely holistic superoganism model of the environmental as a paradigm pregnant with moral implications:

> It is at least not impossible to regard the earth's parts—soil, mountains, rivers, atmosphere, etc.—as organs or parts of organs, of a *co-ordinated whole,* each part with a definite function. And if we could see *this whole, as a whole,* through a great period of time, we might perceive not only organs with coordinated functions, but possibly also that process of consumption and replacement which in biology we call metabolism, or growth. In such a case we would have all the visible attributes of a living thing, which we do not realize to be such because it is too big, and its life processes too slow. And there would also follow that invisible attribute—a soul or consciousness—which . . . many philosophers of all ages ascribe to all living things and aggregates thereof, including the "dead" earth.
>
> Possibly in our intuitive perceptions, which may be truer than our science and less impeded by words than our philosophies, we realize the indivisibility of the earth—its soil, mountains, rivers, forests, climate, plants, and animals—and *respect it collectively* not only as a useful servant but as a living being, vastly less alive than ourselves, but vastly greater than ourselves in time and space. . . . Philosophy, then, suggests one reason why we cannot destroy the earth with moral impunity; namely, that the "dead" earth is an organism possessing a certain kind and degree of life, which we intuitively respect as such.[34]

Had Leopold retained this overall theoretical approach in "The Land Ethic," the land ethic would doubtless have enjoyed more critical attention from philosophers. The moral foundations of a land or, as he might then have called it, "earth" ethic, would rest upon the hypothesis that the Earth is alive and ensouled—possessing inherent psychological characteristics, logically parallel to reason and sentiency. This notion of a conative whole Earth could plausibly have served as a general criterion of intrinsic worth and moral considerability, in the familiar format of mainstream moral thought.

Part of the reason, therefore, that "The Land Ethic" emphasizes more and more the integrity, stability, and beauty of the environment as a whole, and less and less the "biotic right" of individual plants and animals to life, liberty, and the pursuit of happiness, is that the superorganism ecological paradigm invites one, much more than does the community paradigm, to hypostatize, to reify the whole, and to subordinate its individual members.

In any case, as we see, rereading "The Land Ethic" in light of "Some Fundamentals," the whole Earth organism image of nature is vestigially present in Leopold's later thinking. Leopold may have abandoned the "earth ethic" because ecology had abandoned the organism analogy, in favor of the community analogy, as a working theoretical paradigm. And the community model was more suitably given moral implications by the social/sentimental ethical natural history of Hume and Darwin.

Meanwhile, the biotic community ecological paradigm itself had acquired, by the late thirties and forties, a more holistic cast of its own. In 1935 British ecologist Arthur Tansley pointed out that from the perspective of physics the "currency" of the "economy of nature" is energy.[35] Tansley suggested that Elton's qualitative and descriptive food chains, food webs, trophic niches, and biosocial professions could be quantitatively expressed by means of a thermodynamic flow model. It is Tansley's state-of-the-art thermodynamic paradigm of the environment that Leopold explicitly sets out as a "mental image of land" in relation to which "we can be ethical" (214). And it is the ecosystemic model of land which informs the cardinal practical precepts of the land ethic.

The Land Pyramid is the pivotal section of "The Land Ethic"—the section which effects a complete transition from concern for "fellow-members" to the "community as such." It is also its longest and most technical section. A description of the "ecosystem" (Tansley's deliberately nonmetaphorical term) begins with the sun. Solar energy "flows through a circuit called the biota" (215). It enters the biota through the leaves of green plants and courses through plant-eating animals, and then on to omnivores and carnivores. At last the tiny fraction of solar energy converted to biomass by green plants remaining in the corpse of a predator, animal feces, plant detritus, or other dead organic material is garnered by decomposers—worms, fungi, and bacteria. They recycle the participating elements and degrade into entropic equilibrium any remaining energy. According to this paradigm

> land, then, is not merely soil; it is a fountain of energy flowing through a circuit of soils, plants, and animals. Food chains are the living channels which conduct energy upward; death and decay return it to the soil. The circuit is not closed; . . . but it is a sustained circuit, like a slowly augmented revolving fund of life. (216)

In this exceedingly abstract (albeit poetically expressed) model of nature, process precedes substance and energy is more fundamental than matter. Individual plants and animals become less autonomous beings than ephemeral structures in a patterned flux of energy. According to Yale biophysicist Harold Morowitz,

> viewed from the point of view of modern [ecology], each living thing . . . is a dissipative structure, that is it does not endure in and of itself but only as a result of the continual flow of energy in the system. An example might be instructive. Consider a vortex in a stream of flowing water. The vortex is a structure made of an ever-changing group of water molecules. It does not exist as an entity in the classical Western sense; it exists only because of the flow of water through the stream. In the same sense, the structures out of which biological entities are made are transient, unstable entities with constantly changing molecules, dependent on a constant flow of energy from food in order to maintain form and structure. . . . From this point of view the reality of individuals is problematic because they do not exist per se but only as local perturbations in this universal energy flow.[36]

Though less bluntly stated and made more palatable by the unfailing charm of his prose, Leopold's proffered mental image of land is just as expansive, systemic, and distanced as Morowitz's. The maintenance of "the complex structure of the land and its smooth functioning as an energy unit" emerges in The Land Pyramid as the *summum bonum* of the land ethic (216).

From this good Leopold derives several practical principles slightly less general, and therefore more substantive, than the summary moral maxim of the land ethic distilled in The Outlook. "The trend of evolution [not its "goal," since evolution is ateleological] is to elaborate and diversify the biota" (216). Hence, among our cardinal duties is the duty to preserve what species we can, especially those at the apex of the pyramid—the top carnivores. "In the beginning, the pyramid of life was low and squat; the food chains short and simple. Evolution has added layer after layer, link after link" (215–16). Human activities today, especially those, like systematic deforestation in the tropics, resulting in abrupt massive extinctions of species, are in effect "devolutionary"; they flatten the biotic pyramid; they choke off some of the channels and gorge others (those which terminate in our own species).[37]

The land ethic does not enshrine the ecological status quo and devalue the dynamic dimension of nature. Leopold explains that "evolution is a long series of self-induced changes, the net result of which has been to elaborate the flow mechanism and to lengthen the circuit. Evolutionary changes, however, are usually slow and local. Man's invention of tools has enabled him to make changes of unprecedented violence, rapidity, and scope" (216–17). "Natural" species extinction, i.e., species extinction in the normal course of evolution, occurs when a species is replaced by competitive exclusion or evolves into another form.[38] Normally speciation outpaces extinction. Mankind inherited a richer, more diverse world than had ever existed before in the 3.5 billion-year odyssey of life on Earth.[39] What is wrong with anthropogenic species extirpation and extinction is the *rate* at which it is occurring and the *result*: biological impoverishment instead of enrichment.

Leopold goes on here to condemn, in terms of its impact on the ecosystem, "the world-wide pooling of faunas and floras," i.e., the indiscriminate introduction of exotic and domestic species and the dislocation of native and endemic species; mining the soil for its stored biotic energy, leading ultimately to diminished fertility and to erosion; and polluting and damming water courses (217).

According to the land ethic, therefore: Thou shalt not extirpate or render species extinct; thou shalt exercise great caution in introducing exotic and domestic species into local ecosystems, in extracting energy from the soil and releasing it into the biota, and in damming or polluting water courses; and thou shalt be especially solicitous of predatory birds and mammals. Here in brief are the express moral precepts of the land ethic. They are all explicitly informed—not to say derived—from the energy circuit model of the environment.

The living channels—"food chains"—through which energy courses are composed of individual plants and animals. A central, stark fact lies at the heart of ecological processes: Energy, the currency of the economy nature, passes from one organism to another, not from hand to hand, like coined money, but so to speak, from stomach to stomach. Eating *and being eaten,* living *and dying* are what make the biotic community hum.

The precepts of the land ethic, like those of all previous accretions, reflect and reinforce the structure of the community to which it is correlative. Trophic asymmetries constitute the kernel of the biotic community. It seems unjust, unfair. But that is how the economy of nature is organized (and has been for thousands of millions of years). The land ethic, thus, affirms as good, and strives to preserve, the very inequities in nature whose social counterparts in human communities are condemned as bad and would be eradicated by familiar social ethics, especially by the more recent Christian and secular egalitarian exemplars. A "right to life" for individual members is not consistent with the structure of the biotic community and hence is not mandated by the land ethic. This disparity between the land ethic and its more familiar social precedents contributes to the apparent devaluation of individual *members* of the biotic community and augments and reinforces the tendency of the land ethic, driven by the systemic vision of ecology, toward a more holistic or community-per-se orientation.

Of the few moral philosophers who have given the land ethic a moment's serious thought, most have regarded it with horror because of its emphasis on the good of the community and its deemphasis on the welfare of individual members of the community. Not only are other sentient creatures members of the biotic community and subordinate to its integrity, beauty, and stability; so are *we.* Thus, if it is not only morally permissible, from the point of view of the land ethic, but morally required, that members of certain species be abandoned to predation and other vicissitudes of wild life or even deliberately culled (as in the case of alert and sentient whitetail deer) for the sake of the integrity, stability, and beauty of the biotic community, how can we consistently exempt ourselves from a similar draconian regime? We too are only "plain members and citizens" of the biotic community. And our global population is growing unchecked. According to William Aiken, from the point of view of the land ethic, therefore, "massive human diebacks would be good. It is our duty to cause them. It is our species' duty, relative to the whole, to eliminate 90 percent of our numbers." Thus, according to Tom Regan, the land ethic is a clear case of "environmental fascism."[40]

Of course Leopold never intended the land ethic to have either inhumane or antihumanitarian implications or consequences. But whether he intended them or not, a logically consistent deduction from the theoretical premises of the land ethic might force such untoward conclusions. And given their magnitude and monstrosity, these derivations would constitute a *reductio ad absurdum* of the whole land ethic enterprise and entrench and reinforce our current human chauvinism and moral alienation from nature. If this is what membership in the biotic community entails, then all but the most radical misanthropes would surely want to opt out.

The land ethic, happily, implies neither inhumane nor inhuman consequences. That some philosophers think it must follows more from their own theoretical presuppositions than from the theoretical elements of the land ethic itself. Conventional modern ethical theory rests moral entitlement, as I earlier pointed out, on a criterion or qualification. If a candidate meets the criterion—rationality or sentiency are the most commonly posited—he, she, or it is entitled to equal moral standing with others who possess the same qualification in equal degree. Hence, reasoning in this philosophically orthodox way, and forcing Leopold's theory to conform: if human beings are, with other animals, plants, soils, and waters, equally members of the biotic community, and if community membership is the criterion of equal moral consideration, then not only do animals, plants, soils, and waters have equal (highly attenuated) "rights," but human beings are equally subject to the same subordination of individual welfare and rights in respect to the good of the community as a whole.

But the land ethic, as I have been at pains to point out, is heir to a line of moral analysis different from that institutionalized in contemporary moral philosophy. From the biosocial evolutionary analysis of ethics upon which Leopold builds the land ethic, it (the land ethic) neither replaces nor overrides previous accretions. Prior moral sensibilities and obligations attendant upon and correlative to prior strata of social involvement remain operative and preemptive.

Being citizens of the United States, or the United Kingdom, or the Soviet Union, or Venezuela, or some other nation-state, and therefore having national obligations and patriotic duties, does not mean that we are not also members of smaller communities or social groups—cities or townships, neighborhoods, and families—or that we are relieved of the peculiar moral responsibilities attendant upon and correlative to these memberships as well. Similarly, our recognition of the biotic community and our immersion in it does not imply that we do not also remain members of the human community—the "family of man" or "global village"—or that we are relieved of the attendant and correlative moral responsibilities of that membership, among them to respect universal human rights and uphold the principles of individual human worth and dignity. The biosocial development of morality does not grow in extent like an expanding balloon, leaving no trace of its previous boundaries, so much as like the circumference of a tree.[41] Each emergent, and larger, social unit is layered over the more primitive, and intimate, ones.

Moreover, as a general rule, the duties correlative to the inner social circles to which we belong eclipse those correlative to the rings farther from the heartwood when conflicts arise. Consider our moral revulsion when zealous ideological nationalists encourage children to turn their parents in to the authorities if their parents should dissent from the political or economic doctrines of the ruling party. A zealous environmentalist who advocated visiting war, famine, or pestilence on human populations (those existing somewhere else, of course) in the name of the integrity, beauty, and stability of the biotic community would be similarly perverse. Family obligations in general come before nationalistic duties and humanitarian obligations in general come before environmental duties. The land ethic, therefore, is not draconian or fascist. It does not cancel human morality. The land ethic may, however, as with any new accretion, demand choices which affect, in turn, the demands of the more interior social-ethical circles. Taxes and the military draft may conflict with family-level obligations. While the land ethic, certainly, does not cancel human morality, neither does it leave it unaffected.

Nor is the land ethic inhumane. Nonhuman fellow members of the biotic community have no "human rights," because they are not, by definition, members of the human community. As fellow members of the biotic community, however, they deserve respect.

How exactly to express or manifest respect, while at the same time abandoning our fellow members of the biotic community to their several fates or even actively consuming them for our own needs (and wants), or deliberately making them casualties of wildlife management for ecological integrity, is a difficult and delicate question.

Fortunately, American Indian and other traditional patterns of human-nature interaction provide rich and detailed models. Algonkian woodland peoples, for instance, represented animals, plants, birds, waters, and minerals as other-than-human persons engaged in reciprocal, mutually beneficial socio-economic intercourse with human beings.[42] Tokens of payment, together with expressions of apology, were routinely offered to the beings whom it was necessary for these Indians to exploit. Care not to waste the usable parts, and care in the disposal of unusable animal and plant remains, were also an aspect of the respectful, albeit necessarily consumptive, Algonkian relationship with fellow members of the land community. As I have more fully argued elsewhere, the Algonkian portrayal of human-nature relationships is, indeed, although certainly different in specifics, identical in abstract form to that recommended by Leopold in the land ethic.[43]

Ernest Partridge has turned the existence of an American Indian land ethic, however, against the historicity of the biosocial theoretical foundations of the land ethic:

> Anthropologists will find much to criticize in [Leopold's] account. . . . The anthropologist will point out that in many primitive cultures, far greater moral concern may be given to animals or even to trees, rocks, and mountains, than are given to persons in other tribes. . . . Thus we find not an "extension of ethics," but a "leap-frogging" of ethics, over and beyond persons to natural beings and objects. Worse still for Leopold's view, a primitive culture's moral concern for nature often appears to "draw back" to a human centered perspective as that culture evolves toward a civilized condition.[44]

Actually, the apparent historical anomalies, which Partridge points out, confirm, rather than confute, Leopold's ethical sequence. At the tribal stage of human social evolution, a member of another tribe was a member of a separate and independent social organization, and hence of a separate and alien moral community; thus, "[human] persons in other tribes" were not extended moral consideration, just as the biosocial model predicts. However, at least among those tribal people whose world view I have studied in detail, the animals, trees, rocks, and mountains of a tribe's territory were portrayed as working members and trading partners of the local community. Totem representation of clan units within tribal communities facilitated this view. Groups of people were identified as cranes, bears, turtles, and so on; similarly, populations of deer, beaver, fox, etc., were clans of "people"—people who liked going about in outlandish get-ups. Frequent episodes in tribal mythologies of "metamorphosis"—the change from animal to human form and vice versa—further cemented the tribal integration of local nonhuman natural entities. It would be very interesting to know if the flora and fauna living in another tribe's territory would be regarded, like its human members, as beyond the moral pale.

Neither does the " 'draw-back' to a human centered [ethical] perspective as [a] culture evolves toward a civilized condition," noticed by Partridge, undermine the biosocial theoretical foundations of the land ethic. Rather, the biosocial theoretical foundations of the land ethic elucidate this historical phenomenon as well. As a culture evolves toward civilization, it increasingly distances itself from the biotic community. "Civilization" means "cityfication"—inhabitation of and participation in an artificial, humanized environment and a corresponding perception of isolation and alienation from nature. Nonhuman natural entities, thus, are divested of their status as members in good standing of the moral community as civilization develops. Today, two processes internal to civilization are bringing us to a recognition that our renunciation of our biotic citizenship was a mistaken self-deception. Evolutionary science and ecological science, which certainly are products of modern civilization now supplanting the anthropomorphic and anthropocentric myths of earlier civilized generations, have rediscovered our integration with the biotic community. And the negative feedback received from modern civilization's technological impact upon nature—pollution, biological impoverishment, etc.—forcefully reminds us that mankind never really has, despite past assumptions to the contrary, existed apart from the environing biotic community.

This reminder of our recent rediscovery of our biotic citizenship bring us face to face with the paradox posed by Peter Fritzell.[45] Either we are plain members and citizens of the biotic community, on a par with other creatures, or we are not. If we are, then we have no moral obligations to our fellow members or to the community per se because, as understood from a modern scientific perspective, nature and natural phenomena are amoral. Wolves and alligators do no wrong in killing and eating deer and dogs (respectively). Elephants cannot be blamed for bulldozing acacia trees and generally wreaking havoc in their natural habitats. If human beings are natural beings, then human behavior, however destructive, is natural behavior and is as blameless, from a natural point of view, as any other behavioral phenomenon exhibited by other natural beings. On the other hand, we are moral beings, the implication seems clear, precisely to the extent that we are civilized, that we have removed ourselves from nature. We are more than natural beings; we are metanatural—not to say, "supernatural"—beings. But then our moral community is limited to only those beings who share our transcendence of nature, i.e., to human beings (and perhaps to pets who have joined our civilized community as surrogate persons) and to the human community. Hence, have it either way—we are members of the biotic community or we are not—a land or environmental ethic is aborted by either choice.

But nature is *not* amoral. The tacit assumption that we are deliberating, choice-making ethical beings only to the extent that we are metanatural, civilized beings, generates this dilemma. The biosocial analysis of human moral behavior, in which the land ethic is grounded, is designed precisely to show that in fact intelligent moral behavior *is* natural behavior. Hence, we are moral beings not in spite of, but in accordance with, nature. To the extent that nature has produced at least one ethical species, *Homo sapiens*, nature is not amoral.

Alligators, wolves, and elephants are not subject to reciprocal interspecies duties or land ethical obligations themselves because they are incapable of conceiving and/or assuming them. Alligators, as mostly solitary, entrepreneurial reptiles, have no apparent moral sentiments or social instincts whenever. And while wolves and elephants certainly do have social instincts and at least protomoral sentiments, as their social behavior amply indicates, their conception or imagination of community appears to be less culturally plastic than ours and less amenable to cognitive information. Thus, while we might regard them as ethical beings, they are not able, as we are, to form the concept of a universal biotic community, and hence conceive an all-inclusive, holistic land ethic.

The paradox of the land ethic, elaborately noticed by Fritzell, may be cast more generally still in more conventional philosophical terms: Is the land ethic prudential or deontological? Is the land ethic, in other words, a matter of enlightened (collective, human) self-interest, or does it genuinely admit nonhuman natural entities and nature as a whole to true moral standing?

The conceptual foundations of the land ethic, as I have here set them out, and much of Leopold's hortatory rhetoric, would certainly indicate that the land ethic is deontological (or duty oriented) rather than prudential. In the section significantly titled The Ecological Conscience, Leopold complains that the then-current conservation philosophy is inadequate because "it defines no right or wrong, assigns no obligation, calls for no sacrifice, implies no change in the current philosophy of values. In respect of land-use, it urges *only* enlightened self-interest" (207–8, emphasis added). Clearly, Leopold himself thinks that the land ethic goes beyond prudence. In this section he disparages mere "self-interest" two more times, and concludes that "obligations have no meaning without conscience, and the problem we face is the extension of the social conscience from people to land"(209).

In the next section, Substitutes for a Land Ethic, he mentions rights twice—the "biotic right" of birds to continuance and the absence of a right on the part of human special interest to exterminate predators.

Finally, the first sentences of The Outlook read: "It is inconceivable to me that an ethical relation to land can exist without love, respect, and admiration for land, and a high regard for its value. By value, I of course mean something far broader than mere economic value; I mean value in the philosophical sense" (223). By "value in the philosophical sense," Leopold can only mean what philosophers more technically call "intrinsic value" or "inherent worth."[46] Something that has intrinsic value or inherent worth is valuable in and of itself, not because of what it can do for us. "Obligation," "sacrifice," "conscience," "respect," the ascription of rights, and intrinsic value—all of these are consistently opposed to self-interest and seem to indicate decisively that the land ethic is of the deontological type.

Some philosophers, however, have seen it differently. Scott Lehmann, for example, writes:

> Although Leopold claims for communities of plants and animals a "right to continued existence," his argument is homocentric, appealing to the human stake in preservation. Basically it is an argument from enlightened self-interest, where the self in question is not an individual human being but humanity—present and future—as a whole. . . .[47]

Lehmann's claim has some merits, even though it flies in the face of Leopold's express commitments. Leopold does frequently lapse into the language of (collective, long-range, human) self-interest. Early on, for example, he remarks, "in human history, we have learned (I hope) that the conqueror role is eventually *self*-defeating" (204, emphasis added). And later, of the 95 percent of Wisconsin's species which cannot be "sold, fed, eaten, or otherwise put to economic use," Leopold reminds us that "these creatures are members of the biotic community, and if (as I believe) its stability depends on its integrity, they are entitled to continuance" (210). The implication is clear: the economic 5 percent cannot survive if a significant portion of the uneconomic 95 percent are extirpated; nor may *we*. it goes without saying, survive without these "resources."

Leopold, in fact, seems to be consciously aware of this moral paradox. Consistent with the biosocial foundations of his theory, he expresses it in sociobiological terms:

> An ethic may be regarded as a mode of guidance for meeting ecological situations so new or intricate, or involving such deferred reactions, that the path of social expediency is not discernible to the average individual. Animal instincts are modes of guidance for the individual in meeting such situations. Ethics are possibly a kind of community instinct in-the-making. (203)

From an objective, descriptive sociobiological point of view, ethics evolve because they contribute to the inclusive fitness of their carriers (or, more reductively still, to the multiplication of their carriers' genes); they are expedient. However, the path to self-interest (or to the self-interest of the selfish gene) is not discernible to the participating individuals (nor, certainly, to their genes). Hence, ethics are grounded in instinctive feeling—love, sympathy, respect—not in self-conscious calculating intelligence. Somewhat like the paradox of hedonism—the notion that one cannot achieve happiness if one directly pursues happiness per se and not other things–one can only secure self-interest by putting the interests of others on a par with one's own (in this case long-range collective human self-interest and the interest of other forms of life and of the biotic community per se).

So, is the land ethic deontological or prudential, after all? It is both—self-consistently both—depending upon point of view. From the inside, from the lived, felt point of view of the community member with evolved moral sensibilities, it is deontological. It involves an affective-cognitive posture of genuine love, respect, admiration, obligation, self-sacrifice, conscience, duty, and the ascription of intrinsic value and biotic rights. From the outside, from the objective and analytic scientific point of view, it is prudential. "There is no other way for land to survive the impact of mechanized man," nor, therefore, for mechanized man to survive his own impact upon the land (viii).

NOTES

1. Wallace Stegner, "The Legacy of Aldo Leopold"; Curt Meine, "Building 'The Land Ethic' "; both in J. Baird Callicott, ed., *Companion to A Sand County Almanac: Interpretive and Critical Essays* (Madison: University of Wisconsin Press, 1987), 233–245, 172–185, respectively. The oft-repeated characterization of Leopold as a prophet appears traceable to Roberts Mann, "Aldo Leopold: Priest and Prophet," *American Forests* 60, no. 8 (August 1954): 23, 42–43; it was picked up, apparently, by Ernest Swift, "Aldo Leopold: Wisconsin's Conservationist Prophet," *Wisconsin Tales and Trails* 2, no. 2 (September 1961): 2–5; Roderick Nash institutionalized it in his chapter, "Aldo Leopold: Prophet," in *Wilderness and the American Mind* (New Haven: Yale University Press, 1967; revised edition, 1982).
2. John Passmore, *Man's Responsibility for* [significantly not "to"] *Nature: Ecological Problems and Western Traditions* (New York: Charles Scribner's Sons, 1974).
3. H. J. McCloskey, *Ecological Ethics and Politics* (Totowa, N.J.: Rowman and Littlefield, 1983), 46.
4. Robin Attfield, in "Value in the Wilderness," *Metaphilosophy* 15 (1984), writes, "Leopold the philosopher is something of a disaster, and I dread the thought of the student whose concept of philosophy is modeled principally on these extracts. (Can value 'in the philosophical sense' be contrasted with instrumental value? If concepts of right and wrong did not apply to slaves in Homeric Greece, how could Odysseus suspect the slavegirls of 'misbehavior'? If all ethics rest on interdependence how are obligations to infants and small children possible? And how can 'obligations have no meaning without conscience,' granted that the notion of conscience is conceptually dependent on that of obligation?)" (294). L. W. Sumner,

"Review of Robin Attfield, *The Ethics of Environmental Concern*," *Environmental Ethics* 8 (1986):77.

5. Edward O. Wilson, *Sociobiology: The New Synthesis* (Cambridge: Harvard University Press, 1975), 3. See also W. D. Hamilton, "The Genetical Theory of Social Behavior," *Journal of Theoretical Biology* 7 (1964):1–52.
6. Charles R. Darwin, *The Descent of Man and Selection in Relation to Sex* (New York: J.A. Hill and Company, 1904). The quoted phrase occurs on p. 97.
7. See Adam Smith, *Theory of the Moral Sentiments* (London and Edinburgh: A. Millar, A. Kinkaid, and J. Bell, 1759) and David Hume, *An Enquiry Concerning the Principles of Morals* (Oxford:The Clarendon Press, 1777; first published in 1751). Darwin cites both works in the key fourth chapter of *Descent* (pp. 106 and 109, respectively).
8. Darwin, *Descent*, 98ff.
9. Ibid., 105f.
10. Ibid., 113ff.
11. Ibid., 105.
12. See, for example, Elman R. Service, *Primitive Social Organization: An Evolutionary Perspective* (New York: Random House, 1962).
13. See Marshall Sahlins, *Stone Age Economics* (Chicago: Aldine Atherton, 1972).
14. Darwin, *Descent*, 111.
15. Ibid., 117ff. The quoted phrase occurs on p. 118.
16. Ibid., 124.
17. See Donald Worster, *Nature's Economy: The Roots of Ecology* (San Francisco: Sierra Club Books, 1977).
18. Charles Elton, *Animal Ecology* (New York: Macmillan, 1927).
19. Aldo Leopold, *Round River* (New York: Oxford University Press, 1953), 148.
20. Kenneth Goodpaster, "On Being Morally Considerable," *Journal of Philosophy* 22 (1978): 308–25. Goodpaster wisely avoids the term *rights*, defined so strictly albeit so variously by philosophers, and used so loosely by nonphilosophers.
21. Kenneth Goodpaster, "From Egoism to Environmentalism" in *Ethics and Problems of the 21st Century*, ed. K. E. Goodpaster and K. M. Sayre (Notre Dame, Ind.: University of Notre Dame Press, 1979), 21–35.
22. See Immanuel Kant, *Foundations of the Metaphysics of Morals* (New York: Bobbs-Merrill, 1959; first published in 1785); and Jeremy Bentham, *An Introduction to the Principles of Morals and Legislation*, new edition (Oxford: The Clarendon Press, 1823).
23. Goodpaster, "Egoism to Environmentalism." Actually Goodpaster regards Hume and Kant as the cofountainheads of this sort of moral philosophy. But Hume does not reason in this way. For Hume, the other-oriented sentiments are as primitive as self-love.
24. See Peter Singer, *Animal Liberation: A New Ethics for Our Treatment of Animals* (New York: Avon Books, 1975) for animal liberation; and see Tom Regan, *All That Dwell Therein: Animal Rights and Environmental Ethics* (Berkeley: University of California Press, 1982) for animal rights.
25. See Albert Schweitzer, *Philosophy of Civilization: Civilization and Ethics*, trans. John Naish (London: A. & C. Black, 1923). For a fuller discussion see J. Baird Callicott, "On the Intrinsic Value of Non-human Species," in *The Preservation of Species*, ed. Bryan Norton (Princeton: Princeton University Press, 1986), 138–72.
26. Peter Singer and Tom Regan are both proud of this circumstance and consider it a virtue. See Peter Singer, "Not for Humans Only: The Place of Nonhumans in Environmental Issues" in *Ethics and Problems of the 21st Century*, 191–206; and Tom Regan, "Ethical Vegetarianism and Commercial Animal Farming" in *Contemporary Moral Problems*, ed. James E. White (St. Paul, Minn.: West Publishing Co., 1985), 279–94.
27. See J. Baird Callicott, "Hume's Is/Ought Dichotomy and the Relation of Ecology to Leopold's Land Ethic," *Environmental Ethics* 4 (1982): 163–74, and "Non-

anthropocentric Value Theory and Environmental Ethics," *American Philosophical Quarterly* 21 (1984):299–309, for an elaboration.

28. Hume, *Enquiry*, 219.
29. Darwin, *Descent*, 120.
30. I have elsewhere argued that "value in the philosophical sense" means "intrinsic" or "inherent" value. See J. Baird Callicott, "The Philosophical Value of Wildlife," in *Valuing Wildlife: Economic and Social Values of Wildlife*, ed. Daniel J. Decker and Gary Goff (Boulder, Col.: Westview Press, 1986), 214–21.
31. See Worster, *Nature's Economy*.
32. See J. Baird Callicott, "The Metaphysical Implications of Ecology," *Environmental Ethics* 8 (1986): 300–15, for an elaboration of this point.
33. Robert P. McIntosh, *The Background of Ecology: Concept and Theory* (Cambridge: Cambridge University Press, 1985).
34. Aldo Leopold, "Some Fundamentals of Conservation in the Southwest," *Environmental Ethics* 1 (1979): 139–40, emphasis added.
35. Arthur Tansley, "The Use and Abuse of Vegetational Concepts and Terms," *Ecology* 16 (1935):292–303.
36. Harold J. Morowitz, "Biology as a Cosmological Science," *Main Currents in Modern Thought* 28 (1972):156.
37. I borrow the term "devolution" from Austin Meredith, "Devolution," *Journal of Theoretical Biology* 96 (1982): 49–65.
38. Holmes Rolston, III, "Duties to Endangered Species," *Bioscience* 35 (1985): 718–26. See also Geerat Vermeij, "The Biology of Human-Caused Extinction," in Norton, *Preservation of Species*, 28–49.
39. See D. M. Raup and J. J. Sepkoski, Jr., "Mass Extinctions in the Marine Fossil Record," *Science* 215 (1982): 1501–3.
40. William Aiken, "Ethical Issues in Agriculture," in *Earthbound: New Introductory Essays in Environmental Ethics*, ed. Tom Regan (New York: Random House, 1984), 269. Tom Regan, *The Case for Animal Rights* (Berkeley: University of California Press, 1983), 262, and "Ethical Vegetarianism," 291. See also Eliott Sober, "Philosophical Problems for Environmentalism," in Norton, *Preservation of Species*, 173–94.
41. I owe the tree-ring analogy to Richard and Val Routley (now Sylvan and Plumwood, respectively), "Human Chauvinism and Environmental Ethics," in *Environmental Philosophy*, ed. D. Mannison, M. McRobbie, and R. Routley (Canberra: Department of Philosophy, Research School of the Social Sciences, Australian National University, 1980), 96–189. A good illustration of the balloon analogy may be found in Peter Singer, *The Expanding Circle: Ethics and Socibiology* (New York: Farrar, Straus and Giroux, 1983).
42. For an elaboration see Thomas W. Overholt and J. Baird Callicott, *Clothed-in-Fur and Other Tales: An Introduction to an Ojibwa World View* (Washington, D.C.: University Press of America, 1982).
43. J. Baird Callicott, "Traditional American Indian and Western European Attitudes Toward Nature: An Overview," *Environmental Ethics* 4 (1982): 163–74.
44. Ernest Partridge, "Are We Ready for an Ecological Morality?" *Environmental Ethics* 4 (1982): 177.
45. Peter Fritzell, "The Conflicts of Ecological Conscience," *Companion to A Sand County Almanac*, 128–53.
46. Worster, *Nature's Economy*.
47. Scott Lehmann, "Do Wildernesses Have Rights?" *Environmental Ethics* 3 (1981): 131.

Challenges in Environmental Ethics

Holmes Rolston III

Holmes Rolston III is professor of philosophy at Colorado State University. He is the author of Philosophy Gone Wild: Essays in Environmental Ethics *and* Environmental Ethics: Duties to and Values in the Natural World.

Ethicists had settled on at least one conclusion as ethics became modern in Darwin's century: that the moral has nothing to do with the natural. To argue otherwise commits the naturalistic fallacy, moving without justification from what *is* in nature *ought to be* in culture. Science describes natural history, natural law; ethics prescribes human conduct, moral law; and to confuse the two makes a category mistake. Nature simply *is*, without objective value; the preferences of human subjects establish value; and these human values, appropriately considered, generate human duties. Only humans are ethical subjects and only humans are ethical objects. Nature is amoral; the moral community is interhuman.

In the last third of this century, unsettled as we enter the next millennium, there is foreboding revolution. Only the human species contains moral agents, but perhaps conscience on such an earth ought not be used to exempt every other form of life from consideration, with the resulting paradox that the sole moral species acts only in its collective self-interest toward all the rest. There is something overspecialized about an ethic, held by the dominant class of *Homo sapiens*, that regards the welfare of only one of several million species as an object and beneficiary of duty. We need an interspecific ethics. Whatever ought to be in culture, this biological world that *is* also *ought to be*; we must argue from the natural to the moral.

If this requires a paradigm change about the sorts of things to which duty can attach, so much the worse for those humanistic ethics no longer functioning in, nor suited to, their changing environment. The anthropocentrism

This essay was originally prepared for an American Philosophical Association symposium on Rolston's book, *Environmental Ethics*. A revised version appears in *Ecology, Economics, Ethics: The Broken Circle* (Yale University Press, New Haven, London, 1991).

associated with them was fiction anyway. There is something Newtonian, not yet Einsteinian, besides something morally naive, about living in a reference frame where one species takes itself as absolute and values everything else relative to its utility. If true to their specific epithet, ought not *Homo sapiens* value this host of life as something with a claim to care in its own right? Man may be the only measurer of things, but is man the only measure of things? The challenge of environmental ethics is a principled attempt to redefine the boundaries of ethical obligation.

Still there is the sense of anomaly that forebodes paradigm overthrow. An ecological conscience? Sometimes this seems to be a category mistake, joining a scientific adjective with an ethical noun, rather like Christian biochemistry mismatches a religious adjective and a scientific noun. With analysis, we suspect that the relation is three-place. Person A has a duty to person B concerning the environment C, and no one has ever denied that natural things have instrumental value to humans. Humans are helped or hurt by the condition of their environment, and we have duties to humans that concern their valuable environment, an environment they are able to value. So conservatives may shrink back into the persistent refusal of philosophers to think biologically, to naturalize ethics in the deep sense. They will fear that it is logically incoherent to suppose there is a nonanthropogenic value, or that this is too metaphysically speculative ever to be operational and that it does not make any pragmatic difference anyway, claiming that an adequate environmental ethic can be anthropogenic, even anthropocentric.

When we face up to the crisis, however, we undergo a more direct moral encounter. Environmental ethics is not a muddle; it is an invitation to moral development. All ethics seeks an appropriate respect for life, but respect for human life is only a subset of respect for all life. What ethics is about, in the end, is seeing outside your own sector of self-interest, of class interest. A comprehensive ethic will find values in and duties to the natural world. The vitality of ethics depends on our knowing what is really vital, and there will be found the intersection of value and duty. An ecological conscience requires an unprecedented mix of science and conscience, of biology and ethics.

1. HIGHER ANIMALS

We have direct encounters with life that has eyes, at least where our gaze is returned by something that itself has a concerned outlook. The relation is two-place: I-thou, subject to subject. Compared with concern about soil and water, which are instrumentally vital but blind, when we meet the higher animals there is somebody there behind the fur and feathers. "The environment" is external to us all, but where there is inwardness in this environment, perhaps we ought to be conscious of other consciousness. Whatever matters to animals, matters morally.

Wild animals defend their own lives, because they have a good of their own. Animals hunt and howl, seek shelter, build nests and sing, care for their young, flee from threats, grow hungry, thirsty, hot, tired, excited, sleepy, seek out their habitats and mates. They suffer injury and lick their wounds. They can know security and fear, endurance and fatigue, comfort and pain. When they figure out their helps and hurts in the environment, they do not make man the measure of things at all; more, man is not the only measurer of things.

Still, man is the only moral measurer of things, and how should he count these wild, nonmoral things? One might expect classical ethics to have sifted well an ethics for animals. Our ancestors did not think about endangered species, ecosystems, acid rain, or the ozone layer, but they lived in closer association with wild and domestic animals than do we. Nevertheless, until recently, the scientific, humanistic centuries since the so-called Enlightenment have not been sensitive ones for animals. Animals were mindless, living matter; biology was mechanistic. Even psychology, rather than defending animal experience, was behaviorist. Philosophy, as we have already said, thought man the measure of things. Across several centuries of hard science and humanist ethics there has been little compassion for animals. We eat millions of them every year and we use many millions more in industry and research, as though little matters unless it matters to humans.

So far as we got ethically, we rather oddly said that we should be humane toward nonhuman animals. "The question is not," said Bentham, "Can they reason, nor Can they talk? but, Can they suffer?" These nonhumans do not share with humans the capacity to reason or talk, but they do share the capacity to suffer, and human ethics can be extended so far forth to our animal cousins. We may be unsure about insects and fish, but at least we will need an avian and a mammal ethics.

The progress of recent science itself has increasingly smeared the human-nonhuman boundary line. Animal anatomy, biochemistry, perception, cognition, experience, behavior, and evolutionary history are kin to our own. Animals have no immortal souls, but then persons may not either, or beings with souls may not be the only kind that count morally. Ethical progress further smeared the boundary. Sensual pleasures are a good thing, ethics should be egalitarian nonarbitrary, nondiscriminatory. There are ample scientific grounds that animals enjoy pleasures and suffer pains; and ethically no grounds to value these in humans and not in animals. The *is* in nature and the *ought* in ethics are not so far apart after all. We should treat animals humanely, that is, treat animals equally with ourselves where they have equal interests.

Recently, then, there has been a vigorous reassessment of human duties to sentient life. More has been written on this subject in the past fifteen years than in the previous fifteen centuries. The world cheered in the fall of 1988 when humans rescued two whales from the winter ice. A sign in Rocky Mountain National Park enjoins humans not to harass bighorn sheep: "Respect their right to life." We have passed animal welfare legislation and set up animal care committees in our universities. We have made a vital breakthrough past humans, and the first lesson in environmental ethics has been learned.

But the risk of ethical inadequacy here lies in a moral extension that expands rights as far as mammals and not much further, a psychologically based ethic that counts only felt experience. We respect life in our nonhuman but near-human animal cousins, a semi-anthropic and still quite subjective ethics. Justice remains a concern for just-us subjects. Extending our human ethics, we say that the sheep, too, have rights and that we should be humane to the whales. There has, in fact, not been much theoretical breakthrough, no paradigm shift. We do not yet have a biologically based ethics.

We certainly need an ethic for animals, but that is only one level of concern in a comprehensive environmental ethics. When we try to use culturally extended rights and psychologically based utilities to protect the flora or even the insentient fauna, to protect endangered species or ecosystems, we can only stammer. Indeed, we get lost trying to protect bighorns, because in the wild the cougar is not respecting the rights or utilities of the sheep she slays. There are no rights in the wild, and nature is indifferent to the welfare of particular animals. Further, in culture, humans slay sheep and eat them regularly, while humans have every right not to be eaten by either humans or cougars.

A bison fell through the ice into a river in Yellowstone Park; the environmental ethic there, letting nature take its course, forbade would-be rescuers from either saving or mercy killing the suffering animal. A drowning human would have been saved at once. It was as vital to the struggling bison as to any human to get out; the poor thing froze to death that night. Was the Yellowstone ethic callous to life, inhumane? Or had it other vitalities to consider? This ethic seems rather to have concluded that a moral extension is too nondiscriminating; we are unable to separate an ethics for humans from an ethics for wildlife. To treat wild animals with compassion learned in culture does not appreciate their wildness.

Man, said Socrates, is the political animal; humans maximally are what they are in culture, where the natural selection pressures (impressively productive in ecosystems) are relaxed without detriment to the species *Homo sapiens,* and indeed with great benefit to its member persons. Wild and even domestic animals cannot enter culture; they do not have that capacity. They cannot acquire language at sufficient levels to take part in culture; they cannot make their clothing, or build fires, much less read books or receive an education.

Worse, cultural protection can work to their detriment; with too much human or humane care their wildness is made over into a human artifact. A cow does not have the integrity of a deer, a poodle that of a wolf. Culture is a good thing for humans, often a bad thing for animals. Culture does make a relevant ethical difference, and environmental ethics has different criteria from interhuman ethics.

Can they talk? and, Can they reason?, indicating cultural capacities, are relevant questions, not just, Can they suffer? Compassionate respect for life in its suffering is only part of the analysis. Sometimes in an environmental ethic we do need to follow nature, and not so much to treat animals humanely, like we do humans, as to treat animals naturally, for what they are by themselves. Even when we treat them humanely within culture, part of the ethic may also involve treating them naturally.

"Equality" is a positive word in ethics, "discriminatory" a pejorative one. On the other hand, simplistic reduction is a failing in the philosophy of science and epistemology; to be "discriminating" is desirable in logic and value theory. Something about treating humans as equals with bighorns and cougars seems to "reduce" humans to merely animal levels of value, a "no more" counterpart in ethics of the "nothing but" fallacy often met in science. Humans are "nothing but" naked apes. Something about treating sheep and cougars as the equals of humans seems to elevate them unnaturally, unable to value them for what they are. There is something insufficiently discriminating in such judgments—species blind in a bad sense, blind to the real differences between species, valuational differences that do count morally. To the contrary, a discriminating ethicist will insist on preserving the differing richness of valuational complexity, wherever found.

Two tests of discrimination are pain and diet. It might be thought that pain is a bad thing, whether in nature or culture. Perhaps when dealing with humans in culture, additional levels of value and utility must be protected by conferring rights that do not exist in the wild, but meanwhile at least we should minimize animal suffering. That is indeed a worthy imperative in culture where animals are removed from nature and bred, but it may be misguided where animals remain in ecosystems. When the bighorn sheep of Yellowstone caught pinkeye—blinded, injured, and starving in result—300 bighorns, over half the herd, perished. Wildlife veterinarians wanted to treat the disease, as they would have in any domestic herd, and as they did with Colorado bighorns infected with an introduced lungworm, but the Yellowstone ethicists left them to suffer, seemingly not respecting their life. Had they no mercy? Was this again inhumane?

They knew rather that, while intrinsic pain is a bad thing whether in humans or in sheep, pain in ecosystems is instrumental pain, through which the sheep are naturally selected for a more satisfactory adaptive fit. Pain in a medically skilled culture is pointless, once the alarm to health is sounded, but pain operates functionally in bighorns in their niche, even after it becomes no longer in the interests of the pained individuals. To have interfered in the interests of the blinded sheep would have weakened the species. The question, Can they suffer? is not as simple as Bentham thought. What we *ought* to do depends on what *is*. The *is* of nature differs significantly from the *is* of culture, even when similar suffering is present in both.

Some ethicists will insist that at least in culture we can minimize animal pain, and that will constrain our diet. There is predation in nature; humans evolved as omnivores. But humans, the only moral animals, should refuse to participate in the meat-eating phase of their ecology, just as they refuse to live merely by the rules of natural selection. Humans do not look to the behavior of wild animals as an ethical guide in other matters (marriage, truth telling, promise keeping, justice, charity). There they do not follow nature. Why should they justify their dietary habits by watching what animals do?

But the difference is that these other matters are affairs of culture; these are person-to-person events, not events at all in spontaneous nature. By contrast, eating is omnipresent in wild nature; humans eat because they are in nature, not because they are in culture. Eating animals is not an event between persons, but is a human-to-animal event; and the rules for this come from the ecosystems in which humans evolved and which they have no duty to remake. We must eat to live; nature absolutely requires that. We evolved to eat as omnivores; that animal nature underruns over human nature. Even in culture meat eating is still relatively natural; there is nothing immoral about fitting into one's ecology. We follow nature, treat animals naturally, capture nutritional values, and learn our place in the scheme of life and death. This respects life, profoundly so. Humans, then, can model their dietary habits from their ecosystems, though they cannot and should not so model their interpersonal justice or charity. When eating they ought to minimize animal suffering, and they also may gladly affirm their ecology. The boundary between animals and humans has not been rubbed out after all; only what was a boundary line has been smeared into a boundary zone. We have discovered that animals count morally, though we are only beginning to solve the challenge of how to count them.

2. ORGANISMS

In college zoology I did an experiment on nutrition in rats, to see how they grew with and without vitamins. When the experiment was completed, I was told to take the rats out and drown them. I felt squeamish but did it. In college botany I did an experiment on seedlings to test how they grew with this or that fertilizer. The experiment over, I threw out the seedlings without a second thought. While there can be ethics about sentient animals, after that perhaps ethics is over. Respect for life ends somewhere in zoology; it is not part of botany. No consciousness, no conscience. Without sentience, ethics is nonsense.

Or do we want an ethic that is more objective about life? In Yosemite National Park for almost a century humans entertained themselves by driving through a tunnel cut in a giant sequoia. Two decades ago the Wawona tree, weakened by the cut, blew down in a storm. People said: Cut us another drive-through sequoia. The Yosemite environmental ethic, deepening over the years, said no! You ought not to mutilate majestic sequoias for amusement. Respect their life! Indeed, some ethicists count the value of redwoods so highly that they will spike redwoods, lest they be cut. In the Rawah Wilderness in alpine Colorado, old signs read, "Please leave the flowers for others to enjoy." When they rotted out, the new signs urged a less humanist ethic: "Let the flowers live!"

But trees and flowers cannot care, so why should we? We are not considering animals that are close kin, nor can they suffer or experience anything. There are no humane societies for plants. Plants are not valuers with preferences that can be satisfied or frustrated. It seems odd to claim that plants need our sympathy, odd to ask that we should consider their point of view. They have no subjective life, only objective life.

Fishermen in Atlantic coastal estuaries and bays toss beer bottles overboard, a convenient way to dispose of trash. On the bottom, small crabs, attracted by the residual beer, make their way inside the bottles and become trapped, unable to get enough foothold on the slick glass neck to work their way out. They starve slowly. Then one dead crab becomes bait for the next victim, an indefinitely resetting trap! Are those bottle traps of ethical concern, after fishermen have been warned about this effect? Or is the whole thing out of sight, out of mind, with crabs too mindless to care about? Should sensitive fishermen pack their bottle trash back to shore—whether or not crabs have much, or any, felt experience?

Flowers and sequoias live; they ought to live. Crabs have value out of sight, out of mind. Afraid of the naturalistic fallacy, conservative ethicists will say that people should enjoy letting flowers live or that it is silly to cut drive-through sequoias, aesthetically more excellent for humans to appreciate both for what they are. The crabs are out of sight, but not really out of mind; humans value them at a distance. But these ethically conservative reasons really do not understand what biological conservation is in the deepest sense. Nothing matters to a tree, but much is *vital*.

An organism is a spontaneous, self-maintaining system, sustaining and reproducing itself, executing its program, making a way through the world, checking against performance by means of responsive capacities with which to measure success. It can reckon with vicissitudes, opportunities, and adversities that the world presents. Something more than physical causes, even when less than sentience, is operating within every organism. There is *information* superintending the causes; without it the organism would collapse into a sand heap. This information is a modern equivalent of what Aristotle called formal and final causes; it gives the organism a *telos*, "end," a kind of (nonfelt) goal. Organisms have ends, although not always ends-in-view.

All this cargo is carried by the DNA, essentially a *linguistic* molecule. By a serial "reading" of the DNA, a polypeptide chain is synthesized, such that its sequential structure determines the bioform into which it will fold. Ever-lengthening chains (like ever-longer sentences), are organized into genes (like paragraphs and chapters). Diverse proteins, lipids, carbohydrates, enzymes—all the life structures are "written into" the genetic library. The DNA is thus a *logical set*, not less than a biological set, informed as well as formed. Organisms use a sort of symbolic logic, use these molecular shapes as symbols of life. The novel resourcefulness lies in the epistemic content conserved, developed, and thrown forward to make biological resources out of the physicochemical sources. This executive steering core is cybernetic—partly a special kind of cause and effect system, and partly something more: partly a historical information system discovering and evaluating ends so as to map and make a way through the world, partly a system of significances attached to operations, pursuits, resources. In this sense, the genome is a set of *conservation* molecules.

The genetic set is really a *propositional* set—to choose a provocative term—recalling how the Latin *propositum* is an assertion, a set task, a theme, a plan, a proposal, a project, as well as a cognitive statement. From this it is also a motivational set, unlike human books, since these life motifs are set to drive the movement from genotypic potential to phenotypic expression. Given a chance, these molecules seek organic self-expression. They thus proclaim a life way, and with this an organism, unlike an inert rock, claims the environment as source and sink, from which to abstract energy and materials and into which to excrete them. It "takes advantage" of its environment. Life thus arises out of earthen sources (as do rocks), but life turns back on its sources to make resources out of them (unlike rocks). An acorn becomes an oak; the oak stands on its own.

So far we have only description. We begin to pass to value when we recognize that the genetic set is a *normative set*; it distinguishes between what *is* and what *ought to be*. This does not mean that the organism is a moral system, for there are no moral agents in nature; but the organism is an axiological, evaluative system. So the oak grows, reproduces, repairs its wounds, and resists death. The physical state that the organism seeks, idealized in its programmatic form, is a valued state. *Value* is present in this achievement. *Vital* seems a better word for it than *biological*. We are not dealing simply with an individual defending its solitary life but with an individual having situated fitness in an ecosystem. Still, we want to affirm that the living individual, taken as a "point experience" in the web of interconnected life, is *per se* an intrinsic value.

A life is defended for what it is in itself, without necessary further contributory reference, although, given the structure of all ecosystems, such lives necessarily do have further reference. The organism has something it is conserving, something for which it is standing: its life. Organisms have their own standards, fit into their niche though they must. They promote their own realization, at the same time that they track an environment. They have a technique, a know-how. Every organism has a *good-of-its-kind*; it defends its own kind as a *good kind*. In that sense, as soon as one knows what a giant sequoia tree is, one knows the biological identity that is sought and conserved. Man is neither the measurer nor the measure of things; value is not anthropogenic, it is biogenic.

There seems no reason why such own-standing normative organisms are not morally significant. A moral agent deciding his or her behavior, ought to take account of the consequences for other evaluative systems. This does not follow nature, if we mean by that to imitate ethical agents there, for nature is amoral. But it does follow nature, if we mean by that we respect these amoral organic norms as we shape our conduct. Such an ethic will be teleological, I suppose, since it values the *telos* in organisms, but it seems equally deontological, since it owes (Gk: *deont-*) respect for life in itself, intrinsically, and not just instrumentally, consequentially. (Frankly, the classical teleological/deontological distinction seems as troublesome as helpful in moral analysis here.)

Within the community of moral agents one has not merely to ask whether *x* is a normative system, but, since the norms are a personal option, to judge the norm and the consequences. But within the biotic community organisms are amoral normative systems, and there are no cases where an organism seeks a good of its own that is morally reprehensible. The distinction between having a good of its kind and being a good kind vanishes, so far as any faulting of the organism is concerned. To this extent, everything with a good of its kind is a good kind and thereby has intrinsic value.

One might say that an organism is a bad organism if, during the course of pressing its normative expression, it upsets the ecosystem or causes widespread disease, bad consequences. Remember though, that an organism cannot be a good kind without situated environmental fitness. By natural selection the kind of goods to which it is genetically programmed must mesh with its ecosystemic role. Despite the ecosystem as a perpetual contest of goods in dialectic and exchange, it is difficult to say that any organism is a bad kind in this instrumental sense either. The misfits are extinct, or soon will be. In spontaneous nature any species that preys upon, parasitizes, competes with, or crowds another will be a bad kind from the narrow perspective of its victim or competitor.

But if we enlarge that perspective it typically becomes difficult to say that any species is a bad kind overall in the ecosystem. An "enemy" may even be good for the "victimized" species, though harmful to individual members of it, as when predation keeps the deer herd healthy. Beyond this, the "bad kinds" typically play useful roles in population control, in symbiotic relationships, or in providing opportunities for other species. The *Chlamydia* microbe is a bad kind from the perspective of the bighorns, but when one thing dies, something else lives. After the pinkeye outbreak, the golden eagle population in Yellowstone flourished, preying on the bighorn carcasses. For them *Chlamydia* is a good kind instrumentally.

Some biologist-philosophers will say that, even though an organism evolves to have a situated environmental fitness, not all such situations are good arrangements; some can be clumsy or bad. True, the vicissitudes of historical evolution do sometimes result in ecological webs that are suboptimal solutions, within the biologically limited possibilities and powers of interacting organisms. Still, such systems have been selected over millennia for functional stability; and at least the burden of proof is on a human evaluator to say why any natural kind is a bad kind and ought not to call forth admiring respect. Something may be a good kind intrinsically but a bad kind instrumentally in the system; these will be anomalous cases, however, with selection pressures against them. These claims about good kinds do not say that things are perfect kinds, or that there can be no better ones, only that natural kinds are good kinds until proven otherwise.

What is almost invariably meant by a "bad" kind is that an organism is instrumentally bad when judged from the viewpoint of human interests, of humane interests. "Bad" so used is an anthropocentric word; there is nothing at all biological or ecological about it, and so it has no force evaluating objective nature, however much humanist force it may sometimes have.

A really *vital* ethic respects all life, not just animal pains and pleasures, much less just human preferences. In the Rawahs, the old signs, "Leave the flowers for others to enjoy," were application signs using an old, ethically conservative, humanistic ethic. The new ones invite a change of reference frame—a wilder, more logical because more biological ethic, a radical ethic that goes down to the roots of life, that really is conservative because it understands biological conservation at depths. What the injunction, "Let the flowers live!" means is: "Daisies, marsh-marigolds, geraniums, larkspurs are evaluative systems that conserve goods of their kind, and, in the absence of evidence to the contrary, are good kinds. There are trails here by which you may enjoy these flowers. Is there any reason why your human interests should not also conserve these good kinds?" A drive-through sequoia causes no suffering; it is not cruel. but it is callous and insensitive to the wonder of life. The ethically conservative will complain that we have committed the naturalistic fallacy; rather, we invite a radical commitment to respect all life.

3. SPECIES

Certain rare species of butterflies occur in hummocks (slightly elevated forested ground) on the African grasslands. It was formerly the practice of unscrupulous collectors to go in, collect a few hundred specimens, and then burn out the hummock with the intention of destroying the species, thereby driving up the price of their collections. I find myself persuaded that they morally ought not do this. Nor will the reason resolve into the evil of greed, but it remains the needless destruction of a butterfly species.

This conviction remains even when the human goods are more worthy. Coloradans are considering whether to build the Two Forks Dam to supply urban Denver with water. This would require destroying a canyon and altering the Platte River flow, with many negative environmental consequences, including endangering a butterfly, the Pawnee montane skipper, *Hesperia leonardus montana,* as well as endangering the whooping crane downstream. I doubt whether the good of humans who wish more water for development, both for industry and for bluegrass lawns, warrants endangering species of butterflies and cranes.

Sometimes the stakes are alleged to rise even higher. The Bay checkerspot, *Euphydryas editha bayensis,* proposed to be listed as an endangered species, inhabits peripheral tracts of a large facility on which United Technologies Corporation, a missile contractor, builds and tests Minuteman and Tomahawk propulsion systems. The giant defense contractor has challenged the proposed listing and thinks it airy and frivolous that a butterfly should slow the delivery of warhead missile propulsion systems, and so went ahead and dug a water pipeline through a butterfly patch. They operated out of the classical ethics that says that butterflies do not count but that the defense of humans does.

But a more radical, environmental ethics demurs. The good of humans might override the good of butterfly species but the case must be argued. Lest this seem the foolishness of a maverick philosopher, I point out that such conviction has been written into national law. The Endangered Species Act requires that the case must be argued before a high level "God" committee.

A species exists; a species ought to exist. Environmental ethics must make both claims and move from biology to ethics with care. Species exist only instantiated in individuals, yet are as real as individual plants or animals. The claim that there are specific forms of life historically maintained in their environments over time seems as certain as anything else we believe about the empirical world. At times biologists revise the theories and taxa with which they map these forms, but species are not so much like lines of latitude and longitude as like mountains and rivers, phenomena objectively there to be mapped. The edges of these natural kinds will sometimes be fuzzy, to some extent discretionary. One species will slide into another over evolutionary time. But it does not follow from the fact that speciation is sometimes in progress that species are merely made up, not found as evolutionary lines with identity in time as well as space.

A consideration of species is revealing and challenging because it offers a biologically based counterexample to the focus on individuals—typically sentient and usually persons—so characteristic in classical ethics. In an evolutionary ecosystem, it is not mere individuality that counts, but the species is also significant because it is a dynamic life form maintained over time. The individual represents (re-presents) a species in each new generation. It is a token of a type, and the type is more important than the token.

A species lacks moral agency, reflective self-awareness, sentience, or organic individuality. The older, conservative ethic will be tempted to say that specific-level processes cannot count morally. Duties must attach to singular lives, most evidently those with a psychological self, or some analogue to this. In an individual organism, the organs report to a center; the good of a whole is defended. The members of a species report to no center. A species has no self. It is not a bounded singular. There is no analogue to the nervous hookups or circulatory flows that characterize the organism.

But singularity, centeredness, selfhood, individuality, are not the only processes to which duty attaches. A more radically conservative ethic knows that having a biological identity reasserted genetically over time is as true of the species as of the individual. Identity need not attach solely to the centered organism; it can persist as a discrete pattern over time. Thinking this way, the life that the individual has is something passing through the individual as much as something it intrinsically possesses. The individual is subordinate to the species, not the other way around. The genetic set, in which is coded the *telos*, is as evidently the property of the species as of the individual through which it passes. A consideration of species strains any ethic fixed on individual organisms, much less on sentience or persons. But the result can be biologically sounder, though it revises what was formerly thought logically permissible or ethically binding. This is a higher teleological ethic, finding now the specific *telos*, and concerned about consequences at that level; again, it is deontological, duty bound to the dynamic form of life for what it is in itself.

The species line is the *vital* living system, the whole, of which individual organisms are the essential parts. The species too has its integrity, its individuality, its "right to life" (if we must use the rhetoric of rights); and it is more important to protect this vitality than to protect individual integrity. The right to life, biologically speaking, is an adaptive fit that is right for life, that survives over millennia, and this generates at least a presumption that species in niche are good right where they are, and therefore that it is right for humans to let them be, to let them evolve.

Processes of value that we earlier found in an organic individual reappear at the specific level: defending a particular form of life, pursuing a pathway through the world, resisting death (extinction), regeneration maintaining a normative identity over time, creative resilience discovering survival skills. It is as logical to say that the individual is the species' way of propagating itself as to say that the embryo or egg is the individual's way of propagating itself. The dignity resides in the dynamic form; the individual inherits this, exemplifies it, and passes it on. If, at the specific level, these processes are just as evident, or even more so, what prevents duties arising at that level? The appropriate survival unit is the appropriate level of moral concern. This would be following nature specifically.

Sensitivity to this level, however, can sometimes make an environmental ethicist seem callous. On San Clemente Island, the U.S. Fish and Wildlife Service and the California Department of Fish and Game planned to shoot 2,000 feral goats to save three endangered plant species, *Malacothamnus clementinus, Castilleja grisea, Delphinium kinkiense,* of which the surviving individuals numbered only a few dozens. After a protest, some goats were trapped and relocated. But trapping all was impossible and many hundreds were killed. Is it inhumane to count plant species more than mammal lives, a few plants more than a thousand goats?

Those who wish to restore rare species of big cats to the wilds have asked about killing genetically inbred, inferior cats, presently held in zoos, in order to make space available for the cats needed to reconstruct and maintain a population genetically more likely to survive upon release. All the Siberian tigers in zoos in North America are descendants of seven animals; if these were replaced by others nearer to the wild type and with more genetic variability, the species could be saved in the wild. When we move to the level of species, we may kill individuals for the good of their kind.

Or we may now refuse to let nature take its course. The Yellowstone ethicists let the bison drown, callous to its suffering; they let the blinded bighorns die. But in the spring of 1984 a sow grizzly and her three cubs walked across the ice of Yellowstone Lake to Frank Island, two miles from shore. They stayed several days to feast on two elk carcasses, when the ice bridge melted. Soon afterward, they were starving on an island too small to support them. This time the Yellowstone ethicists promptly rescued the grizzlies and released them on the mainland, in order to protect an endangered species. They were not rescuing individual bears so much as saving the species. They thought that humans had already and elsewhere imperiled the grizzly, and that they ought to save this form of life.

Humans have more understanding than ever of the natural world they inhabit, of the speciating processes, more predictive power to foresee the intended and unintended results of their actions, and more power to reverse the undesirable consequences. The duties that such power and vision generate no longer attach simply to individuals or persons but are emerging duties to specific forms of life. The wrong that humans are doing, or allowing to happen through carelessness, is stopping the historical vitality of life, the flow of natural kinds.

Every extinction is an incremental decay in this stopping life, no small thing. Every extinction is a kind of superkilling. It kills forms (*species*), beyond individuals. It kills "essences" beyond "existences," the "soul" as well as the "body." It kills collectively, not just distributively. It kills birth as well as death. Afterward nothing of that kind either lives or dies. A shutdown of the life stream is the most destructive event possible. Never before has this level of question—superkilling by a superkiller—been deliberately faced. What is ethically callous is the maelstrom of killing and insensitivity to forms of life and the sources producing them. What is required is principled responsibility to the biospheric earth.

Several billion years' worth of creative toil, several million species of teeming life, have been handed over to the care of this late-coming species in which mind has flowered and morals have emerged. Life on earth is a many splendored thing; extinction dims its luster. If, in this world of uncertain moral convictions, it makes any sense to claim that one ought not to kill individuals, without justification, it makes more sense to claim that one ought not to superkill the species, without superjustification. That moves from what *is* to what *ought to be*; and the fallacy is not committed by naturalists who so argue but by humanists who cannot draw these conclusions.

4. ECOSYSTEMS

"A thing is right," urged Aldo Leopold, concluding his land ethic, "when it tends to preserve the integrity, stability, and beauty of the biotic community; it is wrong when it tends otherwise." Again, we have two parts to the ethic: first that ecosystems exist, both in the wild and in support of culture; secondly that ecosystems ought to exist, both for what they are in themselves and as modified by culture. Again, we must move with care from the biological claims to the ethical claims.

Classical, humanistic ethics finds ecosystems unfamiliar territory. It is difficult to get the biology right, and, superimposed on the biology, to get the ethics right. Fortunately, it is often evident that human welfare depends on ecosystemic support, and in this sense all our legislation about clean air, clean water, soil conservation, national and state forest policy, pollution controls, oil spills, renewable resources, and so forth is concerned about ecosystem level processes. Further, humans find much of value for themselves in preserving wild ecosystems and our wilderness and park system is accordingly ecosystem oriented.

Still, a comprehensive environmental ethics needs the best, naturalistic reasons, as well as the good, humanistic ones, for respecting ecosystems. The ecosystem is the community of life; in it the fauna and flora, the species have entwined destinies. Ecosystems generate and support life, keep selection pressures high, enrich situated fitness, evolve congruent kinds in their places with sufficient containment. The ecologist finds that ecosystems are objectively satisfactory communities in the sense that organismic needs are sufficiently met for species long to survive, and the critical ethicist finds (in a subjective judgment matching the objective process) that such ecosystems are satisfactory communities to which to attach duty. Our concern must be for the fundamental unit of survival.

Giant forest fires raged over Yellowstone National Park in the summer of 1988, consuming nearly a million acres, despite the efforts of a thousand firefighters. By far the largest fires ever known in the park, the fires seemed a disaster. But the Yellowstone land ethic enjoins: Let nature take its course. Let it burn! So the fires were not fought at first, but in midsummer national authorities overrode that policy and ordered the fires put out. Even then, weeks later, fires continued to burn, partly because they were too big to control, but partly, too, because Yellowstone personnel did not altogether want the fires put out. Despite the evident destruction of trees, shrubs, and wildlife, they believe that fires are a good thing. Fires reset succession, release nutrients, recycle materials, renew the biotic community. (Nearby, in the Teton wilderness, a storm blew down 15,000 acres of trees, and some proposed that the area be declassified as wilderness for commercial salvage of the timber. But a similar environmental ethics said: No, let it rot.)

Aspen are important in the Yellowstone ecosystem. While some aspen stands are climax and self-renewing, many are seral and give way to conifers. Aspen groves support many birds and much wildlife, especially the beavers, whose activities maintain the riparian zones. Aspen are rejuvenated after fires, and the Yellowstone land ethic wants the aspen for its critical role in the biotic community. Elk browse the young aspen stems. To a degree this is a good thing, since it gives elk critical nitrogen, but in excess it is a bad thing. The elk have no predators, since the wolves are gone, and as a result they overpopulate. Excess elk also destroy the willows and this in turn destroys the beavers.

Rejuvenating the aspen might require managers to cull hundreds of elk—all for the sake of a healthy ecosystem.

The Yellowstone ethic wishes to restore wolves to the greater Yellowstone ecosystem. At the level of species, this is partly for what the wolf is in itself, but it is partly because the greater Yellowstone ecosystem does not have its full integrity, stability, and beauty without this majestic animal at the top of the trophic pyramid. Restoring the wolf as a top predator would mean suffering and death for many elk, but that would be a good thing for the aspen and willows, for the beavers and riparian habitat, with mixed benefits for the bighorns and mule deer, whose food the overpopulating elk consume, but who would also be consumed by the wolves. The Yellowstone ethic demands wolves, as it does fires, in appropriate respect for life in its ecosystem.

Letting nature take its ecosystemic course is why the Yellowstone ethic forbade rescuing the drowning bison, but rescued the sow grizzly with her cubs, the latter to insure that the big predators remain. After the bison drowned, coyotes and magpies, foxes and ravens fed on the carcass. Later, even a grizzly bear fed on it. All this is a good thing because the system cycles on. On that account rescuing the whales trapped in the winter ice seems less of a good thing, when we note that rescuers had to drive away polar bears that attempted to eat the dying whales.

An ecosystem, the conservative ethicist will say, is too low a level of organization to be respected intrinsically. Ecosystems can seem little more than random, statistical processes. A forest can seem a loose collection of externally related parts, the collection of fauna and flora a jumble, hardly a community. The plants and animals within an ecosystem have needs, but their interplay can seem simply a matter of distribution and abundance, birth rates and death rates, population densities, parasitism and predation, dispersion, checks and balances, stochastic process. Much is not organic at all (rain, groundwater, rocks, soil particles, air), while some organic material is dead and decaying debris (fallen trees, scat, humus). These things have no organized needs. There is only catch-as-catch-can scrimmage for nutrients and energy, a game played with loaded dice, not really enough integrated process to call the whole a community.

Unlike higher animals, ecosystems have no experiences; they do not and cannot care. Unlike plants, an ecosystem has no organized center, no genome. It does not defend itself against injury or death. Unlike a species, there is no ongoing *telos*, no biological identity reinstantiated over time. The organismic parts are more complex than the community whole. More troublesome still, an ecosystem can seem a jungle where the fittest survive, a place of contest and conflict, beside which the organism is a model of cooperation. In animals, the heart, liver, muscles and brain are tightly integrated, as are the leaves, cambium, and roots in plants. But the ecosystem community is pushing and shoving between rivals, each aggrandizing itself, or else indifference and haphazard juxtaposition, nothing to call forth our admiration.

Environmental ethics must break through the boundary posted by disoriented ontological conservatives, who hold that only organisms are "real," actually existing as entities, whereas ecosystems are nominal—just interacting individuals. Oak trees are real but forests are nothing but collections of trees. But any level is real if it shapes behavior on the level below it. Thus the cell is real because that pattern shapes the behavior of amino acids; the organism because that pattern coordinates the behavior of hearts and lungs. The biotic community is real because the niche shapes the morphology of the oak trees within it. Being real at the level of community only requires an organization that shapes the behavior of its members.

The challenge is to find a clear model of community and to discover an ethics for it—better biology for better ethics. Even before the rise of ecology, biologists began to conclude that the combative survival of the fittest distorts the truth. The more perceptive model is coaction in adapted fit. Predator and prey, parasite and host, grazer and grazed are contending forces in dynamic process where the well-being of each is bound up with the other—coordinated (orders that couple together) as much as heart and liver are coordinated organically. The ecosystem supplies the coordinates through which each organism moves, outside which the species cannot really be located. A species is what it is where it is.

The community connections are looser than the organism's internal interconnections—but not less significant. Admiring organic unity in organisms and stumbling over environmental looseness is like valuing mountains and despising valleys. The matrix the organism requires in order to survive is the open, pluralistic ecology. Internal complexity—heart, liver, muscles, brain—arises as a way of dealing with a complex, tricky environment. The skin-out processes are not just the support, they are the subtle source of the skin-in processes. In the complete picture, the outside is as *vital* as the inside. Had there been either simplicity or lock-step concentrated unity in the environment, no organismic unity could have evolved. Nor would it remain. There would be less elegance in life.

To look at one level for what is appropriate at another makes a categorical mistake. One should not look for a single center or program in ecosystems, much less for subjective experiences. Instead, one should look for a matrix, for interconnections between centers (individual plants and animals, dynamic lines of speciation), for creative stimulus and open-ended potential. Everything will be connected to many other things, sometimes by obligate associations, more often by partial and pliable dependencies and, among other things, there will be no significant interactions. There will be functions in a communal sense: shunts and criss-crossing pathways, cybernetic subsystems, and feedback loops. An order arises spontaneously and systematically when many self-concerned units jostle and seek their own programs, each doing their own thing and forced into informed interaction.

An ecosystem is a productive, projective system. Organisms defend only their selves, with individuals defending their continuing survival and species increasing the numbers of kinds. But the evolutionary ecosystem spins a bigger story, limiting each kind, locking it into the welfare of others, promoting new arrivals, bringing forth kinds and the integration of kinds. Species *increase their kind*; but ecosystems *increase kinds*, superimposing the latter increase onto the former. *Ecosystems are selective systems, as surely as organisms are selective systems.* The natural selection comes out of the system and is imposed on the individual. The individual is programmed to make more of its kind, but more is going on systemically than that; the system is making more kinds.

This extends natural selection theory beyond the merely tautological formulation that the system selects the best adapted to survive. Ecosystems select for those features that appear over the long ranges, for individuality, for diversification, for sufficient containment, for quality supervening on quantity of life. They do this, appropriately to the community level, by employing conflict, decenteredness, probability, succession, spontaneous generation of order, and historicity. Communal processes—the competition between organisms, more or less probable events, plant and animal successions, speciation over historical time—generate an ever-richer community.

Hence the evolutionary toil, elaborating and diversifying the biota, that once began with no species and results today in five million species, increasing over time the quality of lives in the upper rungs of the tropic pyramids. One-celled organisms evolved into many-celled, highly integrated organisms. Photosynthesis evolved and came to support locomotion—swimming, walking, running, flight. Stimulus-response mechanisms became complex instinctive acts. Warm-blooded animals followed cold-blooded ones. Complex nervous systems, conditioned behavior and learning emerged. Sentience appeared—sight, hearing, smell, tastes, pleasure, pain. Brains coupled with hands. Consciousness and self-consciousness arose. Culture was superimposed on nature.

These developments do not take place in all ecosystems or at every level. Microbes, plants, and lower animals remain, good of their kinds, and serving continuing roles, good for other kinds. The understories remain occupied. As a result, the quantity of life and its diverse qualities continue—from protozoans to primates to people. There is a push-up, lock-up, ratchet effect that conserves the upstrokes and the outreaches. The later we go in time the more accelerated are the forms at the top of the tropic pyramids, the more elaborated are the multiple tropic pyramids of earth. There are upward arrows over evolutionary time.

The system is a game with loaded dice, but the loading is a prolife tendency, not mere stochastic process. Though there is no *nature* in the singular, the system has a nature, a loading that pluralizes, putting *natures* into diverse kinds, nature_1, nature_2, nature_3 . . . nature_n. It does so using random elements (in both organisms and communities), but this is a secret of its fertility, producing steadily intensified interdependencies and options. An ecosystem has no head, but it has a "heading" for species diversification, support, and richness. Though not a superorganism, it is a kind of vital field.

Instrumental value uses something as a means to an end; *intrinsic value* is worthwhile in itself. No warbler eats insects to become food for a falcon; the warbler defends its own life as an end in itself and makes more warblers as it can. A life is defended intrinsically, without further contributory reference. But neither of these traditional terms is satisfactory at the level of the ecosystem. Though it has value *in* itself, the system does not have any value *for* itself. Though a value producer, it is not a value owner. We are no longer confronting instrumental value, as though the system were of value instrumentally as a fountain of life. Nor is the question one of intrinsic value, as though the system defended some unified form of life for itself. We have reached something for which we need a third term: *systemic value*. Duties arise in an encounter with the system that projects and protects these member components in biotic community. If you like, that is an ethic that is teleological again, but since we are respecting both processes and products, perhaps a better word for it now is communitarian. We follow nature, this time ecologically.

Ethical conservatives, in the humanist sense, will say that ecosystems are of value only because they contribute to human experiences. But that mistakes the last chapter for the whole story, one fruit for the whole plant. Humans count enough to have the right to flourish there, but not so much that they have the right to degrade or shut down ecosystems, not at least without a burden of proof that there is an overriding cultural gain. Earlier, environmental ethics will say that ecosystems are of value because they contribute to animal experiences or to organismic life. Later, the deeper, more conservative and more radical view sees that the stability, integrity, and beauty of biotic communities are what are most fundamentally to be conserved.

5. VALUE THEORY

In practice the ultimate challenge of environmental ethics is the conservation of life on earth. In principle the ultimate challenge is a value theory profound enough to support that ethic. We need an account of how nature carries value, and an ethics that appropriately respects those values. For subjectivists both the theory and the ethics will be nothing but human constructs; but objectivists in environmental ethics will use such theory to discover facts, how nature carries values, and from this sometimes there will follow what humans ought to do. The values that nature carries belong as much to the biology of natural history as to the psychology of human experience. Some of the values that nature carries are up to us, our assignment. But fundamentally there are powers in nature that move to us and through us. The splendors of earth do not simply lie in their roles as human resources, supports of culture, or stimulators of experience.

There is no value without an evaluator. So runs a well-entrenched dogma. Humans clearly evaluate their world; sentient animals may also. But plants cannot evaluate their environment; they have no options and make no choices. *A fortiori*, species and ecosystems, earth and nature cannot be bona fide evaluators. Value, like a tickle or remorse, must be felt to be there. Its *esse* is *percipi*. Nonsensed value is nonsense. There are no thoughts without a thinker, no percepts without a perceiver, no deeds without a doer, no targets without an aimer. Valuing is felt preferring; value is the product of this process.

If value arrives only with consciousness, experiences where humans find value there have to be dealt with as appearances of various sorts. The value has to be relocated in the valuing subject's creativity as a person meets a valueless world, or even a valuable one—one *able* to be *valued*—but which before the human bringing of value ability contains only possibility and not any actual value. Value can only be extrinsic to nature, never intrinsic to it. Nature offers but the standing possibility of valuation; value is not generated until humans appear with their valuing ability.

But the valuing subject in an otherwise valueless world is an insufficient premise for the experienced conclusions of those who respect all life. Conversion to a biological view seems truer to world experience and more logically compelling. Here the order of knowing reverses—and also enhances—the order of being. This, too, is a perspective, but ecologically better informed. Science has been steadily showing how the consequents (life, mind) are built on their precedents (energy, matter), however much they overleap them. Life and mind appear where they did not before exist, and with this levels of value emerge that did not before exist. But that gives no reason to say that all value is an irreducible emergent at the human (or upper animal) level. Nature does, of course, offer possibilities for human valuation, but the vitality of the system is not something that goes on in the human mind, nor is its value. The possibility of valuation is carried to us by evolutionary and ecological natural history, and such nature is already valuable before humans arrive to evaluate what is taking place.

How do we humans come to be charged up with values, if there was and is nothing in nature charging us up so? Some value is anthropogenic, generated by humans, but some is biogenic, in the natural genesis. A comprehensive environmental ethics reallocates value across the whole continuum. Value increases in the emergent climax, but is continuously present in the composing precedents. The system is *value-able, able* to produce *value.* Human evaluators are among its products. But when we value we must not forget our communal bonds. Sometimes we need to evaluate (appraise the worth of) what we ourselves may not value (personally prefer). Against the standard view that all value requires a beholder, some value requires only a holder, and some value is held within the historic system that carries value to and through individuals.

Here we do not want a subjective morality but an objective one, even though we find that subjectivity is the most valuable output of the objective system. Is there any reason for ethical subjects to discount the vital systemic processes unless and until accompanied by sentience? Perhaps to evaluate the entire biological world on the basis of sentience is as much a categorical mistake as to judge it according to whether justice and charity are found there. The one mistake judges biological places by extension from psychology, the other from culture. What is "right" about the biological world is not just the production of pleasures and positive experiences. What is "right" includes ecosystemic patterns, organisms in their generating, sustaining environments.

Some value depends on subjectivity, yet all value is generated within the geosystemic and ecosystemic community. Systemically, value fades from subjective to objective value, but also fans out from the individual to its role and matrix. Things do not have their separate natures merely in and for themselves, but they face outward and co-fit into broader natures. Value-in-itself is smeared out to become value-in-togetherness. Value seeps out into the system, and we lose our capacity to identify the individual as the sole locus of value.

Intrinsic value, that of an individual "for what it is in itself," becomes problematic in a holistic web. True, the system produces such values more and more with its evolution of individuality and freedom. Yet to decouple this from the biotic, communal system is to make value too internal and elementary; this forgets relatedness and externality. Every intrinsic value has leading and trailing *ands* pointing to value from which it comes and toward which it moves. Adapted fitness makes individualistic value too system independent. Intrinsic value is a part in a whole, not to be fragmented by valuing it in isolation. An isolated *telos* is biologically impossible; the ethic cannot be teleological in that sense, nor can we term it deontological either, if this requires respect for an intrinsic value regardless of ecosystemic consequences. (The classical distinction fails again.)

Everything is good in a role, in a whole, although we can speak of objective intrinsic goodness wherever a good kind defends itself. We can speak of subjective intrinsic goodness when such an event registers as a point experience, at which point humans pronounce both their experience and what it is of good without need to enlarge their focus. The system is a value transformer where form and being, process and reality, fact and value are inseparably joined. Intrinsic and instrumental values shuttle back and forth, parts-in-wholes and wholes-in-parts, local details of value embedded in global structures, gems in their settings, and their setting-situation a corporation where value cannot stand alone. Every good is in community.

This is what is radically wrong with anthropocentric or merely anthropogenic value. It arrogates to humans what permeates the community. Subjective self-satisfactions are, and ought to be, sufficiently contained within the objectively satisfactory system. The system creates life, selects for adaptive fit, constructs increasingly richer life in quantity and quality, supports myriads of species, escalates individually, autonomy, and even subjectivity, within the limits of decentralized community. When persons appraise this natural history, if such land is not a valuable, satisfactory biotic community, why not? Does earth and its community of life not claim their concern and care?

In environmental ethics one's beliefs about nature, which are based upon but exceed science, have everything to do with beliefs about duty. The way the world *is* informs the way it *ought* to be. We always shape our values in significant measure in accord with our notion of the kind of universe that we live in, and this drives our sense of duty. Our model of reality implies a model of conduct. Perhaps we can leave open what metaphysics ultimately underlies our cosmos, but for an environmental ethics at least we will need an earthbound metaphysics, a metaecology. Differing models sometimes imply similar conduct, but often they do not. A model in which nature has no value apart from human preferences will imply different conduct from one where natures projects fundamental values, some objective and others that further require human subjectivity superposed on objective nature.

This evaluation is not scientific description; hence not ecology per se, but we do move to metaecology. No amount of research can verify that, environmentally, the right is the optimum biotic community. Yet ecological description generates this valuing of nature, endorsing the systemic rightness. The transition from *is* to *good* and thence to *ought* occurs here; we leave science to enter the domain of evaluation, from which an ethic follows.

What is ethically puzzling and exciting is that an *ought* is not so much *derived* from an *is* as discovered simultaneously with it. As we progress from descriptions of fauna and flora, of cycles and pyramids, of autotrophs coordinated with heterotrophs, of stability and dynamism, on to intricacy, planetary opulence and interdependence, to unity and harmony with oppositions in counterpoint and synthesis, organisms evolved within and satisfactorily fitting their communities, arriving at length of beauty and goodness, it is difficult to say where the natural facts leave off and where the natural values appear. For some at least, the sharp *is/ought* dichotomy is gone; the values seem to be there as soon as the facts are fully in, and both alike properties of the system. This conviction, and the conscience that follows from it, can yield our best adaptive fit on earth.

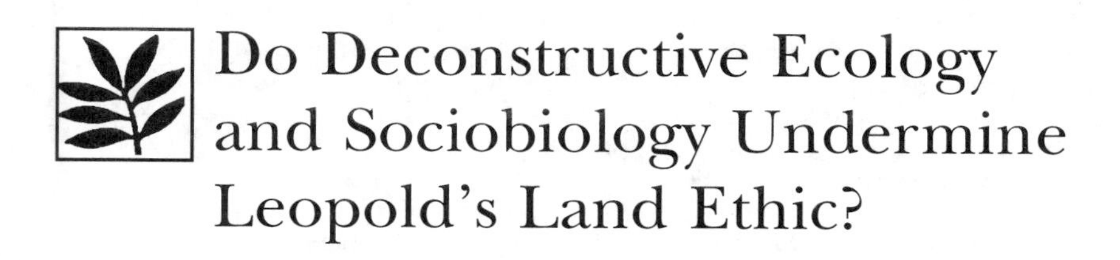

Do Deconstructive Ecology and Sociobiology Undermine Leopold's Land Ethic?

J. Baird Callicott

J. Baird Callicott is professor of philosophy and religious studies at the University of North Texas. He is the author of In Defense of the Land Ethic: Essays in Environmental Philosophy, Beyond the Land Ethic: More Essays in Environmental Philosophy, *and* Earth's Insights: A Multicultual Survey of Ecological Ethics from the Mediterranean Basin to the Australian Outback, *and more than a hundred book chapters, journal articles, and book reviews in environmental philosophy.*

THE ECOLOGICAL SIEGE OF NATURE

In an essay entitled "The Social Siege of Nature," Michael Soulé, one of the architects of conservation biology, directly confronts the insidious challenge to nature conservation posed by poststructuralists. There he defends nature protection from a deconstructive assault by "humanists who feel they must attack and redefine the concept of living nature and its protection as part of the struggle to liberate the less powerful classes of Homo sapiens from oppression by economically and politically stronger subgroups of the species."[1] From the point of view of critical theory, *nature* and its *crisis* are but elements of a "socially constructed" (patriarchal) Western world view that serves to "oppress" various "Others" (including women).

Ironically, however, Soulé is quite complacent about the deconstruction of the popular conception of living nature as a symbiotic, delicately balanced, well-integrated, orderly system which is going on blithely in contemporary ecology. Indeed, he warmly endorses what might be called the new deconstructive ecology.[2]

> Certainly the idea that species live in integrated communities is a myth. So-called biotic communities, a misleading term, are constantly changing in membership.

This essay originally appeared in *Environmental Ethics*, Vol. 18, No. 4 (Winter, 1996), 353–372. Reprinted with permission.

> The species occurring in any particular place are rarely convivial neighbors; their coexistence in certain places is better explained by individual physiological tolerances. Though in some cases the finer details of spatial distribution may be influenced by positive interspecies interactions, the much more common kinds of interactions are competition, predation, parasitism, and disease. Most interactions between individuals and species are *selfish*, not symbiotic. Current ecological thinking argues that nature at the level of local biotic assemblages has never been homeostatic. The principle of balance has been replaced with the principle of gradation—a continuum of degrees of . . . disturbance.[3]

Nature, so described, is not exactly the appealing beneficiary of conservation portrayed by Jacques Cousteau's television programs on the Discovery Channel. With scientific friends like Soulé, nature doesn't need any humanistic enemies. His impassioned call to protect a threatened nature, thus characterized, is about as appealing, morally and politically, as a call to protect endangered street gangs and terrorist organizations. The deconstructive siege of nature that Soulé laments is as much a subversion from within the scientific establishment as an attack from anti-scientific liberal humanists without.[4]

Two of the most fundamental organizing concepts of modern ecology, the ecosystem concept and the biotic community concept, are indeed presently being deconstructed.[5] Just what *are* ecosystems as objects of scientific study? They seem ontologically vague and ambiguously bounded.[6] A community was once believed to be a unit of interdependent species populations which comes and goes as one. But studies of the pollen record suggest that species populations formed very different associations in the past.[7] A hallowed "law" of ecology, that ecological stability depends on biological diversity, has been all but repealed.[8] The very idea that nature is somehow stable—that is, in a static equilibrium of countervailing forces, such as the one once believed to exist between a predator and its prey—is passé.[9] Rather nature is dynamic.[10] It is, moreover, chaotic, changing unpredictably,[11] and disturbance ("perturbation") by wind, flood, fire, pestilence, not freedom from such disruption, is nature's normal state.[12] What implications for environmental ethics have these deconstructive developments in contemporary ecology?

That depends on which environmental ethic you have in mind. The Judeo-Christian stewardship environmental ethic seems to be little affected.[13] From the prevailing autoecological point of view, the planet's complement of species may not be rivets holding Spaceship Earth together, as they were represented to be in Paul and Anne Ehrlich's book, *Extinction*.[14] Nevertheless, they are still God's creatures and He declared each and every one of them to be good—intrinsically valuable—immediately after He created them. Paul W. Taylor's bio entric environmental ethic, which was never very well-informed by ecology, also seems to be little affected.[15] That we ought to respect each and every *individual* shrub, bug, and grub remains just as true as it ever was, whether such teleogical centers of life can be considered members of biotic communities and components of ecosystems or not. The Leopold land ethic, on the other hand, is extremely vulnerable to the current deconstructive turn in ecology.[16] For of all the systems of environmental ethics so far articulated, the Leopold land ethic is the one most thoroughly grounded in evolutionary and ecological biology.[17] From the 1970s through the 1990s, its scientific foundations have undergone a series of seismic tremors. In addition to the recent deconstructive turn taken in ecology, sociobiology has also come along and significantly altered the evolutionary account of the origin and development of human morality upon which Leopold builds the land ethic. Will we find that the land ethic has collapsed into a heap of rubble when we turn around to look at it again?

THE EVOLUTIONARY CORNERSTONE OF THE LAND ETHIC

In *The Descent of Man*, Darwin dealt with what at first glance appears to be an evolutionary anomaly—the existence of ethics. Ethics appears anomalous from an evolutionary point of view because the more aggressively, selfishly, and treacherously inclined specimens of Homo sapiens would otherwise be expected to out compete, on average, their more cooperatively, altruistically, and deferentially inclined conspecifics. Thus, as time goes on, human beings should become more aggressive, selfish, and treacherous rather than more cooperative, altruistic, and deferential; in short, more unethical rather than more ethical. Nevertheless, however normally flawed actual human behavior may be, ethics do exist; and moral sensibilities *seemed* (to Darwin and most of his contemporaries) to be more refined and more broadly cast in nineteenth-century European civilization than among the Stone Age ("savage") peoples that Darwin encountered while voyaging on the Beagle.

Human survival and reproductive success, Darwin argued, grappling with this conundrum, is possible only in a social setting. However, cooperative societies cannot exist if their members do not observe certain limits in the usual course of their interactions with one another. "No tribe," Darwin writes, "could hold together if murder, robbery, treachery, &c., were common; consequently, such crimes, within the limits of the same tribe, are branded with everlasting infamy, but excite no such sentiment beyond these limits."[18] In short, if there is no ethics, there is no community; if there is no community, there is no survival (and, more importantly, no reproduction). Darwin then goes on to imagine the expansion of the moral community as smaller societies merge to form larger, more complex, and more efficient societies:

> As man advances in civilisation, and small tribes are united into larger communities, the simplest reason would tell each individual that he ought to extend his social instincts and sympathies to all the members of the same nation, though personally unknown to him. This point being once reached, there is only an artificial barrier to prevent his sympathies extending to the men of all nations and races.[19]

The literary Leopold is not one to impede the flow of his prose by citing sources. That he is thinking of Darwin's evolutionary scenario of the origin and development of ethics is indicated by allusion in an essay published in 1933 that foreshadows "The Land Ethic," entitled "The Conservation Ethic." After having suggested the existence of an advance in moral sensibilities over the three-thousand-year course of Western civilization from the days of Odysseus down to our own, he writes:

> This extension of ethics, so far studied only by philosophers, is actually a process in ecological *evolution.* Its sequences may be described in *biological* as well as in philosophical terms. An ethic, *biologically,* is a limitation on freedom of action in the *struggle for existence. An ethic,* philosophically, *is a differentiation of social from antisocial conduct.* These are two definitions of one thing. The thing has its origin in the tendency of interdependent individuals or societies to evolve modes of cooperation.[20]

ECOLOGICAL PARADIGMS IN THE LAND ETHIC

To readers of *A Sand Country Almanac,* this quotation from "The Conservation Ethic" should sound familiar. Leopold worked this very passage into "The Land Ethic" with only slight revision.[21] However, in "The Land Ethic" he immediately added a new ecological element: the now problematic "community concept." Basically, Leopold just extends Darwin's reasoning from the correlation of ethics with our various human community memberships—family, clan, tribe, nation, all humanity—to the newly discovered biotic community. Putting Darwin's analysis in a nutshell, Leopold writes, "All ethics so far evolved rest upon a single premise: that the individual is a member of a community of interdependent parts." Ecology, he then goes on to note, "simply enlarges the boundaries of the community to include soils, waters, plants, and animals, or collectively: the land."[22]

In "The Land Ethic," Leopold does not keep his ecological paradigms clearly sorted out. Residual traces of the early twentieth-century Clementsian superorganism paradigm—the ethical implications of which Leopold had flirted with as early as 1923—turn up in the "Land Health and the A-B Cleavage" section of "The Land Ethic."[23] And "The Land Pyramid," the longest section of the "The Land Ethic," is devoted to an exposition of the then state-of-the-art, physics-inspired thermodynamical ecosystem paradigm—introduced in 1935 by Arthur Tansley, operationalized in 1942 by Raymond Lindeman, and then institutionalized in the 1950s and 1960s by Eugene Odum—and to a derivation of the specific land-ethical implications of that paradigm.[24] In the same section of "The Land Ethic"—"The Land Pyramid"—Leopold even uses the phrases *biotic mechanism and land mechanism,* although in "Some Fundamentals of Conservation in the Southwest," published in 1923, he had sharply contrasted an organismic with a "mechanistic conception of the earth."[25]

Two postmodern elements, however, also appear in "The Land Pyramid" section of "The Land Ethic." First, Leopold expressly abjures the balance of nature idea: "The image commonly employed in conservation education is 'the balance of nature,'" he writes. "For reasons too lengthy to detail here, this figure of speech fails to describe accurately what little we know about the land mechanism."[26] In an essay, published in 1933, "A Biotic View of Land," Leopold elaborates his misgivings about the balance-of-nature metaphor:

> To the lay mind, balance of nature probably conveys an actual image of the familiar weighing scale. There may even be danger that the layman imputes to the biota properties which exist only on the grocer's counter. To the ecological mind, balance of nature has merits and also defects. Its merits are that it conceives of a collective total, that it imputes some utility to all species, and that it implies oscillations when balance is disturbed. Its defects are that there is only one point at which balance occurs and that balance is normally static.[27]

Second, Leopold goes on in "The Land Pyramid" section of "The Land Ethic" to emphasize nature's inherent dynamism: "When a change occurs in one part of the circuit," he writes, "many other parts must adjust themselves to it. Change does not necessarily obstruct or divert the flow of energy [through ecosystems]; evolution is a long series of self-induced changes, the net result of which has been to elaborate the flow mechanism and to lengthen the circuit."[28]

LEOPOLD ON THE RELATIONSHIP OF DIVERSITY TO STABILITY

One of the two principal themes of the immediately preceding section, "Substitutes for a Land Ethic," is the dependence of stability on diversity. Speaking of economically worthless wildflowers and songbirds (which had not yet been shadow-priced by industrious neoclassical economists), Leopold avers that "these creatures are members of the biotic community, and if (as I believe) its stability depends on its integrity, they are entitled to continuance."[29] Leopold's scientific scruples are evident in the parenthetical phrase, "as I believe." He does not, that is, state the dependence of stability on diversity as a well-established fact, but as his own well-educated opinion.

Three or four years before Leopold pieced "The Land Ethic" together, he more fully expressed his views on the relationship between diversity and stability in a paper entitled "Conservation: In Whole or in Part?" which remained unpublished until 1991. Stability is a notoriously ambiguous concept in ecology, and has more recently been parceled into several more specific concepts.[30] In "Conservation: In Whole or in Part?" Leopold seems to mean by *stability* what more precisely might be called "community persistence." In the following quote, it is evident that Leopold supposes a typological biotic community to be a persistent unit that comes and goes as such:

> The Wisconsin land was stable . . . for a long period before 1840 [when settled by Europeans]. The pollens imbedded in peat bogs show that the native plants comprising the prairie, the hardwood forest, and the coniferous forest are about the same now as they were at the end of the glacial period, 20,000 years ago. Since that time these major plant communities were pushed alternatively northward and southward several times by long climatic cycles, but their membership and organization remained intact. . . . The bones of animals show that the fauna shifted with the flora, but its composition or membership likewise remained intact.[31]

Leopold then goes on to point out that the biotic communities of the upper Midwest were diverse—that is, they were composed of many different species. And he also points out that while "tooth and claw competition" was the principal mode of interspecies relations, species extinction was rare. From these "facts" Leopold reaches a conclusion, and, though it is that stability (persistence) is caused by (species) diversity, his conclusion is remarkable for its caution:

> The *circumstantial* evidence is that stability and diversity in the native community were associated for 20,000 years, and *presumably* depended on each other. Both now are partly lost, *presumably* because the original community has been partly lost and greatly altered. *Presumably* the greater the losses and alterations, the greater the risk of impairments and disorganizations.[32]

Better resolution of the pollen record now reveals a very different picture. Linda Brubaker sketches it:

> Because species have responded individualistically to climatic variations, plant communities have been transient assemblages, seldom persisting more than 2,000 to 5,000 years. . . . Most of the tree species dominating North America today became common 8,000 to 10,000 years ago when they expanded from ice-age refugia. Most species spread at different rates and in different directions, reaching their current range limits and populations only 3,000 to 5,000 years ago. Thus present-day North American forests should not be considered stable over evolutionary time scales.[33]

Where then does that leave the summary moral maxim of the land ethic, "A thing is right when it tends to preserve the integrity, stability, and beauty of the biotic community; it is wrong when it tends otherwise"? Apparently biotic communities lack integrity. They are mere "transient assemblages" of species that are "individualistically" adapted to the same edaphic and climatic gradients.[34] And apparently they lack stability: Apparently, that is, they do not *persist*; nor, apparently, do they *resist* alteration (species mix and match opportunistically); and, apparently, assemblages do not reconstitute themselves when the climate oscillates back to a former state—they are not *resilient* (at least not in response to long-term climate perturbation cycles). All that seems left to preserve is the beauty of the biotic community. That may satisfy Eugene Hargrove and Mark Sagoff, who ground environmental ethics in natural aesthetics,[35] but the individualistic-dynamic paradigm in deconstructive community ecology seems to undercut two out of three of the land ethic's cardinal values.

A WORD OR TWO OF CAUTION ABOUT SUMMARILY DISMISSING THE DIVERSITY-STABILITY HYPOTHESIS

While the science that informed Leopold's land ethic may be out of date, his scientific epistemology seems to be much more advanced than that of some of the contemporary deconstructive ecologists.[36] Note once more Leopold's caution in asserting a causal relationship between diversity and stability. Surely, an equal degree of caution should accompany the claims of those who assert that there is no such relationship, especially as the environmental risk of their being wrong is very great.

Daniel Goodman reports that ecologists looking for a correlation between diversity and various kinds of stability did not find it, but found instead that *some* monophytic communities (spartina-dominated salt marshes) are remarkably persistent, resistant, and resilient.[37] He also reports that mathematical models involving a few variables are more stable (persistent, resistant, resilient), than multifactored models, with strongly connected variables.[38] But what does that prove? That in *all* biotic communities there is an inverse correlation between diversity and stability? It may only mean that empirical ecologists have not looked hard enough in the right places for a positive correlation between diversity and stability or that mathematico-theoretical ecologists are not clever enough to model the real world correctly. To positively conclude that something does not exist—the correlation between diversity and stability, in this case—because scientists do not observe it or because they cannot model it is to commit the fallacy of argumentum ad ignorantum.

The diversity-stability hypothesis, nevertheless, is currently making a comeback. A recent study of grasslands by David Tilman and John Downing "shows that primary productivity in more diverse plant communities is more resistant to, and recovers more fully from, a major drought."[39] Tilman and Downing explicitly apply their results to the now-classic debate about the diversity-stability hypothesis: "Our results support the diversity-stability hypothesis," they write, "but not the alternative hypothesis that most species are functionally redundant. This study implies that the preservation of biodiversity is essential for the maintenance of stable productivity in ecosystems."[40]

Further, if nature is chaotic—that is, describable by deterministic, nonlinear equations that are sensitive to initial conditions, and we cannot know all the relevant initial conditions, and therefore cannot predict the outcome of changes that we impose upon it—then surely that too calls for erring on the side of caution. If anything, what Donald Worster calls the new "ecology of chaos" makes Leopold's much-quoted cautionary advice more sound now than ever: "To keep every cog and wheel is the first precaution of intelligent tinkering."[41]

EVOLUTIONARY KINSHIP AND THE LAND ETHIC

Although Darwinian evolutionary theory has been refined since mid-century and fundamental challenges to Darwin's gradualism, such as punctuated equilibrium, have been advanced, the idea that all extant species, including Homo sapiens, are descended from one Urform or from very few such forms is not in doubt.[42] Hence, human beings are a part of nature, and we are kin—literally, though more or less distantly kin—to all other kinds of life. These assumptions are common to all secular nonanthropocentric developments in ethics—animal liberation/rights and biocentrism no less than the land ethic.[43] Leopold states the general ethical implication of evolutionary theory with his usual charm and simplicity:

> It is a century now since Darwin gave us the first glimpse of the origin of species. We know now what was unknown to all the preceding caravan of generations: that men are only fellow voyagers with other creatures in the odyssey of evolution. This new knowledge should have given us, by this time, a sense of kinship with fellow creatures; a wish to live and let live; a sense of wonder over the magnitude and duration of the biotic enterprise.[44]

SOCIOBIOLOGY AND THE LAND ETHIC

This statement is as credible now as it was in 1949. However, Darwin's more specialized account of the origin and development of ethics—which is foundational to the Leopold land ethic—has been elaborately developed as "sociobiology," which emerged simultaneously with deconstructive ecology in the mid-1970s. Many of its proponents as well as critics believe that sociobiology reduces altruism to egoism and ethics to reproductive prudence.[45] These conclusions are fallacious. The first involves the fallacy of composition; the second the genetic fallacy (no pun intended).

First, sociobiology takes altruism at the level of organisms at face value. As a matter of fact, some organisms *do* make sacrifices for the sake of others; no doubt about it. The problem for the evolutionary biologist is to account for the existence of genuine altruism in nature consistent with Darwinian principles.[46] Kin selection solves the problem.[47] Since offspring represent their parents' genes in the next generation, natural selection has selected parents who will behave altruistically toward their own offspring, rather than selfishly at the expense of their offspring. For similar reasons—the same genes are represented in siblings, cousins, and so on—altruism toward other close kin also evolved.

Now, let us grant that *genes* are selfish (though using morally charged language to characterize molecular entities is, to say the least, suspect).[48] The point is that our selfish genes have deviously designed genuinely altruistic organisms to further their reproduction. Thus to conclude that, because our genes are selfish, therefore, *we* are selfish is to commit the fallacy of composition—which is, in general, to argue that because some of the parts of a whole have a certain characteristic, therefore, the whole, which the parts compose, also has that characteristic. To argue that we are necessarily selfish because our genes are selfish makes about as much sense, in other words, as to argue that we are necessarily microscopic because our genes are microscopic or that we ourselves necessarily have a nucleus because we are composed of cells and each of our cells have a nucleus.

Doesn't this, however, imply that genuine altruism—and palpable ethical concern by implication—is necessarily limited to *close* kin? As Warwick Fox reports, "J. B. S. Haldane . . . said that he would lay down his life for more than two brothers or sisters, eight cousins, thirty-two second cousins, etc., these numbers corresponding to the proportion of his own genes shared by these relatives."[49] Thus, Fox goes on, "sociobiology explains—and serves to legitimate—the fact that we generally tend to favour our 'nearest and dearest' over against those to whom we are not genetically related."[50]

It may—and rightly—do so. The practical absurdity of the universalism characteristic of modern ethical theory is unwittingly captured by Peter Singer, who argues that he has failed in his duty because he does not donate the greatest portion of his modest income to help alleviate the suffering of hungry people living halfway around the world, even though doing so would sorely impoverish not only himself but his own children.[51] If he actually did what his theory leads him to think he ought to do, Singer would be badly judged—not only by his nearest and dearest, but by practically everyone else as well.

While sociobiology may explain and legitimate moral partiality, it does not, however, preclude a gradated expansion in the embrace of our moral sensibilities, short of indiscriminate universalism.[52] The limited duties, felt by many people, to help alleviate world hunger or save imperiled species are not inconsistent with a sociobiological construction of ethics. On the other hand, such things as imposing hunger on one's nearest and dearest to relieve it elsewhere, or inflicting genocide on a human population to preserve species, are indeed inconsistent with a sociobiological construction of ethics, as well as with commonly accepted morality.

Evolved behavioral dispositions and the emotions that animate them are often blunt as well as blind instruments of inclusive fitness. Altruism evolved in small kinship groups and its expression therefore usually benefited close kin. Nevertheless, adoptive parents may cherish their adopted children no less ardently than if they were their own flesh and blood and make innumerable sacrifices rearing them. How could this behavior be possible and so routine if naturally selected altruism were limited in its range of application to the actual kin which it evolved to benefit? Precisely because our primitive ancestors had no idea that they had genes, any conscious interest in their transmission, or the intellectual sophistication to carry out a benefit-cost analysis in the currency of inclusive fitness (such as that reputedly performed by Haldane); because evolution endowed them with broadcast altruistic feelings and impulses—which originally served to enhance their own genotypic reproduction, but which were deflected to broader social ends in changed circumstances.

Human ethics are complex expressions of naturally selected altruism, but there is a very large cultural component of morality which gives shape and direction to our sympathetic impulses. To argue that a sociobiological analysis of ethics limits the purview of ethical regard to our close kin commits the genetic fallacy (again, no pun intended)—the fallacy of attributing the properties of a cause to its effects. Altruism and eventually ethics may have evolved to serve selfish genes, but that fact does not necessarily limit them to the purpose for which they evolved. Christian preachers regularly declaim, with palpable effect, that we are all brothers and sisters under the skin and address non-relatives in kinship terms—"Brother Jones," "Sister Smith"—and refer to our common Father in Heaven. And contemporary environmental ethicists, including Leopold, point out—with similar moral-rhetorical intentions—that we are kin to other species and that, with them, we are fellow members of a common community: the biotic community.

Science has expanded our world view. The Earth is a "small planet" in an immense, inhospitable universe. We and its other denizens *are*, from a cosmic point of view, *close* kin. And, from the same cosmic point of view, we do in fact depend for our existence—with every breath we take, with every morsel of food we eat—on our fellow voyagers in the odyssey of evolution.

THE COMMUNITY CONCEPT

As noted, our evolutionary kinship with other extant species is not in doubt, in scientific circles, but, in light of contemporary deconstructive ecology, one may well wonder if we and they are really fellow members of a common biotic community.

No poststructuralist ecological theory of which I am aware asserts that organisms are entirely independent of one another. However individualistic and self-seeking each organism may be, consumers cannot exist without producers and producers cannot exist without decomposers.[53] Although James Lovelock's two-species "daisy world" may be of heuristic value in illustrating how the Earth might have evolved an organic thermostat, a world consisting of only two species of the same genus is not ecologically feasible.[54]

The community concept in ecology is a metaphor. The metaphor assimilates the way proximate organisms are mutually dependent to the way proximate human beings are mutually dependent. Now let's consider human communities, the paradigms to which biotic communities are assimilated.

Human communities—at least recent human communities—are neither stable nor typological. They change over time and in the process of change they do not come and go as units.

Take my (now erstwhile) community, Stevens Point, Wisconsin, as an example. It began as a logging community in the 1840s. After the old-growth Wisconsin pinery was leveled, the Scandinavian loggers who cut it down moved on to virgin forests farther west, and the land was settled by Polish dairy farmers. But second growth woods sprang up here and there and some lumber mills hung on, so that while the pestilential Scandinavian arboreal parasites diminished in number, some remained and adapted to the new colonizers, supplying lumber for houses and barns. Loggers and farmers like to drink beer. So an empty niche opened up and German braumeisters invaded the nascent Stevens Point community and established a brewery. Pretty soon, tavern keepers, butchers, bakers, candlestick makers, grocers, farm implement dealers, hardware merchants, Protestant ministers, Catholic priests, doctors, journalists, lawyers, and eventually, college professors, all drifted in. Journalists, lawyers, and college professors use lots of paper. The old pinery was spontaneously growing back to scrubby aspen and jack pine, and the Wisconsin River runs through it. In addition to nearby woody fiber, there was a handy supply of water power and waste transport, so dams went up and paper mills and mill workers came to town.

Notice, none of these invasive species—with the problematic exception of ministers on a mission, priests following a vocation, and doctors being faithful to their Hippocratic oath—were primarily motivated by altruism. Nor did they all move in at once, as a unit. In the formative period each person came because an economic opportunity to which he or she was individually adapted presented itself. Community succession in Stevens Point proceeded from timber mill town to paper mill town. Now Stevens Point has become quite diverse with its social analogue of species populations organized into many economic guilds—paper making, hazard insurance, higher education, retailing, manufacturing, and family farming being most salient. After the community was established, some people who were born there stayed there, others left, and many people who now immigrate to Stevens Point will leave (as did I) when greater oportunity presents itself elsewhere. Further, the boundaries of the town expanded with the passage of time. The posted "city limits" are not helpful in demarcating the actual community, which comprises several smaller adjacent municipalities and includes, more or less, hundreds of people living on nearby ten-to-forty-acre rural estates and eighty-to-one-thousand-acre farms. But does all this mean that there is no such thing, no community *as such*, that we can call Stevens Point, Wisconsin, that all that exists is just a standing crop of various types of transient, selfish individuals who happen to be adapted to similar socioeconomic gradients in an ill-defined place?

Try to tell that to Stevens Pointers, a very community-minded lot. Sure, most people in Stevens Point, like most people everywhere, devote most of their time to private gain and leisure pursuits. Economic competition is vigorous. But the people of Stevens Point nevertheless respect the fellow members of their municipal community: no one is homeless or hungry; every kid who wants to can join the YMCA, whether his or her parents can pay the dues or not (I supported one or two such memberships myself): and the "developmentally challenged" are well integrated into the social mainstream. Stevens Pointers also have respect for the community as such: people root for the home sports teams; a local ordinance prohibiting fringe shopping malls was passed to preserve main street (though, I'm sorry to say, Stevens Point still has tacky strip development); and people impose relatively high property taxes on themselves to support good schools and well-maintained roads, public buildings, and municipal parks.

My point is that paradigmatic human communities are no more integrated, nor less dynamic, nor any easier to demarcate than biotic communities as represented in deconstructive ecology. Yet human communities such as Stevens Point are still recognizable entities and engender moral duties and obligations both to fellow members and to the community as such. On this crucial point my conclusions, therefore, are these. First, that though biotic communities are not now conceived to be so unified and persistent as they once, were, they do exist: proximate plants and animals, however competitive, predatory, and parasitic, are no more independent of one another than are proximate persons. Second, if paradigmatic human communities are sufficiently robust to engender civic duties and obligations both to fellow members and to such communities per se, then biotic communities, which are not less robust than paradigmatic human communities, are, by parity of reasoning, also sufficiently robust to engender analogous environmental duties and obligations.

They would be, at any rate, if we were members of them. I am aware of two environmental philosophers who deny that we are members of biotic as well as of human communities—John Passmore and Brian K. Steverson.

Passmore's example of "bacteria and men" (sic) having no "common interests" is a spectacularly poor choice, given the mutualistic symbiosis between Homo sapiens and the bacteria in our intestines which are essential for our capacity to digest food.[55] In addition, free-living bacteria in the soil are essential to human agriculture, to say nothing of the myriad ecological services performed by bacteria, beautifully documented by Lynn Margulis and her son, Dorion Sagan.[56] Bacteria, those little buggers! We Homo sapiens just couldn't live without them.

Steverson seems to think that we are inhabiting Biosphere Two, hermetically sealed off from Biosphere One. "Human-engineered biotic communities," he writes, meaning agricultural systems, "are, at least structurally, significantly detached from nonengineered ones. Except for some common dependencies on sunshine, soils, and sources of water, human-engineered biotic communities and those resulting from nonhuman processes have essentially distinct structures."[57] This remark is a good object lesson in the need for environmental philosophers to acquire at least a rudimentary ecological literacy before attacking an ecologically grounded environmental ethic such as

Leopold's. Ignorance of the degree to which human-engineered environments—from industrial forests and farms to urban factories and tenements—are integrated into and dependent upon the nonengineered ecosystems that they are imposed on and that they are nestled into is the principal source of concern that they may not be sustainable.[58] Tilled soil is alive with nonengineered microorganisms without whose services plantation forests and food crops would fail. Crops are pollinated by bees and other nonengineered insects, birds, and bats. Steverson wants us to know that he does not think that "humans are totally disconnected from the functioning of nonengineered biotic communities."[59] However, besides the aforementioned "common dependencies on sunshine, soils, and sources of water," the only interface between "human-engineered" and "nonengineered" communities that he acknowledges is "the harvesting of seafood and exotic [as opposed to indigenous?] wild plants."[60] I dont't think further comment from me is needed. Steverson's breathtaking ecological naiveté is self-refuting.

THE LAND ETHIC DYNAMIZED

But *what* environmental duties and obligations does human membership in biotic communities generate? To preserve the integrity, stability, and beauty of the biotic community? These cardinal values of the Leopold land ethic may have to be revised—dynamized, to coin a word—if they are to be ecologically credible. As noted, Leopold was aware of and sensitive to environmental change. He knew that conservation must aim at a moving target. How can we conserve a biota that is dynamic, ever changing, when the very words *conserve* and *preserve*—especially when linked to *integrity* and *stability*—connote arresting change? The key to solving that conundrum is the concept of scale. Scale is a general ecological concept that includes rate as well as scope—that is, the concept of scale is both temporal and spatial. A review of Leopold's "The Land Ethic" reveals that he had the key, although he may not have been aware of just how multiscalar change in nature actually is.

In "The Land Pyramid" section of "The Land Ethic" Leopold writes, "Evolutionary changes . . . are usually slow and local. Man's invention of tools has enabled him to make changes of unprecedented violence, rapidity, and scope." As noted, Leopold was keenly aware that nature is dynamic, but, under the sway of mid-century equilibrium ecology, he conceived of natural change primarily in evolutionary, not in ecological terms. Nevertheless, scale is equally normative when ecological change is added to evolutionary change, that is, when normal climatic oscillations and patch dynamics are added to normal rates of extinction, hybridization, and speciation.

The scale notion is currently being employed to refine the ecosystem concept in ecology. As also noted, a major problem with the ecosystem concept in ecology is the problem of bounding ecosystems.[61] Lindeman's field-defining paper reported his study of Cedar Bog Lake.[62] The influential work of Gene

Likens and Herbert Bormann focused on Hubbard Brook.[63] Thus, one way that ecosystems came to be defined was to regard them as coextensive with watersheds.[64] But such a method of defining ecosystems is crude at best and inapplicable at worst to marine ecosystems and to other study areas that are not easily divisible into watersheds. The watershed method of defining ecosystems is also inapplicable to transwatershed problems such as demarcating the Greater Yellowstone Ecosystem or determining the ecosystemic needs and functions of wide-ranging species like bears and wolves. However, with the development of hierarchy theory in ecology, ecosystems may be defined quite precisely—albeit both abstractly and relativistically—in reference to temporally scaled processes.[65] According to Tim Allen and Tom Hoekstra,

> Ecosystems are not readily defined by spatial criteria. Ecosystems are more easily conceived as a set of interlinked, differently scaled processes that may be diffuse in space, but easily defined in turnover time. . . . Thus a single ecosystem is itself a hierarchy of differently scaled processes. . . . There are differently scaled processes inside a single ecosystem, as well as sets of differently scaled, more inclusive and less inclusive ecosystems. . . . The degree to which processes of different types express themselves and the length of time they do so, are both ways of describing the uniqueness of particular ecosystems. Much of what we observe in ecosystems is better set in time rather than space. . . . The ecosystem is a much richer concept than just some meteorology, soil, and animals, tacked onto patches of vegetation. . . . Ecosystems can be seen more powerfully as sequences of events rather than things in a place. These events are transformations of matter and energy that occur as the ecosystem does its work. Ecosystems are process-oriented and more easily seen as temporally rather than spatially ordered.[66]

Homo sapiens is a part of nature, "a plain member and citizen" of the "land-community"—*pace* Passmore and Steverson—as Leopold puts this evolutionary-ecological point.[67] Hence, anthropogenic changes imposed on nature are no less natural than any other. However, since Homo sapiens is a moral species, capable of ethical deliberation and conscientious choice, and evolutionary kinship and biotic community membership add a land ethic to our familiar social ethics, anthropogenic changes may be land-ethically evaluated. But by what norm? The norm of appropriate scale.

Let me first elaborate Leopold's use of the temporal scale of evolutionary change as a norm for evaluating anthropogenic change. Consider the current episode of abrupt, anthropogenic, mass species extinction, which many people, I included, intuitively regard as the most morally reprehensible environmental thing going on today.[68] Episodes of mass extinction have occurred in the past (though none of those has been attributed to a biological agent).[69] Such events are, however, abnormal. Normally, speciation outpaces extinction—which is the reason why biodiversity has increased over time. So, what is land-ethically wrong with current anthropogenic species extinction? Species extinction is not unnatural. On the contrary, species extinction—anthropogenic or otherwise—is perfectly natural. But the current *rate* of extinction is wildly abnormal. Does being the first biological agent of a geologically significant mass extinction event in the

3.5-billion-year tenure of life on Planet Earth morally become us Homo sapiens? Doesn't that make a mockery of the self-congratulatory species epithet: the sapient, the wise species of the genus Homo?

Earth's climate has warmed up and cooled off in the past. So what's land-ethically wrong with the present episode of anthropogenic global warming? We are a part of nature, so our recent habit of recycling sequestered carbon may be biologically unique, but it is not unnatural. A land-ethical evaluation of the current episode of anthropogenic climate change can, however, be made on the basis of temporal scale and magnitude. We may be causing a big increase of temperature at an unprecedented rate.[70] That's what's land-ethically wrong with anthropogenic global warming.

Temporal and spatial scale in combination are key to the evaluation of direct human ecological impact. Violent nonanthropogenic perturbations regularly occur.[71] Volcanoes bury the biota of whole mountains with lava and ash. Tornadoes rip through forests, leveling trees. Hurricanes erode beaches. Wild fires sweep through forests as well as savannas. Rivers drown floodplains. Droughts dry up lakes and streams. Why therefore are anthropogenic clear cuts, beach developments, hydroelectric impoundments, and the like environmentally unethical? As such, they are not. Once again, it's a question of scale. In general, frequent, intense disturbances, such as tornadoes, occur at small, widely distributed spatial scales. Spatially broadcast disturbances, such as droughts, occur less frequently. Most disturbances at whatever level of intensity and scale are stochastic (random) and chaotic (unpredictable). The problem with anthropogenic perturbations—such as industrial forestry and agriculture, exurban development, drift net fishing, and such—is that they are far more frequent, widespread, and regularly occurring than are nonanthropogenic perturbations.

Stewart Pickett and Richard Ostfeld—exponents of the new natural disturbance/patch dynamics paradigm in ecology, which they dub "the flux of nature" (in contrast to the old "balance of nature")—agree that appropriate scale is the operative norm for ethically appraising anthropogenic ecological perturbation. They note that

> . . . the flux of nature is a dangerous metaphor. The metaphor and the underlying ecological paradigm may suggest to the thoughtless and greedy that since flux is a fundamental part of the natural world, any human-caused flux is justifiable. Such an inference is wrong because the flux in the natural world has severe limits. . . . Two characteristics of human-induced flux would suggest that it would be excessive: fast rate and large spatial extent.[72]

Among the abnormally frequent and widespread anthropogenic perturbations that Leopold himself censures in "The Land Ethic" are the continent-wide elimination of large predators from biotic communities; the ubiquitous substitution of domestic species for wild ones; the ecological homogenization of the planet resulting from the anthropogenic "worldwide pooling of faunas and floras," the ubiquitous "polluting of waters or obstructing them with dams."[73]

CONCLUSION

Biotic communities may be ever-changing assemblages of organisms of various species that happen to be adapted to the same edaphic and climatic gradients. However, that makes them even more analogous to human communities than the old static-holistic representation. Ever-changing, imprecisely bounded communities of human individualists are robust enough to be identifiable entities and to generate special obligations to fellow members and to such communities per se. Why should a communitarian environmental ethic such as Leopold's have to meet any higher standard of community robustness?

The summary moral maxim of the land ethic, nevertheless, must be dynamized in light of developments in ecology since the mid-twentieth century. Although Leopold acknowledged the existence and land-ethical significance of natural environmental change, he seems to have thought of it primarily on a very slow evolutionary temporal scale. But even so, he thereby incorporates the concept of inherent environmental change and the crucial norm of scale into the land ethic. In light of more recent developments in ecology, we can add norms of scale to the land ethic for both climatic and ecological dynamics in land-ethically evaluating anthropogenic changes in nature. One hesitates to edit Leopold's elegant prose, but as a stab at formulating a dynamized summary moral maxim for the land ethic, I hazard the following: "A thing is right when it tends to disturb the biotic community only at normal spatial and temporal scales. It is wrong when it tends otherwise."[74]

NOTES

1. Michael Soulé, "The Social Siege of Nature," in M. Soulé and G. Lease, eds., *Reinventing Nature? Responses to Postmodern Deconstruction* (Washington: Island Press, 1995), p. 138.
2. It might be called *deconstructive ecology* because the old master narratives of ecology—organism, community, ecosystem—are currently being reviled, and there is an apparent contentment with either no organizing paradigm or a plurality of mutually inconsistent organizing paradigms in ecology. See Daniel Simberloff, "A Succession of Paradigms in Ecology: Essentialism to Materialism and Probabilism," *Synthese* 43 (1980): 3–39.
3. Soulé, "Social Siege," p. 143 (emphasis in original).
4. See Donald Worster, "The Ecology of Order and Chaos," *Environmental History Review* 14 (1990): 1–18, for an exposé.
5. For a review of the difficulties with the ecosystem and community concepts, see K. S. Sharader-Frechette and E. D. McCoy, *Method in Ecology: Strategies for Conservation* (Cambridge: Cambridge University Press, 1993).
6. Worster, "Ecology of Order and Chaos," reports that "A survey of recent ecology textbooks shows that the [ecosystem] concept is not even mentioned in one leading work and has a much diminished place in the others" (p. 8). A more sanguine assessment is provided by Frank Benjamin Golley. *A History of the Ecosystem Concept in Ecology* (New Haven, Conn.: Yale University Press, 1994), but even Golley's partisan account reveals the ecosystem concept to be problematic.

7. A severe blow to the community concept was struck by Margaret B. Davis, "Climatic Instability, Time Lags, and Community Disequilibrium," in J. Diamond and T. J. Case, eds., *Community Ecology* (New York: Harper and Row, 1984).
8. Daniel Goodman, "The Theory of Diversity-Stability Relationships in Ecology," *Quarterly Review of Biology* 30 (1975): 237–66, provides a summary of research results through the mid-seventies on the diversity-stability hypothesis. His conclusion drips with sarcasm and contempt: "The diversity-stability hypothesis may have caught the lay conservationists' fancy, not for the allure of its scientific embellishments, but for the more basic appeal of its underlying metaphor. It is the sort of thing that people like, and want, to believe. Thus, though better theories supplant it in scientific usage, we may be certain that the 'hypothesis' will persist for awhile as an element of folk science. Eventually that remnant, too, may vanish in light of discordant facts, and the imagery of this once-scientific hypothesis will recede to a revered position in the popular environmental ethic, where it doubtless will do much good" (p. 261).
9. For a review of the difficulties, see Shrader-Frechette and McCoy, *Method in Ecology*. For a discussion, see Mark Sagoff, "Fact and Value in Ecological Science," *Environmental Ethics* 7 (1985): 99–116.
10. See Daniel Botkin, *Discordant Harmonies: A New Ecology for the Twenty-first Century* (New York: Oxford University Press, 1990).
11. See Robert May, "Biological Populations with Nonoverlapping Generations: Stable Points, Stable Cycles, and Chaos," *Science* 186 (1974): 645–47; James Gleik, *Chaos: The Making of a New Science* (New York: Viking, 1987); H. Degan, A. V. Holden, and L. F. Olsen, *Chaos in Biological Systems* (New York: Plenum Press, 1987).
12. S. T. A. Pickett and P. S. White, *The Ecology of Natural Disturbance and Patch Dynamics* (Orlando, Fla.: Academic Press, 1985).
13. For a representative version of the Judeo-Christian Stewardship environmental ethic see Patrick Dobel, "The Judeo-Christian Stewardship Attitude Toward Nature," in Louis P. Pojman, ed., *Environmental Ethics: Readings in Theory and Application* (Boston; Jones and Bartlett, 1994); 20–24.
14. Paul R. Ehrlich and Anne H. Ehrlich, *Extinction: The Causes and Consequences of the Disappearance of Species* (New York: Random House, 1981). For a discussion of the redundancy of the species most vulnerable to extinction see David Ehrenfeld, "Why Put a Value on Biodiversity?" in E. O. Wilson, ed., *Biodiversity* (Washington: National Academy Press, 1988): 212–16. Also see Sagoff, "Fact and Value."
15. Paul W. Taylor, *Respect of Nature* (Princeton, New Jersey: Princeton University Press, 1986).
16. Harley Cahen, "Against the Moral Considerability of Ecosystems," *Environmental Ethics* 10 (1988): 195–216; Brian K. Steverson, "Ecocentrism and Ecological Modeling," *Environmental Ethics* 16 (1994): 71–88; and Gary L. Comstock, "Do Agriculturalists Need a New, an Ecocentric Ethic?" *Agriculture and Human Values* 12 (1995): 2–15, have anticipated me here. Cahen's argument is more applicable to interest-based ecocentrism, such as that advocated by Lawrence Johnson, *A Morally Deep World* (Cambridge: Cambridge University Press, 1991), than to the communitarian Leopold land ethic. Comstock answers his title question in the negative. I have more to say *infra* about Steverson's critique of ecocentrism.
17. See J. Baird Callicott, "The Conceptual Foundations of the Land Ethic," in J. Baird Callicott, ed., *Companion to* A Sand County Almanac: *Interpretive and Critical Essays* (Madison: University of Wisconsin Press, 1987): 186–217.
18. Charles Darwin, *The Descent of Man and Selection in Relation to Sex* (New York: Modern Library, n.d.), p. 487.
19. Ibid., pp. 491–92.
20. Aldo Leopold, "The Conservation Ethic," *Journal of Forestry* 31 (1933), p. 634 (emphasis added to highlight the allusions to Darwin's account in the *Descent of Man* of the evolutionary origins and cultural development of ethics).

21. One could argue that the revisions—changing *biological* in the second sentence to *ecological* and changing *biologically* in the third sentence to *ecologically*—were ill-advised. Darwin's account of the origin of and evolution of ethics was less an exercise in human ecology than in human evolution, thus it was more generally biological than specifically ecological.
22. Aldo Leopold, *A Sand County Almanac and Sketches Here and There* (New York: Oxford University Press, 1949), pp. 203–04.
23. Aldo Leopold, "Some Fundamentals of Conservation in the Southwest," *Environmental Ethics* 1 (1979):131–41.
24. Arthur Tansley, "The Use and Abuse of Vegetational Concepts and Terms," *Ecology* 16 (1935): 284–307; Raymond L. Lindeman, "The Trophic-Dynamic Aspect of Ecology," *Ecology* 23 (1942):399–418; Eugene Odum, *Fundamentals of Ecology*, 3d ed. (Philadelphia: Saunders, 1971).
25. Leopold *Sand County*, p. 214; "Some Fundamentals," p. 139. The ecosystem paradigm is grounded in physics, not biology, and mechanism had dominated thought in physics since the seventeenth century. Hence, mechanism may be, some have argued, consistent with, if not implied by, the ecosystem paradigm: for a notable example, see Botkin, *Discordant Harmonies*; for an overview, see Stephen Bocking, "Visions of Nature and Society: A History of the Ecosystem Concept," *Alternatives* 20, no. 3 (1994): 12–18.
26. Leopold, *Sand County*, p. 214.
27. Aldo Leopold, "A Biotic View of Land," *Journal of Forestry* 37 (1939): 728. Substantial portions of this essay were incorporated into "The Land Ethic," as were substantial portions of "The Conservation Ethic." See Curt Meine, "Building 'The Land Ethic,'" in J. Baird Callicott, ed., *Companion to* A Sand County Almanac (Madison: University of Wisconsin Press, 1987), pp. 172–85.
28. Leopold, *Sand County*, pp. 216–17.
29. Ibid., p. 210.
30. See Stuart Pimm, *The Balance of Nature?* (Chicago: University of Chicago Press, 1991) for a comprehensive discussion of the principal varieties of stability—persistence, resistance, and resilience. Gordon Orians, "Diversity, Stability, and Maturity in Natural Systems," in H. A. Mooney and J. A. Drake, eds., *Ecology of Biological Invasions of North America and Hawaii* (New York: Springer-Verlag, 1975): 139–50, distinguishes no fewer than seven varieties of stability.
31. Aldo Leopold, "Conservation: In Whole or in Part?" in Susan L. Flader and J. Baird Callicott, eds., *The River of the Mother of God and Other Essays by Aldo Leopold* (Madison: University of Wisconsin Press, 1991), p. 312.
32. Ibid., p. 315 (emphasis added).
33. Linda B. Brubaker, "Vegetation History and Anticipating Future Vegetation Change," in J. K. Agee, *Ecosystem Management for Parks and Wilderness* (Seattle; University of Washington Press, 1988), p. 41.
34. A particularly warm endorsement of reductionism and the individualistic paradigm in ecology is Simberloff, "A Succession of Paradigms in Ecology."
35. See Eugene C. Hargrove, *Foundations of Environmental Ethics* (Englewood Cliffs, New Jersey: Prentice-Hall, 1989); Mark Sagoff, *The Economy of the Earth* (Cambridge: Cambridge University Press, 1988).
36. Goodman, "The Theory of Diversity-Stability Relationships," is incautiously dismissive. Soulé, "The Social Siege of Nature" (p. 143) begins his debunking of the community "myth" with the word *certainly*.
37. Goodman, "The Theory of Diversity-Stability Relationships."
38. Ibid.
39. David Tilman and John A. Downing, "Biodiversity and Stability in Grasslands," *Nature* 367 (1994), 363.
40. Ibid.

41. Luna B. Leopold, ed., *Round River: From the Journals of Aldo Leopold* (New York: Oxford University Press, 1953), pp. 146–47.
42. Soulé, "Social Siege," thus confidently writes, "There is now no question that all life on earth evolved from a common ancestor. The genetic material and the codes embedded within it reveal that every living kind of plant and animal owes its existence to a single-celled ancestor that evolved some three and a half billion years ago. All species are *kin*" (p. 142, emphasis in original).
43. See James Rachels, *Created from Animals* (New York: Oxford University Press, 1990). Paul W. Taylor, "The Ethics of Respect for Nature" *Environmental Ethics* 3 (1981): 197–218 also regards evolutionary kinship to be foundational to his biocentrism.
44. Leopold, *Sand County*, p. 109.
45. For a probative discussion, see John Chandler, "Ethical Philosophy," in M. Maxwell, ed., *The Sociobiological Imagination* (Albany: SUNY, 1991). Among reductive proponents Chandler cites Richard Dawkins, *The Selfish Gene* (New York: Oxford University Press, 1976); Edward O. Wilson, *On Human Nature* (Cambridge, Mass.: Harvard University Press, 1978); and Richard D. Alexander, *The Biology of Moral Systems* (Hawthorn, N.Y.: Aldine, 1987). Among critics, Chandler cites Philip Kitchner, *Vaulting Ambition: Sociobiology and the Quest for Human Nature* (Cambridge, Mass.: MIT Press, 1985).
46. According to Edward O. Wilson, *Sociobiology: The New Synthesis* (Cambridge, Mass.: The Belknap Press of Harvard University, 1975), "the central theoretical problem of sociobiology [is] how can altruism, which by definition reduces personal fitness, possibly evolve by natural selection?" (p. 3).
47. See W. D. Hamilton, "The Genetical Theory of Social Behaviour," *Journal of Theoretical Biology* 7 (1964): 1–52.
48. We are, of course, indebted for this infelicitous phrase to Dawkins, *The Selfish Gene.*
49. Warwick Fox, *Toward a Transpersonal Ecology* (Boston: Shamballa, 1990), p. 264.
50. Ibid.
51. Peter Singer, *The Expanding Circle: Ethics and Sociobiology* (New York: Ferrar, Strauss, and Giroux, 1982).
52. Garret Hardin provides an illuminating discussion in "Discriminating Altruisms," *Zygon* 17 (1982): 163–86.
53. In trying to repair some of the damage done to environmentalism by deconstructive ecology, Worster, in the second edition of *Nature's Economy*, evokes "the principle of interdependency": "No organism or species of organism has any chance of surviving without the aid of others" (p. 429).
54. See Lovelock, *Ages of Gaia.*
55. John Passmore, *Man's Responsibility for Nature: Ecological Problems and Western Traditions* (New York: Scribner's, 1974), p. 116. Passmore intends expressly to criticize the Leopold land ethic with his bacteria counter-example to ethics-generating interspecies community membership.
56. Lynn Margulis and Dorion Sagan, *Microcosmos* (New York: Simon and Schuster, 1986).
57. Steverson, "Ecocentrism," p. 81.
58. Paul R. Ehrlich, "The Limits to Substitution: Meta-resource Depletion and a New Economic-ecological Paradigm," *Ecological Economics* 1 (1989): 9–16.
59. Steverson, "Ecocentrism," pp. 81–82.
60. Ibid.
61. See Shrader-Frechette and McCoy, *Method in Ecology.*
62. Lindeman, "The Tropic-Dynamic Aspect of Ecology."
63. F. H. Bormann and G. E. Likens, "Nutrient Cycling," *Science* 155 (1967): 424–29.
64. For a discussion, see Golley, *The Ecosystem Concept in Ecology.*
65. See R. V. O'Neill, D. L. DeAngelis, J. B. Waide, and T. F. H. Allen, *A Hierarchical Concept of Ecosystems* (Princeton: Princeton University Press, 1986). For an applica-

tion of hierarchy theory in systems ecology to environmental ethics, see Stanley N. and Barbara M. Salthe, "Ecosystem Moral Considerability: A Reply to Cahen," *Environmental Ethics* 11 (1989): 355–61.

66. T. F. H. Allen and T. W. Hoekstra, *Toward a Unified Ecology* (New York: Columbia University Press, 1992), pp. 94, 98–100.
67. Leopold, *Sand County*, p. 204.
68. Others include most of the authors represented in Wilson, *Biodiversity*.
69. D. M. Raup and J. J. Sepkoski, "Periodicity of Extinctions in the Geologic Past," *Proceedings of the National Academy of Sciences USA* 81 (1984): 801–05. For a discussion of causes of these mass extinction events, see D. M. Raup, *Extinction: Bad Genes or Bad Luck?* (New York: W. W. Norton, 1991).
70. See Stephen H. Schneider, *Global Warming: Are We Entering the Greenhouse Century?* (San Francisco: Sierra Club Books, 1989).
71. Pickett and White, *Ecology of Natural Disturbance.*
72. S. T. A. Pickett and Richard S. Ostfeld, "The Shifting Paradigm in Ecology," in R. L. Knight and S. F. Bates, eds., *A New Century for Natural Resources Management* (Washington: Island Press, 1995), pp. 273–74.
73. Leopold, *Sand County*, p. 217.
74. Tom Birch and Holmes Rolston (personal communications) both point out that this reformulation of the summary moral maxim of the land ethic is incomplete (at best). I agree with these reservations. Yet, a summary moral maxim has to be general and pithy to be a summary moral maxim—and general and pithy statements are necessarily incomplete.

PART TWO

Deep Ecology

Introduction

George Sessions

George Sessions is chair of the Department of Philosophy at Sierra College in Rocklin, California. Author of numerous essays about ecophilosophy and deep ecology, and coauthor (with Bill Devall) of Deep Ecology, *Sessions recently published the anthology* Deep Ecology for the 21st Century.

I. THE ECOLOGICAL REVOLUTION OF THE 1960s AND THE RISE OF THE DEEP ECOLOGY MOVEMENT

The decade of the 1960s produced a major ecological revolution—a revolution in consciousness concerning our outlook toward other species and the need to protect the integrity of wild ecosystems, wild evolutionary processes, and what is left of the wild world. Philosophically, the ecological revolution of the 1960s, and the rise of the long-range deep ecology movement, was characterized, at its deepest level, by a move from anthropocentrism to ecocentrism. An ecological critique of anthropocentrism as being at the root of the ecological crisis was pervasive among conservationists and ecologists throughout the 1960s, deriving its impetus from the writings of Henry David Thoreau, John Muir, Robinson Jeffers, Aldo Leopold, and Aldous Huxley and the infusion of Zen Buddhism into conservationist and counterculturalist thinking.

The ecological critique of anthropocentrism received its most explicit and influential statement during the 1960s in the widely reprinted 1966 paper "Historical Roots of Our Ecologic Crisis," written by U.C.L.A. historian, Lynn White, Jr. White argued that Christianity had desacralized nature, encouraged its exploitation, and promoted an anthropocentric worldview in which humans are portrayed as superior to, and in charge of, the rest of nature. Modern science and technology, he claimed, are "permeated with Christian arrogance towards nature." He argued that Marxism and other so-called "post-Christian" ideologies in the West are Judeo-Christian heresies that promote the same exploitive attitudes toward nature. In an effort to reform Christianity ecologically, White proposed a return to the views of Saint Francis, who preached "the equality of all creatures."[1]

The ecocentric change in consciousness of the 1960s also involved a corresponding awareness that the direction of megatechnological, progress-oriented industrial growth societies had to be drastically changed. For example, Stanford ecologist Paul Ehrlich referred to Lynn White's paper and the Zen Buddhism of the 1960s counterculture in his enormously influential *The Population Bomb* in 1968; he claimed that "we've got to change from a growth-oriented exploitive system to one focused on stability and conservation. Our entire system of orienting to nature must undergo a revolution."[2]

II. THOREAU AND THE PRESERVATION OF HUMAN AND NONHUMAN WILDNESS

Thoreau's statements in 1851 that "in wildness was the preservation of the world" and that "all good things are wild and free" were totally revolutionary. It is of crucial importance to realize that Thoreau was referring to both human and nonhuman wildness.[3] During the 1960s, biologists, conservationists, ecotheologians, and ecophilosophers were beginning to realize that the dominant anthropocentric ideology of Western civilization that promotes the technological domination, management, and control of Earth—the domestication, urbanization, and humanization of Earth—in the name of progress was producing a human and ecological disaster. Wildness, autonomy, and freedom (in both humans and nonhumans) were rapidly disappearing. These themes had been dramatically explored earlier in Zamyatin's *We*, Huxley's *Brave New World*, and Orwell's *1984*. Inspired by Thoreau, Muir, and Leopold, conservation leaders such as David Brower (executive director of the Sierra Club, throughout the 1950s and 1960s) began to realize that the protection of wildness was the *key* philosophical and ecological issue. From 1960 through 1964, Brower published highly influential Sierra Club Exhibit Format books publicizing the ecocentric philosophies of Thoreau, Muir, and Jeffers. The 1962 Thoreau book was entitled *In Wildness Is the Preservation of the World.*[4]

In 1972, the environmental textbook writer G. Tyler Miller provided a concise and dramatic overview of the ecological analysis and worldview in the 1960s, claiming that "the ecological . . . revolution will be the most all-encompassing revolution in the history of mankind. It involves questioning and altering almost all of our ethical, political, economic, sociological, psychological, and technological rules or systems."[5]

III. THE 1980s ANTHROPOCENTRIC-ECONOMIC REACTION AND THE RISE OF SUSTAINABLE DEVELOPMENT

The radical and comprehensive thrust of the 1960s ecocentric ecological revolution could not be sustained, however, against the powerful, vested multinational corporate interests and the entrenched Western paradigm of "progress" (and among the left, the achievement of social justice) through unending economic growth and development. Radical environmentalists and ecologists such as Paul Ehrlich have been looked on as "doomsayers" who want to interfere with private property rights and with unlimited corporate expansion and profit making. For growth-oriented economists, modern humanity has created a "second nature" reality of urbanism and stock markets that transcends and replaces the reality of the biological world. Spokespersons for the corporate establishment, such as the economist Julian Simon, argue that there is no human overpopulation problem and that the resources of the Earth, and the limits to human activity, are not determined by the carrying capacity of the Earth's ecological systems but only by the unlimited technological ingenuity and creativity of the human mind and by the free play of market forces.[6] The contemporary vision of the multinational corporations tends toward the development of a deconstructionist, artificial world of "simulacra" and "hyperreality" as they rapidly turn the world (including the last of the wild ecosystems) into an artificial, megatechnological Disneyland theme park and shopper's paradise and as they attempt to create an economic "new world order" through the "globalization of corporate power."[7]

The politically conservative "Reagan reaction" against environmentalism in the United States coincided, during the 1980s, with a change in philosophy toward nature among world leaders in the United Nations. In 1982, the General Assembly had adopted the ecocentric World Charter for Nature, which asserted that the intrinsic value of every form of life is to be recognized: "Nature shall be respected and its essential processes shall not be disrupted." However, by 1987 the U.N. Brundtland Report was based on the increasingly popular but essentially unecological concept of "sustainable development." Ignoring the increasingly frantic warnings of the world's scientists about the ecological state of the world, the Brundtland Report called, instead, for "a new era" of economic growth and development. The concept of sustainable development also became the conceptual basis for the 1992 U.N. Rio environmental conference. As Wolfgang Sachs points out, "The UN Conference in Rio inaugurated environmentalism as the highest state of developmentalism." The Rio conference (and the Brundtland Report) reverted to an anthropocentric, utilitarian "shallow environmentalism" by viewing nature essentially as a "resource base" for unending economic growth and development. For example, in the convention on biodiversity protection, the flora and fauna of the world were treated essentially as genetic raw material for exploitation by biotechnology and pharmaceutical corporations.[8]

The global ecological-overpopulation crisis, warned about with such insistance by Paul Ehrlich and other ecologists in the 1960s, has now reached such proportions that 58 of the National Academies of Sciences throughout the world have issued dire warnings. In 1992, 1,575 of the world's leading scientists released the World's Scientists' Warning to Humanity, claiming that "human beings and the natural world are on a collision course." Anne and Paul Ehrlich now claim that the only realistic solution to the ecological crisis is to "reduce the scale of the human enterprise." The Brundtland Report and Rio conference also fly in the face of recent studies, which show that the majority of Americans (and possibly citizens in other Western industrial countries) already hold the rudiments of a spiritual-ecocentric worldview.[9]

IV. THE ROOTS OF THE 1960s ECOLOGICAL REVOLUTION IN DAVID BROWER AND THE SIERRA CLUB WILDERNESS CONFERENCES

While many historians believe that the ecological revolution began with the publication of Rachel Carson's *Silent Spring* in 1962 (which also critiqued anthropocentrism) and culminated in the major demonstrations of Earthday I in 1970, the roots of post–World War II ecocentric, ecological consciousness extend back much further. Two key books (William Vogt's *The Road to Survival* and Fairfield Osborn's *Our Plundered Planet*, both published in 1948) led to a major debate over issues of human overpopulation, diminishing forests and wildlife, and the ability of technology to solve these problems.[10] Aldo Leopold's *Sand County Almanac* (1949) provided, with its ecocentric "land ethic," a philosophical perspective for these issues. According to Anne and Paul Ehrlich, "The works of Leopold, Vogt and Osborn . . . greatly influenced our own thinking and that of many other ecologists of our generation."[11]

The Sierra Club Wilderness Conferences, beginning in 1949, soon led to discussions of wilderness philosophy, with club leaders such as David Brower and various ecologists coming down on the side of ecocentrism. In so doing, they believed they were following the philosophies of Muir and Leopold. During the 1950s, professional ecologists convinced club leaders at these conferences that wilderness areas should be viewed primarily as wild species habitats and that without stabilization and reduction of the human population the protection of wilderness and the wild would be a lost cause.[12]

Members of the Sierra Club under Brower, and biologists in general, became increasingly radical as the decade of the 1960s progressed. The 1967 annual issue of the *Sierra Club Bulletin* carried an article by Brower calling for an Earth International Park to protect the Earth's remaining wild areas and wild species. Brower claimed, "I believe in wilderness for itself alone. I believe in the rights of creatures other than man." In January 1969, he ran a full-page advertisement promoting the Earth International Park idea in the *New York Times.* A paper by botanist Hugh Iltus, pleading for protection of what was left of the wild world, appeared in the same 1967 issue of the *Bulletin.* Iltus claimed,

> Life's diversity is threatened with imminent destruction . . . it will be all but over in 20 or 30 years for this exuberant biotic wealth. . . . Surely [the graying heads of the National Academy of Sciences] in their wisdom, must see that the living world is falling apart at the seams. . . . One more generation of ecological idiots is one too many.

Iltus also argued that humans have a genetic need for wild environments, a claim that, along with E. O. Wilson's "biophilia hypothesis" and the genetic theories of Paul Shepard, has become the basis of the burgeoning new field of ecopsychology.[13]

While Rachel Carson dramatically focused widespread public attention on environmental problems in 1962, Michael McCloskey (Brower's successor as the Sierra Club's executive director in 1969) has pointed out, correctly in my estimation, that the wilderness movement of the 1950s marks the beginning of the modern environmental-ecological movement. The post–World War II ecological revolution and the clarification of its ecocentric philosophy, according to McCloskey, began with the 1950s Wilderness Conferences and continued with the crusading activism of the Sierra Club during the 1950s and 1960s under Brower's leadership.[14]

The environmental historian Donald Worster summarizes the radical nature of the environmental philosophizing and activism of the ecological revolution:

> [For the most thoughtful environmentalists and ecologists of the 1960s and 1970s] the goal was to save the living world around us, millions of species of plants and animals, including humans, from destruction from our technology, population, and appetites. The only way to do that . . . was to think the radical thought that there must be limits to growth in three areas—limits to population, limits to technology, and limits to appetite and greed.[15]

V. THE ECOLOGICAL REVOLUTION, URBAN-INDUSTRIAL POLLUTION, ENVIRONMENTALISM, AND SOCIAL JUSTICE

Worster suggests, by implication, that there were less thoughtful environmentalists during the decade of the 1960s who didn't see the need for an ecological "revolution" and a philosophical shift to ecocentrism. As urban-industrial pollution developed into a major problem after World War II, "newer man-centered leaders" arose in the environmental ranks during the

1960s, according to environmental historian Stephen Fox, such as the Marxist biologist Barry Commoner and Ralph Nader. These leaders saw industrial pollution as the essence of the environmental problem, while viewing as unimportant the issues of human overpopulation and the necessity for a radical restructuring of the industrial growth paradigm. Further, as Fox points out, they viewed concern for the protection of wilderness and wild species with disdain.[16] Commoner became known as the "pollution man" and appeared on the cover of *Time* magazine in 1970 as "the Paul Revere of ecology." By Earthday 1970, the environmental movement had split essentially into an anthropocentric urban-pollution wing, led by Commoner, Nader, and Murray Bookchin, and an ecocentric wing, centered around Brower, Ehrlich, and most professional ecologists.

In his influential book *The Closing Circle* (1971), Commoner rejected the analyses of Paul Ehrlich and Lynn White concerning the roots of the ecological crisis, thereby refusing to acknowledge the deeper philosophical, religious, and social causes. He claimed instead that the environmental crisis was caused mainly by the replacement of natural fibers and products with synthetic chemicals after World War II. Environmental problems could be solved simply by changing to environmentally benign technologies. Ehrlich countered with his I = PAT formula (that environmental impact is a function of population size, times the level of affluence or consumption, times the nature of the technology employed). Based on this formula, the United States was the world's biggest environmental disaster because of its per capita high-consumption lifestyles and the high levels of industrial chemicals and gases it was spewing into the atmosphere. According to Chris Lewis, in Commoner's more recent book (*Making Peace with the Planet*, 1990), Commoner claims that

> if humanity must give up progress, economic growth, and development—give up the modern world—to end its war against nature and make peace with the planet, it would be a tragic defeat. Commoner refuses to accept calls for controlling population growth, ending economic growth and development, and transforming the modern world. He argues that because humanity lives in two worlds, the natural world or the ecosphere and a social world of its own creation—the technosphere—the environmental crisis is not an ecological problem but a social and political problem.[17]

Chemical pollution and toxic wastes, a very visible and dramatic aspect of the environmental crisis in industrial countries during the 1950s and 1960s, resulted in major air and water pollution and carcinogenic chemicals in foods—all of which posed a significant hazard to human health. It was the pervasive and obvious effects of industrial-chemical pollution on human health that made the environmental crisis a major issue for the public in the 1960s. These problems were close to the daily lives of urban people, and so it was natural for them to identify the environmental crisis with urban pollution and with "cleaning up the environment." The accelerating loss of wildlife habitat, biodiversity, and the Earth's wildness was a far more subtle issue, further removed from their urban lives and difficult to comprehend from their anthropocentric perspective. Carson's *Silent Spring*—which, more than any other single event awakened people to the environmental crisis—was focused on chemical pesticide poisoning. Carson drew a parallel between the atomic radiation being carried by the jetstream from above-ground Russian nuclear testing over the North Pole to the North American continent and the DDT that was similarly being carried into food chains all over the globe. And just as Eskimo children in villages in the Arctic circle had the highest radiation counts in their bones from the fallout, it was discovered that there was DDT in the fatty tissue of penguins in the Antarctic. But as an ecocentric marine biologist, Carson was not interested solely in the issue of human health: she confided to her editor that while her intention in writing the book was to emphasize the menace to human health, nevertheless she was convinced that the dangers pesticides posed to "the basic ecology of all living things . . . outweighs by far . . . any other aspect of the problem."

Beginning in the 1980s, following Bookchin's lead, there has been an explicit attempt to couple anthropocentric social justice with the urban-pollution wing, promoted primarily by social ecologists, eco-Marxists, ecosocialists, postmodern deconstructionists, and others with a leftist anthropocentric political background. For example, ecosocialist David Pepper (in his book, *Eco-socialism: From Deep Ecology to Social Justice*, 1993) claims that "social justice . . . or the increasing global lack of it, is the most pressing of all environmental problems."[18]

In the 1980s, humanity was shocked to learn that industrial-chemical pollution had reached such proportions that the ozone layer was being depleted and that the onset of the greenhouse effect would drastically alter the global climate of the Earth. Designated wild areas and species habitat do not stand apart from such effects as acid rain in the streams and lakes. The greenhouse effect will drastically alter wild ecosystems; ozone depletion causes animals to go blind and could be the cause of the rapid loss of amphibians worldwide. Chemical pesticides could be causing genetic mutations in frogs across the United States. Industrial-chemical pollution and protection of what's left of the wild world can no longer be separated at this point in history. The issue of world overpopulation cannot be separated from levels of consumption, industrial pollution, and continued economic growth and development, as well as from issues concerning the protection of wildlife habitat, biodiversity, and the Earth's wildness. However, as Anne and Paul Ehrlich have recently pointed out, "The ravaging of biodiversity . . . is the most serious single environmental peril facing civilization."[19] But anthropocentric urban-pollution and social justice concerns cannot be allowed to take precedence over the issue of dealing realistically with the urgency of the global ecological crisis. It comes down to a question of priorities and of developing a realistic ecological worldview.

VI. ARNE NAESS AND THE ARTICULATION OF THE DEEP ECOLOGY MOVEMENT

It was the major philosophical split between the anthropocentric industrial-pollution wing and the ecocentric wing in environmentalism during the 1960s that prompted Norwegian ecophilosopher Arne Naess to present his short paper "The Shallow and the Deep, Long-Range Ecology Movements" (in which he coined the term "deep ecology") to a Third World Futures conference in Bucharest in 1972. The shallow movement, Naess claimed, was anthropocentric and was concerned mainly with pollution and resource depletion and "the health and affluence of people in the developed countries." The deep ecology movement had arisen from the experiences of field ecologists such as Rachel Carson and was engaged in deep questioning about the goals and viability of industrial-growth societies. In his paper, Naess was attempting to articulate the philosophical and scientific conclusions and intuitions of the 1960s ecocentric ecological revolution, which, Naess claimed, were similiar all over the world. These included the internal interrelatedness of ecosystems, ecological egalitarianism, appreciation of diversity and symbiosis, ecological complexity, a "deep-seated respect, or even veneration" for wild nature, anticlass posture, and local autonomy and decentralization. The "fight against pollution and resource depletion" was included as one aspect of the overall deep ecology position.[20]

Naess had begun to write and lecture on philosophy and ecology at the University of Oslo in 1968. This early work developed into his book *Okologi, Samfunn og Livsstil* in 1973 (the first ecophilosophy book written by a professional philosopher). It has continued to undergo revisions and, in 1989, it was revised and translated into English as *Ecology, Community and Lifestyle.* The poet Gary Snyder also worked out a unique deep ecology position beginning in the 1960s. Together with fellow Californians Peter Berg and the ecologist Raymond Dasmann, Snyder has developed the foundations for ecocentric bioregionalism. Naess and Snyder are the two most influential international spokespersons for the deep ecology movement.[21]

During the late 1960s, Naess also began to work out his own personal ecological philosophy based on the philosophies of Spinoza and Gandhi, which he calls Ecosophy T (for Tvergastein, his high mountain hut located between Oslo and Bergen). Ecosophy T is based on one ultimate norm, "Self-Realization!"—which refers to the whole of nature (the Tao), and all the human and nonhuman individuals that it comprises, realizing itself. Deep ecology is both a philosophical and social-political activist movement. In 1984, Naess developed the eight-point deep ecology platform, which begins with the basic ecocentric philosophical norms of the deep ecology movement and leads to general policy statements about activism and social change. (Naess's personal Ecosophy T "total view" and the eight-point platform are discussed in detail in Naess's paper, "The Deep Ecology Movement," in this section.)

That there are *three* distinct positions—(1) the 1972 shallow-deep ecology Bucharest paper, (2) Naess's personal Ecosophy T "total view," and (3) the

1984 eight-point platform—has produced considerable confusion over what the deep ecology movement actually stands for. This confusion was further compounded in 1990 when the Australian ecophilosopher Warwick Fox published his book, *Toward a Transpersonal Ecology*, which attempted to identify deep ecology with the concept of "self-realization," which is also essentially Fox's "transpersonal ecology" version of ecopsychology.[22]

Naess intended for the 1984 eight-point platform to replace the 1972 Bucharest paper as a contemporary characterization of the deep ecology movement. Andrew McLaughlin has argued that the eight-point platform is "the heart of Deep Ecology." Some critics of the deep ecology movement have taken exception to remarks made by Earth First! activists, while others have criticized the concept of "self-realization." Most critics, McLaughlin argues, miss the unique logic of the deep ecology position. To criticize this position in a relevant manner, one must criticize some aspect of the eight-point platform. Self-realization is central to Naess' personal Ecosophy T total view, and to Fox's transpersonal ecology, but it is not part of the eight-point platform; therefore it is not representative of the position of the deep ecology movement. Our "urgent task," McLaughlin says, is not needless philosophical quibbling but environmental activism and "social change," designed to bring about what Naess calls *wide* ecological sustainability—by which he means "the protection of the full richness and diversity of life forms on the Earth."[23]

Most deep ecology movement theorists now identify the movement with the deep questioning process, the eight-point platform, and the need for humans to identify with nonhumans and the wild world. Naess has suggested that the movement is also characterized by "spiritual activism": that is, acting from the basis of a fundamental philosophic-religious ecosophy (or "total view") and acting nonviolently.

VII. COMMENTARY ON THE PAPERS

I have included "The Viable Human" by the leading Catholic ecotheologian, Thomas Berry, because it provides a wonderfully concise and comprehensive overview of the contemporary environmental situation. Berry asserts that a spiritual, ecocentric paradigm shift is necessary to come to grips with the global ecological crisis. His ecocentrism is expressed in the claim that "the community of all living species is the greater reality and the greater value."

Industrial entrepreneurs bear a great deal of responsibility for the crisis by promoting an economic-technological-consumerist "wonderworld," whereas in actuality they are creating a "wasteworld." Echoing Orwell's analysis of "Newspeak," Berry claims that contemporary language has been degraded to support the entrepreneur's vision, which includes "the most extravagant modes of commercial advertising to create the illusory world in which the human community is now living." Education has also been warped to the point where it now basically serves as a handmaiden to the entrepreneur's vision. Educational and religious professionals, Berry claims, are failing to adequately address the ecological crisis. Elsewhere, Berry has stated that population stabilization and eventual reduction are ecologically necessary.

Arne Naess's "The Deep Ecological Movement," written in 1986, is the best short, contemporary statement of the position of the deep ecology movement, together with a short description and diagram of Naess's own personal Ecosophy T "total view" (for a more detailed discussion, see Naess, *Ecology, Community, and Lifestyle*). Naess provides illuminating contrasts between shallow and deep ecology on a number of key environmental issues. The essay includes a statement of the 1984 eight-point deep ecology platform, together with what Naess calls the "Apron Diagram," which helps explain what Andrew McLaughlin calls the "unique logic" of the deep ecology position. At Level 1 of the diagram, there is a wide diversity of philosophical and religious positions, such as Christianity, Buddhism, Spinozism, Whiteheadianism, and so forth. Diversity at Level 1 is encouraged to ensure individual and cultural diversity and pluralism. Naess's "Self-Realization!" norm from his personal Ecosophy T position (and Warwick Fox's "transpersonal ecology" position) fit at Level 1 of the Apron Diagram. This diversity of religious and philosophical "fundamentals" or "ultimate norms" *can* (or, it is hoped, *would*) nevertheless converge, at Level 2 of the diagram, to logically support the ecocentric eight-point platform. It is at Level 2 (the platform level) that one looks for ecocentric agreement among philosophical and religious traditions around the world. Level 3 consists of hypotheses and factual statements about the ecological state of the world, such as ozone layer depletion, the rates of species extinction, and so forth. At Level 4, specific environmental actions to be taken would exhibit differences while remaining consistent with and following logically from Levels 2 and 3 of the diagram. At Level 4, the kinds of societies existing around the world that would be consistent with the eight-point platform at Level 2 would reflect considerable cultural diversity, mirroring and paralleling the kind of diversity found at Level 1 (the level of religious-philosophical "fundamentals" or "ultimate premises").

Naess also describes, and provides a logical diagram of, his own personal philosophical "total view," which he calls Ecosophy T. Ecosophy T is logically developed from his single Level 1 norm, "self-realization," and extends down through the various levels of the Apron Diagram.

One environmental ethics textbook author points out that "it sometimes seems that Deep Ecology acts as a lightning rod for environmental criticism and backlash. Because Deep Ecology does critique the dominant worldview, we should not be surprised to find significant critical reaction."[24] In his paper "Demystifying the Critiques of Deep Ecology," the leading deep ecology theorist Harold Glasser goes a long way toward clarifying many of the misconceptions. Glasser distinguishes what he calls "Naess's deep ecology approach to ecophilosophy" (DEA) from the deep ecology movement and from Naess's Ecosophy T. First, Glasser points to four general weaknesses that are common to discussions and critiques of the deep ecology position. Next, he attempts to clarify Naess's approach to the DEA:

> The DEA should be viewed as a *Gestalt*. . . . In my view the DEA consists of at least six coupled elements: (1) the unifying notion of total views, (2) the DEA as a normative-derivational system, the reasoning techniques, (3) "deep questioning" and (4) "loose derivation," (5) the adoption of ultimate premises that incorporate "wide-identification," and (6) the Eight Points of the deep ecology platform.

In "The Deep Ecology–Ecofeminism Debate and Its Parallels," Warwick Fox examines the charges raised against deep ecology by ecofeminists and social ecologists, who have been vociferous critics of deep ecology. This began with the critique by the Australian sociologist and ecofeminist Ariel Salleh in 1984. Social ecologist Murray Bookchin attacked the deep ecology movement at the first meeting of the U.S. Greens in 1987. Much of Bookchin's critique centered around statements made by Dave Foreman and other activists in the Earth First! movement: statements that were not representative of the deep ecology position.[25]

Fox points out that ecocentrism logically and necessarily involves an egalitarian attitude toward all beings; thus it subsumes under its theoretical framework the egalitarian concerns of the various social justice movements, including ecofeminism and social ecology. Ecofeminist criticism is usually directed at deep ecology's analysis of the environmental crisis as rooted in anthropocentrism. But why, Fox asks, should we focus on androcentrism (male-centeredness) as *the* root cause rather than, say, race, Westernization, or social hierarchy? For it is possible to imagine a society that has realized social, racial, and gender equality but is still ecologically exploitive. This holds as well for Bookchin's social hierarchy analysis.

Fox makes the very important point that both ecofeminists and social ecologists tend to remain anthropocentric in practice as well: they continue to focus on their respective social-political agendas while the practical strategies and activism needed to deal with the global ecological crisis itself receive a low priority or are ignored entirely. For example, ecofeminists and social ecologists have displayed very little interest in the crucial Thoreau-Muir dialogue about protecting wildness. They seem to be preoccupied with their respective forms of social justice, often ignoring the larger issues of the contemporary corporate-megatechnological enslavement of humans and the wild in general. Some ecofeminists even extoll the virtues of megatechnology and ever expanding industrial cities. Donna Haraway, for example, encourages women to reject their organic origins and become "cyborgs": a merging of humans with machines and megatechnology that is remarkably like the New Age, artificial worlds vision of Teilhard de Chardin.

Fox also discusses how ecofeminists and social ecologists misinterpret deep ecology's critique of anthropocentrism to mean that *humans in general* are the cause of the environmental crisis, often equating this view with misanthropy. As Fox points out, deep ecology's critique of anthropocentrism is directed at human-centeredness (a legitimating ideology), not at humans per se—a logical mistake that he refers to as "the fallacy of misplaced misanthropy."

Arne Naess has not been very impressed with the tenor of this "debate" (instigated by the ecofeminists and Murray Bookchin) from the very beginning.

He has said, "Away with all single-cause explanations of the ecological crisis!" And, of course, the critique of anthropocentrism is not a part of the eight-point deep ecology platform—the main distinguishing characteristic of the deep ecology movement (along with other distinguishing characteristics identified by Glasser and others). And so, in a strict sense, this "debate" has been largely irrelevant.

A very influential and widely reprinted paper by the Indian social ecologist Ramachandra Guha argues that the deep ecology movement, with its emphasis on the protection of biodiversity and the Earth's wild ecosystems, is not relevant to Third World concerns.[26] The deep ecology movement, he claims, is not relevant to what he sees as "the two fundamental ecological problems facing the globe: (i) overconsumption by the industrialized world and urban elites in the Third World and (ii) growing militarization. . . ." Guha's analysis is incredible in that it ignores what the 1992 World's Scientists' Warning to Humanity, and most ecologists, identify as the major global ecological problems: human overpopulation, ozone layer depletion, greenhouse effect, and biodiversity destruction. Guha sees the wildlife preserves for protecting tigers and other endangered species in India as a form of "elite ecological imperialism" and "a direct transfer of resources from the poor to the rich." Third World environmentalism, Guha claims, should place primary emphasis on human issues of "equality and social justice." The deep ecology movement, he erroneously asserts, has little or no interest in the issues of restructuring society to achieve ecological sustainability and social justice, steady-state economics, and a "radical shift in consumption and production patterns." Guha goes so far as to claim that the deep ecology movement is not relevant even to First World environmentalism: "A truly radical ecology in the American context," he claims, "ought to work toward a synthesis of the appropriate technology, alternate lifestyle, and peace movements." Guha's analysis is an excellent example of how social ecologists and others who put social justice concerns first are ignorant of—and blinded by anthropocentric ideologies to—the realities of the global ecological crisis.

Arne Naess has responded to Guha's paper, arguing basically that biodiversity concerns are very relevant to the Third World and that many people in the Third World are concerned about the multiple aspects of the ecological crisis, including the protection of biodiversity and the wild. Naess claims that Third World people must progress economically, while rich countries must curtail their excessive consumption. The severe overpopulation in the Third World will require that most of the poor live in urban areas in the near future; they cannot continue to destroy tropical forests. Naess refers to Gary Snyder's point that, throughout history, humans have lived in wilderness in moderate numbers without appreciably reducing biological richness and diversity. But this is now not possible in First World countries, where high-consumption lifestyles and other highly destructive practices require the establishment of large designated wilderness areas to protect wildlife habitat and biodiversity.[27]

Guha's paper gave Naess the opportunity to rethink the relationship among ecology, social justice, and "militarization." As a way of heading off the leftist social justice takeover of the environmental-ecology movement, and helping to ensure that these movements cooperate constructively with each other, Naess proposes that the international green movement for social change be thought of as basically comprising three movements: (1) the peace movement, (2) the social justice movement, and (3) the ecology movement. It promotes only confusion, he claims, to identify the entire green movement (and the social justice and peace movements) with the ecology movement. The deep ecology movement strongly supports sustainability for all societies, but sustainability in the ecologically "wide" sense of protecting "the full richness and diversity of life forms on the planet": it is beneath human dignity, Naess claims, to aspire to less. While Naess argues that societies will not have reached full sustainability until significant progress has been made toward attaining all the goals of the green movement, nevertheless a very high priority must be placed on ecological issues: "Considering the accelerating rate of irreversible ecological destruction worldwide, I find it acceptable to continue fighting ecological unsustainability whatever the state of affairs may be concerning the other two goals of Green societies." Supporters of the deep ecology movement, he claims, "should concentrate on specific issues relating to the *ecological* crisis (including its social and political consequences)."[28]

A great deal of current deep ecological literature is concerned with practical biological and political strategies for implementing the ecocentric perspective, bioregionalism, and protection of biodiversity and what remains of the Earth's wildness. In "Ecocentrism, Wilderness, and Global Ecosystem Protection," I discuss recent research by conservation biologists that demonstrates that existing designated wilderness areas and wildlife preserves are ecologically inadequate to protect wild species and allow for continued speciation. It is claimed that the concepts of "ecological restoration" and "mitigation" are often misused by environmental professionals to justify further ecosystem destruction and habitat fragmentation.

Important recent refinements to ecosystem zoning proposals include Arne Naess's concept of "free nature" and Paul Taylor's concept of the "bioculture." Naess claims that an acceptable ecological ideal for the Earth would consist of one-third wilderness, one-third "free nature," and one-third bioculture. Dave Foreman discusses the Wildland Project strategy for protecting biodiversity (endorsed by E. O. Wilson, Paul Ehrlich, and other leading conservation biologists), which consists of greatly expanded wilderness areas and wildlife refuges with interconnecting wildlife corridors.

SELECTED BIBLIOGRAPHY

Barnet, Richard, and John Cavanaugh. *Global Dreams: Imperial Corporations and the New World Order.* New York: Simon and Schuster, 1994.

Cohen, Michael. *The Pathless Way: John Muir and American Wilderness.* Madison: University of Wisconsin Press, 1984. Excellent discussion of the development of Muir's ecocentrism.

———. *The History of the Sierra Club: 1892–1970.* San Francisco: Sierra Club Books, 1988.

Daly, Herman. *Steady State Economics*, 2nd ed. Washington, DC: Island Press, 1991.
Drengson, Alan, and Yuichi Inoue (eds.). *The Deep Ecology Movement.* Berkeley: North Atlantic Books, 1995. Good introductory collection of deep ecology essays.
Eckersley, Robyn. *Environmentalism and Political Theory: Toward an Ecocentric Approach.* Albany: State University of New York Press, 1992. Outstanding political analysis of ecocentrism.
Ehrenfeld, David. *The Arrogance of Humanism.* Oxford: Oxford University Press, 1978. An excellent critique of the technocratic managerial mind-set and a defense of ecocentrism by a professional ecologist.
Ehrlich, Paul, and Anne Ehrlich. *The Population Explosion.* New York: Simon and Schuster, 1990.
______. *Healing the Planet: Strategies for Resolving the Environmental Crisis.* Reading MA: Addison-Wesley, 1991.
______. *Betrayal of Science and Reason: How Anti-environmental Rhetoric Threatens Our Future.* Washington, DC: Island Press, 1996. The Ehrlichs summarize the worldwide consensus among the scientific community on the magnitude and seriousness of the ecological crisis. An appendix includes the warnings by the world's National Academies of Sciences in the 1990s and the 1992 World's Scientists' Warning to Humanity.
Foreman, Dave. *Confessions of an Ecowarrior.* New York: Harmony Books, 1991.
Fox, Stephen. *John Muir and His Legacy: The American Conservation Movement.* Boston: Little, Brown, 1981. Outstanding history of the Muir-inspired American conservation movement.
Fox, Warwick. *Toward a Transpersonal Ecology.* Boston: Shambhala Publications, 1990. Good history and bibliography of the deep ecology movement and exposition of Fox's transpersonal psychology position.
Kellert, Stephen, and E. O. Wilson (eds.). *The Biophilia Hypothesis.* Washington, DC: Island Press, 1993. A scholarly examination of Wilson's hypothesis that humans have a genetic need for wild environments.
LaChapelle, Dolores. *Sacred Land Sacred Sex: Rapture of the Deep.* Durango, CO: Kivaki Press, 1988.
Mander, Jerry. *In the Absence of the Sacred: The Failure of Technology and the Survival of the Indian Nations.* San Francisco: Sierra Club Books, 1991. A devastating critique of contemporary corporate-consumer-megatechnology visions.
———. (ed.). *The Case Against the Global Economy.* San Francisco: Sierra Club Books, 1996. Mander, Ralph Nader, and others take on GATT, NAFTA, and the multinational corporate vision of the global economic "new world order."
McLaughlin, Andrew. *Regarding Nature: Industrialism and Deep Ecology.* Albany: State University of New York Press, 1993.
Naess, Arne. *Ecology, Community, and Lifestyle: Outline of an Ecosophy.* Cambridge: Cambridge University Press, 1989. Naess's main treatise on deep ecology.
Nash, Roderick. *The Rights of Nature: A History of Environmental Ethics.* Madison: University of Wisconsin Press, 1989.
Noss, Reed, and Allen Cooperrider. *Saving Nature's Legacy: Protecting and Restoring Biodiversity.* Washington, DC: Island Press, 1994. Conservation biologists outline the Wildlands Project for protecting wild species and ecosystems.
Oelschlaeger, Max. *The Idea of Wilderness: From Prehistory to the Age of Ecology.* New Haven, CT: Yale University Press, 1991. Excellent account of the ecocentrism of Thoreau, Muir, and Snyder.
______ (ed.). *The Company of Others: Essays in Celebration of Paul Shepard.* Durango, CO: Kivaki Press, 1995. A tribute to Paul Shepard's genius, published just before his recent death.
Sale, Kirkpatrick. *The Green Revolution: The American Environmental Movement 1962–1992.* New York: Hill and Wang, 1993. Good, short history of environmentalism.

———. *Rebels Against the Future.* Reading, MA: Addison-Wesley, 1995. A history of Luddism and discussion of the neo-Luddite movement.

Sessions, George (ed.). *Deep Ecology for the 21st Century.* Boston: Shambhala Publications, 1995. An attempt at a comprehensive and contemporary statement of the deep ecology position. Extensive bibliography.

———. "Postmoderism and Environmental Justice: The Demise of the Ecology Movement?" *The Trumpeter* 12, 3 (1995): 150–54. This article and the next two provide critiques of postmodern deconstructionism and the attempt by some in the social justice movement to coopt the environmental-ecological movement.

———. "Political Correctness, Ecological Realities, and the Future of the Ecology Movement." *The Trumpeter* 12, 4 (1995): 191–96.

———. "Reinventing Nature, The End of Wilderness?: A Response to William Cronon's *Uncommon Ground.*" *The Trumpeter* 13, 1 (1996): 33–38.

———. "Critical Notice of Martha Lee, *Earth First!: Environmental Apocalypse.*" *The Trumpeter* 13, 4 (1996): 197–200.

———. "Comments on Jack Turner's *The Abstract Wild.*" *Wild Duck Review* 3, 1 (February 1997).

Shepard, Paul. *Nature and Madness.* San Francisco: Sierra Club Books, 1982. A classic in the field of ecopsychology.

———. *The Others: How Animals Made Us Human.* Washington, DC: Island Press, 1995.

———. *The Only World We've Got.* San Francisco: Sierra Club Books, 1996.

———. *Traces of an Omnivore.* Washington, DC: Island Press, 1996.

Snyder, Gary. *The Practice of the Wild.* San Francisco: North Point Press, 1990. Snyder's seminal statement on wildness. Snyder and Paul Shepard argue for the human genetic need for the wild and for the move to bioregionalism.

———. *Mountains and Rivers Without End.* Washington, DC: Counterpoint Press, 1996.

Soule, Michael, and Gary Lease. *Reinventing Nature?: A Response to Postmodern Deconstructionism.* Washington, DC. Island Press, 1995. Conservation biologists and others respond to William Cronon and other postmodernists who promote Disneyland-type, urban, hyperreal environments over reinhabitation, bioregionalism, and protection and restoration of the wild.

Turner, Jack. *The Abstract Wild.* Tucson: University of Arizona Press, 1996. A brilliant, uncompromising defense of the wild and critique of the economic paradigm and shallow managerial environmentalism.

Witoszek, Nina (ed.). *Rethinking Deep Ecology.* University of Oslo: Centre for Development and the Environment, 1996.

Witoszek, Nina, and Andrew Brennan, eds. *Philosophical Dialogues: Arne Naess and the Progress of Ecophilosophy.* University of Oslo: Centre for Development and Environment, 1997.

Zakin, Susan. *Coyotes and Town Dogs: Earth First! and the Environmental Movement.* New York, Viking Press, 1993. The best account of the Earth First! movement.

Zimmerman, Michael E. *Contesting Earth's Future: Radical Ecology and Postmodernity.* Berkeley and Los Angeles: University of California Press, 1993.

NOTES

1. Lynn White, Jr., "Historical Roots of Our Ecologic Crisis," *Science* 155 (1967): 1203–7. For discussions of the impact of White's paper, see Stephen Fox, *John Muir and His Legacy: The American Conservation Movement* (Boston: Little, Brown, 1981), pp. 358–74; Roderick Nash, *The Rights of Nature: A History of Environmental Ethics* (Madison: University of Wisconsin Press, 1989), pp. 87–120.

2. Paul Ehrlich, *The Population Bomb* (New York: Ballantine Books, 1968), pp. 169–72.
3. For discussions of Thoreau's concern for protecting wildness in both humans and nonhumans, see Jack Turner, "In Wildness Is the Preservation of the World," and Thomas Birch, "The Incarceration of Wildness," both reprinted in George Sessions (ed.), *Deep Ecology for the 21st Century* (Boston: Shambhala Publications, 1995), pp. 331–55.
4. For a discussion of Brower's Exhibit Format books, see Michael P. Cohen, *A History of the Sierra Club: 1892–1970* (San Francisco: Sierra Club Books, 1988), pp. 254–64, 291–99, 345–52.
5. G. Tyler Miller, Jr., *Replenish the Earth: A Primer in Human Ecology* (Belmont, CA: Wadsworth, 1972), p. 152. Miller's book presents an excellent summary of the ecological-environmental crisis as it was understood by biologists and other scientists at the beginning of the 1970s. See also G. Tyler Miller, Jr., *Living in the Environment: An Introduction to Environmental Science*, 9th ed. (Belmont, CA: Wadsworth, 1996).
6. A vivid presentation of the clash between Ehrlich and Simon and between Ehrlich and Barry Commoner is provided in the excellent Public Broadcasting System (PBS) video "Paul Ehrlich and the Population Bomb," aired in April 1996.
7. On the globalization of corporate power, see Jerry Mander (ed.), *The Case Against the Global Economy* (San Francisco: Sierra Club Books, 1996). For the corporate vision of the world as a megatechnological-consumerist-Disneyland theme park, see Jerry Mander, *In the Absence of the Sacred* (San Francisco: Sierra Club Books, 1991); Paul Shepard, "Virtually Hunting Reality in the Forests of Simulacra," in Michael Soulé and Gary Lease (eds.), *Reinventing Nature?: Responses to Postmodern Deconstruction* (Washington, DC: Island Press, 1995), pp. 17–29.
8. For a discussion of the "Reagan reaction," see Kirkpatrick Sale, *The Green Revolution: The American Environmental Movement 1962–1992* (New York: Hill and Wang, 1993); for critiques of sustainable development, the Bruntland Report, and the 1992 Rio conference, see Donald Worster, "The Shaky Ground of Sustainability," and Wolfgang Sachs, "Global Ecology and the Shadow of 'Development,' " in Sessions, *Deep Ecology*, pp. 417–44.
9. For a statement of the warnings of the National Academies of Sciences and the World's Scientists' Warning to Humanity, see Paul and Anne Ehrlich, *Betrayal of Science and Reason: How Anti-environmental Rhetoric Threatens Our Future* (Washington, DC: Island Books, 1966), pp. 233–50; Anne and Paul Ehrlich, *Healing the Planet: Strategies for Resolving the Environmental Crisis* (Reading MA: Addison-Wesley, 1991), pp. 35–37. For a discussion of the 1995 M.I.T. study of the current attitudes of Americans toward wild nature, see Tom Hayden, *The Lost Gospel of the Earth* (San Francisco: Sierra Club Books, 1996), pp. 232–34.
10. The influence of the Vogt and Osborn books is discussed in Robert Gottlieb, *Forcing the Spring: The Transformation of the American Environmental Movement* (Washington, DC: Island Press, 1993), pp. 36–41, although Gottlieb disparagingly refers to them as "neo-Malthusian" in tone. Both the books by Gottlieb and Mark Dowie, *Losing Ground: American Environmentalism at the Close of the Twentieth Century* (Cambridge MA: M.I.T. Press, 1995) are leftist in orientation; they propose that the environmental movement shift its priorities away from the protection of the Earth's biodiversity, wild ecosystems, and ecological integrity (the position taken by most contemporary ecologists and world scientists' organizations) to an urban pollution and social justice agenda (referred to now as the movement for environmental justice). Those who put social justice issues first or attempt to redirect environmentalism toward an environmental justice agenda remain anthropocentric and apparently fail to fully comprehend the nature and severity of the global ecological crisis.
11. Anne and Paul Ehrlich, *Earth* (New York: Franklin Watts, 1987), pp. 167–68.

12. For a discussion of the Sierra Club Wilderness Conferences and Brower's conversion to ecocentrism, see Cohen, *History of the Sierra Club,* pp. 116–17, 124–34, 214–17, 232–33, 369, 414, 436–37.
13. David Brower, "Toward an Earth International Park," and Hugh H. Iltus, "Whose Fight Is the Fight for Nature?" *Sierra Club Bulletin* 52, 9 (October 1967): 20, 34–39. This issue of the *Bulletin* also published the paper by White, "Historical Roots of Our Ecologic Crisis," pp. 123–27. For a discussion of the *New York Times* ad, see Cohen, *History of the Sierra Club,* pp. 424–26.
14. Cohen, *History of the Sister Club,* pp. 133–34.
15. Donald Worster, "The Shaky Ground of Sustainability," in Sessions, *Deep Ecology,* pp. 417–18.
16. Stephen Fox, *John Muir and His Legacy: The American Conservation Movement* (Boston: Little, Brown, 1981). Chapter 9 of Fox's book is an excellent summary of the conflicting trends in the development of environmentalism throughout the 1960s and early 1970s. For a revealing account of the anthropocentric, social justice–oriented new left approach to environmental issues during this period, see Gottlieb, *Forcing the Spring,* chap. 3. It is illuminating to contrast the environmental concerns of the new left with the little manifesto, "Four Changes," written by the Zen Buddhist counterculturalist and deep ecologist Gary Snyder in 1969 (reprinted in Sessions, *Deep Ecology,* pp. 141–50).
17. Chris Lewis, "Telling Stories About the Future: Environmental History and Apocalyptic Science," *Environmental History Review* 17, 3 (1993): 42–60.
18. For critiques of the attempt by leftists to redirect the environmental movement away from the major problems of the global ecological crisis and toward an urban-pollution–social justice agenda, see George Sessions, "Postmodernism and Environmental Justice: The Demise of the Ecology Movement?" *The Trumpeter* 12, 3 (1995): 150–54; George Sessions, "Political Correctness, Ecological Realities, and the Future of the Ecology Movement," *The Trumpeter* 12, 4 (1995): 191–96; George Sessions, "Reinventing Nature, The End of Wilderness?: A Response to William Cronon's *Uncommon Ground,*" *The Trumpeter* 13, 1 (1996): 33–38.
19. Ehrlich, *Healing the Planet,* pp. 35–37.
20. A summary of the talk was published as Arne Naess, "The Shallow and the Deep, Long-Range Ecology Movements: A Summary," *Inquiry* (Oslo) 16 (1973); reprinted in Sessions, *Deep Ecology,* pp. 151–55.
21. Arne Naess, *Ecology, Community, and Lifestyle: Outline of an Ecosophy,* David Rothenberg (trans.) (Cambridge: Cambridge University Press, 1989); Snyder, "Four Changes"; Gary Snyder, "Re-inhabitation," in *The Old Ways* (San Francisco: City Lights Books, 1977); Raymond Dasmann, *The Destruction of California* (New York: Macmillan, 1965); Peter Berg and Raymond Dasmann, "Reinhabiting California," in Peter Berg (ed.), *Reinhabiting a Separate Country* (San Francisco: Planet Drum Foundation, 1978); Gary Snyder, *The Practice of the Wild* (San Francisco: North Point Press, 1990).
22. Warwick Fox, *Toward a Transpersonal Ecology* (Boston: Shambhala Publications, 1990). For a critique of Fox's attempt to replace deep ecology with "transpersonal ecology," see Harold Glasser, "On Warwick Fox's Assessment of Deep Ecology," *Environmental Ethics* 19, 1 (1997): 69–85; Harold Glasser, "Naess's Deep Ecology Approach and Environmental Policy," *Inquiry* (Oslo) 39, 2 (1996): 157–87.
23. See Andrew McLaughlin, "The Heart of Deep Ecology" and Arne Naess, "Politics and the Ecological Crisis," in Sessions, *Deep Ecology,* pp. 85–93 and 445–53, respectively.
24. Joseph R. DesJardins, *Environmental Ethics: An Introduction to Environmental Philosophy,* 2nd ed. (Belmont, CA: Wadsworth, 1997), p. 215. In his section on deep ecology, unfortunately, DesJardins repeats many of the misconceptions he decries.

25. Ariel Salleh, "Deeper Than Deep Ecology: The Ecofeminist Connection," *Environmental Ethics* 6, 4 (1984): 339–45; Murray Bookchin, "Social Ecology Versus Deep Ecology: A Challenge for the Ecology Movement," *Socialist Review* 88, 3 (1988): 11–29; reprinted in D. VanDeVeer and C. Pierce (eds.), *Environmental Ethics and Policy Book* (Belmont, CA: Wadsworth, 1994), pp. 228–38. See also Steve Chase (ed.), *Defending the Earth: A Dialogue between Murray Bookchin and Dave Foreman* (Boston: South End Press, 1991); George Sessions, "Critical Notice of Martha Lee, *Earth First!: Environmental Apocalypse*," *The Trumpeter* 13, 4 (1996): 197–200.
26. Ramachandra Guha, "Radical American Environmentalism and Wilderness Preservation: A Third World Critique," *Environmental Ethics* 11, 1 (1989): 71–83; reprinted in VanDeVeer and Pierce, *Environmental Ethics and Policy Book*, pp. 548–56.
27. Arne Naess, "The Third World, Wilderness, and Deep Ecology," in Sessions, *Deep Ecology*, pp. 397–407; see also David Johns, "The Relevance of Deep Ecology to the Third World," *Environmental Ethics* 12, 3 (1990): 233–52; Eric Katz and Lauren Oelchsli, "Moving Beyond Anthropocentrism: Environmental Ethics, Development, and the Amazon," *Environmental Ethics* 15, 1 (1993): 49–59.
28. See Arne Naess, "The Third World, Wilderness, and Deep Ecology," "Politics and the Ecological Crisis," and "Deep Ecology for the Twenty-Second Century," in Sessions, *Deep Ecology*, pp. 397–407, 445–53, and 463–67, respectively; see also Arne Naess, "The Three Great Movements, *The Trumpeter* 9, 2 (1992).

The Viable Human

Thomas Berry

Thomas Berry is director of the Riverdale Center for Religious Research in New York and is widely regarded as one of the world's leading ecotheologians. He is the author of The Dream of the Earth *(1988) and many papers in ecotheology.*

To be viable, the human community must move from its present anthropocentric norm to a geocentric norm of reality and value. Within the solar system, the earth is the immediate context of human existence. And we recognize the sun as the primary source of earth's energies. Beyond the sun, however, is our own galaxy, and beyond that is the universal galactic system that emerged some 15 billion years ago through some ineffable mystery.

To establish this comprehensive context is important; it is the only satisfactory referent in our quest for a viable presence of the human within the larger dynamics of the universe. We suppose that the universe itself is *the* enduring reality and *the* enduring value even while it finds expression in a continuing sequence of transformations. In creating the planet Earth, its living forms, and its human intelligence, the universe has found, so far as we know, the most elaborate manifestation of its deepest mystery. Here, in its human form, the universe is able to reflect on and celebrate itself in a unique mode of conscious self-awareness.

Our earliest human documents reveal a special sensitivity in human intellectual, emotional, and aesthetic responses to the natural world. These responses reveal cosmic and biologic realms of thought as well as anthropocentric life attitudes. These realms were all centered in each other, the later dependent on the earlier for survival, the earlier dependent on the later for their manifestation.

Instinctively, humans have always perceived themselves as a mode of being *of* the universe as well as distinctive beings *in* the universe. This was the beginning. The emergence of the human was a transformative moment for the earth as well as for the human. As with every species, the human being needed to establish its niche, a sustainable position in the larger community of life, to

Originally published in *Revision*, Vol 9, No. 2 (Winter/Spring 1987). Reprinted with permission of the Helen Dwight Reid Education Foundation. Published by Heldref Publications, 1319 Eighteenth St., N.W., Washington, D.C. 20036-1802.

fulfill its need for food, shelter, and clothing, for security, for family and community. The need for community was special because of the unique human capacity for thought and speech, aesthetic appreciation, emotional sensitivities, and moral judgment. The fulfilling of these needs resulted in a cultural shaping that established the specific identifying qualities of the human being.

Whatever the cultural elaboration of the human, its basic physical as well as psychic nourishment and support came from the surrounding natural environment. In its beginnings, human society was integrated with the larger life society and the larger earth community composed of all the geological as well as biological and human elements. Just how long this primordial harmony endured we do not know beyond the last hundred thousand years of the Paleolithic period. Some ten thousand years ago, the Neolithic and then the Classical civilizations came into being. It must suffice to say that with the classical and generally literate civilizations of the past five thousand years, the great cultural worlds of the human developed, along with vast and powerful social establishments whereby humans became oppressive and even destructive of other life forms. Alienation from the natural world increased, and new ideals of human well-being neglected the needs of other living species. Because of this human dysfunctional relation with the earth, some of these earlier human cultures became nonsustainable. We can observe this especially in the classical Mediterranean civilizations of Greece and Rome. Even so, the human species as a whole was not seriously endangered; these experiences were regional and limited in their consequences. In recent times, however, this has changed.

A deep cultural pathology has developed in Western society and has now spread throughout the planet. A savage plundering of the entire earth is taking place through industrial exploitation. Thousands of poisons unknown in former times are saturating the air, the water, and the soil. The habitat of a vast number of living species is being irreversibly damaged. In this universal disturbance of the biosphere by human agents, the human being now finds that the harm done to the natural world is returning to threaten the human species itself.

The question of the viability of the human species is intimately connected with the question of the viability of the earth. These questions ultimately arise because at the present time the human community has such an exaggerated, even pathological, fixation on its own comfort and convenience that it is willing to exhaust any and all of the earth's resources to satisfy its own cravings. The sense of reality and of value is strictly directed toward the indulgences of a consumer economy. This nonsustainable situation can be clearly seen in the damage done to major elements necessary for the continued well-being of the planet. When the soil, the air, and the water have been extensively poisoned, human needs cannot be fulfilled. Strangely, this situation is the consequence of a human-centered norm of reality and value.

Once we grant that a change from an anthropocentric to a biocentric sense of reality and value is needed, we must ask how this can be achieved and how it would work. We must begin by accepting the fact that the life community, the community of all living species, is the greater reality and the greater value, and that the primary concern of the human must be the preservation and enhancement of this larger community. The human does have its own distinctive reality and its own distinctive value, but this distinctiveness must be articulated within the more comprehensive context. The human ultimately must discover the larger dimensions of its own being within this community context. That the value of the human being is enhanced by diminishing the value of the larger community is an illusion, the great illusion of the present industrial age, which seeks to advance the human by plundering the planet's geological structure and all its biological species.

This plundering is being perpetrated mainly by the great industrial establishments that have dominated the entire planetary process for the past one hundred years, during the period when modern science and technology took control not only of our natural resources but also of human affairs. If the viability of the human species is now in question, it is a direct consequence of these massive ventures, which have gained extensive control not only of our economies but also of our whole cultural development, whether it be economics, politics, law, education, medicine, or moral values. Even our language is heavily nuanced in favor of the consumer values fostered by our commercial industrial establishment.

Opposed to the industrial establishment is the ecological movement which seeks to create a more viable context for the human within the framework of the larger community. There must, however, be a clear understanding that this question of viability is not an issue that can be resolved in any permanent manner. It will be a continuing issue for the indefinite future.

The planet that ruled itself directly for the past millennia is now determining its future through human decision. Such has been the responsibility assumed by humans when we ventured into the study of the empirical sciences and their associated technologies. In this process, whatever the benefits, we endangered ourselves and every living organism on this planet.

If we look back over the total course of planetary development, we find that there was a consistent fluorescence of the life process in the larger arc of its development over some billions of years. There were innumerable catastrophic events in both the geological and biological realms, but none of these had the distinguishing characteristics or could cause such foreboding as Earth experiences at present.

The total extinction of life is not imminent, though the elaborate forms of life expression in the earth's ecosystems may be shattered in an irreversible manner. What is absolutely threatened is the degradation of the planet's more brilliant and satisfying forms of life expression. This degradation involves extensive distortion and a pervasive weakening of the life system, its comprehensive integrity as well as its particular manifestations.

While there are pathologies that wipe out whole populations of life forms and must be considered pernicious to the life process on an extensive scale, the human species has, for some thousands of years, shown itself to be a pernicious presence in the world of the living on a unique and universal scale. Nowhere has this been more evident than in the Western phase of development of the human species. There is scarcely any geological or biological reality or function that has not experienced the deleterious influence of the human. The survival of hundreds of thousands of species is presently threatened. But since the human survives only within this larger complex of ecosystems, any damage done to other species, or to the other ecosystems, or to the planet itself, eventually affects the human not only in terms of physical well-being but also in every other phase of human intellectual understanding, aesthetic expression, and spiritual development.

Because such deterioration results from a rejection of the inherent limitation of earthly existence and from an effort to alter the natural functioning of the planet in favor of a humanly constructed wonderworld for its human occupants, the human resistance to this destructive process has turned its efforts toward an emphasis on living creatively within the functioning of the natural world. The earth as a bio-spiritual planet must become, for the human, the basic reference in identifying what is real and what is worthwhile.

Thus we have the ecologist standing against industrial enterprise in defense of a viable mode of human functioning within the context of a viable planetary process. This opposition between the industrial entrepreneur and the ecologist has been both the central human issue and the central earth issue of this late 20th century. My position is that the efforts of the entrepreneur to create a wonderworld are, in fact, creating a wasteworld, a nonviable environment for the human species. The ecologist is offering a way of moving toward a new expression of the true wonderworld of nature as the context for a viable human situation. The current difficulty is that the industrial enterprise has such extensive control over the planet that we must certainly be anxious about the future.

But we are tempted to diminish our assessment of the danger lest we be overwhelmed with the difficulty, for indeed, we are caught in a profound cultural pathology. We might even say that, at present, our dominant institutions, professions, programs, and activities are counterproductive in their consequences, addictive to a consumer society; and we are paralyzed by our inability to respond effectively. Such a description is well merited if we consider the extent to which we have poisoned our environment, the air we breathe, the water we drink, and the soil that grows our food.

Having identified the magnitude of the difficulty before us, we need to establish a more specific analysis of the problems themselves. Then we need to provide specific programs leading toward a viable human situation on a viable planet.

The industrial entrepreneur is in possession of the natural resources of the planet, either directly, by corporate control, or indirectly, through governments subservient to the industrial enterprise. This possession is, of course, within limits. Fragmentary regions of the planet have been set aside as areas to be preserved in their natural state or to be exploited at a later time. These regions survive at the tolerance of the industrial establishment. Some controls now exist through governmental and private protection. These must be expanded.

Ecologists recognize that reducing the planet to a resource base for consumer use in an industrial society is already a spiritual and psychic degradation. Our main experience of the divine, the world of the sacred, has been diminished as money and utility values have taken precedence over spiritual, aesthetic, emotional, and religious values in our attitude toward the natural world. Any recovery of the natural world will require not only extensive financial funding but a conversion experience deep in the psychic structure of the human. Our present dilemma is the consequence of a disturbed psychic situation, a mental imbalance, an emotional insensitivity, none of which can be remedied by any quickly contrived adjustment. Nature has been severely, and in many cases irreversibly, damaged. Healing can occur and new life can sometimes be evoked, but only with the same intensity of concern and sustained vigor of action as that which brought about the damage in the first place. Yet, without this healing, the viability of the human is severely limited.

The basic orientation of the common law tradition is toward personal rights and toward the natural world as existing for human use. There is no provision for recognition of nonhuman beings as subjects having legal rights. To the ecologists, the entire question of possession and use of the earth, either by individuals or by establishments, needs to be profoundly reconsidered. The naive assumption that the natural world exists solely to be possessed and used by humans for their unlimited advantage cannot be accepted. The earth belongs to itself and to all the component members of the community. The entire earth is a gorgeous celebration of existence in all its forms. Each living thing participates in the celebration as the proper fulfillment of its powers of expression. The reduction of the earth to an object simply for human possession and use is unthinkable in most traditional cultures. To Peter Drucker, the entrepreneur creates resources and values. Before it is possessed and used, "every plant is a weed and every mineral is just another rock" (*Innovation and Entrepreneurship*, 1985, p. 30). To the industrial entrepreneur, human possession and use is what activates the true value of any natural object.

The Western legal tradition, with its insistance on personal rights and the freedom of the human to occupy and use the land and all its component forms, is the greatest support for the entrepreneur. There is no question of other natural beings having rights over the human. Human use is not limited by any legally recognized rights of other natural beings but only by human determination of the limits that humans are willing to accept.

To achieve a viable human-earth community, a new legal system must take as its primary task to articulate the conditions for the integral functioning of the earth process, with special reference to a mutually enhancing human-earth relationship. Within this context, each component of the earth would be a separate community and together they would constitute the integral expression of the great community of the planet Earth.

In this context, each individual being is also supported by every other being in the earth community. In turn, each contributes to the well-being of every other. Justice would consist in carrying out this sequence of creative relationships. Within the human community there would, of course, be a need for articulating patterns of social relationships, in which individual and group rights would be recognized and defended and the basic elements of personal security and personal property would be protected. The entire complex of political and social institutions would be needed. Economic organizations would also be needed. But these would be so integral with the larger earth economy that they would enhance rather than obstruct each other.

Another significant aspect of contemporary life, wherein the industrial entrepreneur has a dominant position, is language. Since we are enclosed in an industrial culture, the words we use have their significance and validation defined within this industrial framework. A central value word used by our society is "progress." This word has great significance for increasing our scientific understanding of the universe, our personal and social development, our better health and longer life. Through modern technology, we can manufacture great quantities of products with greater facility. Human technology also enables us to travel faster and with greater ease. So on and on, endlessly, we see our increasing human advantage over the natural world.

But then we see that human progress has been carried out by desolating the natural world. This degradation of the earth is the very condition of the "progress" presently being made by humans. It is a kind of sacrificial offering. Within the human community, however, there is little awareness of the misunderstanding of this word. The feeling that even the most trivial modes of human progress are preferable to the survival of the most sublime and even the most sacred aspects of the natural world is so pervasive that the ecologist is at a loss as to how to proceed. The language in which our values are expressed has been co-opted by the industrial establishments and is used with the most extravagant modes of commercial advertising to create the illusory world in which the human community is now living.

One of the most essential roles of the ecologist is to create the language in which a true sense of reality, of value, and of progress can be communicated to our society. This need for rectification of language was recognized very early by the Chinese as a first task for any acceptable guidance of the society. Just now, a rectification is needed for the term "progress." As presently used, this word might be understood more properly to mean "retardation" or "destruction." The meaning of the term "profit" also needs to be rectified. Profit according to what norms and for whom? The profit of the corporation is the deficit of the earth. The profit of the industrial enterprise can also be considered the deficit of the quality of life, even for human society.

Gender has wide implications for our conception of the universe, the earth, and the life process, as well as for the relation of human individuals toward each other and for identifying social roles. The industrial establishment is the extreme expression of a non-viable patriarchal tradition. Only with enormous psychic and social effort and revolutionary processes has this control been mitigated with regard to the rights of serfs, slaves, women and children, ethnic groups, and the impoverished classes of our society. The rights of the natural world of living beings other than humans is still at the mercy of the modern industrial corporation as the ultimate expression of patriarchal dominance over the entire planetary process. The four basic patriarchal oppressions are rulers over people, men over women, possessors over nonpossessors, and humans over nature.

For the ecologist, the great model of all existence is the natural ecosystem, which is self-ruled as a community wherein each component has its unique and comprehensive influence. The ecologist, with a greater understanding of the human as a nurturing presence within the larger community of the geological and biological modes of earth, is closer to the feminine than to the masculine modality of being and of activity.

The purpose of education, as presently envisaged, is to enable humans to be "productive" within the context of the industrial society. A person needs to become literate in order to fulfill some function within the system, whether in the acquisition or processing of raw materials, manufacturing, distributing the product in a commercially profitable manner, managing the process or the finances, or finally, spending the net earnings in acquisition and enjoyment of possessions. A total life process is envisaged within this industrial process. All professional careers now tend toward the industrial-commercial model, especially medicine, law, and the engineering sciences.

In a new context, the primary educator as well as the primary lawgiver and the primary healer would be the natural world itself. The integral earth community would be a self-educating community within the context of a self-educating universe. Education at the human level would be the conscious sensitizing of the human to those profound communications made by the universe about us, by the sun and moon and stars, the clouds and rain, the contours of the earth and all its living forms. All the music and poetry of the universe would flow into the student, the revelatory presence of the divine, as well as insight into the architectural structures of the continents and the engineering skills whereby the great hydrological cycle functions in moderating the temperature of the earth, in providing habitat for aquatic life, in nourishing the multitudes of living creatures. The earth would also be our primary teacher of sciences, especially the biological sciences, and of industry and economics. It would teach us a system in which we would create a minimum of entropy, a system in which there is no unusable or unfruitful junk. Only in such an integral system is the future viability of the human assured.

Much more could be said about the function of the natural world as educator, but this may be sufficient to suggest the context for an education that would be available to everyone from the beginning to the end of life, when the earth that brought us into being draws us back into itself to experience the deepest of all mysteries.

In this ecological context, we see that the problems of human illness are not only increasing but also are being considerably altered in their very nature by the industrial context of life. In prior centuries, human illness was experienced within the well-being of the natural world with its abundance of air and water and foods grown in a fertile soil. Even city dwellers in their deteriorated natural surroundings could depend on the purifying processes of the natural elements. The polluting materials themselves were subject to natural composition and reabsorption into the ever-renewing cycles of the life process.

But this is no longer true. The purifying processes have been overwhelmed by the volume, the composition, and the universal extent of the toxic or non-biodegradable materials. Beyond all this, the biorhythms of the natural world are suppressed by the imposition of mechanistic patterns on natural processes.

The profession of medicine must now consider its role, not only within the context of human society, but in the context of the earth process. A healing of the earth is now a prerequisite for the healing of the human. Adjustment of the human to the conditions and restraints of the natural world constitutes the primary medical prescription for human well-being. Nothing else will suffice.

Behind the long disruption of the earth process is the refusal of our Western industrial society to accept any restraints upon its quest for release—not simply from the normal ills to which we are subject but release from the human condition itself. There exists in our tradition a hidden rage against those inner as well as outer forces that create a challenge or impose a limitation on our activities.

Some ancient force in the Western psyche seems to perceive limitation as the demonic obstacle to be eliminated rather than as a discipline to evoke creativity. Acceptance of the shadow aspect of the natural world is a primary condition for creative intimacy with the natural world. Without this opaque or even threatening aspect of the universe we would lose our greatest source of creative energy. This opposing element is as necessary for us as is the weight of the atmosphere that surrounds us. This containing element, even the gravitation that binds us to the earth, should be experienced as liberating and energizing rather than confining.

Strangely enough, it is our efforts to establish a thoroughly sanitized world that have led to our toxic world. Our quest for wonderworld is making wasteworld. Our quest for energy is creating entropy on a scale never before witnessed in the historical process. We have invented a counterproductive society that is now caught in the loop that feeds back into itself in what can presently be considered a runaway situation. This includes all our present human activities, although it is most evident in the industrial-commercial aspects of contemporary life.

The communications media are particularly responsible for placing the entire life process of the human in an uncontrolled situation. Producer and consumer feed each other in an ever-accelerating process until we experience an enormous glut of basic products. But we see unmatched deprivation for the growing numbers of people living in the shantytowns of the world.

There are no prominent newspapers, magazines, and periodicals that have consistently designated space for commentary on the ecological situation. There are sections for politics, economics, sports, arts, science, education, food, entertainment, and a number of other areas of life, including religion; but only on rare occasions are there references to what is happening to the planet. Of course, these periodicals are supported by the great industrial establishment, and the ecological situation is considered threatening or limiting to the industrial enterprise. In reality, industrial control of the media is among the most devastating forces threatening the viability of the human.

Efforts are made to mitigate the evils consequent to this industrial-commercial process by modifying the manner in which these establishments function, reducing the amount of toxic waste produced as well as developing more efficient modes of storing or detoxifying waste. Yet all of this is trivial in relation to the magnitude of the problem. So, too, are the regulatory efforts of the government; these are microphase solutions for macrophase problems.

We also witness the pathos of present efforts to preserve habitats for wildlife in some areas while elsewhere the tropical rain forests of the earth are being destroyed. Other efforts to alter present destructive activities are made by confrontational groups such as Greenpeace, Earth First!, and People for the Ethical Treatment of Animals. These are daring ventures that dramatize the stark reality of the situation. That such tactics (to save the whales at sea, the wilderness life on the land, and the millions of animals being tortured in laboratories under the guise of scientific research) are needed to force humans to examine and question our behavior is itself evidence of how deep a change is needed in human consciousness.

Beyond the mitigating efforts and confrontational tactics is the clarification of more creative modes of functioning in all our institutions and professions, especially through movements associated with reinhabiting the various bioregions of the world such as the Regeneration Project of the Rodale Institute, The Land Institute in Salina, Kansas, and the two North American Bioregional Congresses. These new and mutually enhancing patterns of human-earth relationships are being developed on a functional as well as a critical-intellectual basis. Among these organizations, the Green movement may be one of the most creative and effective in its overall impact as the years pass. This movement is finding expression in politics, in economics, in education, in healing, and in spiritual reorientation. These recent movements, oriented toward a more benign human relationship with the environment, indicate a pervasive change in consciousness that is presently our best hope for developing a sustainable future.

We might also now recover our sense of the maternal aspect of the universe in the symbol of the Great Mother, especially the Earth as the maternal principle out of which we are born. Once this symbol is recovered, the dominion of the patriarchal system that has brought such aggressive attitudes into our activities will be eliminated. If this is achieved, our relationship with the natural world should undergo its most radical readjustment since the origins of our civilization in classical antiquity.

We might also recover our archetypal sense of the cosmic tree and the tree of life. The tree symbol gives expression to the organic unity of the universe but especially of the earth in its integral reality. Obviously, any damage done to the tree will be experienced through the entire organism. This could be one of our most effective ways of creating not simply conscious decisions against industrial devastation of the earth but a deep instinctive repulsion to any such activity. This instinct should be as immediate as the instinct for survival itself.

In the United States, the educational and religious professionals should be especially sensitive in discerning what is happening to the planet. These professions present themselves as guides for the establishment of our values and interpretors of the significance of our lives. The study of education and religion should awaken an awareness of the world in which we live, how it functions, how the human fits into the larger community of life, and the role that the human fulfills in the great story of the universe, the historical sequence of developments that have shaped our physical and cultural landscape. Along with an awareness of the past and present, education and religion should guide the future.

The pathos of these times, however, is precisely the impasse we witness in our educational and religious programs. Both are living in a past fundamentalist tradition or venturing into New Age programs that are often trivial in their consequences, unable to support or to guide the transformation that is needed in its proper order of magnitude. We must recognize that the only effective program available is the program offered by the earth itself as our primary guide toward a viable human mode of being.

Both education and religion need to ground themselves within the story of the universe as we now understand this story through empirical knowledge. Within this functional cosmology we can overcome our alienation and begin the renewal of life on a sustainable basis. This story is a numinous revelatory story that could evoke the vision and the energy required to bring not only ourselves but the entire planet into a new order of magnificence.

Meanwhile, in the obscure regions of the human unconsciousness, where the primordial archetypal symbols function as ultimate controlling factors in human thought, emotion, and in practical decision making, a profound reorientation toward this integral human-earth relationship is gradually taking place. This archetypal journey must be experienced as the journey of each individual, since the entire universe has been involved in shaping our psyche as well as our physical being from that first awesome moment when the universe began. In the creation of a viable human, the universe reflects on and celebrates itself in conscious self-awareness, and finds a unique fulfillment.

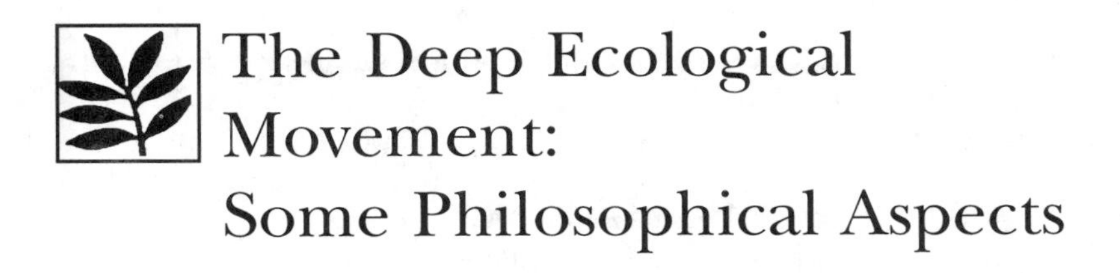

The Deep Ecological Movement: Some Philosophical Aspects

Arne Naess

Arne Naess is professor emeritus at the University of Oslo, Norway, where he was chairman of the philosophy department for many years. Naess coined the term and developed the basic concepts of "deep ecology" in 1972. Widely regarded as one of the leading scholars in Europe, he is the author of Ecology, Community and Lifestyle *(English trans. 1989) and many books and papers on empirical linguistics, Spinoza, Gandhi, and ecosophy.*

1. DEEP ECOLOGY ON THE DEFENSIVE

Increasing pressures for continued growth and development have placed the vast majority of environmental professionals on the defensive. By way of illustration:

The field-ecologist Ivar Mysterud, who both professionally and vigorously advocated deep ecological principles in the late 1960s, encountered considerable resistance. Colleagues at his university said he should keep to his science and not meddle in philosophical and political matters. He should resist the temptation to become a prominent "popularizer" through mass media exposure. Nevertheless, he persisted and influenced thousands of people (including myself).

Mysterud became a well-known professional "expert" at assessing the damage done when bears killed or maimed sheep and other domestic animals in Norway. According to the law, their owners are paid damages. And licensed hunters receive permission to shoot bears if their misdeeds become considerable.[1] Continued growth and development required that the sheep industry consolidate, and sheepowners became fewer, richer, and tended to live in cities. As a result of wage increases, they could not afford to hire shepherds to watch the flocks, so the sheep were left on their own even more than before. Continued growth also

This essay originally appeared in *Philosophical Inquiry* 8, 1–2 (1986). Reprinted with permission.

required moving sheep to what was traditionally considered "bear territory." In spite of this invasion, bear populations grew and troubles multiplied.

How did Mysterud react to these new problems? Did he set limits to the amount of human/sheep encroachment on bear territory? Did he attempt a direct application of his deep ecological perspective to these issues? Quite the contrary. He adopted what appeared to be a shallow wildlife management perspective, and defended the sheepowners: more money to compensate for losses, quicker compensation, and the immediate hiring of hunters who killed mostly "juvenile delinquent" bears accused of killing many sheep.

Protectors of big carnivores noted with concern the change of Mysterud's public "image"; had he really abandoned his former value priorities? Privately he insisted that he hadn't. But in public he tended to remain silent.

The reason for M.'s unexpected actions was not difficult to find: the force of economic growth was so strong that the laws protecting bears would be changed in a highly unfavorable direction if the sheepowners were not soon pacified by accepting some of their not unreasonable demands. After all, it did cost a lot of money to hire and equip people to locate a flock of sheep which had been harassed by a bear and, further, to prove the bear's guilt. And the bureaucratic procedures involved were time-consuming. M. had not changed his basic value priorities at all. Rather, he had adopted a purely defensive compromise. He stopped promoting his deep ecology philosophy publicly in order to retain credibility and standing among opponents of his principles and to retain his friendships with sheepowners.

And what is true of Mysterud is also true of thousands of other professional ecologists and environmentalists. These people often hold responsible positions in society where they might strengthen responsible environmental policy, but, given the exponential forces of growth, their publications, if any, are limited to narrowly professional and specialized concerns. Their writings are surely competent, but lack a deeper and more comprehensive perspective (although I admit that there are some brilliant exceptions to this).

If professional ecologists persist in voicing their value priorities, their jobs are often in danger, or they tend to lose influence and status among those who are in charge of overall policies.[2] Privately, they admit the necessity for deep and far-ranging changes, but they no longer speak out in public. As a result, people deeply concerned about ecology and the environment feel abandoned and even betrayed by the "experts" who work within the "establishment."

In ecological debates, many participants know a lot about particular conservation policies in particular places, and many others have strong views concerning fundamental philosophical questions of environmental ethics, but only a few have both qualities. When these people are silent, the loss is formidable.

For example, the complicated question concerning how industrial societies can increase energy production with the least undesirable consequences is largely a waste of time if this increase is pointless in relation to ultimate human ends. Thousands of experts hired by the government and other big institutions devote their time to this complicated problem, yet it is difficult for the public to find out or realize that many of these same experts consider the problem to be pointless and irrelevant. What these experts consider relevant are the problems of how to stabilize and eventually decrease consumption without losing genuine quality of life for humans. But they continue to work on the irrelevant problems assigned to them while, at the same time, failing to speak out, because the ultimate power is not in their hands.

2. A CALL TO SPEAK OUT

What I am arguing for is this: even those who completely subsume ecological policies under the narrow ends of human health and well-being cannot attain their modest aims, at least not fully, without being joined by the supporters of deep ecology. They need what these people have to contribute, and this will work in their favor more often than it will work against them. Those in charge of environmental policies, even if they are resource-oriented (and growth tolerating?) decision makers, will increasingly welcome, if only for tactical and not fundamental reasons, what deep ecology supporters have to say. Even though the more radical ethic may seem nonsensical or untenable to them, they know that its advocates are, in practice, doing conservation work that sooner or later must be done. They concur with the practice even though they operate from diverging theories. The time is ripe for professional ecologists to break their silence and express their deepest concerns more freely. A bolder advocacy of deep ecological concerns by those working within the shallow, resource-oriented environmental sphere is the best strategy for regaining some of the strength of this movement among the general public, thereby contributing, however modestly, to a turning of the tide.

What do I mean by saying that even the more modest aims of shallow environmentalism have a need for deep ecology? We can see this by considering the World Conservation Strategy—prepared by the International Union for the Conservation of Nature and Natural Resources (IUCN) in cooperation with the United Nations Environmental Programme (UNEP) and the World Wildlife Fund (WWF). The argument in this important document is thoroughly anthropocentric in the sense that all its recommendations are justified exclusively in terms of their effects upon human health and basic well-being.[3]

A more ecocentric environmental ethic is also recommended apparently for tactical reasons: "A new ethic, embracing plants and animals as well as people, is required for human societies to live in harmony with the natural world on which they depend for survival and well-being." But such an ethic would surely be more effective if it were acted upon by people who believe in its validity, rather than merely its usefulness. This, I think, will come to be understood more and more by those in charge of educational policies. Quite simply, it is indecent for a teacher to proclaim an ethic for tactical reasons only.

Furthermore, this point applies to all aspects of a world conservation strategy. Conservation strategies are more eagerly implemented by people who love what they are conserving, and who are convinced that what they love is intrinsically lovable. Such lovers will not want to hide their attitudes and values, rather they will increasingly give voice to them in public. They possess a genuine ethics of conservation, not merely a tactically useful instrument for human survival.

In short, environmental education campaigns can fortunately combine human-centered arguments with a practical environmental ethic based on either a deeper and more fundamental philosophic or religious perspective, and on a set of norms resting on intrinsic values. But the inherent strength of this overall position will be lost if those who work professionally on environmental problems do not freely give testimony to fundamental norms.

The above is hortatory in the positive etymological sense of that word. I seek "to urge, incite, instigate, encourage, cheer" (Latin: *hortari*). This may seem unacademic but I consider it justifiable because of an intimate relationship between hortatory sentences and basic philosophical views which I formulate in section 8. To trace what follows from fundamental norms and hypotheses is eminently philosophical.

3. WHAT IS DEEP ECOLOGY?

The phrase "deep ecology movement" has been used up to this point without trying to define it. One should not expect too much from definitions of movements; think, for example, of terms like "conservatism," "liberalism," or the "feminist movement." And there is no reason why supporters of movements should adhere exactly to the same definition, or to any definition, for that matter. It is the same with characterizations, criteria, or a set of proposed necessary conditions for application of the term or phrase. In what follows, a platform or key terms and phrases, agreed upon by George Sessions and myself, are tentatively proposed as basic to deep ecology.[4] More accurately, the sentences have a double function. They are meant to express important points which the great majority of supporters accept, implicitly or explicitly, at a high level of generality. Furthermore, they express a proposal to the effect that those who solidly reject one or more of these points should not be viewed as supporters of deep ecology. This might result because they are supporters of a shallow (or reform) environmental movement or rather they may simply dislike one or more of the eight points for semantical or other reasons. But they may well accept a different set of points which, to me, has roughly the same meaning, in which case I shall call them supporters of the deep ecology movement, but add that they *think* they disagree (maybe Henryk Skolimowski is an example of the latter). The eight points are:

1. The well-being and flourishing of human and non-human life on Earth have value in themselves (synonyms: intrinsic value, inherent worth). These values are independent of the usefulness of the non-human world for human purposes.

2. Richness and diversity of life forms contribute to the realization of these values and are also values in themselves.
3. Humans have no right to reduce this richness and diversity except to satisfy vital needs.
4. The flourishing of human life and cultures is compatible with a substantially smaller human population. The flourishing of non-human life *requires* a smaller human population.
5. Present human interference with the non-human world is excessive, and the situation is rapidly worsening.
6. Policies must therefore be changed. These policies affect basic economic, technological, and ideological structures. The resulting state of affairs will be deeply different from the present.
7. The ideological change will be mainly that of appreciating life quality (dwelling in situations of inherent value) rather than adhering to an increasingly higher standard of living. There will be a profound awareness of the difference between bigness and greatness.
8. Those who subscribe to the foregoing points have an obligation directly or indirectly to try to implement the necessary changes.

Comments on the Eight Points of the Platform

RE (1): This formulation refers to the biosphere, or more professionally, to the ecosphere as a whole (this is also referred to as "ecocentrism"). This includes individuals, species, populations, habitat, as well as human and non-human cultures. Given our current knowledge of all-pervasive intimate relationships, this implies a fundamental concern and respect.

The term "life" is used here in a more comprehensive non-technical way also to refer to what biologists classify as "non-living": rivers (watersheds), landscapes, ecosystems. For supporters of deep ecology, slogans such as "let the river live" illustrate this broader usage so common in many cultures.

Inherent value, as used in (1), is common in deep ecology literature (e.g., "The presence of inherent value in a natural object is independent of any awareness, interest, or appreciation of it by any conscious being").[5]

RE (2): The so-called simple, lower, or primitive species of plants and animals contribute essentially to the richness and diversity of life. They have value in themselves and are not merely steps toward the so-called higher or rational life forms. The second principle presupposes that life itself, as a process over evolutionary time, implies an increase of diversity and richness.

Complexity, as referred to here, is different from complication. For example, urban life may be more complicated than life in a natural setting without being more complex in the sense of multifaceted quality.

RE (3): The term "vital need" is deliberately left vague to allow for considerable latitude in judgment. Differences in climate and related factors, together with differences in the structures of societies as they now exist, need to be taken into consideration.

RE (4): People in the materially richest countries cannot be expected to reduce their excessive interference with the non-human world overnight. The stabilization and reduction of the human population will take time. Hundreds of years! Interim strategies need to be developed. But in no way does this excuse the present complacency. The extreme seriousness of our current situation must first be realized. And the longer we wait to make the necessary changes, the more drastic will be the measures needed. Until deep changes are made, substantial decreases in richness and diversity are liable to occur: the rate of extinction of species will be ten to one hundred or more times greater than in any other short period of earth history.

RE (5): This formulation is mild. For a realistic assessment, see the annual reports of the Worldwatch Institute in Washington, D.C.

The slogan of "non-interference" does not imply that humans should not modify some ecosystems, as do other species. Humans have modified the earth over their entire history and will probably continue to do so. At issue is the *nature and extent* of such interference. The per capita destruction of wild (ancient) forests and other wild ecosystems has been excessive in rich countries; it is essential that the poor do not imitate the rich in this regard.

The fight to preserve and extend areas of wilderness and near-wilderness ("free Nature") should continue. The rationale for such preservation should focus mainly on the ecological functions of these areas (one such function: large wilderness areas are required in the biosphere for the continued evolutionary speciation of plants and animals). Most of the present designated wilderness areas and game reserves are not large enough to allow for such speciation.

RE (6): Economic growth as it is conceived of and implemented today by the industrial states is incompatible with points (1) through (5). There is only a faint resemblance between ideal sustainable forms of economic growth and the present policies of industrial societies.

Present ideology tends to value things because they are scarce and because they have a commodity value. There is prestige in vast consumption and waste (to mention only several relevant factors).

Whereas "self-determination," "local community," and "think globally, act locally," will remain key terms in the ecology of human societies, nevertheless the implementation of deep changes requires increasingly global action: Action across borders.

Governments in Third World countries are mostly uninterested in deep ecological issues. When institutions in the industrial societies try to promote ecological measures through Third World governments, practically nothing is accomplished (e.g., with problems of desertification). Given this situation, support for global action through non-governmental international organizations becomes increasingly important. Many of these organizations are able to act globally "from grassroots to grassroots" thus avoiding negative governmental interference.

Cultural diversity today requires advanced technology, that is, techniques that advance the basic goals of each culture. So-called soft, intermediate, and alternative technologies are steps in this direction.

RE (7): Some economists criticize the term "quality of life" because it is supposedly vague. But, on closer inspection, what they consider to be vague is actually the nonquantifiable nature of the term. One cannot quantify adequately what is important for the quality of life as discussed here, and there is no need to do so.

RE (8): There is ample room for different opinions about priorities: what should be done first; what next? What is the most urgent? What is clearly necessary to be done, as opposed to what is highly desirable but not absolutely pressing? The frontier of the environmental crisis is long and varied, and there is a place for everyone.

The above formulations of the eight points may be useful to many supporters of the deep ecology movement. But some will certainly feel that they are imperfect, even misleading. If they need to formulate in a few words what is basic to deep ecology, then they will propose an alternative set of sentences. I shall of course be glad to refer to them as alternatives. There ought to be a measure of diversity in what is considered basic and common.

Why should we call the movement "the deep ecological movement"?[6] There are at least six other designations which cover most of the same issues: "Ecological Resistance," used by John Rodman in important discussions; "The New Natural Philosophy" coined by Joseph Meeker; "Eco-philosophy," used by Sigmund Kvaloy and others to emphasize (1) a highly critical assessment of the industrial growth societies from a general ecological point of view, and (2) the ecology of the human species; "Green Philosophy and Politics" (while the term "green" is often used in Europe, in the United States "green" has a misleading association with the rather "blue" Green agricultural revolution); "Sustainable Earth Ethics," as used by G. Tyler Miller; and "Ecosophy" (ecowisdom), which is my own favorite term. Others could be mentioned as well.

And so, why use the adjective "deep"? This question will be easier to answer after the contrast is made between shallow and deep ecological concerns. "Deep ecology" is not a philosophy in any proper academic sense, nor is it institutionalized as a religion or an ideology. Rather, what happens is that various persons come together in campaigns and direct actions. They form a circle of friends supporting the same kind of lifestyle which others may think to be "simple," but which they themselves see as rich and many-sided. They agree on a vast array of political issues, although they may otherwise support different political parties. As in all social movements, slogans and rhetoric are indispensable for in-group coherence. They react together against the same threats in a predominantly nonviolent way. Perhaps the most influential participants are artists and writers who do not articulate their insights in terms of professional philosophy, expressing themselves rather in art or poetry. For these reasons, I use the term "movement" rather than "philosophy." But it is essential that fundamental attitudes and beliefs are involved as part of the motivation for action.

4. DEEP VERSUS SHALLOW ECOLOGY

A number of key terms and slogans from the environmental debate will clarify the contrast between the shallow and the deep ecology movements.[7]

A. Pollution

Shallow Approach: Technology seeks to purify the air and water and to spread pollution more evenly. Laws limit permissible pollution. Polluting industries are preferably exported to developing countries.

Deep Approach: Pollution is evaluated from a biospheric point of view, not focusing exclusively on its effects on human health, but rather on life as a whole, including the life conditions of every species and system. The shallow reaction to acid rain, for example, is to tend to avoid action by demanding more research, and the attempt to find species of trees which will tolerate high acidity, etc. The deep approach concentrates on what is going on in the total ecosystem and calls for a high priority fight against the economic conditions and the technology responsible for producing the acid rain. The long-range concerns are one hundred years, at least.

The priority is to fight the deep causes of pollution, not merely the superficial, short-range effects. The Third and Fourth World countries cannot afford to pay the total costs of the war against pollution in their regions; consequently they require the assistance of the First and Second World countries. Exporting pollution is not only a crime against humanity, it is a crime against life in general.

B. Resources

Shallow Approach: The emphasis is upon resources for humans, especially for the present generation in affluent societies. In this view, the resources of the earth belong to those who have the technology to exploit them. There is confidence that resources will not be depleted because, as they get rarer, a high market price will conserve them, and substitutes will be found through technological progress. Further, plants, animals, and natural objects are valuable only as resources for humans. If no human use is known, or seems likely ever to be found, it does not matter if they are destroyed.

Deep Approach: The concern here is with resources and habitats for all life-forms for their own sake. No natural object is conceived of solely as a resource. This leads, then, to a critical evaluation of human modes of production and consumption. The question arises: to what extent does an increase in production and consumption foster ultimate human values? To what extent does it satisfy vital needs, locally or globally? How can economic, legal, and educational institutions be changed to counteract destructive increases? How can resource use serve the quality of life rather than the economic standard of living as generally promoted by consumerism? From a deep perspective, there is an emphasis upon an ecosystem approach rather than the consideration merely of isolated life-forms or local situations. There is a long-range maximal perspective of time and place.

C. Population

Shallow Approach: The threat of (human) "overpopulation" is seen mainly as a problem for developing countries. One condones or even applauds population increases in one's own country for short-sighted economic, military, or other reasons; an increase in the number of humans is considered as valuable in itself or as economically profitable. The issue of an "optimum population" for humans is discussed without reference to the question of an "optimum population" for other life-forms. The destruction of wild habitats caused by increasing human population is accepted as in inevitable evil, and drastic decreases of wildlife forms tend to be accepted insofar as species are not driven to extinction. Further, the social relations of animals are ignored. A long-term substantial reduction of the global human population is not seen to be a desirable goal. In addition, the right is claimed to defend one's borders against "illegal aliens," regardless of what the population pressures are elsewhere.

Deep Approach: It is recognized that excessive pressures on planetary life stem from the human population explosion. The pressure stemming from the industrial societies is a major factor, and population reduction must have the highest priority in those societies.

D. Cultural Diversity and Appropriate Technology

Shallow Approach: Industrialization of the Western industrial type is held to be the goal of developing countries. The universal adoption of Western technology is held to be compatible with cultural diversity, together with the conservation of the positive elements (from a Western perspective) of present non-industrial societies. There is a low estimate of deep cultural differences in non-industrial societies which deviate significantly from contemporary Western standards.

Deep Approach: Protection of non-industrial cultures from invasion by industrial societies. The goals of the former should not be seen as promoting lifestyles similar to those in the rich countries. Deep cultural diversity is an analogue on the human level to the biological richness and diversity of life-forms. A high priority should be given to cultural anthropology in general education programs in industrial societies.

There should be limits on the impact of Western technology upon present existing non-industrial countries and the Fourth World should be defended against foreign domination. Political and economic policies should favor subcultures within industrial societies. Local, soft technologies should allow for a basic cultural assessment of any technical innovations, together with freely expressed criticism of so-called advanced technology when this has the potential to be culturally destructive.

E. Land and Sea Ethics

Shallow Approach: Landscapes, ecosystems, rivers, and other whole entities of nature are conceptually cut into fragments, thus disregarding larger units and comprehensive gestalts. These fragments are regarded as the properties and resources of individuals, organizations or states. Conservation is argued in terms of "multiple use" and "cost/benefit analysis." The social costs and long-term global ecological costs of resource extraction and use are usually not considered. Wildlife management is conceived of as conserving nature for "future generations of humans." Soil erosion or the deterioration of ground water quality, for example, is noted as a human loss, but a strong belief in future technological progress makes deep changes seem unnecessary.

Deep Approach: The earth does not belong to humans. For example, the Norwegian landscapes, rivers, flora and fauna, and the neighboring sea are not the property of Norwegians. Similarly, the oil under the North Sea or anywhere else does not belong to any state or to humanity. And the "free nature" surrounding a local community does not belong to the local community.

Humans only inhabit the lands, using resources to satisfy vital needs. And if their non-vital needs come in conflict with the vital needs of nonhumans, then humans should defer to the latter. The ecological destruction now going on will not be cured by a technological fix. Current arrogant notions in industrial (and other) societies must be resisted.

F. Education and the Scientific Enterprise

Shallow Approach: The degradation of the environment and resource depletion requires the training of more and more "experts" who can provide advice concerning how to continue combining economic growth with maintaining a healthy environment. We are likely to need an increasingly more dominating and manipulative technology to "manage the planet" when global economic growth makes further environmental degradation inevitable. The scientific enterprise must continue giving priority to the "hard sciences" (physics and chemistry). High educational standards with intense competition in the relevant "tough" areas of learning will be required.

Deep Approach: If sane ecological policies are adopted, then education should concentrate on an increased sensitivity to non-consumptive goods, and on such consumables where there is enough for all. Education should therefore counteract the excessive emphasis upon things with a price tag. There should be a shift in concentration from the "hard" to the "soft" sciences which stress the importance of the local and global cultures. The educational objective of the World Conservation Strategy ("building support for conservation") should be given a high priority, but within the deeper framework of respect for the biosphere.

In the future, there will be no shallow environmental movement if deep policies are increasingly adopted by governments, and thus no need for a special deep ecological social movement.

5. BUT WHY A "DEEP" ECOLOGY?

The decisive difference between a shallow and a deep ecology, in practice, concerns the willingness to question, and an appreciation of the importance of questioning, every economic and political policy in public. This questioning is both "deep" and public. It asks "why" insistently and consistently, taking nothing for granted!

Deep ecology can readily admit to the practical effectiveness of homocentric arguments:

> It is essential for conservation to be seen as central to human interests and aspirations. At the same time, people—from heads of state to the members of rural communities—will most readily be brought to demand conservation if they themselves recognize the contribution of conservation to the achievement of their needs as perceived by them, and the solution of their problems, as perceived by them.[8]

There are several dangers in arguing solely from the point of view of narrow human interests. Some policies based upon successful homocentric arguments turn out to violate or unduly compromise the objectives of deeper argumentation. Further, homocentric arguments tend to weaken the motivation to fight for necessary social change, together with the willingness to serve a great cause. In addition, the complicated arguments in human-centered conservation documents such as the World Conservation Strategy go beyond the time and ability of many people to assimilate and understand. They also tend to provoke interminable technical disagreements among experts. Special interest groups with narrow short-term exploitive objectives, which run counter to saner ecological policies, often exploit these disagreements and thereby stall the debate and steps toward effective action.

When arguing from deep ecological premises, most of the complicated proposed technological fixes need not be discussed at all. The relative merits of alternative technological proposals are pointless if our vital needs have already been met. A focus on vital issues activates mental energy and strengthens motivation. On the other hand, the shallow environmental approach, by focusing almost exclusively on the technical aspects of environmental problems, tends to make the public more passive and disinterested in the more crucial non-technical, lifestyle-related, environmental issues.

Writers within the deep ecology movement try to articulate the fundamental presuppositions underlying the dominant economic approach in terms of value priorities, philosophy, and religion. In the shallow movement, questioning and argumentation comes to a halt long before this. The deep ecology movement is therefore "the ecology movement which questions deeper." A realization of the deep changes which are required, as outlined in the deep ecology eight point platform (discussed in #3 above) makes us realize the necessity of "questioning everything."

The terms "egalitarianism," "homocentrism," "anthropocentrism," and "human chauvinism" are often used to characterize points of view on the shallow-deep spectrum. But these terms usually function as slogans which are often open to misinterpretation. They can properly imply that man is in some respects only a "plain citizen" (Aldo Leopold) of the planet on a par with all other species, but they are sometimes interpreted as denying that humans have any "extraordinary" traits, or that, in situations involving vital interests, humans have no overriding obligations towards their own kind. But this would be a mistake: they have!

In any social movement, rhetoric has an essential function in keeping members fighting together under the same banner. Rhetorical formulations also serve to provoke interest among outsiders. Of the many excellent slogans, one might mention "nature knows best," "small is beautiful," and "all things hang together." But sometimes one may safely say that nature does not always know best, that small is sometimes dreadful, and that fortunately things hang together sometimes only loosely, or not at all.

Only a minority of deep ecology supporters are academic philosophers, such as myself. And while deep ecology cannot be a finished philosophical system, this does not mean that its philosophers should not try to be as clear as possible. So a discussion of deep ecology as a derivational system may be of value to clarify the many important premise/conclusion relations.

6. DEEP ECOLOGY ILLUSTRATED AS A DERIVATIONAL SYSTEM

Underlying the eight tenets or principles presented in section 3, there are even more basic positions and norms which reside in philosophical systems and in various world religions. Schematically we may represent the total views logically implied in the deep ecology movement by streams of derivations from the most fundamental norms and descriptive assumptions (level 1) to the particular decisions in actual life situations (level 4).

The pyramidal model has some features in common with hypothetico-deductive systems. The main difference, however, is that some sentences at the top (= deepest) level are normative, and preferably are expressed by imperatives. This makes it possible to arrive at imperatives at the lowest derivational level: the crucial level in terms of decisions. Thus, there are "oughts" in our premises as well as in our conclusions. We never move from an "is" to an "ought," or vice versa. From a logical standpoint, this is decisive!

The above premise/conclusion structure (or diagram) of a total view must not be taken too seriously. It is not meant in any restrictive way to characterize creative thinking within the deep ecology movement. Creative thinking moves freely in any direction. But many of us with a professional background in science and analytical philosophy find such a diagram helpful.

As we dig deeper into the premises of our thinking, we eventually stop. Those premises we stop at are our ultimates. When we philosophize, we all stop at different places. But we all use premises which, for us, are ultimate. They

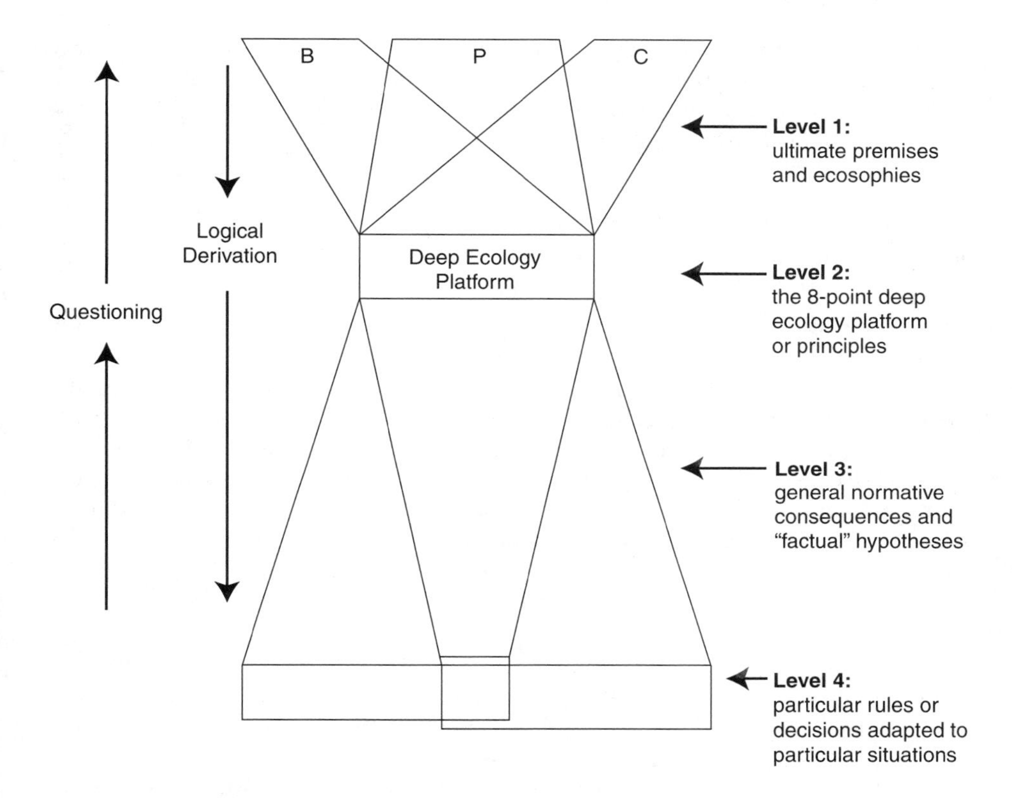

belong to level 1 in the diagram. Some will use a sentence like "Every life form has intrinsic value" as an ultimate premise, and therefore place it at level 1. Others try, as I do, to conceive of it as a conclusion based on a set of premises. For these people, this sentence does not belong to level 1. There will be different ecosophies corresponding to such differences.

Obviously, point 6 of the 8 point deep ecology tenets (see section 3) cannot belong to level 1 of the diagram. The statement "there must be new policies affecting basic economic structures" needs to be justified. If no logical justification is forthcoming, why not just assert instead that ecologically destructive "business as usual" economic policies should continue? In the diagram I have had ecosophies as ultimate premises in mind at level 1. None of the 8 points of the deep ecology principles belong at the ultimate level; they are derived as conclusions from premises at level 1.

Different supporters of the deep ecology movement may have different ultimates (level 1), but will nevertheless agree about level 2 (the 8 points).

Level 4 will comprise concrete decisions in concrete situations which appear as conclusions from deliberations involving premises at levels 1 to 3. An important point: supporters of the deep ecology movement act from deep premises. They are motivated, in part, from a philosophical or religious position.

7. MULTIPLE ROOTS OF THE DEEP ECOLOGY PLATFORM

The deep ecology movement seriously questions the presuppositions of shallow argumentation. Even what counts as a rational decision is challenged, because what is "rational" is always defined in relation to specific aims and goals. If a decision is rational in relation to the lower level aims and goals of our pyramid, but not in relation to the highest level, then this decision should not be judged to be rational. This is an important point! If an environmentally oriented policy decision is not linked to intrinsic values or ultimates, then its rationality has yet to be determined. The deep ecology movement connects rationality with a set of philosophical or religious foundations. But one cannot expect the ultimate premises to constitute rational conclusions. There are no "deeper" premises available.

Deep ecological questioning thus reveals the fundamental normative orientations of differing positions. Shallow argumentation stops before reaching fundamentals, or it jumps from the ultimate to the particular; that is, from level 1 to level 4.

But it is not only normative claims that are at issue. Most (perhaps all) norms presuppose ideas about how the world functions. Typically the vast majority of assertions needed in normative systems are descriptive (or factual). This holds at all the levels.

As mentioned before, it does not follow that supporters of deep ecology must have identical beliefs about ultimate issues. They do have common attitudes about intrinsic values in nature, but these can, in turn (at a still deeper level), be derived from different, mutually incompatible sets of ultimate beliefs.

Thus, while a specific decision may be judged as rational from within the derivational system (if there is such) of shallow ecology, it might be judged as irrational from within the derivational system of deep ecology. Again, it should be emphasized that what is rational from within the deep ecology derivational pyramid does not require unanimity in ontology and fundamental ethics. Deep ecology as a conviction, with its subsequently derived practical recommendations, can follow from a number of more comprehensive world views, from differing ecosophies.

Those engaged in the deep ecology movement have so far revealed their philosophical or religious homes to be mainly in Christianity, Buddhism, Taoism, Baha'i, or in various philosophies. The top level of the derivational pyramid can, in such cases, be made up of normative and descriptive principles which belong to these religions and philosophies.

Since the late 1970s, numerous Christians in Europe and America, including some theologians, have actively taken part in the deep ecology movement. Their interpretations of the Bible, and their theological positions in general, have been reformed from what was, until recently, a crude dominating anthropocentric emphasis.

There is an intimate relationship between some forms of Buddhism and the deep ecology movement. The history of Buddhist thought and practice, especially the principles of non-violence, non-injury, and reverence for life, sometimes makes it easier for Buddhists to understand and appreciate deep ecology than it is for Christians, despite a (sometimes overlooked) blessedness which Jesus recommended in peace-making. I mention Taoism chiefly because there is some basis for calling John Muir a Taoist, for instance, and Baha'i because of Lawrence Arturo.

Ecosophies are not religions in the classical sense. They are better characterized as *general* philosophies, in the sense of total views, inspired in part by the science of ecology. At level 1, a traditional religion may enter the derivational pyramid through a set of normative and descriptive assumptions which would be characteristic of contemporary interpretations (hermeneutical efforts) of that religion.

Supporters of the deep ecology movement act in contemporary conflicts on the basis of their fundamental beliefs and attitudes. This gives them a particular strength and a joyful expectation or hope for a greener future. But, naturally, few of them are actively engaged in a systematic verbal articulation of where they stand.

8. ECOSOPHY T AS AN EXAMPLE OF A DEEP ECOLOGICAL DERIVATIONAL SYSTEM

I call the ecosophy I feel at home with "Ecosophy T." My main purpose in announcing that I feel at home with Ecosophy T is didactic and dialectic. I hope to get others to announce their philosophy. If they say they have none, I maintain that they have, but perhaps don't know their own views, or are too modest or inhibited to proclaim what they believe. Following Socrates, I want to provoke questioning until others know where they stand on basic matters of life and death. This is done using ecological issues, and also by using Ecosophy T as a foil. But Socrates pretended in debate that he knew nothing. My posture seems to be the opposite. I may seem to know everything and to derive it magically from a small set of hypotheses about the world. But both interpretations are misleading! Socrates did not consistently claim to know nothing, nor do I in my Ecosophy T pretend to have comprehensive knowledge. Socrates claimed to know, for instance, about the fallibility of human claims to have knowledge.

Ecosophy T has only one ultimate norm: "Self-realization!" I do not use this expression in any narrow, individualistic sense. I want to give it an expanded meaning based on the distinction between a large comprehensive Self and narrow egoistic self as conceived of in certain Eastern traditions of *atman*.[9] This large comprehensive Self (with a capital "S") embraces all the life forms on the planet (and elsewhere?) together with their individual selves (jivas). If I were to express this ultimate norm in a few words, I would say: "Maximize (long-range, universal) Self-realization!" Another more colloquial way to express this ultimate norm would be to say "Live and let live!" (referring to all of the life forms and natural processes on the planet). If I had to give up the term fearing its inevitable misunderstanding, I would use the term "universal symbiosis." "Maximize Self-realization!" could, of course, be misinterpreted in the direction of colossal ego trips. But "Maximize symbiosis!" could be misinterpreted in the opposite direction of eliminating individuality in favor of collectivity.

Viewed systematically, not individually, maximum Self-realization implies maximizing the manifestations of all life. So next I derive the second term, "Maximize (long-range, universal) diversity!" A corollary is that the higher the levels of Self-realization attained by any person, the more any further increase depends upon the Self-realization of others. Increased self-identity involves increased identification with others. "Altruism" is a natural consequence of this identification.

This leads to a hypothesis concerning an inescapable increase of identification with other beings when one's own self-realization increases. As a result, we increasingly see ourselves in other beings, and others see themselves in us. In this way, the self is extended and deepened as a natural process of the realization of its potentialities in others.

By universalizing the above, we can derive the norm, "Self-realization for every being!" From the norm, "Maximize diversity!" and a hypothesis that maximum diversity implies a maximum of symbiosis, we can derive the norm "Maximize symbiosis!" Further, we work for life conditions such that there is a minimum of coercion in the lives of others. And so on![10] The eight points of the deep ecology platform are derived in a fairly simple way.

A philosophy as a world view inevitably has implications for practical situations. Like other ecosophies, Ecosophy T therefore moves on, without apologies, to the concrete questions of lifestyles. These will obviously show great variation because of differences in hypotheses about the world in which each of us lives, and in the "factual" statements about the concrete situations in which we make decisions.

I shall limit myself to a discussion of a couple of areas in which my "style" of thinking and behaving seem somewhat strange to friends and others who know a little about my philosophy.

First, I have a somewhat extreme appreciation of diversity; a positive appreciation of the existence of styles and behavior which I personally detest or find nonsensical (but which are not clearly incompatible with symbiosis); an enthusiasm for the "mere" diversity of species, or varieties within a genus of plants or animals; I support, as the head of a philosophy department, doctri-

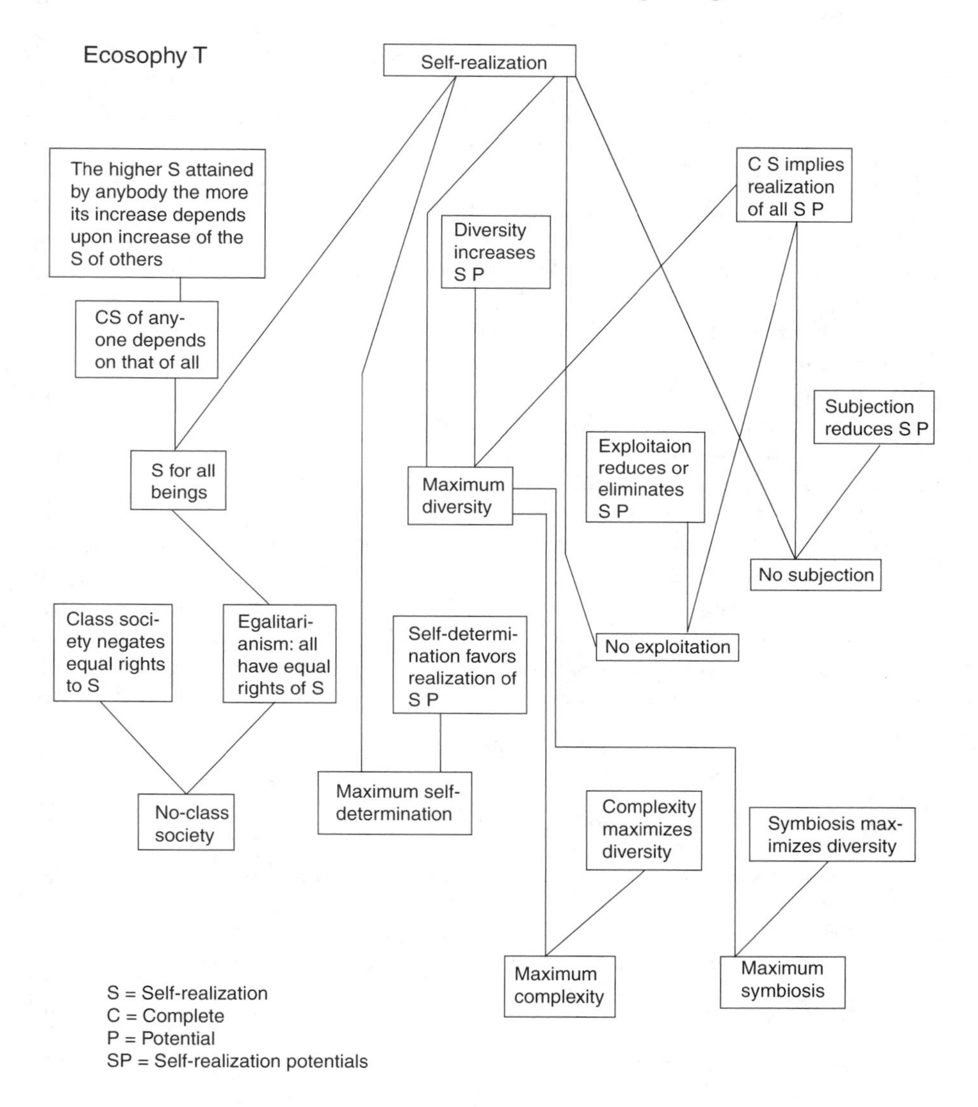

nal theses completely at odds with my own inclinations, with the requirement only that the authors are able to understand fairly adequately some basic features of the kind of philosophy I myself feel at home with; an appreciation of combinations of *seemingly* incompatible interests and behaviors, which makes for an increase of subcultures within industrial states and which might to some extent help future cultural diversity. So much for "diversity!"

Second, I have a somewhat extreme appreciation of what Kant calls "beautiful actions" (good actions based on inclination), in contrast with actions which are performed out of a sense of duty or obligation. The choice of the formulation "Self-realization!" is in part motivated by the belief that maturity in humans can be measured along a scale from selfishness to an increased realization of Self, that is, by broadening and deepening the self, rather than being measured by degrees of dutiful altruism. I see joyful sharing and caring as a natural process of growth in humans.

Third, I believe that multifaceted high-level Self-realization is more easily reached through a lifestyle which is "simple in means but rich in ends" rather than through the material standard of living of the average citizens of industrial states.

The simple formulations of the deep ecology platform and Ecosophy T are not meant primarily to be used among philosophers, but also in dialogues with the "experts." When I wrote to the "experts" and environmental professionals personally, asking whether they accept the eight points of the platform, many answered positively in relation to most or all of the points. And this includes top people in the ministries of oil and energy! Nearly all were willing to let their written answers be widely published. It is an open question, however, as to what extent they will try to influence their colleagues who use only shallow argumentation. But the main conclusion to be drawn is moderately encouraging: there are views of the human/nature relationship, widely accepted among established experts responsible for environmental decisions, which require a pervasive, substantial change of present policies in favor of our "living" planet, and these views are held not only on the basis of shortsighted human interests.

NOTES

1. For more about interspecific community relationships, see Arne Naess, "Self-realization in Mixed Communities of Humans, Bears, Sheep, and Wolves," *Inquiry* 22 (1979): 321–41; Naess and Ivar Mysterud, "Philosophy of Wolf Policies I: General Principles and Preliminary Exploration of Selected Norms," *Conservation Biology* 1, 1 (1987): 22–34.
2. These problems are discussed further in Naess's keynote address to the second international Conference Conservation on Biology held at the University of Michigan in May 1985; published as "Intrinsic Value: Will the Defenders of Nature Please Rise?" *Conservation Biology* (1986): 504–15.
3. IUCN, *World Conservation Strategy: Living Resource Conservation for Sustainable Development* (Gland, Switzerland, 1980), section 13 ("Building Support for Conservation").
4. The deep ecology principles (or platform) were agreed upon during a camping trip in Death Valley, California (April, 1984) and first published in George Sessions (ed.), *Ecophilosophy VI* newsletter (May, 1984). They have subsequently appeared in a number of publications.
5. Tom Regan, "The Nature and Possibility of an Environmental Ethics," *Environmental Ethics* 3 (1981): 19–34, citation on p. 30.
6. I proposed the name "Deep, Long-Range Ecology Movement" in a lecture at the Third World Future Research conference in Bucharest in September 1972. A summary of that lecture ("The Shallow and the Deep, Long-Range Ecology Movement") was published in *Inquiry* 16 (1973): 95–100. Within the deep ecology movement it is fairly common to use the term "deep ecologist," whereas "shallow ecologist," I am

glad to say, is rather uncommon. Both terms may be considered arrogant and slightly misleading. I prefer to use the awkward, but more egalitarian expression "supporter of the deep (or shallow) ecology movement," avoiding personification. Also, it is common to call deep ecology consistently anti-anthropocentric. This has led to misconceptions: see my "A Defense of the Deep Ecology Movement," *Environmental Ethics* 5 (1983).

7. The "shallow/deep" dichotomy is rough. Richard Sylvan has proposed a much more subtle classification; see his "A Critique of Deep Ecology," *Discussion Papers in Environmental Philosophy*, RSSS, Australian National University, No. 12 (1985).
8. *World Conservation Strategy*, section 13 (concluding paragraph).
9. The term *atman* is not taken in its absolutistic senses (not as a permanent indestructible "soul"). This makes it consistent with those Buddhist denials (the *avatman doctrine*) that the *atman* is to be taken in absolutist senses. Within the Christian tradition some thelogians distinguish "ego" and "true self" in ways similar to these distinctions in Eastern religions. See the ecophilosophical interpretation of the gospel of Luke in Stephen Verney's *Onto the New Age* (Glasgow: Collins, 1976), pp. 33–41.
10. Many authors take some steps toward derivational structures, offering mild systematizations. The chapter "Environmental Ethics and Hope" (in G. Tyler Miller, *Living in the Environment*, 3rd ed. [Belmont: Wadsworth, 1983]) is a valuable start, but the derivational relations are unclear. The logic and semantics of simple models of normative systems are briefly discussed in my "Notes on the Methodology of Normative Systems," *Methodology and Science* 10 (1977): 64–79. For a defense of the thesis that as soon as people assert anything at all, they assume a total view, implicitly involving an ontology, methodology, epistemology, and ethics, see my "Reflections about Total Views," *Philosophy and Phenomenological Research* 25 (1964–65): 16–29. The best and wittiest warning against taking systematizations too seriously is to be found in Søren Kierkegaard, *Concluding Unscientific Postscript*.

    For criticism and defense of my fundamental norm ("Self-realization"), together with my answer, see *In Sceptical Wonder: Essays in Honor of Arne Naess* (Oslo: University Press, 1982). My main exposition of Ecosophy T was originally offered in the Norwegian work, *Okologi, samfunn og livsstil* (Oslo: University Press, 5th ed., 1976). Even there, the exposition is sketchy. (Editor's note: Naess's Norwegian book has been revised and reissued as Arne Naess (translated and edited by David Rothenberg), *Ecology, Community and Lifestyle* [Cambridge: Cambridge University Press, 1989].)

Demystifying the Critiques of Deep Ecology

Harold Glasser

Affiliated with the Foundation for Deep Ecology, Harold Glasser is general editor of Selected Works of Arne Naess, *a nine-volume collection that will be published in 1998.*

I. INTRODUCTION

Discussions of Naess's deep ecology approach to ecophilosophy (DEA), while widespread throughout the environmental philosophy literature, are often suffused with misconceptions and misunderstandings. Some of these are relatively trivial, but others, unfortunately, are quite serious. The more serious interpretation errors often result in misrepresentation and distortion of the DEA. When laden with these errors, the weight of even the most penetrating criticisms is diminished.

In this essay I offer an explication of the DEA, Naess's general, philosophical approach for promoting the development of ecologically responsible policies, lifestyles, and concrete decisions. The DEA must be distinguished from both the deep ecology movement and Naess's personal ecosophy (Ecosophy T). I will offer neither an analysis of the deep ecology movement, the loose group of individuals who endorse the deep ecology platform (but may not actually employ the DEA), nor an evaluation of Naess's personal ecosophy (Ecosophy T), formed by his particular implementation of the DEA. Although I regret adding yet another expression to this already confusing stew of terms, I will use the expressions "deep ecology" and "DEA" as shorthand for my particular interpretation of Naess's deep ecology approach to ecophilosophy.

The purposes of this essay are threefold: first, to highlight several of the misconceptions, second, to suggest some possible reasons for their prevalence,

An earlier version of this article appeared in Nina Witoszek (ed.), *Rethinking Deep Ecology* (Oslo: Center for Development and the Environment, University of Oslo, 1996), pp. 88–106. Although an extension and complete revision, this paper also draws liberally from Harold Glasser, "Deep Ecology Clarified: A Few Fallacies and Misconceptions." *The Trumpeter: Journal of Ecosophy* 12 (1995): 138–42.

and, third, to offer an alternative, hopefully clarifying, interpretation of the DEA. I am not suggesting that there are not valid explanations for the misconceptions and misunderstandings, quite the contrary. My primary purpose, however, is to show that while these errors of interpretation are unfortunate, they are frequently avoidable. By sincerely employing the *principle of charity* we can reap both a more insightful understanding of the DEA and a more profound understanding of its problems. And by seriously grappling with these issues, we spontaneously engage in the very process that Naess urges is essential to forging sound, mutually supportive, and pluralistic responses to the ecological crisis.

II. MISCONCEPTIONS AND FALLACIES

People seem either to feel sympathy with the term "deep ecology" and what it conjures up (intrinsic value, a search for "root" causes, efforts to articulate one's total view, Naess and Sessions' "deep ecology platform," etc.) or they tend to feel antipathy towards the term.[1] A dynamic has emerged where supporters frequently neglect to give the DEA a critical eye, while foes often fail to offer it a receptive ear.

While some may argue about whether Naess should be considered as the "father" of deep ecology, he is undeniably the source for the interpretation of deep ecology I consider here. A host of expositions and criticisms of deep ecology (or elements of it) have been put forth.[2] Many of these contain careful and coherent analyses. Even some of these, however, are hindered by one or more forms of four weaknesses common to discussion of deep ecology.[3] My purpose in raising these "weaknesses" is not to criticize particular authors or engage in elaborate refutations, but rather to call attention to the dearth of accessible, thorough, and balanced treatments of Naess's DEA. This problem, regrettably, holds equally for its supporters and critics alike.

The first weakness consists of glossing over details when developing expository discussions. A common instance is the unfortunate use of the term "deep ecologists" for supporters or theoreticians of the deep ecology movement. While at first glance this seems like a relatively trivial use of shorthand, it has significant semantic implications, the most serious of which is that it implicitly suggests the existence of a counterpart to "deep ecologists," namely "shallow ecologists." This is an assertion Naess never intended to make and many times has counseled against. His use of the depth metaphor, following Kierkegaard, was directed at our level of problematizing.[4] Its purpose is to draw attention to the need for publicly questioning all of the practices, policies, values, and assumptions that propel the ecological crisis.

The term "deep" is not meant as a simple modifier to denote a particular branch of ecology. If we attempt to isolate "musical" from "chairs," the phrase "musical chairs" loses its meaning. Furthermore, the existence of a term "musical chairs" does not, by logical necessity, imply the existence of a similarly meaningful converse, "nonmusical chairs." Deep ecology is no more, or less, about *ecology* than economic science is about *science.* "Economic science," as a discipline and as commonly practiced, is not about making hypotheses regarding isolatable phenomena, developing controlled experiments to explain the phenomena, and confirming or refuting the original hypotheses through testing. Deep ecology is merely *informed* by our contemporary understanding of ecology as economic science is *informed* by our contemporary understanding of science. Just as it makes more sense to call a practitioner of economic science an "economist," it might, in many respects, be more apropos to refer to theoreticians or practitioners of the DEA as "deepists"; people who subscribe to, *inter alia,* a philosophy of publicly questioning all of the practices, policies, values, and assumptions that propel the ecological crisis. There is, however, no logical necessity that people subscribing to such a view of "deep questioning" will *necessarily* arrive at more ecologically sound policies, or personal practices, only a sincere *belief* that such reflection might help illuminate contradictions and conflicts. In any case, we cannot deny the obvious possibility of tainting those who do not subscribe to such a perspective with a derogatory sheen. While Naess, as an expert in semantics, cannot be absolved for the unfortunate semantic implications of his terminology, it behooves us to keep in mind his stated intention.

A second, quite common shortcoming results from drawing inferences from a scanty, selective, or dated reading of the literature or relying upon secondary or tertiary sources. The broad range, depth, volume, and evolutionary nature of Naess's philosophical writings demand a particularly labor intensive commitment to comprehensive analysis. Naess's publications on deep ecology[5] draw heavily from earlier work on empirical and applied semantics,[6] total views,[7] normative systems theory,[8] gestalt ontology,[9] scepticism,[10] democracy,[11] Spinoza,[12] Gandhi,[13] and the philosophy of science[14] as well as his lifelong love of the mountains.[15] The DEA represents a culmination and integration of Naess's life of philosophical inquiry fused with his political activism and love of nature. Naess's breadth, many unpublished papers, and tendency to revise, revise, and re-revise, however, make this weakness difficult to avoid even with a commitment to exhaustive analysis.

Examples of the "selective" reading weakness include assertions that deep ecology is inherently fascist, anti-humanist, or anti-feminist because the deep ecology platform and the vast majority of deep ecology writings fail to make explicit reference to denouncing fascism, oppression of women, and the general domination of some humans by other humans. To argue, however, that because Nazis were concerned with the welfare of animals and deep ecology theorists express concern for animals, then deep ecology has Fascist leanings, is simply guilt by association. Furthermore, the first statement of the deep ecology platform (DEP) makes explicit reference to the intrinsic value of *all* life, human and non-human alike and the second platform statement venerates the diversity of all life forms. While the particular means of achieving the goals of the DEP are left open, it seems fairly certain that any means which do not, at a minimum, honor and respect diversity, both human and non-human, will be in direct contradiction to these platform statements.

The deep ecology movement has as its primary focus the reversal of the ecological crisis. This focus, however, in no way precludes or undermines the overlapping concerns of the peace and social justice movements. Quite the contrary, it calls out for collaboration. The DEA is consistent with many possible interpretations of, and responses to, the roots and coevolutionary development of the ecological crisis.

The third, and perhaps most significant weakness, may result from a compounding of the two previous shortcomings, but is not necessarily derivative of them. It arises from incorporating critical misconceptions and methodological or logical fallacies. I will discuss five misconceptions and five methodological or logical fallacies.

The first misconception consists of equating ecocentrism with misanthropy. Ecocentrism refers to a valuation approach that characterizes ecosystems as wholes and defines value in terms of the well-being and flourishing of these ecosystems; it is an assertion of the intrinsic value of both whole ecosystems and every constituent. Misanthropy is literally the hatred of mankind. Clearly, the two terms are not equivalent. Furthermore, since humans are elements of ecosystems, it seems ludicrous to even suggest the conclusion that ecocentrism somehow implies misanthropy.

The second misconception consists of identifying "Self-realization!," the ultimate norm of Naess's personal Ecosophy T, or "biospherical egalitarianism in principle" as singular ultimate norms of deep ecology. Such conclusions, however, are precluded by Naess's repeated emphasis upon the existence of a wide plurality of ultimate norms that are consistent with the DEA.

The third misconception consists of attempting to isolate the DEP as the "heart" of deep ecology, treating the DEP *as* deep ecology, or dismissing the DEP as "non-distinctive." All three conclusions fail to acknowledge the gestalt nature of the DEA as a philosophical system, particularly its emphasis upon total views and its incorporation of normative systems theory.

The fourth misconception consists of pinpointing the genealogy of deep ecology in a stoic attempt to overcome the alienation resulting from the tragic loss of free nature. While this interpretation may be consistent with some supporters' views, it is inconsistent as *the* explanation, given the plurality of other viable explanations. For instance, Naess's repeated emphasis upon: the Pyrrhonian sceptics *ataraxia*,[16] the questioning of technological optimism, economic rationality, costs associated with biodiversity loss, etc., and the importance of learning how to live "rightly," with virtue and simplicity.

The fifth misconception consists of associating Naess's use of "depth" with a statement of an individual's character or the level of their willingness to reject anthropocentrism. While we cannot deny the unfortunate semantic implications of Naess's "depth metaphor," it is clear that his focus was directed at our willingness to raise and take seriously the search for fundamental causes and the consideration of radical responses.

The first methodological or logical fallacy consists of assuming that extension of care and concern to non-humans necessarily implies reducing care for humans. Do parents with nine children necessarily care less for each child than parents with two children?

The second methodological or logical fallacy consists of presuming that discussions of population reduction imply draconian measures. Why should one assume, however, that population cannot be reduced slowly, over centuries, and through democratic means?

The third methodological or logical fallacy consists of surmising that acceptance of "non-instrumental value" or "objective intrinsic value"[17] necessarily imply granting equal moral standing to all entities or the grading of intrinsic value. Naess uses the two terms, "inherent value" and "intrinsic value" interchangeably and in a non-technical sense that is ontological in origin. Efforts to preserve one species over another need not resort to moral arguments, as is often conjectured. Galvanized by an awareness of life's exigencies, these efforts do, however, necessitate accepting and evaluating a broad range of normative, sometimes conflicting criteria. Naess discusses walking in the mountains of Norway where he chooses to place his feet on the more common *Salix herbacea* rather than on the small, incredibly beautiful, and less common *Gentiana nivalis.*[18] His employment of *felt nearness* in no way implies a belief that either plant, or even Naess himself, has more right to live and blossom. Similarly, justification of this act does not necessitate any grading of intrinsic value.

The fourth methodological or logical fallacy consists of inferring that acceptance of intrinsic value necessitates acceptance of moral monism.[19] Again, I must emphasize that Naess's concept of "intrinsic" or "inherent" value is, however, ontological, not ethical or epistemological.[20] The DEA does not rest on a single moral principle, quite the contrary. It assumes both that there cannot exist perfect sets of principles to guide us through all moral dilemmas and that because each problem is context dependent and because a diverse array of viable alternatives usually exists, the existence of single "right" answers for every quandary is illusory.

The fifth methodological or logical fallacy consists of positing that because humans are a part of nature and because "nature knows best," then whatever humans do qualifies as natural, and hence morally unobjectionable. It is certainly true that humans are *a part* of nature and that this belief is consistent with the DEA. The assertion that "nature knows best," that it has an identifiable collective consciousness and some conception of "best" (utilitarian?, individualistic?, democratic?), however, is inconsistent with any theorizing on deep ecology I recognize. Furthermore, the DEP is quite specific about acknowledging that humans are also *apart* from nature, with unique obligations and special responsibilities for preserving the existing endowment of richness and diversity.

The final form of weakness is represented by the few disingenuous attempts at critical analyses that seek to set up deep ecology as a "straw man." These efforts, which often make use of the previously discussed examples, undertake to dismiss deep ecology and its contributions by demonstrating that it has fatal flaws. While some of the other weaknesses are more subtle, and thus insidious, these undertakings are usually "hatchet jobs" with transparent ulterior motives.

This brief review of the significant range of problems associated with the interpretation and exposition of deep ecology highlights the need for more accessible, thorough, and balanced treatments of Naess's DEA.[21] One possible explanation for the scarcity of such treatments rests in the difficulty of tracing Naess's own meanings. Following the zetetic sceptic tradition he eschews dogma by asserting that his own work is searching, "on the way"; it is necessarily fragmentary and ever amenable to improvements, modifications, and elaborations.[22] This evolutionary nature of the DEA along with Naess's tendency for liberal revisions, at times, however, make it truly difficult to pin down his interpretation of particular elements of the DEA.[23]

III. ORIGINS OF THE MISUNDERSTANDINGS: SOME SPECULATION

Additional difficulty in tracing Naess's meanings may result from his philosophical commitment to vagueness as a device for encouraging widespread acceptance of the DEA.[24] "Methodological vagueness" is a sophisticated semantic device for facilitating the acceptance and agreement of statements and notions by emphasizing the positive aspect of ambiguity that is sometimes associated with a high level of generalization. Naess maintains that this device, by leaving open issues of an inconsequential nature, acts to facilitate communication and agreement on the consequential ones. One can readily appreciate the pragmatic merits of eliminating *irrelevant* and contentious details. However, one cannot help but also wonder if in the process of practical decision-making, *relevant* but contentious details might be glossed over. This may, unfortunately, lead some readers to mistake the benign motivation of Naess's methodological vagueness for simple rhetorical vagueness.

While Naess's sincerity, depth of intention, and intellectual integrity are beyond question, the propriety of emphasizing methodological vagueness raises some concern. Methodological vagueness has an antipodal side. As Naess himself has recognized, it can be employed to obfuscate conflicts, as with discussions that fail to point out the oxymoronic nature of the term "sustainable development."[25] As high level goals, sustainability and development (in the sense of access to health care, food, shelter, clean water, education, free nature, etc.) are admirable and certainly worthy of advocating, but coupled they tend to belie links to neoclassical welfare economics and the underlying conflicts between ecological sustainability and perpetual economic growth. Because the border separating issues of a consequential and an inconsequential nature is amorphous and subjective, as well as quite wide, the use of methodological vagueness can introduce a tension between parallel efforts orchestrated to isolate and clarify fundamental conflicts (deep questioning). There is a tradeoff between the benefits associated with positive expressions of ambiguity and the costs associated with its capacity for exploitation or potential for generating further confusion.

Failing to directly address "border" issues, like whether or not privileged ontological perceptions of nature exist, may only beg further speculation, confusion, and misconception. In order to fully reap the benefits of methodological vagueness, readers must be made aware that it has been employed both with deliberation and without attempt to obfuscate. The end result, otherwise, may be to turn away some possible supporters who eschew vagueness or, worse yet, wonder if the technique is being employed to avoid the asperities of deeper analyses.

Also central to the DEA is Naess's antidogmatism and insistence on radical pluralism. Naess, convinced that a successful response to the ecological crisis demands a diversity of perspectives, approaches, and lifestyles, imposes a minimum of external constraints while encouraging individuals to develop their own, critically thought-out total views. By offering little guidance as to whether acceptance or rejection of particular norms or hypotheses is mandatory, this approach, however, also tends to stimulate further confusion over, and criticism of, the DEA. This leads some to believe that Naess makes it unnecessarily difficult for his readers to piece together a coherent picture of the DEA.

Questions arising from the use of methodological vagueness and the insistence upon radical pluralism are bound to generate frustration; they are an inevitable consequence of efforts to comprehend Naess's writings. Multiple readings of Naess's full range of work are necessary to absorb the depth and complexity of his contribution to environmental thought and policy. Readers will, however, be rewarded well for their journey.

IV. THE DEEP ECOLOGY APPROACH: AN ATTEMPT AT CLARIFICATION

Presentations of the DEA as a systematic philosophical framework for supporting the development of ecologically inspired total views (as I attempt to do below) have been largely absent from other discussions of deep ecology.[26] The ontologically inspired DEA asks us to reconsider the notion of fundamental human/environment and spiritual/physical cleavages.[27] It weaves descriptive and prescriptive premises into a normative framework for melding a value system with a world view. A primary goal is to contribute towards arresting the ecological crisis by helping individuals to reason consistently from their ultimate beliefs.

The DEA should be viewed as a Gestalt where not only is the whole more than the sum of its parts, but the parts, as coevolving entities themselves, are more than *mere* parts. In my view the DEA consists of at least six coupled elements: (1) the unifying notion of total views, (2) the DEA as a normative-derivational system, the reasoning techniques, (3) "deep questioning" and (4) "loose derivation," (5) the adoption of ultimate premises that incorporate some form of "wide identification," and (6) the eight points of the deep ecology platform.

Naess argues that humans act as if we have systematic conceptual structures for relating to the world, *total views,* which integrate "our basic assumptions, our life philosophy, and our decisions in everyday life,"[28] whether or not we attempt to make such structures explicit. Contending that each individual's decisions regarding society and nature are guided by total views, Naess asserts that we should strive to clearly articulate them. While the process of articulating one's total view places significant demands upon the individual, Naess argues that we have no choice: "The essential idea is that, as humans, we are responsible in our actions as to motivations and premises relative to any question that can be asked of us."[29] The primary purpose of the DEA is to support individuals in carrying out this responsibility and thereby to facilitate democratic group decision-making.

Naess characterizes the DEA as a normative-derivational system. The systematization of the DEA is normative because it delimits the set of viable ultimate premises. The approach is derivational by virtue of being a logical systematization, where concrete consequences "follow" from premises and hypotheses. Naess's systematization is not derivational in the traditional hypothetico-deductive sense, but derivational only in his sense of being predicated upon an identifiable reasoning process.

The description of the DEA as a normative-derivational system is a pedagogical device for elucidating Naess's process of systematically reasoning from ultimate premises to concrete decisions or actions. The approach employs two reasoning techniques. "Loose derivation" is the synthetic process of building successively more particular norm-hypothesis chains by continually adding new, non-ultimate norms and hypotheses. It is "loose" in the sense that more precise norm and hypothesis statements do not follow *directly* from ultimate premises; they also depend upon the character of the additional, successively more precise norms and hypotheses. The inverse process, "deep questioning," allows norm conflicts to be examined and "deconstructed." It acts as a sort of touchstone to insure that derived consequences are consistent with each higher level norm and hypothesis. New information and insight may, at times, warrant the revision, or even the abandonment, of preceding norms and premises.

The DEA rests upon the assumption that certain, very basic premises are unproven or unprovable; the deep questioning process must eventually grind to a halt. Ultimate premises or ultimate norms are the unavoidable foundations upon which all theories or generalizations are built. Because of their generality, complexity, and inherent lack of preciseness, an almost infinite variety of ultimate norms exist. Naess argues that a wide variety of ultimate norms are consistent with the DEA.[30] As I understand Naess, the only restriction placed upon the set of ultimate norms to insure that they are deep ecological ultimate norms is that the DEP be derivable from them.[31] I use Naess's term, *wide identification,* to refer to this common element of deep ecological ultimate premises. It represents, at a minimum, an expansion of one's sphere of concern to include non-humans. It is often characterized by the perception that all life is interdependent; common goals bind all living beings to the life process. In its most expansive form, wide-identification is the perception that the interests of *all* entities in nature (both living and non-living, ecosystems and individuals) are our own. This is the notion of "Self-realization!" employed by Naess as the ultimate norm in Ecosophy T. While Naess may, in his own personal ecosophy, prefer this most expansive notion of identification, such a wide-reaching perspective is by no means necessary for acceptance of the DEP.

The DEP was worked out and agreed upon by Arne Naess and George Sessions in 1984.[32] It was intended to express "the most general and basic views" that supporters of the deep ecology movement (DEM) have in common.[33] Naess points out that the DEP was *not* supposed to indicate common views in concrete situations.[34] On the level of symbolizing a "call for ecological sustainability," the platform statements can be viewed as representing the general views held by supporters of the DEM. By outlining value priorities and calling for operational constraints on human behavior, the DEP acts as a filter, affecting the derivation process at all levels. On another level, however, the platform is, in some sense, a skeleton outline of a total view and thus represents *more* than basic and general views. For instance the DEP's first statement, representing a belief in the "intrinsic value" of all life, really constitutes an ultimate norm and should not be characterized as simply a "general and basic view."[35] It is relevant to point out that a less controversial first statement, simply advocating the importance of richness and diversity as non-use values, might facilitate a wider acceptance of the other seven platform statements.

Elements two through five of the DEA refer to the general process of reasoning from fundamentals to form total views. The DEP, as a synthetic product of this reasoning process, should be distinguished from it. Figure 1 outlines the *general process* of reasoning from fundamentals to arrive at concrete consequences, a primary element of the DEA. It explicitly leaves out the DEP because it represents a particular collection of norms and hypotheses obtained by engaging in the process. For a priori acceptance of the DEP violates the aim of the DEA; that is, it presupposes the existence of, and active engagement in, a similar process. What I am claiming is that the DEP should be distinguished from the reasoning process itself. In keeping with Naess's original suggestion, it must be put forth, and seen, as one possible precisation that helps to fill out the DEA by acting as a tentative set of guidelines for approaching the derivation of ecologically responsible concrete consequences.[36] Individuals should, however, scrutinize the DEP with the same deep questioning attitude that they would use to analyze any other collections of norms and premises. The goal of the DEA, after all, is to help individuals develop their own deep ecological total views.

Figure 1 Process Diagram of the Normative Systems Aspect of the DEA

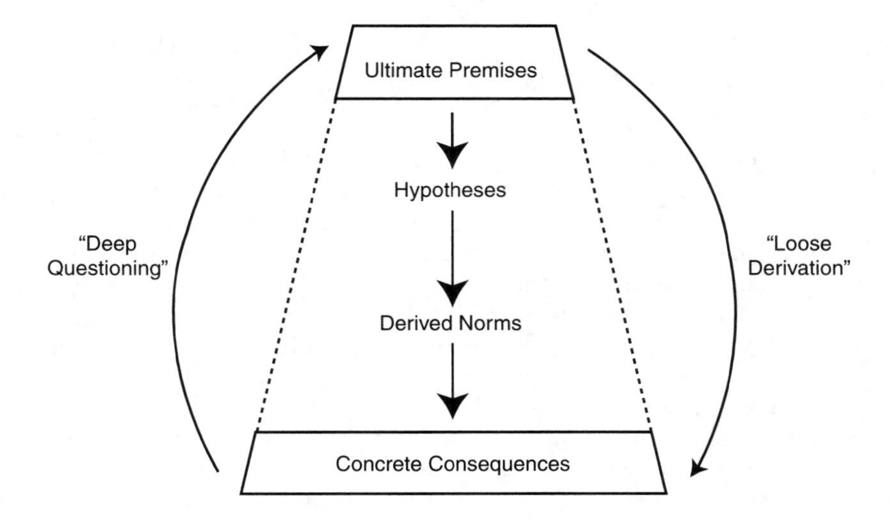

I have deliberately not adhered to Naess's four-level systematization in the process schema because the distinctions between levels 2 and 3, general principles and more or less general consequences derived from the DEP (i.e., lifestyles), are fuzzy. To reflect the vagaries of clearly distinguishing between and ordering these two categories, derived norms and hypotheses that fall under these headings are simply depicted between the dotted lines and the two clear boundaries, ultimate premises (our starting point) and concrete consequences (particular actions or decisions—our end point). My focus here is to draw attention to Naess's process for analyzing normative systems and to emphasize his strategy for helping us to construct our own total views. Naess enjoins us to make this effort to articulate our norms and hypotheses so that the entire decision-making process is readily discernible—to both ourselves and others.

The process figure also draws attention to two crucial techniques for developing a total view, *loose derivation* and *deep questioning*. Figure 1 is intended to show how the two techniques work in unison, enabling individuals to arrive at a variety of concrete rules and decisions that maintain consistency with ultimate premises. As has been mentioned before, a manifold of concrete consequences can follow from this built-in pluralism. The attraction of Naess's derivational structure is that it affords a substantial degree of flexibility. Such a perspective is compatible with a variety of, sometimes dissonant, ultimate norms, including those inspired by Christian stewardship, ecofeminism, creation myths, enlightened self-interest, Buddhism, Hinduism, scientific ecology, ecological integrity, social ecology, Taylor's "Respect for Nature,"[38] biospherical egalitarianism in principle, Wilson's Biophilia Hypothesis,[39] and Naess's "Self-realization!"[40] to name a few. It allows individuals to both maintain divergent fundamental premises and arrive at their own conclusions while still maintaining consistency with the goal of ecological harmony.

In closing, Naess reminds us that "we need to integrate life theory and life practice, clarify our value priorities, distinguish life quality from mere standard of life, and contribute in our own way to diminish unsustainability."[41] This quotation marries Naess's eudaemonic concern with his zetetic sceptic's response to the inherent vagueness of the sustainability notion. Here is where the logic of the DEA shines; society may never agree upon a satisfactory definition of "sustainability," but clear cases of unsustainability can be observed. These should be sought out and redressed while inquiry directed towards clarifying and elaborating the sustainability notion continues. The DEA is strongest on justification for a precautionary principle strategy that argues, in the face of ignorance and uncertainty, to preserve the existing heritage and thereby not foreclose options. It runs into some difficulty, however, in the areas of how to inculcate wide-identification, how to assess "vital needs," and how to inspire value priorities that insure environmental protection in the face of conflicting choices and opportunities.

The DEA's focus upon praxis (individual responsibility and action) separates it from more traditionally descriptive inquiries into ecophilosophy.[42] The significance of the DEA rests in its focus upon improving decision-making. The significance is not in the arguable *correctness* of the approach, but in its ability to help structure and focus our thinking about the environmental implications of individual and collective decisions. Naess's DEA has provided inspiration and one viable foundation for environmental protection, much work awaits us!

NOTES

1. Nina Witoszek, the editor of the Center for Development and the Environment Occasional Papers Volume, argues that many people simply feel ambivalence towards deep ecology. While Witoszek may be correct, my experiences in lecturing on deep ecology and my awareness of the discussions in the literature, however, tend to strongly controvert this assertion.
2. The following discursive bibliographic entry attempts to highlight a few of the more salient expositions and criticisms of deep ecology.

   References focusing upon or highlighting exposition of deep ecology include: Jim Cheney, "Ecology, Community and Lifestyle: An Outline of an Ecosophy (a review of)," *Environmental Ethics* 13 (1991): 263–273; Bill Devall and George Sessions, *Deep Ecology: Living as if Nature Mattered* (Salt Lake City: Gibbs Smith Books, 1985); Arne Naess, *Ecology, Community, and Lifestyle: Outline of an Ecosophy*, translated and edited by David Rothenberg (Cambridge: Cambridge University Press, 1989a); Peter Reed, "Man Apart: An Alternative to the Self-Realization Approach," *Environmental Ethics* 11 (1989): 53–69; Peter Reed and David Rothenberg, ed., *Wisdom and the Open Air: The Norwegian Roots of Deep Ecology* (Minneapolis: University of Minnesota Press, 1993); David Rothenberg, "A Platform of Deep Ecology," *Environmentalist* 7 (1987): 185–190; David Rothenberg, *Is It Painful to Think: Conversations with Arne Naess* (Minneapolis: University of Minnesota Press,

1993); George Sessions, ed., *Deep Ecology for the Twenty-First Century* (Boston: Shambhala, 1995); Warwick Fox, *Toward a Transpersonal Ecology: Developing New Foundations for Environmentalism* (Boston and London: Shambhala, 1990).

Books or articles where criticism or exposition of deep ecology figures centrally in the authors' arguments include: Robin Attfield, "Sylvan, Fox, and Deep Ecology: A View from the Continental Shelf," *Environmental Values* 2 (1993): 21–32; Steve Chase, ed., *Defending the Earth: A Dialog Between Murray Bookchin and Dave Foreman* (Boston: A Learning Alliance Book, 1991); Jim Cheney, "The Neo-Stoicism of Radical Environmentalism," *Environmental Ethics* 11 (1989): 293–325; Luc Ferry, *New Ecological Order* (Chicago: University of Chicago Press, 1995); William C. French, "Against Biospherical Egalitarianism," *Environmental Ethics* 17 (1995): 39–57; Harold Glasser, "Naess's Deep Ecology Approach and Environmental Policy," *Inquiry* 39 (1996): 157–187; Harold Glasser, "On Warwick Fox's Assessment of Deep Ecology," *Environmental Ethics* 19 (1997): 69–85; Al Gore, *Earth in the Balance: Ecology and the Human Spirit* (New York: Houghton Mifflin, 1992); Ramachandra Guha, "Radical Environmentalism and Wilderness Preservation: A Third World Critique," *Environmental Ethics* 11 (1989): 71–83; Martin W. Lewis, *Green Delusions: An Environmentalist Critique of Radical Environmentalism* (Durham: Duke University Press, 1992); Andrew McLaughlin, *Regarding Nature: Industrialism and Deep Ecology* (Albany: State University of New York, 1993); Freya Mathews, "Relating to Nature: Deep Ecology or Ecofeminism?" *The Trumpeter* 11 (1994): 159–166; Charles T. Rubin, *The Green Crusade: Rethinking the Roots of Environmentalism* (New York: Free Press, 1994); Richard A. Watson, "Misanthropy, Humanity, and the Eco-Warriors." *Environmental Ethics* 14 (1992): 95; Michael E. Zimmermam, "Rethinking the Heidegger–Deep Ecology Relationships," *Environmental Ethics* 15 (1993): 195–224; and Michael E. Zimmerman, *Contesting Earth's Future: Radical Ecology and Postmodernity* (Berkeley: University of California Press, 1994).

Criticisms centered on deep ecology include: Murray Bookchin, "Social Ecology Versus 'Deep Ecology': A Challenge for the Ecology Movement," *Green Perspectives: Newsletter of the Green Program Project* (Summer 1987): 1–23; George Bradford, "How Deep Is Deep Ecology," *Fifth Estate* (Fall 1987): 5–30; William Grey, "A Critique of Deep Ecology," *Journal of Applied Philosophy* 3 (1986): 211–216; Ariel Salleh, "The Ecofeminism/Deep Ecology Debate," *Environmental Ethics* 14 (1992): 195–216; Ariel Salleh, "Class, Race, and Gender Discourse in the Ecofeminism/Deep Ecology Debate," *Environmental Ethics* 15 (1993): 225–244; Henryk Skolimowski, "Eco-Philosophy and Deep Ecology," *The Ecologist* 18 (1988): 124–127; Richard Sylvan (formerly Routley), "A Critique of Deep Ecology (Part I)," *Radical Philosophy* 40 (1985): 2–12; Richard Sylvan, "A Critique of Deep Ecology (Part II)," *Radical Philosophy* 41 (1985): 10–22; Richard Sylvan, "A Critique of (Wild) Western Deep Ecology: A Response to Warwick Fox's Response to an Earlier Critique," unpublished manuscript (1990): 57 pages; Richard A. Watson, "A Critique of Anti-Anthropocentric Biocentricism," *Environmental Ethics* 5 (1983): 245–256; Richard A. Watson, "Misanthropy, Humanity, and the Eco-Warriors," *Environmental Ethics* 14 (1992): 95. The most exhaustive compilation of criticisms of deep ecology that I am aware of appears in Fox, 1990, pp. 45–50.

3. This explication of "weaknesses" common to discussions of deep ecology draws from the references cited in note 2.
4. For a discussion of Naess's use of the "depth metaphor," see Harold Glasser, "The Deep Ecology Approach and Environmental Policy," *Inquiry* (1996).
5. Naess has nearly 100 articles on deep ecology, in English alone (numerous Norwegian publications also exist). Close to one-half of the English articles are still unpublished.
6. See Arne Naess, *Interpretation and Preciseness: A Contribution to the Theory of Communicative Action* (Oslo: Jacob Dybwad, 1953) and Arne Naess, *Communication and*

Argument: Elements of Applied Semantics, translated by Alastair Hannay (Oslo: Universitetsforlaget, 1981). These books will be included as volumes II and VII, respectively, of the forthcoming *Selected Works of Arne Naess*, revised and edited by Harold Glasser (Dordrecht: Kluwer, 1998).

7. See Arne Naess, "Reflections About Total Views," *Philosophy and Phenomenological Research* 25 (1964): 16–29.
8. See Arne Naess, "Notes on the Methodology of Normative Systems," *Methodology and Science* 10 (1977): 64–79.
9. See Arne Naess, "The World of Concrete Contents," *Inquiry* 28 (1985): 417–428, and Arne Naess, "Ecosophy and Gestalt Ontology," *The Trumpeter Journal of Ecosophy* 6 (1989b): 134–137, reprinted in Sessions, 1995, pp. 240–245.
10. See Arne Naess, *Scepticism* (London and New York: Humanities Press, 1968); to be included as volume III of the forthcoming *Selected Works of Arne Naess*, revised and edited by Harold Glasser (Dordrecht: Kluwer, 1998).
11. Arne Naess, "The Function of Ideological Convictions," in *Tensions That Cause Wars (Common statement and individual papers by a group of social scientists brought together by UNESCO)*, ed. H. Cantril, pp. 257–298 (Urbana: University of Illinois Press, 1950); Arne Naess, "Appendix I: The UNESCO Questionnaire on Ideological Conflicts Concerning Democracy," in *Democracy in a World of Tensions*, ed. Richard McKeon with the assistance of Stein Rokkan, pp. 513–521 (Chicago: University of Chicago Press, 1951); Arne Naess, Jens Christophersen, and Kjell Kvaløø, *Democracy, Ideology, and Objectivity: Studies in the Semantics and Cognitive Analysis of Ideological Controversy* (Oslo: Universitetsforlaget, 1956); Arne Naess and Stein Rokkan, "Analytical Survey of Agreements and Disagreements," in *Democracy in a World of Tensions*, ed. Richard McKeon and with the assistance of Stein Rokkan, pp. 447–512 (Chicago: University of Chicago Press, 1951).
12. See Arne Naess, *Freedom Emotion and Self-Subsistence: The Structure of a Central Part of Spinoza's Ethics* (Oslo: Universitetsforlaget, 1975); to be included as volume VII of the forthcoming *Selected Works of Arne Naess*, revised and edited by Harold Glasser (Dordrecht: Kluwer, 1998); Arne Naess, "Spinoza and Ecology," *Philosophia* 7 (1977): 45–54; and Arne Naess, "Spinoza and Attitudes Towards Nature," unpublished manuscript (1990).
13. See Johan Galtung and Arne Naess, *Gandhis Politiske Etikk (Gandhi's Political Ethics)*, 2nd edition, 1968 (Oslo: Johan Grundt Tanum, 1955); Arne Naess, *Gandhi and the Nuclear Age*, translated by Alastair Hannay (Totowa, New Jersey: Rowman, 1965b); Arne Naess, "Can Violence Lead to Non-Violence: Gandhi's Point of View," in *Gandhi India and the World: An International Symposium*, ed. Sibnarayan Ray, pp. 287–299 (Philadelphia: Temple University Press, 1970d); Arne Naess, *Gandhi and Group Conflict: An Exploration of Satyagraha* (Oslo: Universitetsforlaget, 1974); to be included as volume VI of the forthcoming *Selected Works of Arne Naess*, revised and edited by Harold Glasser (Dordrecht: Kluwer, 1998); and Arne Naess, "Nonviolent Verbal Communication. The Gandhian Approach," unpublished manuscript (1993a): 9 pages.
14. See Arne Naess, *The Pluralist and Possibilist Aspect of the Scientific Enterprise* (Oslo: Universitetsforlaget, 1972); to be included as volume V of the forthcoming *Selected Works of Arne Naess*, revised and edited by Harold Glasser (Dordrecht: Kluwer, 1998). Two important earlier works, previously unavailable in translation, have been recently translated into English by Ingemund Gullvåg; see Naess, *Erkenntnis und Wissenschaftliches Verhalten (Science as Behavior)* (Oslo: Norwegian Academy of Sciences, Inaugural Dissertation, 1936), and Naess, *Hvilken Verde er den Virkelige? (Which World Is the Real One?)*, Vol. 37, Filosofiske Problemer (Oslo: Universitetsforlaget, 1969). These books will be included as volumes I and IV, respectively, of the forthcoming *Selected Works of Arne Naess*, revised and edited by Harold Glasser (Dordrecht: Kluwer, 1998).

15. See Arne Naess, "Modesty and the Conquest of Mountains," in *The Mountain Spirit*, ed. Michael C. Tobias and H. Drasdo (New York: The Overlook Press, 1979), pp. 13–16; Arne Naess, "Tvergastein: An Example of Place," unpublished manuscript (1992): 13 pages. In a "Letter to the King of Nepal," in *The Autobiography of a Shipping Man*, ed. Erling D. Naess (author), pp. 252–253 (Oslo: Seatrade Publications, 1971), Arne Naess requests that the King consecrate some of the Himalayan Mountains and make them off limits to climbing; and Arne Naess and Johan Brun (Bilder), *Det Gode Lange Livs Far: Hallingskarvet sett fra Tvergastein* (Oslo: N.W. Damm and Son, 1995).

    Additional references to Naess's literary activity on mountaineering are compiled in Arne Naess, "How My Philosophy Seemed to Develop," in *Philosophers on Their Own Work*, ed. Andre Mercier and Maja Svilar (Bern: Peter Lang, 1983), pp. 267–268.
16. *Ataraxia* is the absence of fanaticism concerning matters that cannot be proved and the tranquillity of mind that follows from such an acknowledgment.
17. For an instructive characterization of three different forms of "intrinsic value," see J. O'Neil, "The Varieties of Intrinsic Value," *The Monist* 75 (1992): 119–137. O'Neil makes an important distinction between the value that can be associated with objects that are ends in themselves (non-instrumental) and the value that an object itself possesses *independently* of the valuations of valuers (objective). He alerts us to the relative independence between meta-ethical commitments and ethical ones.
18. Naess discusses this point in "Intuition, Intrinsic Value and Deep Ecology: Arne Naess Replies," *The Ecologist* 14 (1984): 202.
19. This point is addressed in greater detail in Glasser, "Naess's Deep Ecology Approach and Environmental Policy."
20. I believe Naess views the concept of "valuing" as being dependent upon human consciousness, but would argue that some entities have instrumental value, that these entities may also have attributes independent from instrumental value, and that some of these attributes may even be independent from our ability to ascribe value.
21. It was only in 1995 that the first anthologies devoted to deep ecology theoreticians' and supporters' work appeared: George Sessions, ed., *Deep Ecology for the Twenty-First Century* (Boston: Shambhala, 1995), and Alan Drengson and Yuichi Inoue, ed., *The Deep Ecology Movement: An Introductory Anthology* (Berkeley, California: North Atlantic Books, 1995). Even these anthologies, regrettably, carry forth several of the aforementioned weaknesses.
22. Arne Naess, "How My Philosophy Seemed to Develop," in *Philosophers on Their Own Work*, ed. Andre Mercier and Maja Svilar, pp. 209–226 (Bern: Peter Lang, 1983).
23. Recent confusion over the most current and up-to-date version of the DEP and its elaborations testify to this matter.
24. Naess, 1989a, pp. 42–43.
25. See Arne Naess, "Sustainable Development and Deep Ecology," in *Ethics of Environment and Development: Global Challenge, International Response*, ed. R. J. Engel and J. G. Engel, pp. 87–96 (Tucson: University of Arizona Press, 1990a), and Arne Naess, "Sustainability! The Integral Approach," in *Conservation of Biodiversity for Sustainable Development*, ed. O. T. Sandlund, K. Hindar, and A. H. D. Brown, pp. 303–310 (Oslo: Scandinavian University Press, 1992a).
26. See the interpretations of deep ecology presented in: Sessions, 1995; Fox, 1990; Zimmerman, 1994; and Manes, 1990, pp. 139–150. See also Chase, 1991, for a chronicle of Bookchin and Foreman's debate over the meanings and distinctions between *deep ecology* and *social ecology*. Both Manes and Foreman fail to present a complete and coherent picture of the DEA. The misdirected criticism of the DEA, from Bookchin, Ferry, Gore, and many others, may originate, at least in part, from this absence of thoroughness and clarity.

27. Arne Naess, "From Ecology to Ecosophy, From Science to Wisdom," unpublished manuscript (1987): 2.
28. Arne Naess, "The Basics of Deep Ecology," *Resurgence* 126 (1988): 6.
29. Naess, 1989a, p. 38.
30. Arne Naess, "The Deep Ecology Movement: Some Philosophical Aspects," *Philosophical Inquiry* 8 (1986): 10–31.
31. This discussion was inspired, in part, by Naess's response to a question on the role of wide-identification in acceptance of the DEP (personal communication, 5/4/94).
32. Devall and Sessions, 1985, p. 69.
33. Naess, 1989a, p. 28.
34. Naess, 1989a, p. 28.
35. I made this point in an earlier, unpublished manuscript: Harold Glasser, "The Distinctiveness of the Deep Ecology Approach to Ecophilosophy" (1991): 29 pages.
36. Naess has continually emphasized (cf. Naess, 1989a, p. 28) that the DEP is only one of a variety of such formulations that are necessary to account for individual and cultural differences. It is interesting to ask if the DEP, as formulated, represents the most general of such possible formulations.
37. Naess, 1986, p. 23.
38. Paul W. Taylor, *Respect for Nature: A Theory of Environmental Ethics* (Princeton, New Jersey: Princeton University Press, 1986).
39. See E. O. Wilson, *Biophilia* (Cambridge, Massachusetts: Harvard University Press, 1984), and Stephen R. Kellert and E. O. Wilson, ed., *The Biophilia Hypothesis* (Washington, D.C.: Island Press, 1993).
40. See Arne Naess, "A Place of Joy in a World of Fact," *The North American Review* (Summer 1973b): 53–57, reprinted in Sessions, 1995, pp. 249–258; Naess, "Self-Realization: An Ecological Approach to Being in the World" (Keith Roby Memorial Lecture, March 12, 1986a), reprinted in Sessions, 1995, pp. 225–239; and Naess, 1989a.
41. Naess, 1992a, p. 303.
42. Naess, 1989a, pp. 36–38.

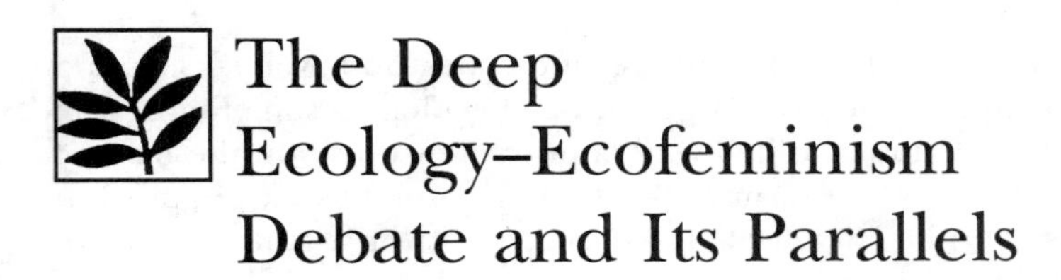

The Deep Ecology–Ecofeminism Debate and Its Parallels

Warwick Fox

Warwick Fox is a fellow at the Center for Environmental Studies, University of Tasmania, Australia. He is the author of Toward a Transpersonal Ecology *(1990), which focuses on the psychological dimensions of deep ecology and ecosophy.*

DEEP ECOLOGY'S ECOCENTRIC EGALITARIANISM

The question of the relative merits of deep ecology and ecofeminism has recently received considerable attention, primarily from an ecofeminist perspective. This question has an obvious significance to anyone concerned with ecophilosophy and ecopolitics since it contrasts two of the most philosophically and socially influential approaches that have developed in response to ecological concerns. For deep ecologists in particular, the ecofeminist critique of deep ecology is of interest for at least two reasons in addition to the direct challenge that it presents to deep ecological theorizing. First, as I argue throughout this paper, the same criticism that can be made of simplistic forms of ecofeminism can be applied with equal force to critiques of deep ecology that proceed from simplistic versions of a broad range of social and political perspectives—the "parallels" of my title. Second, addressing the ecofeminist critique of deep ecology provides an opportunity to further elucidate the nature of deep ecology's concern with anthropocentrism.

Before examining the ecofeminist critique of deep ecology, which centers on deep ecology's negative or critical focus on anthropocentrism, it is important to outline deep ecology's positive or constructive focus. Deep ecology is concerned with encouraging an egalitarian attitude on the part of humans not only toward all *members* of the ecosphere, but even toward all identifiable *entities* or *forms* in the ecosphere. Thus, this attitude is intended to extend, for

This essay originally appeared (in a somewhat longer version) in *Environmental Ethics* 11, 1 (Spring 1989): 5–25. Reprinted with permission.

example, to such entities (or forms) as rivers, landscapes, and even species and social systems considered in their own right. If deep ecologists sometimes write as if they consider these entities to be living entities, they do so on the basis of an extremely broad sense of the term *life*—a sense as broad as that implied in such expressions as "Let the river live!" It is ultimately of little consequence to deep ecologists, however, whether one wishes to consider the kind of egalitarianism they advocate as one that extends only toward living entities (in this extremely broad sense) or as one that extends toward both living and nonliving entities. Either way, the kind of egalitarian attitude they advocate is simply meant to indicate an attitude that, within obvious kinds of practical limits, allows all entities (including humans) *the freedom to unfold in their own way unhindered by the various forms of human domination.*

There are, of course, all sorts of problems involved in defining such things as how far these practical limits should extend or, in many cases, even where one entity ends and another begins. But, against this, it must be remembered that deep ecologists are not *intending* to advocate a specific set of guidelines for action; they are only intending to advocate a *general orientation.* Deep ecologists not only accept but welcome cultural diversity when it comes to effecting the specifics of this general orientation. After all, "the freedom to unfold in their own way unhindered by the various forms of human domination" applies to the unfolding of human cultures too. As Arne Naess puts it, where we draw the limit between justifiable and unjustifiable interference with respect to this general orientation "is a question that must be related to local, regional, and national particularities. Even then a certain area of disagreement must be taken as normal."[1] For deep ecologists, the only overriding consideration is that such limits should always be worked out *in the light of* the general orientation they advocate. Naess captures the sense of this general orientation while also conveying a sense of the cultural (and personal) diversity it allows for: "A rich variety of acceptable motives can be formulated for being *more reluctant* to injure or kill a living being of kind A than a being of kind B. The cultural setting is different for each being in each culture."[2] It is this general attitude of being reluctant, *prima facie,* to interfere with the unfolding of A *or* B—indeed, to desire that both should flourish—that characterizes the general orientation that is advocated by deep ecologists.

Deep ecologists have generally referred to this general orientation or attitude as one of "biospherical egalitarianism" or, more often (in order to suggest the intended comparison with an anthropo*centric* perspective more directly), "biocentric egalitarianism." However, because the prefix *bio-* refers, etymologically, to life or living organisms, it has sometimes been assumed that deep ecology's concerns *are* restricted to entities that are (in some sense) biologically alive. To correct this impression, Arne Naess and George Sessions have, in line with my preceding remarks, often pointed out that their sense of the term *life* is so broad, that it takes in "individuals, species, populations, habitat, as well as human and nonhuman cultures."[3] To avoid the possibility of confusion, however, I prefer to describe the kind of egalitarian attitude subscribed to by deep ecologists as *ecocentric* rather than *biocentric*. While there seems to be little reason for choosing between these terms on the basis of their ecological connotations, there are other grounds for preferring the term *ecocentric* to describe the kind of egalitarianism advocated by deep ecologists.[4] First, the term *ecocentric*, which etymologically means *oikos*-, home, or, by implication, Earth-centered, is more immediately informative than the term *biocentric*, which etymologically means life-centered and so requires an appended explanation of the broad sense in which the term *life* should be understood. Second, the term *ecocentric* seems closer to the spirit of deep ecology than the term *biocentric*, because, notwithstanding their broad usage of the term *life*, the motivation of deep ecologists depends more upon a profound sense that the Earth or ecosphere is *home* than it does upon a sense that the Earth or ecosphere is necessarily alive (you don't have to subscribe to some ecological form of *hylozoism* to be a supporter of deep ecology).

In accordance with this extremely broad, ecocentric egalitarianism, supporters of deep ecology hold that their concerns well and truly subsume the concerns of those movements that have restricted their focus to the attainment of a more egalitarian *human* society. Deep ecologists, in other words, consider their concerns to subsume the egalitarian concerns associated, for example, with feminism (as distinct from *eco*feminism), Marxism, anti-racism, and anti-imperialism.[5] In the eyes of deep ecologists, the emergence of a distinct *eco*feminism, a distinct "green" socialism, and so on, are—at least in their best forms—attempts by feminists, Marxists-cum-socialists, and so on, to redress the human-centeredness of their respective perspectives.[6] Needless to say, deep ecologists welcome these developments and they recognize that ecofeminism, green socialism, and so on have their own distinctive theoretical flavors and emphases because of the different theoretical histories that inform them. Nevertheless, they see no *essential* disagreement between deep ecology and these perspectives, *providing* that the latter are genuinely able to overcome their anthropocentric legacies.

THE ECOFEMINIST CRITIQUE OF DEEP ECOLOGY

With respect to ecofeminism and deep ecology in particular, many observers agree that the two perspectives have much in common—notwithstanding their different theoretical histories.[7] However, some ecofeminist writers have begun to perceive a significant tension between their perspective and that of deep ecology. In an evenhanded examination of ecofeminist criticisms of deep ecology, Michael Zimmerman has presented what is probably the clearest formulation of what I take to be the essential ecofeminist charge against deep ecology: "Feminist critics of deep ecology assert that [deep ecology] speaks of a gender-neutral 'anthropocentrism' [i.e., human-centeredness] as the root of the domination of nature, when in fact *androcentrism* [i.e., male-centeredness] is the real root."[8] There seems to be wide support for the view that this represents the essential ecofeminist criticism of deep ecology. For example, one of the main criticisms made by Janet Biehl in her critique of deep ecology is that, "For ecofeminists the concept of anthropocentrism is profoundly, even "deeply" problematical. . . . By not excluding women from anthropocentrism, deep ecologists implicitly condemn women for being as anthropocentric as they condemn men for being—that is, for presuming to be above nature, for mastering it." Marti Kheel also notes at the outset of her critique of deep ecology that deep ecologists are concerned to "challenge the anthropocentric world view" whereas for ecofeminists "it is the androcentric world view that is the focal point of the needed shift." Likewise, the first difference in emphasis that Charlene Spretnak refers to in her comparison of deep ecology and ecofeminism is that of anthropocentrism versus androcentrism.[9]

Jim Cheney has claimed, nevertheless, in response to an earlier version of this paper, that it is wrong to regard Zimmerman's formulation as representing the essential ecofeminist charge against deep ecology. For Cheney, "The 'essential' [ecofeminist] charge is not that deep ecologists focus on *anthropo*centrism whereas the problem is really with *andro*centrism; rather, the central concern is . . . that deep ecology is *itself* in some sense androcentric."[10] In comparison to what I take to be the essential ecofeminist charge against deep ecology (as formulated concisely by Zimmerman), Cheney's formulation of the essential ecofeminist charge seems to represent a significant (if somewhat confusing) concession to deep ecology, since it suggests that ecofeminists are not overly concerned about deep ecologists' critical focus on anthropocentrism so long as deep ecologists do not formulate their critique of anthropocentrism in a way that is "itself in some sense androcentric." But whether Cheney's formulation represents a significant concession to deep ecology or not, my response to his charge is simple. The charge that I propose to address (as taken from Zimmerman's analysis) is clear-cut and serious—deep ecologists cannot deny that their *negative* focus is concerned, first and foremost, with anthropocentrism and ecofeminists cannot deny that their *negative* focus is concerned, first and foremost, with androcentrism. In contrast, the best that can be said about Cheney's claim that deep ecology is androcentric in its very formulation is that such a claim is entirely contentious.[11] Cheney's own recent attempt in *Environmental Ethics* to establish this claim is essentially based upon a misinterpretation of deep ecology as resting upon a "rights-based foundation."[12] Referring to a brief paper of my own, Cheney even acknowledges in his paper (albeit in a footnote) that if (as Fox claims) deep ecology does not rest upon "the language of intrinsic value and correlated concepts of rights . . . then deep ecology is not subject to some of the criticisms I have offered."[13]

More recently, Cheney has abandoned his previous view of deep ecology and accepted that deep ecologists are primarily concerned with the development of a state of being of wider *identification* and, hence, with the realization of a more expansive (sense of) Self.[14] This understanding of deep ecology appears to have much in common with Cheney's characterization of ecofeminism as being concerned with an ethics of love, care, and friendship as opposed to a theory of rights, justice, and obligation.[15] However, Cheney argues instead that the deep ecological emphasis on the realization of a more expansive (sense of) Self is a "totalizing view" that represents "the desperate endgame of masculine alienation from nature."[16] What Cheney means by his highly abstract and potentially obfuscating reference to a "totalizing view" is that deep ecologists identify "with particulars only in the derivative sense that the logos of the cosmos threads its way through the cosmos, binds it together as a totality, a cosmos. Identification, for the deep ecologist, does not involve seeing or hearing the other or seeing oneself in the other, but rather involves seeing the other *sub specie aeternitas*."[17]

What Cheney seems to object to in deep ecology, then, is not the emphasis on identification *per se* but rather the fact that deep ecologists emphasize identification within a cosmological context—that is, within the context of an awareness that all entities in the universe are part of a single, unfolding process. There is, however, a fundamental problem with arguing, as Cheney seems to want to, for a purely *personal* basis for identification (as opposed to a cosmological and, hence, *transpersonal* basis). Specifically, emphasizing a purely personal basis for identification—one that "leave[s] selves intact"[18]—necessarily implies an emphasis upon identification with entities with which one has considerable personal contact. In practice, this tends to mean that one identifies with *my* self first, *my* family next, *my* friends and more distant relations next, *my* ethnic grouping next, *my* species next, and so on—more or less what the sociobiologists say we are genetically predisposed to do. The problem with this is that, while extending love, care, and friendship to one's nearest and dearest is laudable in and of itself, the *other* side of the coin, emphasizing a purely personal basis for identification (*my*self first, *my* family next, and so on), looks more like the cause of possessiveness, war, and ecological destruction than the solution to these seemingly intractable problems. In contrast, to argue for a cosmological basis for identification is to attempt to convey a lived sense that all entities (including ourselves) are relatively autonomous modes of a single, unfolding process, that all entities are leaves on the tree of life. A lived sense of this understanding means that we strive, insofar as it is within our power to do so, not to identify ourselves exclusively with our leaf (our personal biographical self), our twig (our family), our minor subbranch (our community), our major subbranch (our race/gender), our branch (our species), and so on, but rather to identify ourselves with the tree. This necessarily leads, at the limit, to impartial identification with *all* particulars (all leaves on the tree).[19]

This distinction between personally based identification and cosmologically based identification certainly represents a difference in *theoretical* stance between Cheney's conception of ecofeminism on the one hand and deep ecology on the other. But whether this difference also reflects a basic difference between feminine and masculine modes of approaching the world (as Cheney wants to suggest) is a separate issue. On my reading of the literature, I do not see how anyone can—or why they would want to—deny that many women are *vitally* interested in cultivating a cosmological/transpersonal based sense of identification.[20] The cosmological/transpersonal voice *is* a "different voice" from the personal voice, but it does not seem to respect gender boundaries.

Moreover, as the above discussion suggests, whatever one's view of the relationship or lack of relationship between these approaches and gender, a personally based approach to identification is vulnerable to criticism from an ecocentric perspective in a way in which a cosmological/transpersonal approach is not.

Because this brief examination of Cheney's critique of deep ecology suggests that there are major weaknesses with his claim that the essential ecofeminist charge against deep ecology is actually "that deep ecology is *itself*, in some sense androcentric," in what follows I, therefore, consider the essential ecofeminist charge against deep ecology to be the far more clear-cut and potentially far more serious charge (vis-à-vis Cheney's charge) that deep ecology "speaks of a gender-neutral 'anthropocentrism' as the root of the domination of nature, when in fact *androcentrism* is the real root."[21]

PROBLEMS WITH THE ECOFEMINIST AND OTHER CRITIQUES

Having established the nature of the ecofeminist charge that I am concerned to address in what follows, it is important to note that this charge is *not* directed at deep ecology's positive or constructive task of encouraging an egalitarian attitude on the part of humans toward all entities in the ecosphere, but rather at deep ecology's negative or critical task of dismantling anthropocentrism. This distinction often seems to be overlooked by ecofeminist critics of deep ecology, who, presumably, are in general agreement with the constructive task of deep ecology.[22] But with respect to the critical task of these two perspectives, the fact remains that in the absence of a good answer to the ecofeminist charge, there is no reason—other than intellectual blindness or outright chauvinism in regard to issues concerning gender—why deep ecologists should not make androcentrism the focus of their critique rather than anthropocentrism. In addressing this challenge to the critical focus of deep ecology, I first make some general remarks about a certain style of social and political theorizing and then proceed to the essential deep ecological response to this ecofeminist charge.

To begin with, deep ecologists completely agree with ecofeminists that men have been far more implicated in the history of ecological destruction than women. However, deep ecologists also agree with similar charges derived from other social perspectives: for example, that capitalists, whites, and Westerners have been far more implicated in the history of ecological destruction than precapitalist peoples, blacks, and non-Westerners.[23] If ecofeminists also agree with these points, then the question arises as to why they do not also criticize deep ecology for being neutral with respect to issues concerning such significant social variables as socioeconomic class, race, and Westernization. There appears to be two reasons for this. First, to do so would detract from the priority that ecofeminists wish to give to their own concern with androcentrism. Second, and more significantly, these charges could also be applied with equal force to the ecofeminist focus on androcentism itself.[24] How does one defend the ecofeminist charge against deep ecology (i.e., that androcentrism is "the real root" of ecological destruction) in the face of these charges?[25] For deep ecologists, it is simplistic on both empirical and logical grounds to think that one particular perspective on human society identifies *the* real root of ecological destruction. Empirically, such thinking is simplistic (and thus descriptively poor) because it fails to give due consideration to the multitude of interacting factors at work in any given situation. (While on a *practical* level it can be perfectly reasonable to devote most of one's energy to one particular cause—if only for straightforward reasons to do with time and energy—that, of course, is no excuse for simplistic social *theorizing.*) Such thinking fails, in other words, to adopt an ecological perspective with respect to the workings of human society itself. Logically, such thinking is simplistic (and thus facile) because it implies that the solution to our ecological problems is close at hand—all we have to do is remove "the real root" of the problem—when it is actually perfectly possible to conceive of a society that is nonandrocentric, socioeconomically egalitarian, nonracist, and nonimperialistic with respect to other human societies, but whose members nevertheless remain aggressively anthropocentric in collectively agreeing to exploit their environment for their collective benefit in ways that nonanthropocentrists would find thoroughly objectionable. Indeed, the "green" critique of socialism proceeds from *precisely* this recognition that a socially egalitarian society does not necessarily imply an ecologically benign society.

An interesting example of the failure to recognize this point is provided by Murray Bookchin's anarcho-socialist inspired "social ecology" (I describe this approach as "anarcho-socialist" in inspiration because it advocates decentralism and cooperativeness and stands opposed to all forms of hierarchy). Bookchin is interesting in this context because, on the one hand, he correctly observes in the course of a highly polemical attack upon deep ecology that it is possible for a relatively ecologically benign human society also to be extremely oppressive internally (he offers the example of ancient Egyptian society), and yet, on the other hand, he fails to see that the reverse can also apply—that is, that it is possible for a relatively egalitarian human society to be extremely exploitative ecologically.[26] For Bookchin, to accept this latter point would be to argue against the basis of his own social ecology, since in his view a nonhierarchical, decentralist, and cooperative society is "a society that will live in harmony with nature *because* its members live in harmony with each other."[27] Bookchin's presentation of social ecology thus conveys no real appreciation of the fact that the relationships between the internal organization of human societies and their treatment of the nonhuman world can be as many and varied as the outcomes of any other evolutionary process. One may certainly speak in terms of certain forms of human social organization being more *conducive* to certain kinds of relationships with the nonhuman world than others. Bookchin, however, insists far too much that there is a straightforward, necessary relationship between the internal organization of human societies and their treatment of the nonhuman world. To this extent, his social ecology is constructed upon a logically facile basis. Moreover, it serves to reinforce anthropocentrism, since the assumption that the internal organization of human societies determines their treatment of the nonhuman world carries with it the implication that we need only concentrate on *interhuman* egalitarian concerns for all to become ecologically well with the world—a point I take up again later.[28]

In doing violence to the complexities of social interaction, simplistic social and political analyses of ecological destruction are not merely descriptively poor and logically facile, they are also morally objectionable on two grounds, scapegoating and inauthenticity. Scapegoating can be thought of in terms of overinclusiveness. Simplistic analyses target all men, all capitalists, all whites, and all Westerners, for example, to an equal degree when in fact certain subclasses of these identified classes are far more responsible for ecological destruction than others. Not only that but significant minorities of these classes can be actively engaged in *opposing* the interests of both the dominant culture of their class and those members of their class most responsible for ecological destruction. Inauthenticity, on the other hand, can be thought of in terms of underinclusiveness. Simplistic analyses are inauthentic in that they lead to a complete denial of responsibility when at least partial responsibility for ecological destruction should be accepted. Such theorizing conveniently disguises the extent to which (at least a subset of) the simplistically identified oppressed group (e.g., women or the working class) also benefits from, and colludes with, those most responsible for ecological destruction (e.g., consider the case of animal destruction for furs and cosmetics consumed by Western and Westernized women, or the case of capitalists and unionists united in opposition to the antidevelopment stance of "greenies"). It can, of course, be argued in response that the hegemony of androcentrism or capitalism, for example, is such that women or unionists effectively have *no* power to choose in our society and so should not be burdened with *any* responsibility for ecological destruction. But this surely overplays the role of social determination and to that extent only serves to highlight the charge of inauthenticity. Moreover, attempting to escape the charge of inauthenticity in this way directly contradicts the view of feminists or Marxists, to continue with the same examples, that women or the working class *are* capable of self-conscious direction—of being a class *for* themselves, a revolutionary class.

Yet another kind of objection to simplistic analyses of the kind to which I have been referring is that while claiming to be "ecological" or "green," some of these critics in fact remain anthropocentric—albeit in the passive sense of serving to legitimize our continued preoccupation with interhuman affairs rather than in the aggressive sense of overtly discriminating against the nonhuman world. Advocates of these approaches say in essence: "Since the real root of our problems is androcentrism or capitalism, for example, we must *first* get our interactions between humans right (with respect to gender issues, with respect to the redistribution of wealth, and so on) and then everything else (including our ecological problems) will fall into place." Any form of direct concern with the question of the relationship between humans and the *non-human* world is thus trumped by concerns about the resolution of specific interhuman problems. The nonhuman world retains its traditional status as the background against which the significant action—human action—takes place.

Not surprisingly, deep ecologists find it particularly frustrating to witness representatives of simplistic social and political perspectives waving the banner of ecology while in fact continuing to promote, whether wittingly or unwittingly, the interhuman and, hence, human-centered agenda of their respective theoretical legacies. I have already commented on Bookchin's social ecology in regard to this point. Some ecofeminist writing is also relevant here. For example, the focus of Ariel Kay Salleh's critique of deep ecology is thoroughly interhuman. "To make a better world," she concludes, men have to be "brave enough to rediscover and to love the woman inside themselves," while women simply have to "be allowed to love what we are."[29] This conclusion follows from the fact that, in Salleh's version of feminism, women already "flow with the system of nature" by virtue of their essential nature.[30] Karen Warren and Michael Zimmerman have referred to this kind of approach to ecofeminism, according to which women are supposed to be "closer to nature" than men by virtue of their essential nature, as "radical feminism" (in contrast to liberal, traditional Marxist, and socialist feminism) and "essentialist feminism" respectively.[31] Warren correctly notes that "Radical feminists have had the most to say about ecofeminism," and both she and Zimmerman have made telling criticisms of this approach.[32] All I am drawing attention to here is the fact that this kind of "radical" approach simply serves to legitimize and, hence, to perpetuate our entirely *traditional* preoccupation with interhuman affairs. In accordance with the approach adopted by essentialist feminists, there is no need to give any serious consideration whatsoever to the possibility that women might, for example, discriminate against men, accumulate rather than distribute private wealth, be racist, support imperialism, or be ecologically destructive if the conditions of their historical subjugation were undone and the possibility of exercising genuine social and political power were available to them.[33] The upshot is that there is no need to worry about any form of human domination other than that of androcentrism. For deep ecologists, it's just another variation on the same old song—the song that reassures us that all will become ecologically well with the world if we just put this or that interhuman concern first.

I have objected to simplistic (and, hence, unecologically conceived) social and political analyses on the grounds that they are descriptively poor and logically facile, that they lend themselves to scapegoating on the one hand and are inauthentic on the other, and that even in their ecological guises, they are passively anthropocentric. Many who align themselves with the perspectives to which I have referred might well personally agree with the points I have made so far and consider that in virtue of this agreement, these objections do not really apply to their perspective. Thus, this kind of reaction can be quite common in the face of the sorts of objections I have made: "How could anyone be so stupid as to think that we ecofeminists (for example) are not also concerned about issues concerning socioeconomic class, race, and imperialism?" The problem is, however, that there is often a large gap between the alleged and often genuine personal concerns of members of a social and political movement and the theoretical articulation of the perspective that informs their movement. The fact that individual members of a social and political movement agree with the points I have made provides no guarantee whatsoever that the theoretical articulation of the perspective that informs their movement does not itself fall foul of these objections—and it is with this theoretical articulation that I have been concerned. By way of qualification, however, I do not in any way wish to assert that any of the objections I have made are necessarily fatal to the theoretical prospects of the social and political perspectives to which I have referred, since it is possible, at least in principle, for each of these perspectives to be revised or, at a minimum, suitably qualified so as not to fall foul of these objections.[34] But, that said, one must nevertheless be careful not to underestimate the significance of these objections, since presentations of the social and political perspectives to which I have referred continue to fall foul of them on an all too regular basis.

Variations on some (but not all) of the objections I have outlined would apply just as much to deep ecology if it were the case that deep ecologists were simply saying that humans as a whole have been far more implicated in the history of ecological destruction than nonhumans. (The ecofeminist charge against deep ecology implies that deep ecologists are saying precisely this: it turns on the contention that deep ecologists have been overinclusive in criticizing humanity *in general* for the destruction of the nonhuman world when the target of their critical attack should properly be the class of men and, of course, masculine culture in general.) However, this is *not* the essential point that deep ecologists are making, and it is here that we enter into the essential response by deep ecologists to the essential criticism made of their perspective by ecofeminists.

THE ESSENTIAL DEEP ECOLOGICAL RESPONSE TO THE ECOFEMINIST CRITIQUE

The target of the deep ecologists' critique is not humans *per se* (i.e., a general class of social actors) but rather human-*centeredness* (i.e., a legitimating ideology).[35] It is not just ecofeminist critics who miss this point. Some other critics also miss it in an even bigger way by attacking deep ecologists not simply on the grounds that they *criticize* humanity in general for its ecological destructiveness, but rather on the grounds that deep ecologists are actually *opposed* to humanity in general—that is, that they are essentially misanthropic. According to Murray Bookchin, for example, in deep ecology "'*Humanity*' is essentially seen as an ugly 'anthropocentric' thing—presumably, a malignant product of natural evolution."[36] Henryk Skolimowski also suggests (albeit rather indirectly) that deep ecologists are misanthropic. "I find it rather morbid," he writes in *The Trumpeter*, "when some human beings [and the context suggests that he means deep ecologists] think that the human lot is the bottom of the pit. There is something pathological in the contention that humans are a cancer among the species. This kind of thinking is not sane and it does not promote the sense of wholeness which we need nowadays." In line with my remarks here, Alan Drengson, *The Trumpeter*'s editor and a prominent deep ecology philosopher, intervenes immediately at this point by adding parenthetically: "And it is certainly not the thinking of deep ecologists. Ed."[37]

The extent to which people in general are ready to equate opposition to human-centeredness with opposition to humans per se can be viewed as a function of the dominance of the anthropocentric frame of reference in our society. Just as those who criticize capitalism, for example, are often labeled as "Communists" and, by implication, "the enemy," when, in reality, they may be concerned with such things as a more equitable distribution of wealth in society, so those who criticize anthropocentrism are liable to be labeled as *mis*anthropists when, in reality, they may be (and, in the context of environmentalism, generally are) concerned with encouraging a more egalitarian attitude on the part of humans toward all entities in the ecosphere. In failing to notice the fact that being opposed to human-*centeredness* (deep ecology's critical task) is logically distinct from being opposed to humans per se (or, in other words, that being opposed to anthropo*centrism* is logically distinct from being *mis*anthropic), and in equating the former with the latter, Bookchin and Skolimowski commit what I refer to as *the fallacy of misplaced misanthropy*.[38] Committing this fallacy in the context of criticizing deep ecology involves not just a crucial misreading of deep ecology's critical task, but also the oversight of two other considerations that contradict such a misreading. The first is that deep ecology's *constructive* task is to encourage an egalitarian attitude on the part of humans toward all entities in the ecosphere—including *humans*. The second is that deep ecologists are among the first to highlight and draw inspiration from the fact that not all humans have been human-centered either within the Western tradition or outside it. Far from being misanthropic, deep ecologists celebrate the existence of these human beings.

In making human-*centeredness* (rather than humans per se) the target of their critique, deep ecologists have contended that the assumption of human self-importance in the larger scheme of things has, to all intents and purposes, been the single deepest and most persistent assumption of (at least) all the *dominant* Western philosophical, social, and political traditions since the time of the classical Greeks—notwithstanding the fact that the dominant classes representing these traditions have typically adjudged themselves *more* human than others—and that, for a variety of reasons, this assumption is unwarranted and should be abandoned in favor of an ecocentric outlook.[39] Thus, what deep ecologists are drawing critical attention to is the fact that *whatever* class of social actors one identifies as having been most responsible for social domination and ecological destruction (e.g., men, capitalists, whites, Westerners), one tends at the most fundamental level to find a common kind of legitimation for the alleged superiority of these classes over others and, hence, for the assumed rightfulness of their domination of these others. Specifically, these classes of social actors have not sought to legitimate their position on the grounds that they are, for example, men, capitalists, white, or Western per se, but rather on the grounds that they have most exemplified whatever it is that has been taken to constitute the *essence of humanness* (e.g., being favored by God or possessing rationality). These classes of social actors have, in other words, habitually assumed themselves to be somehow *more fully human* than others, such as women ("the weaker vessel"), the "lower" classes, blacks, and non-Westerners ("savages," "primitives," "heathens"). The cultural spell of anthropocentrism has been considered sufficient to justify not only moral superiority (which, in itself, might be construed as carrying with it an obligation to help rather than dominate those who are less blessed), but also all kinds of domination within human society—let alone domination of the obviously nonhuman world.

That anthropocentrism has served as the most fundamental kind of legitimation employed by *whatever* powerful class of social actors one wishes to focus on can also be seen by considering the fundamental kind of legitimation that has habitually been employed with regard to large-scale or high-cost social enterprises such as war, scientific and technological development, or environmental exploitation. Such enterprises have habitually been undertaken not simply in the name of men, capitalists, whites, or Westerners, for example, but rather in the name of God (and thus our essential humanity—or our anthropocentric projection upon the cosmos, depending upon one's perspective) or simply in the name of humanity in general. (This applies notwithstanding the often sexist expression of these sentiments in terms of "man," "mankind," and so on, and notwithstanding the fact that certain classes of social actors benefit disproportionately from these enterprises.) Thus, to take some favorite examples, Francis Bacon and Descartes ushered in the development of modern science by promising, respectively, that it would lead to "enlarging the bounds of Human Empire" and that it would render humanity the "masters and possessors of nature."[40] Approximately three and a half centuries later, Neil Armstrong's moon walk—the culmination of a massive, politically directed, scientific and technological development effort—epitomized both the literal acting out of this vision of "enlarging the bounds of Human Empire" and the literal expression of its anthropocentric spirit: Armstrong's moon walk was, in his own words at the time, a "small step" for him, but a "giant leap for mankind." Here on Earth, not only do examples abound of environmental *exploitation* being undertaken in the name of humanity, but this also constitutes the fundamental kind of legitimation that is still most often employed for environmental *conservation and preservation*—it is implicit in every argument for the conservation or preservation of the nonhuman world on account of its use value to humans (e.g., its scientific, recreational, or aesthetic value) rather than for its own sake or its use value to *nonhuman* beings.

The cultural pervasiveness of anthropocentrism in general and anthropocentric legitimations in particular are further illustrated when one turns to consider those social movements that have *opposed* the dominant classes of social actors to which I have been referring. With respect to the pervasiveness of anthropocentrism in general, it can be seen that those countermovements that have been most concerned with exposing discriminatory assumptions and undoing their effects have typically confined their interests to the human realm (i.e., to such issues as imperialism, race, socioeconomic class, and gender). With respect to the pervasiveness of anthropocentric legitimations in particular, it can equally be seen that these countermovements have not sought to legitimate their own claims on the basis that they are, for example, women, workers, black, or non-Western per se, but rather on the grounds that they too have exemplified—at least equally with those to whom they have been opposed—either whatever it is that *has* been taken to constitute the essence of humanness or else some redefined essence of humanness. While it would, in any case, be contrary to the (human-centered) egalitarian concerns of these countermovements to seek to legitimate their own claims by the former kind of approach (i.e., on the basis that they are, for example, women, workers, black, or non-Western per se), the pity is (from a deep ecological perspective) that these countermovements have not been egalitarian enough. Rather than attempting to replace the ideology of anthropocentrism with some broader, ecocentrically inclined perspective, these countermovements have only served to reinforce it.

It should be clear from this brief survey that the history of anthropocentrism takes in not only the assumption of the centrality and superiority of humans *in general*, but also the various claims and counterclaims that various classes of humans have made with regard to the exemplification of whatever attributes have been considered to be quintessentially human. Deep ecologists recognize that the actual historical reasons for the domination of one class by another (and here I also refer to the domination that humans as a class now exert over the nonhuman world) cannot be identified in any simplistic manner; they can be as complex as any ecological web or the evolutionary path of any organism. However, deep ecologists also recognize that claims to some form of human exclusiveness have typically been employed to *legitimate* the bringing about and perpetuation of historical and evolutionary outcomes involving unwarranted domination. In consequence, deep ecologists have been attempting to get people to see that historical and evolutionary outcomes simply represent "the way things happen to have turned out"—nothing more—and that self-serving anthropocentric legitimations for these outcomes are just that.

What the ecofeminist criticism of deep ecology's focus on anthropocentrism overlooks, then, is the fact that deep ecologists are not primarily concerned with exposing the *classes of social actors* historically most responsible for social domination and ecological destruction, but rather with the task of sweeping the rug out from under the feet of these classes of social actors by exposing the most fundamental kind of *legitimation* that they have habitually employed in justifying their position. (This distinction between a concern with classes of social actors on the one hand and the most fundamental kind of legitimation they employ on the other hand should be apparent from the fact that deep ecology has been elaborated within a philosophical context rather than a sociological or political context—which is not to suggest that deep ecology does not have profound social and political implications.) Of course, ecofeminists, green socialists, and so on are also concerned with questions of legitimation, but they are generally concerned with these questions in a different sense than deep ecologists are concerned with them. The primary emphasis of ecofeminists, green socialists, and the other social and political analysts to whom I have referred is on the distribution of power in society and the ways in which that distribution is reinforced and reproduced. In this context, references to legitimation tend not to be to the "bottom line" rationale employed by these powerful classes (i.e., to legitimation in the fundamental or philosophical sense), but rather to the ways in which existing power structures utilize their sources of power to back up existing states of affairs (from overtly physical forms of power such as the police and the military to less tangible forms such as economic power and the manipulation of social status). To the extent that ecofeminists, green socialists, and so on *are* concerned to expose the fundamental, philosophical legitimation employed by the classes of social actors whose unwarranted degree of power is the focus of their critique, and to the extent that this concern extends out into a genuinely ecocentric perspective, it becomes difficult to see any significant difference between what they call ecofeminism, green socialism, and so on and what others call deep ecology (such differences as remain are simply differences of theoretical flavor and emphasis rather than differences of substance).

Deep ecologists want to unmask the ideology of anthropocentrism so that it can no longer be used as the "bottom line" legitimation for social domination and ecological destruction by *any* class of social actors (men, capitalists, whites, Westerners, humans generally—or even essentialist feminists!).[41] Thus, those who align themselves with certain perspectives on the distribution of power in human society (e.g., feminism, Marxism, anti-racism, or anti-imperialism) misunderstand the essential nature of deep ecology if they see it in terms of their perspective *versus* deep ecology (e.g., in the case of ecofeminism and deep ecology, androcentrism *versus* anthropocentrism)—or if they criticize deep ecology on the basis that it has "no analysis of power." Rather, just as deep ecologists have learned and incorporated much from, and should be open to, a range of perspectives on the distribution of power in human society, so those who align themselves with these social and political perspectives can learn and incorporate much from, and should be open to, the deep ecologists' critique of the most fundamental kind of legitimation that has habitually been employed by those most responsible for social domination and ecological destruction.

NOTES

1. Arne Naess, "Sustainable Development and the Deep Long-Range Ecological Movement," unpublished manuscript.
2. Arne Naess, "Intuition, Intrinsic Value, and Deep Ecology," *The Ecologist* 14 (1984): 202 (emphasis added). Naess fully accepts that "any realistic praxis necessitates

some killing, exploitation, and suppression" ("The Shallow and the Deep, Long-Range Ecology Movement: A Summary." *Inquiry* 16 [1973]: 95). For more on the relevance of tradition and culture, see Naess's paper "Self-realization in Mixed Communities of Humans, Bears, Sheep, and Wolves," *Inquiry* 22 (1979): 231–41.

3. See the eight point list of "basic principles" of deep ecology proposed by Arne Naess and George Sessions and published in numerous places including Bill Devall and George Sessions, *Deep Ecology: Living as if Nature Mattered* (Layton, Utah: Gibbs M. Smith, 1985), chap. 5; and Arne Naess, "The Deep Ecological Movement: Some Philosophical Aspects," *Philosophical Inquiry* 8 (1986): 10–31.
4. *Biocentric* and *ecocentric* are equally useful in connoting the biosphere and the ecosphere respectively and these latter terms are themselves generally used interchangeably. However, where a distinction *is* made between the terms *biosphere* and *ecosphere*, it is the latter term that is taken as the more inclusive.
5. I am, of course, speaking here of the full realization of deep ecology's concerns, i.e., of the breadth of deep ecology's concerns *in principle*. In practice, however, deep ecologists, like everyone else, can fail to realize the full implications of their own principles.
6. In referring to *green socialism* and to *socialists*. I am aware that the term *socialism*, considered in its own right, is today popularly construed as referring to virtually the whole range of (human) social egalitarian concerns and that the concerns of socialism and green socialism might therefore be considered as subsuming the concerns of feminism and ecofeminism respectively. But there are nevertheless significant differences between these approaches at the level of their theoretical flavors and emphases.
7. There is nothing to suggest that there is any incompatibility between deep ecology and an ecologically informed feminism in any of the works by the following authors, all of whom make explicit reference to both perspectives: Fritjof Capra, *The Turning Point: Science, Society, and the Rising Culture* (New York: Bantam Books, 1983), chap. 12; Don E. Marietta, Jr, "Environmentalism, Feminism, and the Future of American Society," *The Humanist*, May–June 1984, pp. 15–18 and 30; Bill Devall and George Sessions, *Deep Ecology*, chap. 6; Charlene Spretnak, "The Spiritual Dimension of Green Politics," appendix C in Charlene Spretnak and Fritjof Capra, *Green Politics: The Global Promise* (London: Paladin, Grafton Books, 1986); and Patsy Hallen, "Making Peace with Nature: Why Ecology Needs Feminism," *The Trumpeter* 4, No. 3 (1987): 3–14. Even those authors who do see a tension between these perspectives generally acknowledge that these perspectives at least bear a strong apparent similarity to each other. For example, Jim Cheney writes: "On the face of it, that *branch* of environmentalism called the 'deep ecology movement' seems to have answered the [ecofeminist] call for a nonhierarchical, nondomineering attitude toward nature" ("Eco-Feminism and Deep Ecology," *Environmental Ethics* 9 [1987]: 115–45).
8. Zimmerman, "Feminism, Deep Ecology, and Environmental Ethics," *Environmental Ethics* 9 (1987): 21–44.
9. Janet Biehl, "It's Deep, but Is It Broad? An Eco-feminist Looks at Deep Ecology," *Kick It Over*, Winter 1987, p. 2A; Marti Kheel, "Ecofeminism and Deep Ecology," and Charlene Spretnak, "Ecofeminism: Our Roots and Flowering." *The Elmwood Newsletter*, Winter 1988, p. 7.
10. Personal communication, 21 April 1988.
11. Zimmerman ("Feminism, Deep Ecology, and Environmental Ethics," pp. 38–42) provides a thoughtful consideration of the various problems associated with the kind of claim that Cheney makes.
12. Cheney, "Eco-Feminism and Deep Ecology," p. 129.
13. Ibid., p. 133. The brief paper of mine that Cheney refers to is "A Postscript on Deep Ecology and Intrinsic Value," *The Trumpeter* 2, no. 4 (1985): 20–23. For a far more extensive critique of the view that deep ecology rests upon what Cheney refers to as "the language of intrinsic value and correlated concepts of rights," see

my monograph *Approaching Deep Ecology: A Response to Richard Sylvan's Critique of Deep Ecology*, Environmental Studies Occasional Paper, no. 20 (Hobart: Centre for Environmental Studies, University of Tasmania, 1986).

14. Jim Cheney, "The Neo-Stoicism of Radical Environmentalism," unpublished early draft. This version of Cheney's critique of deep ecology follows his reading of my *Approaching Deep Ecology* and is, in large measure, a response to it.
15. See Cheney, "Eco-Feminism and Deep Ecology," p. 128.
16. Cheney, "Neo-Stoicism."
17. Ibid., p. 16.
18. Ibid., p. 15.
19. The fact that cosmologically based identification tends to be more *impartial* than personally based identification does not mean that it need be any less deeply felt. Consider Robinson Jeffers! For Jeffers, "This whole [the universe] is in *all its parts* so beautiful, and is felt by me to be so intensely in earnest, that I am *compelled* to love it" (quoted in Devall and Sessions, *Deep Ecology*, p. 101; emphasis added).
20. See, for example, Dolores LaChapelle, *Earth Wisdom* (Los Angeles: Guild of Tutors Press, 1978); Joanna Macy, "Deep Ecology and the Council of All Beings," and "Gaia Meditations (Adapted from John Seed)," *Awakening in the Nuclear Age*, Summer/Fall 1986, pp. 6–10 (both reprinted in *Revision*, Winter/Spring 1987, pp. 53–57); Freya Matthews, "Conservation and Self-Realization: A Deep Ecology Perspective," *Environmental Ethics* 10 (1988): 347–55; and Frances Vaughan, "Discovering Transpersonal Identity," *Journal of Humanistic Psychology* 25 (1985): 13–38.
21. Zimmerman, "Feminism, Deep Ecology, and Environmental Ethics," p. 37.
22. In a thoughtful analysis of the strengths and shortcomings of several varieties of feminism (liberal, traditional Marxist, radical, and socialist) for the development of a genuinely ecofeminist perspective, Karen J. Warren concurs that an ecologically informed feminism—"a transformative feminism"—would tie "the liberation of women to the elimination of all systems of oppression" ("Feminism and Ecology: Making Connections," *Environmental Ethics* 9 [1987]: 18). Unfortunately, however, many feminists who claim to be ecofeminists do not make their (presumed) commitment to an *ecocentric* egalitarianism particularly explicit, with the result that ecofeminist analyses can sometimes serve to reinforce anthropocentrism rather than overcome it. As for those ecofeminists, such as Warren, who are explicit about their commitment to an ecocentric egalitarianism, it becomes difficult to see any essential difference between their approach and that of deep ecology. As one ecofeminist-cum-deep ecologist said to me after reading Warren's article: "Why doesn't she just call it [i.e., Warren's vision of a transformative feminism] deep ecology? Why specifically attach the label *feminism* to it if she's advocating a genuinely nonprioritizing, biocentric egalitarianism?"
23. When I refer to any class of social actors, I expressly mean also to refer to the culture(s) associated with that class. However, I omit writing "men and their associated cultures," "non-Westerners and their associated cultures," and so on simply for ease of comprehension. In referring to capitalists and, hence, the culture of capitalism, I also mean to refer to "state capitalism" as found in the industrialized communist countries.
24. Indeed, even as I wrote this paper, a significant real-life example of such criticisms was being played out between the women of Greenham Common in the form of a "bitter dispute" over allegations of racism at the camp. Reports suggested that this dispute "threatens the world's most renowned peace camp after six years" (Deborah Smith, "Showdown at Greenham Common," *The Times on Sunday*, 25 October 1987, p. 27). Karen J. Warren similarly criticizes radical feminists—that group of feminists who "have had the most to say about ecofeminism"—for paying "little attention to the historical and material features of women's oppression (including the relevance of race, class, ethnic, and national background)" ("Feminism and Ecology," pp. 14–15).

25. Note that I am borrowing the phrase "the real root" from Michael Zimmerman's previously quoted formulation of what I consider to be the essential ecofeminist charge against deep ecology. I employ this phrase several times in the argument that follows.
26. Murray Bookchin, "Social Ecology Versus 'Deep Ecology,' " *Green Perspectives: Newsletter of the Green Program Project*, Summer 1987.
27. Ibid., p. 2 (emphasis added). This view is central to Bookchin's major statement of social ecology: *The Ecology of Freedom: The Emergence and Dissolution of Hierarchy* (Palo Alto: Cheshire Books, 1982).
28. This observation is in keeping with the anthropocentric flavor that many deep ecologists detect in Bookchin's work notwithstanding his avowed ecological orientation.
29. Salleh, "Deeper than Deep Ecology," p. 345. In another presentation of the ecofeminist sensibility, Don Davis also concludes by reiterating this conclusion of Salleh's ("Ecosophy: The Seduction of Sophia?" *Environmental Ethics* 8 [1986]: 151–62).
30. Salleh, "Deeper than Deep Ecology," p. 340.
31. Warren, "Feminism and Ecology," pp. 13–15, and Zimmerman, "Feminism, Deep Ecology," p. 40.
32. Warren, "Feminism and Ecology," p. 14. See also Alan E. Wittbecker, "Deep Anthropology: Ecology and Human Order," *Environmental Ethics* 8 (1986): 261–70, which provides a number of counterinstances to Salleh's essentialist feminist claim that the suppression of the feminine is "universal."
33. Stunningly obvious instances of these kinds of examples, such as the Prime Minister of England, Margaret Thatcher (the "Iron Lady"), sending warships to the Falklands, are typically explained in terms of the hegemony of androcentrism being such as to have overpowered the offending woman's essential nature. The implication is that if, as Salleh says, women could just "be allowed to love what we are," then it would no longer be possible to find such examples.
34. Where revised, such perspectives would no doubt continue to differ from deep ecology in terms of their theoretical flavors and emphases, but they would not differ from deep ecology in terms of their essential concerns. Whether these revised perspectives would be recognizable or acceptable to their earlier supporters is of course an interesting question.
35. Ecofeminists, green socialists, and so on are also concerned with questions of legitimation, but generally in a different sense than deep ecologists are.
36. Bookchin, "Social Ecology," p. 3 (emphasis added).
37. Henryk Skolimowski, "To Continue the Dialogue with Deep Ecology," *The Trumpeter* 4, no. 4 (1987): 31. Skolimowski has previously been taken to task for the anthropocentrism inherent in his own approach: see George Sessions' review of Skolimowski's *Eco-Philosophy* in *Environmental Ethics* 6 (1984): 167–74. Since then Skolimowski has become a regular critic of deep ecology: see his articles "The Dogma of Anti-Anthropocentrism and Ecophilosophy," *Environmental Ethics* 6 (1984): 283–88 (Skolimowski's response to Sessions' review); "In Defence of Ecophilosophy and of Intrinsic Value: A Call for Conceptual Clarity," *The Trumpeter* 3, no. 4 (1986): 9–12 (this issue of *The Trumpeter* also carried replies from Bill Devall, Arne Naess, and myself); "To Continue the Dialogue with Deep Ecology"; and "Eco-Philosophy and Deep Ecology," *The Ecologist* 18 (1988): 124–27. I defend Sessions' reading of Skolimowski in my "Further Notes in Response to Skolimowski," *The Trumpeter* 4, no. 4 (1987): 32–34.
38. Much of Bookchin's case for his (mistaken) contention that deep ecology is essentially a misanthropic enterprise rests on certain statements by one or two significant figures in Earth First!—especially Dave Foreman and his personal, unhistorical, and abhorrently simplistic views on population control. However, Bookchin overlooks the surely obvious fact that Foreman says elsewhere in the same interview (p. 42), "I am speaking for myself, not for Earth First!," and both

he and Foreman overlook the equally obvious fact that such a view runs contrary to the deep-ecological principle of encouraging an egalitarian attitude on the part of humans toward all entities in the ecosphere. In contrast to Foreman, Arne Naess says in a recent paper: "Sustainable development today means development along the lines of each culture, not development along a common, centralized line. But faced with hungry children humanitarian action is a priority, whatever its relation to developmental plans and cultural invasion" ("Sustainable Development and the Deep-Long-Range Ecological Movement").

39. There are two significant qualifications to be noted in this statement. First, I say "to all intents and purposes" because where these traditions have supposedly been primarily theocentric rather than anthropocentric, it has of course still been humans who have, by divine decree, had "dominion . . . over all the earth [which they are enjoined to 'fill and subdue'] . . . and over every living thing that moves upon the earth" (Genesis 1:26 and 1:28). From a deep ecological perspective, personalistic theocentrisms, in which humans are made in the image of a god to whom they have a privileged personal relationship, are simply anthropocentric projections upon the cosmos. Second, I say "since the time of the *classical* Greeks" (i.e., the Sophists, Socrates, Plato, and Aristotle) as distinct from the *early* Greeks, who initiated Western philosophy (i.e., the early and later Ionians, the Pythagoreans, the Eleatics, and the Atomists—often collectively referred to as the pre-Socratics), because, as Bertrand Russell has pointed out, "What is amiss, even in the best philosophy after Democritus [i.e., after the pre-Socratics], is an undue emphasis on man as compared with the universe" (Bertrand Russell, *History of Western Philosophy* [London: Unwin Paperbacks, 1979], p. 90). Russell's statement is meant to refer to humanity in general, although it also applies, of course, if its sexist expression is read as representing its intended meaning (i.e., if "man" is read as "men"). It should be noted in this regard, however, that the reason why Russell's statement is true in the gender specific sense is, as I argue below, precisely because men have seen themselves as essentially *more* human than women—an observation that returns us to Russell's intended meaning in a dialectical manner. For excellent discussions of the anthropocentric nature of Western philosophy since the time of the pre-Socratics, see George Sessions, "Anthropocentrism and the Environmental Crisis," *Humboldt Journal of Social Relations* 2 (1974): 71–81 and George Sessions, "Spinoza and Jeffers on Man in Nature," *Inquiry* 20 (1977): 481–528.
40. Both quotes are from Brian Easlea's erudite and inspiring book *Liberation and the Aims of Science: An Essay on Obstacles to the Building of a Beautiful World* (London: Chatto and Windus, 1973), p. 253.
41. I include a reference to essentialist feminists here because, as Michael Zimmerman points out ("Feminism, Deep Ecology," p. 40), "In recent years, a number of feminists have favoured . . . an essentialist view [that women are essentially more attuned to nature than men] and have concluded that woman is *better* than man" (my emphasis). Karen Warren criticizes this point of view sharply ("Feminism and Ecology," p. 15): "The truth is that women, like men, are both connected to nature and separate from it, natural and cultural beings . . . locating women either on the nature or on the culture side . . . mistakenly perpetuates the sort of oppositional, dualistic thinking for which patriarchal conceptual frameworks are criticized." But, even more fundamentally (since this is the end that such oppositional, dualistic thinks *serves*), essentialist feminism perpetuates the anthropocentric assumption that some humans are more equal than others by virtue of their essential nature.

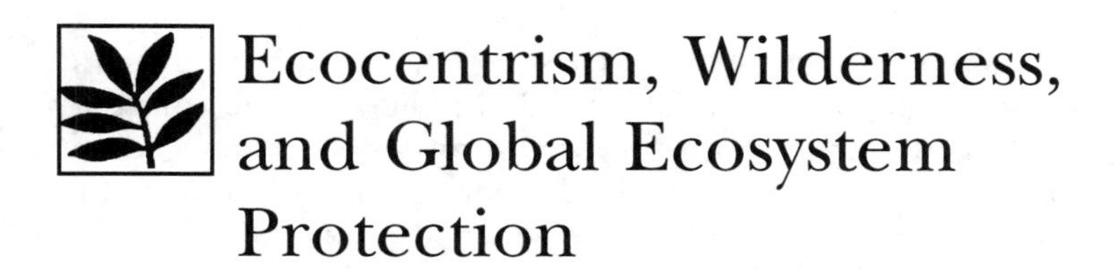

Ecocentrism, Wilderness, and Global Ecosystem Protection

George Sessions

George Sessions is chair of the Department of Philosophy at Sierra College in Rocklin, California. Author of numerous essays about ecophilosophy and deep ecology, and coauthor (with Bill Devall) of Deep Ecology, *Sessions recently published the anthology* Deep Ecology for the 21st Century.

WILDERNESS: FROM MUIR TO PINCHOT TO MUIR

The ecophilosopher Holmes Rolston III has quoted disapprovingly from a 1978 U.S. Forest Service document on "wilderness management" that asserts: "Wilderness is for people. . . . The preservation goals established for such areas are designed to provide values and benefits to society. . . . Wilderness is not set aside for the sake of its flora or fauna, but for people."[1]

It is disappointing to find Forest Service theorists in the late 1970s still promoting narrowly human-centered views of the function and values of wilderness. In so doing, they follow in the footsteps of the U.S. Forest Service founder, Gifford Pinchot, who once claimed "there are just people and resources." As the ideological archival of John Muir at the beginning of the twentieth century, Pinchot promoted the anthropocentrism and utilitarian resource management mentality that has pervaded conservationist and land-use agency policy since the turn of the century.

It is somewhat ironic that Forest Service theorists continue with this unecological anthropocentric approach when we consider that Aldo Leopold (the *founder* of the Forest Service wilderness concept in the 1920s) published his justly famous ecocentric "land ethic" over forty years ago, and when professional ecologists have been promoting the ecological functions of wilderness at the Sierra Club Wilderness Conferences since the late 1950s.

Originally published (in a longer version) in *The Wilderness Condition*, edited by Max Oelschlaeger (San Francisco: Sierra Club Books, 1992). Reprinted with permission.

Unlike the Forest Service, the National Park Service began to implement an ecological approach to its wilderness and wildlife policies in the spring of 1963, following the suggestions of its Advisory Board on Wildlife Management (the so-called Leopold Report, named for its chairman, Starker Leopold, the son of Aldo Leopold and a zoologist at the University of California at Berkeley). The Leopold Report proposed that the wilderness parks, using Yellowstone as a model, be treated as "biotic wholes." Leopold's committee, according to Alston Chase, was proposing "a philosophy of management that could be applied universally" (for instance, to the African wildlife reserves).[2]

Alston Chase blames the wilderness ecosystem approach for the decline of wildlife and ecological deterioration of Yellowstone, and has proposed instead a heavily manipulative scientific wildlife management approach—one that would turn Yellowstone into what some have described as a "natural zoo." Ecologists claim that, like most parks when established, Yellowstone does not comprise a complete ecosystem. For the ecosystem approach to work, a "Greater Yellowstone Ecosystem" must be established and legally protected. In addition, predator/prey balances must be reestablished, as through the reintroduction of the wolf.[3]

When Congress passed the Forest Reserve Act in 1891 enabling President Benjamin Harrison to set aside 13 million acres in "forest reserves," Muir had reason to believe they would be protected as wilderness. But the "forest reserves" later became National Forests, and Pinchot and the Forest Service had other plans for them. Following Pinchot's advocacy of the Resource Conservation and Development position, the Forest Service (as a branch of the Department of Agriculture) sees its primary function as serving as a handmaiden for industrial "resource" exploitation. Ecologically destructive activities such as mining, domestic animal grazing, and sport hunting, are allowed even within National Forest designated wilderness areas. And just as the Pioneers cleared wild forests to make way for agriculture, the Forest Service has facilitated and promoted the destruction of the last unprotected old growth (ancient) forest ecosystems in America to make way for agriculture in the form of biologically sterile monocultural "tree farms"—where the trees consist of one or two commercially valuable species, are even-aged, and grow in nice neat rows like a field of corn.

For the Forest Service, the forests are a *commodity* to be managed, "enhanced," and exploited: either as an agricultural crop to be "harvested" or as designated areas where "the wilderness experience" serves as a human recreational commodity. Forest economists decide these issues by assigning an economic value to the various human "uses" of the forests and computing a cost-benefit analysis.

Further, the forests are to be "enhanced"—and *domesticated*—by replacing ancient forest biodiversity with genetically manipulated "superior" (more economically valuable) trees which grow straighter and faster. One wonders about the wisdom of this now that the genetically "enhanced" domestic grains of the agricultural Green Revolution have turned sour. At present, geneticists are scouring the world for the genetic variability of whatever little pockets of wild grains still remain that have not been genetically tampered with. On the other hand, John Muir has already responded to this genetic tampering with the forests when he claimed that "all wildness is finer than tameness." Similarly, for Thoreau: "In wildness is the preservation of the world."

As early as 1976, John Rodman pointed out:

> The charges frequently made in recent years by Preservationists and others—e.g., that the Forest Service is a captive (or willing) agent of corporate interests, that it allows ecologically-disruptive clear-cutting as well as cutting in excess of official quotas, while permitting grazing corporations to overgraze the land while paying fees far less than they would have to pay for the use of private land, etc.—represent less the latter-day capture of an agency by one or more of its constituents than a maturation of the basic principles of the founder [Pinchot]. The Forest Service is, in effect, a perennial government subsidy, in exchange for certain regulatory controls, to certain types of corporations.[4]

The massive clear-cutting of the last unprotected old-growth coniferous forests along the West Coast of North America (from California to Washington and into the Tongass National Forest in Southeast Alaska) is surpassed in unbridled destruction only by the unrestricted Canadian clear-cutting of British Columbia. At the present rate of clear-cutting along the British Columbia coast, this world's largest remaining temperate rain forest will be gone in fifteen years.[5] Surely, the loss of these last great ancient forest ecosystems in North America will go down as one of the great ecological crimes and blunders of this century, comparable to present rain forest destruction in the Amazon and the rest of Central and South America, Africa, Australia, and Southeast Asia. Japan's thirst for wood products for international markets has been primarily responsible for encouraging the destruction of 80 to 90 percent of the tropical forests in Sri Lanka and Southeast Asia over the last forty years. Japan is also a leading exploiter of the old-growth forests of Central and South America (including Brazil, Peru, and Chile) and the United States (including Southeast Alaska). Japanese corporations are now negotiating with Russia to clear cut the great pine forests of Siberia, the habitat of the Siberian tiger.

The destruction of the biodiversity of the last of the wild ancient forest ecosystems, and their replacement with unstable even-age tree plantations, is now occurring all over the world at an increasing rate.[6] Forestry critic Chris Maser points out that we are nowhere near attaining "sustainable forestry" even on those lands where tree cutting is appropriate, because we are training "plantation managers" instead of foresters. He writes: "We are liquidating our forests and replacing them with short-rotation plantations. Everything Nature does in designing forests adds to diversity, complexity, and stability through time. We decrease this by redesigning forests into plantations."[7] The destruction of ancient forests must cease, and a massive global effort should be made to try to *restore* diverse wild forest ecosystems. Fortunately, wide-scale public pressure is now being applied to modern forestry ideology to bring about major ecological reform. And even Pinchot-trained foresters are beginning to undergo a change of heart. As Canadian forester Bob Nixon recently remarked:

> As a forester, I learned to view forests as a source of industrial fibre. Now, I know that forests are much more than vertical assemblages of lumber, so very much more important than just a source of consumer products. . . . Natural forests, the new research tells us, are no longer something to move through, in the economic sense, in our quest for higher gains, but indeed a key element in the balanced functioning of planetary life.[8]

And how has wildness fared in Muir's National Parks under the anthropocentric orientation of twentieth-century America? The parks do not allow resource extraction within their boundaries, including their newly designated wilderness areas. But many of the parks have been damaged by NPS policies over the years that have catered to dominant American values and lifestyles, which see the parks as essentially natural "scenery" and recreational escapes for city-dwellers. This has encouraged a Disneyland atmosphere of excessive tourism and overdeveloped facilities, upgraded high-speed roads ("scenic drives"), mechanized recreation such as snowmobiling (which disturbs the tranquillity and the wildlife) and human overcrowding: what Edward Abbey called "industrial tourism."[9] In short, there has been a constant push from the commercially motivated to turn them into "theme parks" and international "roadside attractions."

THE IMPLICATIONS OF CONSERVATION BIOLOGY FOR THE EARTH'S EVOLUTIONARY PROCESSES

The adequacy of currently designated wilderness areas and nature reserves throughout the world received a serious jolt in the 1980s from the findings of the new discipline of conservation biology.

In the 1960s, professional ecologists stepped outside their narrow areas of scientific expertise and began warning the public of the impending ecological disaster. They also proposed various public strategies to cope with these problems. The "intellectual activism" begun by these ecologists has been institutionalized into a new branch of ecology called "conservation biology." According to Mitch Friedman:

> Conservation biology considers the application of ecological theory and knowledge to conservation efforts. The development and utilization of this new discipline is a welcome advance in conservation, where ecological considerations tend to be overshadowed by political and economic forces, in part due to poor understanding of the effects of land-use decisions.[10]

Conservation biology has been spearheaded largely by Michael Soulé (an ecologist and a former student of Paul Ehrlich), who refers to conservation biology as a "crisis discipline" that has to apply its findings in the absence of certainty. This new field integrates ethical norms with the latest findings of ecological science.[11]

Soulé has provided scientific definitions for the terms "conservation" and "preservation." In his usage, "preservation" means "the maintenance of individuals or groups, but not for their evolutionary change." He proposes that "conservation" be taken to denote "policies and programs for the long-term retention of natural communities under conditions which provide for the potential for continuing evolution." Mitch Friedman carries this a step further by introducing the concept of "ecosystem conservation." This approach "involves the preservation of ecosystem wilderness: enough of the land area and functional components—the creatures *and* their habitat—to insure the continuation of processes which have co-evolved over immeasurable time."[12]

One can quibble over the choice of terms. "Conservation" has negative associations with Pinchot and the Resource Conservation and Development position. And "preservation" does not necessarily mean trying to maintain something in a static state, such as "preserving jam" or "deep-freezing" a wilderness. Perhaps "protection" would be a more neutral term. However, the term "ecosystem conservation" means protecting the ongoing dynamic continuum of evolutionary processes that constitutes the overall ecological health of the planet, in the sense described by Aldo Leopold.

It is thus clear that the *primary purpose* in setting aside and evaluating wilderness areas and wild nature preserves, from the standpoint of conservation biology and the ecological crisis, is the conservation and protection of wild plants, animals, and ecosystems (biotic diversity) and the continuation of wild evolutionary processes.

Based upon these objectives, we need to look at present global ecological realities. As Friedman points out:

> An element of panic is present within the literature of conservation biology, as well as among the conservation community at large. This panic originates predominately from the present rate of species extinction, and the forecasts for impending mass extinction. We presently have scarcely a clue of even the total number of species on the planet, with estimates ranging between three and thirty-seven million. Yet, some researchers are predicting that anthropogenic extinctions, at current rates (which do not consider military disasters or other unpredictable events), may eliminate as many as a third of the planet's species over the next several decades (Meyers, 1987). This is shocking to anyone who treasures the intrinsic values of Earth's natural diversity and fecundity, or who fears for the fate of humanity and the planet as a whole. While most of these extinctions are occurring as a result of tropical rainforest deforestation, the same processes are occurring in temperate areas, including the United States (Wilcove et al., 1986).[13]

A further crisis that conservation biology has brought to public attention, as the result of ecological research in the 1980s, is that existing nature reserves (namely, national park and forest wilderness areas) do not meet realistic ecological criteria: they are too small and disconnected to protect biodiversity and ecological/evolutionary processes. Friedman claims:

> It is not enough to preserve some habitat for each species if we want to conserve ecosystems; the habitat must remain in the conditions under which the resident species evolved. For this reason, national forests, under present "multiple use" management, may not be effective nature reserves for many species.
>
> Historically, national parks and other reserves have been established according to political, or other nonbiological considerations. . . . To conserve species diversity, the legal boundaries of nature reserves should be congruent with natural criteria (Newmark, 1985). For instance, a reserve may be large [e.g., Everglades National Park] while still not protecting the ecological integrity of the area.
>
> Newmark (1985) suggests that reserves contain not only entire watersheds, but at least the minimum area necessary to maintain viable populations of those species which have the largest home ranges. Others have stated that complete, intact ecosystems should be preserved (Terborgh and Winter, 1980; Noss, 1985).[14]

In the 1970s Michael Soulé examined twenty wildlife reserves in East Africa, including the massive Tsavo and Serengeti national parks. He and his fellow researchers projected that

> all of the reserves will suffer extinctions in the near future. Their study predicts that a typical reserve, if it becomes a habitat island, will lose almost half of its large mammal species over the next 500 years . . . when a habitat island, for instance a national park surrounded by national forest, is reduced in size (i.e., clearcutting along the park boundaries), the number of species in that island will decrease. The empirical evidence for the relaxation effect is alarming, and reflects the urgency with which we must re-evaluate our conservation strategies and remedy the situation.[15]

Edward Grumbine further points out that

> Newmark (1985) investigated eight parks and park assemblages and found that even the largest reserve was six times too small to support minimum viable populations of species such as grizzly bear, mountain lion, black bear, wolverine, and gray wolf. A recent study by Salwasser et al. (1987) looked beyond park boundaries and included adjacent public lands as part of conservation networks. The results were the same. Only the largest area (81,000 square km) was sufficient to protect large vertebrate species over the long term. . . . Virtually every study of this type has reached similar conclusions: No park in the coterminus U.S. is capable of supporting minimum viable populations of large mammals over the long term. And the situation is worsening.[16]

Frankel and Soulé claim that "an area on the order of 600,000 square km (approximately equal to all of Washington and Oregon) is necessary for speciation of birds and large mammals."[17]

Christopher Manes quotes Soulé as saying that "for the first time in hundreds of millions of years significant evolutionary change in most higher organisms is coming to a screeching halt. . . . Vertebrate evolution may be at an end." Manes claims that Soulé's remarks may be as significant as the findings of Copernicus or Darwin in that "only a hundred or so years after Darwin 'discovered' our fundamental relationship to nature in terms of evolution, we are, according to Soulé, putting an end to it."[18]

The inescapable conclusion is this: there needs to be widespread public recognition that current global wilderness and nature preserve protection policies are failing miserably. Past policies and strategies have been based on inadequate ecological understanding. Humans have effectivity clogged the evolutionary arteries of Mother Gaia.

Along with protecting the ozone layer, minimizing the severity of the greenhouse effect, and stabilizing (and then reducing) the growth and size of the human population, the most crucial ecological task facing humanity at this time is to devise and implement realistic nature reserve protection strategies.

APPROACHES TO GLOBAL ECOSYSTEM PROTECTION ZONING

Even before conservation biologists were demonstrating the necessity for greatly expanded nature preserves throughout the world with interconnecting corridors, ecologists and environmentalists over twenty years ago had called for worldwide zoning to protect wild ecosystems and species. The first such proposal was made by David Brower in 1967. Declaring that less than 10 percent of the Earth had, at that time, escaped technological exploitation by humans, he proposed protecting the remaining wilderness and "granting other life forms the right to coexist" in what Jerry Mander called an Earth International Park.[19]

Another major zoning proposal was put forth in 1971 by the noted ecologist Eugene Odum. Odum proposed that:

> *The biosphere as a whole should be zoned,* in order to protect it from the human impact. We must strictly confine the Urban-Industrial Zone and the Production Zone (agriculture, grazing, fishing), enlarge the Compromise Zone, and drastically expand the Protection Zone, i.e., wilderness, wild rivers. Great expanses of seacoasts and estuaries must be included in the Protection Zone, along with forests, prairies and various habitat types. We must learn that the multiple-use Compromise Zone is no substitute, with its mining, lumbering, grazing, and recreation in the national forests, for the scientific, aesthetic, and genetic pool values of the Protection Zone. Such zoning, if carried out in time, may be the only way to limit the destructive impact of our technological–industrial–agri-business complex on earth.

In commenting upon Odum's proposal, John Phillips claimed that "to go so far as to zone the biosphere and set aside an adequate Protection Zone would be a supreme act of rationality by which the rational animal could protect the rest of life on earth, and himself, from his own irrational temptations."[20]

In 1973, Paul Shepard made a daring proposal for global ecosystem protection. In order to allow for the huge expanses of unmanaged wilderness needed "for ecological and evolutionary systems on a scale essential to their own requirements," he proposed that the interiors of continents and islands be allowed to return to the wild. Based on the now optimistic assumption that human population would stabilize by the year 2020 at 8 billion people, he proposed that humans live in cities strung in narrow ribbons along the edges of the continents. Hunting/gathering forays would range into the central wilderness, but there would be no permanent habitation.[21]

Based on his ecocentric orientation, Shepard foresaw the huge amounts of wilderness necessary for the healthy ecological and evolutionary functioning of the Earth. But his proposal has a number of practical and social/political problems, not the least of which would be (1) the physical problems involved in relocating humans to the edges of the continents, and (2) the pressures exerted by these concentrated human populations on the ocean shoreline ecosystems and estuaries. At this stage of history, it is probably more realistic to expand and interconnect ecosystem protection zones with the basically existing patterns of human settlement in mind.

Two other strategies that were developed to protect wild ecosystems are the Biosphere Reserve concept, as part of UNESCO's Man and the Biosphere Program, and the World Heritage Site system. According to Edward Grumbine:

> A model biosphere reserve consists of four integrated zones: a large protected core; a buffer zone; a restoration zone; and a stable cultural area where "indigenous people live in harmony with the environment." . . . the National Park Service has informally adopted the biosphere reserve model as a guide to regional land planning [and] after eighteen years, 41 biosphere reserves exist in the U.S. many of which occupy both national park and forest lands.[22]

Grumbine sees some possibilities with World Heritage Site designations, but he argues that there are serious problems with the Biosphere Reserve concept: the zones are not properly related and the "self-sustaining" core is not large enough to allow for speciation. He suggests that the biosphere reserve model be replaced by a national system of biological reserves.

ECOLOGICAL RESTORATION, MITIGATION, AND STEWARDSHIP

Grumbine further argues that the establishment of biological reserves needs to be supplemented by a major program of *ecological restoration*:

> Restoration of damaged lands must be married to the goal of native diversity. This follows the *wilderness recovery* strategy of Noss (1986) and would include large scale restoration of natural fire cycles, recovery of threatened, endangered, and extirpated species, road closures and reforestation projects, stream rehabilitation to

> increase native anadromous fisheries, and much more (see Berger, 1985). Once an area was restored, nature would take its course with minimal interference from managers. The amount of work to be done would likely offset the loss of jobs in exploitive industries.[23]

The concept of ecological restoration is a crucial one for all of the zones, but serious problems emerge when developers try to use it as a justification for "mitigation" procedures: claiming that we can continue to develop (that is, *destroy*) wild ecosystems, displace wildlife, and then compensate these losses by "restoring" an equivalent area elsewhere. This is a shortsighted foolhardy approach, part of the overall "Disneyland syndrome" and the mentality that "human ingenuity and technological know-how can solve all our problems." This neglects the difficult and expensive process of restoration, together with the probability that restoration projects will be only partially successful. In all likelihood, they cannot reproduce the incredibly complex and diverse wild ecosystems that were destroyed. Further, mitigation procedures and environmental impact reports (EIR's), as they now exist in environmental law and as taught in environmental management programs in colleges and universities, function basically to "grease the skids" of continued growth and development as wildlife habitat is fragmented and destroyed, and wild flora and fauna relentlessly continue to disappear.

The anthropocentric/ecocentric debate has resurfaced in the context of trying to clarify the concept of "ecological restoration." Some restoration theorists argue for a stewardship approach in which restoration areas are to be treated as agricultural farms to be continuously manipulated and "enhanced" by humans (which is similar to the ideology of the Forest Service and their genetically "enhanced" forests). For instance, restoration theorist John Harper proposes the manipulative, interventionist, Baconian/Cartesian model of science as appropriate for ecology and restoration ecology:

> The *raison d'être* for a science of ecology is presumably the development of an understanding of the workings of nature that would enable us to predict its behavior and to manage and control it to our liking. . . . [Thus] the importance of a more manipulative, experimental approach to ecological research such as that represented by restoration ecology.

There is a play on words here, a bit of Orwellian Newspeak, with Harper's concept of ecological restoration. If one is going to continuously manipulate, there is no *ecological* restoration. By proposing the human-dominant managerial stewardship model for restoration ecology (the "participatory happy gardener" image of René Dubos) Harper seems totally unconcerned with the continual extension of human domesticity and the elimination of more wildness while, at the same time he assumes that humans are competent to manage Nature. Professional ecologists such as Frank Egler have countered that "Nature is not only more complex than we think, it is more complex that we *can* think!"[24]

Critics claim that proponents of nature preserves (which are largely free of human intervention and manipulation) view Nature as "static." But from Thoreau and Muir to modern conservation biologists, the protection of wildness in nature (or wilderness) preserves has been seen as the protection of wild evolutionary change: in Soulé's words, as the conservation of "natural communities under conditions which provide for the potential for continuing evolution." Ecological restoration should be followed, as Grumbine suggests, by allowing nature to take its course "with minimal interference from managers." Stewardship concepts of restoration should be confined to the bioculture.

FREE NATURE, BIOCULTURE, AND BIOREGIONALISM

Arne Naess has added an important refinement to zoning proposals and ecosystem protection strategies by distinguishing between *wilderness* protection zones (where people do not live and resource extraction is prohibited) and what he calls *free nature.* "Free nature" consists of areas of relatively sparse human habitation (for example, the foothills of the Sierra, parts of northern Europe, and much of the Third World) where wild natural processes are still essentially intact and dominant. These areas should be zoned to protect natural processes and wildlife while encouraging nonexploitive bioregional living. The remaining Fourth World tribal peoples who are still following traditional ways with minimal impact on wild ecosystems, can be thought of as living in free nature areas.[25]

One of the central features of thinking about ecological sustainable societies is the move toward decentralization and bioregional ways of life, which involves reinhabiting and restoring damaged ecosystems. But Roderick Nash, a major theorist and proponent of wilderness protection, has worried that a total movement toward bioregional reinhabitation of the Earth at this point (what he calls the "garden scenario") would be ecologically disastrous: "The problem, of course, is numbers. There are simply too many people on the planet to decentralize into garden environments and still have significant amounts of wilderness."[26] Elsewhere, Nash characterizes bioregionalism as "the contemporary attempt to 'reinhabit' wilderness areas."[27]

Nash is entirely justified in calling attention to the limitations of an overly ambitious bioregional program at this point in history. It is not clear, however, that the intent of contemporary bioregionalists is to reinhabit wilderness areas. Leading bioregional theorists such as Peter Berg, Gary Snyder, Raymond Dasmann, Thomas Berry, and Kirkpatrick Sale are fully aware of the importance of establishing greatly expanded wilderness/protection zones. Bioregional ways of life are appropriate for "free nature" and for ecologically restructured cities as suggested in such projects as Peter Berg's "green cities."[28] Redesigned ecological cities would contain wild and semiwild areas interspersed with human inhabited areas, either by protecting and expanding upon wild or near-wild areas that now exist near cities, or by restoring such areas.

Roderick Nash points out that "in 1982 [Edward] Abbey expressed his basic belief that humans had no right to use more than a portion of the planet and they had already passed that limit. Wild places must be left wild." In 1985, Stanford ecologist Paul Ehrlich claimed that "in a country like the United States, there is not the slightest excuse for developing one more square inch of undisturbed land." In their 1987 survey of world environmental problems, Anne and Paul Ehrlich proposed that, as a general policy "the prime step [is] *to permit no development of any more virgin lands* . . . whatever remaining relatively undisturbed land exists that supports a biotic community of any significance should be set aside and fiercely defended against encroachment."[29] As the Ehrlichs point out, the 6 billion humans now on Earth have already destroyed or appropriated approximately 40 percent of biomass productivity on the land.[30]

Environmental ethicist Paul Taylor also promotes the idea of the protection of wilderness as species habitat. He claims that we must

> constantly place constraints on ourselves so as to cause the least possible interference in natural ecosystems and their biota. . . . If [humans] have a sufficient concern for the natural world, they can control their own population growth, change their habits of consumption, and regulate their technology so as to save at least part of the Earth's surface as habitat for wild animals and plants.[31]

Taylor finds it necessary to distinguish between the basic needs of humans versus their nonbasic wants. To allow for sufficient amounts of species habitat, humans must reduce their nonbasic wants and consumption habits when these come into conflict with the basic needs of other species for survival and well-being. Taylor's analysis coincides with Naess's distinction between vital and nonvital needs and wants, which is incorporated into the Deep Ecology platform.[32]

Paul Taylor makes another important contribution to the discussion of ecosystem protection zoning with his concept of the *bioculture.* He defines bioculture as "that aspect of any human culture in which humans create and regulate the environment of living things and systemically exploit them for human benefit."[33] Large-scale agriculture, pets, domestic animal and plant breeding, and "tree plantations" all belong to the human bioculture. Wilderness protection zoning, in effect, separates the world of the wild from the exploitive human activities of the bioculture. "Free nature" can be conceived of as a sort of hybrid buffer zone (where wild ecological processes predominate) situated between protection zones and biocultural zones.

Taylor's concept of the bioculture is a useful one. For instance, it helps us see that many movements are primarily involved with an ecological reform of the bioculture. The organic farm movement (inspired by Wendell Berry and Wes Jackson) is one example of this. The animal rights movement, in its concern with the "rights" of *all* animals, has, at least theoretically, failed to distinguish between the conditions of domestic animals in the bioculture and the very different situation of wild animals in wild ecosystems, sometimes with alarmingly anti-ecological results.

The present unecological goals and practices of the Forest Service (and similar practices worldwide) in clear-cutting wild forest ecosystems and replacing them with "tree plantations" can now be seen as an attempt to extend the bioculture at the expense of the wild. Taylor points out that the ethics of the bioculture differs fundamentally from the basically "noninterference" ethics appropriate to wilderness/protection zones. Perhaps some ecologically enlightened version of the "stewardship" model is appropriate for the bioculture, but not for wilderness/protection areas. Different kinds of problems arise when domestic animals gone ferral (and exotics) intrude in wild ecosystems, when wild animals stray from the protection zones into biocultural zones, and when there are mixed communities of wild and domestic as in "free nature."[34]

WILDERNESS PROTECTION IN THE FIRST WORLD

The question still remains concerning how much of the Earth should be protected in wilderness and other ecosystem protection zones. The basic answer to this question has essentially been given by the recent research of the conservation biologists: enough habitat to protect the diversity and abundance of wild species, and the ongoing ecological health of the Earth, which involves, among other things, continued speciation and wild evolutionary change. Along these lines, Arne Naess has provided a future ecological vision toward which we can progress:

> I am not saying that we should have preserved the primordial forest as a whole, but looking back we can imagine a development such that, let us say, one third was preserved as wilderness, one third as free nature with mixed communities, which leaves one third for cities, paved roads, etc. [bioculture]. This would probably be enough, and I guess most people with influence in matters of the environment would agree. But of course, it is a wild fantasy, which is, incidentally, an important kind of wilderness![35]

To realize how ecologically out of balance we are in the United States, based upon Naess's suggestion, we have to consider Thomas Fleischner's point that "over 95% of the contiguous United States has been altered from its original state. Only 2% is legally protected from explosive uses."[36] And even that 2 percent lacks adequate ecological protection. For example, Forest Service legally designated wilderness areas continue to allow mining, sport hunting, and domestic animal grazing within their boundaries. Legislative efforts are now being made to revise existing mining laws that have been the cause of much public land abuse. Some have claimed that, apart from ancient forest destruction, the greatest cause of ecological destruction on public lands (both wilderness and nonwilderness areas) is cattle and sheep grazing. Domestic animal grazing destroys the natural plant and grass communities, causes erosion, damages streams and other water supplies, competes with wildlife, results in federal programs to kill large numbers of large predators (including the poisoning and trapping of huge numbers of "nontarget" wildlife), and should be phased out.[37]

To begin to achieve an ecological land-use balance, once the ecologically destructive uses of now-existing Forest Service wilderness have been eliminated, the remaining 3 percent of *de facto* (nondesignated) wilderness should be placed in protection zones. This would bring the contiguous United States to a total to 5% protected habitat. That still leaves the contiguous United States approximately 30 percent short of a ratio of one-third wilderness, one-third free nature, and one-third bioculture (disregarding, for the present, the zoning of free nature).

Under the provisions of the Wilderness Act of 1964, the congressional battles over legal classification of wilderness in the National Parks and National Forests have already been fought, and mainline reform environmentalists have compromised severely in both cases, particularly the latter. Now the battle to zone land as wilderness is occurring over the 250 million acres administered by the Bureau of Land Management (BLM). The BLM is studying only 10 percent of its land (25 million acres) for possible wilderness designation (most BLM land is contracted out to private corporations and individuals for mining and domestic animal grazing). The projections are that, after the political wrangling and compromises are concluded, only 10 to 15 million acres will be legally protected. It must be remembered that the lands being discussed here (Park Service, Forest Service, and BLM) are *public* lands!

The Wilderness Act of 1964, while framed and successfully lobbied by dedicated conservationists, is nevertheless a pre-ecological document and, accordingly, its stated purposes and provisions do not reflect the huge tracts of wilderness protection zones (and the degree of protection) required for species and wild ecosystem protection, especially for large mammal speciation. A recent news magazine article discussing the Wilderness Act and the upcoming BLM wilderness fight still couches the issues largely in terms of anthropocentric special-interest compromise politics: of wilderness recreation versus "motorized-recreation and commercial interests." The ecological issues are all but ignored.[38]

In order to boost the wilderness protection zone percentages toward the 30 percent figure, it would probably be necessary to place most Forest Service and BLM lands in protection zones and to restore them to wildlife habitat. A recent proposal by Deborah and Frank Popper of Rutgers University to return the Great Plains to buffalo habitat would also greatly increase ecosystem protection areas.

These strategies for protecting wildness and biodiversity have recently been refined and sophisticated. For instance, the Wildlands Project has been working closely with conservation biologists to develop a North American Wilderness Recovery Strategy. According to Dave Foreman:

> Going far beyond current National Park, Wildlife Refuge, and Wilderness Area systems, where individual reserves are discrete islands of wildness in a sea of human-modified landscapes, [conservation biologists] call for large Wilderness cores, buffer zones, and biological corridors. . . . Biological corridors would provide secure travelways between core reserves for the dispersal of wide-ranging species, for genetic exchange between populations, and for migration of organisms in response to climate change. Surrounding the core reserves would be buffer zones where increasing levels of compatible human activity would be allowed away from the cores. . . . Conservation biologists propose to begin with existing National Parks, Wilderness Areas, and other protected or unprotected natural areas [and enlarge and connect them]. . . . The key concept in this new Wilderness Area model is *connectivity*.[39]

Foreman has recently discussed the history of the bioregional/reinhabitation movement beginning with the writings of Gary Snyder, Peter Berg, and Raymond Dasmann. He claims that:

> The centerpiece of every bioregional group's platform should be a great core wilderness preserve where all the indigenous creatures are present and the natural flow is intact. Other wilderness preserves, both large and small, should be established and protected throughout the bioregion, and natural corridors established to allow for the free flow of genetic material between them and to such preserves in other bioregions. . . . These core wilderness preserves should be sacred shrines to us as reinhabitory people, but they transcend even their sacredness to us in simply being what they are—reserves of native diversity.[40]

AN INTERNATIONAL PERSPECTIVE

Increasingly, our environmental problems are being recognized as global in scope and, as such, require effective international cooperation. Noel Brown, director of the United Nations Environmental Program, indicated that an Ecological Council (comparable to the Security Council) could soon be a reality.[41] With the human population predicted to soar to 10 to 15 billion people, if unchecked, by the middle of the next century (population biologists argue that 1 to 2 billion people worldwide, living comfortably at a basic-needs consumption level, would be maximum for what Naess calls "wide" ecological sustainability), the United Nations needs to reorganize its population control agencies and ecological protection programs to reflect a streamlined, effective, integrated biosphere approach to environmental problems. The United Nations General Assembly has already officially adopted an ecocentric orientation when it approved the World Charter for Nature in 1982. The charter asserts: "Every form of life is unique, warranting respect regardless of its worth to man, and, to accord other organisms such recognition, man must be guided by a moral code of action. . . Nature shall be respected and its essential processes shall not be disrupted."[42] The severity of the ecological crisis must be fully appreciated, and the Charter for Nature needs to be reaffirmed and effectively implemented. Humanity has now entered an era of what some ecologists are calling *biological meltdown*!

The urgency of the ecological crisis suggests that the United Nations should give the highest priority to stabilizing the human population in the shortest time possible while ensuring that human dignity and the ideals of justice are protected. Birth control programs, including making contraceptives freely available to all who want them, have *quite recently* proven to be highly effective in dramatically reducing birthrates in certain Third World countries. It is just as important that population be stabilized, and then reduced, in First World countries. The massive funding and implementation of such programs is needed immediately throughout the world. The United Nations should continue to help feed the hungry and improve basic living conditions in Third World countries, and discourage consumerism and further industrialization throughout the world as part of an overall program of ecological and economic sustainability. Major educational programs should be instituted to "ecologize" the peoples of the world.

Unlike First World countries, which are now overdeveloped, overpopulated, and ecologically unsustainable, Third World countries need to improve their overall material standards of living, although along ecologically sustainable paths. It is unrealistic and unjust to expect Third World countries to turn to the protection of their wild ecosystems *at the expense* of the vital needs of their human populations. But the magnitude and severity of the global ecological crisis must be fully appreciated. Third World countries should be encouraged to adopt as high a priority as possible on the establishment of ecosystem protection zones, and the protection of large areas of free nature.

NOTES

1. John Hendee, George Stankey, and Robert Lucas, *Wilderness Management* (Washington: USDA Forest Service Misc. Publication No. 1365, 1978), pp. 140–41; quoted in Holmes Rolston III, "Values Gone Wild," in Rolston, *Philosophy Gone Wild: Essays in Environmental Ethics* (Buffalo: Prometheus Books, 1986), p. 119.
2. Alston Chase, *Playing God in Yellowstone* (Boston: Atlantic Monthly Press, 1986), p. 33.
3. For a critique of Chase's views, see Dave Foreman, Doug Peacock, and George Sessions, "Who's 'Playing God in Yellowstone'?" *Earth First! Journal* 7, 11 (1986): 18–21.
4. John Rodman, "Resource Conservation—Economics and After," unpublished manuscript, Pitzer College, Claremont, Calif., 1976; see also Bill Devall and George Sessions, "The Development of Natural Resources and the Integrity of Nature," *Environmental Ethics* 6, 4 (1984): 293–322.
5. Joel Connelly, "British Columbia's Big Cut: Who Owns the Ancient Forests?" *Sierra* 76, no. 3 (1991): 42–53; see also Gary Snyder, *The Practice of the Wild* (San Francisco: North Point Press, 1990), pp. 116–43.
6. See Bill Devall (ed.), *Clearcut: The Tragedy of Industrial Forestry* (San Francisco: Sierra Club Books, 1994).
7. Chris Maser, *The Redesigned Forest* (San Pedro, Calif.: R&E Miles Publisher, 1988).
8. Bob Nixon, "Focus on Forests and Forestry," *The Trumpeter* 6, 2 (1989): 38.
9. Edward Abbey, *Desert Solitaire: A Season in the Wilderness* (New York: McGraw-Hill, 1968); see also Joseph Sax, *Mountains without Handrails* (Ann Arbor: University of Michigan Press, 1980).

10. Mitch Friedman, "How Much Is Enough?: Lessons from Conservation Biology," in Mitch Friedman (ed.), *Forever Wild: Conserving the Greater North Cascades Ecosystem* (Mountain Hemlock Press [P.O. Box 2962, Bellingham, WA 98227], 1988), p. 34. I have drawn much of the following material on conservation biology from the excellent summaries in this book by Friedman and by Edward Grumbine, "Ecosystem Management for Native Diversity." For further discussions of the importance of conservation biology for environmentalism in the '90s, see James R. Udall, "Launching the Natural Ark," *Sierra* 76, 5 (1991): 80–89; Edward Grumbine, *Ghost Bears: Exploring the Biodiversity Crisis* (Washington, D.C.: Island Press, 1992).
11. Michael Soulé, "What Is Conservation Biology?" *Bioscience* 35 (1985): 727–34; quoted in Friedman, ibid.
12. Friedman, *Forever Wild*, pp. 1–2; see also O. H. Frankel and Michael Soulé, *Conservation and Evolution* (Cambridge: Cambridge University Press, 1981); Michael Soulé and D. Simberloff, "What Do Genetics and Ecology Tell Us about the Design of Nature Reserves?" *Biological Conservation* 35 (1986): 19–40.
13. Friedman, "How Much Is Enough?" p. 39; Norman Myers, "The Extinction Spasm Impending: Synergisms at Work," *Conservation Biology* I (1987): 14–21; A. P. Dobson, C. H. McLellan, and D. S. Wilcove, "Habitat Fragmentation in the Temperate Zone," in M. Soulé (ed.), *Conservation Biology: The Science of Scarcity and Diversity* (Sunderland, Mass.: Sinauer, 1986), pp. 237–56.
14. Friedman, ibid.; A. Runte, *National Parks: The American Experience* (Lincoln: University of Nebraska Press, 1987); W. D. Newmark, "Legal and Biotic Boundaries of Western North American National Parks: A Problem of Congruence," *Biological Conservation* 33 (1985): 197–208; W. D. Newmark, "A Land-Bridge Island Perspective on Mammalian Extinctions in Western North American Parks," *Nature* 325 (1987): 430–32; R. M. May and D. S. Wilcove, "National Park Boundaries and Ecological Realities," *Nature* 324 (1986): 206–7; J. Terborgh and B. Winter, "Some Causes of Extinction," in B. A. Wilcox and Michael Soulé, *Conservation Biology: An Evolutionary-Ecological Perspective* (Sunderland, Mass.: Sinauer, 1980), pp. 19–133; R. F. Noss, "Wilderness Recovery and Ecological Restoration," *Earth First!* 5, no. 8 (1985): 18–19; R. F. Noss, "Recipe for Wilderness Recovery," *Earth First!* 6 (1986): 22, 25.
15. Friedman, "How Much Is Enough?" p. 37; C. Holtby, B. A. Wilcox, and Michael Soulé, "Benign Neglect: A Model of Faunal Collapse in the Game Reserves of East Africa," *Biological Conservation* 15 (1979): 259–70.
16. Grumbine, "Ecosystem Management," p. 46; W. D. Newmark, "Legal and Biotic Boundaries."
17. Friedman, "How Much Is Enough?" p. 43; Frankel and Soulé, *Conservation and Evolution.*
18. Michael Soulé, "Conservation Biology: Its Scope and Challenge," in M. Soulé and B. Wilcox (eds.), *Conservation Biology*, p. 166; quoted in Christopher Manes, *Green Rage: Radical Environmentalism and the Unmaking of Civilization* (Boston: Little, Brown, 1990), pp. 34–35.
19. David Brower, "Toward an Earth International Park," *Sierra Club Bulletin* 52, 9 (1967): 20.
20. Eugene P. Odum, *Fundamentals of Ecology* (Philadelphia: W. B. Saunders, 1971), p. 269; John Phillips, a philosopher/ecologist at St. Cloud State University in Minnesota, developed Odum's proposal in 1974 and presented it in "On Environmental Ethics," read at American Philosophical Association, San Francisco, 1978.
21. Paul Shepard, *The Tender Carnivore and the Sacred Game* (New York: Scribner's, 1973), pp. 260–73.
22. Edward Grumbine, "Ecosystem Management for Native Diversity," pp. 48, 52–53.
23. Grumbine, ibid.; R. F. Noss, "Recipe for Wilderness Recovery"; J. J. Berger, *Restoring the Earth: How Americans Are Working to Renew Damaged Environments* (New York: Knopf, 1985).

24. John Harper, "The Heuristic Value of Ecological Restoration," in William Jordan (ed.), *Restoration Ecology* (Cambridge: Cambridge University Press, 1987), pp. 35–36; C. Mark Cowell, "Ecological Restoration and Environmental Ethics," *Environmental Ethics* 15, no. 1 (1993): 19–32; for critiques of stewardship models of ecological restoration, see Eric Katz, "The Big Lie: Human Restoration of Nature," *Technology and the Environment* (New York: JAI Press, 1992), pp. 231–41; Jamie Sayan, "Notes toward a Restoration Ethic," *Restoration and Management Notes* 7, 2 (1989): 57–59; see also Andrew McLaughlin, *Regarding Nature* (New York: State University of New York Press, 1993), pp. 214–17.
25. Arne Naess, "Ecosophy, Population, and Free Nature," *The Trumpeter* 5, 3 (1988).
26. Roderick Nash, *Wilderness and the American Mind*, 3rd ed. (New Haven: Yale University Press, 1982), pp. 380–84.
27. Roderick Nash, *The Rights of Nature*, pp. 270–71, n. 28.
28. See Peter Berg, Beryl Magilavy, Seth Zuckerman, *A Green City Program* (San Francisco: Planet Drum Books, 1989); Peter Berg (ed.), *Reinhabiting a Separate Country: A Bioregional Anthology of Northern California* (San Francisco: Planet Drum Foundation, 1978); Gary Snyder, "Re-inhabitation," in Snyder, *The Old Ways* (San Francisco: City Lights Books, 1977), pp. 57–66; Thomas Berry, "Bioregions: The Context for Reinhabiting the Earth," in Berry, *The Dream of the Earth*, pp. 163–70; Kirkpatrick Sale, *Dwellers in the Land: The Bioregional Vision* (San Francisco: Sierra Club Books, 1985).
29. Roderick Nash, *The Rights of Nature*, pp. 168–69; Paul Ehrlich, "Comments," *Defenders of Wildlife*, Nov./Dec. 1985; Anne and Paul Ehrlich, *Earth* (New York: Franklin Watts, 1987), p. 242.
30. Ehrlich and Ehrlich, ibid., p. 153.
31. Paul Taylor, *Respect for Nature: A Theory of Environmental Ethics* (Princeton: Princeton University Press, 1986), pp. 288, 310.
32. Ibid., pp. 269–77.
33. Ibid., pp. 53–58.
34. For a critique of the stewardship model as applied to agriculture, see Sara Ebenreck, "A Partnership Farmland Ethic," *Environmental Ethics* 5, 1 (1983): 33–45; Arne Naess, "Self-Realization in Mixed Communities of Humans, Bears, Sheep and Wolves," *Inquiry* 22 (1979): 231–42; Arne Naess and Ivar Mysterud, "Philosophy of Wolf Policies I," *Conservation Biology* 1, 1 (1987): 22–34.
35. Arne Naess, "Ecosophy, Population, and Free Nature," p. 118.
36. Thomas Fleischner, "Keeping It Wild: Toward a Deeper Wilderness Management," in Friedman, *Forever Wild*, p. 79.
37. For proposals to eliminate domestic grazing on public lands, see Denzel and Nancy Ferguson, *Sacred Cows at the Public Trough* (Bend, Ore.: Maverick Publications, 1983).
38. "The Battle for the Wilderness," *U.S. News and World Report* 107, 1 (July 1989): 16–21, 24–25.
39. See Dave Foreman and Howie Wolke, *The Big Outside* (New York: Harmony/Crown Books, 1992); John Davis (ed.), "The Wildlands Project: Plotting a Wilderness Recovery Strategy," *Wild Earth* (1993), special issue; Dave Foreman, "The Northern Rockies Ecosystem Protection Act and the Evolving Wilderness Area Model," *Wild Earth* 3, 4 (1993): 57–62.
40. Dave Foreman, "Who Speaks for Wolf?" in D. Foreman, *Confessions of an Ecowarrior* (New York: Harmony Books, 1991), pp. 37–50; for a bioregional ecologist's plan to save California's ecosystems and wildlife by limiting human population, see Raymond F. Dasmann, *The Destruction of California* (New York: Macmillan, 1965).
41. See W. R. Prescott, "The Rights of Earth: An Interview with Dr. Noel J. Brown," *In Context* 22 (1989): 29–34.
42. *World Charter for Nature. United Nations General Assembly* (New York: United Nations, A/RES/37/7, Nov. 9, 1982); see also Harold W. Wood, Jr., "The United Nations World Charter for Nature," *Ecology Law Quarterly* 12 (1985): 977–96.

PART THREE

Ecofeminism

Introduction

Karen J. Warren

Karen J. Warren is a feminist philospher who has published essays on ecofeminism and edited special issues on ecofeminism for Hypatia: A Journal of Feminist Philosophy *and the* American Philosophical Association Newsletter on Feminism and Philosophy. *She has edited two anthologies on ecological feminism; coedited one anthology on feminism, violence, and nature; and written a book entitled* Quilting Ecofeminist Philosophy. *Warren has given public presentations on ecofeminism throughout the United States, as well as in Australia, Brazil, Canada, Finland, Norway, and Russia. She also conducts workshops on environmental ethics and critical thinking for elementary and secondary school teachers and students.*

The past few decades have witnessed an enormous interest in both the women's movement and the ecology (environmental) movement. Many feminists have argued that the goals of these two movements are mutually reinforcing; ultimately they involve the development of worldviews and practices that are not based on male-biased models of domination. As Rosemary Radford Ruether wrote in 1975 in her book, *New Woman/New Earth*:

> Women must see that there can be no liberation for them and no solution to the ecological crisis within a society whose fundamental model of relationships continues to be one of domination. They must unite the demands of the women's movement with those of the ecological movement to envision a radical reshaping of the basic socioeconomic relations and the underlying values of this [modern industrial] society. (204)

Since the early 1970s, many feminists, especially ecological feminists ("ecofeminists"), have defended Ruether's basic point: the environment is a feminist issue.

Just what makes the environment (ecology) a feminist issue? What are some of the alleged connections between the domination of women and the

An earlier version of this essay appeared in the American Philosophical Association *Newsletter on Feminism and Philosophy*, Fall 1991.

domination of nature? How and why is recognition of these connections important to feminism, environmentalism, and environmental philosophy? Answering these questions is largely what ecofeminism is about.

In this essay I offer an introduction to the literature and issues of ecofeminism. I begin with a characterization of ecofeminism. Then I identify eight sorts of connections—what I call "woman-nature connections"—that ecofeminists claim link the twin dominations of women and nature. Discussion of these alleged connections provides an overview of the scholarly literature in ecofeminism and the sorts of reasons ecofeminists have given for the centrality of ecofeminist insights to environmental philosophy and feminism. It also helps to situate the four essays included in this section (essays by Merchant, Plumwood, Salleh, and Warren) within that range of scholarly positions. I conclude by suggesting that the philosophical significance of ecofeminism is that it challenges feminism to take environmental issues seriously, environmental philosophy to take feminism seriously, and philosophy to take both seriously.

A CHARACTERIZATION OF ECOFEMINISM

Just as there is not one feminism, there is not one ecofeminism. "Ecological feminism" is the name given to a variety of positions that have roots in different feminist practices and philosophies. These different perspectives reflect not only different feminist perspectives (e.g., liberal, traditional Marxist, radical, socialist, black, and Third World feminisms); they also reflect different understandings of the nature of, and solution to, pressing environmental problems (see Warren 1987). So, it is an open question how many, which, and on what grounds any of the various positions in environmental philosophy that acknowledge feminist concerns or claim to be feminist are properly identified as ecofeminist positions. Stated differently, what one takes to be a genuine ecofeminist position will depend largely on how one conceptualizes both feminism and ecofeminism.

What, then, can one say about ecofeminism? What characterizes ecofeminism as a theoretical position and political movement? Despite important differences among ecofeminists and the various feminisms from which they gain their inspiration, there is something all ecofeminists agree about; such agreement provides a minimal condition account of ecofeminism. What all ecofeminists agree about is that there are important connections between the domination of women and the domination of nature, an understanding of which is crucial to feminism, environmentalism, and environmental philosophy (Warren 1987). A main project of ecofeminism, then, is to make visible these "woman-nature connections" and, where harmful to women and nature, to dismantle them.

If woman-nature connections are the backbone of ecofeminism, just what are they? And why is the alleged existence of these connections claimed to be so significant?

WOMAN-NATURE CONNECTIONS

There are at least eight sorts of connections that ecofeminists have identified. These alleged connections provide sometimes competing, sometimes mutually complementary or supportive analyses of the nature of the twin dominations of women and nature. A casual, albeit philosophically uncritical perusal of these eight alleged connections helps to identify the range and variety of ecofeminist positions on woman-nature connections.

1. Historical, Typically Causal Connections. One alleged connection between women and nature is historical. When historical data are used to generate theories concerning the sources of the dominations of women and nature, the alleged connections are also causal. In fact, so pervasive is the historical-causal theme in ecofeminist writings that Ariel Salleh (1988) virtually defines ecofeminism in terms of it: "Eco-feminism is a recent development in feminist thought which argues that the current global environmental crisis is a predictable outcome of patriarchal culture."

What are these alleged historical-causal connections? Some ecofeminists (e.g., Eisler 1988, 1990; Spretnak 1990) trace historical-causal connections to prototypical patterns of domination begun with the invasion of Indo-European societies by nomadic tribes from Eurasia about 4500 B.C. (see Lahar 1991, 33). Riane Eisler describes the time before these invasions as a "matrifocal, matrilineal, peaceful agrarian era." Others (e.g., Griffin 1978; Plumwood 1991, this section; Ruether 1975) trace historical connections to patriarchal dualisms and conceptions of rationality in classical Greek philosophy and the rationalist tradition. Still other feminists (e.g., Merchant 1980, this section) focus on cultural and scientific changes that occurred more recently—during the scientific revolution of the sixteenth and seventeenth centuries. According to these feminists, it was during the sixteenth and seventeenth centuries that an older world order, characterized by an organism metaphor of nature and cooperation between humans and nature, was replaced by a reductionist, "mechanistic world view of modern science." This mechanistic view is claimed to have been "the death of nature" by sanctioning unchecked commercial and industrial expansion and the moral permissibility of environmental destruction.

What prompts and explains these alleged historical and causal woman-nature connections? What else was in place to permit and sanction the twin dominations of women and nature? To answer these questions, ecofeminists, especially ecofeminist philosophers, have turned to the conceptual props that keep these historical-causal dominations in place.

2. Conceptual Connections. Many ecofeminists have argued that, ultimately, historical and causal links between the dominations of women and nature are located in conceptual structures of domination that construct women and nature in male-biased ways. Basically three such conceptual links have been offered.

One account locates a conceptual basis of the twin dominations of women and nature in *value dualism* and *value hierarchies*. These are ways of conceptualizing diversity into disjunctive pairs (value dualisms) and spatial up-down metaphors (value hierarchies), according to which disjuncts are seen as oppositional (rather than as complementary) and as exclusive (rather than as inclusive) and higher value (status, prestige) is attributed to that which is higher ("up") than to that which is lower ("down") (see Gray 1981; Griffin 1978; Plumwood 1991, this section; Ruether 1975). Frequently cited examples of these hierarchically organized value dualisms include reason/emotion, mind/body, culture/nature, human/nature, and man/woman dichotomies. These theorists argue that whatever is historically associated with emotion, body, nature, and women is regarded as "down," or inferior to that which is (historically) associated with reason, mind, culture, human (i.e., male), and men—what is "up."

A second account of conceptual women-nature connections expands on the first by housing the problematic value dualisms and value hierarchies in larger, oppressive conceptual frameworks—ones that are common to *all* social "isms of domination," for example, sexism, racism, classism, heterosexism, and ethnocentrism, as well as "naturism" (i.e., the unjustified domination of non-human nature; see Warren 1987, 1988, 1990, this section). A conceptual framework is a socially constructed set of basic beliefs, values, attitudes, and assumptions that shapes and reflects how one views oneself and others. A conceptual framework is oppressive when it explains, justifies, and maintains unjustified relationships of domination and subordination. An oppressive conceptual framework is *patriarchal* when it explains, justifies, and maintains the subordination of women by men.

Oppressive and patriarchal conceptual frameworks are characterized not only by value dualisms and hierarchies but also by three other features: "*power-over conceptions of power*"; conceptions and relationships of privilege that systematically give an advantage to whatever is "up"; and a *logic of domination*, that is, a structure of argumentation that provides the moral premise that superiority justifies subordination (Warren 1987, 1990, this section). In this second view, it is oppressive and patriarchal conceptual frameworks, and the behaviors that they give rise to, that sanction, maintain, and perpetuate the twin dominations of women and nature.

A third account locates a conceptual basis in sex-gender differences, particularly in differentiated personality formation or consciousness (see Cheney 1987; Gray 1981; Salleh, 1984). The claim is that female bodily experiences (e.g., of reproduction and childbearing), not female biology per se, situate women differently with respect to nature than men. This alleged sex-gender difference is claimed to be revealed in a different consciousness toward nature in women than in men. The claim is that such sex-gender difference is rooted conceptually in "paradigms that are uncritically oriented to the dominant western masculine forms of experiencing the world: the analytic, non-related, delightfully called 'objective' or 'scientific' approaches" (Salleh 1988, 130)—

just those value dualisms that are claimed to separate and inferiorize what is historically female-gender-identified. These sociopsychological factors provide a conceptual link insofar as they are embedded in different conceptualization structures and strategies ("different ways of knowing"), coping strategies, and ways of relating to nature for women and men. In this third view of conceptual connections between the dominations of women and nature, then, a main goal of ecofeminism is to develop gender-sensitive language, theory, and practices that do not further the exploitative experiences and habits of dissociated, male-gender-identified culture toward women and nature.

One project of ecofeminism is to expose and dismantle the conceptual structures of domination that have kept in place various "isms of domination," particularly the dominations of women and nature. Despite differences among ecofeminists about the nature of these conceptual connections, if some such account of the conceptual connections between the domination of women and of nature is correct, many basic philosophical notions (e.g., reason and rationality, knowledge, objectivity, ethics, and the knowing, moral self) will need to be reconceived. A conceptual account of the dominations of women and nature, then, provides a significant challenge to mainstream, dominant Western accounts of the nature of philosophy and philosophical reasoning.

3. Empirical and Experiential Connections. Many ecofeminists have focused on uncovering empirical evidence that links women (as well as children, people of color, and the underclass) with environmental destruction. Some ecofeminists point to various health and risk factors borne disproportionately by women, children, racial minorities, and the poor—risks caused by the presence of low-level radiation, pesticides, toxins, and other pollutants (e.g., Caldecott and Leland 1983; Salleh 1990, this section; Shiva 1988; Warren 1991a). Other ecofeminists provide empirical data to show that First World development policies result in practices regarding food, forest, and water that directly contribute to the inability of women to provide adequately for themselves and their families (e.g., Mies 1986; Shiva 1988; Warren 1988, 1989, 1991a). Still others, most notably ecofeminist animal rights scholars, argue that such practices as factory farming, animal experimentation, hunting, and meat eating are tied to patriarchal concepts and practices (e.g., Adams 1990, 1991; Kheel 1985; Slicer 1991). Some ecofeminists go even further by connecting such social ills as rape and pornography with male-gender-identified abuse of both women and nature (e.g., Collard with Contrucci 1988; Griffin 1981). In all these cases, appeal to such empirical data is intended both to document the very real, felt, lived "experiential" connections between the dominations of women and nature and to motivate the need for joining together feminist critical analysis, generally, with environmental concerns, specifically.

Sometimes, however, the empirical and experiential connections between women and nature are of a different sort: they are intended to reveal important cultural and spiritual ties to the earth, honored and celebrated by (some) women and indigenous peoples. This suggests the fourth sort of women-nature connection, that some woman-nature connections are best understood as features of important symbol systems.

4. Symbolic Connections. Some ecofeminists have explored the symbolic association and devaluation of women and nature that appears in religion, theology, art, and literature. Documenting such connections and making them integral to the project of ecofeminism is often heralded as ecofeminism's promising contribution to the creation of liberating, life-affirming, and postpatriarchal worldviews and earth-based spiritualities or theologies. Ecofeminism is then presented as offering alternative spiritual symbols (e.g., Gaia and goddess symbols), spiritualities or theologies, and even utopian societies (e.g., see Gearhart 1979). Appreciating such symbolic woman-nature connections involves understanding "the politics of women's spirituality" (Spretnak 1982).

Some ecofeminist theorists draw on literature, particularly "nature writing," to unpack the nature of woman-nature, linguistic symbolic connections (see Bell 1988; Kolodny 1975; Murphy 1988, 1991). Literary criticism of the sort offered by Patrick Murphy (1988) claims that patriarchal conceptions of nature and women have justified "a two-pronged rape and domination of the earth and the women who live on it" (p. 87), often using this as background for developing an ecofeminist literary theory (Murphy 1991).

Some ecofeminist theorists focus on language, particularly the symbolic connections between sexist and naturist language, that is, language that debases women and nonhuman nature by naturalizing women and feminizing nature. For example, there are concerns about whether sex-gendered language used to describe "Mother Nature" is, in Ynestra King's (1981) words, "potentially liberating or simply a rationale for the continued subordination of women." There are concerns about connections among the vocabularies used to describe women, nature, and nuclear weaponry (see Cohn 1989; Strange 1989). Women are often described in animal terms (e.g., as cows, foxes, chicks, serpents, bitches, beavers, old bats, pussycats, cats, birdbrains, harebrains). Nature is often described in female and sexual terms: nature is raped, mastered, conquered, controlled, mined. Her "secrets" are "penetrated" and her "womb" is put into the services of the "man of science." "Virgin timber" is felled, "fertile soil" is tilled, and land that lies "fallow" is "barren." The claim is that language that so feminizes nature and naturalizes women describes, reflects, and perpetuates the domination and debasement of both by failing to see the extent to which the twin dominations of women and nature (including animals) are, in fact, culturally (and not merely figuratively) analogous. The development of theory and praxis in feminism and environmental philosophy that does not perpetuate such sexist-naturist language and the power over systems of domination they reinforce is, therefore, taken as a main goal of ecofeminism.

5. Epistemological Connections. The various alleged historical-causal, conceptual, empirical, and symbolic woman-nature connections (discussed above) have also motivated the need for new, ecofeminist epistemologies. Typically these emerging epistemologies build on scholarship currently under way in feminist philosophy; they challenge mainstream philosophical views of reason, rationality, knowledge, and the nature of the knower (see APA 1989). Furthermore, as Val Plumwood (1991, this section) suggests in this section, if one mistakenly construes environmental philosophy as only or primarily concerned with ethics, one will neglect "a key aspect of the overall problem, which is concerned with the definition of the human self as separate from nature, the connection between this and the instrumental view of nature, and broader political aspects of the critique of instrumentalism." For Plumwood and other ecofeminist philosophers, ecofeminist epistemologies must critique rationalism in the Western philosophical tradition and develop views of the ethical, knowing self that do not maintain and perpetuate harmful value dualisms and hierarchies, particularly human-nature ones.

Some ecofeminists (e.g., Mills 1987, 1991) appeal to the critical theory of Horkheimer, Adorno, Balbus, and the Frankfurt circle, claiming that "their epistemology and substantive analysis both point to a convergence of feminist and ecological concerns, anticipating the more recent arrival of eco-feminism" (Salleh 1988, 131). For these feminists, "critical theory" provides a critique of the "nature versus culture" dichotomy and an epistemological structure for critiquing the relationships between the domination of women and the domination of nature.

6. Political (Praxis) Connections. Françoise d'Eaubonne (1974, 213–52) introduced the term "ecofeminisme" in 1974 to bring attention to women's potential for bringing about an ecological revolution. Ecofeminism has always been a grassroots political movement motivated by pressing pragmatic and, as we have seen, empirical concerns (see Lahar 1991). These range from issues of women's and environmental health to science, development, and technology; the treatment of animals; and peace and antinuclear, antimilitarist activism. The varieties of ecofeminist political perspectives on the environment are properly seen as an attempt to take seriously such grassroots activism by developing analyses of domination that explain, clarify, and guide political praxis.

7. Ethical Connections. To date, most of the ecofeminist philosophical literature on woman-nature connections has appeared in the area of environmental philosophy known as "environmental ethics." The ecofeminist philosophical claim is that the interconnections among the conceptualizations and treatment of women, animals, and (the rest of) nature require a feminist ethical analysis and response. Minimally, the goal of ecofeminist environmental ethics is to develop theories and practices concerning humans and the natural environment that are not male-biased and provide a guide to action in the prefeminist present (Warren 1990). This may involve developing an ecofeminist ethic of care and appropriate reciprocity (Cheney 1987, 1989; Curtin 1991; Warren 1988, 1990, this section), ecofeminist kinship ethics (Plumwood 1991, this section), ecofeminist animal rights positions (Adams 1991; Slicer 1991), ecofeminist social ecology (King 1981, 1983, 1989, 1990), or ecofeminist bioregionalism (Plant 1990). As ecofeminist philosophers Plumwood and Warren claim in their essays in this section, mainstream environmental ethics are inadequate to the extent that they are problematically anthropocentric or hopelessly androcentric.

8. Theoretical Connections. The varieties of alleged woman-nature connections discussed above have generated different, sometimes competing theoretical positions in all areas of feminist and environmental philosophy. Nowhere is this more evident than in the field of environmental ethics. Primarily because of space limitations, then, the discussion of theoretical connections offered here is restricted to environmental ethics.

In many respects, contemporary environmental ethics reflects the range of positions in contemporary philosophical ethics. The latter includes traditional consequentialist (e.g., ethical egoist and utilitarian) and nonconsequentialist or deontological (e.g., Kantian, rights-based, and virtue-based) positions, as well challenges to them by nontraditional (e.g., some feminist, existentialist, Marxist, Afrocentric, and non-Western) approaches. This range of positions is also reflected in that field of philosophy known as environmental ethics. There are consequentialist (e.g., ethical egoist, ecoutilitarian, and utilitarian-based animal liberation ethics) and nonconsequentialist (e.g., rights-based animal liberation and stewardship ethics) approaches in environmental ethics that extend traditional ethical considerations to include animals and the nonhuman environment. (Note that some would argue that these are not bona fide environmental ethics since they do not make the natural environment itself deserving of moral consideration.) There also are nontraditional approaches, the sort covered in this anthology (e.g., holistic Leopoldian land ethics, social ecology, deep ecology, and ecological feminism), that raise considerations underplayed or omitted entirely from mainstream philosophical ethics. Feminists who address environmental issues can be found advocating positions within this broad philosophical range. So where does ecological feminism, as a position in feminist theory, fit in?

Not surprisingly, where one thinks ecological feminism fits in will depend largely on what one means by "ecological feminism." If it is an umbrella term for any feminism that raises feminist concerns about the environment, then presumably ecofeminists can be found along the *continuum* of feminist-inspired and -advocated environmental ethics (or environmental philosophy). If, however, the term is used as I am using it in this essay and as it is used by the authors in this section—as the name for a variety of positions expressly committed to exploring alleged woman-nature connections (of the sort identified above) and to developing feminist and environmental philosophies based on these insights—then ecological feminism is best viewed as one of several nontraditional approaches to environmental ethics and philosophy. We are back to where we began this essay: ecological feminism is the name of a variety of positions that make visible different sorts of woman-nature connections, claiming that an understanding of these connections is necessary for any adequate feminism, environmentalism, or environmental philosophy. Whether the connections alleged and the arguments advanced in support of them are accepted on feminist and philosophical grounds is a question the friendly critic must answer.

THE ESSAYS IN THIS SECTION

As the preceding overview of the literature reveals, the four essays in this section provide only a glimpse of the positions advocated by ecofeminists. Still, together they raise issues across all eight categories of woman-nature connections that were identified above. Their inclusion here provides a sample of the philosophically relevant contributions ecofeminist historians, sociologists, and philosophers have made to ecofeminist and environmental philosophy.

A historian of environmental science, Carolyn Merchant published her highly influential book, *The Death of Nature: Women, Ecology and the Scientific Revolution*, in 1980. In it she argues that prior to the seventeenth century, nature was conceived in an organic model as a benevolent female and a nurturing mother; after the scientific revolution, nature was conceived in a mechanistic model as (mere) machine, inert and dead. In both models, nature was female. Merchant argues that the move from the organic to the mechanistic model permitted the justified exploitation of the (female) earth, by removing the sorts of barriers to such treatment that the metaphor of nature as alive previously prevented; the mechanistic worldview of modern science sanctioned the exploitation of nature, the unrestrained commercial expansion, and the socioeconomic conditions that perpetuated the subordination of women. *The Death of Nature* weaves together scholarly material from politics, art, literature, physics, technology, philosophy, and popular culture to show how this mechanistic worldview replaced an older, organic worldview, which provided gendered moral restraints on how one treated nature.

The essay by Merchant in this section, "The Death of Nature," is culled from *The Death of Nature*. This essay represents an edited version of the philosophically significant aspects of Merchant's main argument in her book, sidestepping some of the more technical, literary, or scientific specifics that receive extensive attention there. Inclusion of the Merchant essay in this section ensures representation of an early and classic, although not universally accepted (see Plumwood 1986), historical ecofeminist position on the patriarchal source of the domination of nature.

In "Nature, Self, and Gender: Feminism, Environmental Philosophy, and the Critique of Rationalism," Val Plumwood argues that the key to woman-nature connections in the Western world is found in "rationalism," that long-standing philosophical tradition that affirms the human/nature dichotomy and a network of other related dualisms (e.g., masculine/feminine, reason/emotion, spirit/body) and that offers an account of the human self as masculine and centered on rationality to the exclusion of its contrasts (especially characteristics regarded as feminine, animal, or natural). Plumwood criticizes both deep ecology specifically and environmental philosophy generally for missing entirely the ecofeminist critique that "anthropocentrism and androcentrism are linked." She claims,

> The failure to observe such connections is the result of an inadequate historical analysis and understanding of the way in which the inferiorization of both women and nature is grounded in rationalism, and the connections of both to the inferiorizing of the body, hierarchical concepts of labor, and disembedded and individualist accounts of the self.

Plumwood concludes that "the effect of ecofeminism is not to absorb or sacrifice the critique of anthropocentrism, but to deepen and enrich it."

In "Working with Nature: Reciprocity or Control?" Ariel Salleh gives empirical documentation of women's involvement in the environmental movement. Salleh argues that it is a "patriarchal belief system" that maintains and justifies both the invisibility of what women do and the continued destruction of the natural environment. According to Salleh, the rationale for the exploitation of women and of nature "has been uncovered by the ecofeminist analysis of patriarchy." What is needed, she argues, is that "the unconscious connection between women and nature needs to be made conscious, and the hierarchical fallacies of the Great Chain of Being acknowledged, before there can be any real growth toward a sane, humane, ecological future." Feminists, environmentalists, and philosophers must see that struggles for equality of women and ecological sustainability are interlinked.

In "The Power and the Promise of Ecological Feminism," ecofeminist philosopher Karen J. Warren, like Val Plumwood, focuses on the conceptual connections between the dominations of women and nature. She argues that because the conceptual connections are located in an oppressive patriarchal conceptual framework characterized by a logic of domination, first, the logic of traditional feminism requires the expansion of feminism to include ecological feminism, and, second, ecological feminism provides a distinctively feminist environmental ethic. Appealing to the argumentative significance of first-person narrative and emerging ecofeminist ethics of care, kinship, and appropriate reciprocity, Warren concludes that any feminism, environmentalism, or environmental philosophy that fails to recognize important woman-nature connections is simply inadequate.

why doesn't she just say "I"?

THE SIGNIFICANCE OF ECOFEMINISM

In this essay I have provided eight sorts of connections alleged by ecofeminists to hold between the domination of women and the domination of nature. I also have indicated both generally and specifically (in terms of the four essays included in this section) the nature of the challenges that acceptance of these connections poses for contemporary feminism, environmentalism, and environmental philosophy. But if the power and promise of ecological feminism runs as deep as many ecofeminists suppose, there must be implications of ecofeminism for mainstream philosophy as well. What are some of these?

The historical-causal links alleged between the dominations of women and of nature suggest that data from the social sciences on women, development, and the environment are important to theoretical undertakings in many areas of philosophy. This can be seen by considering some of the main subfields of philosophy: in ethics, for instance, such data raise important issues about anthropocentric and androcentric bias. Can mainstream normative ethical theories generate an environmental ethic that is not male-biased? In epistemology, data on the "indigenous technical knowledge" of women in forestry, water collection, farming, and food production (see Warren 1988, 1991a) raise issues about women's "epistemic privilege" and the need for "feminist standpoint epistemologies." In metaphysics, data on the cross-cultural variability of women-nature connections raise issues about the social constructions of conceptions of both women and nature and the human-nature dichotomy of at least dominant Western philosophy (see Warren 1990, this section). In political philosophy, data on the inferior standards of living of women globally raise issues about political theories and theorizing: what roles do unequal distributions of power and privilege play in the maintenance of systems of domination over both women and nature? How do they affect the content of political theories and the methodology of political theorizing? In the history of philosophy, data on the historical debasement of what is both female-gender- and nature-identified raise issues about the anthropocentric and androcentric biases of philosophical theories in any given time period. In philosophy of science, particularly philosophy of biology, such data raise issues about the relationships between feminism and science, particularly ecological science. As Carolyn Merchant (1985) asks, "Is there a set of assumptions basic to the science of ecology that also holds implications for the status of women? Is there an ecological ethic that is also a feminist ethic?" (p. 229). Are there important parallels between contemporary ecofeminist ethics and ecosystem ecology that suggest ways in which the two are engaged in mutually supportive projects (see Warren and Cheney 1991)? These are the sorts of questions ecofeminism raises for traditional fields in mainstream philosophy.

However, perhaps the most serious challenges to mainstream philosophy are at the level of conceptual analysis and theory. Ecofeminism raises significant issues about the philosophical conceptions of the self, knowledge and the knower, reason and rationality, objectivity, and a host of favored dualisms that form the backbone of philosophical theorizing—indeed, of the very conception of philosophy itself. If ecofeminists are correct, these notions will need to be reexamined for possible male-gender bias. The challenge to philosophy is to replace conceptual schemes, theories, and practices that currently feminize nature and naturalize women, to the mutual detriment of both, with ones that do not. That is what ecofeminists generally, and the authors in this section specifically, argue is needed from feminism, environmentalism, environmental philosophy, and philosophy. It is left to the reader to decide whether ecofeminists are correct.

WORKS CITED

Adams, Carol J. 1990. *The Sexual Politics of Meat: A Feminist-Vegetarian Critical Theory.* New York: Continuum.
______. 1991. "Ecofeminism and the Eating of Animals." *Hypatia* 6: 125–145.
American Philosophical Association (APA). 1989. *Newsletter on Feminism and Philosophy* 88 (2). Special issue on Reason, Rationality, and Gender. Nancy Tuana and Karen J. Warren (eds.).
______. *Newsletter on Feminism and Philosophy.* 1991, 1992. Two-part special issue on Feminism and the Environment (Fall, Winter). Nancy Tuana and Karen J. Warren (eds.).
Bell, Barbara Currier. 1988. "Cable of Blue Fire: Glimpsing a Group Identity for Humankind." *Studies in the Humanities* 15 (2): 90–107. Special Issue on Feminism, Ecology, and the Future of the Humanities. Patrick Murphy (ed.).
Caldecott, Leonie, and Stephanie Leland (eds.). 1983. *Reclaim the Earth.* London: Women's Press.
Cheney, Jim. 1987. "Eco-feminism and Deep Ecology." *Environmental Ethics* 9 (2): 115–45.
______. 1989. "Postmodern Environmental Ethics: Ethics as Bioregional Narrative." *Environmental Ethics* 11 (2): 117–34.
Cohn, Carol. 1989. "Sex and Death in the Rational World of Defense Intellectuals." In *Exposing Nuclear Phallacies,* Diana Russell (ed.). New York: Pergamon Press.
Collard, Andrée, with Joyce Contrucci. 1988. *Rape of the Wild: Man's Violence Against Animals and the Earth.* Bloomington: Indiana University Press.
Curtin, Deane. 1991. "Toward an Ecological Ethic of Care." *Hypatia* 6 (1): 60–74.
d'Eaubonne, Françoise. 1974. *Le Féminisme ou la Mort.* Paris: Pierre Horay.
Eisler, Rianne. 1988. *The Chalice & the Blade: Our History, Our Future.* San Francisco: Harper and Row.
______. 1990. "The Gaia Tradition and the Partnership Future." In *Reweaving the World: The Emergence of Ecofeminism,* Irene Diamond and Gloria Femen Orenstein (eds.). San Francisco: Sierra Club Books.
Gearhart, Sally. 1979. *The Wanderground: Stories of the Hill Women.* Boston: Alyson Publications.
Gray, Elizabeth Dodson. 1981. *Green Paradise Lost.* Wellesley, MA: Roundtable Press.
Griffin, Susan. 1978. *Woman and Nature: The Roaring Inside Her.* San Francisco: Harper and Row.
______. 1981. *Pornography and Silence: Culture's Revenge Against Nature.* New York: Harper and Row.
Griscom, Joan L. 1981. "On Healing the Nature/History Split in Feminist Thought." *Heresies 13, Feminism and Ecology* 4: 4–9.
Kheel, Marti. 1985. "The Liberation of Nature: A Circular Affair." *Environmental Ethics* 7 (2): 135–49.
King, Ynestra. 1981. "Feminism and the Revolt of Nature." In *Heresies 13, Feminism and Ecology* 4 (1): 12–16.
______. 1983. "The Eco-feminist Imperative." In *Reclaim the Earth,* Leonie Caldecott and Stephanie Leland (eds.). London: Women's Press.
______. 1989. "The Ecology of Feminism and the Feminism of Ecology." In *Healing the Wounds: The Promise of Ecofeminism,* Judith Plant (ed.). Santa Cruz, CA: New Society Publishers.

______. 1990. "Healing the Wounds: Feminism, Ecology, and the Nature/Culture Dualism." In *Reweaving the World: The Emergence of Ecofeminism.* Irene Diamond and Gloria Femen Orenstein (eds.). San Francisco: Sierra Club Books.
Kolodny, Annette. 1975. *The Lay of the Land: Metaphor as Experience and History in American Life and Letters.* Chapel Hill: University of North Carolina Press.
Lahar, Stephanie. 1991. "Ecofeminist Theory and Grassroots Politics." *Hypatia* 6 (1): 28–45.
Merchant, Carolyn. 1980. *The Death of Nature: Women, Ecology, and the Scientific Revolution.* San Francisco: Harper and Row.
______. 1985. "Feminism and Ecology." In *Deep Ecology: Living as if Nature Mattered,* Bill Devall and George Sessions (eds.). Salt Lake City: Peregrine Smith Books.
Mies, Maria. 1986. *Patriarchy and Accumulation on a World Scale.* London: Zed Books.
Mills, Patricia Jagentowicz. 1987. *Woman, Nature, and Psyche.* New Haven, CT: Yale University Press.
______. 1991. "Feminism and Ecology: On the Domination of Nature." *Hypatia* 6 (1): 162–78.
Murphy, Patrick. 1988. "Introduction: Feminism, Ecology, and the Future of the Humanities." *Studies in the Humanities* 15 (2): 85–89. Special issue on Feminism, Ecology, and the Future of the Humanities.
______. 1991. "Ground, Pivot, Motion: Ecofeminist Theory, Dialogics, and Literary Practice. *Hypatia* 6 (1): 146–61.
Ortner, Sherry B. 1974. "Is Female to Male as Nature Is to Culture?" In *Woman, Culture and Society,* Michelle Rosaldo and Louise Lamphere (eds.). Stanford, CA: Stanford University Press.
Plant, Judith. 1990. "Searching for Common Ground: Ecofeminism and Bioregionalism." In *Reweaving the World: The Emergence of Ecofeminism,* Irene Diamond and Gloria Femen Orenstein (eds.). San Francisco: Sierra Club Books.
Plumwood, Val. 1986. "Ecofeminism: An Overview and Discussion of Positions and Arguments." *Australasian Journal of Philosophy,* 64 (suppl.): 120–37.
______. 1991. "Nature, Self, and Gender: Feminism, Environmental Philosophy and the Critique of Rationalism." *Hypatia* 6 (1): 3–37.
Roach, Catherine. 1991. "Loving Your Mother: On the Woman-Nature Relation." *Hypatia* 6 (1): 46–59.
Ruether, Rosemary Radford. 1975. *New Woman/New Earth: Sexist Ideologies and Human Liberation.* New York: Seabury Press.
Salleh, Ariel Kay. 1984. "Deeper Than Deep Ecology: The Eco-feminist Connection." *Environmental Ethics* 6 (4): 339–45.
______. 1988. "Epistemology and the Metaphors of Production: An Eco-feminist Reading of Critical Theory." In *Studies in the Humanities* 15 (2): 130–39. Special issue on Feminism, Ecology, and the Future of the Humanities. Patrick Murphy (ed.).
______. 1990. "Living with Nature: Reciprocity or Control?" In *Ethics of Environment and Development,* R. Engel and J. Engel (eds.). Tucson: University of Arizona Press.
Shiva, Vandana. 1988. *Staying Alive: Women, Ecology and Development.* London: Zed Books.
Slicer, Deborah. 1991. "Your Daughter or Your Dog? A Feminist Assessment of Animal Research Issues." *Hypatia* 6 (1): 108–24.
Spretnak, Charlene. 1990. "Ecofeminism: Our Roots and Flowering." In *Reweaving the World: The Emergence of Ecofeminism,* Irene Diamond and Gloria Femen Orenstein (eds.). San Francisco: Sierra Club Books.
______ (ed.). 1982. *The Politics of Women's Spirituality.* Garden City, NY: Anchor Press.
Strange, Penny. 1989. "It'll Make a Man Out of You: A Feminist View of the Arms Race." In *Exposing Nuclear Phallacies,* Diana Russell (ed.). New York: Pergamon Press.
Warren, Karen J. 1987. "Feminism and Ecology: Making Connections." *Environmental Ethics* 9 (1): 3–20.
______. 1988. "Toward an Ecofeminist Ethic." *Studies in the Humanities* 15 (2): 140–56. Patrick Murphy (ed.).

______. 1989, June. "Water and Streams: An Ecofeminist Perspective." *Imprint*, pp. 5–7.
______. 1990. "The Power and the Promise of Ecological Feminism." *Environmental Ethics* 12 (2): 125–46.
______. 1991a. "Taking Empirical Data Seriously: An Ecofeminist Perspective on Woman-Nature Connections." Working Paper, presented at the North American Society for Social Philosophy, Colorado Springs, CO, August 10.
______. 1991b. "Toward a Feminist Peace Politics." *Journal of Peace and Justice Studies* 3 (1): 87–102.
Warren, Karen J., and Jim Cheney. 1991. "Ecological Feminism and Ecosystem Ecology." *Hypatia* 6 (1): 179–97.

The Death of Nature

Carolyn Merchant

Carolyn Merchant is a professor of environmental history, philosophy, and ethics in the Department of Conservation and Resource Studies at the University of California at Berkeley. She is the author of numerous publications on feminism and the environment, including The Death of Nature: Women, Ecology and the Scientific Revolution *and* Ecological Revolutions.

INTRODUCTION: WOMEN AS NATURE

Women and nature have an age-old association—an affiliation that has persisted throughout culture, language, and history. Their ancient interconnections have been dramatized by the simultaneity of two recent social movements—women's liberation, symbolized in its controversial infancy by Betty Friedan's *Feminine Mystique* (1963), and the ecology movement, which built up during the 1960s and finally captured national attention on Earth Day, 1970. Common to both is an egalitarian perspective. Women are struggling to free themselves from cultural and economic contraints that have kept them subordinate to men in American society. Environmentalists, warning us of the irreversible consequences of continuing environmental exploitation, are developing an ecological ethic emphasizing the interconnectedness between people and nature. Juxtaposing the goals of the two movements can suggest new values and social structures, based not on the domination of women and nature as resources but on the full expression of both male and female talent and on the maintenance of environmental integrity.

New social concerns generate new intellectual and historical problems. Conversely, new interpretations of the past provide perspectives on the present and hence the power to change it. Today's feminist and ecological consciousness can be used to examine the historical interconnections between women and nature that developed as the modern scientific and economic world took form in the sixteenth and seventeenth centuries—a transformation that shaped and pervades today's mainstream values and perceptions.

Excerpted from *The Death of Nature*, originally published by Harper and Row (New York, 1980). Reprinted with permission.

The ancient identity of nature as a nurturing mother links women's history with the history of the environment and ecological change. The female earth was central to the organic cosmology that was undermined by the Scientific Revolution and the rise of a market-oriented culture in early modern Europe. The ecology movement has reawakened interest in the values and concepts associated historically with the premodern organic world. The ecological model and its associated ethics make possible a fresh and critical interpretation of the rise of modern science in the crucial period when our cosmos ceased to be viewed as an organism and became instead a machine.

In investigating the roots of our current environmental dilemma and its connections to science, technology, and the economy, we must reexamine the formation of a world view and a science that, by reconceptualizing reality as a machine rather than a living organism, sanctioned the domination of both nature and women.

NATURE AS FEMALE

The world we have lost was organic. From the obscure origins of our species, human beings have lived in daily, immediate, organic relation with the natural order for their sustenance. In 1500, the daily interaction with nature was still structured for most Europeans, as it was for other peoples, by close-knit, cooperative, organic communities.

Thus it is not surprising that for sixteenth-century Europeans the root metaphor binding together the self, society, and the cosmos was that of an organism. As a projection of the way people experienced daily life, organismic theory emphasized interdependence among the parts of the human body, subordination of individual to communal purposes in family, community, and state, and vital life permeating the cosmos to the lowliest stone.

The idea of nature as a living organism had philosophical antecedents in ancient systems of thought, variations of which formed the prevailing ideological framework of the sixteenth century. The organismic metaphor, however, was immensely flexible and adaptable to varying contexts, depending on which of its presuppositions was emphasized. A spectrum of philosophical and political possibilities existed, all of which could be subsumed under the general rubric of *organic.*

Central to the organic theory was the identification of nature, especially the earth, with a nurturing mother: A kindly beneficent female who provided for the needs of mankind in an ordered, planned universe. But another opposing image of nature as female was also prevalent: wild and uncontrollable nature that could render violence, storms, droughts, and general chaos. Both were identified with the female sex and were projections of human perceptions onto the external world. The metaphor of the earth as a nurturing mother was gradually to vanish as a dominant image as the Scientific Revolution proceeded to mechanize and to rationalize the world view. The second image, nature as

Describe at least one of the four reasons that Warren gives to justify the use of 1st person narrative in ecofeminist ethics.

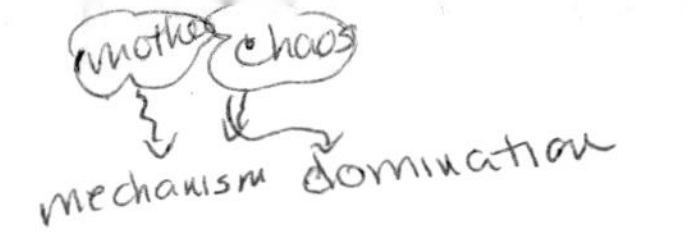

disorder, called forth an important modern idea, that of power over nature. Two new ideas, those of mechanism and of the domination and mastery of nature, became core concepts of the modern world. An organically oriented mentality in which female principles played an important role was undermined and replaced by a mechanically oriented mentality that either eliminated or used female principles in an exploitative manner. As Western culture became increasingly mechanized in the 1600s, the female earth and virgin earth spirit were subdued by the machine.[1]

The change in controlling imagery was directly related to changes in human attitudes and behavior toward the earth. Whereas the nurturing earth image can be viewed as a cultural constraint restricting the types of socially and morally sanctioned human actions allowable with respect to the earth, the new images of mastery and domination functioned as cultural sanctions for the denudation of nature. Society needed these new images as it continued the processes of commercialism and industrialization, which depended on activities directly altering the earth—mining, drainage, deforestation, and assarting (grubbing up stumps to clear fields). The new activities utilized new technologies—lift and force pumps, cranes, windmills, geared wheels, flap valves, chains, pistons, treadmills, under- and overshot watermills, fulling mills, flywheels, bellows, excavators, bucket chains, rollers, geared and wheeled bridges, cranks, elaborate block and tackle systems, worm, spur, crown, and lantern gears, cams and eccentrics, ratchets, wrenches, presses, and screws in magnificent variation and combination.

These technological and commercial changes did not take place quickly; they developed gradually over the ancient and medieval eras, as did the accompanying environmental deterioration. Slowly over many centuries early Mediterranean and Greek civilization had mined and quarried the mountainsides, altered the forested landscape, and overgrazed the hills. Nevertheless, technologies were low level, people considered themselves parts of a finite cosmos, and animism and fertility cults that treated nature as sacred were numerous. Roman civilization was more pragmatic, secular, and commercial and its environmental impact more intense. Yet Roman writers such as Ovid, Seneca, Pliny, and the Stoic philosophers openly deplored mining as an abuse of their mother, the earth. With the disintegration of feudalism and the expansion of Europeans into new worlds and markets, commercial society began to have an accelerated impact on the natural environment. By the sixteenth and seventeenth centuries, the tension between technological development in the world of action and the controlling organic images in the world of the mind had become too great. The old structures were incompatible with the new activities.

Both the nurturing and domination metaphors had existed in philosophy, religion, and literature. The idea of dominion over the earth existed in Greek philosophy and Christian religion; that of the nurturing earth, in Greek and other pagan philosophies. But, as the economy became modernized and the Scientific Revolution proceeded, the dominion metaphor spread beyond the religious sphere and assumed ascendancy in the social and political spheres as well. These two competing images and their normative associations can be found in sixteenth-century literature, art, philosophy, and science.

The image of the earth as a living organism and nurturing mother had served as a cultural constraint restricting the actions of human beings. One does not readily slay a mother, dig into her entrails for gold or mutilate her body, although commercial mining would soon require that. As long as the earth was considered to be alive and sensitive, it could be considered a breach of human ethical behavior to carry out destructive acts against it. For most traditional cultures, minerals and metals ripened in the uterus of the Earth Mother, mines were compared to her vagina, and metallurgy was the human hastening of the birth of the living metal in the artificial womb of the furnace—an abortion of the metal's natural growth cycle before its time. Miners offered propitiation to the deities of the soil and subterranean world, performed ceremonial sacrifices, and observed strict cleanliness, sexual abstinence, and fasting before violating the sacredness of the living earth by sinking a mine. Smiths assumed an awesome responsibility in precipitating the metal's birth through smelting, fusing, and beating it with hammer and anvil; they were often accorded the status of shaman in tribal rituals and their tools were thought to hold special powers.

The Renaissance image of the nurturing earth still carried with it subtle ethical controls and restraints. Such imagery found in a culture's literature can play a normative role within the culture. Controlling images operate as ethical restraints or as ethical sanctions—as subtle "oughts" or "ought-nots." Thus as the descriptive metaphors and images of nature change, a behavioral restraint can be changed into a sanction. Such a change in the image and description of nature was occurring during the course of the Scientific Revolution.

DOMINION OVER NATURE: FRANCIS BACON'S PHILOSOPHY

Francis Bacon (1561–1626), a celebrated "father of modern science," transformed tendencies already extant in his own society into a total program advocating the control of nature for human benefit. Melding together a new philosophy based on natural magic as a technique for manipulating nature, the technologies of mining and metallurgy, the emerging concept of progress and a patriarchal structure of family and state, Bacon fashioned a new ethic sanctioning the exploitation of nature.

Bacon has been eulogized as the originator of the concept of the modern research institute, a philosopher of industrial science, the inspiration behind the Royal Society (1660), and as the founder of the inductive method by which all people can verify for themselves the truths of science by the reading of nature's book.[2] But from the perspective of nature, women, and the lower orders of society emerges a less favorable image of Bacon and a critique of his program as ultimately benefiting the middle-class male entrepreneur. Bacon, of course, was not responsible for subsequent uses of his philosophy. But, because he was in an extremely influential social position and in touch with the important developments of his time, his language, style, nuance, and metaphor become a mirror reflecting his class perspective.

Sensitive to the same social transformations that had already begun to reduce women to psychic and reproductive resources, Bacon developed the power of language as political instrument in reducing female nature to a resource for economic production. Female imagery became a tool in adapting scientific knowledge and method to a new form of human power over nature. The "controversy over women" and the inquisition of witches—both present in Bacon's social milieu—permeated his description of nature and his metaphorical style and were instrumental in his transformation of the earth as a nurturing mother and womb of life into a source of secrets to be extracted for economic advance.

Much of the imagery Bacon used in delineating his new scientific objectives and methods derives from the courtroom, and, because it treats nature as a female to be tortured through mechanical inventions, strongly suggests the interrogations of the witch trials and the mechanical devices used to torture witches.

The new man of science must not think that the "inquisition of nature is in any part interdicted or forbidden." Nature must be "bound into service" and made a "slave," put "in constraint" and "molded" by the mechanical arts. The "searchers and spies of nature" are to discover her plots and secrets.[3]

This method, so readily applicable when nature is denoted by the female gender, degraded and made possible the exploitation of the natural environment. As woman's womb had symbolically yielded to the forceps, so nature's womb harbored secrets that through technology could be wrested from her grasp for use in the improvement of the human condition:

> There is therefore much ground for hoping that there are still laid up in the womb of nature many secrets of excellent use having no affinity or parallelism with anything that is now known . . . only by the method which we are now treating can they be speedily and suddenly and simultaneously presented and anticipated.[4]

Bacon transformed the magical tradition by calling on the need to dominate nature not for the sole benefit of the individual magician but for the good of the entire human race. Through vivid metaphor, he transformed the magus from nature's servant to its exploiter, and nature from a teacher to a slave. Bacon argued that it was the magician's error to consider art (technology) a mere "assistant to nature having the power to finish what nature has begun" and therefore to despair of ever "changing, transmuting, or fundamentally altering nature."[5]

The natural magician saw himself as operating within the organic order of nature—he was a manipulator of parts within that system, bringing down the heavenly powers to the earthly shrine. Agrippa . . . had begun to explore the possibility of ascending the hierarchy to the point of cohabiting with God. Bacon extended this idea to include the recovery of the power over nature lost when Adam and Eve were expelled from paradise.

Due to the Fall from the Garden of Eden (caused by the temptation of a woman), the human race lost its "dominion over creation." Before the Fall, there was no need for power or dominion, because Adam and Eve had been made sovereign over all other creatures. In this state of dominion, mankind was "like unto God." While some, accepting God's punishment, had obeyed the medieval strictures against searching too deeply into God's secrets, Bacon turned the constraints into sanctions. Only by "digging further and further into the mine of natural knowledge" could mankind recover that lost dominion. In this way, "the narrow limits of man's dominion over the universe" could be stretched "to their promised bounds."[6]

Although a female's inquisitiveness may have caused man's fall from his God-given dominion, the relentless interrogation of another female, nature, could be used to regain it. As he argued in *The Masculine Birth of Time*, "I am come in very truth leading you to nature with all her children to bind her to your service and make her your slave." "We have no right," he asserted, "to expect nature to come to us." Instead, "Nature must be taken by the forelock, being bald behind." Delay and subtle argument "permit one only to clutch at nature, never to lay hold of her and capture her."[7]

Nature existed in three states—at liberty, in error, or in bondage.

> She is either free and follows her ordinary course of development as in the heavens, in the animal and vegetable creation, and in the general array of the universe; or she is driven out of her ordinary course by the perverseness, insolence, and forwardness of matter and violence of impediments, as in the case of monsters; or lastly, she is put in constraint, molded, and made as it were new by art and the hand of man; as in things artificial.[8]

The first instance was the view of nature as immanent self-development, the nature naturing herself of the Aristotelians. This was the organic view of nature as a living, growing, self-actualizing being. The second state was necessary to explain the malfunctions and monstrosities that frequently appeared and that could not have been caused by God or another higher power acting on his instruction. Since monstrosities could not be explained by the action of form or spirit, they had to be the result of matter acting perversely. Matter in Plato's *Timaeus* was recalcitrant and had to be forcefully shaped by the demiurge. Bacon frequently described matter in female imagery, as a "common harlot." "Matter is not devoid of an appetite and inclination to dissolve the world and fall back into the old Chaos." It therefore must be "restrained and kept in order by the prevailing concord of things." "The vexations of art are certainly as the bonds and handcuffs of Proteus, which betray the ultimate struggles and efforts of matter."[9]

The third instance was the case of art (techné)—man operating on nature to create something new and artificial. Here "nature takes orders from man and works under his authority." Miners and smiths should become the model for the new class of natural philosophers who would interrogate and alter nature. They had developed the two most important methods of wresting nature's secrets from her, "the one searching into the bowels of nature, the other shaping nature as on an anvil." "Why should we not divide natural philosophy into two parts, the mine and the furnace?" For "the truth of nature lies hid in certain deep mines and caves," within the earth's bosom. Bacon, like some of the practically minded alchemists, would "advise the studious to sell their books and build furnaces" and, "forsaking Minerva and the Muses as barren virgins, to rely upon Vulcan."[10]

The new method of interrogation was not through abstract notions, but through the instruction of the understanding "that it may in very truth dissect nature." The instruments of the mind supply suggestions, those of the hand give motion and aid the work. "By art and the hand of man," nature can then be "forced out of her natural state and squeezed and molded," In this way, "human knowledge and human power meet as one."[11]

Here, in bold sexual imagery, is the key feature of the modern experimental method—constraint of nature in the laboratory, dissection by hand and mind, and the penetration of hidden secrets—language still used today in praising a scientist's "hard facts," "penetrating mind," or the "thrust of his argument." The constraints against penetration in *Natura*'s lament over her torn garments of modesty have been turned into sanctions in language that legitimates the exploitation and "rape" of nature for human good.

Scientific method, combined with mechanical technology, would create a "new organon," a new system of investigation, that unified knowledge with material power. The technological discoveries of printing, gunpowder, and the magnet in the fields of learning, warfare, and navigation "help us to think about the secrets still locked in nature's bosom." "They do not, like the old, merely exert a gentle guidance over nature's course; they have the power to conquer and subdue her, to shake her to her foundations." Under the mechanical arts, "nature betrays her secrets more fully . . . than when in enjoyment of her natural liberty."[12]

Mechanics, which gave man power over nature, consisted in motion; that is, in "the uniting or disuniting of natural bodies." Most useful were the arts that altered the materials of things—"agriculture, cookery, chemistry, dying, the manufacture of glass, enamel, sugar, gunpowder, artificial fires, paper, and the like." But in performing these operations, one was constrained to operate within the chain of causal connections; nature could "not be commanded except by being obeyed." Only by the study, interpretation, and observation of nature could these possibilities be uncovered; only by acting as the interpreter of nature could knowledge be turned into power. Of the three grades of human ambition, the most wholesome and noble was "to endeavor to establish and extend the power and dominion of the human race itself over the universe." In this way "the human race [could] recover that right over nature which belongs to it by divine bequest."[13]

The interrogation of witches as a symbol for the interrogation of nature, the courtroom as a model for its inquisition, and torture through mechanical devices as a tool for the subjugation of disorder were fundamental to the scientific method as power. For Bacon . . ., sexual politics helped to structure the nature of the empirical method that would produce a new form of knowledge and a new ideology of objectivity seemingly devoid of cultural and political assumptions.

Human dominion over nature, an integral element of the Baconian program, was to be achieved through the experimental "disclosure of nature's secrets." Seventeenth-century scientists, reinforcing aggressive attitudes toward nature, spoke out in favor of "mastering" and "managing" the earth. Descartes wrote in his *Discourse on Method* (1636) that through knowing the crafts of the artisans and the forces of bodies we could "render ourselves the masters and possessors of nature."[14] Joseph Glanvill, the English philosopher who defended the Baconian program in his *Plus Ultra* of 1668, asserted that the objective of natural philosophy was to "enlarge knowledge by observation and experiment . . . so that nature being known, it may be mastered, managed, and used in the services of humane life." To achieve this objective, arts and instruments should be developed for "searching out the beginnings and depths of things and discovering the intrigues of remoter nature."[15] The most useful of the arts were chemistry, anatomy, and mathematics; the best instruments included the microscope, telescope, thermometer, barometer, and air pump.

The new image of nature as a female to be controlled and dissected through experiment legitimated the exploitation of natural resources. Although the image of the nurturing earth popular in the Renaissance did not vanish, it was superseded by new controlling imagery. The constraints against penetration associated with the earth-mother image were transformed into sanctions for denudation. After the Scientific Revolution, *Natura* no longer complains that her garments of modesty are being torn by the wrongful thrusts of man. She is portrayed in statues by the French sculptor Louis-Ernest Barrias (1841–1905) coyly removing her own veil and exposing herself to science. From an active teacher and parent, she has become a mindless, submissive body. Not only did this new image function as a sanction, but the new conceptual framework of the Scientific Revolution—mechanism—carried with it norms quite different from the norms of organicism. The new mechanical order and its associated values of power and control would mandate the death of nature.

THE MECHANICAL ORDER

The fundamental social and intellectual problem for the seventeenth century was the problem of order. The perception of disorder, so important to the Baconian doctrine of dominion over nature, was also crucial to the rise of mechanism as a rational antidote to the disintegration of the organic cosmos. The new mechanical philosophy of the mid-seventeenth century achieved a reunification of the cosmos, society, and the self in terms of a new metaphor—the machine. Developed by the French thinkers Mersenne, Gassendi, and Descartes in the 1620s and 1630s and elaborated by a group of English emigrés to Paris in the 1640s and 1650s, the new mechanical theories emphasized and reinforced elements in human experience developing slowly since the late Middle Ages, but accelerating in the sixteenth century.

New forms of order and power provided a remedy for the disorder perceived to be spreading throughout culture. In the organic world, order meant the function of each part within the larger whole, as determined by its nature, while power was diffused from the top downward through the social or cosmic hierarchies. In the mechanical world, order was redefined to mean the predictable behavior of each part within a rationally determined system of laws, while power derived from active and immediate intervention in a secularized world. Order and power together constituted control. Rational control over nature, society, and the self was achieved by redefining reality itself through the new machine metaphor.

As the unifying model for science and society, the machine has permeated and reconstructed human consciousness so totally that today we scarcely question its validity. Nature, society, and the human body are composed of interchangeable atomized parts that can be repaired or replaced from outside. The "technological fix" mends an ecological malfunction, new human beings replace the old to maintain the smooth functioning of industry and bureaucracy, and interventionist medicine exchanges a fresh heart for worn-out, diseased one.

The mechanical view of nature now taught in most Western schools is accepted without question as our everyday, common sense reality—matter is made up of atoms, colors occur by the reflection of light waves of differing lengths, bodies obey the law of inertia, and the sun is in the center of our solar system. None of this was common sense to our seventeenth-century counterparts. The replacement of the older, "natural" ways of thinking by a new and "unnatural" form of life—seeing, thinking, and behaving—did not occur without struggle. The submergence of the organism by the machine engaged the best minds of the times during a period fraught with anxiety, confusion, and instability in both the intellectual and social spheres.

The removal of animistic, organic assumptions about the cosmos constituted the death of nature—the most far-reaching effect of the Scientific Revolution. Because nature was now viewed as a system of dead, inert particles moved by external, rather than inherent forces, the mechanical framework itself could legitimate the manipulation of nature. Moreover, as a conceptual framework, the mechanical order had associated with it a framework of values based on power, fully compatible with the directions taken by commercial capitalism.

The mechanistic view of nature, developed by the seventeenth-century natural philosophers and based on a Western mathematical tradition going back to Plato, is still dominant in science today. This view assumes that nature can be divided into parts and that the parts can be rearranged to create other species of being. "Facts" or information bits can be extracted from the environmental context and rearranged according to a set of rules based on logical and mathematical operations. The results can then be tested and verified by resubmitting them to nature, the ultimate judge of their validity. Mathematical formalism provides the criterion for rationality and certainty, nature the criterion for empirical validity and acceptance or rejection of the theory.

The work of historians and philosophers of science notwithstanding, it is widely assumed by the scientific community that modern science is objective, value-free, and context-free knowledge of the external world. To the extent to which the sciences can be reduced to this mechanistic mathematical model, the more legitimate they become as sciences. Thus the reductionist hierarchy of the validity of the sciences first proposed in the nineteenth century by French positivist philosopher August Comte is still widely assumed by intellectuals, the most mathematical and highly theoretical sciences occupying the most revered position.

The mechanistic approach to nature is as fundamental to the twentieth-century revolution in physics as it was to classical Newtonian science, culminating in the nineteenth-century unification of mechanics, thermodynamics, and electromagnetic theory. Twentieth-century physics still views the world in terms of fundamental particles—electrons, protons, neutrons, mesons, muons, pions, taus, thetas, sigmas, pis, and so on. The search for the ultimate unifying particle, the quark, continues to engage the efforts of the best theoretical physicists.

Mathematical formalism isolates the elements of a given quantum mechanical problem, places them in a latticelike matrix, and rearranges them through a mathematical function called an *operator*. Systems theory extracts possibly relevant information bits from the environmental context and stores them in a computer memory for later use. But since it cannot store an infinite number of "facts," it must select a finite number of potentially relevant pieces of data according to a theory or set of rules governing the selection process. For any given solution, this mechanistic approach very likely excludes some potentially relevant factors.

Systems theorists claim for themselves a holistic outlook, because they believe that they are taking into account the ways in which all the parts in a given system affect the whole. Yet the formalism of the calculus of probabilities excludes the possibility of mathematizing the gestalt—that is, the ways in which each part at any given instant take their meaning from the whole. The more open, adaptive, organic, and complex the system, the less successful is the formalism. It is most successful when applied to closed, artificial, precisely defined, relatively simple systems. Mechanistic assumptions about nature push us increasingly in the direction of artificial environments, mechanized control over more and more aspects of human life, and a loss of the quality of life itself.

HOLISM

Holism was proposed as a philosophical alternative to mechanism by J. C. Smuts in his book *Holism and Evolution* (1926), in which he attempted to define the essential characteristics of holism and to differentiate it from nineteenth-century mechanism. He attempts to show that

> Taking a plant or animal as a type of whole, we notice the fundamental holistic characters as a unity of parts which is so close and intense as to be more than a sum of its parts; which not only gives a particular conformation or structure to the parts but so relates and determines them in their synthesis that their functions are altered; the synthesis affects and determines the parts so that they function toward the "whole"; and the whole and the parts therefore reciprocally influence and determine each other and appear more or less to merge their individual characters.[16]

Smuts saw a continuum of relationships among parts from simple physical mixtures and chemical compounds to organisms and minds in which the unity among parts was affected and changed by the synthesis. "Holism is a process of creative synthesis; the resulting wholes are not static, but dynamic, evolutionary, creative. . . . The explanation of nature can therefore not be purely mechanical; and the mechanistic concept of nature has its place and justification only in the wider setting of holism."

The most important example of holism today is provided by the science of ecology. Although ecology is a relatively new science, its philosophy of nature, holism, is not. Historically, holistic presuppositions about nature have been assumed by communities of people who have succeeded in living in equilibrium with their environments. The idea of cyclical processes, of the interconnectedness of all things, and the assumption that nature is active and alive are fundamental to the history of human thought. No element of an interlocking cycle can be removed without the collapse of the cycle. The parts themselves thus take their meaning from the whole. Each particular part is defined by and dependent on the total context. The cycle itself is a dynamic interactive relationship of all its parts, and process is a dialectical relation between parts and whole. Ecology necessarily must consider the complexities and the totality. It cannot isolate the parts into simplified systems that can be studied in a laboratory because such isolation distorts the whole.

External forces and stresses on a balanced ecosystem, whether natural or man made, can make some parts of the cycle act faster than the systems' own natural oscillations. Depending on the strength of the external disturbance, the metabolic and reproductive reaction rates of the slowest parts of the cycle, and the complexity of the system, it may or may not be able to absorb the stresses without collapsing.[17] At various times in history, civilizations which have put too much external stress on their environments have caused long-term or irrevocable alterations.

CONCLUSION

By pointing up the essential role of every part of an ecosystem, that if one part is removed the system is weakened and loses stability, ecology has moved in the direction of the leveling of value hierarchies. Each part contributes equal value to the healthy functioning of the whole. All living things, as integral parts of a viable ecosystem, thus have rights. The necessity of protecting the ecosystem from collapse due to the extinction of vital members was one argument for the passage of the Endangered Species Act of 1973. The movement toward egalitarianism manifested in the democratic revolutions of the eighteenth century, the extension of citizens' rights to blacks, and finally, voting rights to women was thus carried a step further. Endangered species became equal to the Army Corps of Engineers: the snail darter had to have a legal hearing before the Tellico Dam could be approved, the Furbish lousewort could block construction of the Dickey-Lincoln Dam in Maine, the red-cockaded woodpecker must be considered in Texas timber management, and the El Segundo Blue Butterfly in California airport expansion.

The conjunction of conservation and ecology movements with women's rights and liberation has moved in the direction of reversing both the subjugation of nature and women. In the late nineteenth and early twentieth centuries, the strong feminist movement in the United States begun in 1842 pressed for women's suffrage first in the individual states and then in the nation. Women activists also formed conservation committees in the many women's organizations that were part of the Federation of Women's Clubs established in 1890. They supported the preservationist movement for national, state, and city parks and wilderness areas led by John Muir and Frederick Law Olmsted, eventually splitting away from the managerial, utilitarian wing headed by Gifford Pinchot and Theodore Roosevelt.[18]

Today the conjunction of the women's movement with the ecology movement again brings the issue of liberation into focus. Mainstream women's groups such as the League of Women Voters took an early lead in studying and pressing for clean air and water legislation. Socialist-feminist and "science for the people" groups worked toward revolutionizing economic structures in a direction that would equalize female and male work options and reform a capitalist system that creates profits at the expense of nature and working people.

The March 1979 accident at the Three-Mile Island nuclear reactor near Harrisburg, Pennsylvania, epitomized the problems of the "death of nature" that have become apparent since the Scientific Revolution. The manipulation of nuclear processes in an effort to control and harness nature through technology backfired into disaster. The long-range economic interests and public image of the power company and the reactor's designer were set above the immediate safety of the people and the health of the earth. The hidden effects of radioactive emissions, which by concentrating in the food chain could lead to an increase in cancers over the next several years, were initially downplayed by those charged with responsibility for regulating atomic power.

Three-Mile Island is a recent symbol of the earth's sickness caused by radioactive wastes, pesticides, plastics, photochemical smog, and fluorocarbons. The pollution "of her purest streams" has been supported since the Scientific Revolution by an ideology of "power over nature," an ontology of interchangeable atomic and human parts, and a methodology of "penetration" into her innermost secrets. The sick earth, "yea dead, yea putrified," can probably in the long run be restored to health only by a reversal of mainstream values and a revolution in economic priorities. In this sense, the world must once again be turned upside down.

As natural resources and energy supplies diminish in the future, it will become essential to examine alternatives of all kinds so that, by adopting new social styles, the quality of the environment can be sustained. Decentralization, nonhierarchical forms of organization, recycling of wastes, simpler living styles involving less-polluting "soft" technologies, and labor-intensive rather than capital-intensive economic methods are possibilities only beginning to be explored.[19] The future distribution of energy and resources among communities should be based on the integration of human and natural ecosystems. Such a restructuring of priorities may be crucial if people and nature are to survive.

NOTES

1. On the tensions between technology and the pastoral ideal in American culture, see Leo Marx, *The Machine in the Garden* (New York: Oxford University Press, 1964). On the domination of nature as female, see Annette Kolodny, *The Lay of the Land* (Chapel Hill: University of North Carolina Press, 1975); Rosemary Radford Ruether, "Women, Ecology, and the Domination of Nature," *The Ecumenist* 14 (1975): 1–5; William Leiss, *The Domination of Nature* (New York: Braziller, 1972). On the roots of the ecological crisis, see Donald Hughes, *Ecology in Ancient Civilizations* (Albuquerque: University of New Mexico Press, 1976); Lynn White, Jr., *Medieval Technology and Social Change* (New York: Oxford University Press, 1966); and L. White, Jr., "Historical Roots of Our Ecological Crisis," in White, Jr. *Machina ex Deo* (Cambridge, Mass.: M.I.T. Press, 1968), pp. 75–94; Reijer Hooykaas, *Religion and the Rise of Modern Science* (Grand Rapids, Mich.: Eerdmans, 1972); Christopher Derrick, *The Delicate Creation: Towards a Theology of the Environment* (Old Greenwich, Conn.: Devin-Adair, 1972). On traditional rituals in the mining of ores and in metallurgy, see Mircea Eliade, *The Forge and the Crucible*, trans. Stephan Corrin (New York: Harper & Row, 1962), pp. 42, 53–70, 74, 79–96. On the divergence between attitudes and practices toward the environment, see Yi-Fu Tuan, "Our Treatment of the Environment in Ideal and Actuality," *American Scientist* (May-June 1970): 246–49.
2. Treatments of Francis Bacon's contributions to science include Paolo Rossi, *Francis Bacon: From Magic To Science* (London: Routledge & Kegan Paul, 1968); Lisa Jardine, *Francis Bacon: Discovery and the Art of Discourse* (Cambridge, England: Cambridge University Press, 1974); Benjamin Farrington, *Francis Bacon, Philosopher of Industrial Science* (New York: Schumann, 1949); Margery Purver, *The Royal Society: Concept and Creation* (London: Routledge & Kegan Paul, 1967).
3. Bacon, "The Great Instauration" (written 1620), *Works*, vol. 4, p. 20; "The Masculine Birth of Time," ed. and trans. Benjamin Farrington, in *The Philosophy of*

Francis Bacon (Liverpool, England: Liverpool University Press, 1964), p. 62; "De Dignitate," *Works*, vol. 4, pp. 287, 294.

4. Quoted in Moody E. Prior, "Bacon's Man of Science," in Leonard M. Marsak, ed., *The Rise of Modern Science in Relation to Society* (London: Collier-Macmillan, 1964), p. 45.
5. Rossi, p. 21; Leiss, p. 56; Bacon, *Works*, vol. 4, p. 294; Henry Cornelius Agrippa, *De Occulta Philosophia Libri Tres* (Antwerp, 1531): "No one has such powers but he who has cohabited with the elements, vanquished nature, mounted higher than the heavens, elevating himself above the angels to the archetype itself, with whom he then becomes cooperator and can do all things," as quoted in Frances A. Yates, *Giordano Bruno and the Hermetic Tradition* (New York: Vintage Books, 1964), p. 136.
6. Bacon, "Novum Organum," Part 2, in *Works*, vol. 4, p. 247; "Valerius Terminus," *Works*, vol. 3, pp. 217, 219; "The Masculine Birth of Time," trans. Farrington, p. 62.
7. Bacon, "The Masculine Birth of Time," and "The Refutation of Philosophies," trans. Farrington, pp. 62, 129, 130.
8. Bacon, "De Augmentis," *Works*, vol. 4, p. 294; see also Bacon, "Aphorisms," *Works*, vol. 4.
9. "De Augmentis," *Works*, vol. 4, pp. 320, 325; Plato, "The Timaeus," in *The Dialogues of Plato*, trans. B. Jowett (New York: Random House, 1937), vol. 2, p. 17; Bacon, "Parasceve," *Works*, vol. 4, p. 257.
10. Bacon, "De Augmentis," *Works*, vol. 4, pp. 343, 287, 343, 393.
11. Bacon, "Novum Organum," *Works*, vol. 4, p. 246; "The Great Instauration," *Works*, vol. 4, p. 29; "Novum Organum," Part 2, *Works*, vol. 4, p. 247.
12. Bacon, "Thoughts and Conclusions on the Interpretation of Nature or A Science of Productive Works," trans. Farrington, *The Philosophy of Francis Bacon*, pp. 96, 93, 99.
13. Bacon, "De Augmentis," *Works*, vol. 4, p. 294; "Parasceve," *Works*, vol. 4, p. 257; "Plan of the Work," vol. 4, p. 32; "Novum Organum," *Works*, vol. 4, pp. 114, 115.
14. René Descartes, "Discourse on Method," Part 4, in E. S. Haldane and G. R. T. Ross, eds., *Philosophical Works of Descartes* (New York: Dover, 1955), vol. 1, p. 119.
15. Joseph Glanvill, *Plus Ultra* (Gainesville, Fla.: Scholar's Facsimile Reprints, 1958; first published 1668), quotations on pp. 9, 87, 13, 56, 104, 10.
16. J. C. Smuts, *Holism and Evolution* (New York: Macmillan, 1926), pp. 86, 87. On holism in the biological sciences, see Arthur Koestler, "Beyond Holism and Reductionism: The Concept of the Holon," in *Beyond Reductionism: New Perspectives in the Life Sciences*, ed. A. Koestler and J. R. Smythies (Boston: Beacon Press, 1969).
17. On ecological cycles, see Barry Commoner, *The Closing Circle: Nature, Man, and Technology* (New York; Bantam Books, 1971), Chap. 2.
18. Samuel P. Hays, *Conservation and the Gospel of Efficiency: The Progressive Conservation Movement*, 1890–1920 (Cambridge, Mass.: Harvard University Press, 1959), pp. 142–43.
19. Murray Bookchin, "Ecology and Revolutionary Thought," in *Post-Scarcity Anarchism* (San Francisco: Ramparts Press, 1971), pp. 57–82, and M. Bookchin, "Toward an Ecological Solution" (Berkeley, Cal.: Ecology Center Reprint, n.d.). See also Victor Ferkiss, *Technological Man* (New York: New American Library, 1969), Chap. 9, pp. 205–11; Theodore Roszak, *Where the Wasteland Ends* (Garden City, N.Y.: Doubleday, 1973), pp. 367–71; Paul Goodman and Percival Goodman, *Communitas*, 2nd ed., rev. (New York: Vintage, 1960); Paul Goodman, *People or Personnel* (New York: Random House, 1965); E. F. Schumacher, *Small Is Beautiful: Economics as if People Mattered* (New York: Harper and Row, 1973); Ernest Callenbach, *Ecotopia* (Berkeley, Cal.: Banyan Tree Books, 1976).

Nature, Self, and Gender: Feminism, Environmental Philosophy, and the Critique of Rationalism

Val Plumwood

Val Plumwood is a forest activist, bushwalker, crocodile survivor, and wombat mother. She has published numerous articles on ecofeminism and environmental philosophy and has written Feminism and the Mastery of Nature.

Environmental philosophy has recently been criticized on a number of counts by feminist philosophers. I want to develop further some of this critique and to suggest that much of the issue turns on the failure of environmental philosophy to engage properly with the rationalist tradition, which has been inimical to both women and nature. Damaging assumptions from this tradition have been employed in attempting to formulate a new environmental philosophy that often makes use of or embeds itself within rationalist philosophical frameworks that are not only biased from a gender perspective, but have claimed a negative role for nature as well.

In sections I. through IV. I argue that current mainstream brands of environmental philosophy, both those based in ethics and those based in deep ecology, suffer from this problem, that neither has an adequate historical analysis, and that both continue to rely implicitly upon rationalist-inspired accounts of the self that have been a large part of the problem. In sections V. and VI. I show how the critique of rationalism offers an understanding of a range of key broader issues that environmental philosophy has tended to neglect or treat in too narrow a way. Among these issues are those connected with concepts of the human self and with instrumentalism.

This essay originally appeared in *Hypatia* 6, 1 (Spring 1991): 3–27. Reprinted with permission.

I. RATIONALISM AND THE ETHICAL APPROACH

The ethical approach aims to center a new view of nature in ethics, especially universalizing ethics or in some extension of human ethics. This approach has been criticized from a feminist perspective by a number of recent authors (especially Cheney 1987, 1989). I partly agree with and partly disagree with these criticisms; that is, I think that the emphasis on ethics as the central part (or even the whole) of the problem is misplaced, and that although ethics (and especially the ethics of non-instrumental value) has a role, the particular ethical approaches that have been adopted are problematic and unsuitable. I shall illustrate this claim by a brief discussion of two recent books: Paul Taylor's *Respect for Nature* (1986) and Tom Regan's *The Case for Animal Rights* (1986). Both works are significant, and indeed impressive, contributions to their respective areas.

Paul Taylor's book is a detailed working out of an ethical position that rejects the standard and widespread Western treatment of nature as instrumental to human interests and instead takes living things, as teleological centers of life, to be worthy of respect in their own right. Taylor aims to defend a biocentric (life-centered) ethical theory in which a person's true human self includes his or her biological nature (Taylor 1986, 44), but he attempts to embed this within a Kantian ethical framework that makes strong use of the reason/emotion dichotomy. Thus we are assured that the attitude of respect is a moral one because it is universalizing and disinterested, "that is, each moral agent who sincerely has the attitude advocates its universal adoption by all other agents, regardless of whether they are so inclined and regardless of their fondness or lack of fondness for particular individuals" (41). The essential features of morality having been established as distance from emotion and "particular fondness," morality is then seen as the domain of reason and its touchstone, belief. Having carefully distinguished the "valuational, conative, practical and affective dimensions of the attitude of respect," Taylor goes on to pick out the essentially cognitive "valuational" aspect as central and basic to all the others: "It is *because* moral agents look at animals and plants in this way that they are disposed to pursue the aforementioned ends and purposes" (82) and, similarly, to have the relevant emotions and affective attitudes. The latter must be held at an appropriate distance and not allowed to get the upper hand at any point. Taylor claims that actions do not express moral respect unless they are done as a matter of moral principle conceived as ethically obligatory and pursued disinterestedly and not through inclination, solely or even primarily:

> If one seeks that end solely or primarily from inclination, the attitude being expressed is not moral respect but personal affection or love. . . . It is not that respect for nature *precludes* feelings of care and concern for living things. One may, as a matter of simple kindness, not want to harm them. But the fact that one is so motivated does not itself indicate the presence of a moral attitude of respect. Having the desire to preserve or protect the good of wild animals and plants for

> their sake is neither contrary to, nor evidence of, respect for nature. It is only if the person who has the desire understands that the actions fulfilling it would be obligatory even in the absence of the desire, that the person has genuine respect for nature. (85–86)

There is good reason to reject as self-indulgent the "kindness" approach that reduces respect and morality in the protection of animals to the satisfaction of the carer's own feelings. Respect for others involves treating them as worthy of consideration for their own sake and not just as an instrument for the carer's satisfaction, and there is a sense in which such "kindness" is not genuine care or respect for the other. But Taylor is doing much more than this—he is treating care, viewed as "inclination" or "desire," as irrelevant to morality. Respect for nature on this account becomes an essentially *cognitive* matter (that of a person believing something to have "inherent worth" and then acting from an understanding of ethical principles as universal).

The account draws on the familiar view of reason and emotion as sharply separated and opposed, and of "desire," caring, and love as merely "personal" and "particular" as opposed to the universality and impartiality of understanding, and of "feminine" emotions as essentially unreliable, untrustworthy, and morally irrelevant, an inferior domain to be dominated by a superior, disinterested (and of course masculine) reason. This sort of rationalist account of the place of emotions has come in for a great deal of well-deserved criticism recently, both for its implicit gender bias and its philosophical inadequacy, especially its dualism and its construal of public reason as sharply differentiated from and controlling private emotion (see, for example, Benhabib 1987; Blum 1980; Gilligan 1982, 1987; Lloyd 1983a and 1983b).

A further major problem in its use in this context is the inconsistency of employing, in the service of constructing an allegedly biocentric ethical theory, a framework that has itself played such a major role in creating a dualistic account of the genuine human self as essentially rational and as sharply discontinuous from the merely emotional, the merely bodily, and the merely animal elements. For emotions and the private sphere with which they are associated have been treated as sharply differentiated and inferior, as part of a pattern in which they are seen as linked to the sphere of nature, not the realm of reason.

And it is not only women but also the earth's wild living things that have been denied possession of a reason thus construed along masculine and oppositional lines and which contrasts not only with the "feminine" emotions but also with the physical and the animal. Much of the problem (both for women and nature) lies in rationalist or rationalist-derived conceptions of the self and of what is essential and valuable in the human makeup. It is in the name of such a reason that these other things—the feminine, the emotional, the merely bodily or the merely animal, and the natural world itself—have most often been denied their virtue and been accorded an inferior and merely instrumental position. Thomas Aquinas states this problematic position succinctly:

"the intellectual nature is alone requisite for its own sake in the universe, and all others for its sake" (Thomas Aquinas 1976, 56). And it is precisely reason so construed that is usually taken to characterize the authentically human and to create the supposedly sharp separation, cleavage, or discontinuity between all humans and the nonhuman world, and the similar cleavage within the human self. The supremacy accorded an oppositionally construed reason is the key to the anthropocentrism of the Western tradition. The Kantian-rationalist framework, then, is hardly the area in which to search for a solution. Its use, in a way that perpetuates the supremacy of reason and its opposition to contrast areas, in the service of constructing a supposedly biocentric ethic is a matter for astonishment.

Ethical universalization and abstraction are both closely associated with accounts of the self in terms of rational egoism. Universalization is explicitly seen in both the Kantian and the Rawlsian framework as needed to hold in check natural self-interest; it is the moral complement to the account of the self as "disembodied and disembedded," as the autonomous self of liberal theory, the rational egoist of market theory, the falsely differentiated self of object-relations theory (Benhabib 1987; Poole 1984, 1985). In the same vein, the broadening of the scope of moral concern along with the according of rights to the natural world has been seen by influential environmental philosophers (Leopold 1949, 201–2) as the final step in a process of increasing moral abstraction and generalization, part of the move away from the merely particular—*my* self, *my* family, *my* tribe—the discarding of the merely personal and, by implication, the merely selfish. This is viewed as moral progress, increasingly civilized as it moves further away from primitive selfishness. Nature is the last area to be included in this march away from the unbridled natural egoism of the particular and its close ally, the emotional. Moral progress is marked by increasing adherence to moral rules and a movement away from the supposedly natural (in human nature), and the completion of its empire is, paradoxically, the extension of its domain of adherence to abstract moral rules to nature itself.

On such a view, the particular and the emotional are seen as the enemy of the rational, as corrupting, capricious, and self-interested. And if the "moral emotions" are set aside as irrelevant or suspect, as merely subjective or personal, we can only base morality on the rules of abstract reason, on the justice and rights of the impersonal public sphere.

This view of morality as based on a concept of reason as oppositional to the personal, the particular, and the emotional has been assumed in the framework of much recent environmental ethics. But as a number of feminist critics of the masculine model of moral life and of moral abstraction have pointed out (Blum 1980, Nicholson 1983), this increasing abstraction is not necessarily an improvement. The opposition between the care and concern for particular others and generalized moral concern is associated with a sharp division between public (masculine) and private (feminine) realms. Thus it is part of the set of dualistic contrasts in which the problem of the

Western treatment of nature is rooted. And the opposition between care for particular others and general moral concern is a false one. There *can* be opposition between particularity and generality of concern, as when concern for particular others is accompanied by *exclusion* of others from care or chauvinistic attitudes toward them (Blum 1980, 80), but this does not automatically happen, and emphasis on oppositional cases obscures the frequent cases where they work together—and in which care for particular others is essential to a more generalized morality. Special relationships, which are treated by universalizing positions as at best morally irrelevant and at worst a positive hindrance to the moral life, are thus mistreated. For as Blum (1980, 78–83) stresses, special relationships form the basis for much of our moral life and concern, and it could hardly be otherwise. With nature, as with the human sphere, the capacity to care, to experience sympathy, understanding, and sensitivity to the situation and fate of particular others, and to take responsibility for others is an index of our moral being. Special relationship with, care for, or empathy with particular aspects of nature as experiences rather than with nature as abstraction are essential to provide a depth and type of concern that is not otherwise possible. Care and responsibility for particular animals, trees, and rivers that are known well, loved, and appropriately connected to the self are an important basis for acquiring a wider, more generalized concern. (As we shall see, this failure to deal adequately with particularity is a problem for deep ecology as well.)

Concern for nature, then, should not be viewed as the completion of a process of (masculine) universalization, moral abstraction, and disconnection, discarding the self, emotions, and special ties (all, of course, associated with the private sphere and femininity). Environmental ethics has for the most part placed itself uncritically in such a framework, although it is one that is extended with particular difficulty to the natural world. Perhaps the kindest thing that can be said about the framework of ethical universalization is that it is seriously incomplete and fails to capture the most important elements of respect, which are not reducible to or based on duty or obligation any more than the most important elements of friendship are, but which are rather an expression of a certain kind of selfhood and a certain kind of relation between self and other.

II. RATIONALISM, RIGHTS, AND ETHICS

An extension to nature of the standard concepts of morality is also the aim of Tom Regan's *The Case for Animal Rights* (1986). This is the most impressive, thorough, and solidly argued book in the area of animal ethics, with excellent chapters on topics such as animal intentionality. But the key concept upon which this account of moral concern for animals is based is that of rights, which requires strong individual separation of rights-holders and is set in a framework of human community and legality. Its extension to the natural world raises a host of problems (Midgley 1983, 61–64). Even in the case of individual higher animals for which Regan uses this concept of rights, the approach is problematic. His concept of rights is based on Mill's notion that, if a being has a right to something not only should he or she (or it) have that thing but others are obliged to intervene to secure it. The application of this concept of rights to individual wild living animals appears to give humans almost limitless obligations to intervene massively in all sorts of far reaching and conflicting ways in natural cycles to secure the rights of a bewildering variety of beings. In the case of the wolf and the sheep, an example discussed by Regan, it is unclear whether humans should intervene to protect the sheep's rights or to avoid doing so in order not to violate the wolf's right to its natural food.

Regan attempts to meet this objection by claiming that since the wolf is not itself a moral agent (although it is a moral patient), it cannot violate the sheep's rights not to suffer a painful and violent death (Regan 1986, 285). But the defense is unconvincing, because even if we concede that the wolf is not a moral agent, it still does not follow that on a rights view we are not obliged to intervene. From the fact that the wolf is not a moral agent it only follows that it is not *responsible* for violating the sheep's rights, not that they are not violated or that others do not have an obligation (according to the rights view) to intervene. If the wolf were attacking a human baby, it would hardly do as a defense in that case to claim that one did not have a duty to intervene because the wolf was not a moral agent. But on Regan's view the baby and the sheep do have something like the same rights. So we do have a duty, it seems, (on the rights view) to intervene to protect the sheep—leaving us where with the wolf?

The concept of rights seems to produce absurd consequences and is impossible to apply in the context of predators in a natural ecosystem, as opposed to a particular human social context in which claimants are part of a reciprocal social community and conflict cases are either few or settleable according to some agreed-on principles. All this seems to me to tell against the concept of rights as the correct one for the general task of dealing with animals in the natural environment (as opposed, of course, to domestic animals in a basically humanized environment).[1]

Rights seem to have acquired an exaggerated importance as part of the prestige of the public sphere and the masculine, and the emphasis on separation and autonomy, on reason and abstraction. A more promising approach for an ethics of nature, and also one much more in line with the current directions in feminism, would be to remove rights from the center of the moral stage and pay more attention to some other, less dualistic, moral concepts such as respect, sympathy, care, concern, compassion, gratitude, friendship, and responsibility (Cook 1977, 118–9). These concepts, because of their dualistic construal as feminine and their consignment to the private sphere as subjective and emotional, have been treated as peripheral and given far less importance than they deserve for several reasons. First, rationalism and the prestige of reason and the public sphere have influenced not only the concept of what morality is (as Taylor explicates it, for example, as essentially a rational and cognitive act of understanding that certain actions are ethically obligatory) but of what is *central* to it or what counts as moral concepts. Second, concepts such as respect, care, concern, and so on are resistant to analysis along lines of a dualistic reason/emotion dichotomy, and their construal along these lines has involved confusion and distortion (Blum 1980). They *are* moral "feelings" but they involve reason, behavior and emotion in ways that do not seem separable. Rationalist-inspired ethical concepts are highly ethnocentric and cannot account adequately for the views of many indigenous peoples, and the attempted application of these rationalist concepts to their positions tends to lead to the view that they lack a real ethical framework (Plumwood 1990). These alternative concepts seem better able to apply to the views of such peoples, whose ethic of respect, care and responsibility for land is often based on special relationships with particular areas of land via links to kin (Neidjie 1985, 1989). Finally these concepts, which allow for particularity and mostly do not require reciprocity, are precisely the sorts of concepts feminist philosophers have argued should have a more significant place in ethics at the expense of abstract, malestream concepts from the public sphere such as rights and justice (Gilligan 1982, 1987, Benhabib 1987). The ethic of care and responsibility they have articulated seems to extend much less problematically to the nonhuman world than do the impersonal concepts which are currently seen as central, and it also seems capable of providing an excellent basis for the non-instrumental treatment of nature many environmental philosophers have now called for. Such an approach treats ethical relations as an expression of self-in-relationship (Gilligan 1987, 24) rather than as the discarding, containment, or generalization of a self viewed as self-interested and non-relational, as in the conventional ethics of universalization.[2] As I argue later, there are important connections between this relational account of the self and the rejection of instrumentalism.

It is not that we need to abandon ethics or dispense with the universalized ethical approach entirely, although we do need to reassess the centrality of ethics in environmental philosophy.[3] What is needed is not so much the abandonment of ethics as a different and richer understanding of it (and, as I argue later, a richer understanding of environmental philosophy generally than is provided by ethics), one that gives an important place to ethical concepts owning to emotionality and particularity and that abandons the exclusive focus on the universal and the abstract associated with the nonrelational self and the dualistic and oppositional accounts of the reason/emotion and universal/particular contrasts as given in rationalist accounts of ethics.

III. THE DISCONTINUITY PROBLEM

The problem is not just one of restriction in ethics but also of restriction *to* ethics. Most mainstream environmental philosophers continue to view environmental philosophy as mainly concerned with ethics. For example, instrumentalism is generally viewed by mainstream environmental philosophers as a problem in ethics, and its solution is seen as setting up some sort of theory of intrinsic value. This neglects a key aspect of the overall problem that is concerned with the definition of the human self as separate from nature, the connection between this and the instrumental view of nature, and broader *political* aspects of the critique of instrumentalism.

One key aspect of the Western view of nature, which the ethical stance neglects completely, is the view of nature as sharply discontinuous or ontologically divided from the human sphere. This leads to a view of humans as apart from or "outside of" nature, usually as masters or external controllers of it. Attempts to reject this view often speak alternatively of humans as "part of nature" but rarely distinguish this position from the obvious claim that human fate is interconnected with that of the biosphere, that humans are subject to natural laws. But on the divided-self theory it is the essentially or authentically human part of the self, and in that sense the human realm proper, that is outside nature, not the human as a physical phenomenon. The view of humans as outside of and alien to nature seems to be especially strongly a Western one, although not confined to the West. There are many other cultures which do not hold it, which stress what connects us to nature as genuinely human virtues, which emphasize continuity and not dissimilarity.[4]

As ecofeminism points out, Western thought has given us a strong human/nature dualism that is part of the set of interrelated dualisms of mind/body, reason/nature, reason/emotion, masculine/feminine and has important interconnected features with these other dualisms.[5] This dualism has been especially stressed in the rationalist tradition. In this dualism what is characteristically and authentically human is defined against or in opposition to what is taken to be natural, nature, or the physical or biological realm. This takes various forms. For example, the characterization of the genuinely, properly, characteristically, or authentically human, or of human virtue, in polarized terms to exclude what is taken to be characteristic of the natural is what John Rodman (1980) has called "the Differential Imperative" in which what is virtuous in the human is taken to be what maximizes distance from the merely natural. The maintenance of sharp dichotomy and polarization is achieved by the rejection and denial of what links humans to the animal. What is taken to be authentically and characteristically human, defining of the human, as well as the ideal for which humans should strive is *not* to be found in what is shared with the natural and animal (e.g., the body, sexuality, reproduction, emotionality, the senses, agency) but in what is thought to separate and distinguish them—especially reason and its off-shoots. Hence humanity is defined not as part of nature (perhaps a special part) but as separate from and in opposition to it. Thus the relation of humans to nature is treated as an oppositional and value dualism.

The process closely parallels the formation of other dualisms, such as masculine/feminine, reason/emotion, and spirit/body criticized in feminist thought (see, for example, Ruether 1975, Griffin 1978, Griscom 1981, King

1981, Lloyd 1983, Jaggar 1983) but this parallel logic is not the only connection between human/nature dualism and masculine/feminine dualism. Moreover, this exclusion of the natural from the concept of the properly human is not the only dualism involved, because what is involved in the construction of this dualistic conception of the human is the rejection of those parts of the human character identified as feminine—also identified as less than fully human—giving the masculine conception of what it is to be human. Masculinity can be linked to this exclusionary and polarized conception of the human, via the desire to exclude and distance from the feminine and the nonhuman. The features that are taken as characteristic of humankind and as where its special virtues lie, are those such as rationality, freedom, and transcendence of nature (all traditionally viewed as masculine), which are viewed as not shared with nature. Humanity is defined oppositionally to both nature and the feminine.

The upshot is a deeply entrenched view of the genuine or ideal human self as not including features shared with nature, and as defined *against* or in *opposition* to the nonhuman realm, so that the human sphere and that of nature cannot significantly overlap. Nature is sharply divided off from the human, is alien and usually hostile and inferior. Furthermore, this kind of human self can only have certain kinds of accidental or contingent connections to the realm of nature. I shall call this the discontinuity problem or thesis and I argue later that it plays a key role with respect to other elements of the problem.

IV. RATIONALISM AND DEEP ECOLOGY

Although the discontinuity problem is generally neglected by the ethical stance, a significant exception to its neglect within environmental philosophy seems to be found in deep ecology, which is also critical of the location of the problem within ethics.[6] Furthermore, deep ecology also seems initially to be more likely to be compatible with a feminist philosophical framework, emphasizing as it does connections with the self, connectedness, and merger. Nevertheless, there are severe tensions between deep ecology and a feminist perspective. Deep ecology has not satisfactorily identified the key elements in the traditional framework or observed their connections to rationalism. As a result, it fails to reject adequately rationalist assumptions and indeed often seems to provide its own versions of universalization, the discarding of particular connections, and rationalist accounts of self.

Deep ecology locates the key problem area in human-nature relations in the separation of humans and nature, and it provides a solution for this in terms of the "identification" of self with nature. "Identification" is usually left deliberately vague, and corresponding accounts of self are various and shifting and not always compatible.[7] There seem to be at least three different accounts of self involved—indistinguishability, expansion of self, and transcendence of self—and practitioners appear to feel free to move among them at will. As I shall show, all are unsatisfactory from both a feminist perpective and from that of obtaining a satisfactory environmental philosophy, and the appeal of deep ecology rests largely on the failure to distinguish them.

A. The Indistinguishability Account

The indistinguishability account rejects boundaries between self and nature. Humans are said to be just one strand in the biotic web, not the source and ground of all value and the discontinuity thesis is, it seems, firmly rejected. Warwick Fox describes the central intuition of deep ecology as follows: "We can make no firm ontological divide in the field of existence . . . there is no bifurcation in reality between the human and nonhuman realms . . . to the extent that we perceive boundaries, we fall short of deep ecological consciousness" (Fox 1984, 7). But much more is involved here than the rejection of discontinuity, for deep ecology goes on to replace the human-in-environment image by a holistic or gestalt view that "dissolves not only the human-in-environment concept, but every compact-thing-in-milieu concept"—except when talking at a superficial level of communication (Fox 1984, 1). Deep ecology involves a cosmology of "unbroken wholeness which denies the classical idea of the analyzability of the world into separately and independently existing parts."[8] It is strongly attracted to a variety of mystical traditions and to the Perennial Philosophy, in which the self is merged with the other—"the other is none other than yourself." As John Seed puts it: "I am protecting the rain forest" develops into "I am part of the rain forest protecting myself. I am that part of the rain forest recently emerged into thinking" (Seed et al. 1988, 36).

There are severe problems with these claims, arising not so much from the orientation to the concept of self (which seems to me important and correct) or from the mystical character of the insights themselves as from the indistinguishability metaphysics which is proposed as their basis. It is not merely that the identification process of which deep ecologists speak seems to stand in need of much more clarification, but that it does the wrong thing. The problem, in the sort of account I have given, is the discontinuity between humans and nature that emerges as part of the overall set of Western dualisms. Deep ecology proposes to heal this division by a "unifying process," a metaphysics that insists that everything is really part of and indistinguishable from everything else. This is not only to employ overly powerful tools but ones that do the wrong job, for the origins of the particular opposition involved in the human/nature dualism remain unaddressed and unanalyzed. The real basis of the discontinuity lies in the concept of an authentic human being, in what is taken to be valuable in human character, society, and culture, as what is distinct from what is taken to be natural. The sources of and remedies for this remain unaddressed in deep ecology. Deep ecology has confused dualism and atomism and then mistakenly taken indistinguishability to follow from the rejection of atomism. The confusion is clear in Fox, who proceeds immediately from the ambiguous claim that there is no "bifurcation in reality between the human and nonhuman realms" (which could be taken as a rejection of human discontinuity from nature) to the conclusion that what is needed is that we embrace an indistinguishability metaphysics of unbroken wholeness in the whole of reality. But the problem must be addressed in terms of this specific dualism and its connections. Instead deep ecology proposes the obliteration of all distinction.

Thus deep ecology's solution to removing this discontinuity by obliterating *all* division is far too powerful. In its overgenerality it fails to provide a genuine basis for an environmental ethics of the kind sought, for the view of humans as metaphysically unified with the cosmic whole will be equally true whatever relation humans stand in with nature—the situation of exploitation of nature exemplifies such unity equally as well as a conserver situation and the human self is just as indistinguishable from the bulldozer and Coca-Cola bottle as the rocks or the rain forest. What John Seed seems to have in mind here is that once one has realized that one is indistinguishable from the rain forest, its needs would become one's own. But there is nothing to guarantee this—one could equally well take one's own needs for its.

This points to a further problem with the indistinguishability thesis, that we need to recognize not only our human continuity with the natural world but also its distinctness and independence from us and the distinctness of the needs of things in nature from ours. The indistinguishability account does not allow for this, although it is a very important part of respect for nature and of conservation strategy.

The dangers of accounts of the self that involve self-merger appear in feminist contexts as well, where they are sometimes appealed to as the alternative to masculine-defined autonomy as disconnection from others. As Jean Grimshaw writes of the related thesis of the indistinctness of persons (the acceptance of the loss of self-boundaries as a feminine ideal): "It is important not merely because certain forms of symbiosis or 'connection' with others can lead to damaging failures of personal development, but because care for others, understanding of them, are only possible if one can adequately distinguish oneself *from* others. If I see myself as 'indistinct' from you, or you as not having your own being that is not merged with mine, then I cannot preserve a real sense of your well-being as opposed to mine. Care and understanding require the sort of distance that is needed in order not to see the other as a projection of self, or self as a continuation of the other" (Grimshaw 1986, 182–3).

These points seem to me to apply to caring for other species and for the natural world as much as they do to caring for our own species. But just as dualism is confused with atomism, so holistic self-merger is taken to be the only alternative to egoistic accounts of the self as without essential connection to others or to nature. Fortunately, this is a false choice;[9] as I argue below, nonholistic but relational accounts of the self, as developed in some feminist and social philosophy, enable a rejection of dualism, including human/nature dualism, without denying the independence or distinguishability of the other. To the extent that deep ecology is identified with the indistinguishability thesis, it does not provide an adequate basis for a philosophy of nature.

B. The Expanded Self

In fairness to deep ecology it should be noted that it tends to vacillate between mystical indistinguishability and the other accounts of self, between the holistic self and the expanded self. Vacillation occurs often by way of slipperiness as to what is meant by identification of self with the other, a key notion in deep ecology. This slipperiness reflects the confusion of dualism and atomism previously noted but also seems to reflect a desire to retain the mystical appeal of indistinguishability while avoiding its many difficulties. Where "identification" means not "identity" but something more like "empathy," identification with other beings can lead to an expanded self. According to Arne Naess, "The self is as comprehensive as the totality of our identifications. . . . Our Self is that with which we identify."[10] This larger self (or Self, to deep ecologists) is something for which we should strive "insofar as it is in our power to do so" (Fox 1986, 13–19), and according to Fox we should also strive to make it as large as possible. But this expanded self is not the result of a critique of egoism; rather, it is an enlargement and an extension of egoism.[11] It does not question the structures of possessive egoism and self-interest; rather, it tries to allow for a wider set of interests by an expansion of self. The motivation for the expansion of self is to allow for a wider set of concerns while continuing to allow the self to operate on the fuel of self-interest (or Self-interest). This is apparent from the claim that "in this light . . . ecological resistance is simply another name for self defense" (Fox 1986, 60). Fox quotes with approval John Livingstone's statement: "When I say that the fate of the sea turtle or the tiger or the gibbon is mine, I mean it. All that is in my universe is not merely mine; it is *me*. And I shall defend myself. I shall defend myself not only against overt aggression but also against gratuitous insult" (Fox 1986, 60).

Deep ecology does not question the structures of rational egoism and continues to subscribe to two of the main tenets of the egoist framework—that human nature is egoistic and that the alternative to egoism is self-sacrifice.[12] Given these assumptions about egoism, the obvious way to obtain some sort of human interest in defending nature is through the expanded Self operating in the interests of nature but also along the familiar lines of self-interest.[13] The expanded-self strategy might initially seem to be just another pretentious and obscure way of saying that humans empathize with nature. But the strategy of transferring the structures of egoism is highly problematic, for the widening of interest is obtained at the expense of failing to recognize unambiguously the distinctness and independence of the other.[14] Others are recognized morally only to the extent that they are incorporated into the self, and their difference denied (Warren 1990). And the failure to critique egoism and the disembedded, nonrelational self means a failure to draw connections with other contemporary critiques.

C. The Transcended or Transpersonal Self

To the extent that the expanded Self requires that we detach from the particular concerns of the self (a relinquishment that despite its natural difficulty we should struggle to attain), expansion of self to Self also tends to lead into the third position, the transcendence or overcoming of self. Thus Fox urges us to strive for *impartial* identification with *all* particulars, the cosmos, discarding our identifications with our own particular concerns, personal emotions, and attachments (Fox 1990, 12). Fox presents here the deep ecology version of universalization, with the familiar emphasis on the personal and the particular as corrupting and self-interested—"the cause of possessiveness, war and ecological destruction" (1990, 12).

This treatment of particularity, the devaluation of an identity tied to particular parts of the natural world as opposed to an abstractly conceived whole, the cosmos, reflects the rationalistic preoccupation with the universal and its account of ethical life as oppositional to the particular. The analogy in human terms of impersonal love of the cosmos is the view of morality as based on universal principles or the impersonal and abstract "love of man." Thus Fox (1990, 12) reiterates (as if it were unproblematic) the view of particular attachments as ethically suspect and as oppositional to genuine, impartial "identification," which necessarily falls short with all particulars.

Because this "transpersonal" identification is so indiscriminate and intent on denying particular meanings, it cannot allow for the deep and highly particularistic attachment to place that has motivated both the passion of many modern conservationists and the love of many indigenous peoples for their land (which deep ecology inconsistently tries to treat as a model). This is based not on a vague, bloodless, and abstract cosmological concern but on the formation of identity, social and personal, in relation to particular areas of land, yielding ties often as special and powerful as those to kin, and which are equally expressed in very specific and local responsibilities of care.[15] This emerges clearly in the statements of many indigenous peoples, such as in the moving words of Cecilia Blacktooth explaining why her people would not surrender their land:

> You ask us to think what place we like next best to this place where we always lived. You see the graveyard there? There are our fathers and our grandfathers. You see that Eagle-nest mountain and that Rabbit-hole mountain? When God made them, He gave us this place. We have always lived here. We do not care for any other place. . . . We have always lived here. We would rather die here. Our fathers did. We cannot leave them. Our children were born here—how can we go away? If you give us the best place in the world, it is not so good as this. . . . This is our home. . . . We cannot live any where else. We were born here and our fathers are buried here. . . . We want this place and no other. . . . (McLuhan 1973, 28)

In inferiorizing such particular, emotional, and kinship-based attachments, deep ecology gives us another variant on the superiority of reason and the inferiority of its contrasts, failing to grasp yet again the role of reason and incompletely critiquing its influence. To obtain a more adequate account than that offered by mainstream ethics and deep ecology it seems that we must move toward the sort of ethics feminist theory has suggested, which can allow for both continuity and difference and for ties to nature which are expressive of the rich, caring relationships of kinship and friendship rather than increasing abstraction and detachment from relationship.[16]

V. THE PROBLEM IN TERMS OF THE CRITIQUE OF RATIONALISM

I now show how the problem of the inferiorization of nature appears if it is viewed from the perspective of the critique of rationalism and seen as part of the general problem of revaluing and reintegrating what rationalist culture has split apart, denied, and devalued. Such an account shifts the focus away from the preoccupations of both mainstream ethical approaches and deep ecology, and although it does retain an emphasis on the account of the self as central, it gives a different account from that offered by deep ecology. In section VI, I conclude by arguing that one of the effects of this shift in focus is to make connections with other critiques, especially feminism, central rather than peripheral or accidental, as they are currently viewed by deep ecologists in particular.

First, what is missing from the accounts of both the ethical philosophers and the deep ecologists is an understanding of the problem of discontinuity as created by a dualism linked to a network of related dualisms. Here I believe a good deal can be learned from the critique of dualism feminist philosophy has developed and from the understanding of the mechanisms of dualisms ecofeminists have produced. A dualistically construed dichotomy typically polarizes difference and minimizes shared characteristics, construes difference along lines of superiority/inferiority, and views the inferior side as a means to the higher ends of the superior side (the instrumental thesis). Because its nature is defined oppositionally, the task of the superior side, that in which it realizes itself and expresses its true nature, is to separate from, dominate, and control the lower side. This has happened both with the human/nature division and with other related dualisms such as masculine/feminine, reason/body, and reason/emotion. Challenging these dualisms involves not just a reevaluation of superiority/inferiority and a higher status for the underside of the dualisms (in this case nature) but also a reexamination and reconceptualizing of the dualistically construed categories themselves. So in the case of the human/nature dualism it is not just a question of improving the status of nature, moral or otherwise, while everything else remains the same, but of reexamining and reconceptualizing the concept of the human, and also the concept of the contrasting class of nature. For the concept of the human, of what it is to be fully and authentically human, and of what is genuinely human in the set of characteristics typical humans possess, has been defined oppositionally, by *exclusion* of what is associated with the inferior natural sphere in very much the way that Lloyd (1983), for example, has shown in the case of the categories of masculine and feminine, and of reason and its contrasts.

Humans have both biological and mental characteristics, but the mental rather than the biological have been taken to be characteristic of the human and to give what is "fully and authentically" human. The term "human" is, of course, not merely descriptive here but very much an evaluative term setting out an ideal: it is what is essential or worthwhile in the human that excludes the natural. It is not necessarily denied that humans have some material or animal component—rather, it is seen in this framework as alien or inessential to them, not part of their fully or truly human nature. The human essence is often seen as lying in maximizing control over the natural sphere (both within and without) and in qualities such as rationality, freedom, and transcendence of the material sphere. These qualities are also identified as masculine, and hence the *oppositional* model of the human coincides or converges with a masculine model, in which the characteristics attributed are those of the masculine ideal.

Part of a strategy for challenging this human/nature dualism, then, would involve recognition of these excluded qualities—split off, denied, or construed as alien, or comprehended as the sphere of supposedly *inferior* humans such as women and blacks—as equally and fully human. This would provide a basis for the recognition of *continuities* with the natural world. Thus reproductivity, sensuality, emotionality would be taken to be as fully and authentically human qualities as the capacity for abstract planning and calculation. This proceeds from the assumption that one basis for discontinuity and alienation from nature is alienation from those qualities which provide continuity with nature in ourselves.

This connection between the rationalist account of nature within and nature without has powerful repercussions. So part of what is involved is a challenge to the centrality and dominance of the rational in the account of the human self. Such a challenge would have far-reaching implications for what is valuable in human society and culture, and it connects with the challenge to the cultural legacy of rationalism made by other critiques of rationalism such as feminism, and by critiques of technocracy, bureaucracy, and instrumentalism.

What is involved here is a reconceptualization of the human side of the human/nature dualism, to free it from the legacy of rationalism. Also in need of reconceptualization is the underside of this dualism, the concept of nature, which is construed in polarized terms as bereft of qualities appropriated to the human side, as passive and lacking in agency and teleology, as pure materiality, pure body, or pure mechanism. So what is called for here is the development of alternatives to mechanistic ways of viewing the world, which are also part of the legacy of rationalism.

VI. INSTRUMENTALISM AND THE SELF

There are two parts to the restructuring of the human self in relation to nature—reconceptualizing the human and reconceptualizing the self, and especially its possibilities of relating to nature in other than instrumental ways.

Here the critique of the egoistic self of liberal individualism by both feminist and social philosophers, as well as the critique of instrumental reason, offers a rich set of connections and insights on which to draw. In the case of both of these parts what is involved is the rejection of basically masculine models, that is, of humanity and of the self.

Instrumentalism has been identified as a major problem by the ethical approach in environmental philosophy but treated in a rather impoverished way, as simply the problem of establishing the inherent worth of nature.[17] Connection has not been made to the broader account that draws on the critique of instrumental reason. This broader account reveals both its links with the discontinuity problem and its connection with the account of the self. A closer look at this further critique gives an indication of how we might develop an account that enables us to stress continuity without drowning in a sea of indistinguishability.

We might notice first the strong connections between discontinuity (the polarization condition of dualism) and instrumentalism—the view that the excluded sphere is appropriately treated as a means to the ends of the higher sphere or group, that its value lies in its usefulness to the privileged group that is, in contrast, worthwhile or significant in itself. Second, it is important to maintain a strong distinction and maximize distance between the sphere of means and that of ends to avoid breaking down the sharp boundaries required by hierarchy. Third, it helps if the sphere treated instrumentally is seen as lacking ends of its own (as in views of nature and women as passive), for then others can be imposed upon it without problem. There are also major connections that come through the account of the self which accompanies both views.

The self that complements the instrumental treatment of the other is one that stresses sharply defined ego boundaries, distinctness, autonomy, and separation from others—that is defined *against* others, and lacks essential connections to them. This corresponds to object/relations account of the masculine self associated with the work of Nancy Chodorow (1979, 1985) and also to the self-interested individual presupposed in market theory (Poole 1985, 1990).[18] This self uses both other humans and the world generally as a means to its egoistic satisfaction, which is assumed to be the satisfaction of interests in which others play no essential role. If we try to specify these interests they would make no essential reference to the welfare of others, except to the extent that these are useful to serve predetermined ends. Others as means are interchangeable if they produce equivalent satisfactions—anything which conduces to that end is as valuable, other things being equal, as anything else which equally conduces to that end. The interests of such an individual, that of the individual of market theory and of the masculine self as theorized by Chodorow, are defined as essentially independent of or disconnected from those of other people, and his or her transactions with the world at large consist of various attempts to get satisfaction for these predetermined private interests. Others are a "resource," and the interests of others connect with the interests of such autonomous selves only accidentally or contingently. They are not valued for themselves but for their effects in producing gratification. This kind of instrumental picture, so obviously a misdescription in the case of relations to other humans, is precisely still the normal Western model of what our relations to nature should be.

Now this kind of instrumental, disembedded account of the relation of self to others has been extensively criticized in the area of political theory from a variety of quarters, including feminist theory, in the critique of liberalism, and in environmental philosophy (Benhabib 1987; Benhabib and Cornell 1987; Benjamin 1985; Chodorow 1985; Gilligan 1982, 1987; Grimshaw 1986; Jagger 1983; Miller 1978; Plumwood 1980; Poole 1984, 1985, 1990; Warren 1990). It has been objected that this account does not give an accurate picture of the human self—that humans are social and connected in a way such an account does not recognize. People do have interests that make *essential* and not merely accidental or contingent reference to those of others, for example, when a mother wishes for her child's recovery, the child's flourishing is an essential *part* of her flourishing, and similarly with close others and indeed for others more widely ("social others"). But, the objection continues, this gives a misleading picture of the world, one that omits or impoverishes a whole significant dimension of human experience, a dimension which provides important insight into gender difference, without which we cannot give an adequate picture of what it is to be human. Instead we must see human beings and their interests as *essentially* related and interdependent. As Karen Warren notes "Relationships are not something extrinsic to who we are, not an 'add on' feature of human nature; they play an essential role in shaping what it is to be human" (Warren 1990, 143). That people's interests are relational does not imply a holistic view of them—that they are merged or indistinguishable. Although some of the mother's interests entail satisfaction of the child's interests, they are not identical or even necessarily similar. There is overlap, but the relation is one of intentional inclusion (her interest is *that* the child should thrive, that certain of the child's key interests are satisfied) rather than accidental overlap.

This view of self-in-relationship is, I think, a good candidate for the richer account of self deep ecologists have sought and for which they have mistaken holistic accounts. It is an account that avoids atomism but that enables a recognition of interdependence and relationship without falling into the problems of indistinguishability, that acknowledges both continuity and difference, and that breaks the culturally posed false dichotomy of egoism and altruism of interests;[19] it bypasses both masculine "separation" and traditional-feminine "merger" accounts of the self. It can also provide an appropriate foundation for an ethic of connectedness and caring for others, as argued by Gilligan (1982, 1987) and Miller (1978).

Thus it is unnecessary to adopt any of the stratagems of deep ecology—the indistinguishable self, the expanded self, or the transpersonal self—in order to provide an alternative to anthropocentrism or human self-interest. This can be better done through the relational account of self, which clearly recognizes the distinctness of nature but also our relationship and continuity with it. On this relational account, respect for the other results neither from the containment of self nor from a transcendence of self, but is an *expression* of self in relationship, not egoistic self as merged with the other but self as embedded in a network of essential relationships with distinct others.

The relational account of self can usefully be applied to the case of human relations with nature and to place. The standard Western view of the relation of the self to the nonhuman is that it is always *accidentally* related, and hence the nonhuman can be used as a means to the self-contained ends of human beings. Pieces of land are real estate, readily interchangeable as equivalent means to the end of human satisfaction; no place is more than "a stage along life's way, a launching pad for higher flights and wider orbits than your own" (Berman 1982, 327). But, of course, we do not all think this way, and instances of contrary behavior would no doubt be more common if their possibility were not denied and distorted by both theoretical and social construction. But other cultures have recognized such essential connection of self to country clearly enough, and many indigenous voices from the past and present speak of the grief and pain in loss of their land, to which they are as essentially connected as to any human other. When Aboriginal people, for example, speak of the land as part of them, "like brother and mother" (Neidjie 1985, 51; 1989, 4, 146), this is, I think, one of their meanings. If instrumentalism is impoverishing and distorting as an account of our relations to other human beings, it is equally so as a guiding principle in our relations to nature and to place.[20]

But to show that the self can be essentially related to nature is by no means to show that it normally would be, especially in modern Western culture. What is culturally viewed as alien and inferior, as not worthy of respect or respectful knowledge, is not something to which such essential connection can easily be made. Here the three parts of the problem—the conception of the human, the conception of the self, and the conception of nature—connect again. And normally such essential relation would involve particularity, through connection to end friendship for *particular* places, forests, animals, to which one is particularly strongly related or attached and toward which one has specific and meaningful, not merely abstract, responsibilities of care.

One of the effects of viewing the problems as arising especially in the context of rationalism is to provide a rich set of connections with other critiques; it makes the connection between the critique of anthropocentrism and various other critiques that also engage critically with rationalism, such as feminism and critical theory, much more important—indeed essential—to the understanding of each. The problem of the Western account of the human/nature relation is seen in the context of the other related sets of dualisms; they are linked through their definitions as the underside of the various contrasts of reason. Since much of the strength and persistence of these dualisms derives from their connections and their ability to mirror, confirm, and support one another, critiques of anthropocentrism that fail to take account of these connections have missed an essential and not merely additional feature.

Anthropocentrism and androcentrism in particular are linked by the rationalist conception of the human self as masculine and by the account of authentically human characteristics as centered around rationality and the exclusion of its contrasts (especially characteristics regarded as feminine, animal, or natural) as less human. This provides a different and richer account of the notion of anthropocentrism, now conceived by deep ecology (Fox 1990, 5) in terms of the notion of equality, which is both excessively narrow and difficult to articulate in any precise or convincing way in a context where needs are so different. The perception of the connection as at best accidental is a feature of some recent critiques of ecofeminism, for example the discussion of Fox (1990) and Eckersley (1989) on the relation of feminism and environmental philosophy. Fox misses entirely the main thrust of the ecofeminist account of environmental philosophy and the critique of deep ecology which results or which is advanced in the ecofeminist literature, which is that it has failed to observe the way in which anthropocentrism and androcentrism are linked.[21] It is a consequence of my arguments here that this critique needs broadening—deep ecology has failed to observe (and often even goes out of its way to deny) connections with a number of other critiques, not just feminism, for example, but also socialism, especially in the forms that mount a critique of rationalism and of modernity. The failure to observe such connections is the result of an inadequate historical analysis and understanding of the way in which the inferiorization of both women and nature is grounded in rationalism, and the connections of both to the inferiorizing of the body, hierarchical concepts of labor, and disembedded and individualist accounts of the self.

Instead of addressing the real concerns of ecofeminism in terms of connection, Fox takes ecofeminism as aiming to replace concern with anthropocentrism by concern with androcentrism.[22] This would have the effect of making ecofeminism a reductionist position which takes women's oppression as the basic form and attempts to reduce all other forms to it. This position is a straw woman;[23] the effect of ecofeminism is not to absorb or sacrifice the critique of anthropocentrism, but to deepen and enrich it.

REFERENCES

Benhabib, Seyla. 1987. The generalised and the concrete other. In *Women and moral theory*, 154–77. E. Kittay and D. Meyers, eds. Totowa, N.J.: Rowman and Allenheld.

Benhabib, Seyla and Drucilla Cornell, eds. 1987. *Feminism as critique.* Minneapolis: University of Minnesota Press; Cambridge: Polity Press.

Benjamin, Jessica. 1985. The bonds of love: Rational violence and erotic domination. In *The Future of difference.* H. Eisenstein and A. Jardine, eds. New Brunswick: Rutgers University Press.

Berman, Marshall. 1982. *All that is solid melts into air: The experience of modernity.* New York: Simon & Schuster; London: Penguin.

Biehl, Janet. 1987. It's deep, but is it broad? An ecofeminist looks at deep ecology. *Kick It Over* special supplement (Winter).

Blum, Lawrence A. 1980. *Friendship, altruism and morality.* Boston and London: Routledge & Kegan Paul.

Callicott, J. Baird. 1985. Intrinsic value, quantum theory, and environmental ethics. *Environmental Ethics* 7: 261–62.
Cheney, Jim. 1987. Ecofeminism and deep ecology. *Environmental Ethics* 9: 115–145.
______. 1989. The neo-stoicism of radical environmentalism. *Environmental Ethics* 11: 293–325.
Chodorow, Nancy. 1979. *The reproduction of mothering*. Berkeley: University of California Press.
______. 1985. Gender, relation and difference in psychoanalytic perspective. In *The future of difference*, 3–19. H. Eisenstein and A. Jardine, eds. New Brunswick: Rutgers University Press.
Collard, Andrée. 1988. *Rape of the wild: Man's violence against animals and the earth.* Bloomington: Indiana University Press; London: The Woman's Press.
Cook, Francis. 1977. *Hua-Yen Buddhism: The jewel net of Indra*, 118–119. State College, PA: Pennsylvania State University Press.
Eckersley, Robyn. 1989. Divining evolution: The ecological ethics of Murray Bookchin. *Environmental Ethics* 11: 99–116.
Fox, Warwick. 1982. The intuition of deep ecology. Paper presented at Environment, Ethics and Ecology Conference, Canberra. Also published under the title Deep ecology: A new philosophy of our time? *The Ecologist* 14 (1984): 194–200.
______. 1986. Approaching deep ecology: A response to Richard Sylvan's critique of deep ecology. Environmental Studies Occasional Paper 20. Hobart: University of Tasmania Centre for Environmental Studies.
______. 1989. The deep ecology-ecofeminism debate and its parallels. *Environmental Ethics* 11: 5–25.
______. 1990. *Towards a transpersonal ecology: Developing new foundations for environmentalism.* Boston: Shambala.
Gearhart, Sally Miller. 1982. The Future—if there is one—is female. In *Reweaving the web of life*, 266–285. P. McAllister, ed. Philadelphia and Santa Cruz: New Society Publishers.
Gilligan, Carol. 1982. *In a different voice.* Cambridge: Harvard University Press.
______. 1987. Moral orientation and moral development. In *Women and moral theory*, 19–33. E. Kittay and D. Meyers, eds. Totowa, N. J.: Rowman and Allenheld.
Griffin, Susan. 1978. *Woman and nature: The roaring inside her.* New York: Harper and Row.
Grimshaw, Jean. 1986. *Philosophy and feminist thinking.* Minneapolis: University of Minnesota Press. Also published as *Feminist philosophers.* Brighton: Wheatsheaf.
Griscom, Joan L. 1981. On healing the nature/history split in feminist thought. *Heresies* 4(1): 4–9.
Jaggar, Alison. 1983. *Feminist politics and human nature.* Totowa, N.J.: Rowman & Allenheld; Brighton: Harvester.
Kheel, Marti. 1985. The liberation of nature: A circular affair. *Environmental Ethics* 7: 135–49.
King, Ynestra. 1981. Feminism and revolt. *Heresies* 4(1): 12–16.
______. 1989. The ecology of feminism and the feminism of ecology. In *Healing the wounds.* J. Plant, ed., Philadelphia and Santa Cruz: New Society Publishers.
Leopold, Aldo. 1949. *A sand county almanac*, 201–2. Oxford and New York: Oxford University Press.
Lloyd, Genevieve. 1983a. Public reason and private passion. *Metaphilosophy* 14: 308–26.
______. 1983b. Reason, gender and morality in the history of philosophy. *Social Research* 50(3): 490–513.
______. 1984. *The man of reason.* London: Methuen.
McLuhan, T. C., ed. 1973. *Touch the earth.* London: Abacus.
Midgley, Mary. 1983. *Animals and why they matter.* Athens: University of Georgia Press; London: Penguin.

Miller, Jean Baker. 1976, 1978. *Toward a new psychology of women.* Boston: Beacon Press; London: Penguin
Naess, Arne. 1973. The shallow and the deep, long-range ecology movement: A summary. *Inquiry* 16: 95–100.
______. 1986. Intrinsic value: Will the defenders of nature please rise. In *Conservation Biology.* M. Soule, ed. Sunderland, MA: Sinauer Associates.
______. 1988. *Ecology, community and lifestyle.* Cambridge: University Press.
Neidjie, Bill. 1985. *Kakadu man.* With S. Davis and A. Fox. Canberra: Mybrood P/L.
Neidjie, Bill and Keith Taylor, eds. 1989. *Story about feeling.* Wyndham: Magabala Books.
Nicholson, Linda J. 1983. Women, morality and history. *Social Research* 50(3): 514–36.
Plumwood, Val. 1975. Critical notice of Passmore's *Man's responsibility for nature. Australasian Journal of Philosophy* 53(2): 171–85.
______. 1980. Social theories, self-management and environmental problems. In *Environmental Philosophy,* 217–332. D. Mannison, M. McRobbie, and R. Routley eds. Canberra: ANU Department of Philosophy Monograph Series RSSS.
______. 1986. Ecofeminism: An overview and discussion of positions and arguments. In *Women and philosophy: A radical philosophy reader.* S. Sayers, ed. London: Routledge.
______. 1989. Do we need a sex/gender distinction? *Radical Philosophy* 51: 2–11.
______. 1990. Plato and the bush. *Meanjin* 49(3): 524–36.
______. 1991. Ethics and instrumentalism: A response to Janna Thompson. *Environmental Ethics.* Forthcoming.
Poole, Ross. 1984. Reason, self-interest and "commercial society": The social content of Kantian morality. *Critical Philosophy* 1: 24–46.
______. 1985. Morality, masculinity and the market. *Radical Philosophy* 39: 16–23.
______. 1990. Modernity, rationality and the "masculine." In *Femininity/Masculinity and representation.* T. Threadgold and A. Cranny-Francis, eds. Sydney: George Allen and Unwin, 1990.
Regan, Tom. 1986. *The case for animal rights.* Berkeley: University of California Press.
Relph, Edward. 1976. *Place and placelessness.* London: Pion.
______. 1981. *Rational landscapes and humanistic geography.* London: Croom Helm.
Rodman, John. 1980. Paradigm change in political science. *American Behavioural Scientist* 24(1): 54–55.
Ruether, Rosemary Radford. 1975. *New woman new earth.* Minneapolis: Seabury Press.
Salleh, Ariel. 1984. Deeper than deep ecology. *Environmental Ethics* 6: 339–45.
Seed, John. 1989. Interviewed by Pat Stone. *Mother Earth News* (May/June).
Seed, John, Joanna Macy, Pat Fleming, and Arne Naess. 1988. *Thinking like a mountain: Towards a council of all beings.* Philadelphia and Santa Cruz: New Society Publishers.
Sylvan, Richard. 1985. A critique of deep ecology. *Radical Philosophy* 40 and 41.
Taylor, Paul. 1986. *Respect for nature.* Princeton: Princeton University Press.
Thomas Aquinas. 1976. *Summa contra Gentiles.* Bk. 3, Pt. 2, chap. 62. Quoted in *Animal rights and human obligations,* 56. T. Regan and P. Singer, eds. Englewood Cliffs, N. J.: Prentice Hall.
Thompson Janna. 1990. A refutation of environmental ethics. *Environmental Ethics* 12(2): 147–60.
Warren, Karen J. 1987. Feminism and ecology: Making connections. *Environmental Ethics* 9: 17–18.
______. 1990. The power and promise of ecological feminism. *Environmental Ethics* 12(2):121–46.
Zimmerman, Michael E. 1987. Feminism, deep ecology, and environmental ethics. *Environmental Ethics* 9.

NOTES

1. Regan, of course, as part of the animal rights movement, is mainly concerned not with wild animals but with domestic animals as they appear in the context and support of human society and culture, although he does not indicate any qualification in moral treatment. Nevertheless, there may be an important moral boundary here, for natural ecosystems cannot be organized along the lines of justice, fairness and rights, and it would be absurd to try to impose such a social order upon them via intervention in these systems. This does not mean, of course, that humans can do anything in such a situation, just that certain kinds of intervention are not in order. But these kinds of intervention may be in order in the case of human social systems and in the case of animals that have already been brought into these social systems through human intervention, and the concept of rights and of social responsibility may have far more application here. This would mean that the domestic/wild distinction would demarcate an important moral boundary in terms of duties of intervention, although neither Regan (1986) nor Taylor (1986) comes to grips with this problem. In the case of Taylor's "wild living things" rights seem less important than respect for independence and autonomy, and the prima facie obligation may be nonintervention.
2. If the Kantian universalizing perspective is based on self-containment, its major contemporary alternative, that of John Rawls, is based on a "definitional identity" in which the "other" can be considered to the extent that it is not recognized as truly different, as genuinely other (Benhabib 1987, 165).
3. Contra Cheney, who appears to advocate the abandonment of all general ethical concepts and the adoption of a "contextual" ethics based in pure particularity and emotionality. We do need both to reintegrate the personal and particular and reevaluate more positively its role, but overcoming moral dualism will not simply amount to an affirmation of the personal in the moral sphere. To embrace pure particularity and emotionality is implicitly to accept the dualistic construction of these as oppositional to a rationalist ethics and to attempt to reverse value. In general this reactive response is an inadequate way to deal with such dualisms. And rules themselves, as Grimshaw (1986, 209) points out, are not incompatible with recognition of special relationships and responsibility to particular others. Rules themselves are not the problem, and hence it is not necessary to move to a ruleless ethics; rather it is rules that demand the discarding of the personal, the emotional, and the particular and which aim at self-containment.
4. For example, Bill Neidjie's words "This ground and this earth/like brother and mother" (Neidjie 1985, 46) may be interpreted as an affirmation of such kinship or continuity. (See also Neidjie 1985, 53, 61, 62, 77, 81, 82, 88).
5. The logic of dualism and the masculinity of the concept of humanity are discussed in Plumwood (1986, 1989) and Warren (1987, 1990).
6. Nonetheless, deep ecology's approach to ethics is, like much else, doubtfully consistent, variable and shifting. Thus although Arne Naess (1973, 1986, 1988) calls for recognition of the intrinsic value of nature, he also tends to treat "the maxim of self-realization" as *substituting for* and obviating an ethical account of care and respect for nature (Naess 1988, 20, 86), placing the entire emphasis on phenomenology. In more recent work, however, the emphasis seems to have quietly shifted back again from holistic intuition to a broad and extremely vague "biocentric egalitarianism" which places the center once again in ethics and enjoins an ethic of maximum expansion of Self (Fox 1990).
7. Other critics of deep ecology, such as Sylvan (1985) and Cheney (1987) have also suggested that it shifts between different and incompatible versions. Ecofeminist critics of deep ecology have included Salleh (1984), Kheel (1985), Biehl (1987), and Warren (1990).

8. Arne Naess, quoted in Fox (1982, 3, 10).
9. This is argued in Plumwood (1980), where a relational account of self developed in the context of an anarchist theory is applied to relations with nature. Part of the problem lies in the terminology of "holism" itself, which is used in highly variable and ambiguous ways, sometimes carrying commitment to indistinguishability and sometimes meaning only "nonatomistic."
10. Arne Naess, quoted in Fox (1986, 54).
11. As noted by Cheney (1989, 293–325).
12. Thus John Seed says: "Naess wrote that when most people think about conservation, they think about sacrifice. This is a treacherous basis for conservation, because most people aren't capable of working for anything except their own self-interest . . . Naess argued that we need to find ways to extend our identity into nature. Once that happens, being out in front of bulldozers or whatever becomes no more of a sacrifice than moving your foot if you notice that someone's just about to strike it with an axe" (Seed 1989).
13. This denial of the alterity of the other is also the route taken by J. Baird Callicott, who indeed asserts that "The principle of axiological complementarity posits an essential unity between self and world and establishes the problematic intrinsic value of nature in relation to the axiologically privileged value of self" (1985, 275). Given the impoverishment of Humean theory in the area of relations (and hence its inability to conceive a self-in-relationship whose connections to others are not merely contingent but essential), Callicott has little alternative to this direction of development.
14. Grimshaw (1986, 182). See also the excellent discussion in Warren (1990, 136–38) of the importance of recognition and respect for the other's difference; Blum (1980, 75); and Benhabib (1987, 166).
15. This traditional model of land relationship is closely linked to that of bioregionalism, whose strategy is to engage people in greater knowledge and care for the local areas that have meaning for them and where they can most easily evolve a caring and responsible life-style. The feat of "impartial identification with all particulars" is, beyond the seeking of individual enlightenment, strategically empty. Because it cares "impartially" for everything it can, in practice, care for nothing.
16. Thus some ecofeminists, such as Cheney (1987, 1989) and Warren (1990), have been led to the development of alternative accounts of ethics and ethical theory building and the development of distinctively ecofeminist ethics.
17. Although the emphasis of early work in this area (for example, Plumwood 1975) was mainly directed toward showing that a respectful, noninstrumental view of nature was logically viable since that was widely disputed, it is certainly well past time to move beyond that. Although there is now wider support for a respectful, noninstrumental position, it remains controversial; see, for example, Thompson (1990) and Plumwood (1991).
18. Poole (1984) has also shown how this kind of self is presupposed in the Kantian moral picture, where desire or inclination is essentially self-directed and is held in check by reason (acting in the interests of universality).
19. In the sense of altruism in which one's own interests are neglected in favor of another's, essentially relational interests are neither egoistic nor altruistic.
20. On rationalism and place see Edward Relph (1976, 1981).
21. Fox (1990, 12), in claiming gender neutrality for cosmologically based identification and treating issues of gender as irrelevant to the issue, ignores the historical scholarship linking conceptions of gender and conceptions of morality via the division between public and private spheres (for example, Lloyd [1984] and Nicholson [1983]). To the extent that the ecofeminist thesis is not an essentialist one linking *sex* to emotionality and particularity or to nature but one linking social and historical conceptions of *gender* to conceptions of morality and rationality, it is not

refuted by examples of women who buy a universalizing view or who drive bulldozers, or by Mrs. Thatcher. Fox's argument here involves a sex/gender confusion. On the sex/gender distinction see Plumwood (1989, 2–11).

22. Thus Fox (1990) throughout his discussion, like Zimmerman (1987, 37), takes "the ecofeminist charge against deep ecology" to be that "androcentrism is 'the real root' of ecological destruction" (1990, 14), so that "there is no need to worry about any form of human domination other than androcentrism" (1990, 18). Warren (1990, 144) tellingly discusses Fox's claim that "feminist" is redundant as an addition to a deep ecological ethic.
23. This reductionist position has a few representatives in the literature (perhaps Andrée Collard [1988], and Sally Miller Gearhart [1982]), but cannot be taken as representative of the main body of ecofeminist work. Fox, I believe, is right to resist such a reduction and to insist on the nonliminability of the form of oppression the critique of anthropocentrism is concerned with, but the conclusion that the critiques are unrelated does not follow. Critiques and the different kinds of oppression they correspond to can be distinguishable but, like individuals themselves, still related in essential and not merely accidental ways. The choice between merger (reductive elimination) and disconnection (isolation) of critiques is the same false dichotomy that inspires the false contrasts of holism and atomism, and of self as merged, lacking boundaries, versus self as isolated atom, lacking essential connection to others.

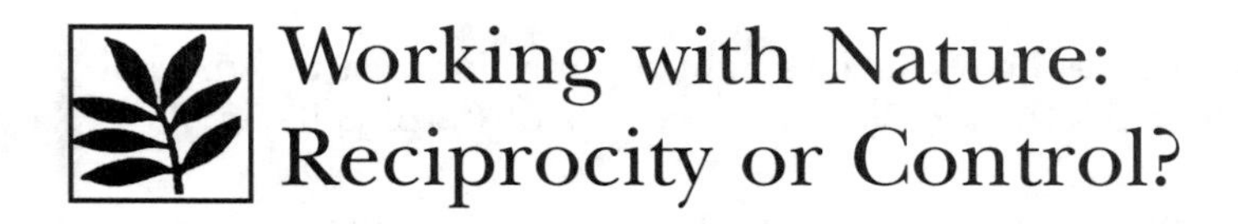

Working with Nature: Reciprocity or Control?

Ariel Salleh

Ariel Salleh is an Australian ecofeminist writer and activist currently affiliated with the University of Western Sydney. She recently published her book, Ecofeminism as Politics: Nature, Marx and the Postmodern.

INTRODUCTION

During the 1980s, international agencies acknowledged close connections between women and the natural world. Now the International YWCA's Geneva-based Y's EYES campaigns not only for health and human rights, but also for issues of energy use, water supply, and appropriate technology. The Environment Liaison Centre in Nairobi, an independent non-governmental organization (NGO), runs sessions for women on forestry, sustainable farming, and pollution control, and urges political recognition of women's traditional farming expertise. The Rome/Santiago International Information and Communication Services (ISIS) facilitates women's education in similar areas. The International Women's Tribune Center in New York provides leadership skills and resource material on conservation and development to a vast female network. In Santo Domingo, the United Nation's International Research and Training Institute for the Advancement of Women (INSTRAW), works on water management programmes. In Bangalore, an innovative group called Development Alternatives with Women for a New Era (DAWN), is critical of the imported 'growth' ethic and the oppressive gender division this ethic reinforces. World WIDE—Women in Defense of Environment—Washington D.C., is also trying to pre-empt superficial 'development' schemes and 'give voice to the voiceless' in policy.[1]

This essay originally appeared in *Ethics of Environment and Development,* ed. J. Ronald Engel and Joan Gibb Engel (Tucson: University of Arizona Press, 1990). Reprinted with permission.

This recognition of women's involvement in, and concern for, the environment is both essential and rare. For, in the words of Carol Gilligan:

> Though we have listened for centuries to the voices of men and the theories of development that their experience informs, we have come more recently to notice not only the silence of women, but the difficulty of hearing what they say when they speak; yet in the different voice of women lies the truth of an ethic of care, the tie between relationship and responsibility, and the origins of aggression in the failure to connect.[2]

Women could bring to discussions of environmental sustainability 'the truth of an ethic of care'. Yet, their 'different voice' is seldom heard. Ecofeminists are attempting to change that. As a grass-roots political movement which honors the different voices of women across culture and class, ecofeminism points to ways in which women's work, itself, models an alternative environmental ethic and practice.

PATRIARCHAL ECONOMICS

At the celebrated 1985 Nairobi Forum on 'Equality, Development, and Peace', the social and environmental impact of cash-cropping and industrialization were discussed thoroughly, after which the conference resolved to counter harmful development by getting more women into pressure groups, management, and education. The media was asked to promote more constructive images of women, and governments were encouraged to research and modify policies which inhibit women's full participation in community life. These resolutions were adopted by delegates from 157 countries, and later, by the fortieth session of the United Nations General Assembly. The resolutions are to be monitored by the appropriate UN agencies up to the year 2000.[3] Still, the problem remains: just as 'most women's work is invisible, so are our Herculean efforts against [that invisibility], North and South, East and West'.[4]

Some impressive grassroots projects—the Chipko movement among Indian peasants to preserve forests and limestone deposits from the 'formal' economy; the Greenbelt Movement of Kenya women, led by Wangari Maathai, which won an Alternative Nobel Prize; and model farming by the Ação Feminea Democrática Gaucha in the Amazon—are internationally acclaimed. In official accounts of development, however, women's activities are often passed over. While the UN Economic Commission on Africa found that women and their children produce 70 percent of the continent's food, are responsible for the transport of that food, and work a 14–16-hour day, the UN Food and Agriculture Organization (FAO) describes only 5 per cent of them as employed. Similarly, national statistics on agricultural production in Peru indicate a female contribution of 2.6 per cent, while local estimates put it at 86 per cent. In Egypt, the same cultural phenomenon occurs: official figures show a 3.6 per cent agricultural contribution by women, whereas local opinion has it at 35–50 per cent. Tourist postcards and agency propaganda shots also tend to portray 'rural workers' as male. Further, while 'women grow half the world's food . . . most agricultural advisors are men—who tend to give advice to men'.[5] And what kind of advice is that? Famine conditions in Ethiopia have resulted from land being taken out of women's hands by those who would render it profitable in terms defined by an abstract and unpredictable global economy.

Sithembiso Nyoni, coordinator of women's rural progress associations in Zimbabwe, believes that consultants and ministers are too concerned about international hobnobbing to remember that 'we are the basis of their power'. Hence, in the South, the debt crisis gets worse as 'aid programmes' open the way for multinational corporations and an increasing concentration of assets among the wealthy. Meanwhile, the female half of the world's population owns less than 1 per cent of world property. Major breadwinners in the Third World, women receive less than 1 per cent of UN aid. Under the present 'relations of production', their access to land is contingent upon marriage, and other forms of credit are invariably blocked by bureaucratic attitudes. A survey of professional staff in environmental agencies and NGOs by Dutch IUCN administrator Irene Dankelman affirms that women are noticeably few at an advisory level.[6] Neither the famous Indian report on the status of women nor India's sixth Five-Year Plan acknowledges problems with water, fuel, and feed. Yet, the daily experience of Third World women gives them an acute knowledge of indigenous species, water holes, drought-resistant seeds, storage methods, and fuel materials.

Beyond this, Hilkka Pietilä, a Finnish ecofeminist, suggests that if women's voices were listened to 'the authentic female approach and value system concerning development [would be] an untapped and fresh resource'.[7] The IUCN has now set up a working party on Women, Environment, and Sustainable Development to assess the World Conservation Strategy (WCS). The committee is to draft a supplement considering how the WCS might be 'adapted' to 'incorporate women's issues'. We might well ask, why a 'supplement'? Why is women's central productive role again being marginalized in this way, even by those with the best of intentions?

Why is it that women's work is not counted—that women are not counted—that women 'don't count'? In her booklet, *The Global Kitchen*, Selma James writes that not only are few women paid for the work they do, but even salaried women receive only two-thirds of what men are paid for the same work. More significantly, most women's labour is left out of that basic government statistic, the gross national product (GNP).[8] A housewife and mother in the 'developed' world completes at least 70 unsalaried hours a week; that is, twice the standard Australian working week of 35 hours. She both *reproduces* the earning labour force, and *produces* use value through cooking, laundry, mending or buying clothes, cleaning, maintenance, and gardening. Then there are the emotional/moral obligations of her open-ended role—helping children, the aged, and sick; sexual relief for the man in her life; and possibly the labour of childbearing consequent to this. Many middle-class women take on a heavy round of voluntary commitments like the Parent-Teacher Association, amnesty work, or resident action. Migrant women use extra energy to absorb the strains put on their families by having continually to rebuild their communities. On top of this, as we have seen, non-metropolitan women in a Two-Thirds world grow the bulk of community food, usually unsupported by men, who are attracted into the urban cash economy. Similarly, in 'advanced' industrialized societies, one family in three is surviving with no male help. North and South, women have more in common than many might think. The general rule is: maximum responsibilities, minimum rights.

The Arusha 1984 United Nations conference on the Advancement of Women in Africa concluded that concrete steps should be taken to quantify the unremunerated contribution of women; to ascertain its exchange value.[9] As Selma James points out, by the logic of the present economy, "the woman who cleans a house is not 'working' but the military man who bombs it, is. However, the work of the same woman, if hired by her husband . . . would pop into the GNP."[10] Interestingly, the compensation of childcare and domestic labour is perceived as a 'gift' from the state, charity, or welfare, but never as 'economic' exchange. James argues that we should allocate domestic hours worked to standard job categories, apply the going wage, then total. Using such a method in the early 1970s, John Kenneth Galbraith estimated that household labour was probably worth 25 per cent of the US GNP. Carnegie, Ford, and Rockefeller Foundation reports in 1985 claimed that housework constituted 33 per cent of the US GNP. No wonder women campaign so vigorously against military involvement; they are defending what they have produced by their labour. Given the predatory structure of the patriarchal economic system, it is not surprising that Norwegian social psychologist, Berit As, should discover that economic growth means more unpaid work being put on women's shoulders.[11] Many examples can be given. The import of tractors to Sri Lanka forces women to pick cotton twice as fast in order to keep wages at the same level. The growing engagement of European women outside the home only locks them into a double shift, for Swedish Central Bureau of Statistics figures show that 70 per cent of men never clean house or cook. According to the sociologist, Ruth Schwartz Cowan, housework in 'advanced' societies takes longer despite new 'labour-saving' gadgets.[12] Home economics and the professionalization of motherhood among educated women has created exacting standards in the quality of care they feel they should give their families. Technology and education may actually reinforce the gender division of labour which restricts women's access to 'economic' work.

The injustice of the global economy also affects women in other ways. Mothers across Europe are picking up the community health costs of nuclear radiation following Chernobyl. In the Third World, female illiteracy rises while a Western middle-class, facing recession, chooses private schooling for its sons. Now the US fast food habit brings deforestation and dispossession to Central American families, where a World Bank-funded enclosure movement subsidizes big cattle ranchers in the hamburger snack business.

Just as the environment is damaged by the growth ethic, so are women's lives. Rural women following men into the cities find themselves in makeshift ghettos, without water, garbage removal, health care, or schools. Lin Nelson, a US occupational health researcher, has documented how those who gain employment in chemical or electronics plants are exposed to toxic contaminants affecting the skin, lungs, and nervous system. Foetal damage, miscarriage, and infant death are frequent among workers in these industries.[13] Elsewhere, women fall victim to dangerous contraceptives. Australian clerical staff suffer an epidemic of neuromuscular repetition strain injury caused by long hours at wordprocessing machines. Female microchip assemblers, employed for their 'dexterity and obedience' in the sweatshops of a rapidly industrializing South Korea, are left blind after two years of intensive production. Finally, in developing countries, an internationally organized tourist trade in sex quietly helps fulfil an urgent need for foreign exchange, while more debt accumulates with the purchase of masculine status symbols, like weapons and oil.

Economic imperialism, not socialism or feminism, is the force most likely to destroy the family. Cecelia Kirkman, who counsels in a battered women's refuge in New York City, describes the neglect of women and children at the apex of the developed world. A marked shift in the tax burden meant that by 1983, the US corporate tax contribution dropped to only 6 per cent of government revenue. Major defence contractors—Boeing, General Dynamics, General Electric, Grumman, and Lockheed—paid no tax at all for a few years in the early 1980s. Yet, in that time, the welfare dollar was severely trimmed. Cuts to social service agencies, schools, hospitals, and day-care centres also badly affected women who work in these major areas of female paid employment. But structural violence is not only economic. To spend the tax dollar on the military is to consent to a dehumanizing brutality. Kirkman has collected statistics which link men's training for war with domestic violence and child abuse.[14] The International Women's Tribune Center is also examining the ties between militarism, male sexuality, and violence toward individual women.[15] The decimation of family life and concurrent feminization of poverty in the military superstate is exposed in Barbara Ehrenreich's *The Hearts of Men.* Ehrenreich reports that in the USA, 'in the mid-sixties and until the mid-seventies, the number of poor adult males actually declined, while the number of poor women heading households swelled by 100,000 a year'.[16] Money that might have sustained women breadwinners went into arms, foreign investments, six-digit executive salaries, glossy playboy lifestyles, and a paper whirlwind of speculation. For the fact is that men, whether in governments, unions, business, or international agencies, hold almost all authority positions. They make choices and set priorities which are comfortable to them. North and South, East and West, the flexible, do-it-yourself, cooperative economy of women is daily subsumed by private and public spheres alike; just as the degraded 'resource base' of nature silently absorbs the longer-term costs of what is called 'development'.[17]

ECOFEMINIST ECONOMICS

Ecofeminist theologians Rosemary Ruether and Elizabeth Dodson-Gray see the patriarchal belief system which justifies all these things as a hierarchy, a 'Great Chain of Being' with God or Allah at the top; next Man, the steward of nature; then women, children, animals, and finally plants and rocks at the base.[18] A deep divide separates the categories of 'Man' and 'Women', and it is this same line which maintains the polarization of 'reality' into the 'truly human' and the 'simply natural'.[19] Traditionally, women, children, animals, and plants have been accorded no rights and have existed solely for the enhancement of God and Man. New modes of industrial production simply extend the underlying logic, as both 'nature' and those who labour with nature are treated as 'resources' without intrinsic value. Modern science, with its devastating tools and techniques, has now absorbed this theology and largely usurped its political function of rationalizing masculine domination.

Why have men chosen to alienate themselves from the rest of life in this way? A growing number of social theorists believe it may have begun with a painful sense of exclusion from the life process, and the realization by men

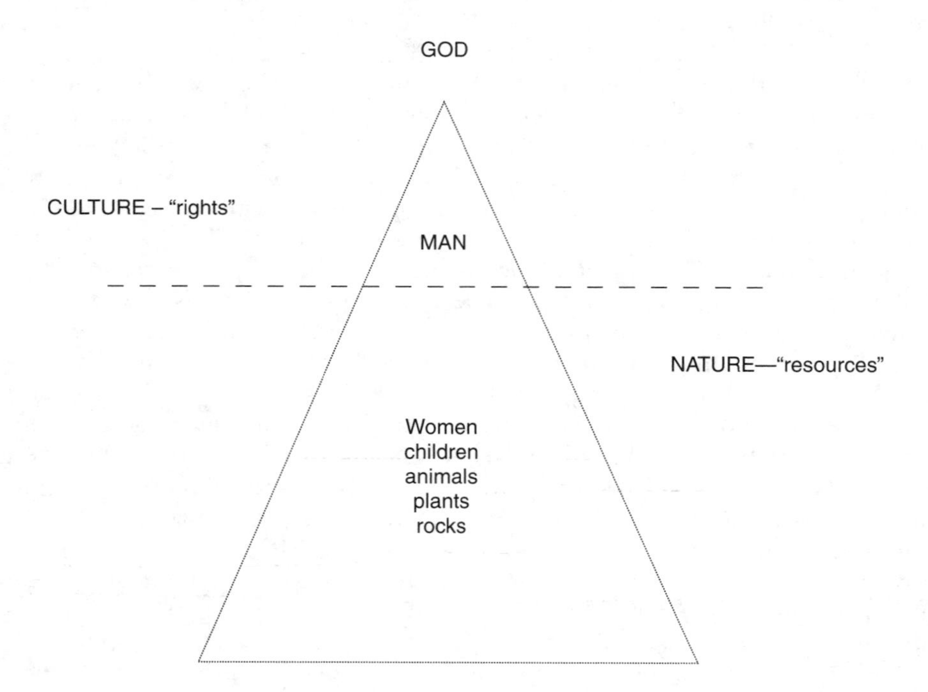

*A modified version of this pyramid by Elizabeth Dodson-Gray was originally published in *Green Paradise Lost,* Rountable Press, Wellesley, MA, 1981, p. 4.

that, while they may 'appropriate' life, they cannot 'produce' it. This hypothesis seems to be substantiated by the work of ecofeminist Maria Mies, who finds the same ancient psychology reappearing in Western economic theory. She notes that the concept of 'labour' is usually reserved for men's work, work that is done with the hands or head. Hands and head are considered 'human' parts of the body, while the womb and breasts are described as 'natural' or 'animal'.[20] Certainly, men's bodily production is not identical with women's. Women may produce in two ways: they may labour with the uterus and/or they may labour with the organs of the head and hands as men do. However, the arbitrary naturalization of women's activities is currently used to foster their exclusion from the paid workforce.

Turning this argument right around to address a future sustainable economy, it is worth noting that not only is there a quantitative difference between men and women's productive contribution, but also a profoundly important qualitative difference. Qualitatively, women's mediation of nature in all its labour forms, is organized around a logic of reciprocity rather than mastery and control. As Mies puts it, women 'are not owners of their own bodies or of the earth, but they cooperate with their bodies and with the earth in order to let grow and to make grow'.[21] This logic of reciprocity is the basis of humankind's first productive economy—invented by women—an informal subsistence economy which is still the mainstay of life for the majority of people on Earth today, despite the superimposition of supposedly more 'efficient' mass-scale modes of production with development.

Under patriarchy then, the things that men do, called 'production' are valued; while the things that women do, especially (re)production, social as well as biological, are not valued. An extract from the Kenya *Standard* illustrates this well:

> As more and more land will be required for food production in order to meet the demand from the population . . . cash crop expansion may stagnate. Given the costs involved in adopting more modern farming *techniques to raise productivity* . . . population growth, if allowed to continue, can only result in more encroachment on vital forest reserves.[22]

The line of reasoning pursued here deflects responsibility away from patriarchal economics and puts the onus for environmental depletion squarely on women. As men see it, women must stop making new life since this is detrimental to economic growth. Investigations by the *New Internationalist* suggest the converse.[23] The reason for Africa's falling food production is not scarcity of land *per se*, nor lack of technology, but the seduction of local men by the formal economy which takes both land and men's labour away from family farming.

The problem of overpopulation is real and needs to be seriously examined. However, given the ethical issues of eugenics/genocide and of a woman's rights over her own body, the targeting of Third World population control by environmentalists has both racist and sexist dimensions. Even as a matter of simple equity, where children provide supplementary farm labour for overworked mothers, it is inappropriate for male elites and their international policy advisors to demand population control. Such programmes originated in a post-World War II middle-class urban desire to protect 'the quality of life'—for which read 'levels of consumerism'. Now the argument for population 'control' is formulated more prudently in terms of protecting Earth's scarce resources. But this injunction as applied to the South exclusively is patently hypocritical. Each infant born into the so-called advanced societies will use about fifteen times more global resources during his or her lifetime than a person born in the Third World.[24] Population restraint may well be called for in the North, hopefully complemented by a scaling back of high-technology excess. On the other hand, subsistence dwellers are producers as much as consumers: As 'prosumers' they are practical examples of human autonomy in a non-exploitative relation to land. To borrow the impoverished language of the dominant materialistic ethos here: in certain circumstances a child born in the South could be seen as an 'asset' rather than a 'liability'. What much of the talk about population 'control' may express is a projection and displacement of the guilt experienced by those who continue to live comfortably off the invisible backs of working women in the Two Thirds World.

Deeper than this, does the constant focus on population control in development debates even reflect a fear of nature or of female power? Fear of that different voice? If not, then why the irrational pursuit by male elites of status in a global economic pecking order and expertise in frankly destructive technologies? Consider this piece from the Kenya *Sunday Nation*:

> Only sound social, economic and political policies that favour or promote indigenous scientific and technological potential will help the continent meet its *basic human needs* . . . the minimum target of 1000 scientists and engineers per million inhabitants.[25]

The iniquitous financial transfer from South to North which imported development involves, the predatory consumption of food and energy resources by an industrialized North, lessons from the green revolution—are all glossed over, although they are surely very good arguments for disengagement from the multinational arena and for concentrating on the wealth in one's own back yard. What is overlooked again and again is that the self-reliant, life-affirming, bioregional labours of women, 'the informal or free economy, the world of nurturance and close human relations, is the sphere where basic human needs are anchored and where models for humane alternatives can be found'.[26]

As things stand, women, half the world's population, put in 65 per cent of the world's work, and get back only 10 per cent of all income paid.[27] The rationale for this institutionalized theft, and that of the exploitation of nature, has been uncovered by ecofeminist analyses of patriarchy. But unless the reality of this cultural process is accepted by environmentalists, their handling of the global predicament will fail to make any sense. *Our Common Future*, the

1987 report by the World Commission on Environment and Development, a collection of environmentalists, economists, politicians, scientists, and engineers, is a classic case in point.[28] The wisdom of 'live simply that others may simply live' is lost. Ultimately, its recommendations collapse back into a 'more growth and trickle-down someday' solution to world poverty. Given the metaphysical premises on which economics is currently organized, the costs of growth will again be passed down to women producers and on to nature. Getting more women in advisory positions is only half of the story. The unconscious patriarchal connection between woman and nature needs to be made conscious, and the hierarchical fallacies of the 'Great Chain of Being' acknowledged, before there can be any real growth towards a sane, humane, ecological future. Once this step is made, the way that women work in reciprocity with nature will become visible as a model to learn from. The result would be a fundamental change in the relations of production, a change summarized by ecofeminist Ynestra King, when she says: 'men must stop trying to control nature and join women in identifying with nature'.[29] The personal is indeed political; and struggles for equality and sustainability are closely interlinked.

NOTES

1. *Women and the Environmental Crisis: A Report of Workshop Proceedings at the Nairobi Forum 85: Women in Development* (Philadelphia: New Society Publishers, 1984).
2. Carol Gilligan, *In a Different Voice* (Cambridge, Mass.: Harvard University Press, 1984), 173–74.
3. *Report of the World Conference to Review and Appraise the Achievements of the United Nations Decade for Women—Equality, Development, and Peace, Nairobi, 15–16 July 1985* (New York: United Nations, 1986).
4. Selma James, *The Global Kitchen* (London: Housewives in Dialogue Archive, 1985), 25; Marilyn Waring, *Counting for Nothing* (Sydney: Allen & Unwin, 1989).
5. FAO statistics and quotation from *Women and the Environmental Crisis*, 45.
6. Irene Dankelman and Joan Davidson, eds., *Women and Environment in the Third World* (London: Earthscan, 1988), Ch. 7.
7. Hilkka Pietilä, 'Women as an Alternative Culture Here and Now', *Development* 4 (1984), 60.
8. James, *The Global Kitchen*, 1.
9. *Forward Looking Strategies for the Advancement of Women in Africa Beyond the End of the United Nations Decade for Women*, Expert Group Meeting, Arusha, United Republic of Tanzania, 4–6 October, 1984 (New York: United Nations Economic and Social Council, 1984).
10. Ibid., 10–11.
11. Berit As, 'A Five Dimensional Model for Change', *Women's Studies International Quarterly* 4 (1981): 111.
12. Ruth Schwartz Cowan, *More Work for Mother* (New York: Basic Books, 1983).
13. Lin Nelson, 'Feminists Turn to Workplace, Environmental Health', *Women and Global Corporations* 7, 1 and 2 (1986).
14. Cecelia Kirkman, 'The War at Home', *The Non-Violent Activist* 3 (1986): 7.
15. International Women's Tribune Center Team and Anne Walker, 'Peace Is No Violence Against Women', *The Tribune, A Women and Development Quarterly* (3rd Quarter, 1985): 32.

16. Barbara Ehrenreich, *The Hearts of Men* (New York: Anchor, 1983), 172.
17. Hazel Henderson, 'Indicators of No Real Meaning', in Paul Elkins, ed., *The Living Economy: A New Economics in the Making* (London: Routledge and Kegan Paul, 1986), 33.
18. Rosemary Ruether, *New Woman New Earth* (New York: Dove, 1975); Elizabeth Dodson-Gray, *Green Paradise Lost* (Wellesley, Mass: Roundtable Press, 1979).
19. For more detailed discussion of this hierarchy, see the essay by Hilkka Pietilä in Engel, *op. cit.*
20. Maria Mies, *Patriarchy and Accumulation on a World Scale* (London: Zed Books, 1986).
21. Ibid., 52.
22. 'How Food Production Is Hit by Population', *The Standard* (2 October 1987): 14.
23. Debbie Taylor, ed., 'Myth Conceptions', *New Internationalist* (October 1987): 8–9.
24. F.E. Trainer, *Abandon Affluence* (London: Zed Books, 1985), 1.
25. Otula Owuor, 'Sound Science Policies Called For', *Sunday Nation* (4 October, 1987): 17 (emphasis added).
26. Hilka Pietilä, *Tomorrow Begins Today* (ICDA/ISIS Workshop, Nairobi Forum, 1985), 26.
27. United Nations International Labour Organization (ILO).
28. World Commission on Environment and Development, *Our Common Future* (Oxford: Oxford University Press, 1987).
29. Ynestra King, Address to the international conference on 'Eco-feminist Perspectives—Culture, Nature, Theory', at the University of Southern California, Los Angeles, 1987.

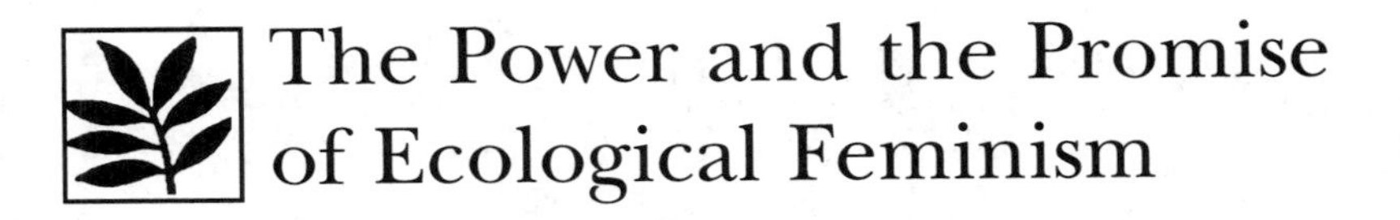

The Power and the Promise of Ecological Feminism

Karen J. Warren

Karen J. Warren is a feminist philosopher who has published essays on ecofeminism and edited special issues on ecofeminism for Hypatia: A Journal of Feminist Philosophy *and the* American Philosophical Association Newsletter on Feminism and Philosophy. *She has edited two anthologies on ecological feminism; coedited one anthology on feminism, violence, and nature; and written a book entitled* Quilting Ecofeminist Philosophy. *Warren has given public presentations on ecofeminism throughout the United States, as well as in Australia, Brazil, Canada, Finland, Norway, and Russia. She also conducts workshops on environmental ethics and critical thinking for elementary and secondary school teachers and students.*

INTRODUCTION

Ecological feminism (ecofeminism) has begun to receive a fair amount of attention lately as an alternative feminism and environmental ethic.[1] Since Françoise d'Eaubonne introduced the term *ecoféminisme* in 1974 to bring attention to women's potential for bringing about an ecological revolution,[2] the term has been used in a variety of ways. As I use the term in this paper, ecological feminism is the position that there are important connections—historical, experiential, symbolic, theoretical—between the domination of women and the domination of nature, an understanding of which is crucial to both feminism and environmental ethics. I argue that the promise and power of ecological feminism is that *it provides a distinctive framework both for reconceiving feminism and for developing an environmental ethic which takes seriously connections between the domination of women and the domination of nature.* I do so by discussing the nature of a feminist ethic and the ways in which ecofeminism provides a feminist and environmental ethic. I conclude that any feminist theory *and* any environmental ethic which fails to take seriously the twin and interconnected dominations of women and nature is at best incomplete and at worst simply inadequate.

This essay originally appeared in *Environmental Ethics* 12, 3 (Summer 1990): 125–46. Reprinted with permission.

FEMINISM, ECOLOGICAL FEMINISM, AND CONCEPTUAL FRAMEWORKS

Whatever else it is, feminism is at least the movement to end sexist oppression. It involves the elimination of any and all factors that contribute to the continued and systematic domination or subordination of women. While feminists disagree about the nature of and solutions to the subordination of women, all feminists agree that sexist oppression exists, is wrong, and must be abolished.

A "feminist issue" is any issue that contributes in some way to understanding the oppression of women. Equal rights, comparable pay for comparable work, and food production are feminist issues wherever and whenever an understanding of them contributes to an understanding of the continued exploitation or subjugation of women. Carrying water and searching for firewood are feminist issues wherever and whenever women's primary responsibility for these tasks contributes to their lack of full participation in decision making, income producing, or high status positions engaged in by men. What counts as a feminist issue, then, depends largely on context, particularly the historical and material conditions of women's lives.

Environmental degradation and exploitation are feminist issues because an understanding of them contributes to an understanding of the oppression of women. In India, for example, both deforestation and reforestation through the introduction of a monoculture species tree (e.g., eucalyptus) intended for commercial production are feminist issues because the loss of indigenous forests and multiple species of trees has drastically affected rural Indian women's ability to maintain a subsistence household. Indigenous forests provide a variety of trees for food, fuel, fodder, household utensils, dyes, medicines, and income-generating uses, while monoculture-species forests do not.[3] Although I do not argue for this claim here, a look at the global impact of environmental degradation on women's lives suggests important respects in which environmental degradation is a feminist issue.

Feminist philosophers claim that some of the most important feminist issues are *conceptual* ones: these issues concern how one conceptualizes such mainstay philosophical notions as reason and rationality, ethics, and what it is to be human. Ecofeminists extend this feminist philosophical concern to nature. They argue that, ultimately, some of the most important connections between the domination of women and the domination of nature are conceptual. To see this, consider the nature of conceptual frameworks.

A *conceptual framework* is a set of *basic* beliefs, values, attitudes, and assumptions which shape and reflect how one views oneself and one's world. It is a socially constructed lens through which we perceive ourselves and others. It is affected by such factors as gender, race, class, age, affectional orientation, nationality, and religious background.

Some conceptual frameworks are oppressive. An *oppressive conceptual framework* is one that explains, justifies, and maintains relationships of domination and subordination. When an oppressive conceptual framework is *patriarchal,* it explains, justifies, and maintains the subordination of women by men.

I have argued elsewhere that there are three significant features of oppressive conceptual frameworks: (1) value-hierarchical thinking, i.e., "up-down" thinking which places higher value, status, or prestige on what is "up" rather than on what is "down"; (2) value dualisms, i.e., disjunctive pairs in which the disjuncts are seen as oppositional (rather than as complementary) and exclusive (rather than as inclusive), and which place higher value (status, prestige) on one disjunct rather than the other (e.g., dualisms which give higher value or status to that which has historically been identified as "body," "emotion," and "female"); and (3) logic of domination, i.e., a structure of argumentation which leads to a justification of subordination.[4]

The third feature of oppressive conceptual frameworks is the most significant. A logic of domination is not *just* a logical structure. It also involves a substantive value system, since an ethical premise is needed to permit or sanction the "just" subordination of that which is subordinate. This justification typically is given on grounds of some alleged characteristic (e.g., rationality) which the dominant (e.g., men) have and the subordinate (e.g., women) lack.

Contrary to what many feminists and ecofeminists have said or suggested, there may be nothing *inherently* problematic about "hierarchical thinking" or even "value-hierarchical thinking" in contexts other than contexts of oppression. Hierarchical thinking is important in daily living for classifying data, comparing information, and organizing material. Taxonomies (e.g., plant taxonomies) and biological nomenclature seem to require *some* form of "hierarchical thinking." Even "value-hierarchical thinking" may be quite acceptable in certain contexts. (The same may be said of "value dualisms" in non-oppressive contexts.) For example, suppose it is true that what is unique about humans is our conscious capacity to radically reshape our social environments (or "societies"), as Murray Bookchin suggests.[5] Then one could truthfully say that humans are better equipped to radically reshape their environments than are rocks or plants—a "value-hierarchical" way of speaking.

The problem is not simply *that* value-hierarchial thinking and value dualisms are used, but *the way* in which each has been used in *oppressive conceptual frameworks* to establish inferiority and to justify subordination.[6] It is the logic of domination, *coupled with* value-hierarchical thinking and value dualisms, which "justifies" subordination. What is explanatorily basic, then, about the nature of oppressive conceptual frameworks is the logic of domination.

For ecofeminism, that a logic of domination is explanatorily basic is important for at least three reasons. First, without a logic of domination, a description of similarities and differences would be just that—a description of similarities and differences. Consider the claim, "Humans are different from plants and rocks in that humans can (and plants and rocks cannot) consciously and radically reshape the communities in which they live; humans are similar to plants and rocks in that they are both members of an ecological community." Even if humans are "better" than plants and rocks with respect to the conscious ability of humans to radically transform communities, one does not *thereby* get any *morally* relevant distinction between humans and nonhumans, or an argument for the domination of plants and rocks by humans. To get *those* conclusions one needs to add at least two powerful assumptions, viz., (A2) and (A4) in argument A below:

(A1) Humans do, and plants and rocks do not, have the capacity to consciously and radically change the community in which they live.
(A2) Whatever has the capacity to consciously and radically change the community in which it lives is morally superior to whatever lacks this capacity.
(A3) Thus, humans are morally superior to plants and rocks.
(A4) For any X and Y, if X is morally superior to Y, then X is morally justified in subordinating Y.
(A5) Thus, humans are morally justified in subordinating plants and rocks.

Without the two assumptions that *humans are morally superior* to (at least some) nonhumans, (A2), and that *superiority justifies subordination,* (A4), all one has is some difference between humans and some nonhumans. This is true *even if* that difference is given in terms of superiority. Thus, it is the logic of domination, (A4), which is the bottom line in ecofeminist discussions of oppression.

Second, ecofeminists argue that, at least in Western societies, the oppressive conceptual framework which sanctions the twin dominations of women and nature is a patriarchal one characterized by all three features of an oppressive conceptual framework. Many ecofeminists claim that, historically, within at least the dominant Western culture, a patriarchal conceptual framework has sanctioned the following argument B:

(B1) Women are identified with nature and the realm of the physical; men are identified with the "human" and the realm of the mental.
(B2) Whatever is identified with nature and the realm of the physical is inferior to ("below") whatever is identified with the "human" and the realm of the mental; or, conversely, the latter is superior to ("above") the former.
(B3) Thus, women are inferior to ("below") men; or, conversely, men are superior to ("above") women.
(B4) For any X and Y, if X is superior to Y, then X is justified in subordinating Y.
(B5) Thus, men are justified in subordinating women.

If sound, argument B establishes *patriarchy,* i.e., the conclusion given at (B5) that the systematic domination of women by men is justified. But according to ecofeminists, (B5) is justified by just those three features of an oppressive conceptual framework identified earlier: value-hierarchical thinking, the assumption at (B2); value dualisms, the assumed dualism of the mental and the physical at (B1) and the assumed inferiority of the physical vis-à-vis the mental at (B2); and a logic of domination, the assumption at (B4), the same as the previous premise (A4). Hence, according to ecofeminists, insofar as an oppressive patriarchal conceptual framework has functioned historically (within at least dominant Western culture) to sanction the twin dominations of women and nature (argument B), both argument B and the patriarchal conceptual framework, from whence it comes, ought to be rejected.

Of course, the preceding does not identify which premises of B are false. What is the status of premises (B1) and (B2)? Most, if not all, feminists claim that (B1), and many ecofeminists claim that (B2), have been assumed or asserted within the dominant Western philosophical and intellectual tradition.[7] As such, these feminists assert, as a matter of historical fact, that the dominant Western philosophical tradition has assumed the truth of (B1) and (B2). Ecofeminists, however, either deny (B2) or do not affirm (B2). Furthermore, because some ecofeminists are anxious to deny any ahistorical identification of women with nature, some ecofeminists deny (B1) when (B1) is used to support anything other than a strictly historical claim about what has been asserted or assumed to be true within patriarchal culture—e.g., when (B1) is used to assert that women properly are identified with the realm of nature and the physical.[8] Thus, from an ecofeminist perspective, (B1) and (B2) are properly viewed as problematic though historically sanctioned claims: they are problematic precisely because of the way they have functioned historically in a patriarchal conceptual framework and culture to sanction the dominations of women and nature.

What *all* ecofeminists agree about, then, is the way in which *the logic of domination* has functioned historically within patriarchy to sustain and justify the twin dominations of women and nature.[9] Since *all* feminists (and not just ecofeminists) oppose patriarchy, the conclusion given at (B5), all feminists (including ecofeminists) must oppose at least the logic of domination, premise (B4), on which argument B rests—whatever the truth-value status of (B1) and (B2) *outside of* a patriarchal context.

That *all* feminists must oppose the logic of domination shows the breadth and depth of the ecofeminist critique of B: it is a critique not only of the three assumptions on which this argument for the domination of women and nature rest, viz., the assumptions at (B1), (B2), and (B4); it is also a critique of patriarchal conceptual frameworks generally, i.e., of those oppressive conceptual frameworks which put men "up" and women "down," allege some way in which women are morally inferior to men, and use that alleged difference to justify the subordination of women by men. Therefore, ecofeminism is necessary to *any* feminist critique of patriarchy, and, hence, necessary to feminism (a point I discuss again later).

Third, ecofeminism clarifies why the logic of domination, and any conceptual framework which gives rise to it, must be abolished in order both to make possible a meaningful notion of difference which does not breed domination and to prevent feminism from becoming a "support" movement based primarily on shared experiences. In contemporary society, there is no one "woman's voice," no *woman* (or *human*) *simpliciter*: every woman (or human) is a woman (or human) of some race, class, age, affectional orientation, marital status, regional or national background, and so forth. Because there are no "monolithic experiences" that all women share, feminism must be a "solidarity movement" based on shared beliefs and interests rather than a "unity in sameness" movement based on shared experiences and shared victimization.[10] In the words of Maria Lugones, "Unity—not to be confused with solidarity—is understood as conceptually tied to domination."[11]

Ecofeminists insist that the sort of logic of domination used to justify the domination of humans by gender, racial or ethnic, or class status is also used to justify the domination of nature. Because eliminating a logic of domination is part of a feminist critique—whether a critique of patriarchy, white supremacist culture, or imperialism—ecofeminists insist that *naturism* is properly viewed as an integral part of any feminist solidarity movement to end sexist oppression and the logic of domination which conceptually grounds it.

ECOFEMINISM RECONCEIVES FEMINISM

The discussion so far has focused on some of the oppressive conceptual features of patriarchy. As I use the phrase, the "logic of traditional feminism" refers to the location of the conceptual roots of sexist oppression, at least in Western societies, in an oppressive patriarchal conceptual framework characterized by a logic of domination. Insofar as other systems of oppression (e.g., racism, classism, ageism, heterosexism) are also conceptually maintained by a logic of domination, appeal to the logic of traditional feminism ultimately locates the basic conceptual interconnections among *all* systems of oppression in the logic of domination. It thereby explains at a *conceptual* level why the eradication of sexist oppression requires the eradication of the other forms of oppression.[12] It is by clarifying this conceptual connection between systems of oppression that a movement to end sexist oppression—traditionally the special turf of feminist theory and practice—leads to a reconceiving of feminism as *a movement to end all forms of oppression.*

Suppose one agrees that the logic of traditional feminism requires the expansion of feminism to include other social systems of domination (e.g., racism and classism). What warrants the inclusion of nature in these "social systems of domination"? Why must the logic of traditional feminism include the abolition of "naturism" (i.e., the domination or oppression of nonhuman nature) among the "isms" feminism must confront? The conceptual justification for expanding feminism to include ecofeminism is twofold. One basis has already been suggested: By showing that the conceptual connections between the dual dominations of women and nature are located in an oppressive and, at least in Western societies, patriarchal conceptual framework characterized by a logic of domination, ecofeminism explains how and why feminism, conceived as a movement to end sexist oppression, must be expanded and reconceived as also a movement to end naturism. This is made explicit by the following argument C:

(C1) Feminism is a movement to end sexism.
(C2) But Sexism is conceptually linked with naturism (through an oppressive conceptual framework characterized by a logic of domination).
(C3) Thus, Feminism is (also) a movement to end naturism.

Because, ultimately, these connections between sexism and naturism are conceptual—embedded in an oppressive conceptual framework—the logic of traditional feminism leads to the embracement of ecological feminism.[13]

The other justification for reconceiving feminism to include ecofeminism has to do with the concepts of gender and nature. Just as conceptions of gender are socially constructed, so are conceptions of nature. Of course, the claim that women and nature are social constructions does not require anyone to deny that there are actual humans and actual trees, rivers, and plants. It simply implies that *how* women and nature are conceived is a matter of historical and social reality. These conceptions vary cross-culturally and by historical time period. As a result, any discussion of the "oppression or domination of nature" involves reference to historically specific forms of social domination of nonhuman nature by humans, just as discussion of the "domination of women" refers to historically specific forms of social domination of women by men. Although I do not argue for it here, an ecofeminist defense of the historical connections between the dominations of women and of nature, claims (B1) and (B2) in argument B, involves showing that within patriarchy the feminization of nature and the naturalization of women have been crucial to the historically successful subordinations of both.[14]

If ecofeminism promises to reconceive traditional feminism in ways which include naturism as a legitimate feminist issue, does ecofeminism also promise to reconceive environmental ethics in ways which are feminist? I think so. This is the subject of the remainder of the paper.

CLIMBING FROM ECOFEMINISM TO ENVIRONMENTAL ETHICS

Many feminists and some environmental ethicists have begun to explore the use of first-person narrative as a way of raising philosophically germane issues in ethics often lost or underplayed in mainstream philosophical ethics. Why is this so? What is it about narrative which makes it a significant resource for theory and practice in feminism and environmental ethics? Even if appeal to first-person narrative is a helpful literary device for describing ineffable experience or a legitimate social science methodology for documenting personal and social history, how is first-person narrative a valuable vehicle of argumentation for ethical decision making and theory building? One fruitful way to begin answering these questions is to ask them of a particular first-person narrative.

Consider the following first-person narrative about rock climbing:

> For my very first rock climbing experience, I chose a somewhat private spot, away from other climbers and on-lookers. After studying "the chimney," I focused all my energy on making it to the top. I climbed with intense determination, using whatever strength and skills I had to accomplish this challenging feat. By midway I was exhausted and anxious. I couldn't see what to do next—where to put my hands or feet. Growing increasingly more weary as I clung somewhat desperately to the rock, I made a move. It didn't work. I fell. There I was, dangling midair above the rocky ground below, frightened but terribly relieved that the belay rope had held me. I knew I was safe. I took a look up at the climb that remained. I was determined to make it to the top. With renewed confidence and concentration, I finished the climb to the top.
>
> On my second day of climbing, I rappelled down about 200 feet from the top of the Palisades at Lake Superior to just a few feet above the water level. I could see no one—not my belayer, not the other climbers, no one. I unhooked slowly from the rappel rope and took a deep cleansing breath. I looked all around me—really looked—and listened. I heard a cacophony of voices—birds, trickles of water on the rock before me, waves lapping against the rocks below. I closed my eyes and began to feel the rock with my hands—the cracks and crannies, the raised lichen and mosses, the almost imperceptible nubs that might provide a resting place for my fingers and toes when I began to climb. At that moment I was bathed in serenity. I began to talk to the rock in an almost inaudible, child-like way, as if the rock were my friend. I felt an overwhelming sense of gratitude for what it offered me—a chance to know myself and the rock differently, to appreciate unforeseen miracles like the tiny flowers growing in the even tinier cracks in the rock's surface, and to come to know a sense of *being in relationship* with the natural environment. It felt as if the rock and I were silent conversational partners in a longstanding friendship. I realized then that I had come to care about this cliff which was so different from me, so unmovable and invincible, independent and seemingly indifferent to my presence. I wanted to be with the rock as I climbed. Gone was the determination to conquer the rock, to forcefully impose my will on it; I wanted simply to work respectfully with the rock as I climbed. And as I climbed, that is what I felt. I felt myself *caring* for this rock and feeling thankful that climbing provided the opportunity for me to know it and myself in this new way.

There are at least four reasons why use of such a first-person narrative is important to feminism and environmental ethics. First, such a narrative gives voice to a felt sensitivity often lacking in traditional analytical ethical discourse, viz., a sensitivity to conceiving of oneself as fundamentally "in relationship with" others, including the nonhuman environment. It is a modality which *takes relationships themselves seriously*. It thereby stands in contrast to a strictly reductionist modality that takes relationships seriously only or primarily because of the nature of the *relators* or parties to those relationships (e.g., relators conceived as moral agents, right holders, interest carriers, or sentient beings). In the rock-climbing narrative above, it is the climber's relationship with the rock she climbs which takes on special significance—which is itself a locus of value—in addition to whatever moral status or moral considerability she or the rock or any other parties to the relationship may also have.[15]

Second, such a first-person narrative gives expression to a variety of ethical attitudes and behaviors often overlooked or underplayed in mainstream Western ethics, e.g., the difference in attitudes and behaviors toward a rock when one is "making it to the top" and when one thinks of oneself as "friends with" or "caring about" the rock one climbs.[16] These different attitudes and behaviors suggest an ethically germane contrast between two different types of relationship humans or climbers may have toward a rock: An imposed conqueror-type relationship, and an emergent caring-type relationship. This contrast grows out of, and is faithful to, felt, lived experience.

The difference between conquering and caring attitudes and behaviors in relation to the natural environment provides a third reason why the use of first-person narrative is important to feminism and environmental ethics: it provides a way of conceiving of ethics and ethical meaning as *emerging out of* particular situations moral agents find themselves in, rather than as being *imposed on* those situations (e.g., as a derivation or instantiation of some predetermined abstract principle or rule). This emergent feature of narrative centralizes the importance of *voice.* When a multiplicity of cross-cultural *voices* are centralized, narrative is able to give expression to a range of attitudes, values, beliefs, and behaviors which may be overlooked or silenced by imposed ethical meaning and theory. As a reflection on a felt, lived experience, the use of narrative in ethics provides a stance from which ethical discourse can be held accountable to the historical, material, and social realities in which moral subjects find themselves.

Lastly, and for our purposes perhaps most importantly, the use of narrative has argumentative significance. Jim Cheney calls attention to this feature of narrative when he claims, "To contextualize ethical deliberation is, in some sense, to provide a narrative or story, from which the solution to the ethical dilemma emerges as the fitting conclusion."[17] Narrative has argumentative force by suggesting *what counts* as an appropriate conclusion to an ethical situation. One ethical conclusion suggested by the climbing narrative is that what counts as a proper ethical attitude toward mountains and rocks is an attitude of respect and care (whatever that turns out to be or involve), not one of domination and conquest.

In an essay entitled "In and Out of Harm's Way: Arrogance and Love," feminist philosopher Marilyn Frye distinguishes between "arrogant" and "loving" perception as one way of getting at this difference in the ethical attitudes of care and conquest.[18] Frye writes:

> The loving eye is a contrary of the arrogant eye.
>
> The loving eye knows the independence of the other. It is the eye of a seer who knows that nature is indifferent. It is the eye of one who knows that to know the seen, one must consult something other than one's own will and interests and fears and imagination. One must look at the thing. One must look and listen and check and question.
>
> The loving eye is one that pays a certain sort of attention. This attention can require a discipline but *not* a self-denial. The discipline is one of self-knowledge, knowledge of the scope and boundary of the self. . . . In particular, it is a matter

> of being able to tell one's own interests from those of others and of knowing where one's self leaves off and another begins. . . .
>
> The loving eye does not make the object of perception into something edible, does not try to assimilate it, does not reduce it to the size of the seer's desire, fear and imagination, and hence does not have to simplify. It knows the complexity of the other as something which will forever present new things to be known. The science of the loving eye would favor The Complexity Theory of Truth [in contrast to The Simplicity Theory of Truth] and presuppose The Endless Interestingness of the Universe.[19]

According to Frye, the loving eye is not an invasive, coercive eye which annexes others to itself, but one which "knows the complexity of the other as something which will forever present new things to be known."

When one climbs a rock as a conqueror, one climbs with an arrogant eye. When one climbs with a loving eye, one constantly "must look and listen and check and question." One recognizes the rock as something very different, something perhaps totally indifferent to one's own presence, and finds in that difference joyous occasion for celebration. One knows "the boundary of the self," where the self—the "I," the climber—leaves off and the rock begins. There is no fusion of two into one, but a complement of two entities *acknowledged* as separate, different, independent, yet *in relationship*; they are in relationship *if only* because the loving eye is perceiving it, responding to it, noticing it, attending to it.

An ecofeminist perspective about both women and nature involves this shift in attitude from "arrogant perception" to "loving perception" of the nonhuman world. Arrogant perception of nonhumans by humans presupposes and maintains *sameness* in such a way that it expands the moral community to those beings who are thought to resemble (be like, similar to, or the same as) humans in some morally significant way. Any environmental movement or ethic based on arrogant perception builds a moral hierarchy of beings and assumes some common denominator of moral considerability in virtue of which like beings deserve similar treatment or moral consideration and unlike beings do not. Such environmental ethics are or generate a "unity in sameness." In contrast, "loving perception" presupposes and maintains *difference*—a distinction between the self and other, between human and at least some nonhumans—in such a way that perception of the other as other *is* an expression of love for one who/which is recognized at the outset as independent, dissimilar, different. As Maria Lugones says, in loving perception, "Love is seen not as fusion and erasure of difference but as incompatible with them."[20] "Unity in sameness" alone is an *erasure of difference.*

"Loving perception" of the nonhuman natural world is an attempt to understand what it means *for humans* to care about the nonhuman world, a world *acknowledged* as being independent, different, perhaps even indifferent to humans. Humans *are* different from rocks in important ways, even if they are also both members of some ecological community. A moral community based on loving perception of oneself *in relationship with* a rock, or with the natural environment as a whole, is one which acknowledges and respects difference, whatever "sameness" also exists.[21] The limits of loving perception are determined only by the limits of one's (e.g., a person's, a community's) ability to respond lovingly (or with appropriate care, trust, or friendship)—whether it is to other humans or to the nonhuman world and elements of it.[22]

If what I have said so far is correct, then there are very different ways to climb a mountain and *how* one climbs it and *how* one narrates the experience of climbing it matter ethically. If one climbs with "arrogant perception," with an attitude of "conquer and control," one keeps intact the very sorts of thinking that characterize a logic of domination and an oppressive conceptual framework. Since the oppressive conceptual framework which sanctions the domination of nature is a patriarchal one, one also thereby keeps intact, even if unwittingly, a patriarchal conceptual framework. Because the dismantling of patriarchal conceptual frameworks is a feminist issue, *how* one climbs a mountain and *how* one narrates—or tells the story—about the experience of climbing also are *feminist issues*. In this way, ecofeminism makes visible why, at a conceptual level, environmental ethics is a feminist issue. I turn now to a consideration of ecofeminism as a distinctively feminist and environmental ethic.

ECOFEMINISM AS A FEMINIST AND ENVIRONMENTAL ETHIC

A feminist ethic involves a twofold commitment to critique male bias in ethics wherever it occurs, and to develop ethics which are not male-biased. Sometimes this involves articulation of values (e.g., values of care, appropriate trust, kinship, friendship) often lost or underplayed in mainstream ethics.[23] Sometimes it involves engaging in theory building by pioneering in new directions or by revamping old theories in gender sensitive ways. What makes the critiques of old theories or conceptualizations of new ones "feminist" is that they emerge out of sex-gender analyses and reflect whatever those analyses reveal about gendered experience and gendered social reality.

As I conceive feminist ethics in the pre-feminist present, it rejects attempts to conceive of ethical theory in terms of necessary and sufficient conditions, because it assumes that there is no essence (in the sense of some transhistorical, universal, absolute abstraction) of feminist ethics. While attempts to formulate joint necessary and sufficient conditions of a feminist ethic are unfruitful, nonetheless, there are some necessary conditions, what I prefer to call "boundary conditions," of a feminist ethic. These boundary conditions clarify some of the minimal conditions of a feminist ethic without suggesting that feminist ethics has some ahistorical essence. They are like the boundaries of a quilt or collage. They delimit the territory of the piece without dictating what the interior, the design, the actual pattern of the piece looks like. Because the actual design of the quilt emerges from the multiplicity of voices of women in a cross-cultural context, the design will change over time. It is not something static.

What are some of the boundary conditions of a feminist ethic? First, nothing can become part of a feminist ethic—can be part of the quilt—that promotes sexism, racism, classism, or any other "isms" of social domination. Of course, people may disagree about what counts as a sexist act, racist attitude, classist behavior. What counts as sexism, racism, or classism may vary cross-culturally. Still, because a feminist ethic aims at eliminating sexism and sexist bias, and (as I have already shown) sexism is intimately connected in conceptualization and in practice to racism, classism, and naturism, a feminist ethic must be anti-sexist, anti-racist, anti-classist, anti-naturist and opposed to any "ism" which presupposes or advances a logic of domination.

Second, a feminist ethic is a *contextualist* ethic. A contextualist ethic is one which sees ethical discourse and practice as emerging from the voices of people located in different historical circumstances. A contextualist ethic is properly viewed as a *collage* or *mosaic*, a *tapestry* of voices that emerges out of felt experiences. Like any collage or mosaic, the point is not to have *one picture* based on a unity of voices, but a *pattern* which emerges out of the very different voices of people located in different circumstances. When a contextualist ethic is *feminist*, it gives central place to the voices of women.

Third, since a feminist ethic gives central significance to the diversity of women's voices, a feminist ethic must be structurally pluralistic rather than unitary or reductionistic. It rejects the assumption that there is "one voice" in terms of which ethical values, beliefs, attitudes, and conduct can be assessed.

Fourth, a feminist ethic reconceives ethical theory as theory in process which will change over time. Like all theory, a feminist ethic is based on some generalizations.[24] Nevertheless, the generalizations associated with it are themselves a pattern of voices within which the different voices emerging out of concrete and alternative descriptions of ethical situations have meaning. The coherence of a feminist theory so conceived is given within a historical and conceptual context, i.e., within a set of historical, socioeconomic circumstances (including circumstances of race, class, age, and affectional orientation) and within a set of basic beliefs, values, attitudes, and assumptions about the world.

Fifth, because a feminist ethic is contextualist, structurally pluralistic, and "in-process," one way to evaluate the claims of a feminist ethic is in terms of their *inclusiveness*: those claims (voices, patterns of voices) are morally and epistemologically favored (preferred, better, less partial, less biased) which are more inclusive of the felt experiences and perspectives of oppressed persons. The condition of inclusiveness requires and ensures that the diverse voices of women (as oppressed persons) will be given legitimacy in ethical theory building. It thereby helps to minimize empirical bias, e.g., bias rising from faulty or false generalizations based on stereotyping, too small a sample size, or a skewed sample. It does so by ensuring that any generalizations which are made about ethics and ethical decision making include—indeed cohere with—the patterned voices of women.[25]

Sixth, a feminist ethic makes no attempt to provide an "objective" point of view, since it assumes that in contemporary culture there really is no such point of view. As such, it does not claim to be "unbiased" in the sense of "value-neutral" or "objective." However, it does assume that whatever bias it has as an ethic centralizing the voices of oppressed persons is a *better bias*—"better" because it is more inclusive and therefore less partial—than those which exclude those voices.[26]

Seventh, a feminist ethic provides a central place for values typically unnoticed, underplayed, or misrepresented in traditional ethics, e.g., values of care, love, friendship, and appropriate trust.[27] Again, it need not do this at the exclusion of considerations of rights, rules, or utility. There may be many contexts in which talk of rights or of utility is useful or appropriate. For instance, in contracts or property relationships, talk of rights may be useful and appropriate. In deciding what is cost-effective or advantageous to the most people, talk of utility may be useful and appropriate. In a feminist *qua* contextualist ethic, whether or not such talk is useful or appropriate depends on the context; *other values* (e.g., values of care, trust, friendship) are *not* viewed as reducible to or captured solely in terms of such talk.[28]

Eighth, a feminist ethic also involves a reconception of what it is to be human and what it is for humans to engage in ethical decision making, since it rejects as either meaningless or currently untenable any gender-free or gender-neutral description of humans, ethics, and ethical decision making. It thereby rejects what Alison Jaggar calls "abstract individualism," i.e., the position that it is possible to identify a human essence or human nature that exists independently of any particular historical context.[29] Humans and human moral conduct are properly understood essentially (and not merely accidentally) in terms of networks or webs of historical and concrete relationships.

All the props are now in place for seeing how ecofeminism provides the framework for a distinctively feminist and environmental ethic. It is a feminism that critiques male bias wherever it occurs in ethics (including environmental ethics) and aims at providing an ethic (including an environmental ethic) which is not male biased—and it does so in a way that satisfies the preliminary boundary conditions of a feminist ethic.

First, ecofeminism is quintessentially anti-naturist. Its anti-naturism consists in the rejection of any way of thinking about or acting toward nonhuman nature that reflects a logic, values, or attitude of domination. Its anti-naturist, anti-sexist, anti-racist, anti-classist (and so forth, for all other "isms" of social domination) stance forms the outer boundary of the quilt: nothing gets on the quilt which is naturist, sexist, racist, classist, and so forth.

Second, ecofeminism is a contextualist ethic. It involves a shift *from* a conception of ethics as primarily a matter of rights, rules, or principles predetermined and applied in specific cases to entities viewed as competitors in the contest of moral standing, *to* a conception of ethics as growing out of what Jim Cheney calls "defining relationships," i.e., relationships conceived in some sense as defining who one is.[30] As a contextualist ethic, it is not that rights, or rules, or principles are *not* relevant or important. Clearly they are in certain contexts and for certain purposes.[31] It is just that what *makes* them relevant or important is that those to whom they apply are entities *in relationship with* others.

Ecofeminism also involves an ethical shift *from* granting moral consideration to nonhumans *exclusively* on the grounds of some similarity they share with humans (e.g., rationality, interests, moral agency, sentiency, right-holder status) *to* "a highly contextual account to see clearly what a human being is and what the nonhuman world might be, morally speaking, *for* human beings."[32] For an ecofeminist, *how* a moral agent is in relationship to another becomes of central significance, not simply *that* a moral agent is a moral agent or is bound by rights, duties, virtue, or utility to act in a certain way.

Third, ecofeminism is structurally pluralistic in that it presupposes and maintains difference—difference among humans as well as between humans and at least some elements of nonhuman nature. Thus, while ecofeminism denies the "nature/culture" split, it affirms that humans are both members of an ecological community (in some respects) and different from it (in other respects). Ecofeminism's attention to relationships and community is not, therefore, an erasure of difference but a respectful acknowledgement of it.

Fourth, ecofeminism reconceives theory as theory in process. It focuses on patterns of meaning which emerge, for instance, from the storytelling and first-person narratives of women (and others) who deplore the twin dominations of women and nature. The use of narrative is one way to ensure that the content of the ethic—the pattern of the quilt—may/will change over time, as the historical and material realities of women's lives change and as more is learned about women-nature connections and the destruction of the nonhuman world.[33]

Fifth, ecofeminism is inclusivist. It emerges from the voices of women who experience the harmful domination of nature and the way that domination is tied to their domination as women. It emerges from listening to the voices of indigenous peoples such as Native Americans who have been dislocated from their land and have witnessed the attendant undermining of such values as appropriate reciprocity, sharing, and kinship that characterize traditional Indian culture. It emerges from listening to voices of those who, like Nathan Hare, critique traditional approaches to environmental ethics as white and bourgeois, and as failing to address issues of "black ecology" and the "ecology" of the inner city and urban spaces.[34] It also emerges out of the voices of Chipko women who see the destruction of "earth, soil, and water" as intimately connected with their own inability to survive economically.[35] With its emphasis on inclusivity and difference, ecofeminism provides a framework for recognizing that what counts as ecology and what counts as appropriate conduct toward both human and nonhuman environments is largely a matter of context.

Sixth, as a feminism, ecofeminism makes no attempt to provide an "objective" point of view. It is a social ecology. It recognizes the twin dominations of women and nature as social problems rooted both in very concrete, historical, socioeconomic circumstances and in oppressive patriarchal conceptual frameworks which maintain and sanction these circumstances.

Seventh, ecofeminism makes a central place for values of care, love, friendship, trust, and appropriate reciprocity—values that presuppose that our relationships to others are central to our understanding of who we are.[36] It thereby gives voice to the sensitivity that in climbing a mountain, one is doing something in relationship with an "other," an "other" whom one can come to care about and treat respectfully.

Lastly, an ecofeminist ethic involves a reconception of what it means to be human, and in what human ethical behavior consists. Ecofeminism denies abstract individualism. Humans are who we are in large part by virtue of the historical and social contexts and the relationships we are in, including our relationships with nonhuman nature. Relationships are not something extrinsic to who we are, not an "add on" feature of human nature; they play an essential role in shaping what it is to be human. Relationships of humans to the nonhuman environment are, in part, constitutive of what it is to be a human.

By making visible the interconnections among the dominations of women and nature, ecofeminism shows that both are feminist issues and that explicit acknowledgement of both is vital to any responsible environmental ethic. Feminism *must* embrace ecological feminism if it is to end the domination of women because the domination of women is tied conceptually and historically to the domination of nature.

A responsible environmental ethic also *must* embrace feminism. Otherwise, even the seemingly most revolutionary, liberational, and holistic ecological ethic will fail to take seriously the interconnected dominations of nature and women that are so much a part of the historical legacy and conceptual framework that sanctions the exploitation of nonhuman nature. Failure to make visible these interconnected, twin dominations results in an inaccurate account of how it is that nature has been and continues to be dominated and exploited and produces an environmental ethic that lacks the depth necessary to be truly *inclusive* of the realities of persons who at least in dominant Western culture have been intimately tied with that exploitation, viz., women. Whatever else can be said in favor of such holistic ethics, a failure to make visible ecofeminist insights into the common denominators of the twin oppressions of women and nature is to perpetuate, rather than overcome, the source of that oppression.

This last point deserves further attention. It may be objected that as long as the end result is "the same"—the development of an environmental ethic which does not emerge out of or reinforce an oppressive conceptual framework—it does not matter whether that ethic (or the ethic endorsed in getting there) is feminist or not. Hence, it simply is *not* the case that any adequate environmental ethic must be feminist. My argument, in contrast, has been that it *does* matter, and for three important reasons. First, there is the scholarly issue of accurately representing historical reality, and that, ecofeminists claim, requires acknowledging the historical feminization of nature and naturalization of women as part of the exploitation of nature. Second, I have shown that the conceptual connections between the domination of women and the domination of nature are located in an oppressive and, at least in Western societies, patriarchal conceptual framework characterized by a logic of domination. Thus, I have shown that failure to notice the nature of this connection leaves at best an incomplete, inaccurate, and partial account of what is required of a conceptually adequate environmental ethic. An ethic which *does not* acknowledge this is simply *not* the same as one that does, whatever else the similarities between them. Third, the claim that, in contemporary culture, one can have an adequate environmental ethic which is *not* feminist assumes that, in contemporary culture, the label *feminist* does not add anything crucial to the nature or description of environmental ethics. I have shown that at least in contemporary culture this is false, for the word *feminist* currently helps to clarify just *how* the domination of nature is conceptually linked to patriarchy and, hence, how the liberation of nature, is conceptually linked to the termination of patriarchy. Thus, because the word 'feminist' has critical bite in contemporary culture, it serves as an important reminder that in contemporary sex-gendered, raced, classed, and naturist culture, an unlabeled position functions as a privileged and "unmarked" position. That is, without the addition of the word *feminist,* one presents environmental ethics as if it has no bias, including male-gender bias, which is just what ecofeminists deny: failure to notice the connections between the twin oppressions of women and nature *is* male-gender bias.

One of the goals of feminism is the eradication of all oppressive sex-gender (and related race, class, age, affectional preference) categories and the creation of a world in which *difference does not breed domination*—say, the world of 4001. If in 4001 an "adequate environmental ethic" is a "feminist environmental ethic," the word *feminist* may then be redundant and unnecessary. However, this is *not* 4001, and in terms of the current historical and conceptual reality the dominations of nature and of women are intimately connected. Failure to notice or make visible that connection in 1990 perpetuates the mistaken (and privileged) view that "environmental ethics" is *not* a feminist issue, and that *feminist* adds nothing to environmental ethics.[37]

CONCLUSION

I have argued in this paper that ecofeminism provides a framework for a distinctively feminist and environmental ethic. Ecofeminism grows out of the felt and theorized about connections between the domination of women and the domination of nature. As a contextualist ethic, ecofeminism refocuses environmental ethics on what nature might mean, morally speaking, *for* humans, and on how the relational attitudes of humans to others—humans as well as nonhumans—sculpt both what it is to be human and the nature and ground of human responsibilities to the nonhuman environment. Part of what this refocusing does is to take seriously the voices of women and other oppressed persons in the construction of that ethic.

A Sioux elder once told me a story about his son. He sent his seven-year-old son to live with the child's grandparents on a Sioux reservation so that he could "learn the Indian ways." Part of what the grandparents taught the son

This ~~argument~~ ecofem argument is antipatriarchy

Some E is ~P

Every fem arg must be antipatriarch

All F are ~P

No F are P

~~Any~~-every fem must be ~~environ~~ ecofem

All F are E

No F are P

Some E are not P

∴ All F are E

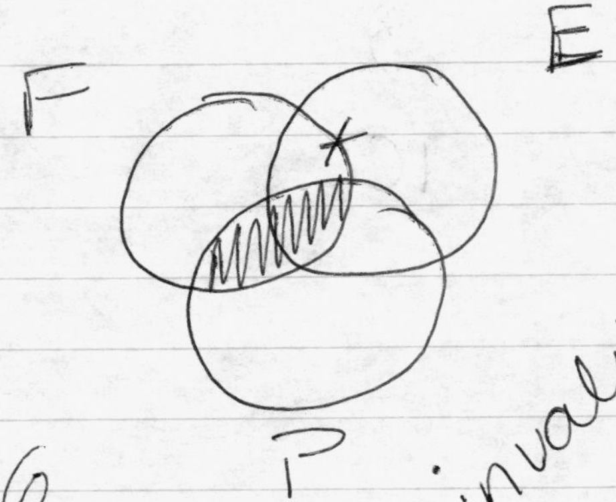

E

F

P

invalid

illicit minor

All S - P

No S - P

Some S - P

Some S - ~P

2

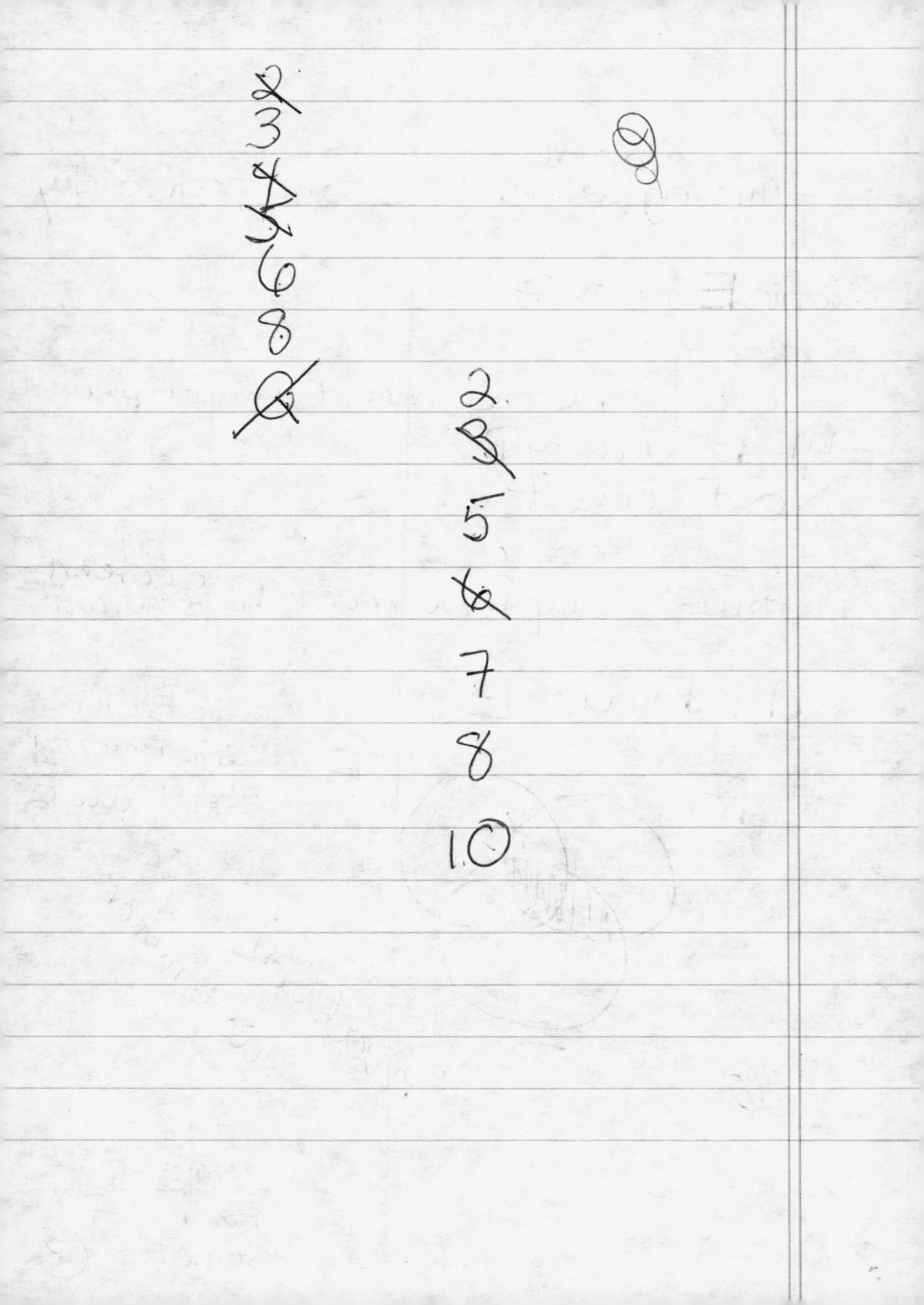

was how to hunt the four leggeds of the forest. As I heard the story, the boy was taught, "to shoot your four-legged brother in his hind area, slowing it down but not killing it. Then, take the four-legged's head in your hands, and look into his eyes. The eyes are where all the suffering is. Look into your brother's eyes and feel his pain. Then, take your knife and cut the four-legged under his chin, here, on his neck, so that he dies quickly. And as you do, ask your brother, the four-legged, for forgiveness for what you do. Offer also a prayer of thanks to your four-legged kin for offering his body to you just now, when you need food to eat and clothing to wear. And promise the four-legged that you will put yourself back into the earth when you die, to become nourishment of the earth, and for the sister flowers, and for the brother deer. It is appropriate that you should offer this blessing for the four-legged and, in due time, reciprocate in turn with your body in this way, as the four-legged gives life to you for your survival." As I reflect upon that story, I am struck by the power of the environmental ethic that grows out of and takes seriously narrative, context, and such values and relational attitudes as care, loving perception, and appropriate reciprocity, and doing what is appropriate in a given situation—however that notion of appropriateness eventually gets filled out. I am also struck by what one is able to see, once one begins to explore some of the historical and conceptual connections between the dominations of women and of nature. A *re-conceiving* and *re-visioning* of both feminism and environmental ethics, is, I think, the power and promise of ecofeminism.

NOTES

1. Explicit ecological feminist literature includes works from a variety of scholarly perspectives and sources. Some of these works are Jim Cheney, "Eco-Feminism and Deep Ecology," *Environmental Ethics* 9 (1987): 115–45; Katherine Davies, "Historical Associations: Women and the Natural World," *Women & Environments* 9, no. 2 (Spring 1987): 4–6; Sharon Doubiago, "Deeper than Deep Ecology: Men Must Become Feminists," in *The New Catalyst Quarterly*, no. 10 (Winter 1987/88): 10–11; Brian Easlea, *Science and Sexual Oppression: Patriarchy's Confrontation with Women and Nature* (London: Weidenfeld & Nicholson, 1981); Ynestra King, "Feminism and the Revolt of Nature," in *Heresies #13: Feminism and Ecology* 4, no. 1 (1981): Greater King 12–16, and "What Is Ecofeminism?" *The Nation*, 12 December 1987; Abby Peterson and Carolyn Merchant, "Peace with the Earth: Women and the Environmental Movement in Sweden," *Women's Studies International Forum* 9, no. 5–6. (1986): 465–79; Judith Plant, ed., *Healing Our Wounds: The Power of Ecological Feminism* (Boston: New Society Publishers, 1989); Kirkpatrick Sale, "Ecofeminism—A New Perspective," *The Nation*, 26 (September 1987): 302–05; Ariel Kay Salleh, "Deeper than Deep Ecology: The Eco-Feminist Connection," *Environmental Ethics* 6 (1984): 339–45, and "Epistemology and the Metaphors of Production: An Eco-Feminist Reading of Critical Theory," in *Studies in the Humanities* 15 (1988): 130–39; Karen J. Warren, "Feminism and Ecology: Making Connections," *Environmental Ethics* 9 (1987): 3–21; Miriam Wyman, "Explorations of Eco-Feminism," *Women & Environments* (Spring 1987): 6–7; Iris Young, " 'Feminism and Ecology' and 'Women and Life on Earth: Eco-Feminism in the 80's,' " *Environmental Ethics* 5 (1983): 173–80.

2. Françoise d'Eaubonne, *Le Féminisme ou la Mort* (Paris: Pierre Horay, 1974), pp. 213–52.
3. I discuss this in my paper "Toward an Ecofeminist Ethic."
4. The account offered here is a revision of the account given earlier in my paper "Feminism and Ecology: Making Connections." I have changed the account to be about "oppressive" rather than strictly "partriarchal" conceptual frameworks in order to leave open the possibility that there may be some patriarchal conceptual frameworks (e.g., in non-Western cultures) which are *not* properly characterized as based on value dualisms.
5. Murray Bookchin, "Social Ecology versus 'Deep Ecology,'" in *Green Perspectives: Newsletter of the Green Program Project,* no. 4–5 (Summer 1987): 9.
6. It may be that in contemporary Western society, which is so thoroughly structured by categories of gender, race, class, age, and affectional orientation, that there simply is no meaningful notion of "value-hierarchical thinking" which does not function in an oppressive context. For purposes of this paper, I leave that question open.
7. Many feminists who argue for the historical point that claims (B1) and (B2) have been asserted or assumed to be true within the dominant Western philosophical tradition do so by discussion of that tradition's conceptions of reason, rationality, and science. For a sampling of the sorts of claims made within that context, see "Reason, Rationality, and Gender," ed. Nancy Tuana and Karen J. Warren, a special issue of the American Philosophical Association's *Newsletter on Feminism and Philosophy* 88, no. 2 (March 1989): 17–71. Ecofeminists who claim that (B2) has been assumed to be true within the dominant Western philosophical tradition include: Gray, *Green Paradise Lost*; Griffin, *Woman and Nature*; Merchant, *The Death of Nature*; Ruether, *New Woman/New Earth.* For a discussion of some of these ecofeminist historical acounts, see Plumwood, "Ecofeminism." While I agree that the historical connections between the domination of women and the domination of nature is a crucial one, I do not argue for that claim here.
8. Ecofeminists who deny (B1) when (B1) is offered as anything other than a true, descriptive, historical claim about patriarchal culture often do so on grounds that an objectionable sort of biological determinism, or at least harmful female sex-gender stereotypes, underlie (B1). For a discussion of this "split" among those ecofeminists ("nature feminists") who assert and those ecofeminists ("social feminists") who deny (B1) as anything other than a true historical claim about how women are described in patriarchal culture, see Griscom, "On Healing the Nature/History Split."
9. I make no attempt here to defend the historically sanctioned truth of these premises.
10. See, e.g., Bell Hooks, *Feminist Theory: From Margin to Center* (Boston: South End Press, 1984), pp. 51–52.
11. Maria Lugones, "Playfulness, 'World-Travelling,' and Loving Perception," *Hypatia* 2, no. 2 (Summer 1987): 3.
12. At an *experiential* level, some women are "women of color," poor, old, lesbian, Jewish, and physically challenged. Thus, if feminism is going to liberate these women, it also needs to end the racism, classism, heterosexism, anti-Semitism, and discrimination against the handicapped that is constitutive of their oppression as black, or Latina, or poor, or older, or lesbian, or Jewish, or physically challenged women.
13. This same sort of reasoning shows that feminism is also a movement to end racism, classism, age-ism, heterosexism and other "isms," which are based in oppressive conceptual frameworks characterized by a logic of domination. However, there is an important caveat: ecofeminism is *not* compatible with all feminisms and all environmentalisms. For a discussion of this point, see my article "Feminism and Ecology: Making Connections." What it *is* compatible with is the minimal condition characterization of feminism as a movement to end sexism that is accepted by all contemporary feminisms (liberal, traditional Marxist, radical, socialist, Blacks and non-Western).

14. See, e.g., Gray, *Green Paradise Lost*; Griffin, *Women and Nature*; Merchant, *The Death of Nature*; and Ruether, *New Woman/New Earth.*
15. Suppose, as I think is the case, that a necessary condition for the existence of a moral relationship is that at least one party to the relationship is a moral being (leaving open for our purposes what counts as a "moral being"). If this is so, then the Mona Lisa cannot properly be said to have or stand in a moral relationship with the wall on which she hangs, and a wolf cannot have or properly be said to have or stand in a moral relationship with a moose. Such a necessary-condition account leaves open the question whether *both* parties to the relationship must be moral beings. My point here is simply that however one resolves *that* question, recognition of the relationships themselves as a locus of value is a recognition of a source of value that is different from and not reducible to the values of the "moral beings" in those relationships.
16. It is interesting to note that the image of being friends with the Earth is one which cytogeneticist Barbara McClintock uses when she describes the importance of having "a feeling for the organism," "listening to the material [in this case the corn plant]," in one's work as a scientist. See Evelyn Fox Keller, "Women, Science, and Popular Mythology," in *Machina Ex Dea: Feminist Perspectives on Technology*, ed. Joan Rothschild (New York: Pergamon Press, 1983), and Evelyn Fox Keller. *A Feeling for the Organism: The Life and Work of Barbara McClintock* (San Francisco: W. H. Freeman, 1983).
17. Cheney, "Eco-Feminism and Deep Ecology," 144.
18. Marilyn Frye, "In and Out of Harm's Way: Arrogance and Love," *The Politics of Reality* (Trumansburg, New York: The Crossing Press, 1983), pp. 66–72.
19. Ibid., pp. 75–76.
20. Maria Lugones, "Playfulness," p. 3.
21. Cheney makes a similar point in "Eco-Feminism and Deep Ecology," p. 140.
22. Ibid., p. 138.
23. This account of a feminist ethic draws on my paper "Toward an Ecofeminist Ethic."
24. Marilyn Frye makes this point in her illuminating paper, "The Possibility of Feminist Theory," read at the American Philosophical Association Central Division Meetings in Chicago, 29 April–1 May 1986. My discussion of feminist theory is inspired largely by that paper and by Kathryn Addelson's paper "Moral Revolution," in *Women and Values: Reading in Recent Feminist Philosophy*, ed. Marilyn Pearsall (Belmont, Calif.: Wadsworth Publishing Co., 1986) pp. 291–309.
25. Notice that the standard of inclusiveness does not exclude the voices of men. It is just that those voices must cohere with the voices of women.
26. For a more in-depth discussion of the notions of impartiality and bias, see my paper, "Critical Thinking and Feminism," *Informal Logic* 10, no. 1 (Winter 1988): 31–44.
27. The burgeoning literature on these values is noteworthy. See, e.g., Carol Gilligan, *In a Different Voice: Psychological Theories and Women's Development* (Cambridge: Harvard University Press, 1982); *Mapping the Moral Domain: A Contribution of Women's Thinking to Psychological Theory and Education,* ed. Carol Gilligan, Janie Victoria Ward, and Jill McLean Taylor, with Betty Bardige (Cambridge: Harvard University Press, 1988); Nel Nodings, *Caring: A Feminine Approach to Ethics and Moral Education* (Berkeley: University of California Press, 1984); Maria Lugones and Elizabeth V. Spelman, "Have We Got a Theory for You! Feminist Theory, Cultural Imperialism, and the Women's Voice," *Women's Studies International Forum* 6 (1983): 573–81; Maria Lugones, "Playfulness"; Annette C. Baier, "What Do Women Want in a Moral Theory?" *Nous* 19 (1985): 53–63.
28. Jim Cheney would claim that our fundamental relationships to one another as moral agents are not as moral agents to rights holders, and that whatever rights a person properly may be said to have are relationally defined rights, not rights possessed by atomistic individuals conceived as Robinson Crusoes who do not exist

essentially in relation to others. On this view, even rights talk itself is properly conceived as growing out of a relational ethic, not vice versa.

29. Alison Jaggar, *Feminist Politics and Human Nature* (Totowa, N.J.: Rowman and Allanheld, 1980), pp. 42–44.
30. Henry West has pointed out that the expression "defining relations" is ambiguous. According to West, "the defining" as Cheney uses it is an adjective, not a principle—it is not that ethics defines relationships; it is that ethics grows out of conceiving of the relationships that one is in as defining what the individual is.
31. For example, in relationships involving contracts or promises, those relationships might be correctly described as that of moral agent to rights holders. In relationships involving mere property, those relationships might be correctly described as that of moral agent to objects having only instrumental value, "relationships of instrumentality." In comments on an earlier draft of this paper, West suggested that possessive individualism, for instance, might be recast in such a way that an individual is defined by his or her property relationships.
32. Cheney, "Eco-Feminism and Deep Ecology," p. 144.
33. One might object that such permission for change opens the door for environmental exploitation. This is not the case. An ecofeminist ethic is anti-naturist. Hence, the unjust domination and exploitation of nature is a "boundary condition" of the ethic; no such actions are sanctioned or justified on ecofeminist grounds. What it *does* leave open is some leeway about what counts as domination and exploitation. This, I think, is a strength of the ethic, not a weakness, since it acknowledges that *that* issue cannot be resolved in any practical way in the abstract, independent of a historical and social context.
34. Nathan Hare, "Black Ecology," in *Environmental Ethics*, ed. K. S. Shrader-Frechette (Pacific Grove, Calif.: Boxwood Press, 1981), pp. 229–36.
35. For an ecofeminist discussion of the Chipko movement, see my "Toward an Ecofeminist Ethic," and Shiva's *Staying Alive.*
36. See Cheney, "Eco-Feminism and Deep Ecology," p. 122.
37. I offer the same sort of reply to critics of ecofeminism such as Warwick Fox who suggest that for the sort of ecofeminism I defend, the word *feminist* does not add anything significant to environmental ethics and, consequently, that an ecofeminist like myself might as well call herself a deep ecologist. He asks: "Why doesn't she just call it [i.e., Warren's vision of a transformative feminism] deep ecology? Why specifically attach the label *feminist* to it . . .?" (Warwick Fox, "The Deep Ecology-Ecofeminism Debate and Its Parallels," *Environmental Ethics* 11, no. 1 [1989]: 14, n. 22). Whatever the important similarities between deep ecology and ecofeminism (or, specifically, my version of ecofeminism)—and, indeed, there are many—it is precisely my point here that the word *feminist* does add something significant to the conception of environmental ethics, and that any environmental ethic (including deep ecology) that fails to make explicit the different kinds of interconnections among the domination of nature and the domination of women will be, from a feminist (and ecofeminist) perspective such as mine, inadequate.

PART FOUR
Political Ecology

Introduction

John Clark

John Clark is professor of philosophy at Loyola University, New Orleans, and currently chairs the Environmental Studies Program. He has long been active in the green and bioregionalism movements. His books include The Anarchist Moment: Reflection on Culture, Nature, and Power; Liberty, Ecology, Geography: The Social Thought of Elisee Reclus; *and a forthcoming reinterpretation of social ecology.*

The field of political ecology has developed rapidly in recent times as political theorists and philosophers have sought to redefine their subject matter in response to an increasing interest in environmental issues, to the intensifying ecological crisis, and to the emergence of the ecological worldview as a major paradigm in contemporary thought. In recent ethical theory, these same factors have produced forms of moral extensionism, in which the principles and methodologies of various traditional ethical theories are applied to environmental questions. They have also inspired ethical theories that are more fundamentally transformed through ecological thinking. Similar developments are now taking place in political theory and social ethics, producing a spectrum of positions that express ecological concerns and embody ecological concepts to widely varying degrees.

The term *environmentalism* is sometimes used to refer to a traditional, human-centered approach that sees the natural world as that which *surrounds* human beings, so that *ecology* is reserved for a more holistic view that rethinks the place of humanity within a larger system or whole. According to such a distinction, most ventures into political ecology have thus far remained at the "environmental" level. Most discussions of ecological questions from conservative, liberal, libertarian, and socialist perspectives have merely applied their preexisting categories to environmental issues with little reflection on the implications of ecology for these categories. Some Marxist theorists have, however, moved further in an ecological direction by exploring the affinities between dialectical and ecological thought. Furthermore, social ecology, bioregionalism, and radical environmentalism have consciously sought to develop a political approach that is grounded in an ecological worldview. As a result of these efforts, political ecology has become a vibrant and rapidly evolving field. Nevertheless, the literature in ecological political theory is only beginning to emerge, and no major work that presents a strong theoretical defense of any position has yet appeared.

As the enormity, complexity, and global nature of today's ecological problems have become increasingly more apparent, the need for a political approach to them has gained ever wider recognition. The growth of political ecology has perhaps been evident in no area more than in the various environmental justice movements. Widespread public attention has been given to the Chipko movement in India, to the struggles of the rubber tappers of the Amazon basin, and to the African-American movement against environmental racism in the United States. The transformation of the American environmental movement has been particularly striking. While it was stereotyped as an exclusive preserve of the white middle class, a large proportion of environmental activism in the United States now occurs in poor, working-class, and minority communities.[1] Furthermore, one finds that throughout the world, political movements among peasants and the urban poor that once seemed focused on social justice issues increasingly define themselves as both social and ecological. The growing international green movement has also been an important expression of interest in political ecology. While the United States has lagged behind many other counties, ecological politics in much of the world is now represented through strong green political parties and movements, a few of which have entered into governing coalitions and many of which have exerted significant influence on ruling parties. Such political developments have been accompanied by a rapidly growing literature on green political theory.[2] In view of these developments, the field of political ecology promises to become an important area of political theory and social philosophy, just as environmental ethics has moved to the center of discussion in applied ethics.

While a thorough survey of political ecology would require a sizable book in itself, this section offers an introduction through these comments and representative selections from seven of the most important viewpoints in the field. These positions are free-market environmentalism, green-market environmentalism, liberal environmentalism, socialist ecology, social ecology, bioregionalism, and radical environmentalism.

FREE-MARKET ENVIRONMENTALISM

Free-market environmentalism applies to environmental issues the general principle that the good of all can be promoted through the unrestricted operation of the market economy.[3] Its proponents contend that the proper function of government is the protection of life, liberties, and property rights. They support a minimal state in which government activity consists primarily of police powers, a judiciary, and a stable monetary framework within which the market can operate smoothly.

Free-market advocates reject the view that market forces have led to ecological degradation in the past or that they will produce any severe ecological crisis in the future. Terry L. Anderson and Donald R. Leal contend that predictions of "serious stresses involving population, resources, and environment" are inaccurate because "all of these forecasts fail to take account of the ability of humans to react to problems of scarcity by reducing consumption, finding substitutes, and improving productivity."[4] Their position is thus close to the "cornucopian" viewpoint of economist Julian Simon, who argues that resources and possibilities for growth are unlimited.[5]

Theorists such as Anderson and Leal maintain that clearly defined property rights are the best assurance of optimal environmental decision making (and, indeed, of the best decision making in every area). In their view, ecological problems seldom result from the exercise of property rights in ways that are, as critics of the market often charge, individually rational but socially and ecologically irrational. Rather, they see these problems as the result of an inadequate definition of property rights or of the absence of such rights over certain natural resources, which are consequently not protected. They accept the economic model of human beings as self-interested rational calculators and consider any reliance on altruistic motivation such as civic responsibility or moral values to be ineffectual. Accordingly, they argue that because of the complexity of ecosystems, they cannot be effectively managed by the state but only by private owners who are more familiar with "natural resources." Owners will make good decisions if they are allowed to benefit fully from their property, if they are expected to pay the costs incurred in their use of the property, and if price mechanisms are not "distorted" through political intervention. Furthermore, free-market advocates claim that political decision making will be biased in favor of groups that are more organized and better informed than the majority, who may not have a strong interest in most decisions and are "rationally ignorant" of the issues. According to this analysis, the market ensures efficiency (which is taken as the major criterion by which to judge decision making), whereas democratic electoral processes do not.

As a major alternative to government regulatory agencies, free-market advocates support the idea of holding polluters legally responsible for the effects of their actions. For example, the government might "register pollutants, monitor the flow of pollutants in the atmosphere, and enforce liability for damages."[6] Government activity would thus follow the minimal state model of using policing powers and the court system to protect life and property rights from invasion.

While most free-market approaches exhibit little evidence of the influence of ecological thought, the recent work of Gus diZerega is an exception.[7] DiZerega claims, following Hayek, that societies in which limited government activity takes place constitute "spontaneous orders" and "self-regulating systems" comparable to naturally functioning ecosystems. This outlook assumes that there are "processes of mutual adjustment maintaining the system as a whole," which are upset by government regulatory activity.[8] DiZerega is also atypical of free-market advocates in his strong rejection of certain property rights. In his view, the "right to ruin soil, create nonrecyclable waste, or seriously reduce genetic diversity within a species are all examples of inappropriate property rights."[9] In general, free-market advocates contend that these activities do not violate any rights if they are carried out by property owners and that they will be eliminated to the extent that the public develops a demand for such environmental goods, so that it will be in the interest of owners to "produce" these commodities.

GREEN-MARKET ENVIRONMENTALISM

The best-known green-market advocate is Paul Hawken, who proposes a market-based approach that differs considerably from that of the "free-market" theorists. Hawken believes that the ecological crisis is much more severe and the risks for the future much greater than the latter are usually willing to admit, and he argues that the unregulated market inevitably creates an ecological crisis. The reason in his view is that enterprises have an economic incentive to reduce expenditures and gain a competitive advantage by externalizing costs as environmental damage. Hawken believes that extensive government action is necessary, but he argues that as little as possible of it should consist of administrative regulation and government planning. Rather, he sees the correct policy to be the enactment of "green taxes" that would internalize ecological costs in prices. On this he follows British economist A. C. Pigou, who proposed the idea of "a 'tax to correct maladjustments' on producers, a tax that would be comparable to the avoided cost or unborne expense."[10] Under such a system, producers would have the same kind of incentives as they presently do to produce profitably and efficiently, but the incentives would work to produce cleaner, more ecologically sound products. In Hawken's view, such a system would make sustainability profitable, while harnessing what he sees as the vast creative abilities of the competitive market and individual initiative. It would also permit the phasing out of much of the present tax system as green taxation is introduced over a twenty-year period.

There are several other elements in Hawken's green-market system. One is "an intelligent product system," in which products are licensed to the consumer for use, while the producer retains ownership and responsibility for ecological consequences during the life of the product. He claims that under such a system "products of service would be designed for complete and easy disassembly for reuse, remanufacture, or reclaiming."[11] Another of his innovative economic proposals is the formation of public "utilities" that are a "hybrid of public-private interests"[12] in areas of important "natural resources." These entities would receive levels of return on investments proportional to their fulfillment of needs in an ecologically sound manner.[13] The result of all these policies would be a market that is both substantially "free" in its principles of operation and ecologically sustainable in its functioning.

LIBERAL ENVIRONMENTALISM

Liberal environmentalism rejects the idea that unrestrained market activity can solve ecological problems and contends that significant government regulatory activity is necessary to prevent environmental damage while respecting human rights and maintaining justice. Liberalism (in the American sense of a moderate social democracy) is the guiding ideological orientation of much of contemporary environmental thinking. This is exemplified, for example, in the extensive publications of the Worldwatch Institute and its director, Lester R. Brown, which focus heavily on expanded government regulatory activity and more effective international environmental agreements.[14] Robert C. Paehlke's analysis of the possibilities for a "progressive environmentalism" is typical of a somewhat greener, less bureaucratic version of liberalism that has increasingly been adopted by environmentalists.[15]

In view of the fact that mainstream environmentalism in the United States and many Western countries has remained steadfastly in the liberal tradition, it is rather surprising that a significant literature on liberal environmental political theory has not yet developed. A notable exception is Avner de-Shalit's recent forthright defense of liberal environmentalism, in which he makes a case for government environmental regulation combined with a strong welfare state based on a liberal conception of the common good.[16]

In de-Shalit's view, the liberal concept of "the general good" can be expanded into a more ecological concept. He contends that "anti-chauvinism" is basic to liberalism and that an extension of liberal principles yields effective environmental politics. He proposes that the liberal principle of concern for the interest and welfare of others can reasonably be expanded "to include non-human animals, 'all sentient creatures,' or even 'all living objects' or 'ecosystems.' "[17]

De-Shalit rejects the green-market approach to ecological problems on the grounds that Pigovian taxes are regressive and therefore unjust. In his view, if producers are charged for "externalities," they will pass on the cost to consumers, and the poor will bear a disproportionate burden since they spend much more of their income on energy and other goods that will taxed most heavily. Advocates of green taxes respond that other taxes and even some of the green fees themselves could be made progressive to offset the undoubtedly regressive nature of taxes on energy and other necessities. Equity could thus be reconciled with full-cost pricing, as some liberals are willing to admit.

However, de-Shalit has a stronger criticism against the very idea that "costs" can be internalized in the market price of a commodity. He points out the difficulty of placing a price on sickness and suffering, and the obvious impossibility of assigning a cost to human lives and the destruction of animal life, not to mention species loss and ecosystem destruction. He also notes that cost-benefit-analysis irrationally "discounts" the value of the lives and experience of future generations. His point, like that of many critics of cost-benefit analysis, is that determination of value is an ethical and political question. Neither an unrestricted market nor even a market that theoretically internalizes estimated external costs can assess value in any "objective" manner.

De-Shalit's version of liberalism advocates a process of public debate and political decision making to limit the amount of pollution and environmental destruction in accord with the public's view of its own interest, whatever the market might otherwise have dictated. He rejects the idea that the community's interest is served by the "free market approach" of suits after the fact by specific individuals whose "property rights" are violated by polluters. He asks why the public should not "prevent pollution before workers breathe in smog, or before people are hurt and the environment is damaged."[18] Such a liberalism espouses a concept of citizenship that has a significant communitarian dimension. De-Shalit holds that "environmental imperatives are basically matters of principle that cannot be bargained away in an economic fashion" and that "not all of us think of ourselves primarily as consumers; many of us regard ourselves as citizens as well."[19] He strongly rejects the value-neutrality of the kind of liberalism popularized by John Rawls, Bruce Ackerman, Ronald Dworkin, and other recent theorists. Instead, he believes that there must be a commitment to a common "idea of the good," flowing from "a theory of value, that is, on the idea of an intrinsic, non-instrumental value."[20]

However, other recent liberal theorists have tried to construct a liberal environmentalism based on Rawlsian principles. Rawls's own recent restatement of his position in *Political Liberalism* gives little encouragement to those interested in developing his theory in an ecological direction.[21] Nevertheless, Brent A. Singer attempts an environmentally oriented reformulation of Rawls's "original position" in which hypothetical contracting agents determine the nature of just political institutions and social practices.[22] According to Rawls, there are certain primary goods that any rationally self-interested person will desire. Singer argues that among these goods will be "regular access to potable water, shelter from freezing temperatures, uncontaminated food supplies, and safe air to breathe."[23] Such goods, in Singer's view, are as fundamental as political liberties, such as free speech on or the right to vote, in that they cannot rationally be traded for "social and economic privileges."[24] Singer contends further that Rawlsian assumptions require the consideration of future generations in an assessment of the need for these primary goods, in addition to a consideration of the interests of "many species of animals as well."[25] Finally, he argues that since many people consider "places of great natural beauty" to have spiritual value, a Rawlsian liberal argument can be made for preserving wilderness and various natural sites on grounds of "spiritual freedom" and "liberty of conscience," unless there are overriding considerations of justice.[26] Such an attempt to apply liberalism to environmental issues may have a somewhat more ecological dimension than the free-market approaches they hope to correct, yet the concern for nature seems much closer to the moral extensionism of animal rights theories than the more thoroughgoing ecological (ecocentric or holistic) viewpoints.

It is noteworthy that while neither free-market environmentalism nor liberalism have been at the center of discussion in political ecology, their theoretical assumptions remain dominant in most analyses of the political dimensions of environmental issues. Most approaches have assumed that some balance between the decision-making processes within a corporate capitalist market economy, planning and regulation by centralized nation-states, and agreements between such states is the context in which approaches to environmental issues and growing ecological crisis must be discussed. However, there are several tendencies in ecological thought that propose deeper changes in political and economic systems and a more radically ecological rethinking of political categories.

SOCIALIST ECOLOGY

A variety of socialist ecologies have sought to demonstrate the relevance of Marxian theory to ecological issues, and a large body of theoretical work has emerged in the process.[27] Much of it can be found in the journal *Capitalism, Nature, Socialism,* which has become a major forum for the development of socialist ecology. In fact, its level of ongoing theoretical discussion of issues in political ecology is unsurpassed by any English-language publication dealing with such issues.

One of the most notable developments in ecosocialist theory is James O'Connor's application of Marx's analysis of conditions of production to environmental issues and his resulting thesis that ecological crisis is "the second contradiction of capitalism." O'Connor explains that "red green politics" assumes that "the ecological crisis cannot be resolved without a radical transformation of capitalist production relationships" and that "economic crisis cannot be resolved without an equally radical transformation of capitalist productive forces."[28] Ecosocialists contend that global competition has led to the "externalization of social and environmental costs," which has resulted in a deterioration of environmental and labor conditions. Since these problems are widespread and overstep regional and national boundaries, they cannot be solved through action at the local level to the extent that many greens, bioregionalists, and social ecologists contend. Even seemingly local problems such as transportation, housing costs, and drugs are in fact "global issues pertaining to the way that money capital is allocated worldwide" and therefore require globally coordinated political action.[29] O'Connor concludes that "the only political form" that "might be eminently suited to both ecological problems of site specificity and global issues, is a democratic state—a state in which the administration of the division of social labor is democratically organized."[30]

John Bellamy Foster applies Barry Commoner's well-known "four laws of ecology" to the Marxist critique of capitalism.[31] Commoner summarizes the principles in *The Closing Circle* as (1) everything is connected to everything else, (2) everything must go somewhere, (3) nature knows best, and (4) nothing comes from nothing.[32] Foster argues that capitalism "breaks" all these "laws" and follows instead the principles that "(1) the only lasting connection between things is the cash nexus; (2) it doesn't matter where something goes as long as it doesn't reenter the circuit of capital; (3) the self-regulating market knows best; and (4) nature's bounty is a free gift to the property owner."[33] In Foster's view, the basic rules of capitalist decision making lead to ecological crisis. The maintenance of the level of profit requires constant growth, so that under capitalism any measures to deal with ecological crisis will only contribute to economic crisis.[34] The only real solution to this problem is "the socialization of nature," by which Foster means environmental protection through "centralized management . . . on a national scale" and, ultimately, a worldwide social revolution that achieves "the democratically organized social governance of both production and nature on a global scale."[35]

David Harvey has also developed one of the most sophisticated versions of ecological Marxism to date.[36] He notes that in a capitalistic money economy, much of what is thought of as "the environment" is assigned a monetary value, which has no necessary relationship to any other kind of value it may have. Monetary value becomes the only universal standard of value available and is the one given most recognition by those who hold decision-making power. This dominance of monetary value does not result from its adequacy as a means of evaluation. It is generally agreed that many realities cannot be quantified in monetary terms if in any way at all, and many find a morally objectionable quality in the assessment of human life, species survival, or ancient ecosystems in monetary terms. Harvey argues that the inappropriateness of economistic values becomes increasingly evident the more we consider realities that are complex wholes rather than discrete entities. While monetary values can be attributed, however inadequately, to individual parts of an ecosystem, ecological value is a function of the complex relationship among the various parts of the whole, as well as the relationship of all these parts to the whole. Harvey argues that economistic value also fails when we expand our evaluation over time. He contends that the economic practice of discounting the value of goods that might exist in the future is ecologically irrational since certain goods in nature are the precondition for any other kind of value. Finally, Harvey argues that the fundamental economistic conceptualization of "environmental consequences" as "externalities" is in basic contradiction to an ecological analysis, which looks on processes as intrinsically interrelated parts of a whole.

Harvey focuses much more directly on the project of a radically dialectical approach than most thinkers in the Marxist tradition, for whom issues of class, economic exploitation, ideology, social crisis, historical agency, and revolutionary social transformation often take theoretical priority. This emphasis gives Harvey's analysis a strongly ecological flavor, which is missing in many versions of political ecology. As he points out, "dialectical thinking prioritizes the understanding of processes, flows, fluxes and relations over the analysis of elements, things, structures and organised systems."[37] Ecological thinking gives priority to these same realities. His efforts to make a connection between the two makes Harvey's approach one of the most successful attempts at ecologizing Marxism.

David Pepper has presented an extensive defense of an ecosocialism that remains much closer in many ways to more traditional Marxism. Marxism is "ecological," in his view, precisely because of its completely anthropocentric concern for human welfare. Since socialist economic growth "must be rational, planned development for everyone's benefit," it will "therefore be ecologically benign."[38] Pepper claims the Enlightenment heritage of Marxism and rejects the "green postmodernist" critique of anthropocentrism and the project of the domination of nature. Marxism, he says, rejects a "mastery" of nature that implies "subjection or destruction" but espouses a "domination" that will in fact solve ecological problems. This "domination" consists of "*collective conscious control by humans of their relationship with nature*" and "implies stewardship rather than destruction."[39] It is not anthropocentrism but "short-term individualist antrhopocentrism" that is ecologically destructive. Pepper espouses the traditional socialist idea that centralized planning must play a large role in social decision making and that purely decentralized solutions are naively utopian. He places heavy emphasis on working-class organizations in the development of an ecosocialist movement, though he also sees as an important role for such transitional steps as municipal and local currency systems.[40]

While some ecosocialist thinkers such as Pepper seek to hold on to much of traditional Marxism while attempting to ecologize it, more strongly ecological socialisms continue to emerge.[41] With the collapse of "actually-existing socialism," Marxist and socialist ideas of praxis are in a state that one might see as either disarray or creative ferment. Accordingly, we find some ecosocialisms that look much like environmental liberalism or social democracy, others that propose radical decentralism and participatory democracy reminiscent of social ecology, some that incorporate more traditional Marxist ideas in the concept of an ecologically responsible centralized workers' state, and still others that propose an eclectic "post-modern" socialism inspired by environmentalism and other "new social movements."

SOCIAL ECOLOGY

Social ecology is the other major dialectical approach to ecopolitics. This ecophilosophy comes out of the tradition of social geography and ecological regionalism of Elisée Reclus, Patrick Geddes, and Lewis Mumford; the libertarian communitarianism of Peter Kropotkin, Gustav Landauer, and Martin Buber; and the teleological and dialectical philosophical tradition of Aristotle, Hegel, and Marx. It is also related to recent evolutionary and process philosophies and holistic traditions of both East and West.

Some have identified social ecology narrowly with the ideas of social theorist Murray Bookchin.[42] Others use the term in a rather amorphous and generic sense. Thus, Carolyn Merchant, in *Radical Ecology*, subsumes under social ecology not only those who explicitly use the term but also those who call themselves "socialist ecologists, green Marxists, and red greens."[43] Contrary to both these views, there is a coherent social ecological tradition that is much larger than any one writer's ideas but that is still quite distinct from most (but not all) socialist and Marxist views.

Social ecology applies an evolutionary, developmental view of history and a holistic conception of social unity-in-diversity to social and political issues. As a dialectical holism, it sees beings in nature as *holons*, that is, as both wholes relative to their parts and parts relative to larger wholes. A holistic account attempts to give adequate consideration to both of these dimensions. Thus, social ecology is concerned with the development in society of both individuality and community, so that each member can achieve personal self-realization while developing a sense of identification with and responsibility toward the larger social and natural whole.

Social ecology sees politics as a branch of ethics, that is, as the pursuit of the good life and of self-realization both for the individual person and for the entire community. It interprets this community not only as the various forms of human community in which we participate but also as the diverse ecological communities of which we are also members, up to the level of the biosphere or earth community. Social ecology has sometimes been thought to naively construct a view of ethics or politics on the model of what is found "in nature." Rather, a social ecological view reinterprets ethics in the light of a holistic outlook that attempts to avoid a dualistic split between humanity and nature. A social ecology of value situates human processes of self-realization and value-experience within a wider context of attainment of good in nature. It holds that there is no purely external nature that can serve as a model for human activity or social organization since both the person and the society are thoroughly ecological in their fundamental nature.

The critique of all forms of domination that hinder the evolutionary processes of human and planetary self-realization occupies a central place in social ecological theory. The objects of this critique include the centralized nation-state, concentrated economic power, patriarchy, the technological megamachine, and various authoritarian and repressive ideologies. While social ecologists hold that there is a *system* of domination in which various hierarchical and authoritarian institutions interact, they find some of these to be more central to the social and ecological crisis than others. They see the dominance of economic power as the most powerful determinant of both social injustice and ecological crisis in our present historical epoch. Moreover, they find this power to be embodied in a vast economic and technological machine (globalized corporate capital) and in an all-pervasive, nihilistic culture of consumption.

The political goal of social ecology is the creation of a free, communitarian society in harmony with the natural world; however, the means to this end are vigorously debated. The politics of social ecology has sometimes been identified with Murray Bookchin's "libertarian municipalism," which aims at creating a movement to establish libertarian municipalities governed by municipal or neighborhood assemblies. While the municipalities are to remain politically sovereign, they will form voluntary "confederations" to organize themselves politically and economically beyond the local level. In Bookchin's view, these confederations will eventually create a condition of "dual power" in which they will be able to challenge the power of the nation-state and the global corporate economic power with which it is allied. A system of libertarian communism, in which distribution will be according to need, will then be established. Private ownership of the means of production will be abolished and replaced by community-controlled enterprises. Hierarchical social institutions, including patriarchy, will be destroyed, and the quest for human domination of nature will come to an end.

Many social ecologists question libertarian municipalism as both effective practical politics and an adequate vision of a future society. Rather, they incorporate some aspects of Bookchin's municipalism in a broader ecological communitarianism. There is general agreement among social ecologists that there must be a decentralization of political power away from the centralized state, and of economic power away from large corporations, and that more human-scale technologies are essential both socially and ecologically. However, many support a variety of social, political, and economic strategies as a means of working toward a free, ecological society. Social ecologists are often interested in creating and promoting producer and consumer cooperatives, land trusts and housing cooperatives, ecological agriculture, ecologically sound technologies, municipal citizens' movements, green political parties, environmental justice groups, publishing projects, environmental defense groups, and many other efforts at social and ecological regeneration.

Social ecologists often take a comprehensive, theoretically grounded but experimental approach to social transformation. They base their efforts on the needs and interests of local communities, the possibilities for social creativity that exist in a historically determinate situation, and the relationship between such diverse particularity and the evolving global whole. Such a nondogmatic, experimental social ecology takes as the measure of its success the organic growth of a compassionate, cooperative, ecological culture, rooted in the specificity of history and place but developing growing interconnections within the entire earth community.

Over the past decade, social ecology has gained some notoriety through Murray Bookchin's often bitter attacks on other philosophical positions, including most notably deep ecology but also ecofeminism and ecosocialism and, more recently, bioregionalism, ecocommunitarianism, and various forms of ecoanarchism. Bookchin gained some attention for his views through his claims of links between deep ecology and racist and politically reactionary ideas.[44] His argument was based primarily on statements by several deep ecologists that supported the withholding of aid to famine victims, opposed immigration on both ecological and cultural grounds, and held that AIDS and other diseases were a natural process of controlling human overpopulation. Interestingly, Bookchin's attack was directed at deep ecological theorists, very few of whom support any of the views he attributes to them, rather than a thinker like Garrett Hardin, who is well known for his essays opposing immigration and aid to famine victims and who has proposed a world government with powers to control population.[45]

The most important political distinction between social and deep ecologists has not in reality been any supposed ecofascist tendencies of the latter. Rather, social ecologists have undertaken a more systematic analysis of social institutions and their relationship to ecological problems. Deep ecologists have in general devoted little attention to social analysis and have adopted a spectrum of political positions, ranging from a rather apolitical emphasis on the need for changes in personal values and "lifestyle," to a liberal and reformist politics, and even to a revolutionary opposition to the megamachine that aims at the overthrow of industrial civilization. Recently, however, deep ecologists have begun to undertake quite serious analyses of social and political issues, as exhibited in the work of Robyn Eckersley and Andrew McLaughlin, and the theoretical gap between social and deep ecology is narrowing considerably.[46] In addition, social ecologists have begun to discuss commonalities with some aspects of deep ecology, and useful dialogue has begun to replace sectarian quarreling.[47]

BIOREGIONALISM

Bioregionalism is the tradition in political ecology that has gone furthest in taking account of the ecological in the most concrete sense. It differs from other ecological approaches in that it goes beyond respect for, identification with, defense of, and general understanding of nature. While it agrees with all of these goals, it focuses on the process of "reinhabitation": the creation of a culture and way of life based on a very specific, detailed knowledge of the ecological realities of the larger natural community in which the human community participates.[48] Furthermore, it explores forms of governance based on such a bioregional consciousness. Its bioregional values call into question the concept of the nation-state and political boundaries, on the one hand, and the homogenizing culture of consumption, on the other. Its vision of social transformation does not appeal to any abstract principles of rights or justice or contentious ideas of individual or group interests. Rather, it is rooted in realities that are very concrete and experiential and, in its view, might form a strong basis for personal and communal identification.

For two decades there has been an organized bioregional movement advocating the rediscovery of a sense of place (reinhabitation), the rooting of culture in the particularities of natural regions, and the development of social and political institutions that reflect bioregional realities. The term *bioregionalism* was first used in this sense by Peter Berg and Raymond Dasmann of the Planet Drum Foundation in San Francisco.[49] That organization's journal, *Raise the Stakes,* has been the most important ongoing arena for the discussion of bioregional ideas. In addition, a series of semiannual Turtle Island (North American) Bioregional Congresses have contributed to the movement's growing cultural and political significance.

Bioregionalism is sometimes described as a "watershed politics" in view of its focus on bioregions (typified by watersheds of rivers and streams) as the context of political activity. Bioregionalism does not stress politics in the electoral and other traditional senses as much as it proposes a broader cultural kind based on the development of local bioregional institutions. However, there have been efforts to draw out its more specific organizational implications. For example, Kirkpatrick Sale compares the "bioregional paradigm" and the dominant "industrioscientific paradigm" and finds the former's conception of "polity" to stress "decentralization, complementarity, and diversity" as opposed to the latter's emphasis on "centralization, hierarchy, and uniformity."[50]

Sale's conception of bioregional political institutions is very similar to that of social ecologist Murray Bookchin (despite harsh attacks on Sale by Bookchin and his colleague Janet Biehl). Sale states that bioregionalism rejects social hierarchy and domination as "unecological," and he proposes an egalitarian, decentralized form of social organization. This would include community ownership of productive enterprises and decision making at the local level, with local units ranging from villages of perhaps 1,000 people up to larger towns and neighborhoods of 5,000 to 10,000 inhabitants. Bioregional politics is to be based on informal decision making by those with competence and experience, the election of a small number of community officials, and the retention of ultimate power by the whole body of citizens.[51] As in Bookchin's municipalism, Sale envisions cooperation on a larger scale through voluntary confederations, although their boundaries would be determined bioregionally.[52] Unlike Bookchin, Sale foresees the persistence of some market exchange between communities alongside barter and cooperative sharing. He does not present any detailed picture of how such a decentralized cooperative economy might operate. He assumes, however, that bioregionalism would require a decentralization not only of political and economic power but also of population. He advocates the voluntary resettlement of the urban population into ecologically balanced cities of much smaller scale than at present,[53] and he notes that "division" is "nature's way" to achieve "salubrity and balance."[54]

Donald Alexander, in "Bioregionalism: Science or Sensibility?" argues that there is a need to overcome the split between those who see bioregionalism, sometimes rather reductively, as a science and those who see it primarily "as an environmental ethic and as a cultural sensibility."[55] Alexander sees Lewis Mumford as the inspiration for a bioregionalism that combines these two aspects in a "dialectical manner." He recommends Mumford's view of the region as "a complex of geographic, economic and cultural elements. Not found as a finished product in nature, not solely the creation of human will and fantasy, the region, like its corresponding artifact, the city, is a collective work of art."[56]

While bioregionalists will certainly benefit from reflection on Mumford's ecological regionalism, the kind of regional vision that he expresses is already present within their tradition. The work of Gary Snyder, the major intellectual influence on the bioregional movement, expresses such a rich conception of natural and cultural regions.[57] Snyder encourages us to learn from the wisdom of "peoples for whom there is no great dichotomy between their culture and nature" and for whom "to be well educated is to have learned the songs, proverbs, stories, sayings, myths (and technologies) that come with [an] experiencing of the nonhuman members of the local ecological community."[58] Bioregional reinhabitation means becoming part of such a culture of nature, rooted in a specific place. Snyder does not spell out the political implications of his regionalism in a programmatic manner, although a strong political critique is implicit in it. For Snyder, on the one hand, it is wild nature and organically rooted local and regional culture that are the source of ecological and social order. On the other hand, "it is the State itself which is inherently greedy, destabilizing, entropic, disorderly, and illegitimate," so that the political question becomes "how the whole human race can regain self-determination in place after centuries of having been disenfranchised by hierarchy and/or centralized power."[59]

RADICAL ENVIRONMENTALISM

Radical environmentalism is a form of political ecology that has emerged from grassroots ecological activism, especially the wilderness preservation movement and the organization Earth First!. It constitutes a distinctive approach to ecological politics, first, because it has an explicit ecophilosophical basis in deep ecology and, second, because of its support for an uncompromising politics of direct action.[60]

Radical environmentalists take two primary approaches to direct action. The first is civil disobedience, which includes such actions as sit-ins at corporate and government offices, blocking logging roads, tree sitting, chaining participants to equipment, and unfurling banners. As Christopher Manes notes, the radical environmentalist conception of civil disobedience is embodied in "the Peaceful Direct Action Code" used in many such protests. In this statement, participants assert that their "attitude is one of openness, friendliness, and respect toward all beings [they] encounter"; that they "will use no violence, verbal or physical, toward any being"; that they "will not damage any property and will discourage others from doing so"; that they "will not run";

and that they "will carry no weapons."[61] Radical environmentalists see such activity as an extension of civil rights and justice movements of the past, so that the rights of nature are now defended through tactics that have long been utilized in struggles for human rights. Environmental civil disobedience is thus in the classical tradition of Thoreauvian and Gandhian nonviolent protest.

The other form of direct action, "monkeywrenching" or "ecotage," has produced much more controversy, with attention focused especially on actual or alleged activities of Earth First! members. As Dave Foreman states, "Monkeywrenching is non-violent resistance to the destruction of natural diversity and wilderness."[62] It is an anarchic, nonhierarchical approach in which small groups of activists prevent ecodestruction by using the simplest, safest, and most effective methods. These methods usually aim at the disablement of equipment used in the ecodestruction. Such actions are not designed to promote social change by example or by influencing public opinion, but rather to achieve immediate pragmatic results. "What is important is stopping the damage; the monkeywrencher, like the guerrilla fighter, is more effective when avoiding capture and being able to return again and again."[63] The ethics and pragmatic value of such tactics of ecodefense continue to be debated in the radical environmental movement and among environmental ethicists.

Manes explains the philosophical basis for radical environmental politics as the "identification with a larger self" proposed by some forms of deep ecology. "If our selves belong to a larger self that encompasses the whole biological community in which we dwell, then an attack on the trees, the wolves, the rivers, is an attack upon all of us. Defense of place becomes a form of self-defense, which in most ethical and legal systems would be ample grounds for spiking a tree or ruining a tire."[64] There is some ambiguity in this concept of ecodefense. If defense of the wild is quite literally interpreted as self-defense, one might conclude that it would justifiably include injury to the attacker since the attackers actually kill trees, wolves, and sometimes whole ecosystems. However, radical environmentalists overwhelmingly reject such retaliation and strongly oppose any sort of injury to human beings. The ethical basis for doing so has not been clarified. If the concept of the larger self and self-defense is not to be taken so literally, further discussion of the nature of such expanded selfhood is necessary.

What is clear is that radical environmentalism is grounded in a deep ecological sensibility that has usually been expressed most strongly in a love of and identification with wilderness. At one time, radical environmentalism was identified almost exclusively with wilderness defense. More recently, however, there has been within the radical environmental movement (particularly in the case of Earth First!) a strong shift toward concern with social and economic issues, even attempts to combine wilderness preservation and ecodefense with labor organizing and campaigns against transnational corporations. The gap between deep ecology-inspired radical environmentalists and social ecologists has therefore narrowed.

Foreman still sees the major concern of radical environmentalism to be the defense of the wild. Manes agrees but argues that defending it successfully requires far-reaching social, economic, and political changes. Foreman has said that radical environmentalism "does not aim to overthrow any social, political, or economic system."[65] However, Manes depicts its goal of social transformation as more far-reaching in many ways that that envisioned by most revolutionary movements. Radical environmentalism, he says, proposes "an end to all commercial logging"; the restoration of "large wilderness areas"; "the banning of all pesticides and toxic wastes"; the "elimination of the automobile, coal-fired power plants, and manufacturing processes using petrochemicals"; "the end of monoculture"; and a considerable "reduction of the human population"—in short, radical environmentalism is willing to contemplate the destruction of "modern industrial society as we know it."[66] As much as ecosocialism or social ecology, it foresees a fundamental transformation of the global power structure, in that its goals "will certainly entail eradicating the relentless engine of environmental decline, the multinational corporation."[67]

NOTES

1. See Jim Schwab, *Deeper Shades of Green: The Rise of Blue-Collar and Minority Environmentalism in America* (San Francisco: Sierra Club Books, 1994).
2. See Dan Coleman, *Ecopolitics: Building a Green Society* (New Brunswick, NJ: Rutgers University Press, 1994); Peter Dickens, *Society and Nature: Toward a Green Social Theory* (London: Harvester Wheatsheaf, 1992); Andrew Dobson, *Green Political Thought* (London: HarperCollins, 1991); Robert Goodin, *Green Political Theory* (Oxford: Polity Press, 1992); Roy Morrison, *Ecological Democracy* (Boston: South End Press, 1995); and Brian Tokar, *The Green Alternative: Creating an Ecological Future* (Philadelphia: New Society Publishers, 1992).
3. This position is sometimes called a "conservative" view, though some of its proponents are careful to identify their position as a classical liberal or libertarian one. It is important to note that there is also a traditionalist conservative position that is much more inclined toward environmental protection and more willing to accept legal regulations. As John R. E. Bliese states in "The Conservative Case for the Environment," *Intercollegiate Review* (1996): 28–36, conservatives should "accept their duty to design our economy so that we produce our goods in a way that does not impair the planet's ability to provide for future generations" and practice the traditionalist virtue of "piety, which includes a proper veneration for this earth" (pp. 33–34). See also Bliese, "Traditional Conservatism and Environmental Ethics," *Environmental Ethics,* 19 (1997), 135–151.
4. Terry L. Anderson and Donal R. Leal, *Free Market Environmentalism* (San Francisco: Pacific Research Institute for Public Policy, 1991), p. 2.
5. See Julian L. Simon, *The Ultimate Resource* (Princeton, NJ: Princeton University Press, 1981), especially chap. 3, "Can the Supply of Natural Resources Really Be Infinite? Yes!"
6. Anderson and Leal, *Free Market Environmentalism,* p. 166.
7. See Gus DiZerega, "Empathy, Society, Nature, and the Relational Self: Deep Ecology and Liberal Modernity," *Social Theory and Practice* 21 (1995): 239–69.
8. Ibid., p. 264.
9. Ibid., pp. 265–66.

10. Paul Hawken, *The Ecology of Commerce: A Declaration of Sustainability* (New York: HarperBusiness, 1993), p. 82.
11. Ibid., p. 68.
12. Paul Hawken, "A Declaration of Sustainability," *The Utne Reader* 59 (September/October 1993): 57.
13. It is not clear how Hawken's desire for minimal regulatory activity can be reconciled with such a proposal.
14. See the annual editions of *State of the World* (New York: Norton, 1984–present).
15. See Robert C. Paehlke, *Environmentalism and the Future of Progressive Politics* (New Haven, CT: Yale University Press, 1989), especially his "core priorities for a contemporary environmental progressivism" (pp. 270–72), and his list of ways in which environmentalists can be distinguished from "neo-conservatives" and "traditional progressives" (pp. 276–77). Paehlke identifies himself as a "moderate social democrat" (p. 311).
16. Avner de-Shalit, "Is Liberalism Environment-Friendly?" *Social Theory and Practice* 21(1995):287–314.
17. Ibid., p. 289.
18. Ibid., p. 301.
19. Ibid., p. 306.
20. Ibid., p. 307.
21. See John Rawls, *Political Liberalism* (New York: Columbia University Press, 1993), pp. 21, 245–46. He states that his theory of justice as fairness does not offer guidance concerning obligations to other species and to "the rest of nature" (p. 21).
22. Brent A. Singer, "An Extension of Rawls' Theory of Justice to Environmental Ethics" *Environmental Ethics* 10 (1988): 217–31.
23. Ibid., p. 219.
24. Ibid.
25. Ibid., pp. 220, 223.
26. Ibid., p. 230.
27. For defenses of the ecological nature of Marx's own thought, see Howard L. Parson (ed.), *Marx and Engels on Ecology* (Westport, CT: Greenwood Press, 1977), and Donald C. Lee, "On the Marxian View of the Relationship Between Man and Nature," *Environmental Ethics* 2 (1980): 3–16. For critiques of this view, see Val Routely [Plumwood], "On Karl Marx as Environmental Hero" *Environmental Ethics* 3 (1981): 237–44, and John Clark, "Marx's Inorganic Body" *Environmental Ethics* 11 (1989): 243–58. Many eco-Marxists now recognize the problematical character of Marx's concept of nature and are attempting to develop a more consistently dialectical view.
28. James O'Connor, "Socialism and Ecology," p. 407. See also James O'Connor, "Capitalism, Nature, Socialism: A Theoretical Introduction" *Capitalism, Nature, Socialism* 1, 1 (1988): 11–38.
29. O'Connor, "Socialism and Ecology," p. 407.
30. Ibid., p. 407.
31. John Bellamy Foster, *The Vulnerable Planet: A Short Economic History of the Environment* (New York: Monthly Review Press, 1995).
32. Barry Commoner, *The Closing Circle: Nature, Man and Technology* (New York: Knopf, 1971), pp. 33–46.
33. Foster, *Vulnerable Planet,* p. 120.
34. Ibid., p. 133.
35. Ibid., p. 142.
36. David Harvey, "The Nature of Environment: The Dialectics of Social and Environmental Change" in Ralph Miliband and Leo Panich (eds.), *Real Problems, False Solutions: Socialist Register 1993* (London: Merlin Press, 1993).
37. Ibid., p. 34.

38. David Pepper, *Ecosocialism: From Deep Ecology to Social Justice* (London: Routledge, 1993), p. 219.
39. Ibid., p. 221 (Pepper's emphasis).
40. Ibid., pp. 222, 229–31.
41. Robyn Eckersley explores the possibility of a convergence between deep ecology and ecosocialism in "The Political Challenge of Left-Green Reconciliation," *Capitalism, Nature, Socialism* 6 (1995): 24. The most theoretically significant development is Joel Kovel's synthesis of ecosocialism with aspects of psychoanalytic theory, phenomenology, social ecology, and Eastern and Western spiritual traditions. See *History and Spirit: An Inquiry Into the Philosophy of Liberation* (Boston: Beacon Press, 1991), and "Ecological Marxism and Dialectic," *Capitalism, Nature, Socialism* 6 (1995): 31–50. See also Ted Benton, *The Greening of Marxism* (New York: Guilford Press, 1996), for a spectrum of ecosocialist approaches, including Eckersley's "Socialism and Ecocentrism: Toward a New Synthesis."
42. See Peter List, *Radical Environmentalism: Philosophy and Tactics* (Belmont, CA: Wadsworth, 1993), p. 11.
43. Carolyn Merchant, *Radical Ecology: The Search for a Livable World* (New York: Routledge, 1992), p. 134.
44. See, for example, Murray Bookchin, "Social Ecology Versus Deep Ecology," *Socialist Review* 88 (1988): 11–29.
45. See Garrett Hardin, "The Tragedy of the Commons," *Science*, 162 (December 1968): 1243–48, and (the article that is probably reprinted most in current applied ethics texts) "Living on a Lifeboat," *Bioscience* 24 (1974): 561–68. For a careful response to what might be seen as ecofascist tendencies in recent ecological thought, see Michael E. Zimmerman, "The Threat of Ecofascism," *Social Theory and Practice* 21 (1995): 207–38.
46. See Robyn Eckersley, *Environmentalism and Political Theory* (Albany: State University of New York Press, 1992), and Andrew McLaughlin, *Regarding Nature: Industrialism and Deep Ecology* (Albany: State University of New York Press, 1993).
47. See Joel Kovel, "The Marriage of Radical Ecologies," and George Bradford, "Toward a Deep Social Ecology," in Michael Zimmerman et al., *Environmental Philosophy: From Animal Rights to Radical Ecology* (Englewood Cliffs, NJ: Prentice Hall, 1993), pp. 406–17 and 418–437, respectively; and John Clark, "How Wide Is Deep Ecology?" *Inquiry* 39 (June 1996): 189–201.
48. For a good sample of bioregional writings, see C. Plant et al., *Home! A Bioregional Reader* (Philadelphia: New Society Publishers, 1990).
49. See Peter Berg (ed.), *Reinhabiting a Separate Country: A Bioregional Anthology of Northern California* (San Francisco: Planet Drum Foundation, 1978).
50. Kirkpatrick Sale, *Dwellers in the Land: The Bioregional Vision* (San Francisco: Sierra Club Books, 1985), p. 50.
51. Ibid., p. 94.
52. Ibid., p. 96.
53. Ibid., p. 116.
54. Ibid., p. 127.
55. Donald Alexander, "Bioregionalism: Science or Sensibility?" *Environmental Ethics* 12 (1990): 164.
56. Ibid., p. 172.
57. Snyder's work plays a very important role in contemporary ecophilosophy and political ecology. While he is a major figure in bioregionalism, he has also had enormous influence on many deep and social ecologists. His broad ecological vision; his exploration of the complex interconnections between nature and culture; his critique of centralized power; and his synthesis of Eastern, Western, and indigenous traditions help one find the common ground in ecophilosophy.
58. Gary Snyder, *The Practice of the Wild* (San Francisco: North Point Press, 1990), p. 18.

59. Ibid., pp. 41–43.
60. The term *radical environmentalism* is sometimes taken in a generic sense to refer to a wide range of ecophilosophies and ecological movements. However, it is used in a narrower sense by direct-actionist groups such as Earth First!, which calls itself a "radical environmental movement," and in Christopher Manes's theoretical defense of the movement, *Green Rage: Radical Environmentalism and the Unmaking of Civilization* (Boston: Little, Brown, 1990).
61. Ibid., pp. 168–69.
62. David Foreman, *Confessions of an Eco-Warrior* (New York: Harmony Books, 1991), p. 113. See also David Foreman and Bill Haywood (eds.), *Ecodefense: A Field Guide to Monkeywrenching* (Tucson, AZ: Ned Ludd Books, 1987). Foreman, well known as a cofounder of Earth First!, left that organization to help start the nature preservation journal *Wild Earth* and is now a national director of the Sierra Club.
63. Foreman, *Confessions*, p. 131.
64. Manes, *Green Rage*, p. 177.
65. Foreman, *Confessions*, p. 115.
66. Manes, *Green Rage*, p. 34.
67. Ibid.

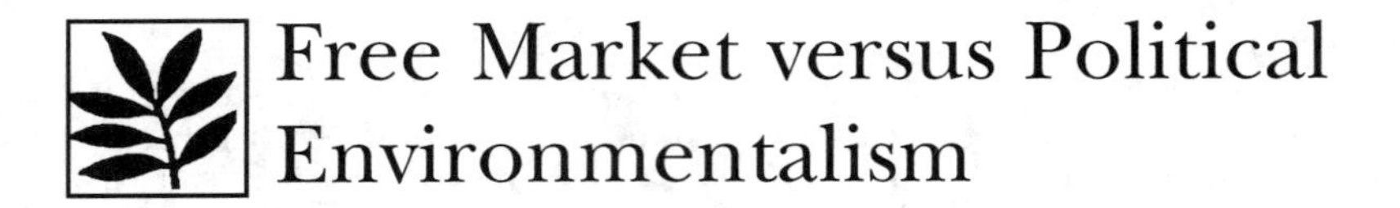

Free Market versus Political Environmentalism

Terry L. Anderson and Donald R. Leal

Terry L. Anderson is executive director for the Political Economy Research Center (PERC) in Bozeman, Montana. David R. Leal is a senior associate at PERC.

In the West it is often said, "Whiskey is for drinkin' and water is for fightin'." These words ring loud and clear when environmental and other demands compete with agricultural needs for water. Fortunately, market-based solutions represent an alternative to this prescription and a possible solution to broader problems of water resource allocation.

A recent incident on Montana's Ruby River illustrates part of the difficulty with present approaches to water resource management. By May of 1987, minimal snowpack, little spring rain, and a heavy demand for irrigation had reduced a 1.5 mile section of the Ruby to a trickle. Hundreds of trout were stranded in overheated pools.[1] Sadly, as fish were dying in the Ruby River, six inches of water was standing in nearby fields, where it was of little or no use. This water could have kept the Ruby flowing and the fish alive if it had been transferred from irrigation to instream flows. Montana's Department of Natural Resources and Conservation and the irrigators eventually agreed to get water flowing again in the Ruby. Unfortunately, the effort was too little and too late to save many of the trout.

Because of the urgency of the situation, legal action would have been largely futile. An alternative would have been to lease from the irrigators some of the water that they were diverting from the river. It would have been relatively easy and inexpensive for a private conservation group like Trout Unlimited to lease the water from irrigators and transfer it to instream flows. Indeed, the amount of water needed to keep the fish alive could have been rented for less than $4,000.[2] With an annual budget of several million dollars, Trout Unlimited could have purchased the water if it had been permitted to do so.[3] Herein lies the problem. At the time of the incident, legitimate use of

This essay originally appeared in the *Harvard Journal of Law and Public Policy*, 15, 2 (Spring, 1992), 297–310. Reprinted with permission.

the water required diversion. Under western water law, private parties were not permitted to use water for instream purposes, except for hydroelectric power generation.[4] Today, the good news is that water marketing is becoming increasingly acceptable in the West. In 1989, conservation groups sought legislation in Montana that would allow water to be purchased or leased from appropriators on a "willing buyer, willing seller" basis. While the groups failed to convince legislators to allow private parties to engage in such transactions, new legislation does allow the Department of Fish, Wildlife, and Parks to experiment with water leasing to enhance instream flows. Colorado, Utah, and Arizona permit private and public entities to acquire existing consumptive rights to augment instream flows.[5]

The market for federal water is also expanding, although much remains to be done.[6] The U.S. Department of Interior in 1987 adopted a policy in support of voluntary transfers of reclamation water, including water markets.[7] Without the typical restrictions on end-use and location, the markets for federal water will ensure correct water prices, thereby promoting greater efficiency and conservation.[8]

Support for water marketing has increased substantially over the last decade, with some of the strongest support coming from environmental groups like the Environmental Defense Fund (EDF). EDF's economist Zach Willey and others have endorsed water markets as a key step in reforming water policy.[9] Even Sandra Postel of Worldwatch Institute, a group not noted for its support of free market environmentalism, has suggested that water markets offer a "promising remedy."[10]

I. "BLISS POINT" ECONOMICS

Despite the growing acceptance of water markets, some environmental officials have failed to embrace the idea. A recent statement by South Africa's Department of Water Affairs (DWA) is one example of this reluctance:

> With the increasing scarcity of water, the hierarchy of priorities for allocation must be further refined by means of appropriate benefit-cost and other economic studies. Within the requirements of contributing to the quality of life, the allocation of water must be based on the economic interests and the social demands of the country as a whole. The optimal utilization of resources, balanced growth and the minimal disruption of the economy are the most important criteria in this regard. . . . The DWA does, however, endeavour to provide for all rightful and reasonable demands within a particular catchment area before considering exports to other areas. The fairness of demands within catchment areas will, however, always be weighed against national requirements.[11]

This analytic approach is rooted in "scientific management," an economic paradigm that stresses marginal analysis by dispassionate "experts," who measure the benefits and costs of alternative allocations with the goal of maximizing social welfare.[12] The paradigm does not consider parties' intentions or the costs of information. Instead, it assumes that benefits and costs are known, and that the process of decisionmaking is simple, if one uses the appropriate model to reach the desired "bliss point" for society.

This same paradigm emphasizes the potential for market failure. In the dominant economics textbook used during the 1960s and the 1970s, Paul Samuelson states:

> Wherever there are externalities, a strong case can be made for supplanting complete individualism by some kind of group action. . . . The reader can think of countless . . . externalities where economics would suggest some kind of limitations on individual freedom in the interest of all.[13]

The emphasis on externalities "contains an implicit bias toward 'intervention solutions' for externalities in the form of taxes, subsidies, regulations, and prohibitions" because it suggests "that externalities necessitate 'corrective' government action."[14]

This emphasis on corrective action often explicitly assumes that governmental decisions will maximize social welfare. In a resource economics textbook, Hartwick and Olewiler write: "'[T]he government' is a separate agent acting in the social interest when activity by individuals fails to bring about a social optimum. . . . [W]e discuss some limits of this approach, but it permits us to abstract from the details of the political process."[15] By abstracting from the details of the political process, however, they ignore the incentives inherent in that process. Because politicians and bureaucrats are rewarded for responding to political pressure groups, there is no guarantee that the values of unorganized interests will be taken into account. Daniel Bromley claims that governmental agencies are

> politically responsible to the citizenry through . . . elections and ministerial direction. However imperfectly this may work, the presumption must be that the wishes of the full citizenry are more properly catered to than would be the case if all environmental protection were left to the ability to pay by a few members of society given to philanthropy.[16]

Compare, however, the factors that influence the relationship between policymakers and bureaucrats with those that influence the relationship between policymakers and voters. First, with most issues, voters face relatively high information costs, creating the phenomenon of "rational ignorance." Second, the only exceptions to this general rule are issues that directly concern the voter. For example, the average urban dweller will likely know more about mass transit issues than agricultural matters. Third, those who are directly affected by policies often find it in their interest to spend time and money trying to influence decisionmaking in the political arena. Thus, because the costs of policies are often diffused and the benefits concentrated, special interest groups (that is, people whose interests are directly affected by a policy) will be well-organized and highly influential in the political arena. Those who have only an indirect or perhaps no interest at stake will remain largely indifferent. This rational indifference and the special interest groups combine to undermine the presumption that in the political arena the full citizenry are more properly catered to by intervention than by market-based incentives.

Government decisionmakers do not necessarily have access to the full information required to maximize society's welfare. As F.A. Hayek has pointed out,

> [T]he economic problem of society is . . . not merely a problem of how to allocate "given" resources—if "given" is taken to mean given to a single mind which deliberately solves the problem set by these "data." It is rather a problem of how to secure the best use of resources known to any of the members of society, for ends whose relative importance only those individuals know. Or, to put it briefly, it is a problem of the utilization of knowledge not given to anyone in its totality.[17]

Assessing the government's "corrective ability" requires only that we examine the record of bureaucratic control of land and water resources in this country. Millions of acres that the U.S. Forest Service manages are denuded of trees at tremendous expense to the environment and to the taxpayer. In Alaska's Tongass National Forest, for example, the federal government spends 98 cents for every 2 cents worth of timber harvested.[18] Another example is water policy. The Bureau of Reclamation built huge dams, flooding vast tracts of land, and delivered the water to farms growing mostly subsidized products. Prices charged for the water seldom cover even the incremental cost of delivering the water, let alone the capital or environmental costs associated with the project. As a result, farmers demand more and more water to produce surplus crops.[19]

Government is not infallible. It is clear, as Castle writes, that "[m]arket 'failure' in some abstract sense does not mean that a nonmarket [*sic*] alternative will not also fail in the same or in some other abstract sense."[20]

II. FREE MARKET ENVIRONMENTALISM

Free market environmentalism considers the potential for market solutions and the problems with political ones. Anthony Fisher summarizes the change in emphasis:

> We have already abandoned the assumption of a complete set of competitive markets. . . . But if we now similarly abandon the notion of a perfect planner, it is not clear, in my judgement, that the government will do any better. Apart from the question of the planner's motivation to behave in the way assumed in our models, to allocate resource [*sic*] efficiently, there is the question of his ability to do so.[21]

Free market environmentalism challenges both the government planner's motivation and his ability. The approach recognizes two facts. First, *incentives affect all human behavior.* Professional managers, no matter how well-intended, respond to the incentives they face. This holds as true for bureaucrats as it does for profit-maximizing owners of firms. We readily accept the argument that business operators would dump wastes into the airways if they did not have to pay for the costs of their action. We often fail, however, to recognize the same elements at work in the political sector. If a politician is not personally accountable for allowing oil development on federal lands or for permitting an agency to dump hazardous wastes into the environment, then we can expect too much development and too much dumping. Moreover, when the beneficiaries of these activities do not have to pay the full costs, they will demand more of each from their political representatives.

Second, *information costs are positive.* In a world of scarcity, private and public decisionmakers must obtain information on the relative values of resource uses. When one use competes with another, tradeoffs are inevitable. Unfortunately, these tradeoffs are complicated when decisionmakers lack value information. In the absence of markets, a resource manager must rely on his own personal valuation of the tradeoffs or on information provided by special interest groups. In either case, there is little reason to believe that these values will necessarily reflect the social good.

With markets for commodities and amenities, prices provide the necessary information for making tradeoffs. Consider the influence a market for recreational and environmental amenities has had on International Paper (IP), one of the nation's largest private timber landowners. When leasing recreational opportunities on its land, IP has systematically improved wildlife habitats. IP's fee hunting and fee recreation programs yield approximately twenty-five percent of the operating profits in the mid-South region, with timber making up the rest. Populations of white-tailed deer, turkeys, rabbits, bobwhite quail, and mourning dove benefit from controlled burns that stimulate forage and from protected riparian zones that preserve cover and food. According to IP's wildlife managers, profits from these programs induced company executives to listen to proposals for improving habitats at the expense of timber production.[22] In contrast, political managers in the Forest Service, who "give away" recreational activities on federal lands, lack this price information and have less incentive to react to changing values.

Free market environmentalism stresses the importance of well-specified property rights as the proper mechanism to provide the incentive for entrepreneurs acting on specific time and space information. Before a landowner can sell access to those interested in recreation or an easement to a land trust, there must be clearly defined and enforceable property rights to the resources. With such rights, imaginative entrepreneurs can capture the value of environmental amenities. For example, a stream owner who can devise ways of charging fishermen can internalize the benefits and costs of improving fishing quality. Similarly, a subdivider who puts covenants on deeds to preserve open space, improve views, and harmonize development with the environment, establishes property rights to these values and captures value in higher asset-prices.

III. FROM THE IMAGINABLE TO THE IMAGINATIVE

Skeptics are quick to point out that harmonizing wildlife needs with timber harvesting or livestock grazing is an easy solution and that free market environmentalism fails to provide solutions to the tougher problems. For example, although wildlife migrate across boundaries, landowners can at least benefit by improved management; in *the open ocean, however, there are no boundaries and no ways to fence in fish.* The result is over-fishing like that which occurs in the North Sea.[23]

The free market environmentalist approach to this problem would establish property rights through individual transferable quotas (ITQs). ITQs give each fisherman a right to a proportion of the catch, thereby eliminating the incentive to over-fish the resource. The market establishes a price for the quota and more efficient fishermen buy quotas from those who are less efficient. The ITQ system has been successfully applied in Australia and New Zealand. Six months after ITQs were applied to Australia's bluefin tuna fishery, fleet capacity dropped by sixty percent, the value of quotas doubled, and the average size of the catch rose as operators with access to larger fish bought out operators with access to smaller fish.[24] Similarly, two years after ITQs were applied to New Zealand's abalone fishery, the value of quotas increased nearly six-fold and abalone numbers increased with the aid of a new breeding program which fishermen financed.[25]

Free market environmentalism can also solve pollution problems through common law tort remedies if property rights are established and polluters can be identified. In England, an association of anglers and clubs has monitored pollution since the 1960s. Angler's Cooperative Association officials point out that the organization was protecting the environment twenty years before the general public became concerned and pressured the government to act:

> The A.C.A. has had an extraordinary record of success. It has fought hundreds of pollution cases (not all of which have gone to court) and only lost one minor one on a legal technicality. The damages it has secured on behalf of members, and member clubs, runs [*sic*] into hundreds of thousands of pounds.[26]

The British experience suggests that pollution could be reduced if private fishing rights were established in the United States. Liability rules would evolve so that owners of fishing rights could bring suit against an upstream polluter whose effluent damaged their fishing resource.[27]

The challenge to the property rights approach occurs when the polluter cannot be identified and damages cannot be assessed. For example, with acid rain, it is clear that sulfur dioxide is the cause, but the actual damage caused by a specific polluter will vary with air currents, moisture, and other climatic conditions. A free market environmentalist solution would require "branding" the pollutants so it would be clear who is causing what damage.

New technology offers the potential for such branding by introducing tracers into the smoke stacks of suspected polluters. This technology was applied in the Winter Haze Intensive Tracer Experiment in Canyonlands National Park, Utah. The park commonly experiences a haze-causing pollutant that some suspected originated from a coal-fired generating plant several hundred miles away. To identify the source, chemical tracers that mimicked the pollutant were introduced into the stack of the plant and a battery of air monitoring stations was set up around the park. The experiment concluded that the plant was contributing to the haze.[28]

The possibility of using tracers has enormous potential for tracking a variety of effluents and media. Tracers can identify users of pesticides and fertilizers, growing contributors to nonpoint sources of pollution. Tracers can also brand chemicals that contaminate groundwater basins. Just as the government requires registration and monitoring of pets to minimize nuisances, the government can require the branding and monitoring of emissions.[29]

Technology has played a key in the evolution of free market environmentalism solutions. Technology provided the means to change dramatically the face of the American West. In the 1870s, homesteaders and ranchers began using barbed wire to define property rights to their land. Previously, the lack of trees and other materials made it very costly to establish property rights. Barbed wire, however, lowered the cost of fencing the western range dramatically.[30]

IV. FROM THEORY TO PRACTICE: ENDANGERED SPECIES

The opening vignette on Montana's Ruby River introduced the free market environmentalism approach as an alternative to political conflicts over water. Similar potential exists in the resource-rich Pacific Northwest, where two major controversies have been brewing over efforts to save several declining species.

The first dispute involves the Northern Spotted Owl, which was declared a threatened species under the Endangered Species Act of 1973[31] in June of 1990.[32] The controversy concerns the amount of federal timberland that would be removed from timber harvesting because of the Act. A government-sponsored plan to increase breeding owl pairs from 739 to 1,180 in the long term would remove from logging perhaps three million acres of timberland. If the plan were implemented, it is estimated that 25,000 to 40,000 timber-related jobs would be lost.[33]

The second controversy surrounds the potential declaration of the sockeye salmon (and possibly other salmon species on the Columbia River) as endangered. Eight federal mainstem dams are located along the Columbia and Snake Rivers, where over ninety percent of the juvenile salmon are killed trying to migrate from their spawning grounds to the ocean. Salmon die when they are shredded or shocked as they are sucked into the giant turbines. They also fall victim to predators, high temperatures, and disease when they are trapped in the slack water behind the dams. According to salmon proponents, the solution is to increase river flows for several months during the spring, the period when juvenile salmon migrate to the sea.

Use of the Endangered Species Act to force a solution has sparked controversy. If sockeye and other salmon are declared endangered, their safety would be given highest priority relative to other uses of the Columbia Basin, such as hydroelectric power generation, shipping, and irrigation. Both hydroelectric power generation and shipping would be severely limited if water is released from the dams to increase river flows. Furthermore, these flows would not be available to fill reservoirs for later power production and irrigation.[34] The Bonneville Power Administration also estimates that rates for Northwestern power could rise by thirty percent or more. Columbia River barge operators predict the possible demise of their industry, and irrigators say farming in Washington and southern Idaho will be devastated if water for irrigation is confiscated.[35]

Why are the Northern Spotted Owl and Columbia River salmon in trouble? The answer is simple: No one owns them or their habitat; thus, no one has the incentive to protect them. In both cases, the federal government controls most of their habitats. The Forest Service and the Bureau of Land Management control the forests that the spotted owl inhabits, and the Bureau of Reclamation and the Army Corps of Engineers control the dams that kill the salmon.

The two cases do differ, however, in the extent of the subsidized destruction of the respective habitats. While federal timber programs run million-dollar deficits or more on many national forests, forests in the Pacific Northwest are moneymakers. The thirteen national forests in Oregon and Washington affected by the spotted owl decision net more than $500 million in timber revenues each year.[36] The government will lose $150 million in revenues on these forests alone, where forest planners project a thirty percent harvest reduction.[37]

The economics of water development in the Columbia River basin are quite different. Here the rule of subsidized development applies to the 6.5 million acre-feet of water used annually for irrigation. The costs of development allocated to irrigation are $745 million. Of this amount, irrigators pay $136 million, while hydroelectric power consumers pay the rest. In addition to the power subsidy, irrigators receive an implicit interest subsidy: They have a ten-year grace period during which they do not have to repay their reclamation loans and they are not charged interest during the forty-year repayment period; this amounts to an interest subsidy of seventy-nine percent.[38] Water supplied for irrigation has made the "desert bloom like a rose," but only at a tremendous cost.

Free market environmentalism can correct these problems. Short of privatizing the national forests, timber leases could be put up for competitive bid with no requirement that timber be harvested; environmentalists could then bid with timber companies. Environmental groups could lease the most critical owl habitat and allow no logging there. On other tracts, they might allow some logging, thus partially offsetting lease costs, but require that logging be done with minimal impact on the owls. Because it owns its timberlands, International Paper has successfully minimized impacts on endangered species such as the red-cockaded woodpecker, and the Audubon Society has demonstrated that oil development can occur on its private preserves without significant damage to bird habitat.[39]

Similarly, efforts to save the sockeye and other species of salmon in the Columbia River basin can be enhanced through water marketing. Environmentalists have embraced water marketing because it raises water prices and reduces water consumption. As the Ruby River example indicates, water leasing for instream purposes offers an innovative way of increasing stream flows to help migrating salmon. If environmental groups, commercial and sports fishermen, and the U.S. Fish and Wildlife Service could negotiate with power producers and irrigators for increased water flows, cooperation would replace conflict. This has happened elsewhere. On the Gunnison River in Colorado, the Nature Conservancy has obtained the rights to 20,000 acre-feet of water to maintain flows for the hump-backed chub, an endangered species with no commercial or sport value.[40] If those who care about the fate of the salmon could lease water for instream flows, they could directly invest their dollars where the salmon are threatened instead of spending time and money on costly lobbying efforts or litigation.

V. CONCLUSION

Critics of free market environmentalism contend that it does not offer a solution to all environmental problems. They contend that although free market environmentalism may work for some recreational and environmental amenities produced from land, it is inconceivable that property rights can be used to solve problems such as ozone depletion or global warming.[41]

If free market environmentalism stimulates environmentalists to apply free market solutions to the easier problems, it can free political resources to work on the tougher problems that, at the moment, seem to be the domain of government. If free market environmentalist solutions spark the imagination of environmental entrepreneurs, technological progress toward fencing the atmosphere may be accelerated. The "free" in free market environmentalism refers to the individual liberty that only markets can provide; and without that human freedom, environmental quality will be of little consequence.

NOTES

1. Eric Wiltse, *Irrigation Spells Death for Hundreds of Ruby River Trout,* BOZEMAN DAILY CHRON., May 12, 1987, at 3.

2. Terry L. Anderson & Donald R. Leal, *A Private Fix for Leaky Trout Streams,* FLY FISHERMAN, June 1988, at 28–31.
3. *Id.*
4. *See* Terry L. Anderson & Ronald N. Johnson, *The Problem of Instream Flows,* 24 ECON. Inquiry 535 (1986).
5. Terry L. Anderson, Water Rights and the Market for Water: The Western USA Experience 21–22 (June 4, 1991) (unpublished manuscript on file with Political Economy Research Center, Bozeman, Montana).
6. Zach Willey, Statement before the Joint Select Committee on Water Resource Policy, Washington State Legislature 6–7 (September 11, 1990) (transcript available from the Environmental Defense Fund, Oakland, California).
7. RICHARD WAHL, MARKETS FOR FEDERAL WATER: SUBSIDIES, PROPERTY RIGHTS, AND THE BUREAU OF RECLAMATION 120–129 (1989).
8. *Id.*
9. *See* Zach Willey, *supra* note 6, at 6–7.
10. Sandra Postel, *Water, Water Everywhere, But Not For Long,* WASHINGTON POST, November 6, 1989, at 23 (National Weekly Edition).
11. DEPARTMENT OF WATER AFFAIRS, MANAGEMENT OF THE WATER RESOURCES OF THE REPUBLIC OF SOUTH AFRICA 2.8 (1986).
12. *See* ALAN RANDALL, RESOURCE ECONOMICS 36 (1981).
13. PAUL A. SAMUELSON, ECONOMICS 450 (11th ed. 1980).
14. John Burton, *Epilogue* to STEVEN N.S. CHEUNG, THE MYTH OF SOCIAL COSTS 76 (1978).
15. JOHN M. HARTWICK & NANCY D. OLEWILER, THE ECONOMICS OF NATURAL RESOURCE USE 18 (1986).
16. DANIEL W. BROMLEY, PROPERTY RIGHTS AND THE ENVIRONMENT: NATURAL RESOURCE POLICY IN TRANSITION 55 (1988).
17. F.A. Hayek, *The Use of Knowledge in Society,* 35 AMER. ECON. REV. 519–520 (1945).
18. U.S. FOREST SERVICE, REGION 10 STATEMENT OF OBLIGATIONS (1984); U.S. FOREST SERVICE, TIMBER SALE PROGRAM ANNUAL REPORT 8–9 (1989).
19. WAHL, *supra* note 7, at 47–67 (1989).
20. Emery N. Castle, *The Market Mechanism, Externalities, and Land Economics,* FARM ECON. 542, 552 (1965).
21. Anthony C. Fisher, RESOURCE AND ENVIRONMENTAL ECONOMICS 54 (1981).
22. Telephone interview with Tom Bourland, Wildlife Biologist, International Paper Company (Sept. 23, 1989); *see also* PRESIDENT'S COUNCIL ON ENVTL. QUALITY, ENVIRONMENTAL QUALITY: 15TH ANNUAL REPORT OF THE COUNCIL ON ENVIRONMENTAL QUALITY 426 (1984).
23. There, British fishermen's income has fallen by six percent in real terms since 1980 and stocks of cod and haddock have fallen by one-half and two-thirds, respectively. *A Sustainable Stock of Fishermen,* ECONOMIST, January 19, 1991, at 17–18.
24. William L. Robinson, *Individual Transferable Quotas in the Australian Southern Bluefin Tuna Fishery,* in FISHERY ACCESS CONTROL PROGRAMS: WORLDWIDE PROCEEDINGS OF THE WORKSHOP IN MANAGEMENT OPTIONS FOR THE NORTH PACIFIC LONGLINE FISHERS 186–205 (Alaska Sea Grant Report No. 86–4, 1986).
25. RODNEY P. HIDE & PETER ACKROYD, DEPOLITICISING FISHERIES MANAGEMENT: CHATHAM ISLANDS' PAUA (ABALONE) AS A CASE STUDY 42, 44 (March 1990) (unpublished report for R.D. Beattie, Ltd., Kaikoura, New Zealand).
26. Esmond Drury, *John Eastwood and the A.C.A.,* ANGLERS' COOPERATIVE ASS'N REV., Summer 1984, at 12, 13.
27. *See, e.g.,* A MITCHELL POLINSKY, AN INTRODUCTION TO LAW AND ECONOMICS 89–94 (1983). With well-specified rights, owners have an incentive to discover innovative ways to detect and monitor pollution. In Britain, the water company for Bournemouth has enlisted the services of twenty West African elephant fish,

Gnathonemus petersii, to monitor water pollution. The four-inch creature emits an easily tracked electrical discharge, the rate of which depends on the pollution level of the water. A contented fish puts out 300 to 500 pulses a minute, but if it becomes distressed by the presence of pollutants, the rate shoots up to more than 1,000 pulses a minute. Sensors in the water supply pick up the pulse rate and pass them on to a computer. If more than half of the fish suddenly increase their pulse rate, an alarm is sounded and scientists step in to assay the water. *See, A Fishy Kind of Pollution Detector,* 249 SCIENCE 983 (1990).

28. Mark Crawford, *Scientists Battle Over Grand Canyon Pollution,* 247 SCIENCE. 911–912 (1990).
29. Former EPA analyst Fred Smith suggests the possibilities:

   > Detection and monitoring schemes would evolve as environmental values mounted and it became appropriate to expend more on fencing. There are exotic technologies that might well play a fencing role even for resources as complex as airsheds. For example, lasimetrics, a technology which can already map atmospheric chemical concentrations from orbit, might in time provide a sophisticated means of tracking transnational pollution flows.

   Fred L. Smith, Jr., Controlling the Global Threat to the Global Liberal Order 10 (November 1989) (unpublished manuscript, on file with the Competitive Enterprise Institute, Washington, D.C.).
30. *See* WALTER PRESCOTT WEBB, THE GREAT PLAINS 309 (1931).
31. Pub. L. No. 93-205, §§ 2–15, 17, 87 Stat. 884 (1973) (codified as amended in scattered sections of 16 U.S.C. (1988)).
32. Determination of Threatened Status for the Northern Spotted Owl, 55 Fed. Reg. 26,114 (1990) (codified in Endangered and Threatened Wildlife, 50 C.F.R. § 17.11 (1991)). *See* David Schaefer & Sylvia Nogaki, *Threatened Wildlife—Agency Makes It Official on Spotted Owl,* SEATTLE TIMES, June 22, 1990, at A1.
33. Robert Nelson, Rethinking Federal Forest Management: A Response to the Designation of the Spotted Owl as a Threatened Species 8–9 (Political Economy Research Center Working Paper No. 90–34, Jan. 1991) (unpublished manuscript, on file at the Political Economy Research Center, Bozeman, Montana).
34. Pat Ford, *How the Basin's Salmon-Killing System Works,* HIGH COUNTRY NEWS, April 22, 1991, at 14–15.
35. Pat Pat Ford, *We've Got An Economic Opportunity Here,* HIGH COUNTRY NEWS, April 22, 1991, at 15.
36. U.S. FOREST SERVICE, TIMBER SALE PROGRAM ANNUAL REPORT 115–16, 162 (1989).
37. When all affected federal forests in Washington, Oregon, and California are taken into account, the loss could be as high as $625 million per year. *See* Nelson, *supra* note 33.
38. Randal R. Rucker & Price V. Fishback, *The Federal Reclamation Program: An Analysis of Rent-Seeking Behavior,* in WATER RIGHTS: SCARCE RESOURCE ALLOCATION, BUREAUCRACY, AND THE ENVIRONMENT 45, 52–63 (Terry L. Anderson ed., 1983) (using a discount rate of 8%).
39. *See* PRESIDENT'S COUNCIL ON ENVTL. QUALITY, *supra* note 21, at 425; *see also* John Baden & Richard Stroup, *Saving the Wilderness,* REASON, July 1981, at 28–36.
40. Steven J. Shupe & John A. Folk-Williams, *Public Interest Perspective,* WATER MARKET UPDATE, March 1987, at 9–10.
41. *But see* ROBERT STAVINS ET AL., PROJECT 88: HARNESSING MARKET FORCES TO PROTECT OUR ENVIRONMENT 10–23 (1988) (recommending a tradeable permit system for phasing out potential ozone depleters, international emissions trading in greenhouse gases, and prevention of deforestation through debt-forest swaps).

A Declaration of Sustainability

Paul Hawken

Paul Hawken is author of the best-selling book The Ecology of Commerce *and of other publications that promote sustainable economic development.*

I recently performed a social audit for Ben and Jerry's Homemade Inc., America's premier socially responsible company. After poking and prodding around, asking tough questions, trying to provoke debate, and generally making a nuisance of myself, I can attest that their status as the leading social pioneer in commerce is safe for at least another year. They are an outstanding company. Are there flaws? Of course. Welcome to planet Earth. But the people at Ben & Jerry's are relaxed and unflinching in their willingness to look at, discuss, and deal with problems.

In the meantime, the company continues to put ice cream shops in Harlem, pay outstanding benefits, keep a compensation ratio of seven to one from the top of the organization to the bottom, seek out vendors from disadvantaged groups, and donate generous scoops of their profits to others. And they are about to overtake their historic rival Häagen-Dazs, the ersatz Scandinavian originator of super-premium ice cream, as the market leader in their category. At present rates of growth, Ben & Jerry's will be a $1 billion company by the end of the century. They are publicly held, nationally recognized, and rapidly growing, in part because Ben wanted to show that a socially responsible company could make it in the normal world of business.

Ben and Jerry's is just one of a growing vanguard of companies attempting to redefine their social and ethical responsibilities. These companies no longer accept the maxim that the business of business is business. Their premise is simple: Corporations, because they are the dominant institution on the planet, must squarely face the social and environmental problems that afflict humankind. Organizations such as Business for Social Responsibility and the Social Venture Network, corporate "ethics" consultants, magazines such as *In Business* and *Business Ethics,* non-profits including the Council on Economic Priorities, investment

This essay originally appeared in *Utne Reader*, #59 (September/October 1993), 54–61. Reprinted with permission.

funds such as Calvert and Covenant, newsletters like *Greenmoney*, and thousands of unaffiliated companies are drawing up new codes of conduct for corporate life that integrate social, ethical, and environmental principles.

Ben and Jerry's and the roughly 2,000 other committed companies in the social responsibility movement here and abroad have combined annual sales of approximately $2 billion, or one-hundredth of 1 percent of the $20 trillion sales garnered by the estimated 80 million to 100 million enterprises worldwide. The problems they are trying to address are vast and unremittingly complex: 5.5 billion people are breeding exponentially, and fulfilling their wants and needs is stripping the earth of its biotic capacity to produce life; a climactic burst of consumption by a single species is overwhelming the skies, earth, waters, and fauna.

As the Worldwatch Institute's Lester Brown patiently explains in his annual survey, *State of the World*, every living system on earth is in decline. Making matters worse, we are having a once-in-a-billion-year blowout sale of hydrocarbons, which are being combusted into the atmosphere, effectively double glazing the planet within the next 50 years with unknown climatic results. The cornucopia of resources that are being extracted, mined, and harvested is so poorly distributed that 20 percent of the earth's people are chronically hungry or starving, while the top 20 percent of the population, largely in the north, control and consume 80 percent of the world's wealth. Since business in its myriad forms is primarily responsible for this "taking," it is appropriate that a growing number of companies ask the question, How does one honorably conduct business in the latter days of industrialism and the beginning of an ecological age? The ethical dilemma that confronts business begins with the acknowledgment that a commercial system that functions well by its own definitions unavoidably defies the greater and more profound ethic of biology. Specifically, how does business face the prospect that creating a profitable, growing company requires an intolerable abuse of the natural world?

Despite their dedicated good work, if we examine all or any of the businesses that deservedly earn high marks for social and environmental responsibility, we are faced with a sobering irony: If every company on the planet were to adopt the environmental and social practices of the best companies—of, say, the Body Shop, Patagonia, and Ben and Jerry's—the world would still be moving toward environmental degradation and collapse. In other words, if we analyze environmental effects and create an input-output model of resources and energy, the results do not even approximate a tolerable or sustainable future. If a tiny fraction of the world's most intelligent companies cannot model a sustainable world, then that tells us that being socially responsible is only one part of an overall solution, and that what we have is not a management problem but a design problem.

At present, there is a contradiction inherent in the premise of a socially responsible corporation: to wit, that a company can make the world better, can grow, and can increase profits by meeting social and environmental needs. It is a have-your-cake-and-eat-it fantasy that cannot come true if the primary cause of environmental degradation is overconsumption. Although proponents of socially responsible business are making an outstanding effort at reforming the tired old ethics of commerce, they are unintentionally creating a new rationale for companies to produce, advertise, expand, grow, capitalize, and use up resources: the rationale that they are doing good. A jet flying across the country, a car rented at an airport, an air-conditioned hotel room, a truck full of goods, a worker commuting to his or her job—all cause the same amount of environmental degradation whether they're associated with the Body Shop, the Environmental Defense Fund, or R. J. Reynolds.

In order to approximate a sustainable society, we need to describe a system of commerce and production in which each and every act is inherently sustainable and restorative. Because of the way our system of commerce is designed, businesses will not be able to fulfill their social contract with the environment or society until the system in which they operate undergoes a fundamental change, a change that brings commerce and governance into alignment with the natural world from which we receive our life. There must be an integration of economic, biologic, and human systems in order to create a sustainable and interdependent method of commerce that supports and furthers our existence. As hard as we may strive to create sustainability on a company level, we cannot fully succeed until the institutions surrounding commerce are redesigned. Just as every act of production and consumption in an industrial society leads to further environmental degradation, regardless of intention or ethos, we need to imagine—and then design—a system of commerce where the opposite is true, where doing good is like falling off a log, where the natural, everyday acts of work and life accumulate into a better world as a matter of course, not a matter of altruism. A system of sustainable commerce would involve these objectives:

1. It would reduce absolute consumption of energy and natural resources among developed nations by 80 percent within 40 to 60 years.
2. It would provide secure, stable, and meaningful employment for people everywhere.
3. It would be self-actuating as opposed to regulated, controlled, mandated, or moralistic.
4. It would honor human nature and market principles.
5. It would be perceived as more desirable than our present way of life.
6. It would exceed sustainability by restoring degraded habitats and ecosystems to their fullest biological capacity.
7. It would rely on current solar income.
8. It should be fun and engaging, and strive for an aesthetic outcome.

STRATEGIES FOR SUSTAINABILITY

At present, the environmental and social responsibility movements consist of many different initiatives, connected primarily by values and beliefs rather than by design. What is needed is a conscious plan to create a sustainable future, including a set of design strategies for people to follow. For the record, I will suggest 12.

1. Take Back the Charter

Although corporate charters may seem to have little to do with sustainability, they are critical to any long-term movement toward restoration of the planet. Read *Taking Care of Business: Citizenship and the Charter of Incorporation,* a 1992 pamphlet by Richard Grossman and Frank T. Adams (Charter Ink, Box 806. Cambridge, MA 02140). In it you find a lost history of corporate power and citizen involvement that addresses a basic and crucial point: Corporations are chartered by, and exist at the behest of, citizens. Incorporation is not a right but a privilege granted by the state that includes certain considerations such as limited liability. Corporations are supposed to be under our ultimate authority, not the other way around. The charter of incorporation is a revocable dispensation that was supposed to ensure accountability of the corporation to society as a whole. When Rockwell criminally despoils a weapons facility at Rocky Flats, Colorado, with plutonium waste, or when any corporation continually harms, abuses, or violates the public trust, citizens should have the right to revoke its charter, causing the company to disband, sell off its enterprises to other companies, and effectively go out of business. The workers would have jobs with the new owners, but the executives, directors, and management would be out of jobs, with a permanent notice on their resumes that they mismanaged a corporation into a charter revocation. This is not merely a deterrent to corporate abuse but a critical element of an ecological society because it creates feedback loops that prompt accountability, citizen involvement, and learning. We should remember that the citizens of this country originally envisioned corporations to be part of a public-private partnership, which is why the relationship between the chartering authority of state legislatures and the corporation was kept alive and active. They had it right.

2. Adjust Price to Reflect Cost

The economy is environmentally and commercially dysfunctional because the market does not provide consumers with proper information. The "free market" economies that we love so much are excellent at setting prices but lousy when it comes to recognizing costs. In order for a sustainable society to exist, every purchase must reflect or at least approximate its actual cost, not only the direct cost of production but also the costs to the air, water, and soil; the cost to future generations; the cost to worker health; the cost of waste, pollution, and toxicity. Simply stated, the marketplace gives us the wrong information. It tells us the flying across the country on a discount airline ticket is cheap when it is not. It tells us that our food is inexpensive when its method of production destroys aquifers and soil, the viability of ecosystems, and workers' lives. Whenever an organism gets wrong information, it is a form of toxicity. In fact, that is how pesticides work. A herbicide kills because it is a hormone that tells the plant to grow faster than its capacity to absorb nutrients allows. It literally grows itself to death. Sound familiar? Our daily doses of toxicity are the prices in the market place. They are telling us to do the wrong thing for our own survival. They are lulling us into cutting down old-growth forests on the Olympic Peninsula for apple crates, into patterns of production and consumption that are not just unsustainable but profoundly short-sighted and destructive. It is surprising that "conservative" economists do not support or understand this idea, because it is they who insist that we pay as we go, have no debts, and take care of business. Let's do it.

3. Throw Out and Replace the Entire Tax System

The present tax system sends the wrong messages to virtually everyone, encourages waste, discourages conservation, and rewards consumption. It taxes what we want to encourage—jobs, creativity, payrolls, and real income—and ignores the things we want to discourage—degradation, pollution, and depletion. The present U.S. tax system costs citizens $500 billion a year in record-keeping, filing, administrative, legal, and governmental costs—more than the actual amount we pay in personal income taxes. The only incentive in the present system is to cheat or hire a lawyer to cheat for us. The entire tax system must be incrementally replaced over a 20-year period by "Green fees," taxes that are added onto existing products, energy, services, and materials so that prices in the marketplace more closely approximate true costs. These taxes are not a means to raise revenue or bring down deficits, but must be absolutely revenue neutral so that people in the lower and middle classes experience no real change of income, only a shift in expenditures. Eventually, the cost of nonrenewable resources, extractive energy, and industrial modes of production will be more expensive than renewable resources, such as solar energy, sustainable forestry, and biological methods of agriculture. Why should the upper middle class be able to afford to conserve while the lower income classes cannot? So far the environmental movement has only made the world better for upper middle class white people. The only kind of environmental movement that can succeed has to start from the bottom up. Under a Green fee system the incentives to save on taxes will create positive, constructive acts that are affordable for everyone. As energy prices go up to three to four times their existing levels (with commensurate tax reductions to offset the increase), the natural inclination to save money will result in carpooling, bicycling, telecommuting, public transport, and more efficient houses. As taxes on artificial fertilizers, pesticides, and fuel go up, again with offsetting reductions in income and payroll taxes, organic farmers will find that their produce and methods are the cheapest means of production (because they truly are), and customers will find that organically grown food is less expensive than its commercial cousin. Eventually, with the probable exception of taxes on the rich, we will find ourselves in a position where we pay no taxes, but spend our money with a practiced and constructive discernment. Under an enlightened and redesigned tax system, the cheapest product in the marketplace would be best for the customer, the worker, the environment, and the company. That is rarely the case today.

4. Allow Resource Companies to Be Utilities

An energy utility is an interesting hybrid of public-private interests. A utility gains a market monopoly in exchange for public control of rates, open books, and a guaranteed rate of return. Because of this relationship and the pioneering work of Amory Lovins, we now have markets for "negawatts." It is the first time in the history of industrialism that a corporation has figured out how to make money by selling the absence of something. Negawatts are the opposite of energy: They represent the collaborative ability of a utility to harness efficiency instead of hydrocarbons. This conservation-based alternative saves ratepayers, shareholders, and the company money—savings that are passed along to everyone. All resource systems, including oil, gas, forests, and water, should be run by some form of utility. There should be markets in negabarrels, negatrees, and negacoal. Oil companies, for example, have no alternative at present other than to lobby for the absurd, like drilling in the Arctic National Wildlife Refuge. That project, a $40 billion to $60 billion investment for a hoped-for supply of oil that would meet U.S. consumption needs for only six months, is the only way an oil company can make money under our current system of commerce. But what if the oil companies formed an oil utility and cut a deal with citizens and taxpayers that allowed them to "invest" in insulation, super-glazed windows, conservation rebates on new automobiles, and the scrapping of old cars? Through Green fees, we would pay them back a return on their conservation investment equal to what utilities receive, a rate of return that would be in accord with how many barrels of oil they save, rather than how many barrels they produce. Why should they care? Why should we? A $60 billion investment in conservation will yield, conservatively, four to ten times as much energy as drilling for oil. Given Lovins' principle of efficiency extraction, try to imagine a forest utility, a salmon utility, a copper utility, a Mississippi River utility, a grasslands utility. Imagine a system where the resource utility benefits from conservation, makes money from efficiency, thrives through restoration, and profits from sustainability. It is possible today.

5. Change Linear Systems to Cyclical Ones

Our economy has many design flaws, but the most glaring one is that nature is cyclical and industrialism is linear. In nature, no linear systems exist, or they don't exist for long because they exhaust themselves into extinction. Linear industrial systems take resources, transform them into products or services, discard waste, and sell to consumers, who discard more waste when they have consumed the product. But of course we don't consume TVs, cars, or most of the other stuff we buy. Instead, Americans produce six times their body weight every week in hazardous and toxic waste water, incinerator fly ash, agricultural wastes, heavy metals, and waste chemicals, paper, wood, etc. This does not include CO_2, which if it were included would double the amount of waste. Cyclical means of production are designed to imitate natural systems in which waste equals food for other forms of life, nothing is thrown away, and symbiosis replaces competition. Bill McDonough, a New York architect who has pioneered environmental design principles, has designed a system to retrofit every window in a major American city. Although it still awaits final approval, the project is planned to go like this: The city and a major window manufacturer form a joint venture to produce energy-saving super-glazed windows in the town. This partnership company will come to your house or business, measure all windows and glass doors, and then replace them with windows with an R-8 to R-12 energy-efficiency rating within 72 hours. The windows will have the same casements, molding, and general appearance as the old ones. You will receive a $500 check upon installation, and you will pay for the new windows over a 10- to 15-year period in your utility or tax bill. The total bill is less than the cost of the energy the windows will save. In other words, the windows will cost the home or business owner nothing. The city will pay for them initially with industrial development bonds. The factory will train and employ 300 disadvantaged people. The old windows will be completely recycled and reused, the glass melted into glass, the wooden frames ground up and mixed with recycled resins that are extruded to make the casements. When the city is reglazed, the residents and businesses will pocket an extra $20 million to $30 million every year in money saved on utility bills. After the windows are paid for, the figure will go even higher. The factory, designed to be transportable, will move to another city, the first city will retain an equity interest in the venture. McDonough has designed a win-win-win-win-win system that optimizes a number of agendas. The ratepayers, the homeowners, the renters, the city, the environment, and the employed all thrive because they are "making" money from efficiency rather than exploitation. It's a little like running the industrial economy backwards.

6. Transform the Making of Things

We have to institute the Intelligent Product System created by Michael Braungart of the EPEA (Environmental Protection Encouragement Agency) in Hamburg, Germany. The system recognizes three types of products. The first are *consumables*, products that are either eaten, or, when they're placed on the ground, turn into dirt without any bio-accumulative effects. In other words, they are products whose waste equals food for other living systems. At present, many of the products that should be "consumable," like clothing and shoes, are not. Cotton cloth contains hundreds of different chemicals, plasticizers, defoliants, pesticides, and dyes: shoes are tanned with chromium and their soles contain lead: neckties and silk blouses contain zinc, tin, and toxic dye. Much of what we recycle today turns into toxic by-products, consuming more energy in the recycling process than is saved by recycling. We should be designing more things so that they can be thrown away—into the compost heap. Toothpaste tubes and other non-degradable packaging can be made out of natural polymers so that they break down and become fertilizer for plants. A package that turns into dirt is infinitely more useful, biologically speaking, than a package that turns into a plastic park bench. Heretical as it sounds, designing for decomposition, not recycling, is the way of the world around us.

The second category is *durables*, but in this case, they would not be sold, only licensed. Cars, TVs, VCRs, and refrigerators would always belong to the original manufacturer, so they would be made, used, and returned within a closed-loop system. This is already being instituted in Germany and to a lesser extent in Japan, where companies are beginning to design for disassembly. If a company knows that its products will come back someday, and that it cannot throw anything away when they do, it creates a very different approach to design and materials.

Last, there are *unsalables*—toxins, radiation, heavy metals, and chemicals. There is no living system for which these are food and thus they can never be thrown away. In Braungart's Intelligent Product System, unsalables must always belong to the original maker, safeguarded by public utilities called "parking lots" that store the toxins in glass-lined barrels indefinitely, charging the original manufacturers rent for the service. The rent ceases when an independent scientific panel can confirm that there is a safe method to detoxify the substances in question. All toxic chemicals would have molecular markers identifying them as belonging to their originator, so that if they are found in wells, rivers, soil, or fish, it is the responsibility of the company to retrieve them and clean up. This places the problem of toxicity with the makers, where it belongs, making them responsible for full-life-cycle effects.

7. Vote, Don't Buy

Democracy has been effectively eliminated in America by the influence of money, lawyers, and a political system that is the outgrowth of the first two. While we can dream of restoring our democratic system, the fact remains that we live in a plutocracy—government by the wealthy. One way out is to vote with your dollars, to withhold purchases from companies that act or respond inappropriately. Don't just avoid buying a Mitsubishi automobile because of the company's participation in the destruction of primary forests in Malaysia, Indonesia, Ecuador, Brazil, Bolivia, Canada, Chile, Canada, Siberia, and Papua New Guinea. Write and tell them why you won't. Engage in dialogue, send one postcard a week, talk, organize, meet, publish newsletters, boycott, patronize, and communicate with companies like General Electric. Educate non-profits, organizations, municipalities, and pension funds to act affirmatively, to support the ecological CERES (formerly *Valdez*) Principles for business, to invest intelligently, and to *think* with their money, not merely spend it. Demand the best from the companies you work for and buy from. You deserve it and your actions will help them change.

8. Restore the "Guardian"

There can be no healthy business sector unless there is a healthy governing sector. In her book *System of Survival*, author Jane Jacobs describes two overarching moral syndromes that permeate our society: the commercial syndrome, which arose from trading cultures, and the governing, or guardian, syndrome that arose from territorial cultures. The guardian system is hierarchical, adheres to tradition, values loyalty, and shuns trading and inventiveness. The commercial system, on the other hand, is based on trading, so it values trust of outsiders, innovation, and future thinking. Each has qualities the other lacks. Whenever the guardian tries to be in business, as in Eastern Europe, business doesn't work. What is also true, but not so obvious to us, is that when business plays government, governance fails as well. Our guardian system has almost completely broken down because of the money, power, influence, and control exercised by business and, to a lesser degree, other institutions. Business and unions have to get out of government. We need more than campaign reform: We need a vision that allows us all to see that when Speaker of the House Tom Foley exempts the aluminum industry in his district from the proposed Btu tax, or when Philip Morris donates $200,000 to the Jesse Helms Citizenship Center, citizenship is mocked and democracy is left gagging and twitching on the Capitol steps. The irony is that business thinks that its involvement in governance is good corporate citizenship or at least is advancing its own interests. The reality is that business is preventing the economy from evolving. Business loses, workers lose, the environment loses.

9. Shift from Electronic Literacy to Biologic Literacy

That an average adult can recognize one thousand brand names and logos but fewer than ten local plants is not a good sign. We are moving not to an information age but to a biologic age, and unfortunately our technological education is equipping us for corporate markets, not the future. Sitting at home with virtual reality gloves, 3D video games, and interactive cable TV shopping is a barren and impoverished vision of the future. The computer revolution is not the totem of our future, only a tool. Don't get me wrong. Computers are great. But they are not an uplifting or compelling vision for culture or society. They do not move us toward a sustainable future any more than our obsession with cars and televisions provided us with newer definitions or richer meaning. We are moving into the age of living machines, not, as Corbusier noted, "machines for living in." The Thomas Edison of the future is not Bill Gates of Microsoft, but John and Nancy Todd, founders of the New Alchemy Institute, a Massachusetts design lab and think tank for sustainability. If the Todds' work seems less commercial, less successful, and less glamorous, it is because they are working on the real problem—how to live—and it is infinitely more complex than a microprocessor. Understanding biological processes is how we are going to create a new symbiosis with living systems (or perish). What we can learn online is how to model complex systems. It is computers that have allowed us to realize how the synapses in the common sea slug are more powerful than all of our parallel processors put together.

10. Take Inventory

We do not know how many species live on the planet within a factor of ten. We do not know how many are being extirpated. We do not know what is contained in the biological library inherited from the Cenozoic age. (Sociobiologist E.O. Wilson estimates that it would take 25,000 person-years to catalog most of the species, putting aside the fact that there are only 1,500 people with the taxonomic ability to undertake the task.) We do not know how complex systems interact—how the transpiration of the giant lily, *Victoria amazonica*, of Brazil's rainforests affects European rainfall and agriculture, for example. We do not know what happens to 20 percent of the CO_2 that is off-gassed every year (it disappears without a trace). We do not know how to calculate sustainable yields in fisheries and forest systems. We do not know why certain species, such as frogs, are dying out even in pristine habitats. We do not know the long-term effects of chlorinated hydrocarbons on human health, behavior, sexuality, and fertility. We do not know what a sustainable life is for existing inhabitants of the planet, and certainly not for future populations. (A Dutch study calculated that your fair share of air travel is one trip across the Atlantic in a lifetime.) We do not know how many people we can feed on a sustainable basis, or what our diet would look like. In short, we need to find out what's here, who has it, and what we can or can't do with it.

11. Take Care of Human Health

The environmental and socially responsible movements would gain additional credibility if they recognized that the greatest amount of human suffering and mortality is caused by environmental problems that are not being addressed by environmental organizations or companies. Contaminated water is killing a hundred times more people than all other forms of pollution combined. Millions of children are dying from preventable diseases and malnutrition.

The movement toward sustainability must address the clear and present dangers that people face worldwide, dangers that ironically increase population levels because of their perceived threat. People produce more children when they're afraid they'll lose them. Not until the majority of the people in the world, all of whom suffer in myriad preventable yet intolerable ways, understand that environmentalism means improving their lives directly will the ecology movement walk its talk. Americans will spend more money in the next 12 months on the movie and tchotchkes of *Jurassic Park* than on foreign aid to prevent malnutrition or provide safe water.

12. Respect the Human Spirit

If hope is to pass the sobriety test, then it has to walk a pretty straight line to reality. Nothing written, suggested, or proposed here is possible unless business is willing to integrate itself into the natural world. It is time for business to take the initiative in a genuinely open process of dialogue, collaboration, reflection, and redesign. "It is not enough," writes Jeremy Seabrook of the British Green party, "to declare, as many do, that we are living in an unsustainable way, using up resources, squandering the substance of the next generation however true this may be. People must feel subjectively the injustice and unsustainability before they will make a more sober assessment as to whether it is worth maintaining what is, or whether there might not be more equitable and satisfying ways that will not be won at the expense either of the necessities of the poor or of the wasting fabric of the planet."

Poet and naturalist W.S. Merwin (citing Robert Graves) reminds us that we have one story, and one story only, to tell in our lives. We are made to believe by our parents and businesses, by our culture and televisions, by our politicians and movie stars that it is the story of money, of finance, of wealth, of the stock portfolio, the partnership, the country house. These are small, impoverished tales and whispers that have made us restless and craven: they are not stories at all. As author and garlic grower Stanley Crawford puts it, "The financial statement must finally give way to the narrative, with all its exceptions, special cases, imponderables. It must finally give way to the story, which is perhaps the way we arm ourselves against the next and always unpredictable turn of the cycle in the quixotic dare that is life: across the rock and cold of lifelines, it is our seed, our clove, our filament cast toward the future." It is something deeper than anything commercial culture can plumb, and it is waiting for each of us.

Business must yield to the longings of the human spirit. The most important contribution of the socially responsible business movement has little to do with recycling, nuts from the rainforest, or employing the homeless. Their gift to us is that they are leading by trying to do something, to risk, take a chance, make a change—any change. They are not waiting for "the solution," but are acting without guarantees of success or proof of purchase. This is what all of us must do. Being visionary has always been given a bad rap by commerce. But without a positive vision for humankind we can have no meaning, no work, and no purpose.

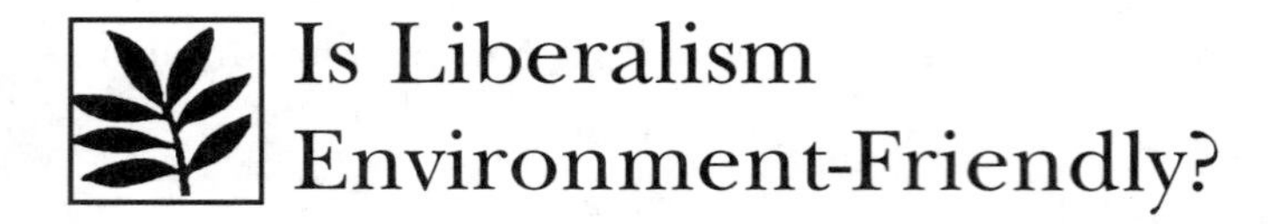

Is Liberalism Environment-Friendly?

Avner de-Shalit

Avner de-Shalit, senior lecturer in political science at the Hebrew University in Jerusalem, is author of Why Posterity Matters.

The state of the environment is a novel issue on the political agenda, yet it is one of the most important. People the world over have begun to realize that the damage to the environment caused by human activities is drastic and at times even irreversible. The pollution of the soil, contamination of water by chemicals, air pollution, the damage to the ozone layer, acid rain, the complications in radioactive waste management, the extinction of certain animal species, deforestation, misguided urban development—all these and other phenomena constitute what is now widely called "the environmental problem."

Some people tend to think that scientists, or engineers, can solve, or at least suggest solutions to all these problems.[1] But although theoretically speaking most environmental problems have scientific solutions, in practice these solutions are thrust aside by economic criteria and considerations. Now, the latter are simply the reflection of social and political ideologies, and so, in fact, environmental policies involve decisions on the allocation of financial resources and time, the distribution of money and political power, and on public priorities. Consequently, the solution to these problems is political,[2] with the result that philosophers and political theorists have tried to find the moral grounds for environment-friendly policies. This paper deals with this attempt. My argument is two-fold: first, that liberalism, for a number of reasons that will be investigated here, has provided a good framework for the evolution of the "Green" ideas and environmental philosophy. But second, that with regard to environmental policies, liberalism nevertheless faces difficulties: while it allows and encourages discussion of environmental issues, it cannot permit its outcome, namely the implementation, maintenance, and justification of environmental policies, and therefore it precludes constructive public action to secure environmental protection.

This ambivalent attitude may confuse the reader, since there is no sharp and unequivocal assertion in favor of or against liberalism in the context of the environment. On the contrary, the intrinsic complexity of liberalism and the gap between the theoretical discussion and praxis reveal the complexity of liberalism's relationship with environmentalism. But this paper may speak to the suggestion that a more "social" liberalism could, perhaps, deliver the goods.[3] In that respect my project calls for further research; however, I am suggesting that theory about the politics of the environment should be placed not merely in its "Greens" or "movement" context, but in a wider framework, that of the liberal tradition in political theory.[4]

LIBERALISM AND ENVIRONMENTAL PHILOSOPHY

It may be argued that at first appearance liberalism and environmental philosophy do not tie in with each other because liberalism's most fundamental feature—the contract—leaves out those who cannot join it, that is, trees, rocks, rivers, animals, and so on. The most prominent of contemporary liberal theorists, John Rawls, for instance, leaves this issue to metaphysics.[5] Others have tried to follow Rawls's path, and yet modify it so that it generates an animal rights ethics,[6] or show that his theory implicitly requires extensive environmental policies.[7] But in this section my aim is not so much to show how liberalism and environmental philosophy can be seen as identical twins or as ideal ideological bedfellows, but rather to argue that liberal societies have become a fertile ground for the promotion of ecological attitudes and environmental philosophy. There are four main reasons for this: the first two reasons lie in the sphere of philosophy, or theory, and involve both the content of the liberal idea and the tradition of liberal thought.

Let us start with the former. One of the main components of liberalism is anti-chauvinism: the moral agent does not automatically exalt its own virtues and discredit those of others. (The moral agent could be a single person or a collective body to which the person belongs, whether it is a voluntary body, for example, a party, firm, or a body into which the person was born, for example, a nation, race, gender, class.) Chauvinists do not consider "others" on equal terms, but liberals have rejected such attitudes and instead propound the idea that all people are equal since they are all human beings cast in the same mold. Hence liberals have contended that all humans deserve equal rights, and that we should follow a policy of "respect for others" and "respecting others as equals."[8] In short, liberalism as a social philosophy has rejected all expressions of chauvinism from national to male chauvinism.

At the same time the situation in which humans deplete resources and damage the environment has been described on several occasions, and quite rightly, as "man (or human) chauvinism"[9] with respect to the ill-treatment of nonhuman animals (sometimes even plants or ecosystems) and their exclusion from the ethical community.

It is only natural, then, that many liberals, both theorists and politicians, have adopted Green ideas and ecological attitudes: the essence of liberalism, as indicated above, is the philosophy of "respect for others." An environmental attitude implies extending the notion of "others" to include nonhuman animals, "all sentient creatures," or even "all living objects" or "ecosystems."

> A land ethic changes the role of homo sapiens from conqueror of the land-community to plain member and citizen of it. It implies respect for his fellow members, and also respect for the community as such.[10]

Most liberals would find it difficult to adhere to "holism" or to Aldo Leopold's "Land Ethic," which rests upon the premise that the individual is a member of a community of interdependent parts; but it is arguable that the elements of antichauvinism and "respect for others" that have characterized liberal thought have influenced and contributed to the emergence of "Green" ideas, at least in their defense of individual entities in the environment. Admittedly, many greens are keener on collections of living objects, for example, species, rather than individual entities. This will be discussed below, where I suggest that a more social type of liberalism suits environmental issues. It also remains to develop a theory of humans' relationship with the nonsentient objects; Christopher Stone has perhaps shown the way.[11] Nevertheless, Roderick Nash has drawn an interesting analogy in this connection between the liberal political campaign against slavery in America and the environmentalists' attempt to persuade the public that the circle of the ethical community should be enlarged to include animals, and even plants, or ecosystems. Just as the Abolitionists were considered radical when they claimed that blacks were being ill-treated and denied any moral status, so the environmentalists are regarded as radical today. Consequently, Nash may be right in claiming that environmental ethics is a "logical extrapolation of the powerful liberal tradition."[12] Liberals in the nineteenth century passed from male chauvinism and racism to moral universalism, environmentalists today pass from a human chauvinism to a broader moral universalism, arguing that "the conscious suffering of a sentient creature is indeed intrinsically bad from that creature's standpoint." Thus, we look at other species

> [as] we look at ourselves, seeing them as beings which have a good they are striving to realize just as we have a good we are striving to realize. . . . [Hence] their lives can be made better or worse by the way humans treat them, and it is possible for humans to take their standpoint and judge what happens to them in terms of *their* well-being [emphasis in original].[13]

Now while liberals in the nineteenth century wished to protect the vulnerable, that is, the potential victims of modernity and progress, environmentalists towards the end of the twentieth century still protect the victims of modernity, but unlike progressive forces in the nineteenth century, they extend the circle of protection to include the natural environment.

So much for the content of liberalism. But there is a second aspect of liberal theory that is built into the tradition of liberal philosophy. Liberals have always subjected their positions, values, ideas and theories to critical scrutiny, and have been the proponents of openness and tolerance, not only in political life, but in the academic and philosophical debate as well.[14] Even philosophers and theorists who attack the liberal tradition for its inability to tackle, understand, or solve ecological problems,[15] must admit that they can do so because they live and work in a liberal and tolerant society.

Moreover, in order to accept environmental philosophy one must be relatively open to new ideas and tolerant of criticism—not only of one's own theory, but also of one's methodology. This is because environmental philosophy is (mostly) biocentric or ecocentric, rather than anthropocentric: that is, it considers nonhuman objects (individual animals, plants, or ecosystems) as moral "clients" as well as human beings, and unlike traditional morality, it discusses the moral relationship between humans and nonhuman entities. So while one should be careful in claiming similarity between liberalism and environmental philosophy (just because the former argues for tolerance), it seems fair to maintain that it is at least partly due to liberalism's rejection of methodological monism and fostering of a philosophical and intellectual milieu in which new ideas can flourish, that environmental philosophy has emerged.[16]

The third reason why liberalism became the breeding ground for a flourishing of ecological attitudes lies in the sphere of internal politics. I refer here to a tradition of defending the individual against the church, the state, large-scale industries and firms. This started in the eighteenth century with the defense of the individual against the state or church, followed by a warning that democracy might still yield despotism. A suspicion of the despotic rule of the majority (thus, liberals defended the minorities—especially the intellectuals—from the masses) grew into the ideology of citizens' rights in the twentieth century. Recently liberalism became the defender of the underdog, a crusader against monopolies and for proper government and universal law.[17]

The same stand is taken today by environmentalists: they must challenge the activities of huge industries and firms, mainly because they are unsustainable. Such firms, for purely profit-making motives, often pollute the air or the water, decimate forests, and in general neglect the right of individuals to a clean environment. The state must impose regulations, but very often the state, for economic and other reasons, also ignores the dangers to individuals. The role of environmentalists, then, is to document the situation, publish warnings, and sometimes take the liberty to act.[18]

Indeed, this stand is taken by many environmentalists. Even Jonathon Porritt, ex-director of Friends of the Earth in Britain and one of the leaders of the British Green Party, who attacks liberal politicians for their lack of support for the Green cause,[19] employs the liberal terminology of rights when presenting his Green philosophy.

> The fact that people's *rights* are being denied is in itself a serious enough problem. . . . And the fact that there are so few . . . who are prepared either to inform people of the denial of their *rights* or to help them to fight for those *rights*, turns a problem of indifference into crisis of inaction [emphasis added].[20]

Last, a fourth reason why ecological attitudes have taken root in liberal societies lies in the sphere of international relations. Here one particular element inherent in liberal thought should be highlighted: internationalism. Admittedly this notion sometimes stands for "free trade," which is not environment-friendly, according to many environmentalists. But at the same time, internationalism embodies a strong belief in and reliance on multilateral agreements and international organizations, together with the conviction that political problems may be solved by sometimes tiresome negotiations and that national interests do not necessarily run counter to international cooperation. While many people consider the international arena as a place where "might is right," and where those whose interests are harmed can only complain post factum, liberals have regarded international relations as a sphere in which it is possible to foresee problems and apply the treatment before the damage is caused.

All these elements are crucial, because environmental problems can and must of course be tackled only through international cooperation. This is precisely the element that is both lacking and needed in contemporary politics in regard to the solution of environmental problems, which are rarely entirely local in character.[21] Indeed, the idea that prevention is better than cure has been the underlying rationale for the 1972 Stockholm Conference on the Human Environment, the Toronto Declaration, the London Dumping Convention, *Our Common Future*, the 1992 UNCED in Rio de Janeiro, and other notable international agreements.

At this point it may be argued that at least a few of the features of liberalism, discussed so far, characterize other currents of thought and ideologies as well, for example, socialism. This may be true, although the second feature, that is, the rejection of methodological monism and advancing academic pluralism is, I believe, characteristic mainly of liberalism. But even if not, my argument is neither that liberalism is a necessary condition for the emergence of environmental philosophy, nor that it is a sufficient condition, but rather that liberalism—as a philosophy and a political attitude—influences, stimulates, and encourages the environmental deliberation and the rise of Green thought.

THE POLITICAL TASK

While in recent years much thought has been given to ecology, it seems that it has nevertheless been too little. The damages to the environment are now of such horrifying proportions that many people think that these problems call for radical and urgent solutions, an approach not necessarily compatible with traditional liberal democracy's reluctance to undertake dramatic changes. And yet, now, in the 1990s the world is witnessing a world-wide democratization and the flourishing of liberal-democratic ideas, and no one should be required to abandon this trend.

The extremely complex political mission for the 1990s, then is two-fold: on the one hand, no longer to relieve ecological "suffering," but rather to introduce reforms radical enough to save the environment and reverse what is still reversible; and on the other hand, to ensure this should not come about at the price of imposing regulations that limit or reduce liberties. Thus, there are two dimensions to this mission: to sustain the growing enthusiasm for democracy and liberty and at the same time to save the environment.

As already indicated above, these two dimensions are closely correlated. Many environmentalists, political theorists, and philosophers, in the light of environmental problems, among them scarcity of resources and pollution, have expressed pessimism and anxiety regarding the future of liberal democracy. Lack of resources on the one hand, and selfish, or self-interested, behavior on the other, has caused them to believe that the only solution might be the imposition of regulations and policies against people's wills. William Ophuls, for example, wrote that "the return of scarcity portends the revival of age-old political evils, for our descendants if not ourselves."[22] As Paehlke points out, all these writers fear that the only possible outcome will be "severe economic restraints, self-discipline beyond that which is likely to develop voluntarily."[23]

But Ophuls's prophecy need not necessarily come to pass. For instance, while his suggestion of replacing the market by political action is, I believe, welcome (see below), it is still questionable whether liberty should give way to authority and egalitarian democracy should be abandoned for the sake of "political competence and status."[24] Ophuls's appeal for a strong leadership[25]—reminiscent of George Bernard Shaw's *Man and Superman*—is not the only alternative.

It seems that democratic societies should be looking for a middle path, which might include, at least prima facie, noncoercive, but planned and consistent policies. These policies must be in line with sustaining and promoting democracy and people's liberties, and yet they may also imply a shift from discussing environmental issues politically to a politics of the environment, and hence state intervention. This leads us to the second main question of the paper.

ENVIRONMENTALISM AND LIBERALISM: INDIVIDUALS' ECONOMIC BEHAVIOR

Why does liberalism outside the debate in the universities fail to justify environmental policies? What happens when it comes to real politics? The debate in the universities has been mainly focused on the question of whether or not there are intrinsic values in nature, or on the issue of animals' rights, because it has never been faced with the actual need to convince the other side, for example, developers, vivisectionists, and so forth. But when politicians come to justify their policies to the general public, they must do this in more traditional, general, and popular terms[26] and it is at this point that liberalism runs into difficulties.

Now, in order to demonstrate this, a distinction should be made between two conceptions of politics that represent two interpretations of liberalism. One, which generally speaking is more common in contemporary mainstream American liberalism, is based on the values of neutrality, minimal state intervention, an opposition to regulations, and a concept of politics as an aggregate of autonomous decisions—all of which are antithetical to environmental policies. The other interpretation, sometimes called "social liberalism," is not hostile to advancing certain ideas of the good (for example, conservation), and is more open to state intervention.[27]

But before we discuss the best conception of politics in the context of ecology, a more radical liberal argument, that the state should not intervene at all because individuals' economic behavior is the best foundation for solving environmental policies, needs to be refuted. I deliberately refrain from claiming to refute the "market approach" to the environment. This is a much debated issue, and had I set out to do this, I should have written a separate article. But I would like to examine the literature on the premises of the market approach in our context, with special attention to the "correct" (not in the sense of politically correct) role of politics.

First of all, many arguments have been put forward against the economic behavior approach with respect to the environment. According to several ecosocialists, we can no longer trust the magic and the invisible hand of the market to do the work for us; we must plan and initiate. Individuals' economic behavior has proved to be both inefficient and inequitable in coping with ecology.

For instance, Jeremy Seabrook, an ex-member of the British Labour Party and currently a Green activist, contends that the market is the best and most efficient mechanism to ruin the entire universe. In spite of this, people all over the world have been attracted to the idea of the market and its promise of a better material future, and so forth, because "the economy became the arena in which the guilt for what had happened [in WW II] was to be assuaged." The market, he argues, became "the object of a superstitious reverence: if only this could be made to work, to grow, to provide, we would surely gain exemption from any recurrence of the barbarities of the recent past." The market, he contends, was successful in doing just this, but it cannot provide what people really need and long for: a pleasant and harmonious life. In the east, he claims, the imported idea of the market ruined the traditional rural way of life and its social manifestations, through the process of urbanization, whereas in the west the market ruined our conception of nature.[28]

But the critique of the economic behavior approach in relation to the environment is also based on economic arguments, using "market" terminology to demonstrate that individuals' behavior cannot tackle the environmental issue. According to those arguments, this will always result in more pollution, because the costs of this pollution are borne by nature as well as by other people who share the environment, rather than by the polluter itself.[29] The polluter does not have to be motivated by ill will: this problem is ingrained in the idea of the market and its very "imperative," as Eckersley calls it—"grow or die."[30] Such private attitudes cannot respect environmental notions of limits to growth and carrying capacity. An environment-friendly product is likely to be more expensive than its rival product, and hence no "rational" (that is, profit-seeking) entrepreneur will consider such products.

At this point, market advocates put forward the idea of penalties for the polluter. Let us intervene slightly in the market, they say, and charge the polluter for what he or she has done.[31] So anybody who pollutes, depletes, or utilizes a certain natural resource beyond a certain degree will have to pay for it one way or another. But how can we assess the damages? Can we do this when the damage is not local, or within national borders, but rather international, for example, acid rain in Canada due to air pollution in the U.S.A.? How do we assess the damage when only a small and very specific section of the society is hurt (for example, the workers in a factory, or those who used to play golf on a ground that is now to be developed)? Moreover, it is very likely that the consumers themselves have to pay for the pollution that the manufacture causes, especially in the cases of monopolies or special products that very few firms, or even only one firm produces. So if all polluting manufactures are charged for the pollution they cause, they will transfer the cost to the consumers. All consumers will then pay the real and full price of energy (including cleaning costs). This, in turn, will increase inequality, because the proportion of income spent on energy declines as income increases, although the use of energy increases. Thus, paying the full price of energy seems unfair for the worst-off.

But there is a further problem with regard to assessing environmental damages. While perhaps it is possible to determine the cost of a certain illness (for example, it is equal to the cost of hospital treatment plus a certain amount for compensations), how can we determine the "cost" of a life? Indeed the very term is strange. We are thinking of the value of life, but can it be translated into the "cost" of life? To estimate a person's probable future earnings or any other criterion of the value of life is obnoxious, because in that case someone who possesses this amount of money would be able to purchase another person's life. But, if, as some advocates of the individuals' economic behavior approach have maintained, this question is too artificial or even irrelevant (for instance, because most environmental problems do not cause death), there is still the question of assessing the value of the lives of nonhumans. Thus, how much is the life of a sea otter worth? David Moberg comments that

> surveying people about how much the animals are worth to them or measuring lost income if sea otters disappeared may keep a few economists employed, but it does not answer the question.

This is indeed a cynical, although a serious reply.

> If only one respondent said it was of infinite value, that would throw off the survey. If you limit the response to how much a person would be willing to spend, the result would obviously be affected by how much money people have, a standard flaw of market preference analysis.[32]

Yet Moberg's response is only part of the answer. The truth of the matter is that any calculation or assessment of the cost/value of animals' lives is, at the end of the day, anthropocentric, and any value in the world of nature is instrumental,[33] just as in the Lockean theory only by mixing human labor with natural objects could these object have some (instrumental) value. Preservation, according to this approach, is a problem only because if humans want to enjoy, say, sea otters, they must first "possess" them. What we should have done instead is to ask the animal itself for the value of its life (for itself). Just as, in the case of human lives, we do not ask a murderer what the value of his victim's life is, but rather ask the victim herself or himself, so should we do in the case of animals' lives. Now I do not wish to slip into the heavily discussed question of the degrees of life, the difference between a virus and a horse, and so on. But if, as indicated above, liberalism has enabled biocentrism to flourish, this is not the right moment to retreat to anthropocentrism. Indeed, this is true not only in cases resulting in the death of animals, but in any case of environmental damage. Evaluating the cost in terms of how much people would pay is totally anthropocentric, and if liberalism follows this path it will not be able to genuinely emerge as "environment-friendly" because environmentalists' criticism of the market approach to valuing is that what makes a certain good valuable is not the state of mind of the consumer who wants that good, but rather something inherent in that good.[34]

Now, some "economic behavior" advocates may remain skeptical with regard to biocentrism. Nonetheless, it is undeniable that these calculations fail to evaluate the cost for some other human beings: those of future generations. The not-yet-born are either ignored or "discounted." The main reason for the latter is that these economists tend to discount the future: a value x in the future is less than x now, because it would be equal to the amount that x would yield in this future if it were invested now and benefited from the interest rate. This, of course, is incompatible with any notion of intergenerational equity.[35]

In addition to the above difficulties with the evaluation of the cost of environmental damages, there is a serious difficulty with the notion that serves the market advocates in their approach to this issue. They assume that all we have to do when we decide on environmental policies is ask people how much they will pay to conserve a forest, save the life of three whales, preserve a certain building, and so forth. Economists call this mechanism the WTP (willingness to pay) test.

But following psychological research that Amos Twersky and Danny Kahaneman conducted in the U.S.A. and Maya Bar-Hillel in Israel, I conducted a simple experiment that reveals the fallacy of the concept of WTP. I told a group of forty students that they should imagine that an ecological disaster has occurred, and that there is an urgent need to clean our country's coast. The first twenty students were given papers in which they were asked whether they would contribute 1% of their salaries this month to clean the coast. All of them replied positively. Then they were asked whether they thought it would be possible to know the average amount that their fellow students would be willing to pay. Ninety percent replied that it would be possible; the average WTP predicted was 1.85% of one's salary.

The second group of twenty students were told the same story, and yet they were asked whether they would be willing to pay 4% of their salaries. They all asserted that they would contribute this amount, and thought that the average WTP would be 6.16% of one's salary.

The results are clear: the concept of WTP reflects nothing about "individuals' autonomous wills." Rather we see that the format of the question and the starting point affect the WTP. Is there no consistent notion of WTP?

So I conducted a similar experiment. This time I told forty students that the department had decided to allow them to use our common room for their coffee breaks. Each student would contribute as much as he or she wishes, in order to run this "coffee shop." They were asked whether they would pay $6 a month. They all answered "yes." When asked about the WTP of their fellow students, their answers varied from $2 to $16 with the average of $7.42.

The second group of twenty students were given the same story, but were asked to contribute $30 a month. 20% agreed, whereas 80% disagreed, but the average evaluations of their fellow students' WTP was $15! My conclusion is that WTP is perhaps interesting, theoretically speaking, but it is not a reliable mechanism for revealing preferences.

It goes without saying that this technical question does not exhaust the discussion of the relationship of liberalism with environmental concern, but it does point to the difficulties with regard to the political and practical implications of liberalism in this context. And beyond all these difficulties with the "economic behavior" approach, there is—according to the critique of the market theory—another, perhaps greater, difficulty. This is the belief that individuals' economic behavior yields the best (sometimes defined in terms of being the most rational) results. Do such results include the difficulties that the people of Athens have in breathing every summer, because of traffic pollution? The problem with the market is that even if it corrects itself, it may be too late, because the damage—sometimes to humans—is irreversible.

Some market advocates answer that the question is not one of metaphysical beliefs, but rather of an ethical belief in the idea of freedom. Since they are aware of the environmental damages in our world, they have suggested that firms should be allowed to react in their own ways and according to their own methods to the changing needs of the market, including the need to be more environment-friendly. This, as Eckersley notes, "is not simply a defense of economic efficiency; it is also linked to a defense of political freedom."[36] Thus, for example, if there must be less pollution, then a system of selling pollution rights should be introduced. Pollution rights will be distributed to firms: if x is the degree of pollution that is tolerable, and n is the number of firms, each firm will get x/n pollution rights. Those who can continue manufacturing and limit the resulting pollution will so do, and cover the cost of doing so by selling pollution rights to other firms.[37]

But while some firms adjust to the new circumstances by limiting pollution, others buy pollution rights, and the problem that remains is the distribution of exposure to hazardous waste and pollution. Third world countries have long been disproportionally exposed to dangerous waste. For instance, in the 1970s it was quite common for African countries to "export" land to Western firms for burying toxic and radioactive waste. And in the Western world the poor find themselves unable to buy houses located in safer areas or to look for safer jobs. Even if taxes are introduced, those who find it most difficult to cope will be, again, the least advantaged.[38] Indeed, why should we wait until the dirt is produced in order to clean it up? Why not prevent pollution before workers breathe in smog, or before people are hurt and the environment is damaged? Why should we let the private sector make the decisions on where to pollute? Are such decisions private at all? Should they be in the hands of those who run the industries and pollute rivers, meadows, and seas?

However, to some Greens and other advocates of the environmental case, the above approach seems too superficial and simplistic. In the final analysis, the world is not ready to give up any form of private initiative, or any expression of political freedom in the sphere of economics. The ultimate opposite to an economy that lacks any state action at all would be an economy lacking any profit-making motive, but many people doubt not only whether full state or public ownership is congruent with liberty, but also whether such a system is better for the environment. As Goodin notes, "the environmental consequences of public ownership in Eastern Europe do not serve as a happy precedent."[39] Thus these people seek to modify, refine, or correct the market, to make it more environment-friendly. They do not reject all that liberalism stands for, but still think that if liberalism implies an "individuals' economic behavior" type of economics, then it is inadequate in the sense that it neglects aspects of ecology, wilderness preservation, and so on. The right question to be asked, these Greens argue, is not how to get rid of the market, but what sort of environmental goods it can deliver, and what it cannot.

The market economy, to start with, does not compensate or reward individuals and firms that do act to conserve the environment. A person who lives in an historic house and preserves it is not usually paid to do so. However, if she sells the house to a developer she may make a lot of money. Similarly, the capitalist who invests huge sums of money in order to recycle his or her industry's waste is not rewarded by his or her neighbor capitalist who pollutes the river that runs next to this industry.

Admittedly the market finds solutions to environmental problems: the quality of the water is bad, so we switch to drinking mineral water; there are no green spots left in town, so a farmer opens her land to the public, and we take our car, drive out into the country, and pay the farmer to enjoy nature; there is too much noise, so there are glass factories that offer us cheaper double windows. But the serious question remains: are we satisfied with these solutions? Is this what we wanted? Can we all afford them? And can the market, even if it does solve one or two problems, become the right solution to the ecological crisis in general?[40]

Moreover, the market may suggest theoretical ways of coping with environmental damages; but can it enforce them? Pollution is a good example. All the more litter and a clean environment is a good that (almost) everybody wants. But some environmental goods (for example, leaving a remote forest untouched) are desired by only a part of the population. Individuals' economic behavior will not save this forest, because its economic value to timber merchants is much greater than the amount that some environmentalists are able to pay to save it for aesthetic reasons.[41]

It seems that this list of goods that individuals' behavior cannot supply in the environmental context is quite long and includes some significant examples. So even if we accept the market as a system relevant to the "environmental era," there is still a strong need for "politics." In other words, we shall eventually realize that the economy is not a genuinely market one. But then, the pro-market economists fail not so much in their economic theory as in their political theory. Therefore, instead of dealing with the issue of a "market or non-market" economy, the right question to consider is that of the more suitable type of politics.

So I now want to return to this question, and argue that liberals must come to terms with the political fact that the need to promote environmental policies reveals: namely, that the state of the environment is closely related to our view of "the political" and the political process, including the debate over the good life, and that the issue of the environment involves the goals of our political life rather than merely the means of achieving certain goals.

ENVIRONMENTALISM AND LIBERALISM: CONCEPTIONS OF POLITICS

When discussing the inadequacy of liberalism's image of politics in the context of ecological policies, I must refer first to the impossibility of neutrality in the context of conservation or any other environmental policy.

The idea of neutrality, as advanced by many prominent liberal theorists, is that the state should stay out of the debate on the nature of the good. Official policies should not promote or reflect any conception of what constitutes the good life; on the contrary, the state should be indifferent to any discrepancies between those ideas. For example, while discussing distributive justice, Gauthier writes:

> An essentially just society . . . does not need to shape individuals in order to afford them justice. . . . In saying that an essentially just society is neutral with respect to the aims of its members, we deny that justice is linked to any substantive conception of what is good, either for the individual or for society.[42]

But can one remain neutral in matters of conservation? A neutral argument in favor of conservation must make a fair political procedure the only criterion for choosing a policy. Suppose a liberal, it is argued, holds a belief about the importance of preservation. This person may hope that a way of life, which in one way or another is related to the environment (for example, to a beautiful forest), will be available to posterity. But this liberal fears that, owing to the destruction of the environment, this way of life will disappear. The destruction of natural objects is, in fact, destructive of the very possibility of certain competing ideas of the good life. The liberal fears that in the future one (that is future generations) may not be in a position to make a neutral choice amongst the ideas of the good life, now available.[43]

But this way of reasoning is misleading. If you and I are choosing between x ideas and I assert that we should choose between $(x + 1)$ ideas, you will probably ask me why I insist upon idea $(x + 1)$. I cannot answer "because it exists," because then you may wonder why I do not advocate idea $(x + 2)$. I therefore have no other choice than to explain why $(x + 1)$ is especially desirable, significant, important and so forth. We wish posterity to enjoy a certain object precisely because it has been "desired and found satisfying in the past." Moreover, we do not preserve—indeed we sometimes try to destroy—what we think is wrong or bad, for example, nuclear weapons. Ironically, according to the above liberal argument we should conserve nuclear weapons—perhaps the idea of war itself as a way of life—so that future generations will be aware of it and have the opportunity to choose between a larger variety of ideas of the good. This, of course, is unwise, if not outrageous. In short, an argument in favor of the conservation of a certain object must be based on the claim that this object is in itself good, especially when conserving it contradicts the interests of certain people at the present time (for example, higher salaries, more jobs, and so on).

It is possible at this point to defend the "neutral liberal" stand by distinguishing between those things that are good in themselves, and those things that are instrumentally valuable, arguing that nuclear weapons fall into the latter category. Leaving aside the empirical question of whether or not there are people who regard nuclear weapons, or wars, as a good, this is exactly the point: "neutral" liberals usually find individuals' well-being the most proper—if not the only—moral basic consideration for social policies. They then tend to define individuals' well-being in terms of satisfying personal individual wants, interpreted as those individuals' subjective wants. But they could have defined them according to objective wants (preferences a person would hold if (s)he were fully informed, not confused and rational).[44] Otherwise it is enough to assume that there may be someone who thinks that wars are good to imply the preservation of this idea. We must therefore assert that wars are not good, but then we should do this according to objective wants. In other words, the challenge of the environment is such that objective wants should also be considered and well-being should be an account of final goods.

In the above liberal argument, however, the concept of neutrality is, in fact, derived from the more fundamental values of choice and autonomy, which are, it has been suggested, basic to American liberalism.[45] The latter is therefore considered very democratic inasmuch as, according to its doctrines, political decisions should reflect nothing other than the aggregate of people's preferences, and respect their choices. For example, environmental policies are congruent with liberalism if and only if a majority (or a winning coalition) is in favor. Thus, private preferences and economic measures, backed by the legitimacy of "rational behavior," have supplanted the debate on political ideals and the image of the good life.[46] This philosophy holds that society is an instrument for the benefit of individuals; all the more, therefore, should nature be subjugated by humans, who through its progressive transformation fulfill their individualistic desires.[47] And according to this idea of politics, everything is reduced to private interests, which are held in balance of a market or exchange.[48]

But if there is any methodological innovation in Green philosophy it is that the wall between what has been considered nature or the environment on the side and culture on the other side falls. The concept of the environment becomes part of our culture, or political. Therefore it is repeatedly argued and widely accepted that what is now needed in environmental politics (which are more than the political discussion of environmental matters) is something more sophisticated: not merely policies that are responsive, whatever the individual preferences are or whatever the outcome may be, but policies that, while responsive, take into account the good of the community as a whole as well, and offer solutions to problems that are rarely considered, and, still less, resolved, by individualistic, self-involved, short-run interests.[49] Moreover, there is a good chance that, in the environmental context, individual and private preferences will contradict the general good. Thus Jonathon Porritt writes:

> There may well have been a time, at the start of the Industrial Revolution, when Adam Smith's assertion that the sum of individual decisions in pursuit of self-interest added up to a pretty fair approximation of public welfare, with the "invisible hand" of the market ensuring that individualism and the general interest of society were one and the same thing. But in today's crowded, interdependent world, these same individualistic tendencies are beginning to destroy our *general* interest and thereby harm us all [emphasis added].[50]

Indeed, economic and self-interested individualistic preferences could easily lead to the continuing depletion of scarce resources, be it oil, clean air, or scenic landscape. As Ted Schrecker writes, the resistance of business to environmental regulations has been "bitter" and firms have fought "long and expensive court battles to avoid conviction," sometimes issuing threats to shut down firms.[51]

Garret Hardin's well-known "Tragedy of the Commons"[52] demonstrates this claim: according to him, the state of the environment resembles a pasture open to all. Each herdsman tries to keep as many cattle on the common as possible, but the carrying capacity of the land is insufficient. Each herdsman seeks to improve his own position. If he asks himself the utility of adding one more animal to his herd, he answers that the advantage is +1 (the herdsman receives all the proceeds from the sale of the additional animal), whereas the disadvantage is only a fraction of –1 (the effects of overgrazing being shared by all other herdsmen). The tragedy, of course, is that all herdsmen reach the same conclusion. Further, the question of how to reduce, say, pollution on the roads, illustrates the fact that environmental issues involve concepts of "public good," "collective action," and "free rider," and that the state is needed to provide the necessary solution: that is, environmental policies.

Thus, one must concede that "environmental imperatives are basically matters of principle that cannot be bargained away in an economic fashion", and that "not all of us think of ourselves primarily as consumers; many of us regard ourselves as citizens as well."[53] And as citizens we are concerned with the public interest, or the good of the community rather than with our own personal interests. As citizens, we have obligations that are not always compatible with our private preferences as individuals, and these obligations must receive priority.

> [The] cost-benefit analysis . . . prevents us from achieving a certain kind of self-determination. . . . It prevents us from deciding who we are, not just what we are. . . . There is a right and a wrong way to manage those national parks. . . . The wrong thing to do is to make a big drive-in for Winnebagos. This has nothing to do with what turns a social profit or maximizes wealth. . . .[54]

Many Greens claim that to live in rural areas, for instance, is "living more in harmony with nature" than living in an urban jungle of cars and industries.[55] In other terms, these Greens may be arguing that there is less alienation in village life, or none at all. So they actually claim that one sort of life is better than another, or, in other words, constitutes the good life. Is it? May they be kept poles apart, the Futurists and George Sorel thought that this type of harmony was merely a form of degeneration and degradation. Although I subscribe to the Greens' view here, this is not relevant to my purpose. The point to be established is that a debate on whether this sort of life is good is perfectly legitimate. One must realize that there *is* a debate here on the idea of the good. In the final analysis, this should be obvious. Any Green or counter-Green argument must make some assumption about the idea of the good, since the argument rests on a theory of value, that is, on the idea of an intrinsic, non-instrumental value.[56] And such a theory of value is simply a theory of the good.

Thus the state of the environment calls for politics of the common and a debate on the good. At this point the objection might be raised that, all the same, the Greens' environmental concern represents nothing but an individual's private preferences. The argument would be that the Greens' claim that the world will be destroyed if their suggestions are not implemented is similar to the warnings issued by an almost unknown candidate for the 1992 American presidential campaign, John Huglin, that if he were not elected and his proposals not taken seriously, there would be a worldwide holocaust, or, more seriously, any religious fanatic's prophecy, and his desire that we should all attend churches, synagogues, mosques, and so on. Moreover—the argument goes—a contractor's wish that a certain valley should be inhabited and developed (which is, for that matter, another private preference) is in no way inferior to the environmentalist demand that all work should stop and the beautiful valley should be preserved.

But this criticism is deceptive. With regard to the last point, the question is not a matter of which standpoint is inferior or superior; both developers and environmentalists express ideas of the good life, images of how this world should be and how humans should live. They even sometimes use the same arguments: for instance, developers put forward the psychological argument that if there are more roads and more jobs, then people will be less tense. And environmentalists argue that since tension is caused by noise, traffic, and the fast rhythm of our lives, if we wish to reduce tension, we must limit growth, build fewer roads, and so on. But the point is that these two programs are not preferences that can be bargained over until a compromise is reached. The two sides represent opposite conceptions of a good world, of what is and what is not desirable.

Now with regard to the fanatics, the challenge is easily answered: environmentalism is based on rational evaluations and scientific, empirical knowledge, whereas religious fanatics do not appreciate such evaluations. Their system is irrational in essence; the environmentalists, on the other hand, base their call for change on scientific grounds and empirical—though controversial—data. So environmentalists do not simply express private preferences, but put forward ideas of the good, based on scientific knowledge and phrased in moral terms.

The next question to ask, then, is the following: isn't there a price to pay for the liberals' insistence on regarding politics as a matter of individuals' autonomous decisions? There must be if it limits a consideration of the good of the community, welfare policies, and so on. For the ecologist, politics must provide the framework in which common and general interests are discussed and protected, if not promoted.

We are speaking, then, of state intervention.[57] Now many liberals would argue that one can remain neutral with regard to the idea of the good, but nonetheless advocate interventionism. You don't have to debate the nature of the good in order to justify state intervention. The Rawlsian theory of justice is neutral, it is argued, but is nevertheless in favor of state intervention. I subscribe to the view that in fact Rawls cannot put forward the idea of interventionism without being committed to some idea of the good.[58] This debate, however, is beyond the scope of this paper. For our purpose it is sufficient to claim that even if Rawls (or any other liberal), basing himself on the idea of neutrality, does justify a certain kind of interventionism, it cannot be the one that suits the case of the environment. As we have seen, where the latter is concerned, interventionism is based on and justified by the debate on the good. Any less weighty reason for interventionism would not justify the dramatic policies that are necessary to deal with the ecological disasters with which we are faced nowadays and the political difficulties that accompany them. Indeed, if such dramatic policies were implemented without being based on a genuine debate concerning the good, they would turn out to be nothing more than what Ophuls fears they would be: that is, regulations imposed on a large section of the population without this section understanding why they are needed.[59]

So although liberalism has been a fertile ground for environmental philosophy, it has a basic difficulty with regard to a public environmental policy and its justification: most liberals adhere to neutrality, and regard liberal-democratic politics primarily as a matter of concerning the wills of individuals, whereas environmental issues call for a politics of the common and consequently for interventionism.

Does this imply that liberal governments cannot tackle the environmental challenge? My argument is that if liberalism limits itself to a policy of neutrality and an aggregate of autonomous decisions, then it is likely to fail in this matter. Ecology implies state intervention, justified by a consideration of the common good, and hence abandoning neutrality as a justification for the liberal state and its policies. A sense of community is needed because in the environmental era social and environmental responsibilities should play a much more important role than self-interested profit-making motivation. If we do not wish to retreat to totalitarian regimes, we must take the opportunity that liberalism as a philosophy provided (as I argued in the first part of this article), and look for a liberalism that is more social: the politics of the aggregate of autonomous decisions and an economics of individuals' preferences are of little benefit. The politics of the common, however, that at the same time does not arbitrarily restrict liberties, can be found in the other, perhaps so far more neglected, tradition of liberalism accompanied by a strong welfare state. This conception of liberalism could, perhaps, allow for a justification of environmental policies in terms of liberal terminology, and is therefore much better suited to the environmental era.[60]

NOTES

1. See Kristin Shrader-Frechette, "Science, Democracy, and Public Policy," *Critical Review* 6 (1993): 255–65.

2. Robert Goodin, "International Ethics and the Environmental Crisis," *Ethics and International Affairs* 4 (1990): 81–105, and "The High Road is Green," *Environmental Politics* 1 (1992): 1–8; Steven Yearley, *The Green Case* (London: Harper Collins Academic, 1991); A. de-Shalit, "Environmental Policies and Justice Between Generations," *European Journal of Political Research* 21 (1992): 307–16.
3. For the debate between individualistic liberalism and communitarianism see M. Sandel, ed., *Liberalism and its Critics* (Oxford: Blackwell, 1984); and S. Avineri and A. de-Shalit, eds., *Communitarianism and Individualism* (Oxford: Oxford University Press, 1992).
4. Throughout this essay I give a very broad and flexible interpretation of liberalism, both in a historical sense (I refer to the liberalisms of the eighteenth, nineteenth, and twentieth centuries) and in an analytical sense.
5. John Rawls, *A Theory of Justice* (Oxford: Oxford University Press, 1973), p. 512. See also M.S. Pritchard and W.L. Wade, "Justice and the Treatment of Animals: A Critique of Rawls," *Environmental Ethics* 3 (1981): 55–62; and Walter Achterberg, "Can Liberal Democracy Survive the Environmental Crisis?" in A. Dobson and P. Lucarde, eds., *The Politics of Nature* (London: Routledge, 1993), pp. 81–101.
6. Brendt Singer, "An Extension of Rawls' Theory of Justice to Environmental Ethics," *Environmental Ethics* 10 (1988): 217–32.
7. R. Taylor, "The Environmental Implications of Liberalism," *Critical Review* 6 (1993):265–83.
8. The latter is Ronald Dworkin's formula. See his "Reverse Discrimination" in his *Taking Rights Seriously* (London: Duckworth, 1981), and his "Liberalism" in his *A Matter of Principle* (Oxford: Clarendon Press, 1986). But see also John Locke ("This equality of men by Nature . . . [is] so evident in itself, and beyond all question . . . ," in his *Second Treatise of Governments*, chap. II, 5), the French first declaration of the rights of man and of citizens ("Men are born, and always continue, free and equal in respect to their rights"), the American Declaration of Independence, Thomas Paine's *Rights of Man*, and Alexis de Tocqueville's *Democracy in America* (since everyone is equal, no one is entitled to be a despotic ruler: part II, chap. 10).
9. This is typical of ecofeminist philosophy. See A. Collard and J. Contrucci, *Rape of the Wild* (London: The Women's Press, 1988). But also of environmental philosophy in general: see R. Routely, "Against the Inevitability of Human Chauvinism," in K. Goodpaster, ed., *Ethics and the Problems of the 21st Century* (Notre Dame: Notre Dame University Press, 1979).
10. Aldo Leopold, *A Sand County Almanac* (Oxford: Oxford University Press, 1987 [1949]).
11. Christopher Stone, "Should Trees Have Standing?," *Southern California Law Review* 45 (1972), and *Earth and Other Ethics* (New York: Harper and Row, 1987).
12. Roderick Nash, *The Rights of Nature* (Madison: University of Wisconsin Press, 1989), p. 200. See also Robert Paehlke, *Environmentalism and the Future of Progressive Politics* (New Haven: Yale University Press, 1989), pp. 8–9.
13. Paul Taylor, "Frankena on Environmental Ethics," *Monist* 64 (1981): 217, and *Respect for Nature* (Princeton: Princeton University Press, 1986), pp. 56–57.
14. J. Horton and S. Mendus, *Aspects of Toleration* (London: Methuen, 1985).
15. For example, Alastair Gunn, "Traditional Ethics and the Moral Status of Animals," *Environmental Ethics* 5 (1983): 133–54.
16. Anna Brammwell traces the origins of environmentalism to romantic philosophy and right-wing political theories. But she fails to distinguish between anti-rational, anti-modern ruralism, and modern, scientific-based and democratic Green environmentalism. See Anna Bramwell, *Ecology in the Twentieth Century* (New Haven: Yale University Press, 1991).

17. Michael Freeden, *The New Liberalism* (Oxford: Clarendon Press, 1978), and Ronald Dworkin, "Liberalism," in his *A Matter of Principle* (Oxford: Clarendon Press, 1986), pp. 187–88.
18. Three good examples of Green publications that warn of the dangers to individuals' rights are the books by Brian Price, *The Friends of the Earth Guide to Pollution* (London: Friends of the Earth, 1983); John May, *The Greenpeace Book of the Nuclear Age* (London: Victor Gollancz Ltd, 1989); and Ferencz and Keyes, *PlanetHood: The Keys to Your Survival and Prosperity* (Oregon: Vision Books, 1988). A famous green act was Greenpeace's attempt to stop French nuclear tests in the Pacific, which ended with the blowing up of the Greenpeace boat by members of French Intelligence in 1985.
19. Jonathan Porritt, *The Coming of the Greens* (London: Fontana, 1988), pp. 71–76.
20. Jonathan Porritt, *Seeing Green* (Oxford: Basil Blackwell, 1984), p. 115.
21. Consider, for instance, the damage being caused by all nations to the ozone layer, the problem of acid rain, or the contamination of the Mediterranean Sea. For a further discussion of the international aspects see G. Porter and J. Brown, *Global Environmental Change* (Boulder: Westview Press, 1991); R.E. Benedick, *Ozone Diplomacy* (Cambridge, Mass.: Harvard University Press, 1992); the Brundtland report, Brundtland Gro Harlem et al.; The World Commission on Environment and Development staff, *Our Common Future* (Oxford: Oxford University Press, 1987); and M. Grubb et al., *The Earth Summit Agreements* (London: Earthscan, 1993).
22. William Ophuls, *Ecology and the Politics of Scarcity* (San Francisco: W.H. Freeman, 1977), p. 145.
23. Robert Paehlke, "Democracy, Bureaucracy, and Environmentalism," *Environmental Ethics* 10 (1988): 293.
24. William Ophuls, op. cit., p. 227.
25. Ibid., p. 159. To be fair, Ophuls denied that he had wanted rule by elite: see his comment in William Ophuls, "On Hoffert and the Scarcity of Politics," *Environmental Ethics* 8 (1986): 287–88.
26. Carolyn Merchant, *Radical Ecology* (London: Routledge, 1992), pp. 159–63, describes such cases and such tendencies among the "big ten" environmental organizations in the U.S.A., and Andrew Dobson, *Green Political Thought* (London: Harper Collins Academic, 1990), discusses the differences between the public and private faces of green argumentation.
27. I discuss the manifestations in Europe of the latter in my article, in Bob Brecher, ed., *Liberalism and the New Europe* (London: Avebury Press, 1993), pp. 149–62.
28. Jeremy Seabrook, *The Myth of the Market* (London: Green Books, 1990), pp. 13–14 and chap. 7.
29. David Moberg, "Environment and Markets," *Dissent* 38 (1991): p. 511.
30. Robyn Eckersley, "Green versus Ecosocialist Economic Programmes: the Market Rules OK?," *Political Studies* 40 (1992): 319.
31. It is interesting to note that John Stuart Mill already thought this could be a solution to air pollution. See *Principles of Political Economy* (New York: The Coloral Press, 1990), p. 7.
32. Moberg, op. cit., p. 512.
33. For a more complicated distinction see Andrew Brennan, "Moral Pluralism and the Environment," *Environmental Values* 1 (1992): 15–33.
34. Robert Goodin, *Green Political Theory* (Oxford: Polity, 1992), p. 25.
35. See Robyn Eckersley, op. cit., p. 319. Some market advocates suggested that future generations' interests are, in fact, represented in any social arrangement that is decided upon now. See David Gauthier, *Morals By Agreement* (Oxford: Clarendon Press, 1986), p. 299. I argue elsewhere that bargaining with the not yet born is impossible, not only literally, but also theoretically. See my *Why Posterity Matters* (London: Routledge, 1994).

36. Robyn Eckersley, op. cit., p. 318.
37. Steidlmeier, for example, argues that pollution permits have a legitimacy as "a second-best solution." See "The Morality of Pollution Permits," *Environmental Ethics* 15 (1993): 133–50.
38. See the statement issued by the Centre for Science and Environment (New Delhi) on global environmental democracy, as a reaction to the "northern agenda," in *Alternatives* 17 (1992): 271–79. Also see J. Moberg, "Who Rules the Market," *Political Studies* 40 (1992): 337.
39. Robert Goodin, op. cit., p. 7, fn. 30.
40. See also Brian Barry, "The Continuing Relevance of Socialism," in Brian Barry, *Liberty and Justice* (Oxford: Clarendon Press, 1991); and Robyn Eckersley, "Free Market Environmentalism: Friend or Foe?," *Environmental Politics* 2 (1993): 1–20.
41. This is related to the question of whether only use value should count, or whether option value (that is, whether I can use and enjoy this environmental good in the future) counts as well. See Alan Randall, "Human Preferences, Economics, and the Preservation of Species," in B. Norton, ed., *The Preservation of Species* (Princeton: Princeton University Press, 1986).
42. David Gauthier, *Morals by Agreement*, p. 341. See also John Rawls, *Political Liberalism* (New York: Columbia University Press, 1993); Bruce Ackerman, *Social Justice in the Liberal State* (New Haven: Yale University Press, 1980); and Will Kymlicka, "Liberal Individualism and Liberal Neutrality," *Ethics* 99 (1989): 883–905. But see Joseph Raz, "Liberalism, Autonomy and the Politics of Neutral Concern," *Midwest Studies in Philosophy* 7 (1980): 89–120.
43. This rationale is put forward in Ronald Dworkin, "Liberalism," op. cit., p. 202.
44. Compare R.M. Hare, "Ethical Theory and Utilitarianism," in A. Sen and B. Williams, eds., *Utilitarianism and Beyond* (Cambridge: Cambridge University Press, 1982).
45. Ronald Beiner, "Liberalism," in his *What's the Matter with Liberalism?* (Berkeley: University of California Press, 1992); and William Galston, *Liberal Purposes* (Cambridge: Cambridge University Press, 1991).
46. See, for example, Kenneth Arrow, *Social Choice and Individual Values* (New York: Wiley, 1962).
47. See also Charles Taylor, *Hegel* (Cambridge: Cambridge University Press, 1975), pp. 540–43.
48. On this see John Elster, "The Market and the Forum: Three Varieties of Political Theory," in J. Elster and A. Hylland, *The Foundations of Social Choice Theory* (Cambridge: Cambridge University Press, 1986).
49. See David Miller's account of energy policies to the two models of politics in his "Deliberative Democracy and Social Choice," *Political Studies* 40 (1992): 54–66.
50. Jonathon Porritt, *Seeing Green*, p. 116.
51. T. Schrecker, "Resisting Environmental Regulations," in R. Paehlke and D. Torgerson, eds., *Managing Leviathan* (London: Belhaven Press, 1991), pp. 165–99; and H. Feiveson, F. Sinden, and R. Socolow, eds., *Boundaries of Analysis* (Cambridge, Mass.: Ballinger Pub., 1976).
52. Garret Hardin, "The Tragedy of the Commons," *Science* 162 (1968): 1243–48.
53. William Ophuls, *Ecology and the Politics of Scarcity*, p. 186; and Mark Sagoff, *The Economy of the Earth* (Cambridge: Cambridge University Press, 1988), p. 27.
54. Mark Sagoff, "Ethics and Economics in Environmental Law," in T. Regan, ed., *Earthbound* (Prospect Heights, Illinois: Waveland Press, 1984), pp. 172–73.
55. For example, Robert Goodin, *Green Political Theory*, p. 51.
56. Arne Naess, *Ecology, Community, and Lifestyle* (Cambridge: Cambridge University Press. 1989); Holmes Rolston III, *Philosophy Gone Wild* (Buffalo: Prometheus Books, 1989).
57. Indeed, it seems that the state "has generally been the only institution with the necessary resources to provide environmental policies." K. Walker, "The State in Environmental Management," *Political Studies* 37 (1980): 25–38.

58. I elaborate on this in "Community and the Rights of Future Generations," *Journal of Applied Philosophy* 9 (1992): 105–17. See also T. Nagel, "Rawls on Justice," in N. Daniels, *Reading Rawls* (Oxford: Basil Blackwell, 1975), pp. 1–16.
59. It is sometimes suggested by environmentalists that international environmental concern is also crucial for the much needed international cooperation in any valid environmental policy. See C. Spretnak and F. Capra, *Green Politics* (London: Paladin, 1985). pp. 157–81. But this forms another issue. See L.K. Caldwell, *International Environmental Policy* (Durham: Duke University Press, 1984).
60. I would like to thank David Miller and my students in the Environmental Ethics seminar for their comments.

Socialism and Ecology*

James O'Connor

James O'Connor is Professor of Sociology and Economics at the University of California, Santa Cruz, and is Editor-in-Chief of Capitalism, Nature, Socialism.

The premise of red green political action is that there is a global ecological and economic crisis; that the ecological crisis cannot be resolved without a radical transformation of capitalist production relationships; and that the economic crisis cannot be resolved without an equally radical transformation of capitalist productive forces. This means that solutions to the ecological crisis presuppose solutions to the economic crisis and vice versa. Another *a priori* of red green politics is that both sets of solutions presuppose an ecological socialism.

The problem is that socialism in theory and practice has been declared "dead on arrival." In theory, post-Marxist theorists of radical democracy are completing what they think is the final autopsy of socialism. In practice, in the North, socialism has been banalized into a species of welfare capitalism. In Eastern Europe, the moment for democratic socialism seems to have been missed over 20 years ago and socialism is being overthrown. In the South, most socialist countries are introducing market incentives, reforming their tax structures, and taking other measures that they hope will enable them to find their niches in the world market. Everywhere market economy and liberal democratic ideas on the right, and radical democratic ideas on the left, seem to be defeating socialism and socialist ideas.

Meanwhile, a powerful new force in world politics has appeared, an ecology or green movement that puts the earth first and takes the preservation of the ecological integrity of the planet as the primary issue. The simultaneous rise of the free market and the greens together with the decline of socialism suggests that capitalism has an ally in its war against socialism. This

*Thanks are due John Ely and Martin O'Connor, in particular, and also Samir Amin, Daniel Faber, Jomo K.S., Brinda Rao, David Sonnenfeld, and Andrew Szasz for helpful criticisms and comments.

This essay originally appeared in *Capitalism, Nature, Socialism,* 2(3), 1991, 1–12. Reprinted with permission.

turns out to be the case. Many or most greens dismiss socialism as irrelevant. Some or many greens attack it as dangerous. Especially are they quick to condemn those who they accuse of trying to appropriate ecology for Marxism.[1] The famous green slogan, "neither left nor right, but out front," speaks for itself.[2]

But most greens are not friends of capitalism, either, as the green slogan makes clear. The question then arises, who or what are the greens allied with? The crude answer is, the small farmers and independent business, i.e., those who used to be called the "peasantry" and "petty bourgeoisie;" "liveable cities" visionaries and planners; "small is beautiful" technocrats; and artisans, cooperatives, and others engaged in ecologically friendly production. In the South, greens typically support decentralized production organized within village communal politics; in the North, greens are identified with municipal and local politics of all types.

By the way of contrast, mainstream environmentalists might be called "fictitious greens."[3] These environmentalists support environmental regulations consistent with profitability and the expansion of global capitalism, e.g., resource conservation for long-run profitability and profit-oriented regulation or abolition of pollution. They are typically allied with national and international interests. In the U.S., they are environmental reformers, lobbyists, lawyers, and others associated with the famous "Group of Ten."

As for ecology, everywhere it is at least tinged with populism, a politics of resentment against not only big corporations and the national state and central planning but also against environmentalism.

Ecology (in the present usage) is thus associated with "localism," which has always been opposed to the centralizing powers of capitalism. If we put two and two together, we can conclude that ecology and localism in all of their rich varieties have combined to oppose both capitalism and socialism. Localism uses the medium or vehicle of ecology and vice versa. They are both the content and context of one another. Decentralism is an expression of a certain type of social relationship, a certain social relation of production historically associated with small-scale enterprise. Ecology is an expression of a certain type of relationship between human beings and nature—a relationship which stresses the integrity of local and regional eco-systems. Together ecology and localism constitute the most visible political and economic critique of capitalism (and state socialism) today.

Besides the fact that both ecology and localism oppose capital and the national state, there are two main reasons why they appear to be natural allies. First, ecology stresses the site specificity of the interchange between human material activity and nature, hence opposes both the abstract valuation of nature made by capital and also the idea of central planning of production, and centralist approaches to global issues generally.[4] The concepts of site specificity of ecology, local subsistence or semi-autarkic economy, communal self-help principles, and direct forms of democracy all seem to be highly congruent.

Second, the socialist concept of the "masses" has been deconstructed and replaced by a new "politics of identity" in which cultural factors are given the place of honor. The idea of the specificity of cultural identities seems to meld easily with the site specificity of ecology in the context of a concept of social labor defined in narrow, geographic terms. The most dramatic examples today are the struggles of indigenous peoples to keep both their cultures and subsistence type economies intact. In this case, the struggle to save local cultures and local eco-systems turns out to be two different sides of the same fight.

For their part, most of the traditional left, as well as the unions, remain focused on enhanced productivity, growth, and international competitiveness, i.e., jobs and wages, or more wage labor—not to abolish exploitation but to be exploited less. This part of the left does not want to be caught any more defending any policies which can be identified with "economic austerity" or policies which labor leaders and others think would endanger past economic gains won by the working class (although union and worker struggles for healthy and safe conditions inside and outside of the workplace obviously connect in positive ways with broader ecological struggles). Most of those who oppose more growth and development are mainstream environmentalists from the urban middle classes who have the consumer goods that they want and also have the time and knowledge to oppose ecologically dangerous policies and practices. It would appear, therefore, that any effort to find a place for the working class in this equation, i.e., any attempt to marry socialism and ecology, is doomed from the start.

But just because something has never happened does not mean that it cannot happen. Or that it is not happening in various ways right now. In the developed capitalist countries, one can mention the green caucuses within Canada's NDP; the work of Barry Commoner, who calls for source reduction, the "social governance of technology," and economic planning based on a "deep scientific understanding of nature;" the anti-toxic and worker and community health and safety movements which bring together labor, community, and ecological issues; various red-green Third World solidarity movements, such as the Third World Network and Environmental Project on Central America; and the new emphasis on fighting ecological racism. One thinks of the Socialist Party's struggle for control of the Upper House of the Diet against the long-entrenched Liberal Democrats, which reflects rising concern about both ecological and social issues in Japan. In Europe, we can see the greening of Labor, Social Democratic, and Communist Parties, even if reluctantly and hesitatingly, as well as the rise of the Green Parties, some of which (as in Germany) are to the left of these parties with respect to some traditional demands of the labor movement. And in the sub-imperialist powers, which are taking the brunt of the world capitalist crisis, e.g., Brazil, Mexico, and Argentina in Latin America, and India and perhaps Nigeria, Korea, and Taiwan, there are new ecological movements in which the traditional working class is engaged. And we cannot forget the Nicaraguan experiment which combined policies aimed at deep environmental reforms with socialism and populism.

There are good reasons to believe that these and other eco-socialist tendencies are no flash in the pan, which permits us to propose that ecology and socialism is not a contradiction in terms. Or, to put the point differently, there are good reasons to believe that world capitalism itself has created the conditions for an ecological socialist movement. These reasons can be collected under two general headings. The first pertains to the causes and effects of the world economic and ecological crisis from the mid-1970s to the present. The second pertains to the nature of the key ecological issues, most of which are national and international, as well as local, issues.

First, the vitality of Western capitalism since World War II has been based on the massive externalization of social and ecological costs of production. Since the slow-down of world economic growth in the mid-1970s, the concerns of both socialism and ecology have become more pressing than ever before in history. The accumulation of global capital through the modern crisis has produced even more devastating effects not only on wealth and income distribution, norms of social justice, and treatment of minorities, but also on the environment. An "accelerated imbalance of (humanized) nature" is a phrase that neatly sums this up. Socially, the crisis has led to more wrenching poverty and violence, rising misery in all parts of the world, especially the South, and, environmentally, to toxification of whole regions, the production of drought, the thinning of the ozone layer, the greenhouse effect, and the withering away of rain forests and wildlife. The issues of economic and social justice and ecological justice have surfaced as in no other period in history. It is increasingly clear that they are, in fact, two sides of the same historical process.

Given the relatively slow rate of growth of world-wide market demand since the mid-1970s, capitalist enterprises have been less able to defend or restore profits by expanding their markets and selling more commodities in booming markets. Instead, global capitalism has attempted to rescue itself from its deepening crisis by cutting costs, by raising the rate of exploitation of labor, and by depleting and exhausting resources. This "economic restructuring" is a two-sided process.

Cost cutting has led big and small capitals alike to externalize more social and environmental costs, or to pay less attention to the global environment, pollution, depletion of resources, worker health and safety, and product safety (meanwhile, increasing efficiency in energy and raw material use in the factories). The modern ecological crisis is aggravated and deepened as a result of the way that capitalism has reorganized itself to get through its latest economic crisis.

In addition, new and deeper inequalities in the distribution of wealth and income are the result of a worldwide increase in the rate of exploitation of labor. In the United States during the 1980s, for example, property income increased three times as fast as wage and salary income. Higher rates of exploitation have also depended upon the ability to abuse undocumented workers and set back labor unions, social democratic parties, and struggles for social justice generally, especially in the South. It is no accident that in those parts of the world where ecological degradation is greatest—Central America, for example—there is greater poverty and heightened class struggles. The feminization of poverty is also a part of this trend of ecological destruction. It is the working class, oppressed minorities, women, and the rural and urban poor worldwide who suffer most from both economic and ecological exploitation. The burden of ecological destruction falls disproportionately on these groups.

Crisis-ridden and crisis-dependent capitalism has forced the traditional issues of socialism and the relatively new issues ("new" in terms of public awareness) of ecology to the top of the political agenda. Capitalism itself turns out to be a kind of marriage broker between socialism and ecology, or, to be more cautious, if there is not yet a prospect for marriage, there are at least openings for an engagement.

Second, the vast majority of economic and social and ecological problems worldwide cannot be adequately addressed at the local level. It is true that the degradation of local ecological systems often do have local solutions in terms of prevention and de-linking (although less so in terms of social transformation). Hence it comes as no surprise to find strong connections between the revival of municipal and village politics and local ecological destruction. But most ecological problems, as well as the economic problems which are both cause and effect of the ecological problems, cannot be solved at the local level alone. Regional, national, and international planning are also necessary. The heart of ecology is, after all, the inter-dependence of specific sites and the need to situate local responses in regional, national, and international contexts, i.e., to sublate the "local" and the "central" into new political forms.

National and international priorities are needed to deal with the problem of energy supplies, and supplies of nonrenewal resources in general, not just for the present generation but especially for future generations. The availability of other natural resources, e.g., water, is mainly a regional issue, but in many parts of the globe it is a national or international issue. The same is true of the destruction of forests. Or take the problem of soil depletion, which seems to be local or site specific. Insofar as there are problems of soil quantity and quality, or water quantity or quality, in the big food exporting countries, e.g., the U.S., the food importing countries are also effected. Further, industrial and agricultural pollution of all kinds spills over local, regional and national boundaries. North Sea pollution, acid rain, ozone depletion, and global warming are obvious examples.

Furthermore, if we broaden the concept of ecology to include urban environments, or what Marx called "general, communal conditions of production," problems of urban transport and congestion, high rents and housing, and drugs, which appear to be local issues amenable to local solutions, turn out to be global issues pertaining to the way that money capital is allocated worldwide; the loss of foreign markets for raw materials and foodstuffs in drug-producing countries; and the absence of regional, national and international planning of infrastructures.

If we broaden the concept of ecology even more to include the relationship between human health and well-being and environmental factors (or what Marx called the "personal condition of production"), given the increased mobility of labor nationally and internationally, and greater emigration and immigration, partly thanks to the way capital has restructured itself to pull out of the economic crisis, we are also talking about problems with only or mainly national and international solutions.

Finally, if we address the question of technology and its transfer, and the relationship between new technologies and local, regional, and global ecologies, given that technology and its transfer are more or less monopolized by international corporations and nation states, we have another national and international issue.

In sum, we have good reasons to believe that both the causes and consequences of, and also the solutions to, most ecological problems are national and international, hence that far from being incompatible, socialism and ecology presuppose one another. Socialism needs ecology because the latter stresses site specificity and reciprocity, as well as the central importance of the material interchanges within nature and between society and nature. Ecology needs socialism because the latter stresses democratic planning, and the key role of the social interchanges between human beings. By contrast, popular movements confined to the community, municipality or village cannot by themselves deal effectively with most of both the economic and ecological aspects of the general destructiveness of global capitalism, not to speak of the destructive dialectic between economic and ecological crisis.

If we assume that ecology and socialism presuppose one another, the logical question is, why haven't they gotten together before now? Why is Marxism especially regarded as unfriendly to ecology and vice versa? To put the question another way, where did socialism go wrong, ecologically speaking?

The standard, and in my opinion correct, view is that socialism defined itself as a movement which would complete the historical tasks of fulfilling the promises of capitalism. This meant two things: first, socialism would put real social and political content into the formal claims of capitalism of equality, liberty, and fraternity. Second, socialism would realize the promise of material abundance which crisis-ridden capitalism was incapable of doing. The first pertains to the ethical and political meanings of socialism; the second, to the economic meaning.

It has been clear for a long time to almost everyone that this construction of socialism failed on two counts. First, instead of an ethical, political society, in which the state is subordinated to civil society, we have the Party bureaucratic state; and thus the post-Marxist attempt to reconcile social justice demands with liberalism.

Second, and related to the first point, in place of material abundance, we have the economic crisis of socialism; and thus the post-Marxist attempt to reconcile not only social justice demands and liberalism but also both of these with markets and market incentives.

However, putting the focus on these obvious failures obscures two other issues that have moved into the center of political debates in the past decade or two. The first is that the ethical and political construction of socialism borrowed from bourgeois society ruled out any ethical or political practice that is not more or less thoroughly human-centered, as well as downplaying or ignoring reciprocity and "discursive truth." The second is that the economic construction of abundance borrowed with only small modifications from capitalism ruled out any material practice that did not advance the productive force, even when these practices were blind to nature's economy. Stalin's plan to green Siberia, which fortunately was never implemented, is perhaps the most grotesque example.

These two issues, or failure, one pertaining to politics and ethics, the other to the relationship between human economy and nature's economy, are connected to the failure of historical materialism itself. Hence they need to be addressed in methodological as well as theoretical and practical terms.

Historical materialism is flawed in two big ways. Marx tended to abstract his discussions of social labor, i.e., the divisions of labor, from both culture and nature. A rich concept of social labor which includes both society's culture and nature's economy cannot be found in Marx or traditional historical materialism.

The first flaw is that the traditional conception of the productive forces ignores or plays down the fact that these forces are social in nature, and include the mode of cooperation, which is deeply inscribed by particular cultural norms and values.

The second flaw is that the traditional conception of the productive forces also plays down or ignores the fact that these forces are natural as well as social in character.

It is worth recalling that Engels himself called Marxism the "materialist conception of history," where "history" is the noun and "materialist" is the modifier. Marxists know the expression "in material life social relations between people are produced and reproduced" by heart, and much less well the expression "in social life the material relations between people and nature are produced and reproduced." Marxists are very familiar with the "labor process" in which human beings are active agents, and much less familiar with the "waiting process" or "tending process" characteristic of agriculture, forestry, and other nature-based activities in which human beings are more passive partners and, more generally, where both parties are "active" in complex, interactive ways.

Marx constantly hammered away on the theme that the material activity of human beings is two-sided, i.e., a social relationship as well as a material relationship; in other words, that capitalist production produced and reproduced a specific mode of cooperation and exploitation and a particular class structure as well as the material basis of society. But in his determination to show that material life is also social life, Marx tended to neglect the opposite and equally important fact that social life is also material life. To put the same point differently, in the formulation "material life determines consciousness," Marx stressed that since material life is socially organized, the social relationships of production determine consciousness. He played down the equally true fact that since material life is also the interchange between human beings and nature, that these material or natural relationships also determine consciousness. These points have been made in weak and strong ways by a number of people, although they have never been integrated and developed into a revised version of the materialist conception of history.

It has also been suggested *why* Marx played up history (albeit to the exclusion of culture) and played down nature. The reason is that the problem facing Marx in his time was to show that capitalist property relationships were historical not natural. But so intent was Marx to criticize those who naturalized hence reified capitalist production relationships, competition, the world market, etc., that he forgot or downplayed the fact that the development of human-made forms of "second nature" does not make nature any less natural. This was the price he paid for inverting Feuerbach's passive materialism and Hegel's active idealism into his own brand of active materialism. As Kate Soper has written, "the fact is that in its zeal to escape the charge of biological reductionism, Marxism has tended to fall prey to an antiethical form of reductionism, which in arguing the dominance of social over natural factors literally spirits the biological out of existence altogether."[5] Soper then calls for a "social biology." We can equally call for a "social chemistry," "social hydrology," and so on, that is, a "social ecology," which for socialists means "socialist ecology."

The greens are forcing the reds to pay close attention to the material interchanges between people and nature and to the general issue of biological exploitation, including the biological exploitation of labor, and also to adopt an ecological sensibility. Some reds have been trying to teach the greens to pay closer attention to capitalist production relationships, competition, the world market, etc.—to sensitize the greens to the exploitation of labor and the themes of economic crisis and social labor. And feminists have been teaching both greens and reds to pay attention to the sphere of reproduction and women's labor.

What does a green socialism mean politically? Green consciousness would have us put "earth first," which can mean anything you want it to mean politically. As mentioned earlier, what most greens mean in practice most of the time is the politics of localism. By contrast, pure red theory and practice historically has privileged the "central."

To sublate socialism and ecology does not mean in the first instance defining a new category which contains elements of both socialism and ecology but which is in fact neither. What needs to be sublated politically is localism (or decentralism) and centralism, i.e., self-determination and the overall planning, coordination, and control of production. To circle back to the main theme, localism per se won't work politically and centralism has self-destructed. To abolish the state will not work; to rely on the liberal democratic state in which "democracy" has merely a procedural or formal meaning will not work, either. The only political form that might work, that might be eminently suited to both ecological problems of site specificity and global issues, is a democratic state—a state in which the administration of the division of social labor is democratically organized.[6]

Finally, the only *ecological* form that might work is a sublation of two kinds of ecology, the "social biology" of the coastal plain, the plateau, the local hydrological cycle, etc., and the energy economics, the regional and international "social climatology," etc., of the globe—that is, in general, the sublation of nature's economy defined in local, regional and international terms. To put the conclusion somewhat differently, we need "socialism" *at least* to make the social relations of production transparent, to end the rule of the market and commodity fetishism, to end the exploitation of human beings by other human beings; we need "ecology" at least to make the social productive forces transparent, to end the degradation and destruction of the earth.

NOTES

1. This is a crude simplification of green thought and politics, which varies from country to country, and which are also undergoing internal changes. In the U.S., for example, where Marxism historically has been relatively hostile to ecology, "left green" is associated with anarchism or libertarian socialism.
2. This slogan was coined by a conservative co-founder of the German Greens and was popularized in the U.S. by anti-socialist "New Age" greens, F. Capra and C. Spretnak. Needless to say, it was never accepted by left greens of any variety.
3. "Mainstream environmentalists" is used to identify those who are trying to save capitalism from its ecologically self-destructive tendencies. Many individuals who call themselves "environmentalists" are alienated by, and hostile to, global capitalism, and also do not necessarily identify with the "local" (see below).
4. Martin O'Connor writes, "One of the striking ambivalencies of many writers on 'environmental' issues is their tendency to make recourse to authoritarian solutions, e.g., based on ethical elitism. An example is the uneasy posturings found in the collection by Herman Daly in 1973 on *Steady-State Economics.*"
5. Quoted by Ken Post, "In Defense of Materialistic History," *Socialism in the World,* 74/75, 1989, p. 67.
6. I realize that the idea of a "democratic state" seems to be a contradiction in terms, or at least immediately raises difficult questions about the desirability of the separation of powers; the problem of scale inherent in any coherent description of substantive democracy; and also the question of how to organize much less plan a nationally and internationally regulated division of social labor without a universal equivalent for measuring costs and productivity (however "costs" and "productivity" are defined) (courtesy of John Ely).

A Social Ecology

John Clark

John Clark is professor of philosophy at Loyola University, New Orleans, and currently chairs the Environmental Studies Program. He has long been active in the green and bioregionalism movements. His books include The Anarchist Moment: Reflections on Culture, Nature, and Power; Liberty, Ecology, Geography: The Social Thought of Elisée Reclus; *and a forthcoming reinterpretation of social ecology.*

Humanity is Nature achieving self-consciousness.
—Elisée Reclus[1]

In its deepest and most authentic sense, a social ecology is the awakening earth community reflecting on itself, uncovering its history, exploring its present predicament, and contemplating its future.[2] One aspect of this awakening is a process of philosophical reflection. As a philosophical approach, a social ecology investigates the ontological, epistemological, ethical, and political dimensions of the relationship between the social and the ecological and seeks the practical wisdom that results from such reflection. It seeks to give us, as beings situated in the course of real human and natural history, guidance in facing specific challenges and opportunities. In doing so, it develops an analysis that is both holistic and dialectical and a social practice that might best be described as an ecocommunitarianism.

THE SOCIAL AND THE ECOLOGICAL

A social ecology is, first of all, an *ecology*. There are strong communitarian implications in the very term *ecology*. Literally, it means the *logos*, the reflection on or study of the *oikos*, or household. Ecology thus calls on us to begin to think of the entire planet as a kind of community of which we are members. It tells us that all of our policies and problems are in a sense "domestic" ones. While a social ecology sometimes loses its bearings as it focuses on specific social concerns, when it is consistent it always situates those concerns within the context of the earth household, whatever else it may study within that community. The dialectical approach of a social ecology requires social ecologists to consider the ecological dimensions of all "social" phenomena. There are no "nonecological" social phenomena to consider apart from the ecological ones.

In some ways, the term *social* in *social ecology* is the more problematical one. There is a seeming paradox in the use of *social* for what is actually a strongly *communitarian* tradition. Traditionally, the "social" realm has been counterposed to the "communal" one, as in Tönnies's famous distinction between society and community, *Gesellschaft* and *Gemeinschaft.* Yet this apparent self-contradiction may be a path to a deeper truth. A social ecology is a project of reclaiming the communitarian dimensions of the social, and it is therefore appropriate that it seek to recover the communal linguistic heritage of the very term itself. *Social* is derived from *socius,* or "companion." A *society* is thus a relationship between companions—in a sense, it is itself a household within the earth household.

AN EVOLVING THEORY

Over the past quarter-century, a broad social and ecological philosophy has emerged under the name social ecology. While this philosophy has recently been most closely associated with the thought of social theorist Murray Bookchin, it continues a long tradition of ecological communitarian thought going back well into the nineteenth century. The lineage of social ecology is often thought to originate in the mutualistic, communitarian ideas of the anarchist geographer Kropotkin. One can certainly not deny that despite Kropotkin's positivistic tendencies and his problematical conception of nature, he has an important relationship to social ecology. His ideas concerning mutual aid, political and economic decentralization, human-scaled production, communitarian values, and the history of democracy have all made important contributions to the tradition.[3] However, it is rooted much more deeply in the thought of another great anarchist thinker, the French geographer Elisée Reclus (1830–1905). During the latter half of the last century and into the beginning of the present one, Reclus developed a far-ranging "social geography" that laid the foundations of a social ecology as it explored the history of the interaction between human society and the natural world, starting with the emergence of *homo sapiens* and extending to Reclus's own era of urbanization, technological development, political and economic globalization, and embryonic international cooperation.

Reclus envisioned humanity achieving a free, communitarian society in harmony with the natural world. His extensive historical studies trace the long record of experiments in cooperation, direct democracy, and human freedom from the ancient Greek polis through Icelandic democracy, medieval free cities, and independent Swiss cantons to modern movements for social transformation and human emancipation. At the same time, he depicts the rise and development of the modern centralized state, concentrated capital, and authoritarian ideologies. His sweeping historical account includes an extensive critique of both capitalism and authoritarian socialism from an egalitarian and antiauthoritarian perspective and an analysis of the destructive ecological effects of modern technology and industry allied with the power of capital and the state. It is notable that a century ago Reclus's social theory attempted to reconcile a concern for justice in human society with compassionate treatment of other species and respect for the whole of life on earth—a philosophical problematic that has only recently reemerged in ecophilosophy and environmental ethics.[4]

Many of the themes in Reclus's work were developed further by the Scottish botanist and social thinker Patrick Geddes (1854–1932), who described his work as "biosophy," the philosophical study of the biosphere. Geddes focuses on the need to create decentralized communities in harmony with surrounding cultural and ecological regions and proposes the development of new technologies (neotechnics) that would foster humane, ecologically balanced communities. He envisions an organically developing cooperative society, based on the practice of mutual aid at the most basic social levels and spreading throughout society as these small communities voluntarily federate into larger associations. Geddes orients his work around the concepts of "Place, Work, and Folk," envisioning a process of incorporating the particularities of the natural region and humane, skillful, and creative modes of production and organically developing local culture into his "Eutopia," or good community. Geddes calls his approach a "sociography," or synthesis of sociological and geographical studies. He applies this approach in his idea of the detailed regional survey as a means of achieving community planning that is rooted in natural and cultural realities and grows out of them organically. He thus makes an important contribution in developing the empirical and bioregional side of the social ecological tradition.[5]

Many of Geddes's insights were later integrated into the expansive vision of society, nature, and technology of his student, the American historian and social theorist Lewis Mumford (1895–1992), who is one of the most pivotal figures in the development of the social ecological tradition. Ramachandra Guha is certainly right when he states, "The range and richness of Mumford's thought mark him as the pioneer American social ecologist. . . ."[6] Most of the fundamental concepts to which Bookchin later attached to the term *social ecology* were borrowed from Mumford's much earlier ecological regionalism.[7] The philosophical basis for Mumford's social analysis is what he calls an "organic" view of reality, a holistic and developmental approach he explicitly identifies as an "ecological" one.[8] In accord with this outlook, he sees the evolution of human society as a continuation of a cosmic process of organic growth, emergence, and development. Yet he also sees human history as the scene of a countermovement within society and nature, a growing process of mechanization.

Much like Reclus before him, Mumford depicts history as a great struggle between freedom and oppression. In Mumford's interpretation of this drama, we find on one side the forces of mechanization, power, domination, and division, and on the other, the impulse toward organism, creativity, love, and unification. The tragedy of history is the increasing ascendancy of mechanism and the progressive destruction of our organic ties to nature and to one another. The dominant moment of history, he says, has been "one long retreat from the vitalities and creativities of a self-sustaining environment and a stimulating and balanced communal life."[9]

Mumford describes the first decisive step in this process as the creation in the ancient world of the Megamachine, in the form of regimented, mechanized massing of human labor power under hierarchical control to build the pyramids as an expression of despotic power. While the Megamachine in this primal barbaric form has persisted and evolved over history, it reemerges in the modern world in a much more complex, technological manifestation, with vastly increased power; diverse political, economic, and cultural expressions; and apparent imperviousness to human control or even comprehension. Mumford sees the results of this historical movement as the emergence of a new totalitarian order founded on technological domination, economic rationality, and profit and fueled by a culture of obsessive consumption. The results are a loss of authentic selfhood; a dissolution of organic community; and a disordered, destructive relationship to the natural world.

Mumford's vision of the process of reversing these historical tendencies is a social-ecological one. He foresees a process of social decentralization in which democratic institutions are re-created at local and regional levels as part of organic but diverse communities. "Real human communities," he contends, are those that combine unity with diversity and "preserve social as well as visual variety."[10] Following Geddes and prefiguring bioregionalism, Mumford believes that the local community must be rooted in the natural and cultural realities of the region. "Strong regional centers of culture" are the basis for "an active and securely grounded local life."[11] Regionalism is not only an ecological concept but also a political and cultural one, and it is the crucial link between the most particular and local dimensions and the most universal and global ones. "The rebuilding of regional cultures" Mumford says, "will give depth and maturity to the world culture that has likewise long been in the process of formation."[12] Mumford contends that an epochal process of personal and social transformation is necessary if the course of history is to be redirected toward a humane, ecological, life-affirming future. Much in the spirit of communitarian philosopher Martin Buber, he foresees a humanized, cooperative world culture emerging out of regenerated regional cultures that arise in turn out of a regenerated human spirit.[13]

While he begins with a general perspective on society and nature that is close to Mumford's, Bookchin makes a number of crucial contributions to the further development of a social ecology.[14] Most significantly, he broadens the theoretical basis of the communitarian, organicist, and regionalist tradition developed by Reclus, Geddes, and Mumford by making dialectical analysis a central focus. He thereby opens the way for more critical and theoretically sophisticated discussions of concepts like holism, unity-in-diversity, development, and relatedness. He also develops Mumford's defense of an organic worldview into a more explicitly ecological theoretical perspective. Mumford's analysis of the historical transformation of organic society into the Megamachine is expanded in Bookchin's somewhat broader account of the emergence of diverse forms of domination and of the rise of hierarchical society. He devotes more detailed attention to the interaction of the state, economic classes, patriarchy, gerontocracy, and other factors in the evolution of domination. Of particular importance is Bookchin's emphasis on the central role of the developing global capitalist economy in ecological crisis, which corrects Mumford's tendency to overemphasize the technical at the expense of the economic.[15] He also adds some additional chapters to the "history of freedom," especially in his discussions of the mutualistic, liberatory, and ecological dimensions of tribal societies, millenarian religious movements, and utopian experiments. Finally, while his predecessors presented a rather general vision of a politics that was antiauthoritarian, democratic, decentralist, and ecological, Bookchin gives a concrete political direction to the discussion of such a politics in his proposals for libertarian municipalism and confederalism.

Some of these contributions have come at a considerable cost. Although Bookchin develops and expands the tradition of social ecology in important ways, he has at the same time also narrowed it through dogmatic and nondialectical attempts at philosophical system building, through an increasingly sectarian politics, and through intemperate and divisive attacks on "competing" ecophilosophies and on diverse versions of his own tradition.[16] To the extent that social ecology has been identified with Bookchinist sectarianism, its potential as an ecophilosophy has not been widely appreciated.

Fortunately, the fundamental issues posed by a social ecology will not fade away in the smoke of ephemeral (and eminently forgettable) partisan skirmishes. Inevitably, a broad, vibrant, and inherently self-critical tradition like social ecology will resist attempts to restrict it in a manner that contradicts its most fundamental values of holism, unity-in-diversity, organic growth, and dialectical self-transcendence. Thus, despite its temporary setbacks, the project of a social ecology continues to develop as a general theoretical orientation, as an approach to the analysis of specific problems, and as a guide to practical efforts at social and ecological regeneration.

A DIALECTICAL HOLISM

A social ecology, as a holistic vision, seeks to relate all phenomena to the larger direction of evolution and emergence in the universe as a whole. Within this context, it also examines the course of planetary evolution as a movement toward increasing complexity and diversity and the progressive emergence of value. According to Mumford, an examination of the "creative process" of "cosmic evolution" reveals it to be "neither random nor predetermined" and shows that a "basic tendency toward self-organization, unrecognizable until billions of years had passed, increasingly gave direction to the process."[17]

This outlook is related to the long teleological tradition, extending from ancient Greek thought to the most recent organicist and process philosophies. It is in accord with Hegel's insight that "substance is subject," if this is interpreted in an evolutionary sense. There is no complete and "given" form of either subject or substance but rather a universal process of substance-becoming-subject. Substance tends toward self-organization, life, consciousness, self-consciousness, and finally transpersonal consciousness (although the development takes place at all levels of being and not merely in consciousness). Social ecology is thus linked to theories of evolutionary emergence. Such a position remains implicit in Hegel's dialectical idealism,[18] receives a more explicit expression in Samuel Alexander's cosmic evolutionism,[19] underlies the metaphysics of Whitehead and contemporary process philosophy,[20] is given a rather technocentric and antinaturalist turn in Teilhard de Chardin,[21] is synthesized with Eastern traditions in Radhakrishnan and Aurobindo,[22] and finds its most developed expression in Ken Wilber's recent effort at grand evolutionary synthesis.[23]

A social ecology interprets planetary evolution and the realization of social and ecological possibilities as a holistic process, rather than merely as a mechanism of adaptation. This evolution can only be understood adequately by examining the interaction and mutual determination between species and species; between species and ecosystem; and among species, ecosystem, and the earth as a whole and by studying particular communities and ecosystems as complex, developing wholes. Such an examination reveals that the progressive unfolding of the potentiality for freedom (as self-organization, self-determination, and self-realization) depends on the existence of symbiotic cooperation at all levels—as Kropotkin pointed out almost a century ago. We can therefore see a striking degree of continuity in nature, so that the cooperative ecological society that is the goal of a social ecology is found to be rooted in the most basic levels of being.

Some critics of social ecology have claimed that its emphasis on the place of human beings in the evolutionary process betrays a nonecological anthropocentrism. While this may be true of some aspects of Bookchin's thought, it does not describe what is essential to a social ecology. Although we must understand the special place that humanity has within universe and earth history, the consequences of such understanding are far from being hierarchical, dualistic, or anthropocentric. A dialectical analysis rejects all "centrisms," for all beings are at once centers (of structuration, self-organization, perceiving, feeling, sensing, knowing, etc.) and also expressions of that which exists at a distance since from a dialectical perspective, determination is negation, the other is immanent in a being, and the whole is immanent in the part. There exists not only unity-in-diversity and unity-in-difference but also unity-in-distance. We must interpret our place in nature in accord with such an analysis, comprehending the ways in which our being is internally related, we might say "vertically," to more encompassing realms of being and, we might say "horizontally," to wider realms of being. By exploring our many modes of relatedness we discover our social and ecological responsibility—our capacity to respond to the needs of the human and natural communities in which we participate.[24]

The use of metaphors such as *community* and *organism* in a dialectical and holistic account of diverse phenomena is certainly not unproblematical. There has rightly been much debate in ecophilosophy concerning the status of such images, and their function and limitations must be a subject of continuing reflection.[25] A dialectical approach assumes their provisional nature, the importance of avoiding their use in a rigid, objectifying way, and the necessity of allowing all theoretical concepts to develop in the course of inquiry. Thus, there are certainly senses in which the earth or the biosphere cannot be described as a community. One might define community as a relationship existing between beings who can act reciprocally in certain ways, taking the criterion for reciprocity to be showing respect, carrying out obligations, or some other capacity. If one adopts such a "model" of a community, the earth is certainly not one, any more than it is an organic whole, if that term is taken to mean having the qualities of a biological organism. Yet the term *community* has in fact much more expansive connotations than those just mentioned. A community is sometimes thought to include not only competent adult human beings (moral agents) but also infants and children, the mentally incompetent, past generations, future generations, domesticated animals, artifacts, architecture, public works, values and ideals, principles, goals, symbols, imaginary significations, language, history, customs and traditions, territory, biota, ecosystems, and other constituents that are thought essential to its peculiar identity. To be a member of a community is often thought to imply responsibilities of many kinds in relation to some or all of the categories listed.

Questions are also raised about the totalizing implications of holism. Critics of holism sometimes identify it with an extreme organicism that denies the significance, reality, or value of the parts.[26] It is important, therefore, to understand that "holism" does not refer exclusively to a view in which the whole is ontologically prior to the part, more metaphysically real than the part, or deserving of more moral consideration than the part. In fact, a dialectical holism rejects the idea that the being, reality, or value of the parts can be distinguished from that of the whole in the manner presupposed by such a critique.

This is sometimes misunderstood when critics overlook an important distinction within a dialectical holism. In its comprehensively holistic analysis, the parts of a whole are not *mere parts* but rather *holons*, which are themselves relative wholes in relation to their own parts.[27] The good of the part can therefore not be reduced to a function of its contribution to the good of the whole. Its good can be also be considered in relation to its *participation* in the attainment of the good of a whole that it helps constitute. But beyond this, to mention what is most relevant to the critiques of holism, its attainment of its *own* good as a unique expression of wholeness must also be considered. There is a striking irony here. An authentic holism is capable of appreciating the value of kinds of wholeness (realized form, self-organization, attainment of good) that are often ignored by "individualisms" that defend *one* level of wholeness against its possible dissolution in some larger whole. Holism does not mean the fetishization of some particular kind of whole, which would constitute a version of the fallacy of misplaced concreteness, but rather an exploration of the meaning of many kinds of wholeness that appear in many ways and on many levels within developing unity-in-diversity.

NO NATURE[28]

So much for the truth of the whole. However, a *dialectical* holism refuses to objectify, reify, or absolutize any whole, including the whole of nature. Just as our experience of objects or things points to the reality of that which escapes objectification and reification, our experience of the whole of nature points to the reality of that which cannot be reduced to nature.

Since the beginnings of philosophical reflection, dialectical thinkers of both East and West have proposed that beneath all knowing and objects of knowledge there is a primordial continuum, the eternal one-becoming-many, the ground of being. It is what Lao Tzu described in the *Tao te Ching* as the reality that precedes all conceptualization, or "naming," and all determination, or "carving of the block":

> The Tao (Way) that can be told is not the eternal Tao;
> The name that can be named is not the eternal name.
> The Nameless is the origin of Heaven and Earth. . . .[29]

This reality is ontologically prior to ecological differentiation and, indeed, to "nature" itself—which is one reason that a mere "naturalism" can never be adequately dialectical. It is an apprehension of the conditional reality of all phenomena that drives dialectical thought to an affirmation of both the being and nonbeing of all objects, categories, and concepts. This ground is what social ecological theorist Joel Kovel refers to as the "plasma of being." It is also what mystical philosophers like Böhme have, quite dialectically, called "the groundless Ground," attempting to express the idea that it is a nonobjectifiable grounding of being rather than an objectified ground, or substance, on which anything can be thought to stand, or which "underlies" other realities. If we wish to attach any concept to this ultimate, it should perhaps be (following Whitehead) "creativity."

As Kovel points out, contemporary science has shown that such a continuum underlies the diversity of beings: "In the universe as a whole, there is no real separation between things; there are only, so far as the most advanced science can tell us, plasmatic quantum fields; one single, endlessly perturbed, endlessly becoming body."[30] Kovel's account of our relation to this primordial ground is both phenomenological and psychoanalytic. It reveals the ways in which we are ecological beings, and indeed spiritual beings, because our being extends beyond the limits of the ego or socially constructed selfhood. Much of our experience reveals to us that this self is not sufficient, or primary, "but is rather that ensemble of social relations which precipitates out of a primordium which comes before social causation—a core which, crucially, remains active throughout life. Before the self, there is being; and before being is the unconscious primordium. Society intersects with the individual through a set of cultural representations. It is a naming, a designation, an affixing from without. Without this naming, the stuff of a person would never take form. But the unconscious, in its core, is prerepresentational."[31] Thus, there are fundamental aspects of being that connect us, physically, psychologically, and ontologically, with greater (or deeper) realities—with other living beings, with our species, with the earth, with the primordial ground of being.

This idea of connectedness leads us to the question of the place of the concept of spirit in a dialectical holism. The most radical "critical" and dialectical views after Hegel, beginning with the Young Hegelians—Feuerbach, Stirner, Marx, and their peers—were intent on banishing Hegel's central category from the philosophical realm. The post-Hegelian dialectical tradition has been dominated by a reductive materialism that has dogmatically rejected the possibility of dialectical inquiry into the most fundamental ontological questions. Some versions of social ecology have inherited this antispiritual tendency of Western materialism. Thus, while Bookchin has sometimes invoked the concept of "ecological spirituality" in his writings, it has usually been in the weak sense of a vague ecological or even ethical sensibility, and he has increasingly sought to banish any strong conception of "spirit" from his social ecological orthodoxy.

It is becoming evident, however, that the most radically dialectical and holistic thinking restores the ontological and political significance of the concept of spirit. Without implying any of the dogmatic and one-sided idealist aspects of Hegel's conception of spirit, a social ecology can find in the concept an important means of expressing our relationship to the evolving, developing, unfolding whole and its deeper ontological matrix. Kovel begins his discussion of spirit with the statement that it concerns "what happens to us as the boundaries of the self give way."[32] The negation of ego identity that he intends by this concept takes place when we discover our relationship to the primordial continuum and to its expressions in the processes of life, growth, development, and the striving toward wholeness. A social ecology can give meaning to an ecological spirituality that will embody the truth of the religious consciousness,[33] which is a liberatory truth, however mystified and distorted it may have been for purposes of domination and social conformism. Such a spirituality is the synthesis and realization of the religion of nature and the religion of history. It consists of a response to the sacredness of the phenomena, of the multiplicity of creative expressions of being, and of the whole that encompasses all beings. It is also an expression of wonder and awe at the mystery of becoming, the unfolding of the universe's potentiality for realized being, goodness, truth, and beauty.

THE ECOLOGICAL SELF

A social ecology applies its holistic and dialectical approach of the question of the nature of the self. While it emphasizes wholeness, it does not accept the illusory and indeed repressive ideal of a completely harmonious, fully integrated selfhood. Rather it sees the self as a developing whole, a relative unity-in-diversity, a whole in constant process of self-transformation and self-transcendence. The very multiplicity of the self, "the chaos within one," is highly valued since it attests to the expansiveness of selfhood and to our continuity with the larger context of being, of life, of consciousness, of mind. Such a view of selfhood shows a respect for the uniqueness of each person and for the striving of each toward a highly particularized (in some ways incomparable) good that flows from his or her own nature. But it also recognizes that personal self-realization is incomprehensible apart from one's dialectical interaction with other persons, with the community, and with the larger natural world. The development of authentic selfhood means the simultaneous unfolding of both individuality and social being. The replacement of the voracious yet fragile and underdeveloped ego of consumer society with such a richly developed selfhood is one of the preeminent goals of social ecology.

Within this general orientation, there remain many areas for development of the social-ecological conception of the self. As Kovel points out, the realm of signification creates an imaginary sphere in which there is a necessary degree of separation from nature, and even from oneself as nature. He explains that "we are at one time part of nature, fully participating in natural processes; and at the same time we are radically different from nature, ontologically destined by a dialectic between attachment and separation to define ourselves in a signified field which by its very 'nature' negates nature."[34] Because of this "basic negativity" in the human standpoint toward the world, "the relationship between the self and nature cannot be comprehended though any simple extrapolation of an ecological model grounded in unity in diversity."[35] Moreover, the "thinglike" aspects of the self—the realm of the preconceptual and of the most primordial layers of desire—can never be fully transcended in either thought or experience. Part of the social ecological project of comprehending "unity-in-diversity" is to theorize adequately this duality and the necessary experiential and ontological moments of alienation, separation, and distance within a general nondualistic, holistic framework (rather than merely to explain these moments away).

In doing so, social ecology will delve more deeply into those inseparable dimensions of body and mind that dualism has so fatefully divided. As we explore such realities as thought, idea, image, sign, symbol, signifier, and language, on the one hand, and the feeling, emotion, disposition, instinct, passion, and desire, on the other, the interconnection between the two "realms" will become increasingly apparent. The abstract "naturalism" of Bookchin's social ecology will be transformed into a richer, more dialectical, and many-sided naturalization. As Abram notes, "We can experience things—can touch, hear, and taste things—only because, as bodies, we are ourselves included in the sensible field, and have our own textures, sounds and tastes. We can perceive things at all only because we are entirely a part of the sensible world that we perceive! We might as well say that we are organs of this world, flesh of its flesh, and that the world is perceiving itself *through* us."[36] Such a holistic concept of human-nature interaction is a necessary complement to the conception of humanity as "nature becoming self-conscious" or "nature knowing itself," which might otherwise be taken in a one-sidedly intellectual, objectifing, and ultimately idealist sense.

A SOCIAL ECOLOGY OF VALUE

For a social ecology, our ecological responsibility as members of the earth community arises from both our relationship to the interrelated web of life on earth and also from our place as a unique form of nature's and the earth's self-expression. As we accept the responsibilities implied by our role in "nature becoming self-conscious," we can begin to reverse our presently antirevolutionary and ecocidal direction and begin to contribute to the continuation of planetary natural and social evolution. We can also cooperate with natural evolution through our own self-development. The overriding ethical challenge to humanity is to determine how we can follow our own path of self-realization as a human community while at the same time allowing the entire earth community to continue its processes of self-manifestation and evolutionary unfolding.[37] A crucial link between these two goals is the understanding of how the flourishing of life on earth is constitutive of the human good, as we dialectically develop in relation to the planetary whole. As Thomas Berry has noted, a central aspect of the human good is to enjoy and indeed celebrate the goodness of the universe, a goodness that is most meaningfully manifested for us in the beauty, richness, diversity, and complexity of life on earth (the social and ecological unity-in-diversity).

A dialectical and holistic theory of value attempts to transcend atomistic theories, without dissolving particular beings (including human beings) into the whole, whether the whole of nature or of the biosphere. Holmes Rolston's holistic analysis, and especially his critique of the conventional division of value into intrinsic and instrumental varieties, can contribute much to the development of a social ecology of value. When value is generated in a system (or, as a social ecology would state it, within a *whole* that is not reducible to a mere sum of parts), we find that it is not generated in an "instrumental" form, for there is no specific entity or entities for the good of which the value is generated as a means. Nor do we find "intrinsic" value in the sense that it there is a single, coherent, definable good or *telos* for the system. Therefore, we must posit something like what Rolston calls "systemic value." According to this conception, the value that exists within the system "is not just the sum of the part-values. No part-values increase of kinds, but the system promotes such increase. Systemic value is the productive process; its products are intrinsic values woven into instrumental relationship."[38]

Such a holistic analysis helps us to reach an authentically ecological understanding of value within ecosystems or ecocommunities. For Rolston, the "species-environment complex ought to be preserved because it is the generative context of value."[39] The ecosystem—that is, the ecocommunity that has shaped the species, is internally related to it, and is embodied in its very mode of being—is a value-generating whole. Ultimately, the earth must be comprehended as, for us, the most morally significant value-generating whole. We must fully grasp the conception of a planetary good that is realizing itself through the greatest mutual attainment of good by all the beings that constitute that whole—in terms of both their own goods and their contribution to shared systemic goods of the various wholes in which they participate.

AN ECOLOGY OF THE IMAGINATION

If a social ecology is to contribute to radical ecological social transformation, it must address theoretically all the significant institutional dimensions of society. It must take into account the fact that every social institution contains organizational, ideological, and imaginary aspects (moments that can be separated from one another only for purposes of theoretical analysis). An economic institution, for example, includes a mode of organizing persons and groups, their activities and practices, and of utilizing material means for economic ends. It also includes a mode of discourse and a system of ideas by which it understands itself and seeks to legitimate its ends and activities. Finally, it includes a mode of self-representation and self-expression by which it symbolizes itself and imagines itself. The social imaginary is part of this third sphere and consists of the system of socially shared images by which the society represents itself to itself.

One essential task of a social ecology is to contribute to the creation of an ecological imaginary, an endeavor that presupposes an awareness of our own standpoint within the dialectical movement of the social world. A social ecology of the imagination therefore undertakes the most concrete and experiential investigation of the existing imaginary. To the extent that this has been done, it has been found that we live in an epoch that is defined above all by the dominant economistic institutions. This dominance is exercised through all the major institutional spheres: economistic forms of social organization, economistic ideology, and an economistic imaginary. But the dominant economism is far from simple and monolithic. Most significantly, it is divided into two essential moments that interact in complex and socially efficacious ways.

These two essential moments, productionism and consumptionism, are inseparable and mutually interdependent. As Marx pointed out long ago in the classical dialectical inquiry on this subject, "Production, distribution, exchange and consumption . . . all form the members of a totality, distinctions within a unity."[40] While Marx's analysis was profoundly shaped by the productionist era in which he lived, all subsequent inquiry is a continuation of the dialectical project that he suggests in this passage. A social ecology ignores none of the moments Marx identifies but rather looks at distribution and exchange as mediating terms between production and consumption. But it will focus on the contemporary world as the scene of a strange dialectic between abstract, systemic rationality and social and ecological irrationality. The economistic society drives relentlessly toward absolute rationality in the exploitation of natural and human resources, in the pursuit of efficiency of production, in the development of technics, in the control of markets through research, and in the manipulation of behavior through marketing. At the same time, it rushes toward complete irrationality in the generation of infinite desire, in the colonization of the psyche with commodified images, in the transformation of the human and natural world into a system of objects of consumption, and most ultimately and materially in undermining the ecological basis for its own existence. Whatever the shortcomings of Marx as economist and political theorist, he is unsurpassed as a prophet insofar as he revealed that the fundamental irrationality of economistic society is in its *spirituality*—the fetishism of commodities.

AN ECOLOGICAL IMAGINARY

One result of the careful study of the social imaginary is the realization that a decisive moment in social transformation is the development of a counter-imaginary. Success in the quest for an ecological society will depend in part on the generation of a powerful ecological imaginary to challenge the dominant economistic one. While this process is perhaps in an embryonic stage, we have in fact already developed certain important elements of an emerging ecological imaginary.

The image of the region poses a powerful challenge to the economistic, statist, and technological imaginaries. Regions are a powerful presence yet have no clearly definable boundaries. This is the case whether these regions are ecoregions, georegions, bioregions, ethnoregions, mythoregions, psychoregions, or any other kind. Regionalism evokes a dialectical imagination that grasps the mutual determination between diverse realms of being, between culture and nature, between unity and multiplicity, between form and formlessness, between being and nothingness. The concept of regionality implies an interplay between the overlapping, evolving boundaries of natural spaces and the flowing, redefining boundaries of imaginary spaces.[41]

The region is intimately connected to another powerful ecological image—that of the wild. The wild is present in the spontaneous aspects of culture and nature. We find it in forms of wild culture, wild nature, and wild mind: in the poetic, in the carnvalesque, in dreams, in the unconscious, in wilderness. We find it in the living earth and in the processes of growth and unfolding on the personal, communal, planetary, and cosmic levels. The point is not to find the wild in any "pristine" state; it is always intermixed with civilizations, domestication, and even domination. The discovery of the wild within a being or any realm of being means the uncovering of its self-manifestation, its creative aspects, its relative autonomy. It is the basis for respect for beings but, even more, for wonder, awe, and a sense of the sacred in all things. The revolts and individualisms of the dominant culture appear quite tame when civilization is subjected to the critique of the wild.[42]

The image of the earth as "Home," or planetary household, and humans as members of the earth community has great imaginary power. As we develop greater knowledge of ecological complexity and as we rediscover the marvelous richness of place, the earth image begins to incorporate within itself a rich regional and local specificity and become a holistic representation of planetary unity-in-diversity. As the horror of economistic-technocratic globalism becomes increasingly apparent, and as the world is remade in the image of the factory, the prison, and the shopping mall, the rich, dialectical counterimage of the earth will necessarily gain increasing imaginary force.

The ecological imaginary can be expanded further to cosmic or universal dimensions. All cultures have felt the need to imagine the macrocosm and orient themselves in relation to the whole. Brian Swimme and Thomas Berry contend that the universe story, taken from contemporary cosmology and transformed into a culturally orienting narrative, "is the only way of providing, in our times, what the mythic stories of the universe provided for tribal peoples and for the earlier classical civilizations in their times."[43] Through the universe and earth story, people see themselves as part of larger processes of development and "unfolding of the cosmos." They thus achieve "a sense of relatedness to the various living and nonliving components of the earth community."[44] These powerful, indeed sublime narratives relativize cultural absolutes and shake the dominant imaginary, just as they give new imaginary meaning to human existence, consciousness, and creativity.

FREEDOM AND DOMINATION

The larger processes of self-realization and unfolding of potentialities have often (since Hegel) been described as the emergence of freedom in the history of humanity, the earth, and the universe. A social ecology carries on this tradition and seeks to give an ecological meaning to such a conception of freedom. It rejects both the "negative freedom" of mere noncoercion or "being left alone" of the liberal individualist tradition, as well as the "positive freedom" of the "recognition of necessity" found in many strongly organicist forms of holism. A social ecological conception of freedom focuses on the realization of a being's potentialities for identity, individuality, awareness, complexity, self-determination, relatedness, and wholeness. In this sense, freedom is found to some degree at all levels of being: from the self-organizing and self-stabilizing tendencies of the atom to the level of the entire universe, evolving to higher levels of complexity and generating new levels of being. In our own planetary history, embryonic freedom can be found in the directiveness of all life, and it takes on increasingly complex forms, including, ultimately, the possibility of humans as complex social beings attaining their good through a highly developed and respectful relationship to other humans and the natural world. The realization of such freedom requires that humanity attain consciousness of its place in the history of the earth and of the universe, that it develop the ethical responsibility to assume its role in larger processes of self-realization, and that human social institutions be reshaped to embody the conditions that would make this knowledge and ethical commitment into practical historical forces. Bookchin's conception of "free nature" focuses on the way in which human self-realization, culminating in creation of an ecological society, establishes a growing planetary realm of freedom. This occurs as humanity "add[s] the dimension of freedom, reason, and ethics to first [i.e., nonhuman] nature and raise[s] evolution to a level of self-reflexivity. . . ."[45] The *activity* of humanity and human self-realization are thus seen as central to the achievement of freedom in nature.

But there is another, larger ecological dimension to freedom. The realization of planetary freedom requires not only the human self-realization that is emphasized in Bookchin's "free nature" but also the human recognition of limits and the human forbearance that is expressed in Arne Naess's usage of that same term.[46] In this sense, "free nature" is the spontaneous, creative nature that has given rise to the entire rich, diverse system of self-realizing life on this planet. It has also given rise to humanity itself, dialectically shaped humanity through our interaction with all the other expressions of this free activity, and made us the complex beings that we are. As necessary as it is for humanity to rectify its disastrous disruptions of natural processes and although a restorative ecological practice is undoubtedly required, a social ecology must also help humanity regain its capacity for creative nonaction, for the Taoist *wu wei*, for "letting-be." The social-ecological conception of freedom as spontaneous creative order points to the need for a larger sphere of wild nature so that biodiversity can be maintained and evolutionary processes can continue their self-expression, not only in human culture and humanized nature, but also in the natural world substantially free of human influence and control. A social ecology therefore implies the necessity not only for wilderness preservation but also for an extensive expansion of wilderness (and relative wilderness) areas where they have been largely destroyed.

A social ecology's vision of human freedom and "free nature" is closely related to its fundamental project of critique of the forms of domination that have stood in the way of human and planetary self-realization. However, there have been some widespread misconceptions about the social-ecological analysis of domination. These result in part from Bookchin's definition of social ecology as the view that "ecological problems arise from deep-seated social problems"[47] and his claims that the "quest to dominate nature" results from actual domination within human society. In a sense, contemporary ecophilosophies in general assert that ecological problems stem from social ones. For example, deep ecology holds that ecological problems result from the social problem of anthropocentrism, and ecofeminism holds that ecological problems result from the social problem of patriarchal ideologies and social structures. But there remains a fundamental dispute between those who, like Bookchin, give causal priority in the creation of ecological crisis to social *institutions* (like capitalism or the state) and others who stress the causal priority of social *ideologies* (like dualism, anthropocentrism, or patriarchal values).

But both sides in this dispute have often seemed less than dialectical in their approach. The roots of ecological crisis are at once institutional and ideological, psychological and cultural. A critical approach to the issue will avoid both one-sided materialist explanations (identifying economic exploitation or other "material conditions" as "the problem") and one-sided idealism (identifying a system of ideas like anthropocentrism as "the problem.") It is indeed tempting to see the emergence of certain hierarchical institutions as the precondition for human destructiveness toward the natural world. Yet these very institutions could only emerge because of the potential for domination, hierarchical values, objectification, and power seeking that have roots in the human psyche and are actualized under certain historical conditions. Furthermore, as a system of domination develops, it does so through its dialectically interacting institutional, ideological, and imaginary spheres, all of which are related to a "transhistorical" human nature developed over a long history of species evolution. Any account of the origins of hierarchy and domination and of their possible "dissolution" must therefore address *at once* the material, institutional, psychological, and even ontological moments of both the development of these phenomena and the process of reversing it.

ECOCOMMUNITARIAN POLITICS

A social ecology seeks to restore certain elements of an ancient conception of the political and to expand the limits of the concept. According to a classic account, if ethics is the pursuit of the good life, or self-realization, then politics is the pursuit of the good life *in common* and self-realization for *the whole community*. A social ecology affirms the political in this sense but reinterprets it in ecological terms. It seeks to recover our long-obscured nature as *zoön politikon* and to explore new dimensions of that nature. By this term is meant not simply the "political animal" who participates in civic decision-making processes but also the social and communal being whose selfhood is developed and expressed through active engagement in many dimensions of the life of the community.

A social ecology investigates the ways in which we can encourage the emergence of humane, mutualistic, ecologically responsible institutions in all areas of social life. It sees not only "politics" but also all areas of social interaction, including production and consumption, personal relationships, family life, child care, education, the arts, modes of communication, spiritual life, ritual and celebration, recreation and play, and informal modes of cooperation, to be *political* realms in the most profound sense. Each is an essential sphere in which we can develop our social being and communal individuality and in which a larger communitarian reality can find much of its basis. Such a conception of the political requires that practices and institutions be humane in spirit and scale, life affirming, creative, decentralized, nonhierarchical, rooted in the particularity of people and place, and based on grassroots, participatory democracy to the greatest degree practically possible.

The social ecological tradition has long emphasized the importance of local democracy. Reclus and Kropotkin both wrote extensively about its history, and Mumford argues that "the neighborhood . . . must be built again into an active political unit, if our democracy is to become active and invigorated once more, as it was two centuries ago in the New England village, for that was a superior political unit. The same principles apply again to the city and the interrelationship of cities in a unified urban and regional network or grid."[48] This conception of regional democracy based in local democracy is a corrolary of the general social-ecological conception (expressed by Geddes) of regional and larger communities growing out of household, neighborhood, and local communities.

Bookchin has carried on this tradition in arguing for the liberatory potential of the town or neighborhood assembly, and he has given his libertarian predecessors' ideas of social and political decentralization a more specific and concrete expression. He and other social ecologists point out the ways in which such an assembly offers the community an arena in which its needs and aspirations can be formulated publicly in an active and creative manner and in which a strong and vital citizenship can be developed and exercised in practice. The community assembly offers a means through which a highly valued multiplicity and diversity can be unified and coordinated, as the citizens engage practically in the pursuit of the good of the whole community. It is also on a scale at which the community's many-sided relationship to its specific ecological and bioregional milieu can be vividly grasped and achieve political expression.

What is debated vigorously among social ecologists is the validity of a "libertarian municipalism" that would make a program of creating local assembly government and federations of libertarian municipalities into a privileged politics of social ecology. In this ideology, the citizens (as Bookchin defines them) and the municipalist movement assume much of the historical role of the working class and the party in classical Marxist theory, and they are endowed with a similar mystique. Yet, it seems clear that the municipalist program and Bookchin's new "revolutionary subject" cannot be uniquely deduced from the general premises of social-ecological analysis, nor can they be shown to be the only plausible basis for an ecological politics. It is therefore not surprising that most activists influenced by social ecology do not direct most of their efforts into municipalism but rather work in many political, economic, and cultural realms.[49]

A social ecology recognizes that political forms, as important as they may be, are given meaning and realize whatever liberatory and communitarian potential they may have within a larger political culture. The political culture is thus both historically and theoretically more fundamental. Consequently, when contemplating a promising political form, a social ecology will consider the ways in which the political culture may limit or liberate the potentials in that form. The institution of the assembly, for example, possesses not only the potential to foster freedom, authentic democracy, solidarity, and civic virtue but also considerable potential for the generation of elitism, egotism, domineering personality traits, and power-seeking behavior. Such dangers are avoided not only through procedures within assemblies themselves but above all by the creation of a communitarian, democratic culture that will express itself in decision-making bodies and in all other institutions. For assemblies and other organs of direct democracy to contribute effectively to an ecological community, they must be purged of the competitive, agonistic, masculinist aspects that have often corrupted them. They can fulfill their democratic promise only if they are an integral expression of a cooperative community that embodies in its institutions the love of humanity and nature.

Barber makes exactly this point when he states that "strong" democracy "attempts to balance adversary politics by nourishing the mutualistic art of listening" and, going beyond mere toleration, seeks "common rhetoric evocative of a common democratic discourse" that should "encompass the affective as well as the cognitive mode."[50] Such concerns echo recent contributions in feminist ethics, which have pointed out that the dominant moral and political discourse have exhibited a one-sided emphasis on ideas and principles and neglected the realm of feeling and sensibility. In this spirit, a social ecology must explore the ways in which the transition from formal to substantive democracy depends not only on the establishment of more radically democratic forms but also on the establishment of cultural practices that foster a democratic sensibility.

SOCIAL ECONOMICS

In view of the dominance of the economic in contemporary society and the importance of the economic in any society, a social ecology must devote considerable attention to the means of creating a socially and ecologically responsible system of production and consumption. Bookchin has stressed the contribution that can be made by such alternatives as community credit unions, community-supported agriculture, community gardens, "civic banks to fund municipal enterprises and land purchases," and community-owned enterprises.[51] In a discussion of how a municipalist movement might be initiated practically, he presents proposals that emphasize cooperatives and small, individually owned businesses. He suggests that the process could begin with the public purchase of unprofitable enterprises (which would then be managed by the workers), the establishment of land trusts, and the support for small-scale productive enterprises. He concludes that in such a system, "cooperatives, farms, and small retail outlets would be fostered with municipal funds and placed under growing public control."[52] Taken together, such suggestions describe the beginnings of a "green economics" that could have a major transformative effect on society.[53]

One of the most compelling aspects of Bookchin's political thought is the centrality of his ethical critique of the dominant economistic society and his call for the creation of a "moral economy" as a precondition for a just ecological society. He asserts that such a "moral economy" implies the emergence of "a productive community" to replace the amoral "mere marketplace" that currently prevails. It requires further that producers "explicitly agree to exchange their products and services on terms that are not merely 'equitable' or 'fair' but supportive of each other."[54] Such an analysis assumes that if the prevailing system of economic exploitation and the dominant economistic culture based on it are to be eliminated, a sphere must be created in which people find new forms of exchange to replace the capitalist market, and this sphere must be capable of continued growth. Bookchin sees this realm as a municipalized economy, in which property becomes "part of a larger whole that is controlled by the citizen body in assembly as citizens."[55]

However, for the present at least, it is not clear why the municipalized economic sector should be looked on as the primary realm rather than as one area among many in which significant economic transformation might begin. It is possible to imagine a broad spectrum of self-managed enterprises, individual producers, and small partnerships that would enter into a growing cooperative economic sector that would incorporate social-ecological values. The extent to which the strong communitarian principle of distribution according to need could be achieved would be proportional to the degree to which cooperative and communitarian values had evolved—a condition that would depend on complex historical factors that cannot be predicted beforehand.

Bookchin suggests that in a transitional phase the "rights" of the small businesses will not be infringed on,[56] though his goal is a fully developed municipalist system in which these businesses will not be allowed to exist. It is far from obvious, however, why these enterprises should not continue to exist in the long term, alongside more cooperative forms of production, as long as the members of the community choose to support them. There is no conclusive evidence that such small enterprises are necessarily exploitative or that they cannot be operated in an ecologically sound manner. Particularly if the larger enterprises in a regional economy are democratically operated, the persistence of such small individual enterprises does not seem incompatible with social-ecological values. This possibility is even more plausible to the degree that the community democratically establishes just and effective parameters of social and ecological responsibility. The dogmatic assertion that in an ecological society only one form of economic organization can exist (whether municipalized enterprises or any other form) is incompatible with the affirmation of historical openness and social creativity and imagination that is basic to a social ecology.

THE NEW LEVIATHAN

If a social ecology cannot be dogmatic in its economic prescriptions for the future, it must be entirely forthright in its judgment concerning the dominant role of global corporate capital in today's intensifying social and ecological crisis. While some social ecologists have repeated vague clichés about the market and capitalism (sometimes confusedly conflating the two), social-ecological analysis consistently results in the inescapable conclusion that the growing global dominance of corporate power is the major *institutional* factor in the crisis. Whatever good intentions individual employees, managers, executives, and stockholders may have, large corporations operate according to the constraints built into their organizational structures and according to the requirements of global economic competition. To the degree that the prevailing conception of global "free trade" is realized in practice, a corporation that operates according to ecologically optimal decision-making processes will be devoured by its more ruthlessly rational competitors. While there are in some cases strong incentives for transnational corporations to appear socially and ecologically responsible, there are stronger pragmatic requirements of rational self-interest that they act in socially and ecologically irresponsible ways. A social ecology must therefore concern itself with the various means by which more responsible decision making might be achieved. This might include regulation by local, regional, and national government bodies; organization of consumers; organization of workers; transformation of organizational structures of existing enterprises; creation of new and more responsible forms of economic organization; and various forms of citizens' direct action. The effectiveness of any of these approaches can only be determined through experience and experimentation. There has been no convincing demonstration that changes in personal and cultural values, changes in individual behavior, regulatory legislation, structural political and economic reform, citizens' direct action, voluntary association, and large-scale resistance movements do not each have roles to play in social-ecological transformation under various historical conditions.

To date, the best general assessment of economic globalization and corporate power from a social-ecological perspective is Athanasiou's *Divided Planet: The Ecology of Rich and Poor.*[57] Athanasiou points out how the link between systemic social issues and ecological crisis is increasingly becoming evident. He notes, for example, that while until recently "only a few isolated radicals saw the Third World's crushing international debt as a green issue, it is well known as a key link in the fiscal chains strangling the world's ecosystems."[58] Athanasiou presents a model of social-ecological analysis that goes far beyond generalizations about a human "quest for domination" or a "grow or die" economy. For example, he explains how in return for loans, the International Monetary Fund and the World Bank impose on poor countries "Structural Adjustment Programs" (SAPs) that are socially and ecologically disastrous, as rational they may seem from a narrow economistic perspective. The SAPs demand drastic reductions in public spending for education, health, housing, and other social goods; eliminate subsidies for agriculture, food, and social services; encourage production for export; eliminate trade barriers; raise interest rates; and lower wages. The result is a more rationalized and superficially stable economy in which poverty increases, the quality of life declines for most people, and environmental destruction accelerates to fuel export-based production.

The phenomenon of globalization shows with increasing clarity the link between transnational capital, the state, the technological system, and the growing and intimately interrelated social and ecological crises. There is no better example of the power of broad social-ecological analysis.

THE FUTURE OF SOCIAL ECOLOGY

Future research in social ecology will consist of much more detailed study of these issues and many other questions related to the development of the global economic, political, and technological systems and the resulting social and ecological consequences. The critical theoretical framework of social ecology will become richer and more highly articulated as it incorporates these empirically based studies. At the same time, its theoretical vision of a communitarian regionalism will be enriched and rendered more determinate by the proliferation of empirical, experiential projects in the tradition of Geddes's regional survey, and its political and economic theory will be transformed as evidence is assimilated from continuing experiments in ecological and communitarian organization and social practice.

Social ecology is at the present moment in a stage of rapid transformation, self-reflection, and expansion of its theoretical horizons. It is in the process of escaping from the dogmatic tendencies that have threatened its theoretical vitality and practical relevance and the sectarian narrowness that has reactively defined it in opposition to other ecophilosophies. It is ready to withdraw from the "contest of ecologies" and move forward in its theoretical development, in creative dialogue with other philosophies.[59] It is now in a position to realize its potential as a holistic and dialectical philosophy that seeks greater openness and opportunity for growth, works toward a more adequate synthesis of theoretical reflection and empirical inquiry, attains an increasingly comprehensive theoretical scope, and strives for a truly dialectical relation to creative social practice—offering the guidance of reflection and remaining open to guidance by the truth of experience.

The project of a social ecology will certainly gain impetus through the growing awareness of global ecological crisis and deterioration of the ties of the human community. Yet it will be moved and inspired most by its affirmative ecological faith—by its love of humanity in all its magnificent expressions, its wonder at the diverse manifestations of life on earth, and its awe at the mystery of being. It will also learn to accept human limitations and the tragic dimension of history and put aside the illusions of shallow progressivism, revolutionary fantasy, and Promethean heroism. It will find hope rather in a vision of the human community—freed from its quest for domination of self, of others, of objects, of nature—realizing its own good by participating in and contributing to the good of the larger community of life. In pursuing this vision, social ecology realizes its deepest meaning as a reflection on the Earth household, a reflection that reveals our place as companions in our common journey.

NOTES

1. Elisée Reclus, *L'Homme et la Terre*, 6 vol. (Paris: Librairie Universelle, 1905–8), Vol. I, p. i.
2. "Social ecology" is also an interdisciplinary field of academic study that investigates the interrelationship between human social institutions and ecological or environmental issues. It is closely related to human ecology, the area of the biological sciences that deals with the role of human beings in ecosystems. However, studies in social ecology are much broader in scope, incorporating many areas of social and natural science in their analysis. This interdisciplinary social ecology offers much of the empirical data which philosophical social ecology utilizes in its theoretical reflection.
3. See especially *Fields, Factories and Workshops* (New York: Benjamin Blom, 1968) and *Mutual Aid: A Factor in Evolution* (Boston: Extending Horizons, 1955) for important discussions of many of these topics, as well as his pamphlet, *The State: Its Historic Role* (London: Freedom Press, 1970) on communitarian and democratic traditions.
4. For the first English translation of some of Reclus's most important texts and an extensive commentary on his thought, see John Clark and Camille Martin, *Liberty, Equality, Geography: The Social Thought of Elisée Reclus* (Littleton, CO: Aigis Publications, 1997). For a concise discussion of Reclus's relevance to contemporary ecological thought, see John Clark, "The Dialectical Social Geography of Elisée Reclus," *Philosophy and Geography* 1 (1997): 117–142.
5. For discussions of Geddes's guiding values of "Sympathy, Synthesis and Synergy" and his regional concepts of "Place, Work, and Folk," see Murdo Macdonald, "Patrick Geddes in Context," *The Irish Review*, (Autumn/Winter 1994,) and "Art and the Context in Patrick Geddes' Work," *Spacioe Societá/Space and Society*, October–December 1994, pp. 28–39.
6. Ramachandra Guha, "Lewis Mumford, the Forgotten American Environmentalist: An Essay in Rehabilitation," in David Macauley (ed.), *Minding Nature: The Philosophers of Ecology* (New York: Guilford Press, 1996), p. 210.
7. Mumford did not choose to coin any convenient term to epitomize his social theory. I take the term "ecological regionalism" from Mark Luccarelli's very helpful study, *Lewis Mumford and the Ecological Region* (New York: Guilford Press, 1995).

8. *The Pentagon of Power* (New York: Harcourt Brace Jovanovich, 1970), p. 386.
9. "The Human Prospect" in *Interpretations and Forecasts: 1922–1972* (New York: Harcourt Brace Jovanovich, 1973), p. 465.
10. Ibid., p. 471
11. *The Condition of Man* (New York: Harcourt Brace Jovanovich, 1944), p. 403.
12. Ibid., p. 404.
13. An adequate account of the ecocommunitarian tradition would explore Buber's enormous contribution. See his major political work, *Paths in Utopia* (Boston: Beacon Press, 1958), including his chapters on his predecessors Kropotkin and Landauer and, especially, his essay "In the Midst of Crisis." Significantly, Buber defines the "social" in terms of the degree to which the "center" extends outward and is "earthly," "creaturely," and "attached" (p. 135).
14. Bookchin's best presentation of his version of social ecology is found in *The Ecology of Freedom: The Emergence and Dissolution of Hierarchy* (Palo Alto, CA: Cheshire Books, 1982).
15. Unfortunately, he lapses into the undialectical "fallacy that technology is a neutral tool to be used or abused by the one who wields it," as David Watson notes in *Beyond Bookchin: Preface for a Future Social Ecology* (Brooklyn, NY, and Detroit, MI: Autonomedia and Black & Red, 1996), p. 119. See the entire chapter, "The Social Ecologist as Technocrat" (pp. 119–167) for a careful dissection of Bookchin's technological optimism from a social-ecological perspective.
16. All done in the name of such values as "mutuality" and "cooperation" and on behalf of an "ethics of complementarity"!
17. Mumford, *Pentagon of Power*, p. 390.
18. "But God does not remain stony and dead; the stones cry out and raise themselves to Spirit." Hegel, *Encyclopedia of the Philosophical Sciences* 247, cited in Errol E. Harris, *The Spirit of Hegel* (Atlantic Highlands, NJ: Humanities Press, 1993), p. 103.
19. See Alexander's classic evolutionary treatise, *Space, Time, and Deity*, 2 vols. (New York: Dover Publications, 1966).
20. The ecological and cosmic evolutionary implications that are implicit in a Whiteheadian "philosophy of organism" are elaborated eloquently in Charles Birch and John B. Cobb, Jr., *The Liberation of Life* (Denton, TX: Environmental Ethics Books, 1990).
21. See Pierre Teilhard de Chardin, *The Phenomenon of Man* (New York: Harper and Row, 1961), and *The Future of Man* (New York: Harper and Row, 1969).
22. See S. Radhakrishnan, *An Idealist View of Life* (New York: Barnes and Noble, 1964), chap. vi., "Matter, Life and Mind," and Sri Aurobindo, *The Essential Aurobindo* (New York: Schocken Books, 1973), part 1, "Man in Evolution."
23. Seen Ken Wilber, *Sex, Ecology, Spirituality* (Boston: Shambhala, 1995), and *A Brief History of Everything* (Boston: Shambhala, 1996).
24. We do not simply "identify" with a larger whole but rather explore specific modes of relatedness and develop our outlook and feelings in relation to what we discover about self and other. In this analysis, a dialectical social ecology has more in common with ecofeminist thought than with those ecological theories that stress "expanded" selfhood.
25. As in Eric Katz's very useful discussion in "Organism, Community, and the 'Substitution Problem'" in *Environmental Ethics* 7 (1985): 241–56. Katz raises many important issues, though he overstates the opposition between the two approaches by interpreting them as rather rigid "models."
26. The most flagrant case is Tom Regan's attack on "Holism as Environmental Fascism" in his essay "Ethical Vegetarianism and Commercial Animal Farming," reprinted in James White (ed.), *Contemporary Moral Problems* (St. Paul, MN: West Publishing, 1988), pp. 327–41. Note Mumford's severe critique, from a holistic, "organicist" perspective, of the extreme, totalizing holism of Teilhard de Chardin in *Pentagon of Power*, pp. 314–19.

27. The concept of the "holon" was first proposed by Arthur Koestler in *The Ghost in the Machine* (Chicago: Henry Regnery, 1967), chap. 3 and passim. Its fundamental importance has recently been defended by Ken Wilber. For a concise discussion of Wilber's analysis of holons; their characteristics of "identity," "autonomy," and "agency"; and their constitution of "holarchies," see *A Brief History of Everything,* chap. 1.
28. One of the most dialectical moves in recent ecological thought is Gary Snyder's choice of the title "No Nature" for his collected poems. Starting out from Hakuin's allusion to "self-nature that is no nature," he reminds us corrigible logocentrists, "Nature is not a book." *No Nature* (New York: Pantheon Books, 1992), pp. v, 381.
29. *Tao te Ching* 1 (Chan trans.) in Wing-Tsit Chan, *A Sourcebook in Chinese Philosophy* (Princeton, NJ: Princeton University Press, 1963), p. 139.
30. *History and Spirit: An Inquiry into the Philosophy of Liberation* (Boston: Beacon Press, 1991), p. 161. It is in relation to this idea of the primordial continuum of being that Merleau-Ponty's dialectical phenomenology can make an important contribution to a social ecology. David Abram, *The Spell of the Sensuous: Perception and Language in a More-Than-Human World* (New York: Pantheon Books, 1996), p. 66, explains Merleau-Ponty's concept of "the Flesh" as "the mysterious tissue or matrix that underlies and gives rise to both the perceiver and the perceived as interdependent aspects of its spontaneous activity." This concept unites subject and object dialectically as determinations within a more primordial reality. Merleau-Ponty himself refers to "that primordial being which is not yet the subject-being nor the object-being and which in every respect baffles reflection. From this primordial being to us, there is no derivation, nor any break; it has neither the tight construction of the mechanism nor the transparency of a whole which precedes its parts." See "The Concept of Nature, I," in *Themes from the Lectures at the Collège de France 1952–1960* (Chicago: Northwestern University Press, 1970), pp. 65–66.
31. Kovel, *History and Spirit,* pp. 166–67.
32. Ibid., p. 1.
33. Harris describes Hegel's view that religion "as the felt awareness and conviction of the infinite immanent and potent in all reality, in both nature and history, and transcendent above all finite existence, is one form of that final self-realization of the whole which is the truth, and without which there would be no dynamic to propel the dialectical process. To repudiate spirit and reject all religion is thus to paralyze the dialectic, and in effect to abandon it." Harris, *Spirit of Hegel,* p. 54. If we are careful to read "transcendent" as "trans-finite" and not as "supernatural," and if we remember that no self-realization of the whole is "final," then this also describes an important aspect of the meaning of "spirituality" for a dialectical holism.
34. "The Marriage of Radical Ecologies," in Zimmerman et al., *Environmental Philosophy: From Animal Rights to Radical Ecology* (Englewood Cliffs, NJ: Prentice Hall, 1993), pp. 410–11. While social ecology and other Western ecophilosophies have come to terms with unity-in-diversity, perhaps they would do well to consider the radically dialectical concept of difference-nondifference, the *bhedabhedavada* of Indian philosophy.
35. "Human Nature, Freedom, and Spirit," in John Clark (ed.), *Renewing the Earth: The Promise of Social Ecology* (London: Green Print, 1990), p. 145.
36. Abram, *Spell of the Sensuous,* p. 68.
37. This is precisely the social ecological problematic first proposed by Lao Tzu two and a half millenia ago.
38. Holmes Rolston III, *Environmental Ethics: Duties to and Values in the Natural World* (Philadelphia: Temple University Press, 1988), p. 188.
39. Ibid., p. 154.
40. Karl Marx, *Grundrisse: Foundations of the Critique of Political Economy* (New York: Vintage Books, 1973), p. 99.

41. For a discussion of the radical implications of regionalism, see Max Cafard, "The Surre(gion)alist Manifesto," *Exquisite Corpse* 8 (1990): 1, 22–23.
42. See Gary Snyder's classic essay, "Good, Wild, Sacred," in *The Practice of the Wild* (San Francisco: North Point Press, 1990).
43. Thomas Berry and Brian Swimme, *The Universe Story: From the Primordial Flaring Forth to the Ecozoic Era* (New York: HarperCollins, 1992), p. 3.
44. Ibid., p. 5.
45. Murray Bookchin, *The Philosophy of Social Ecology* (Montreal: Black Rose Books, 1990), p. 182.
46. The extent to which Bookchin holds a Promethean view of human activity is suggested when he asks how humanity is "to organize a 'free nature.' " "What Is Social Ecology?" in Zimmerman et al., *Environmental Philosophy*, p. 370.
47. Ibid., p. 354.
48. Mumford, "Human Prospect," p. 471.
49. Bookchin's reduction of ecocommunitarian politics to libertarian municipalism is a deeply flawed, undialectical, and fundamentally dogmatic political problematic, and it is not possible to discuss most of its shortcoming here. For a detailed critique, see John Clark, "Municipal Dreams: Murray Bookchin's Idealist Politics," in Andrew Light (ed.), *Anarchism, Nature, and Society: Critical Perspectives on Murray Bookchin's Social Ecology* (New York: Guilford Publications, forthcoming).
50. Benjamin Barber, *Strong Democracy: Participatory Politics for a New Age* (Berkeley: University of California Press, 1984), p. 176.
51. Murray Bookchin, *The Rise of Urbanization and the Decline of Citizenship* (San Francisco: Sierra Club Books, 1987), p. 276, and "Libertarian Municipalism: An Overview," *Green Perspectives* 24 (1991): 4.
52. Ibid.
53. Brian Tokar, in his book *The Green Alternative*, has sketched an even more extensive green economic program, based on what is fundamentally a social-ecological analysis. Tokar's concise and well-written introduction to the green movement should be consulted for a clear example of an experimental, nondogmatic social-ecological politics and economics. See *The Green Alternative: Creating an Ecological Future* (San Pedro, CA: R. & E. Miles, 1992).
54. Murray Bookchin, *The Modern Crisis* (Philadelphia: New Society Publishers, 1986), p. 91.
55. Bookchin, *Rise of Urbanization*, p. 263.
56. Ibid., p. 275.
57. Tom Athanasiou, *Divided Planet: The Ecology of Rich and Poor* (Boston: Little, Brown, 1996).
58. Ibid., p. 9.
59. I have suggested some of the ways in which dialogue between social ecology and deep ecology might be usefully explored in "How Wide Is Deep Ecology?" *Inquiry* 39 (June 1996): 189–201.

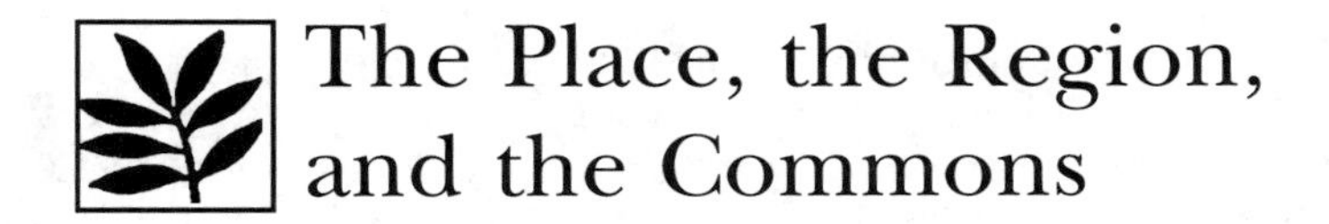

The Place, the Region, and the Commons

Gary Snyder

Pulitzer Prize–winning poet and essayist Gary Snyder teaches in the Department of English at the University of California, Davis.

When you find your place where you are, practice occurs.
DŌGEN

THE WORLD IS PLACES

We experience slums, prairies, and wetlands all equally as "places." Like a mirror, a place can hold anything, on any scale. I want to talk about place as an experience and propose a model of what it meant to "live in place" for most of human time, presenting it initially in terms of the steps that a child takes growing into a natural community. (We have the terms *enculturation* and *acculturation,* but nothing to describe the process of becoming placed or re-placed.) In doing so we might get one more angle on what a "civilization of wildness" might require.

For most Americans, to reflect on "home place" would be an unfamiliar exercise. Few today can announce themselves as someone *from* somewhere. Almost nobody spends a lifetime in the same valley, working alongside the people they knew as children. Native people everywhere (the very term means "someone born there") and Old World farmers and city people share this experience of living in place. Still—and this is very important to remember—being inhabitory, being place-based, has never meant that one didn't travel from time to time, going on trading ventures or taking livestock to summer grazing. Such working wanderers have always known they had a home-base on earth, and could prove it at any campfire or party by singing their own songs.

This essay originally appeared in Gary Snyder, The *Practice of the Wild* (San Francisco: North Point Press, 1990). Reprinted with permission.

The heart of a place is the home, and the heart of the home is the firepit, the hearth. All tentative explorations go outward from there, and it is back to the fireside that elders return. You grow up speaking a home language, a local vernacular. Your own household may have some specifics of phrase, of pronunciation, that are different from the *domus,* the *jia* or *ie* or *kum,* down the lane. You hear histories of the people who are your neighbors and tales involving rocks, streams, mountains, and trees that are all within your sight. The myths of world-creation tell you how *that mountain* was created and how *that peninsula* came to be there. As you grow bolder you explore your world outward from the firepit (which is the center of each universe) in little trips. The childhood landscape is learned on foot, and a map is inscribed in the mind—trails and pathways and groves—the mean dog, the cranky old man's house, the pasture with a bull in it—going out wider and farther. All of us carry within us a picture of the terrain that was learned roughly between the ages of six and nine. (It could as easily be an urban neighborhood as some rural scene.) You can almost totally recall the place you walked, played, biked, swam. Revisualizing that place with its smells and textures, walking through it again in your imagination, has a grounding and settling effect. As a contemporary thought we might also wonder how it is for those whose childhood landscape was being ripped up by bulldozers, or whose family moving about made it all a blur. I have a friend who still gets emotional when he recalls how the avocado orchards of his southern California youth landscape were transformed into hillside after hillside of suburbs.

Our place is part of what we are. Yet even a "place" has a kind of fluidity: it passes through space and time—"ceremonial time" in John Hanson Mitchell's phrase. A place will have been grasslands, then conifers, then beech and elm. It will have been half riverbed, it will have been scratched and plowed by ice. And then it will be cultivated, paved, sprayed, dammed, graded, built up. But each is only for a while, and that will be just another set of lines on the palimpsest. The whole earth is a great tablet holding the multiple overlaid new and ancient traces of the swirl of forces. Each place is its own place, forever (eventually) wild. A place on earth is a mosaic within larger mosaics—the land is all small places, all precise tiny realms replicating larger and smaller patterns. Children start out learning place by learning those little realms around the house, the settlement, and outward.

One's sense of the scale of a place expands as one learns the *region.* The young hear further stories and go for explorations which are also subsistence forays—firewood gathering, fishing, to fairs or to market. The outlines of the larger region become part of their awareness. (Thoreau says in "Walking" that an area twenty miles in diameter will be enough to occupy a lifetime of close exploration on foot—you will never exhaust its details.)

The total size of the region a group calls home depends on the land type. Every group is territorial, each moves within a given zone, even nomads stay within boundaries. A people living in a desert or grassland with great visible spaces that invite you to step forward and walk as far as you can see will range across tens of thousands of square miles. A deep old-growth forest may rarely be traveled at all. Foragers in gallery forests and grasslands will regularly move broadly, whereas people in a deep-soiled valley ideal for gardens might not go far beyond the top of the nearest ridge. The regional boundaries were roughly drawn by climate, which is what sets the plant-type zones—plus soil type and landforms. Desert wastes, mountain ridges, or big rivers set a broad edge to a region. We walk across or wade through the larger and smaller boundaries. Like children first learning our homeland we can stand at the edge of a big river, or on the crest of a major ridge, and observe that the other side is a different soil, a change of plants and animals, a new shape of barn roof, maybe less or more rain. The lines between natural regions are never simple or clear, but vary according to such criteria as biota, watersheds, landforms, elevation. (See Jim Dodge, 1981.) Still, we all know—at some point—that we are no longer in the Midwest, say, but in the West. Regions seen according to natural criteria are sometimes called bioregions.

(In pre-conquest America people covered great distances. It is said that the Mojave of the lower Colorado felt that everyone at least once in their lives should make foot journeys to the Hopi mesas to the east, the Gulf of California to the south, and to the Pacific.)

Every region has its wilderness. There is the fire in the kitchen, and there is the place less traveled. In most settled regions there used to be some combination of prime agricultural land, orchard and vine land, rough pasturage, woodlot, forest, and desert or mountain "waste." The de facto wilderness was the extreme backcountry part of all that. The parts less visited are "where the bears are." The wilderness is within walking distance—it may be three days or it may be ten. It is at the far high rough end, or the deep forest and swamp end, of the territory where most of you all live and work. People will go there for mountain herbs, for the trapline, or for solitude. They live between the poles of home and their own wild places.

Recollecting that we once lived in places is part of our contemporary self-rediscovery. It grounds what it means to be "human" (etymologically something like "earthling"). I have a friend who feels sometimes that the world is hostile to human life—he says it chills us and kills us. But how could we *be* were it not for this planet that provided our very shape? Two conditions—gravity and a livable temperature range between freezing and boiling—have given us fluids and flesh. The trees we climb and the ground we walk on have given us five fingers and toes. The "place" (from the root *plat*, broad, spreading, flat) gave us far-seeing eyes, the streams and breezes gave us versatile tongues and whorly ears. The land gave us a stride, and the lake a dive. The amazement gave us our kind of mind. We should be thankful for that, and take nature's stricter lessons with some grace.

UNDERSTANDING THE COMMONS

I stood with my climbing partner on the summit of Glacier Peak looking all ways round, ridge after ridge and peak after peak, as far as we could see. To the west across Puget Sound were the farther peaks of the Olympic Mountains. He said: "You mean there's a senator for all this?" As in the Great Basin, crossing desert after desert, range after range, it is easy to think there are vast spaces on earth yet unadministered, perhaps forgotten, or unknown (the endless sweep of spruce forest in Alaska and Canada)—but it is all mapped and placed in some domain. In North America there is a lot that is in public domain, which has its problems, but at least they are problems we are all enfranchised to work on. David Foreman, founder of the Earth First! movement, recently stated his radical provenance. Not out of Social Justice, Left Politics, or Feminism did I come—says David—but from the Public Lands Conservation movement—the solid stodgy movement that goes back to the thirties and before. Yet these land and wildlife issues were what politicized John Muir, John Wesley Powell, and Aldo Leopold—the abuses of public land.

American public lands are the twentieth-century incarnation of a much older institution known across Eurasia—in English called the "commons"—which was the ancient mode of both protecting and managing the wilds of the self-governing regions. It worked well enough until the age of market economies, colonialism, and imperialism. Let me give you a kind of model of how the commons worked.

Between the extremes of deep wilderness and the private plots of the farmstead lies a territory which is not suitable for crops. In earlier times it was used jointly by the members of a given tribe or village. This area, embracing both the wild and the semi-wild, is of critical importance. It is necessary for the health of the wilderness because it adds big habitat, overflow territory, and room for wildlife to fly and run. It is essential even to an agricultural village economy because its natural diversity provides the many necessities and amenities that the privately held plots cannot. It enriches the agrarian diet with game and fish. The shared land supplies firewood, poles and stone for building, clay for the kiln, herbs, dye plants, and much else, just as in a foraging economy. It is especially important as seasonal or fulltime open range for cattle, horses, goats, pigs, and sheep.

In the abstract the sharing of a natural area might be thought of as a matter of access to "common pool resources" with no limits or controls on individual exploitation. The fact is that such sharing developed over millennia and always within territorial and social contexts. In the peasant societies of both Asia and Europe there were customary forms that gave direction to the joint use of land. They did not grant free access to outsiders, and there were controls over entry and use by member households. The commons has been defined as "the undivided land belonging to the members of a local community as a whole." This definition fails to make the point that the commons is both specific land *and* the traditional community institution that determines the carrying capacity for its various subunits and defines the rights and obligations of those who use it, with penalties for lapses. Because it is traditional and *local,* it is not identical with today's "public domain," which is land held and managed by a central government. Under a national state such management may be destructive (as it is becoming in Canada and the United States) or benign (I have no good examples)—but in no case is it locally managed. One of the ideas in the current debate on how to reform our public lands is that of returning them to regional control.

An example of traditional management: what would keep one household from bringing in more and more stock and tempting everyone toward overgrazing? In earlier England and in some contemporary Swiss villages (Netting, 1976), the commoner could only turn out to common range as many head of cattle as he could feed over the winter in his own corrals. This meant that no one was allowed to increase his herd from outside with a cattle drive just for summer grazing. (This was known in Norman legal language as the rule of *levancy and couchancy*: you could only run the stock that you actually had "standing and sleeping" within winter quarters.)

The commons is the contract a people make with their local natural system. The word has an instructive history: it is formed of *ko,* "together," with (Greek) *moin,* "held in common." But the Indo-European root *mei* means basically to "move, to go, to change." This had an archaic special meaning of "exchange of goods and services within a society as regulated by custom or law." I think it might well refer back to the principle of gift economies: "the gift must always move." The root comes into Latin as *munus,* "service performed for the community" and hence "municipality."

There is a well-documented history of the commons in relation to the village economies of Europe and England. In England from the time of the Norman Conquest the enfeoffed knights and overlords began to gain control over the many local commons. Legislation (the Statute of Merton, 1235) came to their support. From the fifteenth century on the landlord class, working with urban mercantile guilds and government offices, increasingly fenced off village-held land and turned it over to private interests. The enclosure movement was backed by the big wool corporations who found profit from sheep to be much greater than that from farming. The wool business, with its exports to the Continent, was an early agribusiness that had a destructive effect on the soils and dislodged peasants. The arguments for enclosure in England—efficiency, higher production—ignored social and ecological effects and served to cripple the sustainable agriculture of some districts. The enclosure movement was stepped up again in the eighteenth century: between 1709 and 1869 almost five million acres were transferred to private ownership, one acre in every seven. After 1869 there was a sudden reversal of sentiment called the "open space movement" which ultimately halted enclosures and managed to preserve, via a spectacular lawsuit against the lords of fourteen manors, the Epping Forest.

Karl Polanyi (1975) says that the enclosures of the eighteenth century created a population of rural homeless who were forced in their desperation to become the world's first industrial working class. The enclosures were tragic both for the human community and for natural ecosystems. The fact that England now has the least forest and wildlife of all the nations of Europe has much to do with the enclosures. The takeover of commons land on the European plain also began about five hundred years ago, but one-third of Europe is still not privatized. A survival of commons practices in Swedish law allows anyone to enter private farmland to pick berries or mushrooms, to cross on foot, and to camp out of sight of the house. Most of the former commons land is now under the administration of government land agencies.

A commons model can still be seen in Japan, where there are farm villages tucked in shoestring valleys, rice growing in the *tanbo* on the bottoms, and the vegetable plots and horticulture located on the slightly higher ground. The forested hills rising high above the valleys are the commons—in Japanese called *iriai,* "joint entry." The boundary between one village and the next is often the very crests of the ridges. On the slopes of Mt. Hiei in Kyoto prefecture, north of the remote Tendai Buddhist training temples of Yokkawa, I came on men and women of Ohara village bundling up slender brush-cuttings for firewood. They were within the village land. In the innermost mountains of Japan there are forests that are beyond the reach of the use of any village. In early feudal times they were still occupied by remnant hunting peoples, perhaps Japanese-Ainu mixed-blood survivors. Later some of these wildlands were appropriated by the government and declared "Imperial Forests." Bears became extinct in England by the thirteenth century, but they are still found throughout the more remote Japanese mountains, even occasionally just north of Kyoto.

In China the management of mountain lands was left largely to the village councils—all the central government wanted was taxes. Taxes were collected in kind, and local specialties were highly prized. The demands of the capital drew down Kingfisher feathers, Musk Deer glands, Rhinoceros hides, and other exotic products of the mountains and streams, as well as rice, timber, and silk. The village councils may have resisted overexploitation of their resources, but when the edge of spreading deforestation reached their zone (the fourteenth century seems to be a turning point for the forests of heartland China), village land management crumbled. Historically, the seizure of the commons—east or west—by either the central government or entrepreneurs from the central economy has resulted in degradation of wild lands and agricultural soils. There is sometimes good reason to kill the Golden Goose: the quick profits can be reinvested elsewhere at a higher return.

In the United States, as fast as the Euro-American invaders forcefully displaced the native inhabitants from their own sorts of traditional commons, the land was opened to the new settlers. In the arid West, however, much land was never even homesteaded, let alone patented. The native people who had known and loved the white deserts and blue mountains were now scattered or enclosed on reservations, and the new inhabitants (miners and a few ranchers) had neither the values nor the knowledge to take care of the land. An enormous area was de facto public domain, and the Forest Service, the Park Service, and the Bureau of Land Management were formed to manage it. (The same sorts of land in Canada and Australia are called "Crown Lands," a reflection of the history of English rulers trying to wrest the commons from the people.)

In the contemporary American West the people who talk about a "sagebrush rebellion" might sound as though they were working for a return of commons land to local control. The truth is the sagebrush rebels have a lot yet to learn about the place—they are still relative newcomers, and their motives are not stewardship but development. Some westerners are beginning to think in long-range terms, and these don't argue for privatization but for better range management and more wilderness preservation.

The environmental history of Europe and Asia seems to indicate that the best management of commons land was that which was locally based. The ancient severe and often irreversible deforestation of the Mediterranean Basin was an extreme case of the misuse of the commons by the forces that had taken its management away from regional villages (Thirgood, 1981). The situation in America in the nineteenth and early twentieth centuries was the reverse. The truly local people, the Native Americans, were decimated and demoralized, and the new population was composed of adventurers and entrepreneurs. Without some federal presence the poachers, cattle grazers, and timber barons would have had a field day. Since about 1960 the situation has turned again: the agencies that were once charged with conservation are increasingly perceived as accomplices of the extractive industries, and local people—who are beginning to be actually local—seek help from environmental organizations and join in defense of the public lands.

Destruction extends worldwide and "encloses" local commons, local peoples. The village and tribal people who live in the tropical forests are literally bulldozed out of their homes by international logging interests in league with national governments. A well-worn fiction used in dispossessing inhabitory people is the declaration that the commonly owned tribal forests are either (1) private property or (2) public domain. When the commons are closed and the villagers must buy energy, lumber, and medicine at the company store, they are pauperized. This is one effect of what Ivan Illich calls "the 500-year war against subsistence."

So what about the so-called tragedy of the commons? This theory, as now popularly understood, seems to state that when there are open access rights to a resource, say pasturage, everyone will seek to maximize his take, and overgrazing will inevitably ensue. What Garrett Hardin and his associates are talking about should be called "the dilemma of common-pool resources." This is the problem of overexploitation of "unowned" resources by individuals or corporations that are caught in the bind of "If I don't do it the other guy will" (Hardin and Baden, 1977). Oceanic fisheries, global water cycles, the air, soil fertility—all fall into this class. When Hardin et al. try to apply their model to the historic commons it doesn't work, because they fail to note that the commons was a social institution which, historically, was never without rules and did not allow unlimited access (Cox, 1985).

In Asia and parts of Europe, villages that in some cases date back to neolithic times still oversee the commons with some sort of council. Each commons is an entity with limits, and the effects of overuse will be clear to those who depend on it. There are three possible contemporary fates for common pool resources. One is privatization, one is administration by government authority, and the third is that—when possible—they become part of a true commons, of reasonable size, managed by local inhabitory people. The third choice may no longer be possible as stated here. Locally based community or tribal (as in Alaska) landholding corporations or cooperatives seem to be surviving here and there. But operating as it seems they must in the world marketplace, they are wrestling with how to balance tradition and sustainability against financial success. The Sealaska Corporation of the Tlingit people of southeast Alaska has been severely criticized (even from within) for some of the old-growth logging it let happen.

We need to make a world-scale "Natural Contract" with the oceans, the air, the birds in the sky. The challenge is to bring the whole victimized world of "common pool resources" into the Mind of the Commons. As it stands now, any resource on earth that is not nailed down will be seen as fair game to the timber buyers or petroleum geologists from Osaka, Rotterdam, or Boston. The pressures of growing populations and the powers of entrenched (but fragile, confused, and essentially leaderless) economic systems warp the likelihood of any of us seeing clearly. Our perception of how entrenched they are may also be something of a delusion.

Sometimes it seems unlikely that a society as a whole can make wise choices. Yet there is no choice but to call for the "recovery of the commons"—and this in a modern world which doesn't quite realize what it has lost. Take back, like the night, that which is shared by all of us, that which is our larger being. There will be no "tragedy of the commons" greater than this: if we do not recover the commons—regain personal, local, community, and peoples' direct involvement in sharing (in *being*) the web of the wild world—that world will keep slipping away. Eventually our complicated industrial capitalist/socialist mixes will bring down much of the living system that supports us. And, it is clear, the loss of a local commons heralds the end of self-sufficiency and signals the doom of the vernacular culture of the region. This is still happening in the far corners of the world.

The commons is a curious and elegant social institution within which human beings once lived free political lives while weaving through natural systems. The commons is a level of organization of human society that includes the nonhuman. The level above the local commons is the bioregion. Understanding the commons and its role within the larger regional culture is one more step toward integrating ecology with economy.

BIOREGIONAL PERSPECTIVES

> The Region is the elsewhere of civilization
> –Max Cafard

The little nations of the past lived within territories that conformed to some set of natural criteria. The culture areas of the major native groups of North America overlapped, as one would expect, almost exactly with broadly defined major bioregions (Kroeber, 1947). That older human experience of a fluid, indistinct, but genuine home region was gradually replaced—across Eurasia—by the arbitrary and often violently imposed boundaries of emerging national states. These imposed borders sometimes cut across biotic areas and ethnic zones alike. Inhabitants lost ecological knowledge and community solidarity. In the old ways, the flora and fauna and landforms are *part of the culture.* The world of culture and nature, which is actual, is almost a shadow world now, and the insubstantial world of political jurisdictions and rarefied economies is what passes for reality. We live in a backwards time. We can regain some small sense of that old membership by discovering the original lineaments of our land and steering—at least in the home territory and in the mind—by those rather than the borders of arbitrary nations, states, and counties.

Regions are "interpenetrating bodies in semi-simultaneous spaces" (Cafard, 1989). Biota, watersheds, landforms, and elevations are just a few of the facets that define a region. Culture areas, in the same way, have subsets such as dialects, religions, sorts of arrow-release, types of tools, myth motifs, musical scales, art styles. One sort of regional outline would be floristic. The coastal Douglas Fir, as the definitive tree of the Pacific Northwest, is an example. (I knew it intimately as a boy growing up on a farm between Lake Washington and Puget Sound. The local people, the Snohomish, called it *lukta tciyats,* "wide needles.") Its northern limit is around the Skeena River in British Columbia. It is found west of the crest through Washington, Oregon, and northern California. The southern coastal limit of Douglas Fir is about the same as that of salmon, which do not run south of the Big Sur River. Inland it grows down the west slope of the Sierra as far south as the north fork of the San Joaquin River. That outline describes the boundary of a larger natural region that runs across three states and one international border.

The presence of this tree signifies a rainfall and a temperature range and will indicate what your agriculture might be, how steep the pitch of your roof, what raincoats you'd need. You don't have to know such details to get by in the modern cities of Portland or Bellingham. But if you do know what is taught by plants and weather, you are in on the gossip and can truly feel more at home. The sum of a field's forces becomes what we call very loosely the "spirit of the place." To know the spirit of a place is to realize that you are a part of a part and that the whole is made of parts, each of which is whole. You start with the part you are whole in.

As quixotic as these ideas may seem, they have a reservoir of strength and possibility behind them. The spring of 1984, a month after equinox. Gary Holthaus and I drove down from Anchorage to Haines, Alaska. We went around the upper edge of the basin of the Copper River, skirted some tributaries of the Yukon, and went over Haines Summit. It was White and Black Spruce taiga all the way, still frozen up. Dropping down from the pass to saltwater at Chilkat inlet we were immediately in forests of large Sitka Spruce, Skunk Cabbage poking out in the swamps, it was spring. That's a bioregional border leap. I was honored the next day by an invitation to Raven House to have coffee with Austin Hammond and a circle of other Tlingit elders and to hear some long and deeply entwined discourses on the responsibilities of people to their places. As we looked out his front window to hanging glaciers on the peaks beyond the saltwater, Hammond spoke of empires and civilizations in metaphors of glaciers. He described how great alien forces—industrial civilization in this case—advance and retreat, and how settled people can wait it out.

Sometime in the mid-seventies at a conference of Native American leaders and activists in Bozeman, Montana, I heard a Crow elder say something similar: "You know, I think if people stay somewhere long enough—even white people—the spirits will begin to speak to them. It's the power of the spirits coming up from the land. The spirits and the old powers aren't lost, they just need people to be around long enough and the spirits will begin to influence them."

Bioregional awareness teaches us in *specific* ways. It is not enough just to "love nature" or to want to "be in harmony with Gaia." Our relation to the natural world takes place in a *place*, and it must be grounded in information and experience. For example: "real people" have an easy familiarity with the local plants. This is so unexceptional a kind of knowledge that everyone in Europe, Asia, and Africa used to take it for granted. Many contemporary Americans don't even *know* that they don't "know the plants," which is indeed a measure of alienation. Knowing a bit about the flora we could enjoy questions like: where do Alaska and Mexico meet? It would be somewhere on the north coast of California, where Canada Jay and Sitka Spruce lace together with manzanita and Blue Oak.

But instead of "northern California" let's call it Shasta Bioregion. The present state of California (the old Alta California territory) falls into at least three natural divisions, and the northern third looks, as the Douglas Fir example shows, well to the north. The boundaries of this northern third would roughly run from the Klamath/Rogue River divide south to San Francisco Bay and up the delta where the Sacramento and San Joaquin rivers join. The line would then go east to the Sierra Crest and, taking that as a distinct border, follow it north to Susanville. The watershed divide then angles broadly northeastward along the edge of the Modoc Plateau to the Warner Range and Goose Lake.

East of the divide is the Great Basin, north of Shasta is the Cascadia/Columbia region, and then farther north is what we call Ish River country, the drainages of Puget Sound and the Straits of Georgia. Why should we do this kind of visualization? Again I will say: it prepares us to begin to be at home in this landscape. There are tens of millions of people in North America who were physically born here but who are not actually living here intellectually, imaginatively, or morally. Native Americans to be sure have a prior claim to the term native. But as they love this land they will welcome the conversion of the millions of immigrant psyches into fellow "Native Americans." For the non-Native American to become at home on this continent, he or she must be *born again* in this hemisphere, on this continent, properly called Turtle Island.

That is to say, we must consciously fully accept and recognize that this is where we live and grasp the fact that our descendants will be here for millennia to come. Then we must honor this land's great antiquity—its wildness—learn it—defend it—and work to hand it on to the children (of all beings) of the future with its biodiversity and health intact. Europe or Africa or Asia will then be seen as the place our ancestors came from, places we might want to know about and to visit, but not "home." Home—deeply, spiritually—must be here. Calling this place "America" is to name it after a stranger. "Turtle Island" is the name given this continent by Native Americans based on creation mythology (Snyder, 1974). The United States, Canada, Mexico, are passing political entities; they have their legitimacies, to be sure, but they will lose their mandate if they continue to abuse the land. "The State is destroyed, but the mountains and rivers remain."

But this work is not just for the newcomers of the Western Hemisphere, Australia, Africa, or Siberia. A worldwide purification of mind is called for: the exercise of seeing the surface of the planet for what it is—by nature. With this kind of consciousness people turn up at hearings and in front of trucks and bulldozers to defend the land or trees. Showing solidarity with a region! What an odd idea at first. Bioregionalism is the entry of place into the dialectic of history. Also we might say that there are "classes" which have so far been overlooked—the animals, rivers, rocks, and grasses—now entering history.

These ideas provoke predictable and usually uninformed reactions. People fear the small society and the critique of the State. It is difficult to see, when one has been raised under it, that it is the State itself which is inherently greedy, destabilizing, entropic, disorderly, and illegitimate. They cite parochialism, regional strife, "unacceptable" expressions of cultural diversity, and so forth. Our philosophies, world religions, and histories are biased toward uniformity, universality, and centralization—in a word, the ideology of monotheism. Certainly under specific conditions neighboring groups have wrangled for centuries—interminable memories and hostilities cooking away like radioactive waste. It's still at work in the Middle East. The ongoing ethnic and political miseries of parts of Europe and the Middle East sometimes go back as far as the Roman Empire. This is not something that can be attributed to the combativeness of "human nature" per se. Before the expansion of early empires the occasional strife of tribes and natural nations was almost familial. With the rise of the State, the scale of the destructiveness and malevolence of warfare makes a huge leap.

In the times when people did not have much accumulated surplus, there was no big temptation to move in on other regions. I'll give an example from my own part of the world. (I describe my location as: on the western slope of the northern Sierra Nevada, in the Yuba River watershed, north of the south fork at the three-thousand-foot elevation, in a community of Black Oak, Incense Cedar, Madrone, Douglas Fir, and Ponderosa Pine.) The western slope of the Sierra Nevada has winter rain and snowfall and a different set of plants from the dry eastern slope. In pre-white times, the native people living across the range had little temptation to venture over, because their skills were specific to their own area, and they could go hungry in an unfamiliar biome. It takes a long education to know the edible plants, where to find them, and how to prepare them. So the Washo of the Sierra east side traded their pine nuts and obsidian for the acorns, yew bows, and abalone shells of the Miwok and Maidu to the west. The two sides met and camped together for weeks in the summer Sierra meadows, their joint commons. (Dedicated raiding cultures, "barbarians," evolve as a response to nearby civilizations and their riches. Genghis Khan, at an audience in his yurt near Lake Baikal, was reported to have said: "Heaven is exasperated with the decadence and luxury of China.")

There are numerous examples of relatively peaceful small-culture coexistence all over the world. There have always been multilingual persons peacefully trading and traveling across large areas. Differences were often eased by shared spiritual perspectives or ceremonial institutions and by the multitude of myths and tales that cross language barriers. What about the deep divisions caused by religion? It must be said that most religious exclusiveness is the odd specialty of the Judeo/Christian/Islamic faith, which is a recent and (overall) minority development in the world. Asian religion, and the whole world of folk religion, animism, and shamanism, appreciates or at least tolerates diversity. (It seems that the really serious cultural disputes are caused by different tastes in food. When I was chokersetting in eastern Oregon, one of my crew was a Wasco man whose wife was a Chehalis woman from the west side. He told me that when they got in fights she would call him a "goddamn grasshopper eater" and he'd shout back "fish eater"!)

Cutural pluralism and multilingualism are the planetary norm. We seek the balance between cosmopolitan pluralism and deep local consciousness. We are asking how the whole human race can regain self-determination in place after centuries of having been disenfranchised by hierarchy and/or centralized power. Do not confuse this exercise with "nationalism," which is exactly the opposite, the impostor, the puppet of the State, the grinning ghost of the lost community.

So this is one sort of start. The bioregional movement is not just a rural program: it is as much for the restoration of urban neighborhood life and the greening of the cities. All of us are fluently moving in multiple realms that include irrigation districts, solid-waste management jurisdictions, long-distance area code zones, and such. Planet Drum Foundation, based in the San Francisco Bay Area, works with many other local groups for the regeneration of the city as a living place, with projects like the identification and restoration of urban creeks (Berg and others, 1989). There are groups worldwide working with Third and Fourth World people revisualizing territories and playfully finding appropriate names for their newly realized old regions (*Raise the Stakes*, 1987). Four bioregional congresses have been held on Turtle Island.

As sure as impermanence, the nations of the world will eventually be more sensitively defined and the lineaments of the blue earth will begin to reshape the politics. The requirements of sustainable economies, ecologically sensitive agriculture, strong and vivid community life, wild habitat—and the second law of thermodynamics—all lead this way. I also realize that right now this is a kind of theater as much as it is ecological politics. Not just street theater, but visionary mountain, field, and stream theater. As Jim Dodge says: "The chances of bioregionalism succeeding . . . are beside the point. If one person, or a few, or a community of people, live more fulfilling lives from bioregional practice, then it's successful." May it all speed the further deconstruction of the superpowers. As "The Surre(gion)alist Manifesto" says:

> Regional politics do not take place in Washington, Moscow, and other "seats of power." Regional power does not "sit"; it flows everywhere. Through watersheds and bloodstreams. Through nervous systems and food chains. The regions are everywhere & nowhere. We are all illegals. We are natives and we are restless. We have no country; we live in the country. We are off the Inter-State. The Region is against the Regime—any Regime. Regions are anarchic. (Cafard, 1989)

FINDING "NISENAN COUNTY"

This year Burt Hybart retired from driving dump truck, backhoe, grader, and Cat after many years. Roads, ponds, and pads are his sculpture, shapes that will be left on the land long after the houses have vanished. (How long for a pond to silt up?) Burt still witches wells, though. Last time I saw him he was complaining about his lungs: "Dust boiling up behind the Cat you couldn't see from here to there, those days. When I worked on the Coast. And the diesel fumes."

Some of us went for a walk in the Warner Range. It's in the far northeast corner of California, the real watershed boundary between the headwaters of the Pit River and the *nors* of the Great Basin. From the nine-thousand-foot scarp's high points you can see into Oregon, Goose Lake, and up the west side of the Warners to the north end of Surprise Valley. Dry desert hills to the east.

Desert mountain range. A touch of Rocky Mountain flora here that leapfrogs over desert basins via the Steens Mountains of south-eastern Oregon, the Blue Mountains, and maybe the Wallowas. Cattle are brought up from Eagleville on the east side, a town out of the 1880s. The proprietor of the

Eagleville Bar told how the sheepherders move their flocks from Lovelock, Nevada, in early March, heading toward the Warners, the ewes lambing as they go. In late June they arrive at the foot of the range and move the sheep up to the eight-thousand-foot meadows on the west side. In September the flocks go down to Madeline—the lambs right onto the meat trucks. Then the ewes' long truck ride back to Lovelock for the winter. We find the flock in the miles-long meadow heavens of Mule-ear flowers. The sheep business is Basque-run on all levels. Old aspen grove along the trail with sheepherder inscriptions and designs in the bark, some dated from the 1890s.

Patterson Lake is the gem of the Warners, filling an old cirque below the cliffs of the highest peak. The many little ledges of the cliffs are home to hawks. Young raptors sit solemnly by their nests. Mt. Shasta dominates the western view, a hub to these vast miles of Lodgepole and Jeffrey Pine, lava rock, hayfield ribbons, rivers that sink underground. Ha! This is the highest end of what we call "upriver"—and close to where it drains both ways, one side of the plateau tipping toward the Klamath River, the other to the Pit and the Sacramento. Mt. Shasta visible for so far—from the Coast Range, from Sierra Buttes down by Downieville—it gleams across the headwaters of all of northern California.

Old John Hold walks up a streambed talking to it: "So that's what you've been up to!" Reading the geology, the wash and lay of the heavy metal that sinks below the sand, never tarnishing or rusting—gold. The new-style miners are here, too, St. Joseph Minerals, exploring the "diggings," the tertiary gravels. The county supervisors finally approved the EIR and the exploratory drilling begins. This isn't full-scale mining yet, and they'll come back in eighteen months with their big proposal (if they do). The drilling's not noticeable: a little tower and a trailer lost in the gravel canyons and ridges that were left from the days of hydraulicking.

There were early strong rains this fall, so the springs started up. Then the rain quit and the springs stopped. A warm December. Real rains started in January, with heavy snows above six thousand feet and not much below that. This year more kids go skiing. Resistance to it (as a decadent urban entertainment) crumbles family by family. Most adults here never were mountain people, didn't climb, ski, or backpack. They moved up from the city and like to think they're in a wilderness. A few are mountain types who moved down to be here, and are glad to be living where there are some neighbors. The kids go to Donner Pass to be sliding on the white crystals of future Yuba River waters. I get back to downhill skiing myself; it feels wonderful again. Downhill must have provided one of the fastest speeds human beings ever experienced before modern times. Cross-country ski trips in Sierra Buttes too. On the full moon night of April (the last night of the month) Bill Schell and I did a tour till 2 A.M. around Yuba Pass, snow shining bright in the moonlight, skis clattering on the icy slabs. Old mountain people turned settlers manage to finally start going back into the mountains after the house is built, the garden fenced, the drip-systems in. February brought ten inches of rain in six days. The ponds and springs stream over, the ground's all silvery with surface glitter of a skin of water. Fifteen feet of snow at Sugarbowl near Donner Pass.

Two old gents in the Sacramento Greyhound station. I'm next to an elder who swings his cane back and forth, lightly, the tip pivoting on the ground—and he looks about the room, back and forth, without much focus. He has egg on his chin. A smell of old urine comes from him, blows my way, time to time. Another elder walks past and out. He's very neat: a plastic-wrapped waterproof blanket-roll slung on his shoulder, a felt hat, a white chin beard like an Amish. Red bandanna tied round his neck, bib overalls. Under the overall bottoms peep out more trousers, maybe suit pants. So that's how he keeps warm, and keeps some clothes clean! Back in my traveling days men said, "Yeah, spend the winter in Sac."

I caught the bus on down to Oakland. In Berkeley, on the wall of the Lucas Books building, is a mural that shows a cross section of Alta California from the Northwest Coast to the Mojave Desert. I walked backward through the parking lot to get a look at it whole, sea lions, coyote, redtail hawk, creosote bush. Then noticed a man at one corner of it, touching it up. Talked to him, he is Lou Silva, who did the painting. He was redoing a mouse, and he said he comes back from time to time to put in more tiny fauna.

Spring is good to the apples, much fruit sets. Five male deer with antler velvet nubs walk about the meadow in the morning. High-country skiing barely ends and it's time to go fishing. Planting and building. This area is still growing, though not as rapidly as several years ago. The strong spirit of community of the early seventies has abated somewhat, but I like to think that when the going gets rough this population will stick together.

San Juan Ridge lies between the middle and south forks of the Yuba River in a political entity called Nevada County. New settlers have been coming in here since the late sixties. The Sierra counties are a mess: a string of them lap over the mountain crest, and the roads between the two sides are often closed in winter. A sensible redrawing of lines here would put eastern Sierra, eastern Nevada, and eastern Placer counties together in a new "Truckee River County" and the seat could be in Truckee. Western Placer and western Nevada counties south of the south fork of the Yuba would make a good new county. Western Sierra County plus a bit of Yuba County and northern Nevada County put together would fit into the watershed of the three forks of the Yuba. I would call it "Nisenan County" after the native people who lived here. Most of them were killed or driven away by the gold rush miners.

People live on the ridges because the valleys are rocky or brushy and have no level bottoms. In the Sierra Nevada a good human habitat is not a valley bottom, but a wide gentle *ridge* between canyons.

REFERENCES

Berg, Peter, and others. 1989. *A Green City Program for San Francisco Bay Area Cities and Towns.* San Francisco: Planet Drum.

Cafard, Max. 1989 (Autumn). "The Surre(gion)alist Manifesto." *Mesechabe.*

Cox, Susan Jane Buck. 1985 (Spring). "No Tragedy in the Commons." *Environmental Ethics.*

Dodge, Jim. 1981 (Winter). "Living by Life." *CoEvolution Quarterly.*

Hardin, Garrett, and John Baden. 1977. *Managing the Commons.* San Francisco: W.H. Freeman.

Kroeber, A.L. 1947. *Cultural and Natural Areas of Native North America.* Berkeley: University of California Press.

Netting, R. 1976. What Alpine Peasants Have in Common: Observations on Communal Tenure in a Swiss Village." *Human Ecology.*

Polanyi, Karl. 1975. *The Great Transformation.* New York: Octagon Books.

Raise the Stakes. 1987. Journal of the Planet Drum Foundation. P.O. Box 31251, San Francisco, CA, 94131.

Snyder, Gary. 1974. *Turtle Island.* New York: New Directions.

Thirgood, J.V. 1981. *Man and the Mediterranean Forest: A History of Resource Depletion.* New York: Academic Press.

ECOTAGE

Christopher Manes

Author of Green Rage, *Christopher Manes has also written* Other Creations; Rediscovering the Spirituality of Animals, *as well as numerous essays on environmental philosophy.*

I think we're morally justified to resort to whatever means are necessary in order to defend our land from destruction, from invasion.

—Edward Abbey

How far should a person go in defending the natural world? This is likely to become an increasingly pressing question as the pernicious consequences of deforestation, the greenhouse effect, and atmospheric ozone depletion merge into an endless hot summer of environmental discontent affecting everyone. All but the most retrograde critics of radical environmentalism allow for the use of civil disobedience as a legitimate means of environmental protest (perhaps because the protesters usually end up in jail). The attitude changes, however, when ecotage is at issue. The practice of damaging property to prevent ecological damage is unanimously condemned by government agencies, industry, and the mainstream environmental organizations. It has become a litmus test of sorts, separating the radical from the mainstream environmental movement, the socially acceptable defense of nature from the intolerable. "Monkeywrenching," Foreman contends, "symbolizes our fundamental strategy for dealing with the mad machine."[1] And in many ways the opposition it evokes says as much about our culture as it does about radical environmentalism.

Commenting on the monkeywrenching of a uranium mining operation on the south rim of the Grand Canyon, one newspaper editorial asked, "Does a road across public land or a mine on public land do more damage than spikes in trees, or tires ruined, or a life marred by injury or taken?"[2] The question concisely states the ethical issue that ecotage raises for radical environmentalists. Excluding the alternatives of injury and death, which have to be

This essay is excerpted from a chapter of Christopher Manes's book, *Green Rage* (Boston: Little, Brown and Company, 1990). Reprinted with permission.

discussed separately, radical environmentalists have no difficulty answering in the affirmative: property damage in defense of the environment is a justifiable, even potentially heroic action. As Peter Steinhart says, this is the heart of monkeywrenching, "the reminder that we need more than profits, that we need meaning, wit, vision, dreams. . . . When forests are cut because a financier has ingested too many junk bonds, someone deserves at least a pie in the face."[3] The ethics of satire has real utility to a society when some of its more powerful members pursue self-interest at the expense of the whole community, as many feel the resource industry is doing. Resisting those "alien forces from Houston, Tokyo, Washington DC, and the Pentagon" is, according to Foreman, not only ethical, but also "fun."[4]

In Roderick Nash's view, radical environmentalism attempts to claim a more elevated station for ecotage as part of the liberal tradition of the defense of minority rights, with the complication that the minority in this case is the unprotected animal and plant communities being destroyed. Like the abolitionists of pre-Civil War America, radical environmentalists break the law out of opposition to a moral wrong. "Many tree-spikers would argue," writes George Wuerthner, "that the U.S. Forest Service does not and can not 'own' the old growth trees any more than a southern plantation owner could own slaves."[5] In this same spirit, Bill Devall makes the comparison between ecoteurs and resistance to Nazism: "I don't think anyone would have any qualms about committing sabotage against concentration camps, and yet everything done at Auschwitz was 'legal' under Nazi law. Ecotage also responds to principles higher than secular law in the defense of place."[6]

Those higher principles may be part of the liberal tradition, but they also flow out of the particular ethical implications of Deep Ecology itself. In defining ecotage, Foreman remarks, "It's basically a means of self-defense. It's becoming part of the wilderness, and saying don't go any further, don't go into this place [to destroy it]."[7] This position follows from the idea of the Ecological Self articulated by Arne Naess, Devall, and other Deep Ecologists. If our selves belong to a larger self that encompasses the whole biological community in which we dwell, then an attack on the trees, the wolves, the rivers, is an attack upon all of us. Defense of place becomes a form of self-defense, which in most ethical and legal systems would be ample grounds for spiking a tree or ruining a tire.

Self-defense as an argument for ecotage becomes less compelling to radical environmentalists, however, when defense of place involves injury to other persons. The subject arose in 1987 when a worker in Louisiana-Pacific's Cloverdale mill was lacerated by fragments from a saw that shattered on a tree spike. Although the incident almost certainly had nothing to do with radical environmentalism, it produced a firestorm of criticism from all sides, and even some Earth First!ers felt obliged to distance themselves from monkeywrenching. Mainstream environmentalists like Harold Gilliam saw it as the evil fruit of Deep Ecology, whose biological egalitarianism led to the "implication" that "although spiking could kill mill workers, it would serve them right for killing trees."[8] Industry reaction has been less subtle. The editor of *Forest Industries*,

David Pease, advises his readers that "as for the spikers, if I could warp logic and law to my own notions like they do, I would shoot them down (apologies to Hunter Thompson) like the yellow curs they are."[9] President of Louisiana-Pacific Harry Merlo remarks, "Terrorism is the name of the game for radical environmental goals."[10]

Because tree spikers are trying to prevent logging, not hurt people, the issue is the risk of *unintentional* harm, rather than the willful attack on innocent parties that defines terrorism. "To use the word 'terrorism' for monkeywrenching is to totally cheapen the real meaning of what terrorism is all about," Roselle says, "and what people do when they are really desperate."[11] Real terrorists would not be spiking trees, he adds, but spiking Merlo. Some radical environmentalists find that any risk of harm to humans is unacceptable, while others do not, so long as every reasonable precaution is taken to make sure no one is hurt. "Risk to humans hasn't stopped the timber industry from cutting old growth," Roselle points out, referring to the fact that the forest-products industry has the worst safety record of any enterprise in the United States, which frequently leads to disputes between management and workers over safety conditions. "It's strange they should use that as an argument against responsible monkeywrenching."[12]

Nevertheless, if ecotage raises ethical questions for radical environmentalism, questions its critics are eager to explore and its advocates explain, it also raises questions about the environmental ethics—or lack thereof—held by society at large. With growing numbers of people willing to break the law to protect the environment, our culture is forced to confront the fact that its own ethical choices concerning ecotage sometimes seem strangely out of place in the context of an environmental crisis unparalleled in history. In the long run this illumination may be a much more important consequence than any amount of dollar damages done to bulldozers.

Under present law a timber company can purchase the trees in an old-growth forest, cut them down (often at taxpayers' expense), and leave the forest biome so disrupted that the animal and plant communities it previously supported perish or migrate. Erosion may make local streams unsuitable for the spawning of salmon and therefore affect the ocean food chain hundreds of miles away. Pursued on a large scale, as is certainly happening today, the fragmentation of forests will increase global warming and inevitably lead to a higher rate of extinction, as the findings of island biogeography demonstrate. All this is totally legal. In contrast, those who try to preserve the forest by spiking the trees are guilty of vandalism under present law. If there is something slightly absurd about a scenario in which those who want to destroy a forest can accuse those trying to preserve it of property damage, it is an absurdity we may no longer be able to afford. The notion that the world is an assemblage of interchangeable resources to be sold to the highest bidder may satisfy the nostalgia for 1950s-style endless growth, but it is belied by the gravity of the environmental crisis we face. The world is a web of interdependent living communities, not a department store.

And yet, when faced with a choice between ecotage and environmental havoc, between spiking trees and losing an old-growth forest, our society—or at least those who speak for it in government, industry, and mainstream environmental organizations—continues to condone the latter and condemn the former. This conclusion is usually reached by an appeal to two principles: the rule of law and property rights.

In a very thoughtful discussion of ecotage, Peter Steinhart explores its affinity with the American values of independence and fairness but concludes that it must not be condoned, since "one form of lawlessness tends to invite the other."[13] This is the most common argument mainstream environmentalists use to criticize ecotage, and it may indeed be true. But the charge of indiscriminate lawbreaking can also be made against many critics of monkeywrenching. Ecotage itself has arisen against a vast backdrop of illegal practices on the part of the resource industry and government agencies. . . .

In violation of the Multiple Use–Sustained Yield Act and the National Forest Management Act, one third of the forests in the Pacific Northwest (private and public) were understocked (either inadequately or never replanted) in 1982. Steinhart himself cites the fact that when the California Water Resources Control Board reviewed one hundred timber-harvest plans, it concluded that more than half violated forestry rules and in many cases had been approved without a forester's even having visited the site. While Harry Merlo complains of the lawlessness of radical environmentalists, his own Louisiana-Pacific Corporation has been convicted of antitrust violations and forced to pay $1.5 million in damages. In this context of rampant disrespect for environmental law, the refrain that lawlessness begets lawlessness seems to be an argument *for* ecotage, not against it. Taking the point to an extreme, Devall even suggests that "there are already existing laws on the books to protect the environment, and in a certain sense, strongly supporting those laws means that you *have* to engage in sabotage because the government is not supporting them at the present time."[14]

Of course, radical environmentalists feel obliged to commit ecotage even where environmental laws are being obeyed if in their estimation the statutes are inadequate to preserve natural diversity. This position has led a number of critics to compare radical environmentalists with such an interesting array of characters as Lenin, Oliver North, radical antiabortionists, and others perceived to hold the Machiavellian position that the ends justify the means. As the last chapter showed, however, statutory law has always had an ambiguous status in America. Most everyone agrees we would be a poorer people indeed if we had allowed appeals to the rule of law to quell the civil rights movement or the antiwar protests, where in retrospect the ends did indeed seem to justify the means. As a general proposition, Americans have never had an obsequious attitude toward the law per se, but rather a respect for the many good laws the democratic process tends to produce. The rule-of-law argument against ecotage really comes down to an assertion that a defense of the natural world is not of the same caliber as ending discrimination or stopping a senseless war. Whether that contention will continue to be intelligible as the consequences of environmental degradation begin to be felt in people's everyday lives remains to be seen. But it tells us something about how industrial society values property over the natural world and its efflorescence of life.

In 1983 Eugene Hargrove, the editor of *Environmental Ethics*, condemned the use of monkeywrenching as a tool for environmental protection, noting that even if breaking the civil law was defensible under some natural rights theory, Locke himself had included property as among the most precious natural rights. Needless to say, industry has consistently made even stronger arguments that ecotage is an assault on that most American of values, property. In fact, the sanctity of property in the extreme forms Locke and industrialists have maintained has never been accepted by American jurisprudence. It was intentionally left out of the Declaration of Independence's list of inalienable rights—"Life, Liberty and the pursuit of Happiness"—since Jefferson had a genuine distrust of the mercantile tenor behind property law. It failed to appear in the Preamble to the Constitution, alongside justice, tranquillity, general welfare, and liberty, as one of the purposes of the document. It emerges as a right for the first time in the Fourteenth Amendment's due-process clause. Even here, however, American jurisprudence never recognized property as an inalienable right, but rather as a "bundle of rights" (to use the Supreme Court's words) and responsibilities.[15] The most unregenerate industrialist would have to admit that if everyone used their property as they wanted, by polluting the air and water, for instance, everyone's rights would be impaired in the long run. Congress and state legislatures have already spoken, no doubt not forcefully enough, on the right of the public to regulate private property to prevent pollution and other forms of environmental degradation. The harvesting of trees on the private forests of timber companies is likewise subject to state regulation, inadequate though it may be.

The right to property in its abstract, metaphysical form is not at issue in the ecotage debate, but instead what kinds of property rights society should recognize in relation to environmental protection. Ecotage compels our culture to face the fact that it currently considers a bulldozer of higher value than a living, intact ecosystem that supports a diverse community of plants and animals. In the future, as more and more species become extinct and forests are recognized for their role in maintaining a livable biosphere, this value system may be judged equal to such historic extravagances as the burning of women suspected of witchcraft or the internment of loyal Asian-Americans during World War II.

As the Cloverdale incident demonstrated, ecotage also seems inescapably to invite some examination of the morality of violence in the defense of nature. Sue Joerger of the Southern Oregon Timber Industries Association raises the issue in its starkest terms, claiming that "until these people start saying 'We don't think it's worth human life to save these areas,' they're in a sense condoning murder for saving a roadless area."[16] As already mentioned, Roselle has pointed out the equivocation in this position: the timber industry is quite willing to risk human lives in order to develop a roadless area, and can actually predict fairly accurately how many workers are going to get hurt or die during the course of an operation (an ability not unique to timber companies but possessed by all industries). This does not make timber executives murderers, in the usual sense of the word, any more than ecotage makes radical environmentalists terrorists. But it does define a curious ethical stance: our society—or at least that portion of it in control of industry—is willing to risk injury to humans for economic reasons, but not to preserve the natural world.

Even this almost sacrosanct position that human and nonhuman life are not on the same par is undergoing change, however, in some parts of the world as the biological meltdown raises troublesome questions about the value of the wild and wildlife. Faced with the imminent extinction of Africa's black rhino population at the hands of poachers who sell the horns for their supposed aphrodisiac properties, the government of Zimbabwe instituted a shoot-to-kill policy against the poachers in 1988. More than sixty poachers have been killed. In response to the criticism the policy has generated, the head of the antipoaching patrol said, "When a group of Arabs makes an assault on the British crown jewels there is a skirmish and lots are killed—to protect rocks—and nobody minds. Here we're protecting a world heritage, but it happens to be animals and that hangs people up."[17] The moral choice here is complicated by the fact that the government has a considerable economic stake in ensuring the survival of the rhinos, since wildlife tourism is big business in Zimbabwe. It should be remembered that medieval feudal lords also executed poachers, for reasons somewhat less magnanimous than the love of nature. Still, this new "lesser of two evils" problem, with its choice between watching a species become extinct or using violence to prevent it, is likely to confront society in different forms again and again in years to come, and there is no guarantee events will deal kindly with Joerger's moral certitude. A century from now the children of ecological scarcity may look back and consider the powerful interests that run the resource industry the real terrorists. . . .

REFERENCES

1. Interview with Dave Foreman, Grand Canyon, Ariz., July 8, 1987.
2. "Who Is the Real Rapist?," *Southern Utah News*, July 15, 1987.
3. Peter Steinhart, "Respecting the Law," *Audobon* 89 (November, 1987), p.13.
4. Foreman, ed., *Ecodefense: A Field Guide to Monkeywrenching* (Tucson: Ned Ludd Books, 1987), p. 16.
5. George Wuerthner, "Tree-Spiking and Moral Maturity," *Earth First!*, August 1, 1985 p. 20.
6. Interview with Bill Devall, Grand Canyon, Ariz., July 10, 1987.
7. Interview with Foreman.
8. Harold Gilliam, "Violence Begets Violence," *San Francisco Chronicle*, November 1, 1987.
9. *Forest Industries*, June 1987, p. 2.
10. As quoted in Steinhart, "Respecting the Law," p. 12.
11. Interview with Mike Roselle, Grand Canyon, Ariz., July 9, 1987.

12. Interview with Roselle, San Francisco, July 7, 1989.
13. Steinhart,"Respecting the Law," p. 13.
14. Interview with Devall.
15. The issue is directly addressed by the Supreme Court in Andrus v. Allard, 444 U.S. 51 (1979).
16. Interview with Sue Joerger, Grants Pass, Oreg., September 11, 1987.
17. As quoted in Margaret L. Knox, "Horns of a Dilemma," *Sierra*, November/December 1989, p. 61.